Canadian Politics in the 1990s

Canadian Politics in the 1990s

Third Edition

Edited by
Michael S. Whittington and Glen Williams

Nelson Canada

© Nelson Canada,
A Division of International Thomson Limited

Published in 1990 by
Nelson Canada,
A Division of International Thomson Limited
1120 Birchmount Road
Scarborough, Ontario   M1K 5G4

Canadian Cataloguing in Publication Data

Main entry under title:

Canadian politics in the 1990s

Rev.
Rev. ed. of: Canadian politics in the 1980s.
Includes index.
ISBN 0-17-603456-0

1. Canada—Politics and government—1984-   .
I. Whittington, Michael S., 1942-   .
II. Williams, Glen, 1947-   .

FC630.C363 1990   971.064'6   C89-094474-1
F1034.2.C363 1990

Printed and Bound in Canada

1 2 3 4 5 6   GP   5 4 3 2 1 0

Contents

Introduction

It has been nearly a decade since the publication of the first edition of this book. Our collection has found widespread acceptance from both general readers and specialists and is now generally recognized as the leading volume of its type in Canada. The book's success has been the result of both its distinguished selection of recognized authorities and its uniquely accessible format.

All our authors have been directed to construct a clear and uncluttered introduction to their fields of specialization. The goal here has not been to dazzle the reader with extensive footnotes or elaborate theoretical frameworks. Rather our objective has been to present often complex and always important issues to people who, while generally aware of Canadian politics, do not have the training of professional political scientists or political economists. Our aim has been to simplify a complex set of problems so that a wide readership can benefit from the analytical skills and substantive knowledge of our authors.

This edition goes far beyond a simple update of the previously published chapters. Where appropriate, authors have also reconsidered their earlier work and written essentially new chapters. A formerly overlooked topic area, gender, now has its own chapter. Finally, an entirely new section, "The Regions in National Perspective," has been added to the volume.

Canada's politics has most typically found expression in a spatial dimension with regional identities and regional conflicts organizing Canadian political life. This reality is explored in the book's first section through a series of highly original chapters on the political organization of region within the nation and the continent by Williams, Whittington, Marchak, Gibbins, Nelles, McRoberts, and Boswell. Although approaching the question from distinctly different territorial and theoretical perspectives, these authors all agree that regional issues will continue to dominate the political agenda of the 1990s.

The second section of our volume shifts the focus from region to five aspects of the sociocultural milieu within which the Canadian political process must operate. The chapter by Bell outlines the basic political attitudes and values of Canadians—our political culture. In the same vein, Clarke and Mishler examine the immediate behavioural reflections of our political culture in the levels and kinds of political participation that characterize Canadian liberal democracy. Panitch discusses the distribution of social power in Canada in terms of elite and class. Burt extends this analysis to include gender. The media's role in transmitting political messages is plotted by Fletcher and Taras.

The third section of our book contains three chapters which survey the main "linkage" institutions that connect the political system with its societal environment. These linkage institutions are important because the manner in which they operate can significantly affect the issues that are brought to the attention of the political elites. Brodie and Jenson discuss Canadian political parties from a unique perspective and offer a way to come to terms with the last decade's structural and ideological changes in our partisan politics. Pammett uses the data from the most recent federal elections to suggest how the trends that emerge from his analysis may be manifested in future partisan contests. The final chapter by Pross investigates the increasingly important role of pressure groups in the policy process.

The book's concluding section concentrates on governmental structures and institutions, the traditional meat and potatoes of political science. In an important new chapter, Milne places current constitutional debates in the context of Canada's historic incorporation within the British Empire. Atkinson's chapter assesses the current role of the Canadian Parliament in the light of recent reforms in parliamentary practices. In a complementary chapter, Smith places the leadership role of the Cabinet in the parliamentary system within its historical context.

The next three chapters in this final section all admirably demonstrate the strengths of a political economy approach to the examination of governmental structures and institutions: Stevenson on federalism, Layton on urban politics, and Bakker on the size of government. The final pieces in our collection deal with two of the more bureaucratic aspects of our political system and are written, appropriately, by political scientists who have had extensive practical experience inside the Canadian bureaucracy. Van Loon and Whittington discuss the role of central agencies in the policy process and Schultz surveys the debates surrounding one of the major functions of government, the making of regulations.

Contributors

Michael M. Atkinson, Chairman, Department of Political Science, McMaster University, Hamilton, Ontario

David V.J. Bell, Professor of Political Science and Dean of Graduate Studies, York University, Downsview, Ontario

Isabella Bakker, Assistant Professor, Department of Political Science, York University, Downsview, Ontario

Peter Boswell, Associate Professor, Department of Political Science, Memorial University, Newfoundland

M. Janine Brodie, Associate Professor, Department of Political Science, York University, Downsview, Ontario

Sandra Burt, Associate Professor, Department of Political Science, University of Waterloo, Ontario

Harold Clark, Professor, Department of Political Science, North Texas State University

Frederick J. Fletcher, Director of Mass Communications, Department of Political Science, York University, Downsview, Ontario

Roger Gibbins, Head of Department of Anthropology and Sociology, University of British Columbia, Vancouver, British Columbia

Jane Jenson, Professor, Department of Political Science, Carleton University, Ottawa, Ontario

Jack Layton, Professor, Department of Politics, Ryerson Polytechnical Institute and Senior Alderman, Ward 6, Toronto City Council

Patricia Marchak, Professor, Department of Anthropology and Sociology, University of British Columbia, Vancouver, British Columbia

Ken McRoberts, Graduate Director, Professor, Department of Political Science, York University, Downsview, Ontario

David Milne, Associate Professor, Department of Political Studies, University of Prince Edward Island, Charlottetown, Prince Edward Island

William Mishler, Professor, Department of Political Science, Department of Government and International Studies, University of South Carolina

H.V. Nelles, Interim Chairman, Ontario Council on University Affairs

Jon H. Pammett, Chairman, Department of Political Science, Carleton University, Ottawa, Ontario

Leo V. Panitch, Chairman, Department of Political Science, York University, Downsview, Ontario

A. Paul Pross, Professor, Department of Public Administration, Dalhousie University, Halifax, Nova Scotia

Richard Schultz, Director, Centre for the Study of Regulated Industries, McGill University, Montreal, Quebec

David E. Smith, Professor, Department of Political Science, University of Saskatchewan, Saskatoon, Saskatchewan

Garth Stevenson, Professor, Department of Politics, Brock University, St. Catharines, Ontario

Daphne Gottlieb Taras, Research Coordinator, Canada-China Relations Project, York University, Downsview, Ontario

Michael S. Whittington, Professor, Department of Political Science, Carleton University, Ottawa, Ontario

Glen Williams, Associate Professor, Department of Political Science, Carleton University, Ottawa, Ontario

Richard J. Van Loon, Senior Assistant, Department Minister of Indian and Northern Affairs

PART 1

THE REGIONS IN NATIONAL PERSPECTIVE

1

Regions within Region: Canada in the Continent

GLEN WILLIAMS

An atlas portrays an uncomplicated image of the lines that divide northern North America: two colours, two nations; on one side of the border forty-nine states, on the other ten provinces and two territories. This seeming clarity obscures one of the most complex bilateral relationships in the world. In the twentieth century, the informal evolution of our continental role in relation to the United States has paralleled along a number of important dimensions the formal incorporation of the Canadian colonies into the French and British empires during the seventeenth to nineteenth centuries. Just as the evolution of modern Canada has been marked by the development of a dense system of interregional relations, so too have Canada's regions developed in relation to specific, usually geographically adjacent, local areas in the United States. And, insofar as Canada is more than simply the sum of its southward-facing parts, over time the country as a whole has taken on many of the properties of a northernmost region of the United States.

The continental spatial structures that give meaning to Canada's North American regional identity are most readily visible within Canadian economic life: when investment, production, and trade are considered, the Canadian economy appears more like a *zone* within the American economy than a distinct national economy. For the last four decades, more than two-fifths of Canadian manufacturing and mining industries have been owned by foreign (mostly American) interests (see Table 1.1). This imposing level of foreign ownership is not approached within any other advanced industrial nation.

Also outside of a typical national profile is the nearly exclusive territorial focus of Canadian trade. Approximately three-quarters of Canadian exports are destined for the United States, and the United States is also the source of seven-tenths of Canadian imports. Not surprisingly, there is a direct link between high levels of American ownership of Canadian industry and Canada's extensive trade with the United States. Intrafirm trade between U.S. parent firms and their Canadian branch plants manifests itself in many cases as the essence of Canadian "international" trade. Foreign firms ship 75 percent of the exports of industrial-

Table 1.1
Foreign Control of Canadian Industry, 1971 and 1986 (percent of total)

	Assets		Sales	
	1971	1986	1971	1986
Food	46	34	34	27
Beverages	31	33	32	44
Tobacco products	85	100	78	99
Rubber products	93	89	91	88
Leather products	23	15	21	12
Textile mills	54	47	51	48
Knitting mills	22	12	16	7
Clothing industries	12	12	9	9
Wood industries	31	16	24	14
Furniture industries	19	17	16	13
Paper and allied industries	46	23	43	26
Printing, publishing and allied industries	11	10	11	10
Primary metals	41	20	37	18
Metal fabricating	42	25	43	26
Machinery	75	47	77	50
Transport equipment	82	75	91	87
Electrical products	67	52	65	61
Non-metallic mineral products	62	68	51	52
Petroleum and coal products	99	53	99	67
Chemicals and chemical products	79	72	81	76
Miscellaneous manufacturing	50	35	51	36
Total Manufacturing	**59**	**44**	**57**	**49**
Mineral fuels	81	37	91	50
Total Mining	**69**	**31**	**76**	**41**
Total Non-financial industries	**37**	**24**	**38**	**28**

Source: Statistics Canada, *Annual Reports*, 1972 and 1986; Corporations and Labour Unions Returns Act, Part I, Corporations, March 1975 and December 1988.

ized Ontario's fifty leading exporters. (These fifty firms are alone responsible for two-thirds of the province's exports.) Forty-four percent of the exports of Canada's fifty leading exporters come from foreign-owned enterprises. This compares to less than 5 percent for France, Germany, Sweden, Japan, and the United States.[1]

Overall, the Canadian provinces ship a somewhat greater proportion of their goods outside the country (mainly to the United States) than to each other. They also import more from outside the country—again, mainly the United States—than from each other.[2] Further, as Table 1.2 demonstrates, each of Canada's five geographic regions has developed its own intensive, deeply pervasive, north–south trading relationship with its closest American regional neighbour or neighbours. The spatial concentration of Canada–U.S. trade in many leading commodities is even

Table 1.2
Trade of Canadian Regions with U.S. Regions* They Directly Border (percent of
total trade with the United States of each Canadian region), 1984

	Exports	Imports
Atlantic	90	47
Quebec	62	55
Ontario	90	88
Prairies	65	58
British Columbia	51	60

* Bordering U.S. regions are Atlantic, Midwest, Mountain, and Pacific.
Source: Calculated from Canada, Statistics Canada, International Trade Division, *Canadian International Trading Patterns* (Ottawa: Supply and Services, 1985), pp. 74–
75.

more pronounced than Table 1.2 suggests. In 1984, for example, over 70 percent of Atlantic Canada's meat and fish exports to the United States were destined for just three Atlantic states, while over one-half of British Columbia's meat and fish exports were received by just three Pacific states. Half of Quebec's American wood and paper exports went to only six states, and over three-fifths of both petroleum and natural gas shipments to the United States from the prairies also went to six states. Over 70 percent of Ontario's American-bound iron and steel and 80 percent of that province's U.S. exports of transport equipment were shipped to just five states.[3]

DEFINING A REGIONAL IDENTITY

Canada's regional identity within its continental space is not only visible from an economic perspective, but is also manifested at the focal points of Canadian politics, society, and culture. It was after the Second World War that Canadians were first warned that their nation had moved from "colony to nation to colony."[4] Similar sentiments are still being expressed, although it is hard for many today either to picture clearly our British colonial past or to understand fully the significance of this often repeated figure of speech. It is, however, helpful to realize that in the earliest part of this century, Canadians, especially English Canadians, were privileged members of the world's most powerful empire, and their identity and sense of "nationalism" grew out of that association. Colonial, rather than indigenous, symbols and institutions defined both Canadians' view of themselves and Canada's position on the international stage. Indeed, when our Department of External Affairs was created in 1909, it was the supremacy of the British Colonial Office in the conduct of our imperial and foreign relations that designated Canada's international business as "external" rather than "foreign."

Today, mirroring our British colonial experience, more than two-thirds of our bilateral relations are conducted with one country, the United States.[5] Although the requirements of managing the extensive and complex continental economic relationship go a long way toward explaining this concentration, there are also important cultural and ideological factors at play. Just as most Canadians were content in the early part of the century to accept the primacy of Britain in defining the boundaries of imperial foreign policy, so now the United States is usually given the lead. Deference, of course, is not to be confused with the abrogation of national sovereignty. If there was any cause for doubt on this question, periodic disengaged moments in the conduct of Canada's foreign policy serve to demonstrate to both American and Canadian audiences that Canada retains the capacity to be something more than a U.S. satellite. A list of such episodes would include Canada's maintenance of trade ties with China and Cuba during the Diefenbaker years, Prime Minister Pearson's 1965 call for a pause in the U.S. bombing of North Vietnam, the "Third Option" of the early 1970s that called for reducing Canada's dependence on the United States by expanding its relations with other countries, and Canada providing development aid to Nicaragua during the 1980s.

Living comfortably (for the most part) under the roof of U.S. foreign and defence policy while still asserting sovereignty is a position fraught with contradictions. One 1975 survey of some three hundred members of Canada's foreign policy elites showed that nearly two-thirds saw the United States as Canada's best friend and one-half defined Canada as a "partner" in North America, suggesting that on most issues in international affairs Canadian and American interests are essentially the same. Even so, 52 percent also felt that the continental economy "significantly limited" Canadian autonomy in domestic affairs, and only 28 percent believed that, compared to most other countries, Canada acts independently in international relations.[6]

Elite opinions and mass opinions on this subject closely coincide. Seventy percent of Canadians in the 1980s viewed the United States as Canada's best friend, and one-half between 1977 and 1986 expressed "very great" or "considerable" confidence in the ability of the Americans to deal wisely with world problems.[7] Only one-quarter of Canadians were prepared to agree that we should withdraw from the North Atlantic Treaty Organization (NATO) and our defence agreements with the United States and adopt a policy of neutrality when asked in the mid-1970s and again in the mid-1980s.[8] At least a plurality of Canadian public opinion usually backs controversial U.S. foreign policy initiatives such as Star Wars research in Canada, the 1986 bombing of Libya, or employing the American fleet to confront Iran in the Persian Gulf in 1987.[9] Even so, and reflecting the ambiguous approach of the state elite to this subject, two-thirds of Canadians in the mid-1980s believed that their government's views on international affairs were "unduly affected" by another country, and three-fifths identified the United States as that country.[10]

The gradual unfolding of Canada's status as a U.S. economic region, the virtual absence of a pre-existing anti-colonial tradition, and federalism have all played their parts in fostering relatively deferential international policies. Canada's politicians have no need to be reminded of the U.S. capacity to deliver economic rewards or punishments for Canadian behaviour in international affairs. Ultimately more decisive, however, has been the failure of Canadians to transmit through the generations enthusiasm for, or even knowledge about, their own unique national experience.[11] This failure has been magnified by the way in which Canadians, during the twentieth century, have eagerly absorbed U.S. popular culture during successive intensive bombardments from American print, radio, movie, and television media. Finally, the Canadian political system's obsessive promotion of domestic regional particularisms has also dampened possibilities for the articulation of pan-national voices and projects.

Canadians realize that volunteering to be an extension of the American political economy carries with it certain costs to national independence in world affairs. We earlier observed that both the foreign policy elite and the public agree on this point. However, this sense of realism and deference to U.S. leadership in the world does not carry over to the expression of what are perceived to be Canadian *regional* issues within North America. Here, autonomy is jealously guarded. Territory is a good example of a subject where Canadian national sensibilities will readily engage American interests. Whether it is the Northwest Passage, Georges Bank, the diversion of rivers, or acid rain from the industrial states, Canadians display uncharacteristic enthusiasm in tracing the physical border between the two countries with some measure of precision. Less than 10 percent would favour Canada becoming "a part of the United States of America," and in 1988 only one-quarter thought it would become so within the next fifty years.[12]

National identity as manifested through the preservation of images of distinctiveness in social culture or lifestyle is another no-go area. An important cultural legacy of the British colonial past has been the quiet conviction of many Canadians that they are more civilized than the avaricious and quarrelsome republicans to the south. However pronounced the similarity of the two national cultures in a world perspective, Canadians want very much to believe that they are different. Accordingly, they continually define and measure (at least rhetorically) their social practices and policies against what is frequently perceived to be a negative American yardstick. So, in addition to territory, the Canadian region currently draws its sociocultural frontier by characterizing itself as possessing higher levels of societal order and urban cleanliness as well as a greater willingness to deliver goods and services collectively through the state.[13]

Unlike geographical or sociocultural territory, most Canadians have failed to recognize the economy as a terrain on which the promotion of a significant measure of national autonomy was necessary. In keeping with their behaviour in the foreign and defence fields, Canadians, especially Canada's business and state elites, have seemed mostly content to define their economic interests within the confines of empire. While accepting American economic leadership, Canadians have at times still been able to recognize specific points of divergence between their own and U.S. economic interests. Nonetheless, as we will now see, the development of Canada's economy as a *zone* within the U.S. economy has been facilitated by the relative weakness of economic nationalism within Canadian society during this century.

CONTINENTAL RESOURCE DEVELOPMENT

Countries reliant on natural resource production have been more vulnerable to upheavals in the world economy in the twentieth century than manufacturing countries because resource products suffer from wildly irregular cycles of demand and competitors can rather easily replace traditional suppliers. Historically, Canada's response to these marketplace uncertainties has been to seek special concessionary trading relationships with its largest customers. Until the latter half of the nineteenth century, Canadian fish, fur, lumber, and agricultural resources found shelter in Great Britain behind a system of imperial tariff preferences. When this privileged access was lost, many important Canadian business leaders signed a petition to annex Canada to the United States. The Reciprocity Treaty of 1854, which allowed American market access for resource products from the British North American provinces, was an attempt to forestall any growth in annexationist sentiment.

Although the Reciprocity Treaty was only in effect from 1854 to 1866, these years were subsequently to be romanticized by Canadian merchants and resource producers as "golden years" of prosperity. For many decades after the abrogation of reciprocity by the Americans, its memory was honoured in widespread and persistent calls for the renegotiation of a free trade arrangement with the United States. As it turned out, however, through westward expansion and development of the wheat economy, Canada gradually re-established its pattern of resource staple export dependence on Britain. At the end of the first decade of the twentieth century, nearly one-half of Canadian exports were agricultural exports destined for Britain.

With these renewed commercial links to Great Britain, it is perhaps not altogether surprising that under a Canada–U.S. free trade banner Laurier's Liberals were unable to carry the country in the 1911 election. This result, however, marked only a setback, not a defeat, for the fuller integration of Canadian resource producers into the U.S. market. The growing sophistication of American industry was in part predicated on ready access to Canada's new staple resources: pulp and paper, minerals, and energy. And it is hardly surprising that U.S. direct investment in Canadian resource industries sought to secure this access. As early as 1926, Americans owned one-third of Canadian mining and smelting. By 1963 they owned one-half.

After the Second World War, U.S. investment flowed into Canadian resource industries that were complementary to its own manufacturing sector. Through investment and trade in Canadian natural resources, a continental division of labour was forged in which Canada's role became that of "a specialized (resource producing) adjunct to the American political economy."[14] The logic of profitability guided individual business decisions by private firms that cumulatively promoted the development of Canada's continental role as a resource storehouse. These decisions were also made within a supportive atmosphere fostered by government officials on both sides of the border who sought to establish resource security for the "free world" in the context of the Cold War of the 1940s and 1950s. Furthermore, Canadian politicians and bureaucrats were eager to promote an economic formula that had stimulated, in their view, the post-war economic boom.

Canadian producers of industrial raw materials have enjoyed remarkable success within this century's continental marketplace. Resource companies now overwhelmingly dominate the list of Canada's top exporters and supply approximately one-third of U.S. imports of nickel, one-half of imported iron ore, lead, and zinc, two-thirds of imported sulphur, and four-fifths of imported potash. In the mid-1980s, two-thirds of Canada's pulp and paper output was exported to the United States, and Canadian lumber exports supplied one-third of the American market.[15]

CONTINENTAL INDUSTRIAL PRODUCTION

The other side of its impressive strength in resource industries has been Canada's relative failure in manufacturing. Manufactured products, not resource goods, have established themselves as the most dynamic sector of world trade during the twentieth century. Moreover, among manufactures, the most technologically advanced and highly finished categories have led the way. In the beginning of the 1980s, at least one-half of the exports of countries such as Japan, West Germany, Sweden, and the

United States were of such "finished" manufactures. Canada's proportion was only one-third.

By 1986 Canada's proportion of finished goods had risen to a more respectable 48 percent of its total exports. However, four factors have to be considered before we conclude that there has been any significant recent improvement in the international competitiveness of Canadian manufacturing. First, other countries have also been moving ahead; the new bench mark for Sweden and the United States is three-fifths of total exports.[16] It is also important to recognize that while most industrial countries are either in surplus or break even in their international trade in these strategic products, Canada, the world's largest per capita importer of manufactured goods, is in perpetual deficit. Between 1970 and 1987, Canada's trade deficit in end products amounted to a staggering $245 billion (in unadjusted dollars), of which $105 billion was incurred during the last five years of that period alone.[17] These figures dramatically underline Canada's role as a *resource-producing*, rather than a *manufacturing*, zone in the U.S. economy.

A third factor that must be taken into account in assessing the recent surge in Canadian finished exports is the historical absence of the kind of innovative capacity in Canadian industry that would provide for the creation of internationally competitive products. Studies in the early 1960s first began to warn that Canada was near the bottom of the pile in industrial research and development (R&D). Little has changed. A recent Ontario government report noted that Canada currently ranks "tenth out of twelve in total R&D intensity among the largest industrial economies." Even some newly industrialized economies such as Korea have higher R&D intensities than Canada.[18]

Finally, the peculiar effects resulting from the 1965 Canada–U.S. Auto Pact must also temper any enthusiasm for recent apparent advances in the international competitiveness of Canadian industry. While massive in volume, this trade in automobiles and parts tells us very little about the ability of Canadian firms to develop and market internationally competitive production. The Auto Pact provides mainly for the intrafirm transfers of very similar goods between U.S. manufacturers and their Canadian subsidiary factories, which incidentally pass over an international frontier. As well, until the early 1980s, trade under the Auto Pact had generally favoured the United States. It was only the radical devaluation of the Canadian dollar during this period, significantly lowering Canadian labour costs, that made Canada attractive as a production site to American automakers. If, then, an adjustment is made to remove Auto Pact exchanges, Canada's proportion of finished manufactured exports falls to a dismal 30 percent of its remaining total trade in 1986. This is about one-half the current Swedish level.

As in the resource industries, the considerable structural anomalies of Canadian manufacturing can only be explained through a model of non-autonomous economic development and continental specialization. The base for Canada's modern industrial establishment was laid in the late nineteenth and early twentieth centuries. This era marked the height of the British connection through the wheat economy and the sentiments of imperial nationalism. The politics and economics of Canada's location *within* empire both contributed to the evolution of an autarkic industrial strategy and stifled the subsequent unfolding of a world-competitive manufacturing sector. It was a strategy that provided for a modest industrial base unlikely to challenge British industry on its own turf; whose relatively humble capital requirements did not interfere with the massive investment program required to finance the wheat economy's transcontinental transportation infrastructure; and that even argued that it was strengthening the empire by transferring to Canada the production of "foreign" (U.S.) commodities.

The industrial strategy employed by early Canadian manufacturers has become known as "import substitution industrialization" (isi). It is characterized by unchallenged technological dependence through the nearly exclusive use of foreign machinery and production processes and a disinterest in production for anything but domestic consumption. The state is involved through setting tariff levels high enough to make feasible the domestic production of goods that would otherwise be imported. Canadian manufacturers, seeking a cheap and effective shortcut, licensed American industrial processes rather than developing their own. In contrast to industrialists in other countries who initially borrowed technology and then assimilated, adapted, and innovated from this knowledge base, the use of foreign machinery and production processes became a permanent part of the early Canadian industrial pattern, thus tying it in an important structural way to the evolution of industry in the United States.

With geographic proximity, a tariff-protected domestic market, and concessionary tariff privileges within the British Empire, Canada was an obvious location for the establishment of U.S. branch plants. Through takeovers of existing Canadian manufacturing firms (often already linked to them through licensing arrangements), and the establishment of new subsidiaries, American industrialists consolidated a place of prominence in Canada's most dynamic industrial sectors by the 1920s. Canadian-owned manufacturing became concentrated in the technologically backward and less capital-intensive industries such as textiles, clothing and footware, food processing, and furniture manufacturing. As Table 1.1 indicates, foreign control of Canadian manufacturing reached its peak in the early 1970s and has since returned to its late-1940s level of somewhat more than two-fifths of total ownership.

Three production patterns have marked the seven decades of hegemony for U.S. manufacturing branch plants in Canada. None of these production patterns have broken the original mould that we have seen cast Canadian industries as mere ancillaries to staples resource extraction. All three have contributed to a spatial division within North American manufacturing that accounts for the failure of Canadian industry to become world competitive. The first period, from the 1920s to the late 1940s, consolidated the worst features of the previous import substitution behaviour of Canadian-owned industries. U.S. firms established a presence in Canada in order to gain access to a tariff-protected market for products they would otherwise have shipped from their southern factories. There was no provision in their Canadian branch plants for the development of distinct product lines for world markets save for the transfer of some export business from their U.S. operations to take advantage of the preferential tariff access that Canada enjoyed in Great Britain and the white Dominions.

The second period, from the 1950s to the late 1970s, further institutionalized the import substitution model and, with it, Canada's industrial role in the continent. With the collapse of imperial preferences, Canadian branch plants ceased even this limited export role. Increasingly, American firms viewed the Canadian market as part of their *domestic* operations. Typically, an administrative division of the North American market would establish a Canadian "satellite" plant to satisfy regional demand in this country, just as, say, a Chicago plant would fill demand in the U.S. Midwest, while research and development as well as exports were centred in the U.S. parent plant.

Production in the contemporary period, the 1980's, continues to be organized on a continental basis. Instead of "satellite" plants that produce a large range of miniature-replica lines for a limited territory, however, North American plants are now becoming "rationalized." Following the relatively successful Auto Pact model, this means specialization in the production of a limited range of lines for the entire continent. Falling Canada–U.S. tariffs under the General Agreement on Tariffs and Trade (GATT) made rationalization possible and increasing international competitive pressure made it necessary. Nevertheless, continental rationalization does not change the rules of the game. Canadian factories are no closer to becoming technologically advanced plants capable of autonomously generating world-competitive products. Under the Auto Pact model, managerial authority, research and development, and export marketing all remain the prerogatives of the U.S. parent firms.

POLITICS OF CONTINENTAL ECONOMIC
INTEGRATION

The political climate remained consistently favourable to continental interests during the ongoing process that fashioned Canada's resource and manufacturing industries as regional extensions of the U.S. economy. In some measure, this was due to the growing ability of foreign investors to reward or punish politicians. This could be accomplished directly through the provision of funding for political parties and corporate directorships for retired politicians or indirectly through manipulating the levers of economic expansion or contraction. Politicians, even when they understood the structural limitations in the performance of foreign firms in Canada, became understandably loathe to threaten what they believed to be the motor of the economic growth on which their electoral fortunes depended.

Ultimately more decisive than the considerable power of foreign investors to promote or protect their own interests in the Canadian political system, however, has been the nature of the Canadian discourse on continental economic integration. Two competing interpretations have defined the context for the political management of this issue. These interpretations both begin from a general recognition of the inevitability of some extensive measure of Canadian integration into the continental economy. Both, however, propose distinct sets of policy prescriptions that they believe should govern our association with the Americans. Significantly, more radical political options, such as annexation of Canada to the United States at one extreme or Cuban-style expropriation of all American interests in Canada at the other, have had almost no impact on the course of the debate.

Continentalism has favoured the elimination of trade and investment barriers between Canada and the United States. The unhindered play of continental market forces, according to this view, will maximize Canadian prosperity. The continentalist school has been unready to distinguish between Canadian and foreign-owned firms and typically accords the same Canadian "corporate citizenship" to both. *Nationalism* has promoted greater Canadian control over the pace and extent of continental integration. Foreign investment, according to this view, has prevented Canada from reaching its considerable economic potential. The nationalist school would have Canada's state system institute an industrial strategy to promote Canadian-owned enterprises and to coerce a better deal from American investors in Canada.

Continentalist assumptions went virtually unchallenged among Canada's economic, political, bureaucratic, and academic elites for almost two decades immediately following the Second World War. They were also hegemonic among the population as a whole. Canada–U.S. economic integration was championed by such dynamic political personalities as C. D. Howe, a Liberal Cabinet minister during the 1940s and 1950s, who was the driving force behind taxation and investment policies designed to lure American dollars to Canada. Those few in this era who worried about the long-term consequences of foreign economic domination were accused of attacking the standard of living of ordinary Canadians and/or of trying to turn Canada into a "banana republic." Even prominent political personalities who dared champion a modest degree of economic or military nationalism, such as Prime Minister Diefenbaker or Liberal Cabinet minister Walter Gordon, met a storm of public condemnation and were destined to be marginalized within their own political parties.

By the late 1960s, however, nationalist concerns were no longer easily dismissed. Reinforced by the publication of a number of widely publicized government and academic studies, public and even a minority of elite opinion had shifted. These studies documented the structural limitations imposed on Canada as a result of continental economic integration and even suggested that the capacity of Canadians to maintain themselves as a distinct social formation had been undermined. As Table 1.3 indicates, in the 1970s two-thirds of Canadians thought there was sufficient U.S. capital invested in Canada, and approximately one-half were prepared to countenance schemes to buy back majority control of U.S. companies in Canada *even if this were to reduce living standards*. It should nonetheless be noted that even during this peak of nationalist sentiment, popular misgivings about continental economic integration were far from universal, with approximately one-third disapproving of a buy-back.

The public unease with the high level of American control over the Canadian economy had some limited resonance within the Trudeau Cabinets of the 1970s and early 1980s. Following the 1971 publication of the widely discussed *Foreign Direct Investment in Canada* (Gray Report), the Foreign Investment Review Agency (FIRA) was created. The creation of this new agency was more an exercise in symbolic politics than a genuine effort to regulate foreign businesses in Canada. The massive existing stock of foreign investment that had originally sparked nationalist concerns was left undisturbed. The "new" foreign investment coming under the FIRA mandate typically enjoyed annual approval rates of 90 percent or greater. Nevertheless, from FIRA's inception, the agency had to fight its way through a host of hostile and powerful critics. Foreign investors believed that FIRA had established a dangerous precedent for future Canadian governments who might choose to be even more interventionist. Business leaders and conservative economists railed against the intrusion of state power into the free market. Provincial governments

Table 1.3
Public Perceptions of Foreign Investment

"Now thinking about U.S. capital investment in Canada—Do you think there is enough now or would you like to see more U.S. capital investment in this country?"

	Enough Now	Like to See More	Don't Know
1988	61%	30%	10%
1986	53	34	14
1984	50	35	14
1982	56	36	8
1980	64	20	17
1978	69	23	9
1975	71	16	13
1970	62	25	13

"Some experts are suggesting that Canada should buy back a majority control—say 51%—of U.S. companies in Canada. Even though it might mean a big reduction in our standard of living, would you approve of this or not?"

	Approve	Disapprove	Qualified/Don't Know
1988	36%	50%	14%
1986	36	50	14
1984	36	45	20
1982	43	46	12
1980	48	34	18
1978	52	34	13
1975	58	26	16
1970	46	32	22

Note: Percentages may not add exactly to 100, due to rounding.
Source: Canadian Institute of Public Opinion, *The Gallup Report*, 2 July 1987 and 16 June 1988.

argued that the federal government was restricting their ability to pursue their region's economic development.

The high-water mark of the influence of the nationalist school occurred just after the 1980 federal election. In winning a number of key Ontario seats, the Liberals were helped by their promises of an industrial strategy for Canada and a tougher line on foreign investment. Strong new proposals, significantly broadening the restricted FIRA mandate to ensure that multinational manufacturers operating in Canada performed industrial R&D here and that they had export freedom, were discussed in Cabinet. In the resource sector, the National Energy Program (NEP) sought to Canadianize ownership and control of the critical oil and natural gas industry through a far-reaching package of programs that discriminated against foreign investors. However, tough talk about

"NEPing" other industrial sectors dissolved rapidly in the face of a determined onslaught led by continentalist Cabinet ministers and senior civil servants supported by U.S. government officials and business interests. Key provincial governments and the federal Conservative Party also added their most forceful voices to the chorus of opposition.

The continentalist counterattack coincided with the severe economic recession of the early 1980s. Not only did this make any additional nationalist initiatives impractical, but it also had a critical effect on changing public attitudes toward continentalism. As Table 1.3 demonstrates, the percentage of Canadians wanting to see more U.S. capital in Canada increased after the recession, and the 1970s majority favouring a "buy-back" reversed to become by the mid-1980s a majority who disapproved of this strategy. With the election in 1984 of a Conservative government committed not only to improving commercial relations with the United States, but to the immediate dismantling of FIRA and the NEP as well, the continentalist school unmistakably re-established its traditional political ascendancy in Ottawa.

THE 1987 FREE TRADE AGREEMENT

After the spectacular failure of the Canada–U.S. reciprocity agreement in the 1911 election, Canadian politicians avoided dealing so openly again with an issue obviously bonded to the electorate's fears of territorial surrender and/or loss of sociocultural distinctiveness. Prime Minister William Lyon Mackenzie King established a pattern, in the mid-1930s, of depoliticizing continental commercial relations by presenting movement toward Canada–U.S. tariff liberalization as a disjointed series of technical, bureaucratic adjustments to tariff schedules. Under the post–Second World War General Agreement on Tariffs and Trade, this bureaucratic process of tariff reduction continued. Particularly through the 1967 Kennedy and 1979 Tokyo rounds of GATT negotiations, something very close to *de facto* Canada–U.S. free trade was established. By 1987, 95 percent of Canadian goods were to enter the United States with duties of 5 percent or less, and 91 percent of U.S. exports to the Canadian market were to be in an equivalent position.

From being a deeply buried public issue for at least half a century, Canada–U.S. free trade was catapulted by the Mulroney government to the head of Canada's political agenda through a 1985 announcement that it would begin treaty negotiations with the Americans. Considering the already existing liberalized continental tariff regime, three factors seem to have been responsible for the surprising re-entry of the potentially explosive free trade question into the Canadian political atmosphere: (1) the desire of the continentalists to consolidate their recent victories over the nationalists through seizing the policy initiative; (2) the rise of an

American protectionism that threatened to disrupt, through the use of non-tariff barriers, a Canadian resource and manufacturing production system that, as we have previously described, had become largely based by the mid-1980s on assumed low-tariff access to U.S. markets; and (3) the particular partisan appeal of this initiative to both the neo-liberal right and the populist western wing within the Conservative Party at a time when the party was demoralized by policy paralysis and petty scandals.

In the end, all three of these factors also figured in the resolution of this issue. The 1987 Canada–U.S. free trade agreement (FTA), although it removed remaining tariffs between the two countries, achieved only symbolic relief to Canada from the American non-tariff barriers that had initially prompted Canadian business to press the Tories for the negotiations. Chapter 19 of the FTA establishes that each country will retain its domestic anti-dumping and countervailing duty laws, although appeals on whether these laws have been properly applied may be made to a binational countervail panel. Of significance as well for the trade side, Canada gave up the tariff safeguards under the 1965 Auto Pact, which obligated U.S. automakers to retain a base share of their North American production in Canada.

Of far more import than the sections of the FTA that specifically address tariff matters is the way in which the continentalists have used the agreement to hobble their Canadian opponents. The FTA entrenches a number of key continentalist policy positions and attempts to preclude institutionally any future Canadian challenge to the continentalist status quo from the nationalist school. To illustrate, the FTA is clearly designed to make considerations of the kind that took place in the 1980 Trudeau Cabinet about an enhanced FIRA, with real policy muscle, and the NEP impossible for any future Canadian government. Articles 105, 1402, and 1602 forbid discrimination between foreign and Canadian firms in regard to establishment, investment, operations, and sale. Pertaining to manufacturing, article 1603 forbids performance requirements such as export quotas or domestic sourcing for foreign firms. Pertaining to resources, articles 408 and 409 forbid export taxes and export restrictions, and articles 903 and 904 restate these prohibitions with specific reference to the energy sector. At the conclusion of the negotiations, then Deputy Prime Minister Donald Mazankowski described the energy provisions to Calgary oil executives as "insurance against your own government" by preventing the NEP from being reintroduced.[19]

The ensuing 1988 election was a direct confrontation over ratification of the FTA between forces carrying nationalist and continentalist banners. Business influence, as well as a highly favourable regional distribution of the Tory vote, delivered a narrow plurality victory to the Conservatives. Business and the media elite strongly supported the Tories, not because the FTA delivered secure access to the U.S. market (as it did not), but because they feared that its defeat would allow the state-interventionist nationalists to seize the initiative. The remarkable strength of the nationalists in the free trade debate stands in sharp contrast to their historically weaker position within Canadian political culture. Indeed, right up to the vote, public opinion was running against the trade agreement.

Two factors help explain the relative success of the nationalist forces. First, they were able to break out of their traditionally narrow leadership base in the cultural and intellectual elites and in the trade union movement. The disadvantageous terms of the FTA fractured the continentalist camp, detaching from it the largest portion of the Liberal Party. Many of those who had previously strongly supported continental economic integration, and would have been themselves most unlikely to have sponsored a NEP or a strengthened FIRA, nevertheless believed that formally surrendering these powers unnecessarily weakened the capacity of the Canadian state system to bargain effectively with the Americans in the future.

Second, the nationalist forces enjoyed great success because they centred their attack on the FTA on precisely those two elements of the continental relationship where, as we earlier argued, Canadian autonomy has been jealously guarded: territory and the distinctiveness of the sociocultural milieu. In regard to territory, the nationalists repeatedly warned the public that Canada's political independence was at stake and Canada was about to become the fifty-first state. It is no accident that one of the campaign's most effective television advertisements purported to show the FTA negotiators taking an eraser to the Canada–U.S. border on a map of North America. In respect to national identity, the nationalists argued effectively that traditional Canadian cultural and social values were in jeopardy from direct threats posed by the FTA to Canada's social welfare programs as well as regional and cultural subsidies. So powerful were these nationalist arguments that the continentalists could not simply respond by stressing what they believed were to be the considerable economic benefits of the FTA. In order simply to hold their own, they were forced to protest vigorously that the nationalists were "liars," incautiously promise that social, cultural, and regional programs would not be endangered by the FTA, and air their own television advertisements that pointedly redrew the Canada–U.S. border on a map of North America.

CONCLUSION: MANAGING THE CONTINENTAL RELATIONSHIP

As a regional extension of a larger and more powerful political economy, the Canadian social formation faces special problems in self-management. The politics of issues such as the environment, economic expansion, social welfare, labour, and regional development have by necessity both a domestic and a bilateral dimension. This duality creates basic instability in the economic management capacity of the Canadian political economy: an instability that is further exaggerated by the spatial dispersion of power within a federal system of government. In the context of this instability, then, the Canadian state system is called upon to play the role of a point of balance by focusing, mediating, protecting, and developing the regional position of the Canadian social formation within the continental political economy.

The management of regional relations within the continent is far from easy. For one thing, the point of balance must continually shift to take account of the continuing changes that result from economic expansion and transformation. For another, finding balance within the political environment is also difficult with the fortunes of political ideas such as nationalism/continentalism and province-building/centralization and parties that articulate them constantly on the rise and fall. Finally, there are underlying centripetal and centrifugal forces at play in the Canadian federation with respect to continentalism.

The recent debates surrounding the FTA and the Meech Lake Accord have led many observers to place considerable stress on the centrifugal tendencies in the Canadian federation. Both of these arrangements weaken the policy leadership capacity of the national government at the same time as provincial economies will be strengthening what we have seen to be their already remarkably pronounced southward orientations. In this continentalized free trade environment, historic resentments rooted in the regional economic inequities of Confederation along with a more recent legacy of bitterness from federal–provincial disputes over resource and industrial policy could prove to be a highly volatile mix. Indeed, the FTA leaves provincial elites relatively free to pursue balkanizing regional economic development strategies without having to measure them against any national programs developed by the federal government. The provinces may increasingly find that political decisions taken in Washington have as much, or even more, relevance for their local economies as decisions taken in Ottawa. Demands may grow in some areas for the direct political representation that would come with annexation.

Before succumbing to alarmism, a number of additional factors need to be considered. To begin, direct political representation in the U.S. political system would not necessarily be more effective than the current "special relationship." Canada's state system has given considerable advantage to Canadian elites over other regional elites in the continental economy both by bringing Canadian elites together to recognize their joint interests and by providing them with a common vehicle for promoting these interests. Although the Canadian social formation is not electorally represented in the U.S. political system, Canada's state system has developed considerable means for the "external" political expression of its regional interests to the U.S. executive, Congress, and state governments through diplomacy, treaty, and the advocacy of private interest groups. Private advocacy is primarily energized by American businesses fostering and protecting their Canadian investments, but may also include strategic alliances with indigenous forces within U.S. politics whose issue positions are similar to Canadian ones.

Without exception, the population of each of Canada's regions is only a small fraction of the population of their contiguous American counterparts. When it is remembered that all of Canada's regions share common interests in resource production and export to U.S. markets, sometimes shipping the same products, the utility of constructing a common Canadian position through a separate federal order is clear. It should also be remembered that the burden of providing the highly expensive transportation infrastructure necessary for resource export has traditionally been shared by all of Canada's regions through the federal state. Weaker Canadian regions can also use the federal state to capture some of the benefits of the uneven development of the continental economy from the stronger Canadian regions through equalization payments and social transfers. As well, while it may be shrinking in relative importance, the national market provided by trade between the Canadian regions will likely remain a factor of some significance for all the provinces. For some influential sectors, such as the Canadian communications industry, a protected national market is key. Finally, and perhaps essentially, the maintenance of a federal state allows Canadians a means to affirm symbolically their autonomous national self-definition through preserving their territorial and sociocultural distinctiveness within the continent.

NOTES

1. Ontario, Premier's Council, *Competing in the New Global Economy* (Toronto: Queen's Printer for Ontario, 1988), vol. 1: 69, 73.
2. Canada, *Report of the Royal Commission on the Economic Union and Development Prospects for Canada*, 3 vols. (Ottawa: Supply and Services, 1985), 3: 104, 106. In 1979, 29 percent of provincial goods were exported, while 27 percent were sent to other provinces. Imports were the source of 32 percent of provincial goods, while 26 percent came from other provinces.
3. Calculated from Canada, Statistics Canada, *Exports by Countries*, January–December 1984, March 1985.
4. H. A. Innis, "Great Britain, the United States and Canada," in *Essays in Canadian Economic History*, ed. Mary Q. Innis (Toronto: University of Toronto Press, 1956), p. 405.

5. P. V. Lyon and B. W. Tomlin, *Canada as an International Actor* (Toronto: Macmillan, 1979), p. 71.
6. Ibid., p. 85.
7. Canadian Institute of Public Opinion, *The Gallup Report*, 4 July 1985 and 6 March 1986.
8. Ibid., 19 June 1976 and 26 May 1986.
9. Ibid., 8 July 1985, 5 June 1986, and 3 December 1987. When the Americans downed an Iranian passenger airbus in the summer of 1988 with the loss of over three hundred lives, 49 percent of Canadians believed that "the U.S. acted in good faith to protect an American naval ship and lives," while only 31 percent felt that the U.S. military presence in the area made such an event "inevitable" (21 July 1988).
10. Ibid., 27 November 1986.
11. The classic study here is A. B. Hodgetts, *What Culture? What Heritage? A Study of Civic Education in Canada* (Toronto: Ontario Institute for Studies in Education, 1968).
12. Canadian Institute of Public Opinion, *The Gallup Report*, 15 November 1988.
13. See S. M. Lipset, "Canada and the United States: The Cultural Dimension," in *Canada and the United States: Enduring Friendship, Persistent Stress*, ed. C. Doran and J. Sigler (Englewood Cliffs, N.J.: Prentice-Hall, 1985), and D. Bell and L. Tepperman, *The Roots of Disunity: A Look at Canada's Political Culture* (Toronto: McClelland and Stewart, 1979).
14. M. Clark-Jones, *A Staple State: Canadian Industrial Resources in Cold War* (Toronto: University of Toronto Press, 1987), p. 11.
15. W. Clement, "A Political Economy of Resources," in *The New Canadian Political Economy*, ed. W. Clement and G. Williams (Montreal: McGill-Queen's University Press, 1989), Tables 3 and 4, p. 50.
16. Calculated from United Nations, *Yearbook of International Trade Statistics*, various years.
17. Calculated from Canada, Statistics Canada, *Summary of External Trade*, various years.
18. Ontario, Ministry of Industry, Trade and Technology, *A Commitment to Research and Development: An Action Plan*, January 1988, pp. 9–10.
19. *The Globe and Mail*, 17 October 1987, p. A4.

FURTHER READINGS

Britton, J., and J. Gilmour. *The Weakest Link*. Background Study No. 43. Ottawa: Science Council of Canada, 1978.

Clark-Jones, Melissa. *A Staple State: Canadian Industrial Resources in Cold War.* Toronto: University of Toronto Press, 1987.

Clarkson, Steven. *Canada and the Reagan Challenge*, 2nd ed. Toronto: Lorimer, 1985.

Clement, Wallace. *Continental Corporate Elites.* Toronto: Macmillan, 1977.

Clement, W., and G. Williams, eds. *The New Canadian Political Economy.* Montreal: McGill-Queen's University Press, 1989.

Innis, Harold A. *Essays in Canadian Economic History*, ed. Mary Q. Innis. Toronto: University of Toronto Press, 1956.

Laxer, James. *Leap of Faith: Free Trade and the Future of Canada.* Edmonton: Hurtig, 1986.

Levitt, Kari. *Silent Surrender.* Toronto: Macmillan, 1970.

Lipsey, R. G., and R. C. York. *Evaluating the Free Trade Deal: A Guided Tour through the Canada–U.S. Agreement.* Toronto: C. D. Howe Institute, 1988.

Maslove, A., and S. Winer, eds. *Knocking on the Back Door: Canadian Perspectives on the Political Economy of Freer Trade with the United States.* Halifax: Institute for Research on Public Policy, 1987.

Panitch, Leo. "Dependency and Class in Canadian Political Economy." *Studies in Political Economy* (Autumn 1981).

Williams, Glen. *Not for Export: Toward a Political Economy of Canada's Arrested Industrialization*, updated ed. Toronto: McClelland and Stewart, 1986.

2

Canada's North in the 1990s

MICHAEL S. WHITTINGTON

A cursory glance at a map of Canada will reveal that a very large percentage of our total land mass lies north of the 60th parallel and outside the boundaries of the ten provinces. However, while Yukon and the Northwest Territories make up almost 40 percent of Canada, their combined population is only 80,000. Long viewed as a trackless wasteland or barren wilderness by Canadians living in the ten provinces, during the 1950s these northern territories came to be viewed both as a frontier and as a vast storehouse of mineral and petroleum resources. The goal of "opening up the North" and tapping its resources for southern industries was made explicit during the 1960s and 1970s, and federal government policies such as Diefenbaker's "Roads to Resources" were directed at conquering the northern wilderness.

The 1970s, however, also witnessed an awakening of people's consciousness that the North, while a wilderness to southern Canadians, was in fact home to the Indians, Inuit, and many long-term white residents. The Berger Inquiry in the 1970s revealed to southern Canadians that the people of the North are very committed to their land and feel a deep and justifiable resentment that their homeland is seen simply as a resource warehouse for southern industries.

In the 1980s, it seems that the native peoples of the North have come to realize non-renewable resource development projects will inevitably proceed if they are seen to be in the national interest. Hence, they have shifted from a position of outright opposition to one of insuring that when such projects proceed, they do so in a manner that minimizes the impact on the traditional lifestyle of the original residents of the North. As well, through joint ventures, training, and employment opportunities, the native peoples in the Northwest Territories and Yukon are attempting to share in the economic benefits of development to a degree commensurate with the stake they have in the lands affected.

Thus, as we enter the 1990s, the fate of the North, its resources, and its people and the ultimate relationship that will exist between the northern territories and the rest of Canada remain central policy concerns, and the settlement of these issues will continue to be a dominant item on the agenda for political decision making to the turn of the century.

THE NORTHERN ENVIRONMENT: POPULATION
AND RESOURCES

The population of the North, while tiny numerically, is extremely diverse culturally and linguistically. The total population of the Northwest Territories is approximately 53,000, of which 17 percent are Dene, 35 percent Inuit, 6 percent Métis, and 42 percent non-native. A significant percentage of the white population of the Northwest Territories is composed of people who are only temporary residents or transients and who will ultimately return to southern parts of Canada. The population of Yukon is approximately 27,000, of which approximately one-quarter are Indians and the remainder non-native. One significant difference between the whites in Yukon and those of the Northwest Territories is that a much larger percentage of the former are long-time residents of the North.

A common error made by southern Canadians when they speak of the North is lumping the aboriginal populations of the territories together in the category of "natives." This leads to a very distorted perception of the diversity, both cultural and linguistic, that exists among the native communities. In the first place, the Inuit and the Indians have very little in common with each other and traditionally were bitter enemies when they came into contact. The Inuit language, Inuktitut, is as different from the Athapaskan or Dene languages spoken in the Mackenzie Valley as English is from, say, Finnish. On the other hand, while there are several distinct dialects of Inuktitut spoken in Canada's North, in fact they are similar enough that communication is possible among members of various dialect groups. There are several Indian languages spoken in the Mackenzie Valley, all of which share the Athapaskan root. However, Dogrib, Hare, Slavey, Chipewyan, and Loucheux (or Kutchin) are distinct languages that are related to each other in the same way that the romance languages of Europe are related to each other. In Yukon, while there are virtually no Inuit, there are several Athapaskan dialects spoken, as well as Tlingit, which is a different language related to the languages spoken by the natives of Alaska and British Columbia. Moreover, of the Athapaskan languages spoken in Yukon, only one, Loucheux, is shared by natives of the Northwest Territories.

A second common error committed by southern Canadians is to try to generalize about the two northern territories. As we shall see in the remainder of this chapter, while there are some similar problems shared by the two northern territories, there are also significant differences in the patterns of constitutional and political development, in the cultures, and in the economies of Yukon and the Northwest Territories.

The economies of Canada's northern territories, while still developing, are very diverse but generally founded upon primary resources. The traditional economy of the Northwest Territories and Yukon was based on hunting and fishing. In other words, before the whites arrived, the northern economy was one of subsistence, depending on renewable resources such as wildlife, fish, and wild plants to provide food, fuel, shelter, and clothing to the original inhabitants. The first exposure to Europeans occurred in the northeast, where whalers and explorers, and later missionaries, made the initial intrusions. While these contacts produced some important cultural changes among the Inuit, they did not significantly alter the basic subsistence economy.

In the western Arctic, by contrast, the first exposure to whites was through the fur trade. Here, contact with the European culture actually had a very immediate effect on the traditional economy, for the fur traders taught the natives that they could exchange pelts for goods unattainable locally, such as metal tools and weapons, manufactured textiles, and rum. In effect, the subsistence economy was modified to the extent that the notion of furs as a medium of exchange that could be used to obtain valuable commodities was introduced to the Athapaskan peoples. Nevertheless, basic needs such as food and shelter were still supplied by the subsistence economy, and in fact the fur trade was compatible and even complementary to the traditional way of life of the northern people. Again the missionaries, and later the RCMP, wrought significant cultural (and, it is alleged, genetic) changes on the people of the Mackenzie Valley, but had little independent effect on the traditional economy.

The first direct exposure of Yukon natives to white people came considerably later, and as with the native people of the Mackenzie Valley, the Yukon Indians had their subsistence economy altered to some extent by the incursion of the fur trade. The more significant economic changes in Yukon, however, occurred with the discovery of placer deposits of gold in 1896 and the subsequent "gold rush" of 1898. This brief period of large-scale non-native immigration was to alter the economy and the lifestyle of Yukon natives profoundly and irreversibly. Where in the rest of the North the native contact with European culture was through "the Bay," the church, and the RCMP—and the individuals associated with these three venerable institutions tended to be only transient residents of the North—in Yukon, a significant number of the whites who migrated to the territory with hopes of "striking it rich" in the gold fields actually stayed on after the bonanza days.

In the Northwest Territories, the churches had come to bring the natives "salvation," the RCMP had come to bring them "law and order," and "the Bay" had come to exploit them in a commercial relationship. In Yukon, the whites who stayed set about to "civilize" the territory itself without much serious concern for the original inhabitants at all. Thus, in the Northwest Territories the whites were there to a large extent because of the natives, whereas in Yukon the natives tended to be an incidental fact of the environment and often were thus effectively ignored and left alone by the permanent white settlements at Dawson and Whitehorse.

In the Northwest Territories there was very little change in the basic lifestyle of the natives throughout the first half of the twentieth century. The discovery of oil at Norman wells in the 1920s did not produce significant changes in the economy, though the Canol pipeline was built from Norman Wells to Yukon during the Second World War as a strategic response to the possibility of a Japanese invasion of the West Coast and consequent severing of supplies to Alaska. Gold was discovered near Yellowknife in the 1930s, and since that period mines have operated at varying levels of production in the Great Slave Lake region of the territory. However, while these enterprises may have had localized effects on the natives in the immediate vicinity of the projects, there was no attempt to include the local inhabitants in the work force. In the eastern Arctic there was still less development, and in fact, with the exception of some mineral exploration and the occasional visit of an RCMP patrol (sometimes with a public health nurse in tow), the Inuit were left to the tender mercies of either the Anglican or Roman Catholic Church (depending upon who got there first). As a result, the economy of the Inuit did not alter very much. However, where there was contact with the Church and where, therefore, the Inuit received some European education and expo- sure to the values of Christianity, a number of the traditional values of their culture may have been weakened or erased.

Again, the experience of Yukon was different. While there has been constant gold mining since the turn of the century, and while there has been a permanent white population throughout this period, significant new development did not occur until the building of the Alaska Highway during the Second World War. The construction period itself caused social disorientation in the native communities along the way, but in addition, because many settlements were physically relocated along the highway by the government so that they would be easier to administer, many people were separated from their traditional communities. In the long run, however, the most significant impacts were to occur as a result of Yukon becoming accessible by road to the south. Not only did this open up opportunities for mineral exploration, but tourism began to evolve as a significant component of the economy of the territory. The local white inhabitants welcomed this development as an opportunity to "civilize" still further their chosen homeland and to open up new commercial opportunities. Here, as before, while there was little inten- tional meddling with the native culture or economy, the incidental impacts on traditional lifestyles were extensive.

By the 1960s, the pace of northern development had speeded up considerably. The construction of a string of defensive radar bases across the Far North, the Distant Early Warning (DEW) line, and related military operations in the Arctic had brought white people into local contact with native communities. As well, the Conservative government's "Roads to Resources" program had helped stimulate the construction of all-season roads to once-remote communities such as Inuvik in the Mackenzie Delta (the Dempster Highway, completed in 1978) and Yellowknife, Pine Point, Hay River, Fort Smith, and Fort Simpson in the Great Slave region (the Mackenzie Highway). Moreover, a series of Canadian governments had come to the realization that there were vast and significant potential petroleum and mineral resources in the Far North that could be utilized to supply the raw materials for growing industries in southern Canada. Here, the presumption was that such development was to the advantage of *all* Canadians and that, in fact, it would even by welcomed by the natives of the North, who would benefit from being brought into the mainstream of Canadian life with all of its economic opportunities, access to education, health care, and cultural benefits. To the amazement of southern Canadian politicians, the northern natives have not always welcomed this southern-style development and have often become outspoken in their opposition to it.

The economic development of the North is continuing, but as we look to the decade of the 1990s the problems of northern development transcend the engineering and technological problems of building roads and pipelines through regions of discontinuous permafrost, of operating heavy and delicate machinery in extremes of temperature, and of building tankers that have "class ten" icebreaking capacities. These problems of technology and engineering have in many cases become second-order, incidental problems when compared to the social and political challenges of developing and transporting resources in a manner that is beneficial and acceptable to the indigenous population.

NATIVE VALUES: THE LAND

There are great cultural differences not only between the native and non-native communities, but even among the various native groups in the North. Perhaps the most significant difference between white and native values and attitudes is that the natives, in this case the Indians as well as the Inuit, place a far higher valuer on the collectivity and the community. The notion of private property is underdeveloped, and the principle of community sharing of the wealth of the band, settlement, or extended family is very important. The concept of possession, which is such an important cornerstone of liberal societies, is replaced as well by the simpler notion of "use" of things valued. The sharing ethic and the replacement of the liberal notion of private ownership with the shared inherent right of individuals simply to *use* a resource are nowhere more prominent than in the native concept of *the land*.

In the native culture, Indian and Inuit alike, the land holds a very special place, for it is the land upon which the community must depend for its survival. All of the requirements for existence must somehow be extracted from the land. Conversely, in a mystical way, the native peoples feel a "oneness" with the land. Unlike the whites' view of the North as a wilderness and a frontier to be pushed back and altered to serve their needs, the natives of the North view it as a homeland to which they must adapt in order to survive. The native religions all espouse the notion of human respect for the land and of the spiritual connections between people and the land that provides their livelihood. Thus, the native culture has had difficulty accommodating the very idea of extracting non-renewable resources from the wealth of the land. For the most part, the native economy extracted only resources that could be renewed—in this sense the natives used the resources of the land, but they have never permanently alienated any of its wealth.

Finally, the natives of the North have been, and continue to be, uneasy about many of the resource development schemes, not simply because the notion of resource extraction is culturally alien to them, but for very practical reasons. The natives have learned from hard experience that all too often the whites leave a trail of waste and destruction behind them when they undertake to develop the North. (It has been said in ironic jest that the symbol of the North should be a fuel drum because of the large numbers of them abandoned in even the most remote parts of the North.) In this respect, the natives have been suspicious of development, not simply because the concept of non-renewable resource extraction is foreign to them, but because the activity associated with resource development can alter or even destroy the renewable resources—the fish, wildlife, and flora—upon which the native economy and the traditional way of life ultimately depend.

THE NATIVE POLITICAL CULTURE

Southerners often mistakenly assume that the natives of the Far North have no indigenous political culture—that until the coming of the Europeans the North lacked political institutions. However, the northern people successfully governed themselves since their arrival on this continent centuries before the European explorers. While the native political cultures are less institutionalized than ours, the fact remains that the basic political functions were performed in traditional native communities. One of the features that distinguishes our political culture from that of the Yukon Indians, the Dene, and the Inuit is their egalitarianism. An extension of the "sharing" ethic described above, when transposed into the political context—the right of all members of a community to express their views and to have an influence on the decisions that affect them—is an ancient and deeply rooted political value.

This egalitarianism, however, does not eliminate the need for leadership in the traditional communities. But where we tend to think of political leadership as a highly unitary concept—that is, a concept that features a sovereign institution or individual with the ultimate power to make final decisions on all aspects of social and political life—the native concept of leadership is both *diffuse* and *functional*. It is diffuse because native communities follow different leaders for different kinds of community activities. There are often totally different power structures in a traditional native community, depending upon whether the decisions to be taken involve hunting, war, spiritual matters, settlement of internal disputes, or punishment of wrongdoers. Native leadership is functional because the choice of leader in any given situation depends upon who is best suited to lead in that particular circumstance. There are the top hunters in the communities who will dominate decision making in one area, shamans who will dominate in another, and tribal elders who may assume authority for still others.

These leaders are not elected in the sense that liberal democratic politics defines elections, but rather they come to lead almost automatically, through a sort of community consensus that they are the people most able to do so. Thus it is that sometimes even the most well-meaning attempts of white people to give the natives the best of our political institutions—institutions such as representative democracy—have met with only marginal acceptance. The partial failure of some of these experiments, such as elected municipal councils, must be viewed not so much as an indication of the lack of political development of the native peoples, but more as simply a reluctance to replace the political values and decision-making instruments that they have applied for centuries with a new set imposed from outside. This point must be kept in mind when we discuss the basic political institutions that operate in the North today.

CONSTITUTIONAL HISTORY OF THE NORTH

Although it would be possible to write an extensive article on the constitutional development of the North, the aim here is simply to outline the major events in order to place the current situation in context. Ironically, both the Northwest Territories and Yukon enjoyed a status closer to responsible government in the past than they do today. The older Northwest Territories, composed of Yukon and the modern Northwest Territories as well as territory that is now the provinces of Alberta and Saskatchewan, had a fully elected legislative assembly by 1881 and responsible government from 1897. In 1898 the Yukon Territory was carved out of the Northwest Territories and a commissioner was appointed. Originally the commissioner was advised by an appointed six-member council, but gradually the number of elected members of the council was increased until, by 1908, all members were elected. The territory seemed virtually on the brink of full responsible government and well on the way to provincial status at this time. But after the Klondike boom collapsed, the population declined, and by the end of the First World War the territory had come to be administered almost totally at the whim of the federally appointed commissioner.

Although the Yukon Territorial Council declined in size as the boom period faded away, the council continued to be wholly elected, and both the commissioner and the council continued to sit in the territory rather than in Ottawa. Any hope for a gradual evolution to responsible government and ultimately provincehood was shelved effectively until the decade of the 1970s when the slow movement in that direction began again.

The modern Northwest Territories did not even enjoy the short period of boom that Yukon experienced. When the provinces of Alberta and Saskatchewan were created in 1905, the remaining lands of the territory and the people who lived there reverted to full colonial status, ruled by public servants in Ottawa. In 1921 a council was appointed to advise the commissioner, but all six of the councillors as well as the commissioner himself were federal bureaucrats in the national capital. This status remained essentially unchanged until 1951 when the first members were elected to the council and the first sitting of the council was held in the territory. The territorial franchise was originally limited to the residents of the Mackenzie Valley, but in 1966 three ridings were created in the eastern Arctic. However, the commissioner still ruled very much as a colonial governor, residing in Ottawa and dividing his attention between his responsibilities as commissioner and other obligations as a senior bureaucrat in the Department of Northern Affairs. Moreover, in his decisions regarding the territory, he listened to his elected councillors more as a matter of protocol than through any constitutional obligation. In 1965 a three-member commission was established to look at the political future of the territory. The Carrothers Commission made a number of recommendations about the conduct of government, with the result that the council was enlarged to sixteen members in 1967, and the seat of government and the commissioner of the territory took up permanent residence in Yellowknife. By 1975 the Northwest Territories had the first totally elected council since 1905, and since then the council has been converted to a legislative assembly.

POLITICAL INSTITUTIONS OF THE NORTHWEST TERRITORIES AND YUKON

In spite of all the pressure for more responsible government emanating from the territories and in spite of the gains that have been made in that direction, constitutionally the territories are still subordinate entities. The legislative assemblies, although now fully elected in both territories, do not have sovereign powers. Their authority is a result of delegation to them by the Parliament of Canada and by the Department of Indian Affairs and Northern Development (DIAND) and could be taken away at the whim of the federal government. In this sense the constitutional status of the territorial legislatures is analogous to the status of a municipality vis-à-vis the province.

The Yukon legislative assembly is composed of sixteen members elected by constituency, and the executive council in Yukon is composed of five ministers. While the system is not yet one that can be called full responsible government, the practice of the executive council at present is very close to that. As a result of a letter of instruction from the Minister of Northern Affairs in 1979, the commissioner is now instructed to operate as though he or she is a lieutenant-governor and must take the advice of the elected ministers. The commissioner no longer sits on the executive council, which is chaired by the government leader, and the legislative assembly may vote non-confidence in the executive in the same way that a legislature can defeat a government in the provinces. Also like the provinces, Yukon politics is organized through a party system.

The Northwest Territories progressed more slowly than Yukon along the road to responsible government, but today it is not far behind its western neighbour. Its legislative assembly is composed of twenty-four members elected by constituency from across the territory. While political parties have not yet evolved in territorial elections, a large number of current MLAS are active in, and committed to, federal political parties. There was a short-lived attempt before the 1983 election to form a "Northern Party" out of a coalition of Liberal and Progressive Conservative candidates. However, the idea did not receive much support outside of Yellowknife and was ultimately abandoned. While future territorial elections may eventually be fought along party lines, the current divisions in the territorial assembly are factional ones, reflecting regional, ethnic, and urban–rural differences rather than partisan ones.

There is an executive council in the Northwest Territories as in Yukon, which is composed of eight elected members chosen by the legislative assembly. The commissioner of the Northwest Territories was an active member of the executive council until the 1987 election and, in fact, still acted as the chairman of that body until 1986. The chairperson of the executive council today is the government leader, a position established during the Ninth Assembly and clearly designed to evolve ultimately into a "proto-premiership." While, unlike the case of Yukon, there was no magical letter from Ottawa instructing the commissioner of the Northwest Territories to "back off" and let the elected people take the initiative, because of the personality of the commissioner of the time, John Parker, who always supported responsible government, the position of the commissioner in the territory has evolved to a role virtually identical to that of the commissioner of Yukon.

In the absence of a party system in the Northwest Territories, some of the conventions of "Cabinet government" that have evolved are unique in Canada. The system in place, often referred to as "consensus government," sees the selection of the members of the executive council through a wide-open "election at large" within the "caucus" of the assembly. The caucus, in the absence of political parties, includes the entire assembly sitting *in camera* and casting votes as twenty-four independents. This means that the members of the executive council sit there as Independents—there is no collective responsibility and consequently no clear procedure for voting non-confidence in the government. Unless the members of the executive can be held collectively responsible for their actions there can be no responsible government in any conventional sense.

Before 1987 the government leader was selected by caucus from among the eight ministers-elect. However, in an attempt to make the leader more directly responsible to the caucus, and to give him a stronger mandate than his Cabinet colleagues, a new forum was instituted. After the 1987 election, the caucus met and, after several ballots, selected a government leader. Then, in a second round of balloting, the caucus voted in seven additional ministers to complete the Cabinet. The effect has been to give the leader more clout vis-à-vis the ministers and, in fact, a major say in the allocation of portfolios.

While "consensus government" has its critics, and an inside view might indicate that consensus is not always an easy commodity to achieve, even in Cabinet, the current system *is* working. The various regional, ethnic, and urban–rural factions form issue-specific coalitions within the caucus before controversial matters are raised formally in the assembly. As a result, there is a constantly shifting pattern of alliances and subcoalitions within the legislature and within the executive council itself that permit the continuation of the government and the conduct of the legislature's business on an issue-by-issue basis. Moreover, because there is no party discipline, the system in the Northwest Territories is responsive to the "backbench" MLAs to an extent that is unheard of in legislatures elsewhere in Canada.

There are three federal constituencies in the North: Yukon, held by

Audrey McLaughlin (NDP); Western Arctic in the Mackenzie Valley, held by Ethel Blondin (Lib); and Nunatsiaq in the eastern Arctic, held by Jack Anawak (Lib). While the representatives of the Northwest Territories and Yukon are only three out of 295, they have been able to score some points for their constituents from Ottawa's backbenches. Moreover, because both members from the Northwest Territories are native people, they are in a position to speak with some non-partisan authority on both northern and aboriginal issues. Finally, although the Senate is not a particularly dominant institution in the business of government in Canada, it must be noted that Yukon and the Northwest Territories are each represented by a senator, and the one from the Northwest Territories, Willie Adams, is an Inuk, appointed in 1977.

Having reviewed the evolution of the territories toward responsible government and the extent to which the territories are represented in the Parliament of Canada, it is still necessary to point out that in some important respects the relationship of the territories to the federal government remains essentially colonial. Ultimately, we must ask whether it matters if there is responsible government within the Northwest Territories and Yukon if the territorial governments have only limited power vis-à-vis the colonial parent in Ottawa. The issue of primary concern to northerners in the long run, therefore, is that of devolution of authority to the territorial governments and ultimately the achievement of provincial status. The most promising trend in that regard can be seen best, perhaps ironically, in an examination of trends in the territorial bureaucracies.

BUREAUCRACY IN THE TERRITORIES

A dominant if declining bureaucratic force in the Northwest Territories and Yukon to this day is the federal Department of Indian Affairs and Northern Development (DIAND), which functions as a kind of "colonial office" for the North. It is a vast, sprawling organization, sometimes at war with itself when its "Development" mandate collides with its "Indian Affairs" mandate, but with important residual responsibility within the two northern territories.

Until the mid-1960s Carrothers Commission, DIAND was virtually unchallenged in its control over all matters in the Northwest Territories. Some specific functions were performed by branches of several federal departments such as Transport, Health and Welfare, and National Defence, but where "provincial-type" responsibilities had to be carried out, it was Northern Affairs that dominated. Until 1967 there was virtually no territorial bureaucracy at all, for the simple reason that the territorial government was given very little to do. As a result of recommendations of the Carrothers Report, the federal government began a policy of gradual devolution of legislative authority to the territorial council. Naturally this meant that there would have to be an expanded territorial public service to carry out the ordinances of that council, and since then we have seen a fairly rapid growth to the territorial bureaucracy. In Yukon the territorial bureaucracy evolved earlier than in the Northwest Territories. Because there was a significant number of white residents who demanded a level of political control closer to their experience in southern Canada, the federal government was forced to make concessions in the name of the principle of self-government.

By 1981 the territorial assemblies had been delegated responsibility for education, social development, municipal affairs, public works, and the administration of justice. All health services have been transferred in the Northwest Territories, and the devolution of these responsibilities is being negotiated in Yukon. In the economic areas, the territories have been given control over some matters such as tourism, small businesses, and the regulating and licensing of sport fishing and hunting. By 1988 there were agreements signed with both territories that will see the negotiation of a Northern Accord on oil and gas. This Accord will permit the transfer of management responsibilities and royalty revenues to the Northwest Territories and Yukon for oil and gas "on shore" and a sharing of such responsibilities and revenues with the federal government with respect to the offshore.

When outstanding land claims are settled in the two northern territories, the federal government is committed to the devolution of the remaining provincial-type responsibilities. The most important of these are the management of mineral development and Crown lands and the responsibility for Crown prosecutions in the territorial justice systems.

While traditionally the budgets of Yukon and the Northwest Territories were passed as part of DIAND's estimates, as of 1980 the territorial councils submitted their estimates directly to the Treasury Board in Ottawa. Since 1984 there has been in place a system of formula financing whereby the two territories receive multiyear block-funding commitments from the federal government. With this system, the territorial governments can set their own spending priorities according to local needs, and at the same time they can be held directly responsible for the efficient and economical management of their budgets.

Not surprisingly, a concomitant result of the growth of the territorial bureaucracies has been a reduction of the dominance of DIAND. This has been achieved as well by marginal increases in the northern establishments of other federal departments, but the DIAND presence in Whitehorse and Yellowknife has not been significantly decreased in terms of human resources. The rapid growth of the territorial public service and continued presence of the federal government coupled with the fact that white southerners tend to dominate the positions in both the federal and territorial bureaucracies is resulting in a shift in the ratio of whites to natives in both territories. While, particularly in the Northwest Territories, there has been a strong effort to recruit native people, and to provide special employment opportunities through native on-the-job training programs and affirmative action, native people are still seriously under-represented on the government pay rolls in both territories. The realization that they might one day become—or, as in the Yukon, have already become—a minority in their own land has been an important catalyst in the evolution of Indian and Inuit political movements. It is to a consideration of this phenomenon and related issues that we must now address ourselves.

THE NORTH IN THE 1990s: ISSUES AND DILEMMAS

The North has been evolving very slowly over many decades, and while changes have occurred, there was never perceived to be any real rush about dealing with northern issues. Why then, one might well ask, is there any urgency today, and why would this chapter suggest that northern development is going to be a significant item on the agenda for decision making in the remainder of the twentieth century? The answer is simply that, at last, the mainstream Canadian economic and political elites now see a need to develop the resources that for more than a century have been permitted to lie in "cold storage," undiscovered or a least unexploited. The North (and its people), traditionally ignored by southern politicians, has become economically significant to the rest of Canada.

The initial assumption of southern Canadians was that development would be welcomed by the people of the North, who at last were to be given the full benefits of southern industrialized society and all of the luxuries associated with "civilization." When the first development schemes were unwrapped, the objections of a few outspoken northerners were dismissed as the bleatings of a minority of cranks—crackpots who dared to stand in the way of progress. However, the process of the Berger Inquiry clearly brought home the point that the northern natives were very much in agreement in expressing their fears of large-scale development projects. The natives of the North wish to ensure that resource development projects will not destroy their way of life and ultimately wipe out the native culture. The native culture is very fragile when compared to the cultures of complex industrial societies, and in fact the social and economic uniqueness of the native culture rests to a large extent upon the land. If the land and its resources are taken away or destroyed by large-scale development, the culture, the traditional economy, and the way of life of the native people will perish.

While the original position of the northern native groups was that there should be no development until land claims are settled, there are some indications of a softening in that position. All of the major native groups in the North have set up development corporations that are becoming involved directly in resource development projects. As examples, the economic arm of the Committee for Original Peoples' Entitlement (cope), the Inuvialuit Development Corporation, has become involved in ventures with the oil industry in the Beaufort Sea and Mackenzie Delta; the Denendeh Development Corporation has entered a joint drilling venture with Esso Resources in the Norman Wells area; and the Inuit Tapirisat's Nunasi Corporation has established a number of small businesses and has become directly involved in oil and gas exploration and mining enterprises in the eastern Arctic. The people of Fort Good Hope have entered into a long-term joint venture with Chevron that will see oil and gas exploration in their traditional territory in return for an economic share in the benefits. While this heralds a radical departure from the strongly anti-development position of the native groups in the mid-1970s, the efforts to reap some benefits from what they see as inexorable trends has not lessened their commitment to a fair settlement of land claims.

While settlement of land claims is the central issue in northern development for the natives, white northerners have a different axe to grind. The long-range goal of the non-native northerners is for territorial control over land and resources and ultimately provincial status. There are steps in the general direction of provincehood, but the final thrust cannot proceed until it is clear that such a move will not impose inordinate fiscal demands on an already beleaguered economy. Moreover, the terms of the Meech Lake Accord would make it still more difficult to secure the necessary constitutional amendment conferring provincial status when northerners are ready for that step in economic terms.

In the past it has been on the question of provincial status that native and non-native northerners have disagreed fundamentally. The natives fear provincial status if it occurs before the settlement of land claims. In Yukon, the Indians see that they are in a minority situation and that provincial status would put them at the mercy of the territory's white majority. They prefer to negotiate the land claims with the federal government, to put in place constitutionally guaranteed self-government rights, and to secure some kind of political guarantees of native representation in public government institutions before they accede to provincial status. In the Mackenzie Valley, the feelings of the Dene are much the same. The bureaucratization of the northern government and non-renewable resource development projects have led to an influx of southern whites and reduced the native people of the western Northwest Territories to a minority situation. Further development would only accentuate this trend, and provincial status for the Northwest Territories without guarantees of native representation in local institutions would put the Dene in a position where they would be unable to control their own destiny.

As we can see, therefore, there are a great many issues and points of view about the appropriate direction and the timetable for political, constitutional, and economic development in the North. Many of the options seem mutually exclusive, and some, such as the settlement of land claims, may be preconditions for all other development options. Nonetheless, because land claims loom as the central concern for native northerners and the autonomy of the northern territories in the federation is the main focus of non-native interests, each of these bears further elaboration.

LAND CLAIMS

There were originally four aboriginal claims identified in the North: the Inuvialuit claim in the Mackenzie Delta–Beaufort Sea region; the Council for Yukon Indians (CYI) claim in the Yukon Territory; the Dene–Métis claim in the Mackenzie Valley; and the Tungavik Federation of Nunavut (TFN) claim in the eastern Arctic.

The Inuvialuit claim was settled in 1984. The deal that was negotiated between the Committee for Original Peoples' Entitlement (COPE) and the federal government provided the approximately 2,500 people of the region a wide range of benefits in return for extinguishment of their aboriginal claims and titles to the land in their traditional homeland. The Inuvialuit received title to 35,000 square miles of land, 5,000 square miles of which include the subsurface. In addition, the federal government agreed to pay financial compensation of $45 million (1977 dollars) as well as a $10-million Economic Enhancement Fund and a $7.5-million Social Development Fund. The right of the Inuvialuit to continue to hunt, trap, and fish within their traditional territory was protected, and they were guaranteed representation on land and resource management and environmental assessment boards. The Inuvialuit Final Agreement therefore is a *comprehensive* one that deals with a wide range of topics beyond simply the swap of extinguishment of aboriginal title for land and cash.

In 1988 both the CYI and the Dene–Métis concluded agreements-in-principle with federal and territorial governments. The Dene–Métis agreement is similar to the Inuvialuit deal in that the 13,000 native people of the Mackenzie Valley give up their aboriginal claims to the land in return for clear title to land, cash compensation, and a wide range of other guarantees and benefits. The Dene and Métis are to receive 70,000 square miles of land, $500 million (1990 dollars) as compensation, guaranteed wildlife harvesting rights, guaranteed representation on a wide range of renewable resource management regimes, and guaranteed participation in environmental assessment and review processes. While, as with the Inuvialuit, subsurface ownership of land is limited to a small amount near their communities, the Dene–Métis managed to negotiate a special arrangement whereby they will share in resource revenues throughout their traditional territory.

The Dene–Métis agreement-in-principle also leaves open the possibility of negotiating self-government arrangements before the final land claim agreement is completed, although very little detail is provided. The Dene–Métis and the governments are now proceeding to the very complex process of land selection, which is expected to take up to two years to complete. However, with the agreement-in-principle in place, it seems fairly certain the land claim of the people of the Mackenzie Valley will be settled by early in the 1990s.

The CYI agreement-in-principle is somewhat different from either that of the Dene–Métis or the Inuvialuit Final Agreement in a number of respects. Because of the much larger non-native population in Yukon, the 6,500 Yukon Indians will receive only 16,000 square miles of land in their settlement. (This is only two and a half square miles per person as opposed to five square miles for the Dene and almost fourteen miles for the Inuvialuit.) However, the CYI claim provides that 10,000 of the 16,000 square miles will include the subsurface. The CYI financial package is very similar to that provided to the Dene–Métis, including $250 million (1990 dollars) and a resource revenue sharing arrangement. As well, the CYI also have agreed to give up their special income tax exemptions under section 97 of the Indian Act in return for a "buy out" of approximately $24 million. As with the other two claims, the CYI claim provides for a wide range of guarantees of participation on boards and councils with renewable resource management responsibilities, special harvesting rights, and some economic development opportunities.

However, the CYI agreement-in-principle differs from either that of the Dene–Métis or the Inuvialuit in three significant areas. First, the Yukon wide agreement will be supplemented and elaborated by a separate Yukon First Nation Final Agreement to be negotiated with each of the thirteen Yukon bands. These "band-specific" deals will allow for special provisions that apply to bands with needs and preferences that are unique, and at the same time tie all Yukon Indians into the benefits of the overall package.

The second unique feature of the CYI agreement-in-principle is that a self-government agreement is to be negotiated hand in hand with the bands' final land claim agreement. This is very attractive to the Yukon Indian people because as a minority in the territory they want to have their own local institutions protected from political encroachment by public government institutions.

The third and perhaps most important difference between the CYI agreement-in-principle and the other two concluded to date is that the Yukon Indians are not required to completely extinguish their aboriginal title. While they must give up their land-related aboriginal rights to lands that they do not retain, any aboriginal rights, titles, etc. on the 16,000 square miles that they are keeping will be allowed to continue. The Dene–Métis were not able to seek this option because legal opinion was that, as signatories to treaties, they had already extinguished their aboriginal title, and that aboriginal title cannot be re-created once ceded. Because much of the land selection in Yukon has been concluded already, it is expected that up to five of the Yukon bands will have a final agreement by the end of 1989. The rest of the Yukon bands are expected to conclude their final agreements within two years.

The original land claims proposal of the Inuit of the eastern Arctic, entitled *Nunavut*, was presented to the federal government in 1976 by the Inuit Tapirisat of Canada (ITC), the organization that represents all of the Inuit in Canada. While the ITC originally included the Inuvialuit, COPE eventually broke away from ITC and proceeded with its own land claims proposal. The Nunavut proposal demanded approximately 250,000 square miles of the land in the eastern Arctic, along with royalties and compensatory payments for the past use of Inuit lands. The document was received with considerable criticism from the regions of the eastern Arctic because it saw the land claim settlement as ultimately extinguishing aboriginal title and because it did not provide for political and constitutional guarantees of the rights of the Inuit after settlement of the land claims. The result was what amounted to a withdrawal and redrafting of the original proposal.

The position of the Inuit of the Northwest Territories is based on the simple fact that they form a solid majority in the territory above the tree line in the eastern Arctic, which the people themselves refer to as Nunavut. The long-run solution, as the Inuit see it, is simply to secure the division of the current Northwest Territories into two separate territories, with the creation, in the east, of the territory of Nunavut. The ultimate goal is for Nunavut to eventually become a province with all of the rights of other provinces in Confederation, which of course implies the ownership of "Crown lands." The Inuit have considered options such as fixing the franchise for elections in Nunavut to ensure that only people who have resided in the region for a set number of years and who have indicated a long-term commitment to living there may vote. In this way, the Inuit majority would be protected for the foreseeable future, and the potential danger of dilution of the native political presence by the sudden influx of southern whites would be eliminated. While the Inuit are realistic enough to see that they are not yet ready for total economic or constitutional independence, they do feel that the creation of a new territory could be achieved fairly quickly.

The federal response to the division of the Northwest Territories was at the outset rather cautious. The Drury Commission on constitutional development in the Northwest Territories came out in opposition to such a plan, and in the 1970s the territorial government was also cool toward it. However, the territorial assembly voted in late 1980 to approve in principle the proposal for a divided territory. A plebiscite was held in the Northwest Territories in 1982, and a majority of the voters were in favour of division. The Honourable John Munro announced in November 1982 that the federal government was "in favour in principle" of division, but set the following strict conditions on its implementation: (1) land claims must be settled first; (2) a boundary must be agreed upon; (3) there must be continued support for division by the people of the Northwest Territories; and (4) there must be a general agreement on the basic governmental structure, location of the capital, etc., within the new territories.

While research, public hearings, and negotiations between representatives of the western Northwest Territories were pursued over a number of years through the Nunavut Constitutional Forum (NCF) and the Western Constitutional Forum (WFC), the progress toward division still faces the major hurdle of finding consensus on a boundary. The stakes here are high, and neither the people of Nunavut nor the people of the western Northwest Territories are willing to give up the potential resource wealth in the region where the boundary overlaps. Because agreement on a boundary is a condition for any further movement toward division, and because the boundary will likely coincide with the boundary between the Inuit and the Dene–Métis in the land claims, the division issue has to remain on a back burner at least until the two land claims are settled.

The eastern Arctic or TFN claim is still several months away from an agreement-in-principle, but there is steady progress. The parties have agreed on a quantum of land (although it has not been made public) and the financial package will likely be fairly similar to that negotiated in the Dene–Métis and CYI claims. Self-government, while important, will likely be sought more through the division of the territory and less through commodity self-government packages as in the Yukon deal.

CONSTITUTIONAL DEVELOPMENT: THE TERRITORIES AND FEDERALISM

As we enter the 1990s, it is possible to be optimistic about a timely settlement of all outstanding aboriginal claims in the Northwest Territories and Yukon. With the aboriginal rights of northern native people secure and the achievement of certainty over the tenure of lands north of the 60th parallel, the door will be opened to further economic development in the North that will benefit native and non-native northerners alike. Thus, with native rights issues settled, it may well be that the focus of concern in the 1990s will shift more to the constitutional and political relationship between the two (or three) northern territories and the rest of the federation.

While provincehood has to be seen as the ultimate constitutional goal of the northern territories, there are a number of obstacles that must first be overcome before that goal can be realistically approached. Perhaps the first prerequisite for moving to provincehood is the political will to do so among northerners themselves. At the present time, most people in the Northwest Territories and Yukon feel that provincehood is not an urgent concern. They understand that land claims must be settled first, but even when that happens, northerners, both native and non-native, realize there are some very practical concerns, such as a stable fiscal base, that must be addressed as well. It can be argued that the potential for resource revenues in the Northwest Territories and Yukon could ultimately give the northern governments a tax base that would be healthier than that of many of the provinces. Similarly, the question of small populations is not in itself an obstacle to provincial status, although diseconomies of scale, coupled with high transportation costs, make government a more expensive enterprise in per capita terms in the North than in, for instance, Prince Edward Island.

The federal government is committed to a northern development strategy that foresees the transfer of all provincial-type powers to the territorial governments within the next five or six years. This process of devolution is well under way, and with the exception of land management, mineral development, and criminal prosecutions, most provincial-type programs are either already in the hands of the Northwest Territories and Yukon, or are in the process of being transferred.

The territorial government leaders are now permitted to attend the annual Premiers' Conferences as non-voting participants, and in most federal–provincial forums, with the exception of First Ministers' Conferences, territorial ministers and officials participate virtually as equals with provincial and federal colleagues. As the territories gain control of more and more provincial-type programs, they are granted full membership on the intergovernmental bodies that deal with those subjects.

In summary, there are fully equipped governments in place in Yukon and the Northwest Territories, governments that pass laws, deliver services, pay taxes, and in general act much like governments elsewhere in Canada. When the territories feel they are ready for it, the leap to provincehood should be a small one. That the leap isn't small is in part due to recent developments in federal–provincial summitry, most notably the Meech Lake Accord.

The most obvious obstacle to provincehood served up by the Meech Lake Accord is the new requirement for unanimous agreement of the provinces for the admission of new provinces to the federation. This is clearly a break with the practice up until 1982, where the creation of new provinces out of federal territory was a prerogative of the federal Parliament acting alone. All of the provinces admitted after 1867 acquired this new status without the consent of, or even consultation with, the existing partners to the federation.

The rules changed in 1982 with the Constitution Act of that year. Under the amending formula that then came into effect, the creation of new provinces or the extension of provincial boundaries into federal territories required the consent of two-thirds of the provinces. The latter provision was more alarming to the Northwest Territories and Yukon than was the two-thirds rule for provincehood, for it meant essentially that the North could be annexed to the existing provinces without the consent of the people of the territories.

The Meech Lake Accord will change the rules again, by requiring unanimity for either the extension of the provinces northward or for the creation of new provinces. This is good news for Yukon and the Northwest Territories in that annexation by the provinces is more difficult. However, it is bad news in that the goal of provincehood would seem to be almost unattainable. Federal officials have argued that when the time is right for provincehood, the older "members of the club" will not stand in the way of the new applicant. However, the admission of two or three new provinces would upset the regional veto that is in the amending formula through the two-thirds rule. With the existing formula, either the four western provinces or the four Atlantic provinces, acting together, can stop any amendment; with twelve instead of ten provinces, it would take five provinces to kill an amendment. Full provincial status, therefore, may be difficult to obtain for the northern territories when the cost to the existing provinces is a loss or dilution of their constitutional power in the federation.

Possibly northerners could come to understand that the stakes are high for the existing provinces, and that the creation of new provinces *should* only occur if there is unanimous agreement. Northerners are accustomed to having to convince federal and provincial governments that they too have something of value to say and should be listened to. However, the Meech Lake Accord would go further than simply making membership in the federal club more difficult. That pact also provides for regular First Ministers' Conferences that will deal with most of the major national issues of the day, and it is quite clear that the presence of territorial leaders in such meetings is precluded.

The catch-22 argument with respect to keeping territorial leaders out of First Ministers' Conferences is that the northern territories are not provinces. Now, northerners could likely live with an indefinite postponement of provincehood if they were given a voice in the sorts of discussions that occur at First Ministers' Conferences. However, when the Accord that was so carefully and nobly crafted to guarantee a "distinct society" for Canadians in Quebec also discriminates in such a blatant fashion against 80,000 Canadians who happen to live north of the 60th parallel, the high moral impact of the exercise is softened considerably.

Northerners argue that residents of the provinces are doubly represented at First Ministers' Conferences—their special regional interests are voiced by their provincial premiers and their broad pan-Canadian interests are represented by the prime minister. But if the prime minister is tasked with "thinking nationally" in this forum, how can he also respond to the special regional interests of his northern constituents who have only the federal government to speak for them in such august assemblages?

The insults added to the very real injury of exclusion from provincehood and from representation at First Ministers' Conferences are the provisions of the Meech Lake Accord with respect to Senate and Supreme Court appointments. There is no avenue for territorial input into the appointment of the northern senators, even though the provinces will have the power to nominate their senators for federal approval. Similarly, a member of the bar or bench of the Northwest Territories or Yukon can never aspire to the highest judicial office in the country, the Supreme Court of Canada, unless he or she is also the member of a provincial bar and happens to be nominated by that provincial government. It is small wonder that many northerners are beginning to speak of being "second-class citizens" or of being consciously discriminated against simply because of their place of residence.

CONCLUSION

Great strides have been made in the economic and political development of the North. It is unfortunate that the successes are often overshadowed by the imposition of new injustices by successive governments in Ottawa. Often these "warts" that appear on the face of northern development policy are the result of oversight or omission, but all too often they result from clear decisions to sacrifice northern interests to what are perceived to be national ones. The flaw in this process is that equity and justice for all Canadians must itself *be* the national interest.

Certainly the North is important to all Canadians because it is a land of vast potential wealth, not only in terms of natural resources, but also in terms of the cultural and linguistic diversity that has become a hallmark of the Canadian political identity. The manner in which the world and future generations of Canadians judge Canada's worth as a nation may well come to rest upon the manner in which the present generation of political leaders resolves the poignantly human dilemmas of northern development in the last decade of the twentieth century.

FURTHER READINGS

Berger, Thomas R. *Northern Frontier, Northern Homeland.* Vancouver: Douglas and McIntyre, 1988.

Dacks, Gurston. *A Choice of Futures.* Toronto: Methuen, 1981.

Page, Robert. *Northern Development: The Canadian Dilemma.* Toronto: McClelland and Stewart, 1986.

Whittington, Michael S., ed. *The North.* Toronto: University of Toronto Press, 1985.

3

British Columbia: "New Right" Politics and a New Geography

M. Patricia Marchak

British Columbia is unlike the rest of Canada in two significant respects: it is located on the Pacific Rim, and since the early 1980s its provincial government has openly espoused the "new right" ideology. On the first of these, a global shift in fortunes toward the Pacific Basin countries and away from the Atlantic countries in the past decade has given British Columbia a new geopolitical situation. Much of what is occurring, including the growth of a strong "new right" movement, is related to this change.[1]

The "new right" movement has grown throughout the world, and British Columbia is not the exception in being influenced by it; but within Canada the province has been exceptional in the strength of its political commitment to that ideology. With the downturn in economic fortunes in the early 1980s, the Social Credit government adopted a language, political postures, and finally policies that were no longer consistent with the prevailing (small "l") liberal, Keynesian welfare state premises that had dominated Canadian public life since the 1940s.

In 1983 the government introduced legislation to "downsize" the public sector, "restrain" public expenditures, "privatize" public properties, "deregulate" industry, and centralize government decision making. These words had been used first in Britain under the Thatcher government, then in the United States under the Reagan administration, and were also in vogue within libertarian and right-wing political movements throughout Australia and Europe. They were frequently employed in publications of the Fraser Institute, a corporate-funded "think tank" established in British Columbia in the early 1970s. Members of the B.C. government added their own unique flavour to the neo-conservative discourse in such statements as "unemployment insurance creates unemployment," and "welfare for single mothers creates single mothers."[2] The thrust of the legislation and overall policies was to reduce welfare, abandon minimum wage laws and other income securities for labour, decrease funding for public education, and remove restrictions on capital. As well, the B.C. government removed the condition that contractors be union firms for all government-financed construction, thus opening the way for a more general attack on labour unions and wage demands.

The government's own explanation for its "new right" policies was an impending fiscal crisis combined with loss of international competitive capacities because of high labour costs. I will argue that the government's explanation is manifestly inappropriate since there was no fiscal crisis, although there was a depression, and British Columbia's labour costs, while high, were not germane to international competition. I will also argue that while the "new right" ideology, neo-conservative Social Credit personalities, and the activities of the Fraser Institute were important contributors to the policy changes of the early 1980s, the more fundamental cause of change lay in two conditions: first, the impacts on a resource economy of global economic changes centring around the Pacific Rim; and second, the particular nature of a provincial society dependent on resource exports.

To advance this argument, I will first provide a brief historical sketch and a description of contemporary society in British Columbia, then examine the nature of the global changes that are affecting this society and its economy.

HISTORICAL DEVELOPMENT

British Columbia came into Confederation as a frontier society, still embedded in the fur trade and linked to the Hudson's Bay Company. From the beginning, its fortunes were tied to large corporations from central Canada and the United States, first in mining, then in the forest industry. Its specialized economic role throughout its first century was to supply raw materials to more advanced manufacturing regions.[3] For such a society it is appropriate to use the descriptive term "periphery," meaning one that survives on the edges of central, manufacturing economies. Peripheral societies by their nature are especially vulnerable to changes in the demand for their products by central economies because they lack the capacity to generate autonomous economic growth. Typically, such societies are politically weak because governments have less control over their destinies than do the large companies engaged in the export of their resources. A pattern tends to emerge for peripheral political units, characterized by accommodation to the investment interests of external capital; since such economies are dependent on the export of staples, these accommodations over time tend to lock the society into what Watkins has called "a staples trap."[4]

Peripheries are rarely wealthy, but British Columbia, and Canada more generally, are exceptions. Between 1950 and 1980, British Columbia became a wealthy resource region integrated into the continental economy by virtue of its softwood forests and proximity to the enormous

American market. The U.S. market for standard-sized construction lumber, pulp, and newsprint was greater than could be supplied by U.S. forest companies. A tariff-free border for raw and semi-processed goods (but not for end products), together with Canadian hospitality to foreign investment, encouraged American companies, as well as central Canadian companies, to establish subsidiaries in British Columbia to produce these relatively unsophisticated goods for the American market.

All but 5 percent of the forest lands in British Columbia are owned by the provincial government as "Crown lands." As is so elsewhere, the government leases timber-harvesting rights on Crown lands to private companies under various licensing systems. In British Columbia, a stated government preference for large and vertically integrated companies led to high concentration of timber-harvesting rights in the post-war period.[5] By the early 1970s, eight large companies controlled 83 percent of the available timber land.[6] These companies logged the land, then cut the timber at their sawmilling units, and processed both the chips from the sawmills and whole logs in their pulp mills. There were over two thousand independent sawmills in the province in the 1950s, but fewer than three hundred by the 1970s. Very few medium-sized or small manufacturing companies survived, because they could not obtain supplies of timber, and those that had timber-cutting rights were bought out by the large companies.

In return for these leases, the Crown received rents known as "stumpage." But the stumpage rates were low by comparison with those in neighbouring United States. While they were supposed to be based on the market value of timber, there was actually no "free" log market. Logs were cut by divisions of the large integrated companies or by contractors without independent market capacities.[7] The major companies operating under these conditions included only one B.C.-owned firm. The remainder were owned variously by large Canadian resource companies, American companies, or some combination of the two, with some shares owned in Europe and Japan.[8] With cheap resources and tariff-free borders for pulp and lumber, these companies could obtain their raw materials in British Columbia and process as well as market them in the United States. There was no requirement for them to increase the manufactured content in Canada, and the tariff penalty for end products was, in any event, a disincentive to manufacturing in British Columbia. The cheapness of the resource and the generosity of the provincial government provided no incentives for resource conservation, and by 1980 it was apparent that the lush green forests of British Columbia were becoming seriously depleted.

A similar profile could be made of the mining sector, British Columbia's second largest industry. The largest non-resource industry in the province was, and still is, the Alcan aluminum smelter at Kitimat. The provincial government provided both a new townsite and highly favourable terms for the damming of the Nechako River to generate the smelter's essential electricity.

In a province so dominated by resource industries, and with so small a genuine manufacturing sector, it is not surprising that the occupational profile of the society was skewed toward labour in resource and preliminary processing sectors. The resource towns throughout the province were "two class" communities: managers of firms owned elsewhere, and workers. They had relatively small populations engaged independently in business or other occupations. Only on the lower mainland, in Vancouver and Victoria, was there a substantial "middle class" of clerical, skilled, technical, administrative, and professional workers. Employers for this class included the banks, merchant businesses, and regional head offices of resource companies, and most particularly, the public sector: government directly, or the educational, judicial, and social welfare sectors.

Over the post-war period, unions played a dominant role in establishing relatively high wages,[9] especially in the forest, construction, and mining industries. A higher proportion of the labour force was unionized than elsewhere in Canada. In the two immediate post-war decades, the International Woodworkers of America, representing sawmill and logging workers, dominated the labour movement; but by 1970 the public sector workers became organized, and throughout the 1970s their unions gained bargaining power.[10]

Within this polarized socio-economic context, British Columbia's politics had also become polarized. The New Democratic party (NDP) regularly garnered just under 50 percent of the vote in provincial elections, and a coalition of centre and right-wing parties under the banner of the Social Credit Party garnered just over 50 percent. Only for a brief period between 1972 and 1975, when the other parties split their vote, did the NDP form a government. Before and after that period, the Liberal and Conservative parties all but disappeared in British Columbia, their members merging with the Social Credit Party at the provincial level.

During the early 1980s, the provincial forest economy collapsed. The Canadian economy as a whole also went into a recession, but British Columbia's situation was more accurately described as depression. The immediate cause, but not the only one, was high interest rates in the United States, and the consequent drop in housing construction. Another cause was "glutted markets," brought about by the establishment of more lumber and pulp facilities than justified by market demand. The mining economy had collapsed earlier in the 1970s for similar reasons. For a period of three years, the B.C. economy was severely depressed, and while it has since picked up it seems clear that the heady "boom" days are past. Indices of economic health in British Columbia continued through the 1980s to suggest serious problems; for example, the proportion of the population living below the poverty line increased, and unemployment and bankruptcy rates continued to be higher than elsewhere in Canada. Before discussing the political responses to these events, we need to consider the global context for them.

GLOBAL CONTEXT

From the end of the Second World War until the mid-1960s, the United States was the pre-eminent political and economic power in the world. Canada was pulled further into the American orbit during this time, its energy and other resources being essential to the growth of American industries. From the mid-1960s onward, however, American economic power declined relative to the rejuvenated countries of the European Economic Community (Common Market) and to Japan. The world monetary system established in the 1940s began to unravel in the late 1960s, and the gold standard pegged to the value of the American dollar was abandoned by the United States in 1972.

One of the contributing factors in this decline was the growth of "offshore" sourcing by American companies, especially in the garments, automobile, machine parts, and electronics industries, including the chip manufacturers in the computer industry. These companies moved assembly-line operations to South Asia (Taiwan, South Korea, and Singapore most particularly), to Mexico and Central American countries, and to Brazil in order to obtain cheap labour, tax advantages, special "free export" zone locations, and other conditions not available in the advanced industrial countries. Japanese companies also moved many assembly-line operations offshore to nearby Asian countries and to Brazil. Sourcing assembled products from these low-wage areas, these companies "invaded" the American market, undercutting domestic producers (including subsidiaries of the same companies). The domestic producers, unable to compete (often with themselves in another form), began to close plants in the manufacturing heartland of the northeastern United States and to some extent in central Canada; this process became known as "de-industrialization."[11] By the end of the 1970s, major competitors in key industries such as automobiles began establishing joint-venture companies, linking capital from Japan, the United States, and European countries. Some of these companies established "new" firms in de-industrialized North American regions suffering high unemployment.[12] By 1980 more trade was crossing the Pacific than the Atlantic, Japan was the world's chief creditor nation, the United States had created an enormous national debt, and it was clear on all economic indices that the United States was no longer an unchallenged power on the global stage.

In addition to this reorganization of capital, new technologies had come on stream. Integrated circuitry technology radically altered most industrial production systems, and plants had to be retooled and lines restructured. These numerous changes fundamentally altered the way industries operated, the kinds of products they put out, the employment levels, and the locations of plants. In the forest industry there were also changes. Foremost among these was the development of new pulping technologies to utilize hardwoods and fast-growing pines grown in southern climates, and the manufacture of high-grade papers from these new fibre sources.

Two further changes must be noted. In 1973-74, the Organization of Petroleum Exporting Countries (OPEC) successfully challenged American control of Middle Eastern oil supplies. Thereafter, other industrial countries, including Japan and the members of the European Economic Community, gained more control over their own sources of energy. And in the same period, the United States left Vietnam as a "defeated" power; defeated as much by world and domestic public opinion as by guerrilla forces. These events had political as well as economic impacts, and by 1980 the United States had considerably less political and economic power than it had two decades earlier.

BRITISH COLUMBIA IN THE 1980S

These global events impacted on British Columbia in several ways. Resource markets declined as U.S. buyers either reduced purchases or moved elsewhere. Five major U.S. companies sold their holdings in British Columbia. Their reasons included internal financial problems and reorganization of their global production systems. Some had reduced future returns from the B.C. forests because of over cutting and failure to replant. Remaining companies took substantial losses, closed units either temporarily or permanently, laid off workers and, if they could obtain sufficient funds, began to restructure their operations. This restructuring took the form of reducing investments in mass-production facilities and installing computerized, smaller production plants. Gradually it began to take another form as well: increased joint financing with Japanese and Chinese firms, accompanied by market contracts for logs and pulp in the home countries of these Asian investors.

It was in the midst of this depression and restructuring that the re-elected Social Credit government introduced its "new right" policies favouring capital at the expense of labour. Within two months of the 1983 legislation, approximately 37,000 jobs had disappeared, and some 53,000 persons had dropped out of the B.C. labour force. The unemployment rate continued to increase, approaching 16 percent by the spring of 1984. In this context, provincial legislation that reduced social welfare and public sector employment resulted in the further political polarization of B.C.'s population. But mass rallies and demonstrations had little effect, and by the time the economy began to pick up (though it never improved to the extent of the Ontario economy in that same period), permanent reductions in public sector employment and welfare provisions had been put in place. As well, anti-union legislation had affected the construction industry during the building of Expo '86, and unions in that sector as well as in forestry lost bargaining power and membership. When the forest industry, now considerably restructured, began again to show some life, it was with a much reduced labour force.

PACIFIC RIM INVESTMENTS

The "new right" political agenda proved of particular value to Japanese and New Zealand investors in the coal and forestry industries, to Korean and Hong Kong investors in construction and real estate industries, and to the banking, service, and contracting companies linked to these international investors.

The government signed market agreements with Japanese steel manufacturers for coal from the northeastern region, and in anticipation of long-term sales to Japan it had extended the B.C. railway from the northeast some three hundred kilometres to the newly constructed port at Prince Rupert, and invested in the construction of an "instant" townsite called Tumbler Ridge. It did this despite expert advice from engineers and others, who correctly argued that the process of making steel was changing, so that much less coal was required for production; that the particular coal deposits in the Northeast were inferior to those elsewhere (including the southeast of British Columbia, Alberta, and Australia); and that the Japanese marketing contract was "soft" in that it allowed the Japanese to renegotiate both prices and quantities according to global market trends. Since the same Japanese companies had similar contracts elsewhere, they were creating a surplus of coal, the likely outcome of which would be declining prices. By the time Tumbler Ridge was in place, all of these arguments were proven true, and the B.C. government was obliged to subsidize the companies producing coal and to accept a substantial loss on the B.C. rail extension and port.

Japanese investors also moved into the forest industry. Daishowa, in particular, created joint-venture pulp corporations with American companies where the Americans had timber-cutting licences and sawmills. Through these mills, Japanese newsprint manufacturers obtain semi-processed pulp for further manufacturing in Japan, without having to devote capital to long-term reforestation and with relatively small and short-term investments in plant.

Another Pacific Rim investor moved into British Columbia in the mid-1980s: Fletcher-Challenge of New Zealand. This giant forest company first purchased the properties of the exiting Crown Zellerbach, then, in 1987, purchased B.C. Forest Products. These purchases made it the largest forestry firm in the province and provided it with softwoods to complement its already substantial holdings elsewhere of pines and hardwoods.

The major construction projects in British Columbia in the 1980s have been financed or supported by the government: Expo '86, Tumbler Ridge, and the railway extension and Prince Rupert port. Construction workers were not organized during the 1970s into one union like the forestry workers, but a condition for their work was that only unionized contractors could work on publicly financed projects. Among the Social Credit government's early actions was to remove this condition, and much of the construction on these sites in the 1980s was done by non-union labour. Once the unions were undermined in the construction sector, labour both there and elsewhere became vulnerable to declining wages and deteriorating conditions. According to the government, this was essential to make the province "internationally competitive." In fact, these workers were not competing internationally: the projects were specific to British Columbia. But the government expected that a decline in union bargaining power would improve more generally the investment climate in British Columbia, and in particular would bring in investment from the Pacific Rim countries. It was, however, the international political climate that actually had more to do with the increased investments from Asia. For example, Hong Kong money is attracted to Canada for safekeeping while the long-term fate of Britain's former colony is determined. It has moved into real estate, the hotel and tourist industries, and the banking industry.

Economic links with Pacific Rim countries have greatly increased in the 1980s. A quarter of all exports from British Columbia now go to Japan, a third to Pacific Rim countries altogether, and less than a half to the United States. British Columbia accounts for over half of Canada's exports to non-U.S. Pacific Rim markets. Of all Canadian exports from the Pacific ports, nearly 41 percent are destined for Asia, 26 percent of these to Japan, and the proportion is steadily increasing.[13]

Vancouver, with its port and service industries attached to the Pacific trade, has renewed its identity as a frontier city—but now it is the far northeastern frontier, rather than the western one. The Hong Kong interests that purchased Husky Oil in Alberta, headed by international financier Li Ka-shing, took over the ailing Bank of British Columbia during the depression of the early 1980s. In 1988 Li Ka-shing obtained the Expo '86 site, a highly desirable location in the centre of Vancouver. Recent immigration trends are also reinforcing Vancouver's position on the Asian frontier.

THE ARGUMENT

The Social Credit government argued that its "new right" agenda was justified both by the inability of the province to finance its social spending obligations and by the fact that B.C. workers had priced themselves out of international markets. However, *there was no fiscal crisis*, even though there certainly was a substantial economic depression for a period of three years. This was demonstrated by analyses of the provincial budgets by academic economists. Tellingly, overall government expenditures were not reduced. Funds were simply redirected from social targets toward infrastructure for new industries and toward aids for corporate restructuring. Economists also noted that while the provincial coffers were indeed depleted by the loss of taxes and resource rents during these lean years, the treasury was not in immediate danger of suffering a genuine fiscal crisis.[14]

As well, international competition involving wage costs was not a genuine factor in the B.C. case. British Columbia had a unique resource in its softwood forests; that is what made it affluent throughout the post-war period. Its companies, enabled by public policy, depleted much of the forest resource and failed to adequately replant it. In consequence, the long-term future for mass-production wood and pulp products was in doubt. While this certainly had a negative effect on the economy, it was not the result of competition or wage costs. The development of new wood fibres in the Southern Hemisphere affected British Columbia's competitive position in pulp products, but again this was not something that could be altered by an attack on trade unions or workers since it was not related to wage costs.

If B.C. products were competing with similar items produced in lower-wage countries, then high wages would have presented a competitive disadvantage. But British Columbia was not selling finished manufactured products in any quantity, and thus was not competing with low-wage countries in the global marketplace. Further, the evidence is that wages in manufacturing and service industries were on a par with other regions of Canada—it was in the resource sectors and construction trades that wages were high.[15] These wages, common throughout North America, are high compared to those in South Asia and newly industrializing countries, but since British Columbia's manufactured products were sold mainly within Canada, the B.C. wages would not present a handicap in that market.

The often repeated suggestion by Social Credit's opponents, that the government's "new right" agenda was simply a manifestation of a particular ideology held by specific politicians, ignores the economic context of the ideology. To begin with, the Fraser Institute did not emerge accidentally: it, and other institutes like it elsewhere, was very well funded by the major banks, insurance firms, and resource companies resident in the province.[16] Such corporations do not financially support an economic institute without some expectation of returns on their investment. The message of the Fraser Institute has consistently been in favour of corporate "free enterprise" and in opposition to publicly funded welfare programs. Thus, the Fraser Institute provided many of the arguments, and sometimes even the particular texts, enunciated by members of the government.

To explain the attacks on the public sector, welfare recipients, and unions, we need to keep in mind the polarized electorate, the strength of unions in British Columbia, and the occupational profile of the citizenry. Government services, especially those that do not directly enable private investors to increase their wealth and to provide employment, are costs against general revenue. They must be paid for out of taxes, both individual and corporate. When rents from resource companies virtually disappeared from provincial revenues between 1980 and 1984, the taxation base and accumulated savings had to provide the wherewithal for services. But at this precise time, the major economic units were demanding an infusion of public funds to enable them to undertake retooling of their plants, and the Japanese markets for resources were opening up. For companies resident, even if not owned, in British Columbia to claim these markets and retool plants, the government needed to provide the infrastructure. To meet corporate demands, then, the government had to reduce social service demands on limited funds. The claim of fiscal crisis and the frontal attacks on union wages were means of "legitimating" these priorities, rather than genuine explanations.

The timing was important in the sequence of events. The forest economy went into a slump, large American companies exited, and labour was suffering high unemployment. The major forestry union was unable to mount a strong battle in these circumstances; its own membership was falling because unemployed workers sought alternative employment or moved elsewhere. In fact, its membership went from a reported 48,000 to about 32,000 within half a dozen years.[17]

At the same time, the public sector unions were growing in strength. The continuing wage security of public sector workers in 1983 may have been resented by industrial workers experiencing unemployment, and the government may have anticipated that such resentment would diminish the capacity of labour to mount strong opposition. If there was resentment, it failed to surface in that way, since public sector and industrial workers joined in the "B.C. Solidarity" movement against the government. Apart from private sector morale, a major reason for attacking public sector workers was that their job commitments, wage rates, and unionized strengths inhibited the overall changes in welfare, education, and social services that the government proposed. Apart from welfare recipients, those who administered provincial social services had the strongest vested interest in the maintenance of the welfare state.

The attacks on social services had essentially the same underlying cause as similar attacks elsewhere. The welfare state was beneficial to capital as well as labour in the post–Second World War period, when the industrial economies were rapidly expanding. Income securities were possible with the expanding gross national incomes, and were useful in sustaining a stable yet elastic labour supply for expanding industries. With the restructuring of industries, fewer workers were needed. Industry generally has been unwilling to support the unemployed unless there is a continuing need for an elastic labour supply. With a surplus of labour willing to take jobs at reduced wages, the restructured industries are well placed to construct new plants, unimpeded by existing unions, unhindered by welfare state legislation, and unobstructed by a strong public sector.

In summary, then, I have argued that the Social Credit government was influenced by the "new right" movement elsewhere and by the resident "think tank," but that its basic reason for attacking the welfare system, public sector, and unions was the global restructuring of industry. The impacts of this restructuring were felt most immediately in the major resource sectors. The government, responding to external events and international capital in its traditional manner, sought ways of accommodating the changing requirements of global capital through reduced operating costs, reduced union-bargaining capacities, and increased funding for infrastructure.

IDEOLOGY

Having advanced that structural argument, however, I do not wish to imply that ideology plays no role in the restructuring process. As suggested above, the government advanced the "fiscal crisis" explanation by way of assuring the population that its actions were essential. All the buzzwords noted above, and further ones such as "high technology," "productivity," and "new economic reality," were persistently produced in government speeches. Since the 1983 election, a central campaign organizer for the government of that time has openly explained the strategies used to persuade the public that "restraint" was necessary.[18] While it was a profoundly cynical strategy, involving the deliberate creation of the appearance of crisis, it may be that members of the government fully believed the "new right" message. They clearly had some success in persuading the population to accept it, since they were re-elected.

However, we must keep in mind that this was already a polarized electorate. It remains so, as evidenced in the 1988 federal election, where British Columbia elected nineteen New Democrats and twelve Conservatives, with John Turner as the only Liberal—a maverick result in an election elsewhere dominated by Conservatives and Liberals. It seems very likely that as long as British Columbia remains a peripheral resource region, with a small middle class linked largely to government services, the polarization will be maintained. The federal results may indicate a move to the left, especially because Premier Bill Vander Zalm has recently lost popularity, but more likely the next provincial election will be a seesaw again, between the combined forces of "free enterprise" parties and the social democratic left.

Finally, one must ask why British Columbia, of all Canadian regions, moved so far, so fast toward the "new right." To begin with, this can be overstated: B.C. politicians espoused the "new right" rhetoric and intro- duced its program in a heavy-handed way, but the Conservative federal government and several other provincial governments since 1983 have introduced similar programs and made similar statements in somewhat less aggressive language. Even so, it is true that British Columbia was the first to experience the political impacts of global restructuring, and the explanation is embedded in the argument given above. It has a polarized electorate, where each side already saw the other as an implacable foe; it has a relatively small middle class, and much of that class is attached to the public sector; and above all, it was already fully adapted to being a periphery of more central economies. Its governments had accommo- dated international capital in the resource sectors from the beginning, and its entire economy was directed toward the export of raw materials.

Now that British Columbia is becoming the periphery to new, Pacific Rim countries, it may well become even less similar in political behaviour to the rest of Canada. Its ties to the United States are declining, its ties to Japan, China, and New Zealand are increasing, and its politics are likely to reflect that changed geopolitical position.

NOTES

1. This chapter updates and revises an argument earlier presented in "The Rise and Fall of the Peripheral State: The Case of British Columbia," in *Regionalism in Canada*, ed. Robert J. Brym (Toronto: Irwin, 1986), pp. 123–59.
2. See Fraser Institute publications, including Walter E. Block and Michael Walker, eds., *Discrimination, Affirmative Action, and Equal Opportunity* (Vancouver: Fraser Institute, 1982); Herbert G. Grubel, *Free Market Zones: Deregulating Canadian Enterprise* (Vancouver: Fraser Institute, 1983); and regular columns in *The Financial Post* by Michael Walker.
3. See Rennie Warburton and David Coburn, eds., *Workers, Capital, and the State in British Columbia: Selected Papers* (Vancouver:

University of British Columbia Press, 1988), for useful historical studies.

4. Mel Watkins, "A Staples Theory of Economic Growth," *Canadian Journal of Economics and Political Science* 29, no. 2 (May 1963): 141–58; and "A Staples Theory of Capitalist Growth," paper presented at the Three Nations Conference in New Zealand, November 1980. See for political extensions of this argument, Glen Williams, *Not for Export: Toward a Political Economy of Canada's Arrested Industrialization* (Toronto: McClelland and Stewart, 1983).

5. For details on government policies, see Patricia Marchak, *Green Gold: The Forest Industry in British Columbia* (Vancouver: University of British Columbia Press, 1983), Part I.

6. Peter Pearse, Commissioner, *Timber Rights and Forest Policy in British Columbia*, 2 vols., Royal Commission on Forest Resources (Victoria: Queen's Printer, 1976), 1:42.

7. Pearse, *Timber Rights*, 1:298; and Province of British Columbia, *Timber Appraisal: Policies and Procedures for Evaluating Crown Timber in British Columbia*, second report of the Task Force on Crown Timber Disposal (Victoria: Queen's Printer, 1974).

8. The major companies up to the early 1970s were the following: MacMillan Bloedel, dispersed Canadian ownership with Canadian Pacific as the largest single shareholder; Canadian Forest Products, wholly owned by the Bentley and Prentice families resident in British Columbia; B.C. Forest Products, co-owned by Noranda, Mead of Ohio, and Scott Paper of Philadelphia; Weyerhauser, Crown Zellerbach, Columbia Cellulose, and International Paper, all owned by U.S. parents of the same name; Rayonier, owned by U.S. parent International Telephone and Telegraph; and Northwood, owned by Noranda. As this list demonstrates, only the privately owned Canadian Forest Products was under the control of B.C. residents.

9. For discussion, see Laurence Copithorne, "Natural Resources and Regional Disparities: A Skeptical View," *Canadian Public Policy* 5, no. 2 (1979):181–94.

10. Details are given in Marchak, "The Rise and Fall of the Peripheral State," pp. 123–59.

11. See Barry Bluestone and Bennett Harrison, *The Deindustrialization of America* (New York: Basic Books, 1982); also Robert B. Reich, *The Next American Frontier* (New York: Penguin, 1983); and for corresponding analyses in Britain, see Bill Jordan, *Mass Unemployment and the Future of Britain* (Oxford: Basil Blackwell, 1982).

12. For data on employment and investment trends, see especially Samuel Bowles, David Gordon, and Herbert Gintis, *Beyond The Wasteland* (New York: Doubleday, 1983).

13. Peter N. Nemetz, ed., *The Pacific Rim: Investment, Development and*

Trade (Vancouver: University of British Columbia Press, 1987), Table 1.15a.

14. The budgets and programs were scrutinized by a team of economists at the University of British Columbia in publications distributed by the B.C. Economic Policy Institute, including: Robert C. Allen, "Investment and Education in British Columbia: A Review of the Evidence in Restraint and Recovery," No. 84-4 (1984); Jonathan R. Kesselman, "Revenue Sources for Maintaining Social Services in B.C.," No. 84-1 (1984); Angela Redish, "Is There a Social Policy in British Columbia?" No. 84-7 (1984); Gideon Rosenbluth and William Schworm, "British Columbia's Budgets and the Need for Restraint," No. 84-08 (1984); and William Schworm, "Economic Impact of the British Columbia 'Restraint' Budget," No. 84-09 (1984).

15. For discussion, see Robert C. Allen, "The B.C. Economy: Past, Present, Future," B.C. Economic Policy Institute Paper No. 85-7 (Vancouver: UBC Department of Economics, 1985); also Robert C. Allen "Trade Unions and the B.C. Economy," Institute Paper No. 85-04 (1985); and Statistics Canada, *Average Weekly Earnings*, Cat. No. 72–002.

16. Details of funding and a complete list of contributors are published in Cliff Stainsby and John Malcolmson, "The Fraser Institute, the Government and a Corporate Free Lunch," report prepared for the Solidarity Coalition, 1983; see also annual reports of the Fraser Institute.

17. International Woodworkers of America, *Layoff Survey* (November 1982); and Ministry of Labour, *B.C. Labour Directory* (annual).

18. Patrick Kinsella, in a speech to the Simon Fraser University Student Marketing Association, 28 November, as cited in the *Sun* (Vancouver), 29 November 1984.

FURTHER READINGS

Allen, Robert C. "Investment and Education in British Columbia: A Review of the Evidence in Restraint and Recovery." Vancouver: B.C. Economic Policy Institute, University of British Columbia, Paper No. 84-4, 1984.

———. "The B.C. Economy: Past, Present, Future." Vancouver: B.C. Economic Policy Institute, University of British Columbia, Paper No. 85-7, 1985.

Drushka, Ken. *Stumped: The Forest Industry in Transition.* Vancouver: Douglas and McIntyre, 1985.

Kesselman, Jonathan R. "Revenue Sources for Maintaining Social Services in B.C." Vancouver: B.C. Economic Policy Institute, University of British Columbia, Paper No. 84-1, 1984.

Marchak, Patricia. *Green Gold: The Forest Industry in British Columbia.* Vancouver: University of British Columbia Press, 1983.

———. "The Rise and Fall of the Peripheral State: The Case of British Columbia." In *Regionalism in Canada*, ed. Robert J. Brym. Toronto: Irwin, 1986.

Nemetz, Peter N., ed. *The Pacific Rim: Investment, Development and Trade*. Vancouver: University of British Columbia Press, 1987.

Redish, Angela. "Is There a Social Policy in British Columbia?" Vancouver: B.C. Economic Policy Institute, University of British Columbia, Paper No. 84-7, 1984.

Rosenbluth, Gideon, and William Schworm. "British Columbia's Budgets and the Need for Restraint." Vancouver: B.C. Economic Policy Institute, University of British Columbia, Paper No. 84-08, 1984.

Stainsby, Cliff, and John Malcolmson. "The Fraser Institute, the Government and a Corporate Free Lunch." Report prepared for the Solidarity Coalition, 1983.

Warburton, Rennie, and David Coburn, eds. *Workers, Capital, and the State in British Columbia: Selected Readings*. Vancouver: University of British Columbia Press, 1988.

4

The Prairie Provinces

Roger Gibbins

One of the most striking characteristics of regional politics is to be found in the deeply embedded memories that Canadian voters bring to contemporary political events. Such memories provide a powerful lens or prism through which individuals view and assess both their present condition and their future options. In this sense, Canadians are a historical people at heart, shaped as much by our past as by our visions of the future. Poised on the edge of the twenty-first century, we seek political direction and landmarks by glancing back over our shoulders at a road travelled time and time again in our collective memories.

Admittedly, this observation may seem self-evident in many regions of the country. In Quebec, for example, even licence plates carry the evocative phrase "Je me souviens," and thus as commuters work their way slowly through the freeway system of Montreal, they encounter a gentle reminder to cast their thoughts back to the Conquest, back to the early historical roots of the contemporary Québécois society and provincial state. The old saying in Prince Edward Island, that you are an outsider unless you can show people your grandmother's grave on the island, speaks to a deeply rooted historical sense of place. In the urban heartland of southern Ontario, students at the University of Toronto are surrounded by an architecture and a nomenclature evocative of the nineteenth century when Upper Canada was settled by the United Empire Loyalists.

Initially, however, it might seem that such a historical, rear-view vision would be less evident on the Canadian prairies, where non-aboriginal settlement has much shallower roots. Certainly a sense of history is not evoked by standing next to the wave pool in West Edmonton Mall, or by gazing up at the freshly uncrated skyline of Calgary, or by strolling through Winnipeg's newly refurbished city centre. If anything, the new urban face of the prairie West appears to reflect a popular culture that underscores the innovative and the new, that stresses boosterism and economic growth rather than tradition or reverence for the past. And, yet, I would argue that, as western Canadians on the prairies turn to face the 1990s and beyond, their *political* perspectives are firmly rooted in the past. There is a rich, regional mythology that infuses itself into every nook and cranny of prairie political life, a mythology that is used as much to explain the present and predict the future as it is to account for the past.

This regional mythology of political discontent is best captured by the phrase "western alienation," a term that expresses a sense of political, economic, and cultural estrangement from the Canadian heartland.[1] In essence, western alienation serves as a historical shorthand for the interlocking themes that western Canada has always been outgunned in national politics, and that *as a consequence* western Canadians have been subjected to varying degrees of economic exploitation by central Canada.

To assert the importance of western alienation for an understanding of political life on the Canadian prairies is not to endorse the tenets of the creed in their entirety. The point to be stressed is not that the mythology accurately captures the political and economic relationship between the prairies and the Canadian heartland (although in many respects it does), but rather that the mythology must be captured, examined, and savoured if one is to understand the contemporary contours of political life on the prairies. Thus, as we look forward in this chapter to the 1990s, we must begin by looking back to the economic and political evolution of the prairies. It is against the historical backdrop of the prairie West, albeit a backdrop necessarily painted here in sweeping strokes with little attention to detail, that the political present and future begin to take on form and substance. For a region now bound together more by collective memories than by geography, we must start in the past.

LOOKING BACK

When the settlement of the prairie West began in earnest around the turn of the century, the past counted not at all and geography was everything; the sweep of the prairie landscape and the richness of the prairie soil bound together a region being settled by Canadians pushing west from Ontario and eastern Canada, by Americans and expatriate Canadians coming up from the south, and by a kaleidoscopic array of ethnic groups drawn from across Western and Eastern Europe. The common geography not only set the prairie region apart from British Columbia to the west and from the Canadian Shield to the east; it also underlay a distinctive regional economy that led in turn to a common set of political grievances, and thus to the common political mythology embraced by the phrase "western alienation." The prairie grain economy was the crucible within which a distinctive political style was forged, a style that both knit the region together and set it apart from the rest of Canada.

In the early decades of the twentieth century, wheat was both king on the Canadian prairies and a mainstay of the national economy:

As the annual wheat crop moved from the western farm to the loading ports of the East, it served to justify an expensive system of transcontinental railroads, while the proceeds of its sale enabled the farmer in the West both to buy eastern manufacturers, which in turn became the westbound traffic on the railroads, and to pay for the financial services offered him by banks, grain traders, and mortgage companies. Almost the whole Canadian economy was vitally affected by, and organized around, the movement of the annual grain crop into world markets.[2]

With the introduction of new strains of wheat that would thrive in the relatively harsh environment of the Canadian prairies, with the completion of a transcontinental railway north of the 49th parallel, the closing of free land in the American West, and the easing of a world-wide economic depression, immigration began to pour into the Canadian prairies. Wheat production and grain exports, primarily to European markets, increased dramatically. Within the prairie economy, the dominance of grain farmers was unquestioned; over half the work force was employed directly in agriculture, while most other incomes on the prairies were heavily dependent upon agriculture, and more specifically upon the price of wheat. Thus, the wheat economy bound the prairie provinces into a single economic unit within which individuals shared the same interests and faced the same problems; it supported a distinctive "regional way of life"[3] that extended naturally to the political arena.

One of the outstanding characteristics of the early wheat economy was its dependency on markets external to the region, and largely external to Canada. While the prairie combination of a staples economy coupled with a sparse population was not all that unique to the Canadian experience, market dependency on a one-crop economy was more acute and the resultant economic instability more pronounced than elsewhere in Canada. Certainly the national economy was more diversified, enjoyed a proportionately larger domestic market, and was placed less at risk by the vagaries of the Canadian climate. As a consequence, market-induced swings in the national economy tended to be less-pronounced, and thus to have less political impact, than did such swings in the regional economy. On the prairies, however, boom-and-bust conditions prevailed; when the demand for western Canadian products was strong, when prices were high and the climate favourable, the region prospered, but when demand faltered, when prices fell and the climate turned, the region suffered. In the words of Ogden Nash, "When times were good, they were very, very good, and when times were bad, they were awful."

There is no question that the roller-coaster nature of the prairie economy destabilized political life in the region. In large part, this happened because the host of economic problems that afflicted prairie grain producers—freight rates on grain going out of the region and consumer goods coming in, tariffs on imported agricultural implements, transportation bottlenecks, inequities in the weighing and grading of grain, the massive debt load typical of pioneer societies, fixed interest rates that could not accommodate the variable nature of the grain economy, monopolistic grain exchanges that siphoned off profits, and so on— were seen to have a political explanation, and thus, potentially, a political cure. Simply put, the argument was that western Canadians were outnumbered in national parliamentary institutions, that a combination of party finances drawn almost exclusively from the central Canadian business community, tight party discipline, an enfeebled Senate, secrecy in both Cabinet and caucus, and the legislative majorities generated by the Ontario and Quebec electorates all prevented the effective representation of western Canadian interests in Ottawa.

In somewhat more analytical terms, western Canadians have argued that the national political process exacerbates rather than alleviates regional problems. The central difficulty lies less with any deliberate attempt by the national community to frustrate the interests and ambitions of western Canadians (although at times such intent has been manifest) than with an inherently flawed set of political institutions. By their very design, parliamentary institutions are majoritarian in character and operation. As a consequence, they inhibit rather than facilitate the effective representation of the less-populated regions; they yield policies that are not as sensitive to regional interests as they might be, policies that are not truly national at all. Thus, Sir John A. Macdonald's "National Policy" of tariff protection for central Canadian manufacturing interests became an enduring symbol of regional political impotence. From a prairie perspective, the tariffs and discriminatory freight rates of the National Policy imposed an unconscionable financial burden on western grain producers, who were being forced to buy the necessities of life on the protected domestic market while selling their crops on open international markets.

Western Canadians, therefore, agreed that parliamentary institutions were part of the problem faced by the West rather than the means through which solutions could be found. However, beyond this basic consensus on the nature of the problem, there was very little agreement on the appropriate cure. In the search for the holy grail of an effective regional voice in national political affairs, the political knights of western Canada rode off in all directions, pursuing at different times and in different provinces quite divergent and even contradictory cures. A surprising number were content simply to support the Conservatives when the Liberals were in power, and the Liberals when the Conservatives were in power. Some created new, regionally based protest parties such as the Progressives, Social Credit, the Co-operative Commonwealth Federation, and the Western Canada Concept, the corpses of which litter the politico-historical landscape of the prairies. Others tried, with very little success, to weaken party discipline through such devices as the recall of sitting members, referendums, and direct legislative initiatives from the electorate. Some, such as supporters of the Nonpartisan League and Alberta advocates of group government, sought the abolition of parties altogether. Others, including many contemporary champions of Senate reform, gazed with envy at American congressional institutions or looked farther afield to elected upper houses in Europe and Australia. In what might be termed the "Quebec Strategy," many tried to shore up and increase the powers of provincial governments, even though provincial governments in the West would never have the leverage on national economic policy that Quebec governments were able to secure on cultural and linguistic policies. Still others, although never more than a few in number, contemplated political independence for the West, a notion that was generously, if somewhat presumptuously, extended to embrace British Columbia, Yukon, and the Northwest Territories.

The point to stress is that no consensus prevailed as to the appropriate political cure for the political problems, and thus to the economic problems, facing the prairie West. As a consequence, decades of political protest and often quite radical political experimentation left little permanent mark on Canadian parliamentary institutions and did little to change the underlying dynamics of the prairie economy. When John Diefenbaker swept the prairie West into the Progressive Conservative fold in 1958, and thus brought to an end a tumultuous period of political challenge and discontent, western Canadians had not succeeded in transforming the political face of Canada. Furthermore, it appeared that any prospect of their being able to do so in the future was fading rapidly as the prairie provinces seemed to slide toward the margins of Canadian political and economic life. The lasting scars of the Great Depression, altered patterns of post-war immigration that all but bypassed the prairies in favour of Toronto, Montreal, and Vancouver, a farm population that was shrinking rapidly in the face of mechanization, and an expanding national economy in which agriculture was playing a progressively diminishing role all testified to the marginalization of the prairie West. The new symbols of Canada were not to be found in the grain elevators and rows of combines etched against the prairie sky, but rather in the urban, industrial landscapes of central Canada.

THE NEW WEST

After an extended period of regional quiescence during the late 1950s and 1960s, a period when national political attention was focused almost exclusively on events taking place in Quebec, the prairies swept again onto the national stage during the early 1970s. The "New West" had arrived, garbed no longer in the regalia of the grain economy, but now sporting an upbeat and up-market wardrobe purchased with rapidly increasing, if OPEC-induced, natural resource wealth. While the prairie

West certainly did not displace Quebec from the centre of the political stage, a resurgence and buoyant regional economy made western Canadians leading players.

The "New West" differed from the older, agrarian West in a number of important ways. The population base of the region had stabilized after four decades of relative decline,[4] and there were even signs of a significant westward shift in the national population as Canadians elsewhere began to eye a rapidly expanding natural resource pie in the West. While agriculture still played a very important role in the regional economy, most western Canadians now lived in rapidly expanding urban environments that differed only at the margins from similar communities across Canada. In their work and social lives, relatively few western Canadians were still touched by the rural landscape. The new western Canadians were aggressively urban, white-collar, technocratic, and contemporary; although nostalgia for the rural West lingered on in wine bars, ski resorts, and country-and-western nightclubs, the West no longer stood apart as a distinctive regional community. At the same time, however, the region had not shed its dependency on both external markets and national economic policies. Although both agriculture and the economic base of the prairies more broadly defined were much more diversified than in the past, and even though much of the New West's wealth was generated beneath, rather than from, the prairie soil, the dependency on unstable world markets continued.

The most dramatic illustration of this underlying continuity comes from the history of Alberta over the past two decades. In the early 1970s, both individuals and corporate capital poured into Alberta as OPEC-led increases in the price of oil touched off an economic boom. While the boom was most explosive in Calgary and Edmonton, it was also felt across the province, and indeed across the region, as world markets improved for a wide range of western Canadian resources including coal, natural gas, grains, potash, and uranium. Then, in the early 1980s, softening export markets coupled with the impact of the National Energy Program (NEP) led to a crippling recession, and by the thousands people began leaving the province rather than moving in. After a brief recovery from 1983 through 1985, the economy sagged again as the world price for oil all but collapsed. In the late 1980s, reasonably strong oil and natural gas markets, albeit combined with depressed prices, produced an economic environment that was relatively stable yet far from expansive. While Alberta and the prairie region today are far from destitute, and while the long-term market prospects for western resources, apart from grain, look reasonably bright, the economic mood of the region remains much more subdued than it was during the heydays of the New West.

Economic dependency was not the only thread that linked the "new" West to the old, for continuity also came through ongoing themes of

western alienation. Western Canadians continued to see economic prosperity as the product of their own sweat and blood (helped out, of course,
by the region's natural resource bounty), whereas economic adversity was
seen as the result of external interference. More specifically, they were
quick to blame federal government action or inaction as the immediate
cause of any economic hardship faced by the region, and in the federal–
provincial disputes over the pricing and taxation of energy resources that
dragged on through the 1970s and early 1980s, Ottawa co-operated in this
exercise by providing ample raw material with which disenchanted
western Canadians could work. Certainly the Liberal government's introduction of the National Energy Program in the fall of 1980 provided a
graphic symbol of national policies designed to expropriate western
wealth, and of national policies reflecting the weakness of parliamentary
institutions in providing effective regional representation and protection.
In the minds of western Canadians, and particularly of Albertans, it was
no coincidence that the NEP followed directly on the heels of the 1980
defeat of the Progressive Conservative government and its replacement
by a Liberal government with only two prairie MPs, both elected from
Manitoba. Albertans still talk heatedly and bitterly of the $50 billion (or is
it $100 billion?) that the province lost as a result of the NEP and its cap on
the price of oil. There is little question that the NEP, although now
dismantled, will live on into the indefinite future as a symbol of western
discontent, playing the same role in the years ahead that freight rates and
the Canadian Pacific Railway played in the past.

Here it should be noted, however, that the implementation of the NEP
coincided with the collapse of continental and world oil markets. While
the NEP did not cause the market collapse, there is little doubt that the
federal program exacerbated the impact of the collapse on the energy
industry in western Canada. At the very least, the entanglement between
the two made it all but impossible for western Canadians to separate the
effects of the NEP *per se* from independent market effects. In most cases,
people gave up or could not be bothered to make the effort in the first
place; the economic collapse of the early 1980s was simply attributed to
the NEP, and thus to the Liberal federal government of the day. It was a
convenient explanation that fit well with the political mythology of
western Canada, if less well with the economic realities of the day.

Unfortunately, the NEP also coincided with the intensive intergovernmental negotiations leading up to the Constitution Act, 1982. Although
the Quebec-induced national unity crisis of the late 1970s and early 1980s
had potentially opened up the constitutional and institutional framework
of the Canadian federal state to substantial reform, western Canadians
were unable to exploit the opening. Against the backdrop of the NEP, and
what was widely perceived as a central government and central Canadian
raid on the region's natural resource wealth, western premiers went into

the constitutional negotiations in a defensive posture. From this perspective, they were successful; the Constitution Act did marginally strengthen provincial ownership and control of natural resources, and the Act's new amending formula closely reflected the constitutional aspirations of the western premiers. At the same time, however, the underlying and ongoing institutional sources of western Canadian discontent were not addressed by the Act; parliamentary institutions were not reformed so as to provide more effective forums for regional representation. Executive federalism was still the first line of regional defence as provincial governments remained the primary conduit for the flow of regional interests into the national political process, and as provincial premiers rather than MPs or senators remained the champions of regional interests on the national stage. While this outcome had considerable appeal for provincial governments in the West, it did not address the estrangement many individual western Canadians felt with the national government and the national political process.

Constitutional politics during the heydays of the New West highlighted the role that regional opposition to bilingualism, and to Quebec's growing power and influence more broadly defined, was coming to have within the complex set of emotions and values encapsulated by the term "western alienation." From the outset, bilingual and bicultural conceptions of Canada had never enjoyed a very receptive audience in the unilingual and multicultural environment of the prairies, where francophones were seen as simply one of many ethnic groups having to adjust to a linguistic milieu in which English was, and would always be, the dominant language. However, beyond this historically rooted unease with bilingualism there was also increased resentment of Quebec's growing influence in national political life. Given the country's preoccupation with Quebec-based problems of national unity, there was concern that the economic problems faced by western Canadians were being overlooked and, indeed, that sound economic management had been subordinated to cultural considerations centred on Quebec. There was also a fear that the bilingual version of Canada championed by national political elites was one in which western Canadians would necessarily be marginalized, that the aspirations of western Canadians to play a larger role in Canadian life were at odds with a bilingual vision of the country. In a world in which elites would have to function effectively in both official languages, people brought up in the unilingual prairies would be at a distinct disadvantage.

During this period, the raw emotions of political partisanship reinforced other elements of western alienation. Since 1958, when John Diefenbaker ended a long Tory drought on the prairies, western Canadians had remained in the Conservative camp regardless of party fortunes outside the region. Throughout the Liberal administrations of Lester

Pearson (1963–68) and Pierre Trudeau (1968–84), prairie voters were faithful to the Tory cause, or when they strayed, it was to suitors of the New Democratic Party. As a consequence, prairie MPS were overwhelmingly on the opposition side of the House as the Liberals dominated the federal election scene in Quebec and, to a somewhat lesser extent, Ontario. Thus, regional antagonism toward the national government stemmed not only from policies that Ottawa did or did not pursue, but also from the fact that, with the exception of nine months in 1979, the national government was Liberal while the prairie electorate was resolutely, even grimly, Conservative. For their part, Liberal governments lacked elected representatives who could both enhance the regional sensitivity of national policies and explain national policies to the regional electorate. For the most part, prairie voters saw the national government and national policies through the hostile eyes of opposition MPS and provincial premiers.

It is for these reasons that the 1984 election, in which thirty-nine of the forty-nine prairie MPS ended up on the government side of the House, set up such an important test for parliamentary institutions. For the first time in a long time, western Canadians faced a national government in which their region enjoyed plentiful representation, and in which western Conservative MPS such as Joe Clark, Jake Epp, Ray Hnatyshyn, and Don Mazankowski controlled many of the key command posts. Thus, prairie voters would be able to see how well parliamentary institutions worked in the best of times, rather than in the worst of times under the Liberal governments of Pierre Trudeau. Perhaps, it was argued, Canada's federal institutions were not inherently flawed, and that given the right party and the right leader, they could indeed deliver national policies and programs that could be sold in the West. Certainly this had been the Conservatives' constitutional message during the late 1970s and early 1980s, and the hypothesis could now be put to the test.

THE PRAIRIE WEST AND THE EARLY MULRONEY YEARS

Although western expectations were initially very high, the new Mulroney government appeared to be up to the challenge. Strong regional support was evident for the ideological tenor of Conservative economic policy, and the government moved, albeit slowly, toward greater privatization and deregulation. The Western Energy Accord completed the dismantling of the NEP, and natural gas sales to the United States were deregulated. Through the Western Grain Stabilization Fund and a variety of special measures, $10 billion was spent over the first four years of the Mulroney government to protect farmers facing drought, falling world grain prices, and a crushing debt load.[5] In August 1987, Ottawa established the Western Diversification Office (WDO), and the minister responsible, William McKnight, promised funding of $1.2 billion over the next five years to help diversify the western economy. Despite some question whether this was new money or repackaged old money, the WDO was well received in the West. By mid-October 1988, the federal government had pumped $121.6 million into almost five hundred diversification projects in the three prairie provinces, with another $149 million having been committed to systematic projects of potential benefit to more than one of the four western provinces.

Admittedly, not all of the economic news was good. Oil prices remained low, and although the demand for natural gas was strong, prices were not high. The long-term agricultural outlook remained bleak as many of Canada's traditional wheat markets had become net exporters, and as it became apparent that there would be no early end to the agricultural subsidy war being waged between the United States and the European Economic Community. It was also apparent that the centre of economic growth was again to be found in central Canada, and that national monetary policies designed to dampen growth in Ontario were hurting agricultural and resource industries in the West. On balance, however, the first four years of the Mulroney administration were good years for the prairie West. At the very least, the problems that did emerge in the wake of drought, weak grain markets, and falling oil prices were not worsened by actions taken, or not taken, by the federal government.

Of course, the economic centrepiece of the Mulroney government was the free trade agreement (FTA) with the United States. Here the government also enjoyed substantial support across the prairie West, although in this case support was more pronounced in Alberta than elsewhere. (The wheat pools in Saskatchewan and Manitoba expressed concern about the threat the FTA might pose to Canada's agricultural supply-management program.) An Environics poll taken shortly before the November 1988 election showed that 40 percent of western Canadians (including British Columbians) supported the FTA while 48 percent opposed it, a regional split that was very close to the total national sample in which 39 percent of Canadians supported the FTA and 51 percent opposed it. In Alberta, support for the FTA climbed to 56 percent, the highest in the country.[6]

It is interesting to note, however, that western Canadian support for free trade is built upon a much broader foundation than mere economic self-interest. Indeed, the FTA is likely to have a marginal impact at best on a prairie economy largely driven by domestic and world demand for natural resources, demand that will not be significantly affected by free trade.[7] Free trade may even exacerbate the locational problems faced by prairie industries, located as they are on the very margins of the continental economy, thousands of kilometres away from major markets. Nevertheless, support for the FTA has become entangled with some of the important threads of western alienation, including the institutional critique discussed above. There is no question, for example, that support comes in part from a regional mythology, dating back to the early days of prairie settlement, which maintains that tariffs of the National Policy imposed a particularly onerous burden on western Canada, and that the benefits of the tariffs accrued largely to central Canadian business interests. (This mythology seemed to be confirmed when the government of Ontario opposed the FTA.) *Ipso facto*, any agreement that would reduce tariffs "must" be good for the West.

In Alberta, support for the FTA was also tied to the legacy of the National Energy Program. In a Calgary speech to the Canadian Petroleum Association and the Independent Petroleum Association of Canada, Treasury Board President Patricia Carney was very explicit in drawing this linkage:

> Critics say the problem with the free trade agreement is that under its terms Canada can never impose another National Energy Program on the country. The critics are right. That was our objective in these negotiations.[8]

In a speech to the annual convention of the Alberta Progressive Conservative Party, Premier Don Getty developed the same theme, arguing that the FTA would ensure that "no one is ever going to shove anything down Alberta's throat again."[9] In short, the FTA was good for Alberta because it would restrict Canadian sovereignty by tying the hands of the federal government. In the future, Washington and the marketplace would provide the political protection from central Canada, and from the government of Canada, that parliamentary institutions had failed to provide in the past.

At least, then, on the economic front, the Mulroney government seemed to pass the test set up by the 1984 election; national institutions did appear to work given the right partisan conditions. And yet, here we encounter a major irony, in that sound economic management did not result in solid western Canadian support for the incumbent Conservative government. Western alienation did not disappear, but instead flared up in potentially virulent forms. In the 1988 election, the Progressive Conservatives lost ground on the prairies, dropping from thirty-nine of forty-nine seats (79.6 percent) in 1984 to thirty-six of fifty-four seats (66.7 percent) in 1988. While the long-standing Tory monopoly in Alberta remained virtually unscathed, with twenty-five of twenty-six Conservative candidates being elected, only four of fourteen Conservative candidates were elected in Saskatchewan, and only seven of fourteen in Manitoba. Perhaps more important, the new Reform Party of Canada fought an energetic campaign across the West. Reform candidates, led by Preston Manning, provided an often articulate expression of both traditional western grievances, including opposition to any expansion of official bilingualism, and more contemporary concerns, including opposition to the Meech Lake Accord and support for Senate reform. Although the Reform Party had some difficulty getting its concerns onto a campaign agenda dominated by debate over the FTA, which the party endorsed, and although no Reform candidates were elected in the 1988 campaign. The party nevertheless left a significant mark on the political landscape of the prairies. In Alberta, where the party fought its most energetic campaign, Reform candidates picked up 15.3 percent of the popular vote and finished second in nine of the province's twenty-six constituencies. And in a March 1989 by-election, Deborah Grey, representing Alberta's Beaver River riding, became the first member of the Reform Party to win election to the House of Commons. If nothing else, the Reform Party demonstrated that the ghost of western alienation had not been laid to rest by four years of Conservative government in Ottawa.

LOOKING AHEAD

The resiliency of western alienation in the wake of the 1984 election, and the western Canadian outcome in the 1988 election, may be puzzling to many Canadians living outside the prairie region. Given that both economic prosperity during the late 1970s and seemingly effective regional representation within the national government during the mid-1980s coincided with widespread alienation, one might well ask whether western Canadians will ever be satisfied. Or will western alienation continue as background noise, as static in the Canadian political system, regardless of the region's economic and political fortunes?

In deciding whether western Canadians are habitual malcontents beyond even the pale of institutional reform, it is important to note another important change that occurred with the 1984 election, and which was reinforced to a degree by the 1988 results. In the 1979 and 1980 clashes between the Liberal Party, led by Pierre Trudeau, and the Progressive Conservative Party, led by Joe Clark, prairie voters formed the Conservative heartland. More important, there was no Quebec counterpart or counterweight to Conservative strength in the West. In the 1979 election, which produced a minority Conservative government, 27.9 percent of the Conservative seats came from the prairie provinces while less than 2 percent (two seats) came from Quebec. In the 1980 election, which produced a majority Liberal government, 32 percent of the Conservative seats came from the prairies while less than 1 percent (a single seat) came from Quebec. Thus, the Progressive Conservative Party had a distinctively western Canadian flavour, with no offsetting aromatic contribution from Quebec.

This situation changed rather dramatically in 1984 with Brian Mulroney's landslide victory. The prairie contribution to the Conservative caucus in the House of Commons fell to 18.5 percent while Quebec's jumped to 27.5 percent. In the 1988 election, the proportion of Conservative MPS elected from the prairies increased marginally to 21.4 percent, but the proportion from Quebec increased even more, to 37.5 percent. In the wake of the 1988 election, Conservative MPS from Quebec outnumber those from the prairie West by a margin of almost two to one; Conservative MPS from "central Canada" more broadly defined outnumber prairie Conservative MPS by a margin of three to one. Clearly and inevitably, the centre of gravity for the Progressive Conservatives shifted eastward as the party moved from opposition to government. In the process, western Canadians gained a government, but lost a party. Prior to the Mulroney years, and dating back to the leadership of John Diefenbaker, prairie voters had been able to use the Conservative Party as a regional vehicle of political discontent. Admittedly, it was not an ideal vehicle, given that Conservative MPS habitually found themselves on the opposition side of the House, but at least it was a homegrown, regionalized vehicle that reflected western Canadian political visions. However, since Mr. Mulroney's accession to the Tory throne, the Conservative Party has been nationalized in terms of both policy outlook and electoral support.

This change in the nature of the Conservative Party is linked to two important political developments in the prairie West. The first entails a perennial yet growing unease with Quebec's influence in the national scheme of things. Every federal contract that is awarded to a Quebec firm rather than to one in the West, every extension of official bilingualism outside Quebec or official unilingualism inside Quebec, is taken as evidence that western Canadians are not playing on a level playing field, that the rules of national political life are stacked in favour of Quebec. Although Conservative governments have certainly not ignored western Canadian interests, there is a widespread suspicion that Mr. Mulroney's perception of the national community differs only in nuance from that of Mr. Trudeau. (During the 1988 election, Reform Party literature referred to "the Trudeau/Mulroney vision of Canada.") The perceived focus of Prime Minister Mulroney and his government on Quebec is not only opposed in principle; it is also taken as a measure of just how far the Progressive Conservative Party has drifted from the roots it sank into the western Canadian soil during the 1960s and 1970s.

The second development is growing regional support for Senate reform, and more specifically for Senate reform following the "elected, equal, and effective" precepts of the Triple-E reform lobby. In large part, support for Senate reform reflects a judgment on the results of the 1984 "experiment," a perception that effective regional representation requires something beyond that provided by Progressive Conservative MPS and Cabinet ministers. The argument is that regional representation cannot be achieved through party mechanisms alone, that any party with national ambitions will necessarily downplay the regional concerns of western Canadians in the search for seats in Ontario and Quebec. Correctly or not, the track record of the Mulroney government is used as evidence that effective regional representation requires institutional reform, and not simply the replacement of a Liberal government by a Conservative government.

Both developments have become entangled in turn with the regional debate over the Meech Lake Accord. Although the Accord was initially embraced by provincial governments in the West, it enjoyed a less enthusiastic public reception; individual western Canadians had more difficulty finding their reflection in Meech Lake than did their provincial governments. From a prairie perspective, although admittedly not from a Quebec perspective, the Accord compounded, rather than corrected, problems with the Constitution Act of 1982. As noted above, western premiers had adopted a defensive posture in the constitutional negotiations leading up to the Act, and perhaps as a consequence, the Act did little to advance western Canadian interests through constructive institutional reform. Then came the "Quebec round" and, once again, western Canadian institutional concerns were placed on the back burner; Senate reform was placed on the constitutional agenda, but not addressed. While the Meech Lake Accord addressed the constitutional concerns and aspirations of Quebec, those of the West were put on hold.

Eventually, of course, there may be a "western round" in the constitutional process. This, indeed, is the off-cited promise of the Meech Lake Accord; Senate reform has been placed on the agenda and will be addressed in the future once Quebec's place in the constitution has been secured. However, the dynamics of Meech Lake offer little hope of such an eventuality. If the Accord is ratified, there will be little if any incentive for Quebec and Ontario to address the constitutional aspirations of western Canadians. There is no bargain to be struck because, with the ratification of the Accord, western Canadians would have nothing left with which to bargain. If the Accord is not ratified, if it is grounded on mounting opposition in Manitoba, then further constitutional and institutional change is also precluded. In short, there are good reasons to expect that the Quebec round will be the last round for some time to come.

Where, then, does this leave the prairie West? In addressing this question, it is important to note the continued disintegration of the prairie West as a regional community. With the decline of the grain economy, the diversification of the regional economy, and the growth of provincial governments having limited regional interests, the region is becoming unstitched. More and more, the appropriate points of reference are three quite distinct provincial communities that have evolved from, and thus dissolved, the earlier regional community sweeping from the Lakehead to the Rockies. This disintegration finds reflection in the increased partisan heterogeneity both within and across the three prairie provinces; the partisan environments of the prairie provinces are no more similar than what one might expect from any three randomly selected provinces.

To the extent that there is some partisan glue binding the region together, that glue is provided by the national Progressive Conservative Party. However, as that party becomes more national in composition and orientation, it will serve less well as a regional bond. Moreover, it seems unlikely that the electoral alliance between Quebec and the West can be sustained once the free trade debate subsides, and once Canadian political debate returns to the staples of language and regional economic development. Indeed, the free trade agreement itself may weaken the alliance as western Canadians are asked to embrace a continental economy and a continental future. The more western Canadians see themselves and their future in continental terms, the less supportive they may be of the delicate linguistic agreements required to stitch together the national community. Western Canadians who argued that the French language received undue emphasis within a Canadian context will find that argument even more compelling when placed within the continental context of free trade.

What should we expect politically as the prairie West turns to face the twenty-first century? At the very least, western alienation is likely to continue as western Canadians confront an uncertain economic future, as the Progressive Conservative Party rebuilds its central Canadian roots, and as the quest for Senate reform founders in the murky waters of Meech Lake. At the same time, while political discontent in the West may strain the fabric of national unity, it is unlikely to tear that fabric. The underlying goal of western Canadians has always been to play a more active role in Canadian political, economic, and cultural life. Two questions, however, have not been answered. First, what are the most effective institutional vehicles through which such a role could be played? Is the answer to be found in continued support for the Progressive Conservatives, in a reformed Senate, in the intergovernmental arena, or in the more radical program of the Reform Party? Second, how can Canadian life be shaped to reflect western interests and aspirations while at the same time accommodating the interests and aspirations of Quebec? These questions have been addressed time and time again in the history of the prairie West, and without resolution. Little prospect for their immediate resolution is apparent on the horizon as the prairie provinces enter the 1990s.

NOTES

1. For an expanded discussion, see Roger Gibbins, *Prairie Politics and*

Society: Regionalism in Decline (Toronto: Butterworths, 1980), p. 169ff.

2. J. R. Mallory, *Social Credit and the Federal Power in Canada* (Toronto: University of Toronto Press, 1953), p. 39.

3. Vernon C. Fowke, *The National Policy and the Wheat Economy* (Toronto: University of Toronto Press, 1957), p. 282.

4. At the time of the 1931 census, 22.7 percent of the Canadian population lived on the prairies. That proportion declined steadily thereafter, falling to 16.4 percent in the 1971 and 1976 census. At the time of the 1986 census, 17.5 percent of the national population resided on the prairies; 53.3 percent of the regional population then lived in Alberta compared to 23.9 percent in Manitoba and 22.7 percent in Saskatchewan.

5. "Painting the Farm Tory Blue," *Alberta Report*, 17 October 1988, p. 49.

6. *The Globe and Mail*, 11 November 1988. The Environics poll, which included only 120 Alberta respondents, was conducted between 3 and 8 November 1988. A much larger Alberta survey conducted at approximately the same time showed a more even provincial split; 40 percent of the 1,629 respondents supported the FTA while 39 percent opposed it. *The Calgary Sun*, 6 November 1988.

7. "Evaluating the Fine Print...The Free Trade Agreement and Western Canada," report published by the Canada West Foundation, April 1988.

8. Drew Fagan, "Carney Warms Oil Patch with Free-Trade Promotion," *The Globe and Mail*, 7 July 1988, p. B1.

9. *Calgary Herald*, 10 April 1988, p. A2.

FURTHER READINGS

Conway, J. F. *The West: The History of a Region in Confederation*. Toronto: James Lorimer, 1983.

Francis, R. Douglas, and Howard Palmer. *The Prairie West: Historical Readings*. Edmonton: Pica Pica Press, 1985.

Friesen, Gerald. *The Canadian Prairies: A History*. Toronto: University of Toronto Press, 1984.

Gibbins, Roger. *Regionalism: Territorial Politics in Canada and the United States*. Toronto: Butterworths, 1982.

Gibbins, Roger, ed. *Meech Lake and Canada: Perspectives from the West*. Edmonton: Academic Printing and Publishing, 1989.

Nikiforuk, Andrew, Sheila Pratt, and Don Wanagas. *Running on Empty: Alberta After the Boom*. Edmonton: NeWest Press, 1987.

Smith, David E. *The Regional Decline of a National Party: Liberals on the Prairies*. Toronto: University of Toronto Press, 1981.

5

"Red Tied": Fin de Siècle Politics in Ontario

H. V. NELLES

During the 1980s a fundamental realignment of political forces occurred in Canada. The Conservative Party crafted an electoral strategy that made it possible for a stable national government to be formed based upon solid support in Quebec and a significant majority in the West. At about the same time in Ontario, a forty-two-year-old Conservative dynasty fell from power. The two events were not unrelated. The federal government could, if it chose, govern without Ontario, or even against Ontario. Henceforth, Ontario could no longer assume, as it had become accustomed to doing in the past, that Ottawa naturally represented its interests.

It will take some time for the full implications of this change to be fully understood. In any event, either subtly or dramatically, the new federal game of isolating Ontario so as to form a coalition of national reconciliation in the regions is certain to have profound and lasting effects upon Ontario politics.

At the end of the 1980s Ontario is self-absorbed in the politics of growth. The federal government is more fully committed to a politics of redistribution, both of political power and of economic gains. Up to a certain point, these divergent agendas can be mutually accommodated. However, should the national and provincial interests be seen to come into conflict over fundamental matters, Ontario will most certainly shed its mantle of statesmanship and renew instead its historical role as the spoilt child of Confederation.

For this reason the question of what Ontario wants will likely be posed with greater urgency during the next decade.[1] It is also a two-part question. First, it asks what the province of Ontario will want from the federal system. Second, it asks what the citizens of Ontario will demand of their provincial government. The first is more readily answerable than the second, but both lines of inquiry are likely to lead to the conviction—internally at least—that Ontario, by virtue of its economic power and social complexity, is a distinct society too.

I

Growth must be the starting point for any consideration of Ontario politics. Economic growth changed the face of Ontario during the 1980s and, incidentally, altered its relationship with the other provinces and the federal government. The political systems of many other provinces had to cope with recession, stagnation, and industrial decline. In Ontario the problems of restructuring were absorbed within a rapidly growing, latterly hyperventilated economy. The intensity of the economic growth in the late 1980s clearly differentiated Ontario from the other provinces. While on the one hand growth cushioned adjustment, on the other hand it entailed a degree of social change that imposed political imperatives not widely shared within the federation. Others might envy Ontario its problems, but it had problems nonetheless.

At the beginning of the 1980s other regions of the country were expanding more rapidly than Ontario. It was commonplace then to hear talk of the economic centre of gravity shifting westward, especially as banks moved more aggressively into the oil patch.[2] However, the simultaneous collapse of oil prices and the shuddering recession of the early 1980s had a profound impact upon the relative fortunes of the various provinces. As energy and commodity prices fell in real terms, the burdens of adjustment were borne primarily by the regions.

Ontario reeled from a general contraction in demand, but also from a crisis in the strategic auto and auto-parts sector. However, unlike many other provinces, it then recovered, and the relative strength of that recovery has been truly staggering. At first the takeoff was auto driven; buoyant automobile exports led the way. In the second phase domestic consumer spending kicked in. And in the final years of the 1980s housing and business investment fuelled the boom.

In both absolute and relative terms the recent growth of Ontario has been remarkable. Real Gross Domestic Product (GDP) rose by over 33 percent between 1983 and 1988. During the late 1980s the Ontario economy outpaced the national growth rate (itself heavily influenced by Ontario's performance) by over 40 percent. Indeed, real annual average output growth in Ontario in those years (5.9 percent) exceeded that of Japan (3.8 percent), the United States (3.8 percent), the United Kingdom (3.3 percent), Italy (2.5 percent), Germany (2.2 percent), and France (1.5 percent).[3] If Ontario were a country—and with a population of 9.4 million that would be a plausible assumption—it would have one of the fastest-growing economies in the industrialized world.

Ontario's economic good fortune can be measured in relative terms by any number of indicators. Once again its population is growing, mainly through immigration and interprovincial migration, much faster than the national rate. The reasons for this are abundantly clear—jobs. Ontario has added more than almost 900,000 new jobs over the past decade. During the 1980s, 47 percent of all new jobs created in Canada were located in Ontario. Population growth notwithstanding, unemployment rates are

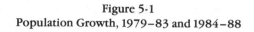

Figure 5-1
Population Growth, 1979–83 and 1984–88

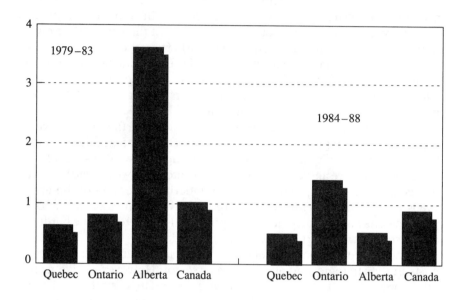

now the lowest in the country, and personal income per capita is the highest (see Figures 5.1, 5.2, and 5.3).

A significant turnaround in the comparative welfare of the provinces occurred during the 1980s. Ontario's relative decline, which was a function of mainly energy-related western growth in the 1970s, was halted and then reversed. Over the decade the economy got bigger in absolute and relative terms, changed its character, and in the process the pace of social change in Ontario also picked up. Ontario in the 1990s will be socially as well as economically a fundamentally different entity than the old familiar Ontario of myth and regional resentment.

Those who imagine Ontario has grown fat and rich selling expensive tariff-protected manufactured goods to the rest of the country had better look again. That may have been true in the hoary past, but it is no longer the case. Ontario is the least reliant of all the provinces upon the national market. That, of course, was one of the greatest ironies of the 1970s. At the time Quebec sought its independence, it was the province most dependent upon the rest of Canada for its income and employment.[4] It was this underlying flaw in the logic of separatism that drove the post-referendum Parti Québécois and then the Quebec Liberals toward what Tom Cour-

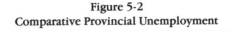

Figure 5-2
Comparative Provincial Unemployment

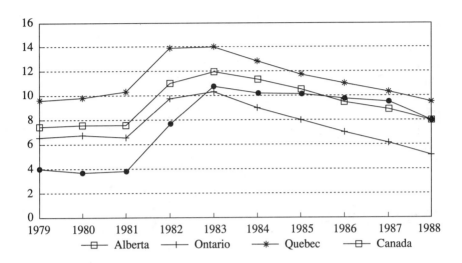

chene calls "market nationalism."[5] In this, as in other things, Quebec was merely catching up with what had been going on for some time in Ontario, where without the patina of language and culture the strategy bore the more prosaic title "continentalism."

Ontario, we are gradually beginning to discover, has always depended primarily upon itself.[6] That is something outsiders have always suspected, but in the psychological realm, not the economic. Ontario was never economically autarkic, but the mere size of its local market ensured that it produced goods and services mainly for local consumption and depended upon itself for supplies. Over time, tariff protection became less and less important to Ontario's employment. During the 1970s Ontario could be said to have become Canada's most economically independent province. Industrial restructuring in the 1980s furthered the process.

Researchers for the Royal Commission on the Economic Union and Development Prospects for Canada (Macdonald Commission) have compiled the most graphic evidence of this state of affairs.[7] Of all the provinces, only British Columbia and Newfoundland shipped smaller percentages of their output to the rest of Canada, and Ontario was by far

Figure 5-3
Provincial Income as a Percent of Canadian Average

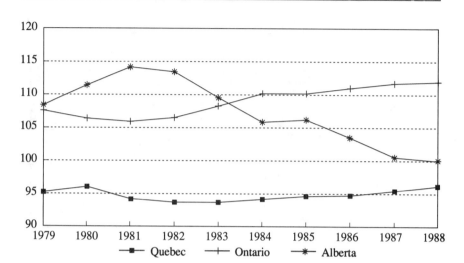

the province that relied least upon the rest of the country for its goods. By contrast, the prairie provinces are much more dependent upon the Canadian market than Ontario (see Table 5.1).

Exports to the United States have grown to a position of much greater importance in the provincial economy since the 1965 Auto Pact. Automobiles and auto parts have been Ontario's leading exports (23 percent and 12 percent respectively) for some time. The Ontario government estimates that exports of goods and services account for 47 percent of its GDP, and over 60 percent of those exports are bound for the United States. The era of continental economic integration has been well advanced in Ontario for a generation.

As a consequence, the implementation of the free trade agreement will likely not have much of an overall adverse impact on Ontario. Certainly some industries will be affected, but generally the agreement has already been anticipated and adjustments made in the wake of the severe recession of the early 1980s. Nevertheless, for some lagging sectors there will be some pain and suffering still to come. Some, but by no means all, of this dislocation will hit Ontario, but so too will most of

Table 5.1
Destination and Sources of Goods by Province, 1979

	Destination of Goods			Source of Goods		
Province	Local %	Canada %	Exports %	Local %	Canada %	Imports %
Nfld.	28	21	51	25	59	16
P.E.I.	40	39	21	25	65	10
N.S.	40	34	26	29	37	33
N.B.	29	29	42	22	43	34
Que.	48	28	24	43	25	32
Ont.	47	25	28	46	17	37
Man.	35	41	24	30	45	24
Sask.	25	29	46	26	52	22
Alta.	39	34	27	47	33	20
B.C.	45	15	40	45	28	27
Canada	44	27	29	43	26	32

Source: Canada, *Report of the Royal Commission on the Economic Union and Development Prospects for Canada*, 3 vols. (Ottawa: Supply and Services, 1985), 3: 104, 106.

the free trade agreement's benefits, especially those having to do with the services sector.

The movement of goods back and forth across space may no longer be an accurate indicator of economic activity because economic development has moved Ontario more than most other regions out of goods production and into the provision of services as the main source of its livelihood. Manufacturing accounted for a mere 19 percent of the Canadian labour force in 1981, a figure that fell even lower following the recession of the early 1980s and its subsequent shake-out. Service-producing industries are more than twice as important in the Ontario economy as goods-producing industries.

In summary, the Ontario economy has already been substantially restructured away from goods-producing to mainly service-producing industries. Second, despite noises to the contrary, the process of thoroughgoing continental economic integration is well advanced. Ontario is more closely connected with the U.S. economy than it is with the rest of Canada. As a result of these changes and its strategic geographical location, Ontario has been booming, almost obscenely so. It is conceivable that within another decade it might account for as much as half the total national economy. Rather than think of Ontario as the great factory of Confederation, it is probably more accurate these days to think of it as that quintessential symbol of the open service economy, a sprawling international airport under constant construction.

II

All of this growth and development has induced equally dramatic social change as well. If Ontario is no longer the tariff-protected manufacturing centre of prairie populist and Atlantic regionalist mythology, it is no longer the WASPish citadel of sainted memory. Post-war immigration has fundamentally altered the social structure of Ontario. For example, in 1981 Ontario was only barely a Protestant province (51.8 percent), and it will undoubtedly become less so by the next census as the Catholic and non-Christian religions continue to grow.[8]

The second-largest ethnic group in Ontario in 1986 was "Other." Presently immigrants from more than 22 percent of the Ontario population, and Ontario's immigrant population is more than half the Canadian total. As traditional sources of immigrants continue to give way to Asia, Latin America, and the Caribbean, and as more than half of Canada's immigrants, lured by the booming economy, have settled in Ontario, the province has developed a rapidly growing population of visible minorities. In the mid-1980s Vietnam, Hong Kong, the Philippines, El Salvador, Jamaica, and China provided 40 percent of immigrants.[9] Ontario has resumed its post-war place as the Canadian magnet for international migrants with this difference: these days immigration produces not just a multi-ethnic society, but also a multiracial society.

Both the economic boom and its social consequences have been concentrated in the metropolitan areas. The Census Metropolitan Area of Toronto, which extends from Pickering in the east to Milton in the west and now as far north as Orangeville, contains 37 percent of the provincial population. Municipal councils, developers, and road builders cannot keep up to the demand for accommodation, as mind-boggling house prices never cease to remind us. The Lake Ontario shoreline has become one massive interconnected conurbation. A graphic illustration of the scale of urban sprawl may be grasped from a currently popular poster, a high-resolution satellite photo taken from an altitude of seven-hundred kilometres that shows the entire sweep of what used to be called the "Golden Horseshoe" from Niagara Falls, through Hamilton, and eastward to Oshawa. Observers of that photo can find themselves, their pinpoint of land, their place to stand, in a geographical mosaic that contains as many as five million people. That picture is almost entirely urban.

There are in reality two Ontarios: the metropolitan regions and the rest of the province. The urban centres are growing and changing much faster than the province as a whole. "Metro-Ontario" is more foreign born, polyglot, ethnic, younger, and multiracial than the rest of the province. Women from a higher proportion of the labour force, and there are more single-parent families. Incomes, tastes, occupations, and many behavioural characteristics, including educational participation rates, differ greatly on either side of this cultural divide. It is important to bear this internal division in mind. Ontario is to some extent a reflection of the country as a whole. Its outlying regions are growing less rapidly; its natural resource and agricultural sectors are in relative decline; it has a large, geographically concentrated francophone minority in the north, the east, and increasingly in metropolitan areas demanding recognition. The rise of Metro-Ontario has cast a long shadow over rural and small-town Ontario. Differential growth and social change drive the political process within Ontario as well as within the federation.

The political challenge in Ontario is, first, to service growth with schools, hospitals, roads, subdivisions; second, to mediate social conflict with equity, welfare, and distributional social policies that integrate disparate groups; and third, to direct change in such a way so as not to alienate the vested majority. And all of this must be done with taxes raised at home.

III

A successful governing party in Ontario must bridge the old and the new Ontarios. The Conservative Party proved remarkably adept at this contortionist activity for forty-two years of fairly dramatic social and economic transformation. The Tories might have gone on forever had they not defeated themselves with two uncharacteristic mistakes: the inept handling of a divisive separate school funding issue, and a bungled leadership transition. Under the weight of those two blunders, the Tory bridge collapsed.

The secrets of political longevity, when reduced to words on a page, seem too trite to be true. In Ontario the rules of the political game as practised by the Conservative Party for forty-two years were accordingly quite simple: make change cautiously; seek consensus and blunt conflict; identify the leader with the province; protect provincial interests; and attract marginal support through leadership changes. In short, accommodate change *within* the party.

The Ontario Progressive Conservatives mastered the knack of accommodating great change without giving the impression that anything had changed at all. For example, the quiet revolution in governing Ontario was so quiet no one noticed. A statist, socializing, bureaucratic government slipped into being without a corresponding political revolution. Conservatives attracted their marginal support through policy changes without alienating their core support. As Ontario grew during the postwar era, a formerly laissez-faire, imperialist party attracted the support of both the new business and bureaucratic elites and the ethnic votes. The thousands of migrants to Ontario and first-time voters *learned* to vote Progressive Conservative, they were not born Tory. [10]

Ontario Tories in power instinctively avoided confrontation, minimized differences, and smothered conflict. This meant never getting too far out in front of public opinion on any issue or, indeed, making clear statements on any issue. Premiers governed by soothing the electorate; politics was an intellectual comfort food. No one in Ontario ever had to take valium for political reasons. Leslie Frost was known as "the Great Tranquillizer"; John Robarts put himself to sleep with his speeches.[11] William G. Davis was transformed into "Bland Bill" for the smooth, monotonous, soporific, content-free quality of his delivery. It was a style that infuriated the opposition, journalists, and all right-thinking academics who like their politics with cleavage. Elections took place in a cloud of pipesmoke, a low drone of bafflegab and mindless radio jingles. Excitement and politics in Ontario were antithetical concepts—on purpose. As Bill Davis taunted the much-reduced opposition after he had sleepwalked to victory in 1981, "Bland Works!"[12]

The party went to great and sophisticated lengths to ensure the identification of the leader with the province and its aspirations. Stately Leslie Frost became "Old Man Ontario," the epitome of the wise and patient elder. John Robarts, in his trimmer years with his three-piece suits, bushy eyebrows, salt and pepper mustache, and gravel voice, fit the progressive, modernizing image of a "management man." His grooming and style proclaimed him more loudly than mere words to be Chairman of the Board of Ontario Incorporated. Bill Davis cultivated a more folksy, suburban image. At home he never let anyone forget he was from Brampton, the archetypical suburb, once a leafy town, then a dormitory suburb, and soon to be a city in its own right. Abroad, his innocent, complacent, pudgy, unflappable suburbanite style symbolized Ontario.

In the federal arena, successive Ontario premiers pursued Ontario's interests with ruthless efficiency all the while insisting that they were primarily concerned about Canada's well-being. At first there were rules in the gentlemen's club of executive federalism. The provinces should not gang up on Ottawa; no single province should be isolated in a discussion, especially Quebec, and Ontario's self-appointed role was to be the interpreter of Quebec to the rest of the country. But as the stakes got higher, the rules fell by the wayside. Ontario changed from being the leading advocate of provincial rights and decentralism to the stoutest supporter of centralized federalism when its interests were put in jeopardy by high energy costs on one side and Quebec separatism on the other. Again, this dramatic realignment occurred without notice at home. When it came to a choice between Joe Clark's government and low energy prices for Ontario consumers, the Ontario Tories abandoned their fellow Tories with almost indecent haste.

Finally, the party handled leadership transitions with enviable skill. At precisely the right moment the elder Frost gave way to a younger, more urbane John Robarts, and the party renewed its association with new elites and immigrants.[13] A tired John Robarts stepped gracefully aside for boyish Bill Davis, who reassembled the key personnel of his opponents' campaign organizations into the fabled Big Blue Machine. Guided now by professional pollsters, full-time political organizers, and advertising agents in close touch with popular preferences, the Tories positioned themselves in the centre of the political spectrum.

These were the rules of exercising power, not gaining it. As long as the Tories occupied the strategic centre, marginalizing the Liberals to the right and the New Democratic Party (NDP) to the left, as long as the opposition vote remained split in this fashion, the Tories need not worry about having to gain power. Two terms of minority government in the 1970s put enough fear of defeat into the organization to focus its mind upon the problem of garnering just enough marginal support to win a majority. But once installed with a majority, after 1981 the Davis government seemed to lose that competitive edge.

Premier Davis's startling announcement of full funding for Roman Catholic separate schools late in his term damaged his party not so much because the policy was flawed—the growing Catholic minority could no longer be denied with impunity and all parties favoured the change—but by the way the change was handled. His even more surprising resignation a few months later left many of his erstwhile supporters feeling angry and betrayed. He had handed them a political liability that could no longer be counteracted with his personal popularity. The abrupt policy change did not win the support of Catholics for whom it was intended, while it alienated other religious groups who either opposed the move or were offended by the high-handed manner with which the decision was taken. In the shadow of this controversy and with a provincial election looming, the leadership contest did not produce the accustomed result of renewal, recruitment, and youthful rejuvenation. Instead, the choice of Frank Miller, a tartan-clad small-town, right winger, an avatar of the old conservatism, fatally wounded the party in Metro-Ontario. The fusion of the old and the new right behind Frank Miller splintered the party into ideological factions that could not, or would not, reunify behind the new leader. The subterranean separate school funding issue sapped even die-hard confidence in the regime; the unattractive, apparently reactionary leadership cost the government support among swing voters in Metro-Ontario.

Politics, like nature, abhors a vacuum. The Liberal Party moved deftly into the centre vacated by the Tories. With a leader from London, Ontario, professionally groomed to appeal to metropolitan constituencies, his identity secured in the media by his trademark red neckties, and a platform largely borrowed from the NDP, the Liberal Party after years in the wilderness began to build much more effective bridges between the two Ontarios than the Tories. In the 1985 election a rise in both Liberal and NPD support denied the Conservatives a majority. Under Frank Miller's leadership, Conservative Party popularity fell by 14 percent in the greater Toronto region. It fell to the third-place NDP to decide whether to prop up the ancien régime or put the Liberals into power. It was a lose/lose situation for the NDP. Subsequently, an unprecedented written accord between the NDP and the Liberals on an agenda for a minority government without the threat of election catapulted the Liberals unexpectedly into power armed with a broadly popular, progressive platform. Stiffened by this accord with the NDP, the Liberals won their spurs in a showdown with the province's doctors over the issue of extra-billing. With the Treasury awash with cash in the boom, the minority government loosened the purse strings after years of fiscal restraint.

These policies greatly enhanced the party's popularity in Metro-Ontario. While party veterans such as Robert Nixon and Sean Conway managed to keep the faith among bedrock Grits in rural Ontario, the telegenic Premier David Peterson, along with colleagues such as Ian Scott, Elinor Caplan, René Fontaine, Robert Wong, Alvin Curling, and later Chaviva Hosek, brought the new cosmopolitan urban constituencies into the fold. Shrewdly, the Liberals siezed for themselves whatever credit accrued from the accord with the NDP. When the accord expired and a general election ensued, the voters returned ninety-five Liberals, as opposed to nineteen New Democrats and a mere sixteen Tories. Thus, with considerable assistance of the NDP the Peterson Liberals moved leftward and cityward into the centre. As we enter the 1990s it is the Liberal Party that has strength in virtually every Ontario electoral constituency, and among all social groups; it is the Conservatives and the NDP who are marginalized (see Figure 5.4A, 5.4B, 5.4C and Table 5.2).

Ironically, the more competitive the political process in Ontario, the less real choice the party system offers the electorate. At various times in the 1980s all three parties held plausible claims to forming the government. In such circumstances the party system, even a three-party system, does not offer much substantive choice to the electorate. Centripetal forces drive all parties toward the centre. For example, all three parties opposed free trade in 1987. There was all-party agreement on a ban on extra-billing, rent control, abortion clinics, Meech Lake, and full funding for separate schools. Party strategists all read the same polls and the census results, and as a result, differences between them turn on matters of nuance and timing, and style, not fundamental principle.

Ontario's aggressive opposition to the free trade agreement during

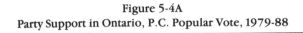

Figure 5-4A
Party Support in Ontario, P.C. Popular Vote, 1979-88

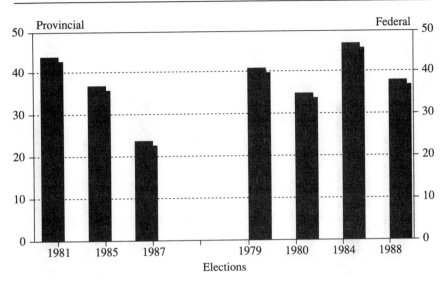

the last provincial election, and in more muted tones during the federal election, had more to do with electoral strategy and federal–provincial bargaining than underlying economic interest. Free trade presents a difficult management problem to a governing party in Ontario because, while economic elites greatly favour the agreement, a majority of the population is either opposed to it or confused by it. At present, the electoral process is socially rather than economically driven. Narrow economic interest may lead in one direction; forces emanating from mass electoral politics lead in another. A governing party must broker this issue between elites and the masses. Initially, when in a minority position dependent upon NDP support, Premier Peterson appeared to provide decisive leadership at a time when it was lacking in Ottawa. He opposed the agreement for tactical reasons when it seemed safe to do so, that is, when the deal seemed dead. Who could predict that Ottawa would back itself into such a bad deal, one that even free trade's most ardent defenders were reduced to referring to as better than no deal at all? Ontario's persistence in opposition, albeit *sotto voce*, had mainly to do with not alienating the support of the newly won majority and ensuring that it would be Ottawa that would eventually pay the dislocation com-

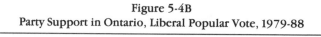

Figure 5-4B
Party Support in Ontario, Liberal Popular Vote, 1979-88

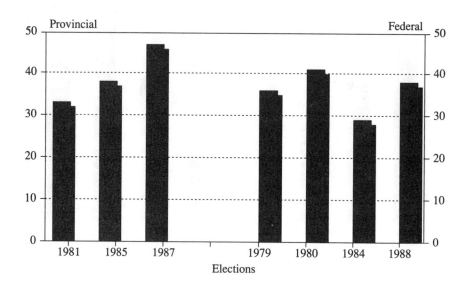

pensation. The truth is that Ontario can live with a good deal or a bad deal, free trade or the National Policy, and everything in between. It is that big and prosperous.

Currently, two issues peculiar to Ontario pervade the domestic political agenda: race relations and Sunday shopping. These two issues symbolize the tensions within and between the two Ontarios. Sunday shopping represents a conflict between the new and the old Ontario. The old Ontario is still there, clustered in its small towns, in the countryside, and in increasingly embattled urban neighbourhoods. Sunday is part of the old order; indeed, it might be thought of as a symbol of that order, though of course as tastes have changed certain lapses toward movies, drinking, and baseball have been grudgingly tolerated. However, in a pluralistic society no real principle sets Sunday apart. Old Ontario—and with it some unions and merchants too—is reluctant to complete the transformation of a majoritarian religious day of rest to a secular holiday, one that will unite rather than divide a religiously pluralistic, consumption-driven population.

Racial tension has become a permanent feature of the Ontario polity just as in the United States and Great Britain. The competition for jobs,

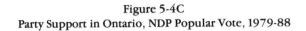

Figure 5-4C
Party Support in Ontario, NDP Popular Vote, 1979-88

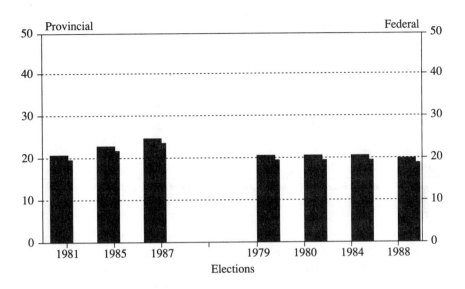

housing, and status among groups, and differential patterns of integration into the labour force, frequently manifest themselves in conflict among races. A heightened sense of racial tension, along with a general deterioration of the urban environment, are the principal political issues of Metro-Ontario. We are likely to hear less of that insufferable twaddle about "the city that works" and rather more about a metropolis that more closely resembles the American pattern.[14]

All three parties are doing their utmost to forge links with the visible minorities and the new urban constituencies. In a time-honoured Ontario tradition, the minority has become an effective majority. But at the same time, political parties are not ideal instruments to effect change. They can either broker interethnic tensions or merely provide another theatre for them. In the last national election the federal Liberal Party in Ontario experienced some of the agony of this association with fiercely contested nomination meetings that pitted rival ethnic organizations against one another and left old-time Liberals alienated and the party bruised and divided in the ensuring election.[15] That is a foretaste of what may be in the offing for all parties as the new constituencies demand not only representation, but also power.

Table 5.2
Ontario Provincial Elections

Election	Candidates Elected			% Popular Vote				% Turnout
	PC	Lib	NDP	PC	Lib	NDP	Other	
1981	70	34	21	44.4	33.7	21.1	0.8	58.0
1985	52	48	25	37.0	37.9	23.8	1.3	61.5
1987	16	95	19	24.7	47.3	25.7	2.3	62.7

Ontario Federal Elections

Election	Candidates Elected			% Popular Vote				% Turnout
	PC	Lib	NDP	PC	Lib	NDP	Other	
1979	57	32	6	41.7	36.3	21	1	78
1980	38	52	5	35.3	41.7	21.7	1.3	72
1984	67	14	13	47.7	29.9	20.8	1.6	76
1988	46	43	10	38.2	38.9	20.1	2.8	75

Source: All statistics except 1988 from published records of provincial and federal chief
electoral officers.

There can be no denying the very real crosscurrents of social unrest in Ontario. The NDP is well equipped by its traditions to address such issues. However, on the social equity front the NDP does not have the franchise on virtue. Its freedom of expression is constrained somewhat by its affiliation with the union movement. Unions are part of the power structure that stands in newcomers' way. Second, unions are constitutionally compelled to protect the interests of the workers they represent; this is normally thought to be against employers, but it could just as readily be against politicians. If the police are accused of racism, their strongest defenders will be their union. If affirmative action means quotas, preferential promotion, and discrimination—albeit for the very best of reasons—the unions will be the most vigorous opponents. The Liberals, unencumbered by union affiliation, have no hostages in that quarter.

To a certain extent these issues can be jawboned. Being seen to be against racism and in favour of improving welfare and education can be enough, for a time. The "spin doctors" and issue managers are adept at positioning politicians to be on the right side of hot issues. But on other questions, what matters is not what you say, but what you spend. In the long run, fiscal priorities have to match rhetorical commitments or the voters will lose interest.

The imperatives of electoral politics have moved the Liberal Party into the left–centre of the political spectrum. Electorally the governing party cannot afford serious competition to its left. The NDP, which provided the Liberals in the accord with a reformist agenda that will likely last a generation, is its most serious threat. The problem is that left–centre on the political spectrum, however warm it might be to the heart, is a very expensive place to be.

Equal pay, indexed pensions, day care, home care, and subsidized housing all cost money. Moreover, with an aging population and socialized medicine, health-related costs are soaring. Meanwhile, education at all levels and social services demand more money. In the boom, especially in glitzy Toronto, abject poverty is growing. And expansion requires massive expenditures on infrastructure.

To the consternation of business groups and economists, Ontario has not made much of a dent in its mounting deficit, notwithstanding the economic boom. Expenditures compete with deficit reduction. Here is another tradeoff that has to be negotiated. How can the deficit be addressed and expensive new programs launched without massive tax increases? The difficulty is compounded by the federal strategy of shifting the burden of funding established programs onto the provincial governments. In Ontario the provincial government must raise the bulk of its revenues itself. Federal transfers represent a much lower proportion of the provincial budget total than all other provinces but resource-rich Alberta.[16]

In Ontario growth and social change demand more expenditures. Sound fiscal management, on the other hand, seems to require spending cuts. The fiscal management side of the government is thus counterpoised against the social agenda side. The electoral requirements of office demand spending; financial affairs on the other hand are more powerfully driven by the intellectual currents emanating from Washington and London to downsize government, privatize the delivery of services, deregulate, reduce taxes for more productive employment, and let markets prevail. The alternative, tax increases, is of dubious merit both economically and electorally. Ontario is a very rich province, and by various measures slightly undertaxed compared with other Canadian jurisdictions.[17] Nevertheless, raising taxes has its risks. The Liberals have already grabbed another 1 percent on the sales tax. The genial treasurer managed that without courting too much unpopularity, but he cannot raise taxes indefinitely and still keep friends.

Because Ontario must pay for whatever it decides to do out of revenues it collects itself, it is unlikely to be a vigorous social policy innovator. It never has been, perhaps for this very reason. Nevertheless, it will have to do just enough to keep its marginal votes to the left or surrender more ground to the NDP. Whether the Liberals continue to govern in Ontario will depend upon how well they have learned the lessons of exercising power perfected by the Tories before them, and how successfully they broker conflicts and bridge social divisions. Already newspapers have begun to print acute-angle photographs that seem to suggest that Premier Peterson has begun to develop a striking physical resemblance to Bill Davis. Delays and policy drift have been seized upon by the opposition as indications of political sclerosis. If true, these symptoms may well be indications of the opposite.

IV

Strains resulting from rapid growth will likely continue to drive the political process in Ontario during the 1990s. If Ontario continues to grow at a rate markedly different from the rest of the country, as seems likely to be the case for the intermediate term, then federal politics will likely take on a more redistributive or equilibrating function. In that case, Ontario will develop a clear set of interests that set it apart within the federation. It will then become necessary for the government of Ontario to articulate these objections and perhaps even defy federal power. Intimations of this behaviour may be sensed in Ontario's resistance to the proposed federal sales tax and the General Agreement on Tariffs and Trade decision on wine markups.

To a certain extent this casting of Ontario as the problem child of Confederation will represent a reversion to a former role. During the late nineteenth century, Ontario more than Quebec was responsible for shaping the extent of provincial powers through its adversarial relationship with the federal government. During the 1930s Ontario and Quebec provided the effective opposition to federal incursions into traditional provincial jurisdiction. And during the 1960s, of course, John Robarts made common cause with Quebec's Jean Lesage and Daniel Johnson and lent legitimacy to their efforts to decentralize Confederation. Ontario, at its televised Confederation of Tomorrow conference, gave Quebec a prime-time opportunity in friendly company to challenge federal power, something the host quietly but firmly supported.

We have recently become accustomed to thinking of Ontario as the most centralist of the provinces. That is in part because of the aberrant behaviour required by the energy crisis on the one hand and the threat of the breakup of the country by Quebec separatism on the other. And in the 1970s Ontario residents tended to identify themselves more strongly with the federal government than the province.[18] This only confirmed eastern and western suspicions that deep down inside Ontario really thought of itself as Canada, suspicions often felt though rarely voiced.[19] In such extremes Ontario's federalist interests were clear. But in more conventional circumstances Ontario is by nature decentralist.

Its objectives in federal–provincial negotiations are fairly straightforward. First and foremost Ontario expects the federal government to manage the Quebec problem without destabilizing the economy. Quebec is no longer as directly important to Ontario employment and income as it once was. Nevertheless, separation would certainly damage the Ontario economy in numerous indirect ways simply by virtue of the market instability that would ensue. However, when Quebec's decentralizing goals are framed within a recognizable federalist outcome, they more or less correspond to Ontario's self-interest. Thus, the prospects for a renewal of the Ontario–Quebec alliance of yore are very good.

With Quebec safely into the federal fold, Ontario wants mainly to be left alone to conduct its internal and economic affairs as it sees fit. That means Ontario is prepared to pay a price for Confederation, but it would prefer to pay as little as possible. In practical terms, this means minimizing federal equalization and other transfer payments to the "have-not" provinces.

This desire to accommodate Quebec and be left alone is perfectly reflected in the Ontario attitude toward the Meech Lake Accord. The government quite genuinely wants Quebec brought into the constitution, whatever that may mean. That this could be done at the expense of federal power is all the better. Meech Lake was, after all, a deal cut between Ontario and Quebec, with the prime minister present more as a broker than a principal. Moreover, by virtually putting to an end all possibility of major federal cost-sharing programs, Ontario protects itself against federal expansion into its jurisdiction and, more important, into its tax base. Buying Quebec at federal expense and ending shared-cost programs conform nicely with Ontario's self-interest. As an added bonus, Meech Lake also puts an end to senate reform—a potentially serious threat to Ontario's remaining power—for a lifetime.

The combination of free trade and Meech Lake also virtually eliminates the possibility of a revival of the National Energy Program. Alberta gloated about this coup because it meant that henceforth there could be no possibility of Ontarians heating their homes at Alberta's expense. The converse, though it has not been noticed, is also true. Under these circumstances there is no compelling reason why Ontario should be made to pay more than the prevailing North American price for its oil simply to provide energy security for the United States. In the event that Alberta continues to be a high-cost oil producer, its purchase upon central Canadian conscience in the interest of national development is correspondingly reduced.

Federal Conservatives were elected partly in reaction against a perceived central Canadian dominance under the Liberal government. The Conservative victory and subsequent reconfiguration of political support occurred in part because of regional dissatisfaction with the distribution of economic benefits and political power within Confederation. Since the election of Brian Mulroney's Conservatives, federal policies have been directed toward a redistribution of national political power and, by inference, economic power. To a certain extent, federal election campaigns have become the instruments of economic redistribution within the federation. At election time Saskatchewan gets a heavy oil upgrader, Quebec a smelter, and so forth. The federal government gives out aircraft-maintenance contracts and space agencies to gain or reward political support in the regions—but not in Ontario. Montreal and Vancouver are made international banking centres, but not Toronto. It is the conventional wisdom that this represents an attempt to bribe voters with their own money. In Canada that is not the case; the regions can be bribed with someone else's money, taxes raised in other provinces, namely Ontario. The regions bridle at the suggestion of bribery, replying indignantly that these federal programs are necessary to give them only what they are properly due from a confederation biased hugely in favour of Ontario.

To some extent the Ontario provincial government can rise above the fray. But not if the price of being a Canadian hurts, or if Ontario is seen to be getting shafted. When a province begins to feel itself alienated, traditional electoral support for the federal party drops and identification with the provincial government increases. During the 1980s Ontarians did begin to shift their allegiances. When asked to choose between the federal and provincial governments in the early 1970s, 51 percent of Ontario respondents identified more closely with the federal government, only 34 percent with the provincial level of government—almost exactly the reverse of the national average. A decade later only 28 percent identified more strongly with the federal government, whereas 48 percent chose the provincial government as the one most likely to represent their concerns.[20] And while participation has been falling in federal elections—even the emotional free trade election—the participation rate in provincial contests has been rising. These surely are intimations of creeping provincial nationalism. In this respect Ontario may be becoming a province more like the others.

But as long as the boom continues and growth absorbs conflict and there is enough wealth to share, the potential federal–provincial conflict along these lines will be muted. In the event of a serious recession, and much sharper conflict between levels of government over revenues, and should redistributive policies be seen to cut too deeply into Ontario's well-being, undoubtedly the provincial government will rise up. Either that or it will be changed.

The most likely field of conflict will be the arcane but explosive field of tax policy, for it is in this area that Ontario has both its greatest needs and its greatest leverage over the federal government and the rest of the country. Ontario can break away and establish its own income tax system as Quebec has already done. If Ottawa continues to cut its deficit by shifting the burden of established-program financing onto the provinces, while at the same time moving deeper into provincial direct tax jurisdiction, Ontario is likely to lead the provincial revolt.

Should the present federal conservative strategy continue, in all likelihood Ontario will emerge as the leading opponent. Effective opposition, however, will require that Ontario not become isolated in the process. However, it is not inconceivable that Ontario might well become the Quebec of the 1990s.

In any event, Ontario will likely become much more assertive and determined to pursue its own agenda in national and international councils. In the process, Ontario' self-conscious identity as a distinct society, with imperatives separate from those of other provinces in the federation, will grow. Finally, the most likely theatre of conflict will be tax sharing. Stripped of self-serving rhetoric, the coming fight between Ontario and Ottawa will be over money—money that Ottawa wants to share with the rest of the country, money that Ontario needs to service its burgeoning society.

NOTES

1. Thomas J. Courchene, "What Does Ontario Want?" Robarts Lecture, York University, April 1988.
2. It is always a salutary if humbling exercise to revisit some of your own prose on these matters. In 1981 I attempted to explain Ontario's response to this geopolitical shift within Confederation in a magazine article, "The Politics of Anaesthesia," *Saturday Night*, September 1981. What I did not realize at that time was how temporary the realignment would be. Readers of this piece should bear the misapprehensions of that earlier essay in mind.
3. *1988 Ontario Budget*, 20 April 1988, pp. 1–2, 32–41; *Economic Outlook and Fiscal Review* (Toronto: Ministry of Treasury and Economics, December 1988), pp. 2–16.
4. Carmine Nappi, *The Structure of Quebec's Exports* (Montreal: C. D. Howe Research Institute, 1978), pp. 8, 27–36; Economic Council of Canada, *Looking Outward: A New Trade Strategy for Canada* (Ottawa: Queen's Printer, 1970), p. 42.
5. Courchene, "What Does Ontario Want?" pp. 16–19; Thomas J. Courchene, "Entrepreneurship: A Mind of State," Robarts Centre For Canadian Studies Working Paper, 1987, and "The Free Trade Agreement: Reflections of a Market Nationalist," Robarts Centre for Canadian Studies Working Paper, 1988.
6. See, for example, Ian Drummond, et al., *Progress Without Planning: The Economic History of Ontario from Confederation to the Second World War* (Toronto: University of Toronto Press, 1987).
7. The data are presented fully in Kenneth Norrie, Richard Simeon, and Mark Krasnick, *Federalism and the Economic Union in Canada* (Toronto: University of Toronto Press, 1986), pp. 222–33.

8. George Mori, "Religious Affiliation in Canada," *Canadian Social Trends* (Ottawa: Statistics Canada, Autumn 1987), pp. 12–16.

9. Statistics Canada, *1986 Census Profiles, Toronto*, Part 2 (Cat. 95-164), Table 1, and *1986 Census Profiles, Ontario*, Part 2 (Cat. 94-112), Table 1; Mary Ann Burke, "Immigration," *Canadian Social Trends* (Ottawa: Statistics Canada, Autumn 1986), pp. 23–27.

10. The best study of Ontario voting behaviour during the 1970s is to be found in Robert J. Drummond, "Voting Behaviour: Casting the Play," in *The Government and Politics of Ontario*, ed. Donald C. Macdonald (Toronto: Van Nostrand Reinhold, 1980), pp. 272–90.

11. An inkling of the Robarts avuncular style may be gleaned from A. K. Macdougall, *John P. Robarts: His Life and Government* (Toronto: University of Toronto Press, 1986). Some of the mingled fury and admiration of being in opposition to such men may be savoured in Donald C. Macdonald's aptly titled memoir, *The Happy Warrior* (Markham, Ont.: Fitzhenry and Whiteside, 1988).

12. See Rosemary Speirs, *Out of the Blue: The Fall of the Tory Dynasty in Ontario* (Toronto: Macmillan, 1986), p. 11, for a splendid, succinct account of the Davis years; Jonathan Manthorpe develops these themes at greater length for an earlier period in *The Power and the Tories* (Toronto: Macmillan, 1987). Bill Davis proved sufficiently shapeless and amiable that not even Claire Hoy's perverse talents could turn him into a total skunk; see Claire Hoy, *Bill Davis: A Biography* (Toronto: Methuen, 1985). For a collection of academic studies on various aspects of this period, see Donald C. Macdonald's edited collection, *The Government and Politics of Ontario.*

13. Peter Oliver in his biography of Allan Grossman documents the effort the Tories made to come and to keep in touch with the growing ethnic communities of Toronto, *Unlikely Tory: The Life and Politics of Allan Grossman* (Toronto: Lester & Orpen Dennys, 1985).

14. Early warning of this trend may be found in the November 1988 issue of *Toronto Life* entitled, "Are We Screwing Up?"

15. For a revealing account of some of these contested nominations by a superb investigative reporter, see Elaine Dewar's essay, "The Inside Story of the Ethnic Takeover of the Liberal Party," *Toronto Life*, December 1988.

16. Canada, *Report of the Royal Commission on the Economic Union and Development Prospects for Canada*, 3 vols. (Ottawa: Supply and Services, 1985), 3:222–29.

17. Norrie, Simeon, and Krasnick, *Federalism and the Economic Union*, pp. 113–14.

18. David J. Elkins and Richard Simeon, eds., *Small Worlds: Provinces and Parties in Canadian Political Life* (Toronto: Methuen, 1980), pp. 1–76.

19. Although in the last federal election, Monte Kwinter, the then Minister of Consumer and Commercial Relations, got himself into hot water by claiming that in trade matters what was good for Ontario was also good for the country.

20. Norrie, Simeon, and Krasnick, *Federalism and the Economic Union*, p. 167.

FURTHER READINGS

Rae, Kenneth. *The Prosperous Years: The Economic History of Ontario, 1939-1975.* Toronto: University of Toronto Press.

Armstrong, Christopher. *The Politics of Federalism: Ontario's Relations with the Federal Government, 1867-1942.* Toronto: University of Toronto Press, 1981.

Chandler, Marsha, and William Chandler. *Public Policy and Provincial Politics.* Toronto: Methuen, 1979.

Bellamy, D., J. Pammet, and D. Rowat, eds. *The Provincial Political Systems.* Toronto: Methuen, 1976.

Robin, Martin, ed. *Canadian Provincial Politics.* Toronto: Prentice-Hall, 1972.

Hall, Roger, William Westfall, and Laurel Sefton MacDowell, eds. *Patterns of the Past.* Toronto: Dundurn Press, 1988.

Nelles, H. V., *The Politics of Development.* Toronto: Macmillan, 1974.

Also, see a special issue of the *Journal of Canadian Studies*, vol. 18, Spring, 1983, for comparative essays on state development in Quebec and Ontario.

6

Quebec: Province, Nation, or "Distinct Society"?

KENNETH MCROBERTS

Any attempt to situate Quebec vis-à-vis the other provinces must begin with the fact that many Québécois themselves would be highly uncomfortable with such an enterprise: they do not see Quebec as simply one of the provinces. They would insist that, both as a society and as a polity, Quebec is distinctive from other provinces in fundamental ways. The phrase "distinct society" has acquired a certain notoriety through its incorporation in the controversial Meech Lake Accord. But it is only one among many different formulations of the same theme: *pas une province comme les autres, statut particulier*, etc. If there is room for debate over the constitutional propriety and implications of the "distinct society" clause, there can be little argument regarding the underlying social and political reality it is intended to recognize.

Clearly, Quebec is "distinct" in the sense of being "distinctive" or "different." Most obviously, it is different in terms of the first language of its residents: Quebec is the only province in which the population is primarily francophone. In 1981, 82 percent of its residents spoke French at home. In New Brunswick, the province with the next largest francophone presence, only 31 percent spoke French at home. In Ontario, the figure was 4 percent; while in all other provinces it was 3 percent or less. In fact, Quebec contained 89 percent of Canadians who use French at home.[1] The specifically cultural distinctiveness of French Quebec may be less obvious than it was in the heyday of the Church when its leaders declared French Canadians to be a pre-eminently Catholic people with no less than a providential mission to preserve French, Catholic civilization. Now the French language is no longer "gardienne de la foi," thanks to the pervasive secularization that Quebec society has experienced over the last thirty years. Nonetheless, subtle cultural differences clearly remain.

Moreover, Quebec's political life is distinctive in a great many ways. In terms of political institutions, Quebec civil law is based on the Civil Code rather than common law as in all the other provinces, and the symbols of the Crown have been markedly downplayed, as with replacing the Speech from the Throne with an Inaugural Address. Quebec provincial governments have pursued policies strikingly different from those of the other provinces. Concern with maintaining Quebec's cultural distinctiveness has led the provincial government to assume a much more important role than have the other provinces in selecting and settling immigrants and in supporting and regulating cultural activities, such as book publishing and the distribution of films. Other areas of governmental activity also seem to reflect the impact of a distinctive balance of social forces. In labour relations, Quebec was the first government in North America to grant the right to strike in the public sector and still remains the only government with an "anti-scab" law. Quebec pioneered in Canada the establishment of multifunctional public clinics, or Centres locaux de services communautaires, which seek to combine health and social services in a highly innovative fashion.

Beyond differences such as these, Quebec also is "distinct" in terms of its separateness from the other provinces. This separateness is evident, for instance, in the sources of news and entertainment to which most of its population turns: French-language media that are institutionally separate from English Canadian counterparts. Even the public broadcasting system, ostensibly responsible to the Canadian Parliament and committed by statute to further national unity, has always been divided between a French-language system, Radio-Canada, which is headquartered in Montreal, the vital cultural centre of francophone cultural activity, and is geared primarily to Quebec, and an English-language system, the CBC, which is headquartered in Toronto, the English Canadian metropolis. But institutional separateness can be seen in other areas than culture. For instance, unlike their counterparts in the other provinces, most labour union members belong to federations, the Confédération des syndicats nationaux (CSN) and the Corporation des enseignants du Québec, which are not affiliated with the Canadian Labour Congress (CLC). Relations between the CLC and the Fédération des travailleurs du Québec (FTQ), which groups together the Quebec union locals that are linked to the CLC, have always been difficult: FTQ leaders have regularly complained that the CLC's English Canadian leadership cannot comprehend the distinctive concerns and needs of the FTQ's membership.

As one might expect, this manifest distinctiveness of Quebec society, and the sense of distinctiveness associated with it, has supported distinct political loyalties. Quebec's political institutions command an allegiance among Quebec francophones that has no clear parallel in the other provinces. Underlying this allegiance is the simple fact that while the federal government is responsible to a predominantly anglophone electorate, the Quebec government, and only the Quebec government, is responsible to a predominantly francophone electorate. Thus, it has been commonly argued (and believed) in Quebec, only the Quebec government can be entrusted with the distinctive interests of Quebec francophones.

This argument, and the attachment to Quebec that it supported, was most dramatically manifested during the 1960s and 1970s in the movement to secure political sovereignty for Quebec. No other part of Canada has produced a serious movement calling for parity between it and the rest of Canada, as under sovereignty-association, let alone for independence. But the contention that Quebec francophones must rely first and foremost on their provincial government has been a constant theme of Quebec politics since Confederation. Indeed, it was primarily because of French Canadian fears that Confederation took a federal form: affording Quebec French Canadians an autonomous government in which they could place their full confidence. Thus, one can trace back over the decades a strong commitment among Quebec's political activists to defend Quebec's provincial autonomy and to support the Quebec government over the federal government when the two are in conflict. By and large, Quebec provincial governments have themselves taken this stance.

In fact, so profound is this sense of Quebec's distinctiveness vis-à-vis the other provinces that by the 1970s the very term "province" had fallen into disuse. Some Quebec nationalists even claimed that it harkened back to the days of the British Empire when it was used to designate divisions within such other imperial holdings as India. But whatever its connotations, "province" served to equate Quebec with Canada's other territorial units when, at least in the eyes of nationalists, Quebec manifestly was not. Thus, the Quebec provincial government became *l'État du Québec*. For the Quebec legislature, only the rather grandiloquent term *Assemblée nationale* would do.

This later change goes to the nub of the matter: for many Quebec francophones Quebec is not just a province with a difference, it's a *nation* and deserving of recognition as such. Since the early nineteenth century, nationalism has provided the set of assumptions through which francophone intellectuals have defined their collectivity and interpreted its historical fate. To be sure, over the decades the dominant form of this nationalism has changed radically in terms not only of the geographical boundaries of the nation, but even of the nation's fundamental characteristics and goals. In part, these changes have reflected changes in the historical condition of the nation as a whole. But they also have reflected alterations in the balance of social forces within the nation, as members of different classes succeed in imposing their brand of nationalism—which invariably has reflected the particular preoccupations and ambitions of their class. If the central theme of this nationalism has been the necessity of maintaining cultural distinctiveness against British and English Canadian threats, a recurrent theme has been the desire to break down the structures of anglophone economic and political domination. In each case, different nationalist leaderships have approached these themes in very different ways.

To understand why Quebec's society is distinctive, and how a "national consciousness" has developed out of this distinctiveness, we need to trace Quebec's historical development.

THE HISTORICAL ROOTS OF DISTINCTIVENESS AND NATIONALISM

Unlike the rest of Canada, Quebec society first emerged within the framework of the French Empire. This formative experience as the colony of New France established forms of distinctiveness that were to endure long after Quebec ceased to be a French colony. A common *Canadien* dialect was created out of the several French dialects that the colonists brought with them, predating the emergence of a national dialect in the mother country. The Catholic Church was afforded a privileged position within the formal institutions of the ancien régime, laying the basis for the central role that it was to play throughout so much of French Canada's history. And the Civil Code was entrenched within the ancien régime legal structures. The colonists soon acquired a sense of collective identity, and destiny, as they faced the common challenges of a harsh climate and periodic threats from native peoples and from the British colonies to the south. They began to call themselves *Canadiens* or *habitants* so as to distinguish themselves from the metropolitan French, as well as from English-speakers. In fact, they periodically expressed resentment against the metropolitan Frenchmen who were nominated to senior positions within the colony.

The colony was never the quasi-feudal society or theocracy that was portrayed by latter-day historians. The Bishop and his colleagues regularly had to spar with secular colonial authorities over policy. Commercial values and interests were actively pursued by some secular elites who amassed considerable personal wealth through the fur trade. And the regularity with which the *habitants* challenged the authority of parish priests or resisted paying their tithes gives the lie to images of a "priest-ridden" society. Thus, social tensions and conflict have marked French Canada from its beginning.

If Quebec emerged as part of the French Empire, it was a relatively unimportant and neglected one. In 1759 it fell under British control and lost forever its formal linkage with France. It was within the structures of the British Empire that the *Canadiens* would have to secure a future for themselves. If they were to maintain their distinctiveness, it would be on terms acceptable to the British authorities, and the English-speaking population that soon established itself within the colony. Moreover, it would be under the direction of a greatly shrunken *Canadien* leadership. With the Conquest, administrative and military structures fell into the hands of the British. And the replacement of France by England as

Quebec's metropole ensured that the colony's trade would be controlled by the British rather than *Canadiens*. In short, all that remained by way of a viable leadership for the *Canadiens* was the Church and, to a lesser extent, the seigneurs: the two classes that had a strong interest in the *Canadiens* defining their distinctiveness in the most traditional of terms.

Initially, British authorities were determined to destroy all forms of cultural distinctiveness for the *Canadiens*. The Royal Proclamation of 1763 was designed to do just that. However, the Proclamation was not put into effect. With time, the colonial authorities determined that the imperial interest would be better served by winning the collaboration of the *Canadien* leadership and thus, presumably, of the *Canadiens* as a whole. Under the Quebec Act of 1774, the seigneurial system was re-established, the Church was once again empowered to collect tithes, Catholics were spared the need to renounce their faith to assume office, and French civil law was re-established. At the same time, a representative assembly was not created out of deference to the *Canadien* clergy and seigneurs who feared a challenge to their own positions.

Ostensibly, the survival of *Canadien* society was assured. Yet, it was a particular *kind* of *Canadien* society that was so assured. In effect, the Quebec Act served to reinforce traditional structures and values within *Canadien* society. And it formalized a cultural division of labour that was to mark Quebec for the next two centuries. *Canadiens* could count upon being able to assume ecclesiastical and legal functions, at least to service the needs of their compatriots, but there was nothing to challenge the firm control over the colony's economic life that English-speakers had secured in the wake of the Conquest. Much of the history of the next two centuries, including the nationalist upsurge of the 1960s and 1970s, can be seen as a struggle by various groups to break French Canadian society out of this mould, and out of the political and economic bonds that supported it, imposed by the British colonial regime in close collaboration with French Canadian traditional elites.

It was in the early nineteenth century that French Canada's first nationalist movement took form. It was spawned by a new class of *Canadiens*, a petite bourgeoisie of liberal professionals and small merchants that coalesced in the legislative assembly that the Constitutional Act of 1791 had created (while at the same time dividing the British colony of Quebec in two). Within the new colony of Lower Canada, French Canadians were clearly preponderant, and even with an overrepresentation of anglophones in the assembly, the *Canadiens* still had a commanding majority. In part, the nationalism of this new *Canadien* petite bourgeoisie was a response to the continuing assimilationist projects of the colony's anglophone population. In part, it was a response to the English bourgeoisie's ambitious plans for development of the colonial economy:

the *Canadiens* would not benefit directly from the projects even though they would have to assume part of the financial burden through taxation.

But the petite bourgeoisie's nationalism also reflected its own class position. It was quite appropriate that this nationalist leadership should champion liberal political reforms and the rights of the representative assembly, given their own dominance of that assembly and relative exclusion from executive and administrative office within the colony. At the same time, the *Canadien* liberal professionals began to challenge clerical pre-eminence over the francophone population by sponsoring such projects as a secularized school system. Out of this protracted conflict emerged the *Patriote* movement, which championed an autonomous state for Quebec and, in 1837, staged an armed uprising in order to secure it. With overwhelming military superiority, the British authorities had no difficulty putting down the rebellion. For good measure, they had the vigorous support of the French Canadian clergy, which had long been alarmed by some of the liberal notions that the *Patriotes* had propagated.

With the defeat of the Rebellions of 1837 the more traditional forces within French Canadian society, led by the Church, were able to secure a new ascendancy. The Church strengthened itself through importing priests from France, refugees from French liberalism, and expanding the religious orders and educational institutions. In the process, a new, apolitical version of French Canadian nationalism became hegemonic. In clerical hands, the essence of the French Canadian nation became its Catholicism. National greatness was to lie in Godliness and spirituality, best achieved in a rural setting, rather than material accomplishments. For this, French Canadians were to rely upon the institutions of the Church rather than governments and politicians, corroded as they were by liberalism and corruption. By definition, within this world view, anglophone dominance of Quebec's economic development was not a problem.

In the immediate aftermath of the Rebellions the very survival of French Canadian society was placed in question by the British authorities. Under the Act of Union, inspired by the Durham Report, Lower Canada and Upper Canada were joined so as to encourage the assimilation of the troublesome *Canadiens*. However, French Canada survived yet another assimilationist threat as French Canadian politicians from Canada East formed an alliance with English Canadian reformers in Canada West and, on that basis, secured recognition of the French fact. In effect, duality became enshrined in the institutions of the United Canadas: French was made an official language along with English, hyphenated ministries were held by representatives of each of the two original colonies, and to some extent, voting was based on a double-majority principle.

Eventually, this situation became unacceptable to many English

Canadians, with the result that French Canadians of Quebec had to trade dualism for federalism. First, Canada West's population began to exceed Canada East's. In 1840 Canada East had been much more populous than Canada West; the two Canadas had been assigned an equal number of seats so as to prevent Canada East's dominance. Now, the residents of Canada West had become eager converts to "rep by pop." Second, the English Canadian bourgeoisie found that its economic projects were being frustrated in the United Canadas assembly by French Canadians and their reformist allies. Thus, the campaign began to join the several British colonies in a common union. There, French Canadians clearly would be in a minority; central political institutions would be dominated by English Canadians. To be acceptable to them Confederation had to be based upon federalism, which would afford Quebec an autonomous state for certain purposes. Thus, a central premise of Confederation was that French Canadians could not entrust their distinctive interests to an English Canadian majority.

Nonetheless, the notion of "distinctive interests" contained in the division of powers quite closely reflects the ascendancy of the Church within French Canadian society. Quebec, and the other provincial governments, were granted jurisdiction over matters that were central to its cultural survival, such as education, or that might affect the prerogatives of the Church and its institutions, such as health, welfare, and the solemnization of marriage. On the other hand, economic responsibilities were effectively lodged with the federal government along with exclusive access to the then primary source of government revenue, indirect taxes. In this sense, the terms of Confederation further formalized the cultural division of labour that underlay the Quebec Act of 1774. The same division of labour was reproduced within the federal government itself. In the Cabinet, anglophones effectively monopolized the major economic portfolios. In the upper levels of the bureaucracy, francophones were seriously underrepresented.

THE ECONOMIC AND SOCIAL TRANSFORMATION OF QUEBEC: SEEDS OF POLITICAL CRISIS

By the turn of the century, social changes were underway in Quebec that eventually would result in serious challenges to these political arrangements, and even to Confederation itself. Industrialization can be traced back as far as the 1870s. At that time, Montreal was producing as much iron and steel products as Toronto and Hamilton combined and had a large number of manufacturing enterprises.[2] With the turn of the century, industrialization spread to other parts of Quebec. For its part, urbanization can be traced to the first part of this century. In fact, by 1921 half of Quebec's population as a whole was urban. The level of urbanization among francophones alone was not quite as high, but by 1931 it had reached 58 percent.

Until the 1960s, the full impact of these changes on Quebec's political life was delayed. Typically, industrialization entails an expansion of the role of the state to assist capital in its undertakings and to placate an expanded working class. And the social and economic problems of urban life usually raise demands for new government services. Moreover, one might well expect demands for state intervention to arise from the way in which English Canadian and American capital dominated Quebec's industrialization. Not only were francophone enterprises marginal in industry, as they had been in commerce and finance, but to a large extent the growing francophone proletariat was employed by "foreigners."

Yet, especially when compared with the neighbouring province of Ontario, which was also being transformed through industrialization and urbanization, the economic and social role of the Quebec state remained quite limited. The provision of education and social services remained effectively under the control of the Church and its orders. Even the weakly developed public schools were subject to clerical domination through the Conseil de l'instruction publique; there was no Ministry of Education. As for the economy, the Quebec government played a largely passive role. Industrial development was encouraged primarily by making natural resources available to American and English Canadian firms at nominal royalty levels. As one might expect, the administrative structures of the Quebec government remained poorly developed. Relatively few personnel had expertise in social sciences. By and large, they were political appointees.

There had been some significant reforms during the Liberal regime of Adélard Godbout (1939–44). The government made school attendance compulsory and granted women the right to vote, in both cases over the strong opposition of the clergy. It also established Hydro-Québec, through the nationalization of Montreal Light, Heat & Power. But upon its return to power in 1944, the Union Nationale regime of Maurice Duplessis was little inclined to follow suit by further expanding the economic and social role of the Quebec government. It did, however, intervene vigorously in one area: labour relations. Through a variety of legislative measures and through deployment of the provincial police, it sought to curtail the actions of unions.

In short, the Duplessis regime faithfully reproduced the historical cultural division of labour in Quebec's economy and did little to address the mounting need of the francophone population for higher levels of education and social services than the Church-related institutions were able, or willing, to provide. Needless to say, the Duplessis administration had the close support of English Canadian and American capitalists who highly prized Duplessis's ability to maintain labour peace and keep taxes low. However, by the 1950s two social groups had emerged within French Quebec that had a clear interest in changing this state of affairs.

First, the post-war years saw the emergence within French Canada of a "new middle class" of salaried professionals. Within the French-language universities, formally under Church control, the numbers of lay faculty had grown rapidly both in the physical sciences and the social sciences. Especially important in the development of a critique of the passivity of the Duplessis regime was the Faculté des sciences sociales at Université Laval where lay faculty openly advocated a variety of reforms, earning Duplessis's bitter emnity in the process. Francophone intellectuals also gained a new base, and popular influence, as Radio-Canada began television broadcasting. At the same time, lay administrators and professionals acquired a new prominence in the Church-related institutions that provided health and social services. Finally, as they had for many years, l'École polytechnique continued to train francophone engineers and l'École des hautes études commerciales continued to graduate accountants and business specialists.

Uniting these different strata of the "new middle class" was a common interest in greater state intervention, whether it be to attenuate clerical control of education and social services or to expand opportunity for francophones within the anglophone-dominated economy. This interest found expression in a variety of new-middle-class movements and organizations. During the 1950s, proposals along these lines appeared readily in such publications as *Cité libre* or *Le Devoir*, and in the annual conferences of the Institut Canadien des affaires publiques. The Quebec Liberal Party, where influence of the new middle class was growing, adopted many of them. The Rassemblement pour l'indépendance nationale (RIN), the first Quebec *indépendantiste* party, was founded in 1960. Based within the francophone new middle class, the RIN called for state intervention on a variety of fronts. In 1960 francophone social workers formed a distinct professional organization in order to reduce clerical domination of their activities and carry on their lobbying for state intervention. And in 1961, many francophone academics and teachers joined in the Mouvement laïque de la langue française, which forthrightly advocated a secularization of Quebec's educational system.[3]

As well, from the 1950s, Quebec's union movements displayed a new militancy. Thanks to post-war prosperity, their memberships increased rapidly. The Confédération des travailleurs catholiques du Canada (CTCC), founded by the Church in 1921, came under a new leadership that was much more forthright in its advocacy of workers' interests and began to distance the CTCC from the Church. Evidence of the CTCC's new militancy was a series of bitter strikes, including the celebrated Asbestos strike of 1949, when the CTCC took on American mining interests as well as Duplessis and the Quebec provincial police. This militancy was echoed by the Fédération des unions industrielles du Québec (FUIQ), which grouped together Quebec locals linked to the Canadian Labour Congress and the American CIO. The CTCC and the FUIQ regularly called upon the Quebec government not only to handle labour relations in a more even-handed manner, but to meet the needs of labour directly through a variety of initiatives such as public health insurance, improved social security, increased state involvement in education, stricter regulation of working conditions, and complete public ownership of hydro production and distribution in the province.

Finally, support for much more limited state initiatives came from the precarious francophone business class, which feared it would be further marginalized by American and English Canadian capital. In the late 1950s the Chambre de commerce du Québec began to call upon the Quebec government to establish an economic advisory council, with strong business representation. In particular, it was hoped that the Quebec state could help French Canadian firms to find much-needed capital.

With the death of Duplessis in 1959, the subsequent disintegration of the Union Nationale, and the election to power of the Liberals under Jean Lesage in 1960, the steadily widening demands for a major expansion of the role of the Quebec state finally found an outlet. The Liberal govern-ment was keen to project an image of progressive change, in contrast with the Duplesssis regime. Moreover, unlike the Union Nationale, the Liberal Party was itself based primarily in urban Quebec. Elements of the new middle class had secured considerable influence in the Liberal Party, and the CTCC leadership had a good working relationship with Lesage and other party figures. In short, the conditions were right for what was to become a fundamental recasting of the Quebec state, and of Quebec politics in general. Over the next few years, Quebec underwent its "Quiet Revolution," a period of unprecedented intellectual and political fer-ment. In the process, all the long-established assumptions about French–English relations and Quebec's place within Confederation were placed in question.

THE QUIET REVOLUTION: STATE BUILDING AND NATION BUILDING

The Quiet Revolution represented first and foremost an ideological change, a transformation of mentalities. Within the new ideology, Que-bec was to be clearly seen as the urban, industrial society that it had become. The state had to assume fully the social and educational func-tions that thus far the Church had been able to retain, just as it had to assume responsibility for planning the direction of the Quebec economy and undertaking the measures needed to modernize it and make it more competitive. In effect, the Quebec state was to assume the functions of a

Keynesian state. But it was Keynesianism with a difference, since the Quebec state was also to be a "national state." With the 1960s, French Canadian nationalism was recast into a more explicitly Québécois nationalism. The greatness of this Quebec nation was to lie not in the past, as with traditional French Canadian nationalism's glorification of the ancien régime, but with the future, as an urban, industrial, and secular society. The Quebec state, responsible to a primarily francophone electorate, was the one institution that could enable the Qubécois to achieve these objectives. In particular, it was the indispensable lever to undoing the cultural division of labour within the Quebec economy, and making Québécois "maîtres chez nous"—"masters in our own house."

As with earlier formulations of nationalist ideology, the Quebec neo-nationalism of the 1960s bore the clear imprint of the class that fashioned and supported it: the francophone new middle class.[4] Qualified as they were to assume managerial and technical positions, they could only be affronted by the anglophone dominance of the economy. By the same token, they had every interest in the transfer of responsibilities from the Church to an expanded Quebec state, with a modern bureaucracy. And they had every reason to support the Quebec government in its struggles with Ottawa, where opportunities for the francophone new middle class were few and far between. Yet, resentment over anglophone domination, the desire for better educational and social services, and suspicion of the federal government were shared by a great many francophones. The various initiatives of the Lesage Liberals enjoyed the unvarying support not only of the new middle class, but of organized labour, especially the CSN. And they were supported on a more qualified basis by francophone business and traditional liberal professional nationalists. With steady propagation by the Quebec government and intellectuals, neo-nationalism acquired a certain degree of hegemony in Quebec. Thus, young francophones entering political life in the 1960s were massively socialized to it.

Beyond ideological change, however, the 1960s did witness real change in the structures and role of the Quebec state. In 1963 Quebec's private hydro-electrical enterprises were nationalized so as to give Hydro-Québec a virtual monopoly over the production and distribution of electricity in the province. In 1968 a publicly owned steelmill, SIDBEC, was established. A Société générale de financement was created to inject capital into enterprises owned by French Canadians. On the basis of funds created through the Quebec Pension Plan, the Caisse de dépôt et de placement du Québec became a major institutional investor and, when needed, purchaser of government securities. In 1964 a Ministry of Education was created, and over subsequent years many of the collèges classiques were transformed into secular, government-administered Collèges d'enseignement général et professionnel (CEGEPS). Control over health and social services moved steadily from Church-related institutions to the Quebec bureaucracy.

Nonetheless, the overall effect of the Quiet Revolution reforms was uneven. Secularization of Quebec society progressed rapidly: as Church-held educational and social functions were transferred to the state, clerical influence in Quebec society declined at an astounding rate. However, much more limited progress was made in reversing the historical anglophone dominance of the Quebec economy, the expansion of Hydro-Québec notwithstanding. Moreover, by the mid-1960s, the uneasy coalition of social forces that had supported the initiatives of the Lesage government had succumbed to its own contradictions. With the return of the Union Nationale to power in 1966, the government fell to a party that had a different social base. Financially, it was increasingly constrained. Thus, while the momentum of change in the Quebec state was not halted, it was markedly slowed. By the same token, mid-1960s relations between Quebec City and Ottawa became increasingly polarized. Initially, the federal government had sought to accommodate Quebec's demands to occupy its jurisdictions to the maximum, as with the establishment of a Quebec Pension Plan in 1964 and other "opting out" schemes. However, misgivings arose in federal circles. With the accession to power in 1968 of Pierre Trudeau, the emphasis clearly shifted to other approaches to Quebec nationalism, such as extension of French-language rights outside Quebec.

In sum, during the 1960s a great many Québécois had been converted to the Quiet Revolution conception of a dynamic, interventionist Quebec state. By the late 1960s, however, the Quebec state no longer seemed able to pursue the neo-nationalist agenda of economic and social change; it had reached its limits. Yet, the original agenda was expanding as new concerns arose. Quebec nationalists began to fear that the continuing anglicization of immigrants threatened francophone predominance in Montreal, if not all of Quebec. New demands arose for restriction of access to English-language schools. At the same time, the relative failure of the Quebec state to carve out new opportunities for francophones in the upper levels of the Quebec economy fostered demands for state intervention to establish French as the language of work. These demands became all the more urgent as the 1960s expansion of the Quebec state structures wound down and fewer new positions were available to francophone university graduates. Finally, working-class organizations began to articulate their own vision of an agenda for Quebec that was not bound by the preoccupations of the new middle class. These concerns acquired urgency as labour relations in the public sector became increasingly conflict-prone.

THE PARTI QUEBECOIS AND QUEBEC
INDEPENDENCE

All these forms of political frustration provided ready grounds for the cause of Quebec independence. Independence bore the promise of a Quebec state that would have the capacity, and resolve, to discharge this much larger agenda. Thus, it became the essential remedy for a wide variety of grievances. In addition, independence had more direct appeal. For the many francophones, especially among the youth, who had come to see themselves as pre-eminently *Québécois*, independence constituted the formal recognition of their own identity. As a result, the Quebec independence movement and its preoccupations were to colour, if not dominate, Quebec politics throughout the 1970s and early 1980s.

In 1968 the Parti Québécois (PQ), under the leadership of René Lévesque, emerged as the primary vehicle of the *indépendantiste* cause. The PQ proposed to repatriate the economic "centres of decision" through state enterprises and regulation of non-Quebec ownership in the financial sector. At the same time, this "technocratic" thrust was coupled with "populist" measures to help a variety of socially deprived groups. All this would be made possible by Quebec becoming a sovereign state. Quebec would be linked to the rest of Canada through a vaguely defined economic association, but Quebec would nonetheless achieve the full-fledged national status to which its centuries-old distinctiveness entitled it. Members of the new middle class dominated the PQ leadership; the party program clearly bore their imprint. But the Parti Québécois emerged as a broad-based coalition of social forces committed to Quebec sovereignty.[5]

The pressures to reinforce Quebec's distinctiveness only grew with the return of the Liberals to power in 1970, this time under Robert Bourassa. In the October Crisis of 1970 the Quebec government was effectively subordinated to Ottawa as the federal government proceeded with its hard-line response to the Front de libération du Québec (FLQ). The following year, efforts to revise the Canadian constitution ground to a halt after the Bourassa government concluded that the Victoria Charter was insufficient to meet Quebec's needs. The government's efforts through Bill 22 to satisfy nationalist demands for the pre-eminence of French within Quebec foundered over rejection of the bill by franco-phones and anglophones alike. At the same time, through its retreat from state economic intervention, the government seemed to be treating as inconsequential the issue of ownership within the Quebec economy. And dramatic confrontations between the Bourassa government and the union movement, especially with respect to public sector workers, further served to weaken the legitimacy of the existing order. As the Parti Québécois dominated opposition forces, its option of Quebec sovereignty emerged as the logical remedy to all these problems. Accordingly, the PQ was able to win power in 1976.

The election of a party formally committed to sovereignty for Quebec served to demonstrate more clearly than ever before the distinctiveness of Quebec politics. Never before had a province elected a government committed to withdrawal from Canada (with the possible exception of the 1867 election of an anti-Confederation government in Nova Scotia). The PQ had not spelled out the precise nature of sovereignty; it remained committed to some notion of economic association. Moreover, the party had declared that a PQ government would first need to obtain popular approval in a referendum before it could proceed to secure sovereignty. Nonetheless, mere evocation of sovereignty was sufficient to plunge the Canadian political system into its gravest crisis.

As it happened, the Lévesque government moved slowly on the question of sovereignty. Three years passed until the government fully defined its proposal; another year passed before it staged its referendum. Instead, the PQ became consumed with the task of running a provincial government. In both areas, the PQ's prudence reflected the new-middle-class base of its leadership. Over the previous twenty years, this class had already made very substantial gains; thus it had little disposition toward, or interest in, needless risk.

The Lévesque government first moved on the language front, with its Bill 101. In its final version, Bill 101 did not differ radically from Bill 22. But it did tighten up access to English schools by non-anglophones and it was more stringent in requiring enterprises to *francisize* their operations. Also, through requiring French-only commercial signs it sought to give Quebec an unmistakably French face. Moreover, coming from an *indépendantiste* government, the measures carried much more credibility than had Bill 22. In addition, the Lévesque administration reformed electoral funding practices and passed a variety of social measures, such as public automobile insurance, labour relations reform, a limited guaranteed income scheme and free medication for the elderly. In effect, the PQ went about providing "good" provincial government. In fact, when it came to routine federal–provincial relations, the PQ government agreed to a wide variety of joint programs with Ottawa.

This emphasis upon providing "good government" was rationalized in terms of the PQ's *étapiste* strategy: as the population acquired confidence in the ability of the party to provide good provincial government, so it would be more prepared to support the party's option of independence. Yet, this strategy carried risks common to all movements that, while committed to global change, assume office within existing structures. As party leaders, and militants, come to enjoy the concrete benefits associated with holding office, their own commitment to more radical change may be tempered. Party militants may become estranged from their leaders, who now have a separate base of power outside of the party. Most important, efforts to provide "good" government may serve to make the existing system more tolerable to the discontented parts of the population, thus undercutting rather than reinforcing support for more radical change. All of these processes appear to have affected the PQ and support for the independence option. Especially striking is the extent to which Bill 101 may have served to rehabilitate the existing federal order by appearing to resolve the language question to nationalists' satisfaction.

In addition, the PQ leadership applied *étapiste* logic to the goal of sovereignty itself, surrounding it with a very comprehensive economic association and committing the government to yet another referendum. In seeking to minimize the prospect of change, the government seemed to acknowledge that true independence would have catastrophic effects. On this basis, it could not address the fears of much of the population, which clearly believed that the PQ's real goal was independence. At the same time, the credibility of its option depended upon whether English Canada was likely to accept it; English Canadian politicians spared no effort to convince Québécois that this would not be the case. Whatever the explanation, the PQ government was unable to broaden support much beyond its primary electoral clientele of younger francophones, especially based within the public sector. Thus, with only 40 percent in favour (not quite 50 percent of francophones), the referendum proposition was soundly defeated.

QUEBEC IN THE 1980S: THE COLLAPSE OF THE NEO-NATIONALIST PROJECT

The failure of the referendum was to have a devastating effect on the nationalist movement. Even if the Parti Québécois was able to secure re-election in 1981, it appeared that what had once seemed to be an inexorable movement to Quebec independence was permanently halted. Pessimism was only confirmed by the 1982 constitutional revision, which not only failed to meet Quebec's long-standing constitutional demands, but was approved over the objections of the Quebec government.

Moreover, the 1980s have seen the widespread repudiation within Quebec of what had been a central premise of the *indépendantiste* movement: the capacity of the state to bring about social and economic improvement. In part this was merely a reflection of international trends: the new intellectual fashionability of neo-liberal doctrines and the early 1980s crisis of Western capitalism. But the attacks were also fuelled by conditions specific to Quebec itself: the unusually high level of tax burden resulting from the ambitious state building of the 1960s and 1970s and, in particular, the emergence of a dynamic francophone business class. By the 1980s, two decades of efforts by the Quebec state to expand francophone economic ownership clearly had borne fruit. A substantial number of firms had become important actors on North American and even international markets: the Banque national, Power Corporation, and the Laurentian Group in finance; Lavalin and SNC in engineering; Bombardier in manufacturing; Provigo in food retailing; and Culinar in food processing. In most cases, these firms were no longer dependent upon intervention by the Quebec state. In fact, francophone business leaders became increasingly critical of all forms of state intervention. The second Lévesque administration clearly reflected these forces. Not only did the government proceed to wind down some state enterprises, but in an effort to reduce spending growth it cut back in social programs and, in particular, engaged in a bitter confrontation with public sector unions.

In short, by the mid-1980s Quebec politics appeared to have gone full circle. The neo-nationalist project that had so dominated the 1960s and 1970s, celebrating and even reinforcing Quebec's distinctiveness, seemed to have been fatally undermined, as had the notion of state intervention that had underlain it. Moreover, with the election in 1985 of a renewed Bourassa Liberal government it appeared that Quebec would be further propelled along a process of "normalization" through which it would become more and more a province like the others. Yet, the experience of the last few years has demonstrated that substantial proportions of Quebec francophones remain very much committed to social and economic roles that the Quebec state assumed during the 1960s and 1970s. They are even more committed to the distinct Québécois identity that these measures served to legitimize.

QUEBEC IN THE 1990S: THE CONTINUING LEGACY OF THE QUIET REVOLUTION

Initially, the way seemed wide open for the 1985 Bourassa government to "roll back" the Quebec state, as demanded by the francophone and anglophone business class to which it is so closely linked. In fact, three reports commissioned by the government mapped out ways to do precisely that. Nonetheless, during the first few years of power the results were uneven. The Bourassa government's proposal to streamline the administrative structures of Bill 101 provoked such an outcry among francophone nationalists that the government was forced to drop the measure (although it did pass a measure to strengthen anglophone access to English-language health and social services). While the government privatized a large number of state enterprises and initiated an overhaul of social programs, it also expanded community clinics (CLSCS) and resisted revising labour law in the ways that business demanded. Quebec remained the only North American jurisdiction with an "anti-scab" law. Clearly, the Bourassa government placed a high price on "restoring political and social stability." Thus, it hesitated to launch the direct attack on organized labour and its allies that would be necessary to fully "normalize" the role of the Quebec state. Undoing the Quiet Revolution would be no easy task, even if it were the intention of the Bourassa government to do so.

This same lesson emerges with respect to the primary legacy of the Quiet Revolution: Quebec nationalism. In recent years, some observers have argued that the bases of Quebec nationalism have effectively disappeared. First, it has been claimed that such forces as cultural and economic continentalization and the integration of immigrants to French Quebec have so weakend Quebec's distinctiveness as to eliminate the basis of a national identity. [6] Second, it has been contended that the grievances that gave rise in the first place to Quebec nationalism, and *Indépendantisme*, have been eliminated through such measures as Bill 101, the reinforcement of the francophone presence outside Quebec, and the repatriation of the Canadian constitution in 1982, and well as through the emergence of a dynamic francophone business class.

Yet, ample bases for a sense of Quebec national identity clearly do persist. The French language continues to distinguish over 80 percent of Quebec's population, and to have at best a secondary presence in the nine other provinces. Language provides a continuing basis not only for distinctiveness, but for social and institutional separateness from other Canadians. Moreover, the persistence of French reflects over two centuries of struggle: a legacy that contemporary Québécois will not easily forget. Even if Quebec francophones were to be distinguished by language alone, they would have more than enough reason to see themselves as members of a "distinct society" and to see the Quebec state as having a primary responsibility to preserve this distinctiveness. Yet, linguistic distinctiveness continues to be reinforced by subtle cultural differences, as well as by the palpable differences in economic and political interest that separate Quebec from, in particular, neighbouring Ontario. This continuing strength of Quebec identity emerges clearly from a 1988 survey that asked Quebec residents how they identified themselves. The response of "above all Québécois" was selected by a full 49 percent of Quebec francophones (the same proportion as had voted "yes" in the 1980 referendum). Another 39 percent defined themselves as "French Canadian." But only 11 percent said they were simply "Canadian." [7]

By the same token, it is far from certain that the grievances that fuelled Quebec nationalism, and *indépendantisme*, during the 1960s and 1970s have been fully resolved. The various linguistic reforms that the federal government undertook to strengthen the French presence outside Quebec have had very mixed results. Francophones clearly have assumed more prominent roles in federal Cabinets, but their presence in the upper levels of the federal bureaucracy remains uneven. Nor has French assumed equal status as a language of work. And despite federal efforts to strengthen the francophone minorities, in all provinces but Quebec the proportion of residents whose first language is French has continued to decline. In fact, most demographers predict that by the year 2000 Quebec will contain close to 95 percent of Canada's French-speaking population. Thus, in the future Quebec will be even more distinguished linguistically from the rest of Canada.

To be sure, the successful efforts of Quebec governments to strengthen the role of French within Quebec itself probably were much more important in easing the discontents of Quebec nationalists than were the federal programs, focused as they were outside Quebec. However, recent events have dramatically demonstrated that even here many Quebec francophones continue to share deep concerns. In December 1988 the Supreme Court of Canada determined that the Bill 101 provision requiring French-only commercial signs was in conflict with the Charter of Rights and Freedoms (as well as Quebec's own Human Rights Act). The Bourassa government responded with a complex measure (Bill 178) restricting outdoor signs to French, but allowing French to be accompanied by another language in advertising within stores. On the basis of the Supreme Court decision, even this compromise measure violated the Charter. Thus, the Bourassa government was obliged to invoke the notwithstanding clause in order to protect Bill 178 from constitutional challenge. Yet, for many Quebec francophones any deviation from the Bill 101 formula was unacceptable. In a dramatic demonstration of the linguistic division within Quebec, a January 1989 survey found that 69 percent of Quebec francophones felt that the provincial government had the right to restrict the freedom of expression of Quebec anglophones in order to protect the French language; 81 percent of non-francophones disagreed.[8] In effect, not only has the pre-eminence of French within Quebec become a *sine qua non* for most Quebec francophones, but Bill 101 itself has acquired a certain sanctity in their eyes ("ne touche pas le Bill 101"). Any threat to the bill's integrity is sufficient to arouse deeply rooted fears about the future of a French Quebec.

By the same token, the 1982 revision of the Canadian constitution clearly did not respond to the long-standing demand of Quebec francophones for a reinforcement of the status and powers of the Quebec government. In fact, it can be argued that the Quebec government's position was weakened through the Constitution Act, 1982. The Charter of Rights and Freedoms limits the Quebec government's prerogatives in such matters as regulating access to English-language schools and restricting access to government services by migrants from other provinces. And the amendment formula denies Quebec (for most purposes) the veto that past Quebec governments (although not the Lévesque administration) had always insisted upon and which, by some scholarly interpretations, Quebec had always enjoyed as a matter of convention. In fact, the Lévesque government refused to accede to the agreement, as did its Liberal successor.

The Meech Lake Accord was designed to remedy this major failing. However, even the Accord is very guarded in its enhancement of Quebec's position. A provision declaring Quebec to be a "distinct society" is carefully balanced by a preceding provision invoking a linguistic duality that extends throughout Canada and is further constrained by a provision declaring that the federal government's "powers, rights or privileges" cannot be diminished. A provision allows Quebec, and the other provinces, to opt out with compensation from federal spending programs within exclusive provincial jurisdictions, but only if they establish initiatives or programs of their own that are compatible with "national objectives" to be set by Ottawa. The area of constitutional amendment over which Quebec, and the other provinces, can exercise a veto is only marginally expanded. A provision allowing Quebec, and the other provinces, to enter into agreements with Ottawa over immigration essentially formalizes existing practice within a concurrent jurisdiction. Quebec, and the other provinces, would set the lists from which the federal government would select nominees for the Supreme Court and the Senate, but would, of course, exercise no leverage over these individuals once they assume office. Certainly, the Meech Lake Accord is a far cry from the substantial programs of constitutional change that such bodies as the Quebec Liberal Party and Ottawa's own Task Force on National Unity had devised in the late 1970s when the Lévesque government was seeking to mobilize support for sovereignty-association. Arguably, it falls short of the Victoria Charter, which all governments but Quebec had agreed to in 1971. In effect, it constitutes the minimal basis upon which Quebec's formal adhesion to the constitution might be secured. Nonetheless, it would appear that even a purely symbolic recognition of the distinctiveness of Quebec society is sufficient to render the Accord suspect in the eyes of many English Canadians and to make its eventual passage highly problematic.[9]

Finally, beyond the continuing tensions surrounding the status of French within Quebec and the apparent impasse regarding the accommodation of Quebec within the Canadian constitutional order, Quebec nationalism may also be reinforced by reorientation of Quebec's economic relationships. Increased economic integration with the United States, under the Canadian–U.S. free trade agreement, may well serve to reduce the relative significance of Quebec's economic linkages with the rest of Canada. To take the extreme scenario, a renewed Quebec independence movement seeking to situate Quebec sovereignty within a larger economic association would no longer need to secure the highly problematic assent of the rest of Canada to such an agreement; it could rely upon the American connection. (For that matter, the equanimity with which Quebec nationalists, and most Québécois, viewed the free trade agreement, in sharp contrast with English Canadian nationalists, is vivid evidence of Quebec's "distinctiveness.")

To be sure, a renewed independence movement would have to draw upon a different configuration of social forces than did the *péquiste* independence movement of the 1970s. Thanks to the mishaps of the second Lévesque administration and, more fundamentally, the generalized attack upon state intervention that has marked the 1980s, the PQ brand of technocratic nationalism has lost its credibility and its coalition of public sector and working-class forces led by the new middle class seems to be beyond repair. A serious resurgence of Quebec *indépendantiste* would have to be based upon a new national project. While there has been a certain resurgence of linguistic concerns, especially among younger francophones, it is not yet clear whether there exists the necessary leadership for a dynamic *indépendantiste* movement. Despite some claims, the ascendant francophone business class would seem to be a most unlikely candidate.

Nonetheless, even if a new *indépendantiste* movement should not emerge within the next few years, Quebec francophones will continue to be concerned about the viability of their society and about the status of Quebec within the Canadian constitutional order. Many will continue to see themselves as first and foremost *Québécois*. At a minimum, Quebec francophones will continue to see Quebec as a distinct society, and Quebec will continue to be one.

NOTES

1. Derived from *Census of Canada*, 1981, 92-911, Table IV.
2. John McCallum, *Unequal Beginnings: Agriculture and Economic Development in Quebec and Ontario until 1870* (Toronto: University of Toronto Press, 1980), p. 104.
3. These developments are traced in Michael D. Beheils, *Prelude to Quebec's Quiet Revolution* (Montreal: McGill-Queen's University Press, 1985). See also Kenneth McRoberts, *Quebec: Social Change and Political Crisis*, 3rd ed. (Toronto: McClelland and Stewart, 1988), ch. 4.
4. The leading role of the new middle class within the Quiet Revolution coalition is discussed at length in McRoberts, *Quebec: Social Change and Political Crisis*, ch. 5. For a critique of this interpretation, see William D. Coleman, *The Independence Movement in Quebec, 1945–1980* (Toronto: University of Toronto press, 1984).
5. Competing approaches to classifying and explaining the ideology and

class bases of the Parti Québécois are assessed in McRoberts, *Quebec: Social Change and Political Crisis*, pp. 242–59.

6. This argument has been made forcefully in Coleman, *The Independence Movement in Quebec.*

7. Among Quebec non-francophones the pattern was reversed: "Canadian"—75 percent; "Québécois"—10 percent; and "English Canadian"—10 percent. "Le francophone est Québécois, l'anglophone 'Canadian,' " *Le Devoir* 25 juin 1988, p. 1.

8. "Language Law Poll Finds Most Opposed," *The Toronto Star*, 22 January 1989, p. A19.

9. The Meech Lake Accord is analyzed in Peter W. Hogg, *Meech Lake Constitutional Accord Annotated* (Toronto: Carswell, 1988) and Katherine E. Swinton and Carol J. Rogerson, eds., *Competing Constitutional Visions: The Meech Lake Accord* (Toronto: Carswell, 1988). See also, McRoberts, *Quebec: Social Change and Political Crisis*, pp. 394–404.

FURTHER READINGS

Balthazar, Louis. *Bilan du nationalisme au Québec.* Montréal: Éditions del'Hexagone, 1986.

Behiels, Michael D., ed. *Quebec Since 1945: Selected Readings.* Toronto: Copp Clark Pitman, 1987.

Bourque, Gilles, and Anne Legaré. *Le Québec: la question nationale.* Paris: Maspero, 1979.

Coleman, William D. *The Independence Movement in Quebec, 1945–1980.* Toronto: University of Toronto Press, 1984.

Dion, Léon. *Á la recherche du Québec.* Québec: Presses de l'Université Laval, 1987.

Gagnon, Alain G., ed. *Quebec: State and Society.* Toronto: Methuen, 1984.

Guindon, Hubert. *Tradition, Modernity and Nationhood: Essays on Quebec Society.* Toronto: University of Toronto Press, 1988.

McRoberts, Kenneth. *Quebec: Social Change and Political Crisis.* 3rd ed. Toronto: McClelland and Stewart, 1988.

Monière, Denis. *Le développement des idéologies au Québec des origines á nos jours.* Montréal: Editions Québec/Amérique, 1977. English-language version: *Ideologies in Quebec.* Toronto: University of Toronto press, 1981.

Renaud, Gilbert. *A l'ombre du rationalisme: la société québécoise, de sa dépendance á sa quotidienneté.* Montréal: Editions Saint-Martin, 1984.

7

The Atlantic Provinces

PETER G. BOSWELL

Contrary to the impression frequently left by the "national" media and many "coast to coast" expeditions, Canada does not end at Halifax. Nor are the Atlantic provinces the same as the Maritimes. There may even be some room for doubt that an Atlantic region actually exists at all.

For the purposes of analysis, Canada is frequently divided into five regions; the four provinces whose land mass is largely or completely surrounded by the waters of the Atlantic Ocean are commonly grouped together and referred to as the Atlantic provinces.[1] While the people, politics, and economics of Newfoundland, Prince Edward Island, Nova Scotia, and New Brunswick may have more in common with each other than with those in other parts of Canada, each of the Atlantic provinces is nonetheless unique.[2]

In addition to the differences *between* the Atlantic provinces, significant regional differentiations exist *within* them. Newfoundland has both its "beyond the overpass" syndrome with much of the province being resentful of St. John's and the northeast Avalon Peninsula, and many residents of Labrador who feel that they are neglected and exploited by those on the island. The divisions between Cape Breton and the rest of Nova Scotia are deep and of long standing, and New Brunswick's two major ethnic groups tend to be located in geographically and economically distinct clusters within the province. Only Prince Edward Island has no major internal regional divisions, although it has been split by issues such as school consolidation and economic development.[3]

Throughout the Atlantic provinces, despite a number of recent initiatives, residents have been slow to identify with the region as opposed to their provinces. While it may be true that the bayman from a Newfoundland outport has more in common with a Nova Scotia fisherman than he does with a St. John's lawyer, both bayman and lawyer are likely to regard themselves as Canadians first, Newfoundlanders second, and maybe if they think about it long enough, residents of Atlantic Canada last.[4] Organizations as diverse as Atlantic Loto, the Atlantic Provinces Economic Council, Atlantic Plus, and the Atlantic Provinces Political Studies Association have all contributed to increased recognition and pride in the region, yet provincial boundaries are in no danger of collapse.

THE PLACE AND THE PEOPLE

For anyone who has driven from other parts of Canada into the Atlantic provinces, there is a perceptible difference once across the Quebec–New Brunswick border, a difference that grows the deeper into Atlantic Canada the traveller proceeds. It is not just that the style of the houses and towns is different, or that people seem to be less hurried and, while friendly enough, somewhat reserved and wary of strangers. The language is familiar, even if spoken with strange accents, the shopping malls look the same as those in the rest of Canada, the banks and the fast-food outlets are identical, yet there is a difference.

Part of the distinctiveness of the Atlantic region is, of course, the physical setting. From the St. John River valley in New Brunswick, through the Annapolis Valley in Nova Scotia, to Cavendish Beach in Prince Edward Island, and Bonavista Bay in Newfoundland, there is a unique beauty. While the Atlantic region cannot boast of the majestic heights of the Rocky Mountains, nor the vast open spaces of the prairies, its gentle, rolling valleys, picturesque fishing villages, and spectacular ocean frontage possess a quality and charm found nowhere else in Canada.

In terms of land mass, the Atlantic provinces are together about as large as the province of Ontario. In 1986 the combined population of the Atlantic provinces made up about 8.5 percent of Canada's total, compared with about 9.4 percent in 1976. As Table 7.1 indicates, there has been slight growth in the population of all four Atlantic provinces in the past decade, although Newfoundland's population declined as a percentage of the region's as a whole.

As Table 7.2 demonstrates, the Atlantic provinces receive very few immigrants, most choosing to settle in the more prosperous central Canadian cities with their greater opportunities for employment. This limited inflow of immigrants, with their contributions of new ideas and ways of doing things, has bequeathed to the Atlantic region a relatively static society with a consequent wariness of outsiders.[5] The data in Table 7.2 also indicate that residents of the Atlantic provinces tend to have lower rates of intraprovincial movement that do other Canadians.

At least part of this wariness of outsiders has its roots in the largely homogeneous ethnic background of most Atlantic Canadians. The majority of residents in Newfoundland, Nova Scotia, and Prince Edward Island are of British stock; and even in New Brunswick, with its population of approximately one-third French background, only about 10 percent of the remainder are of non-British origin.[6]

The relative isolation of the Atlantic region from the rest of English-speaking Canada may also contribute to the wariness of outsiders. Most of Atlantic Canada is surrounded by water; the only land link to the rest of

Table 7.1
Population Figures by Province

	1986 Population	Percent of 1986 Atlantic Population	Percent of 1986 Canadian Population	1976 Population	Percent of 1976 Atlantic Population	Percent of 1976 Canadian Population
Newfoundland	568,350	24.9	2.3	557,725	25.6	2.4
P.E.I.	126,650	5.6	.5	118,229	5.4	.5
Nova Scotia	873,175	38.3	3.5	828,571	37.9	3.6
New Brunswick	709,440	31.1	2.8	677,250	31.0	2.9
Canada	25,309,330			22,992,604		

Source: Statistics Canada, 1986 Census and 1976–77 *Canada Year Book.*

Table 7.2
Population Movement (1986 Census)

	Percent of Canadian Population	Percent of Immigrant Population	Percent of Total Movers*
Newfoundland	2.3	.2	29.1
P.E.I.	.5	.1	27.1
Nova Scotia	3.5	1.0	37.1
New Brunswick	2.8	.7	33.9
Rest of Canada	90.9	98.0	45.7

* "Movers" are those who have changed residence during the previous five years.
Source: Statistics Canada, 1986 Census.

Canada is through New Brunswick by way of either the United States or Quebec. For most people in the Atlantic region, perhaps excluding the Acadians of New Brunswick, Quebec is almost as foreign as is the United States—for some, even more so. The isolation is not only physical, but psychological as well.

Given the isolation, the generally homogeneous ethnic background, and the relatively static population, is there a distinct regional culture that can be identified and that has engendered a distinct political culture? If so, is it equally applicable to all Atlantic provinces?

Atlantic Canadians have been described as having "underdeveloped" political cultures and as being "disaffected" societies.[7] Unfortunately, the reputation of these central Canadian analyses has persisted, long after the data (and perhaps the methodology) on which they were based were out of date. More recent studies have demonstrated that "measures of political participation and efficacy exhibited very little provincial variation."[8]

As an example, the distinct political culture frequently attributed to Newfoundland has rapidly been changing.[9] While some of the old traditions and attitudes remain at the sociocultural level, political culture has moved much more in line with the rest of Canada. Religion, for instance, no longer plays a dominant role in Newfoundland politics, and even the denominational educational system is now supported by less than half of the population.[10] The defeat of the Smallwood government in 1972 brought an end to the worst of the patronage and corruption at the provincial level. Subsequent Conservative administrations have acted to regularize civil service appointments through a Public Service Commission, introduced stringent public tendering procedures, and initiated procedures to reduce conflict-of-interest situations.[11] The political apathy and lack of efficacy frequently attributed to Newfoundlanders in the past also decreased with the political demise of Smallwood. Especially since

Table 7.3
1986 Census Unemployment Rate
(by percentage)

	15–24 Age Group	25 and Over Age Group
Newfoundland	38.9	21.6
P.E.I.	22.6	13.4
Nova Scotia	22.2	10.9
New Brunswick	25.8	14.3
Canadian average	17.0	8.5

Source: Statistics Canada, 1986 Census.

the start of former premier Brian Peckford's government, interest in political matters has been high.

Similar developments have occurred in the other Atlantic provinces, throwing into question many of the stereotypes frequently applied to the region. While a few recent articles have criticized the continued use of outdated stereotypes based on obsolete data,[12] comprehensive current data to thoroughly exorcise the outmoded interpretations are not yet available.

ECONOMIC REALITIES

While it would be misleading to suggest that there is an "Atlantic" economy, some generalizations can be made about the region's economy. Standard indicators, such as unemployment and per capita income, indicate a region that is comparatively poor by national standards. As Table 7.3 indicates, unemployment rates are generally well above the national average, although it should be stressed that there is significant variation within each province as well as within the region as a whole.

Table 7.4 shows that average family income is generally below the national average, although here again there are variations within individual provinces as well as throughout the region. The need to re-examine many of the stereotypes about Atlantic Canada is reinforced by the pattern of incidence of low family income. Prince Edward Island has fewer low-income families than the national average, and Nova Scotia is just at the national level; only Newfoundland and New Brunswick have significantly greater than average numbers of low-income families.

The Atlantic provinces' economies are highly reliant on primary industry. Fishing, mining, agriculture, and forestry together with their related industries are the greatest contributors to the provinces' Gross Domestic Product. Since most of the product from these primary indus-

Table 7.4
1986 Average Family Income and Incidence of Low Income

	Average Family Income	Incidence of Low Income (by percent)
Newfoundland	$28,880	21.5
P.E.I.	$30,451	12.6
Nova Scotia	$32,938	14.3
New Brunswick	$30,527	17.0
Canadian average	$37,827	14.3

Source: Statistics Canada, 1986 Census.

tries is exported as raw or semi-processed materials, the Atlantic provinces are particularly susceptible to the vagaries of national and international markets. This can be seen not only in the fluctuating prices that the products command, but also in vulnerability to the production decisions of international corporations. The economic life of towns and regions can be seriously threatened by the decision of a corporation to obtain raw materials elsewhere in the world and to close down a mine or other operation. One-industry towns, in particular, are defenceless against this. While such closures happen in all provinces, the economies of most non-Atlantic provinces are sufficiently buoyant to be able to absorb such blows with less impact.

The importance of the fishery to the economies of the Atlantic provinces cannot be overstated, particularly in the cases of Newfoundland and Nova Scotia. It is crucial in terms of both income and employment. This is the reason some provincial politicians in the Atlantic region are so concerned about jurisdiction over the fisheries. It is a source of continuing frustration that the Constitution Act, 1867, allocates control and management of the region's fishery resources to the federal government; and it is particularly galling when it appears that foreign access to Canadian fish stocks is being traded for continued access of manufactured goods from central Canada into foreign markets. The setting of Total Allowable Catch limits and the division of the total quota between inshore and offshore sectors and among the Atlantic provinces is the subject of considerable ongoing controversy. The placement of the fishery on the agenda for First Ministers' Conferences flowing from the Meech Lake Accord recognizes the importance of this issue to the region.

For Newfoundland and Nova Scotia, the promise of offshore energy resource development threatened to reproduce the federal–provincial jurisdictional problems of the fishery. The federal right to ownership of offshore resources was confirmed by the Supreme Court of Canada in 1984, following a series of legal manoeuvres by both federal and

Table 7.5

Percentage of Total Provincial Revenue Received as Transfers from the Federal
Government

	1987–88 (est.)	1986–87 (est.)	1977–78
Newfoundland	45.7	46.8	47.1
P.E.I.	45.6	46.3	54.8
Nova Scotia	38.4	38.6	46.6
New Brunswick	43.4	42.7	47.6
Canadian average	19.7	20.2	15.1

Source: Canadian Tax Foundation, *Provincial and Municipal Finances, 1987.*

Newfoundland governments. While Nova Scotia reached an agreement with the federal government in 1982, it was not until 1985 that the Atlantic Accord settled the jurisdictional dispute between Ottawa and Newfoundland.[13] While there were major differences between the Nova Scotia and Newfoundland agreements, in both cases the federal government retained ownership of the resources while providing a share in management and revenue to the provinces. The 1982 Nova Scotia agreement contained a clause allowing that province to sign a new agreement if any other province obtained a better deal. Consequently, in 1986 Nova Scotia signed a second agreement with Ottawa based on the Atlantic Accord.

The full effect of offshore resource development on the Nova Scotian and Newfoundland economies is not yet clear. In both provinces, exploration activities have contributed to economic growth, and it is predicted that the Newfoundland economy will be given a significant boost when the Hibernia development and production agreement between the federal and provincial governments and the oil consortium is signed in 1989.

The impact of revenues from offshore oil in Newfoundland and gas in Nova Scotia will not, however, be enough to create any "have" provinces in the Atlantic region. The "have-not" status and heavy dependence on the federal government for financial assistance is deeply ingrained. While the proportion of Atlantic provincial revenue coming from the federal government has decreased slightly in recent years, as can be seen in Table 7.5, the major source of revenue for the Atlantic provinces remains equalization payments and other federal transfers.

It has been argued that Atlantic Canada's dependence and persistently poor economic performance result not from the region's lack of valuable natural resources, nor from its geographical position. Rather, its flourishing nineteenth-century industries were increasingly brought under central Canadian control after Confederation, and the economic collapse of the 1920s "not only wiped out many of the region's industrial achievements but weakened staple trades such as fishing and forestry."[14]

Some analysts lay the blame for this economic collapse squarely on the shoulders of the federal government, which they suggest succumbed to pressure from central Canadian business interests to disproportionately increase maritime freight rates, thus preventing manufacturers in the Atlantic region from being able to sell their goods in central and western Canadian markets at prices competitive with central Canadian manufacturers.[15] It is further argued that part of the reason why the Atlantic region never really recovered from the de-industrialization that occurred in the wake of the 1920s economic collapse is because the major thrust of new entrepreneurial development was not directed toward secondary manufacturing or industry, but on the expansion of the service sector and on the monopolization of trade.[16]

If the causes of underdevelopment in the Atlantic region remain in dispute, so too do assessments of the effectiveness of a variety of post–Second World War federal programs designed to stimulate regional development. From the establishment in 1961 of the Agricultural Rehabilitation and Development Agency (ARDA), through the 1969 founding of the Department of Regional Economic Expansion (DREE) and its 1982 expansion into the Department of Regional Industrial Expansion (DRIE), to the creation in 1987 of the Atlantic Canada Opportunities Agency (ACOA), federal funds have poured into the region in an attempt to stimulate its economies and provide long-term development.

It is frequently suggested that the failure of these federal programs to create lasting economic growth in the Atlantic region has been the result of federal capitulation to political pressures to provide similar funding for other regions of the country. As an example, 53 percent of DREE's spending in 1969–70 was directed to the Atlantic region; by 1984–85 this had shrunk to 16.1 percent, with 42.6 percent going to Quebec and 23 percent going to Ontario.[17] Other criticisms have been based on the misdirection and inappropriateness of programs, inefficiency of delivery mechanisms, and overall inadequacy of funding.[18]

Perhaps partially as the result of the limited success of the federal development schemes, Atlantic Canadian politicians have had a fascination with high-tech and grandiose development projects as quick economic fixes. Such schemes are usually inappropriate to the physical and economic settings and doomed to early failure. Each of the Atlantic provinces has had its share, and the leaders of both major political parties have fallen prey to the quixotic dreams of desperate economic gambles. Among some of the more spectacular failures have been Newfoundland's experiments in rubber boot and chocolate factories, the Come by Chance refinery, and most recently, the Sprung Greenhouse; Prince Edward Island had its Bathurst Marine and Garden Gulf Foods; Nova Scotia suffered its Clairtone Sound and Glace Bay heavy water plant; and New Brunswick's most colourful debacle was the Bricklin sports car fiasco.

In retrospect, the absence of sound economic planning, good management, and solid marketing analysis that surrounded these projects seems evident, but so too does the enthusiasm of provincial leaders desperate to find some way of providing employment and growth for their provinces. Unfortunately, in most cases a great deal of scarce money was wasted by provincial premiers who tended to operate with too few controls placed on them by their acquiescent legislatures.

POLITICAL INSTITUTIONS AND PROCESSES

The provincial legislatures in the Atlantic provinces are very similar to those in other provinces. Although the three Maritime provinces started out with bicameral legislatures, upper houses have long since disappeared. The legislatures meet for only part of the year and many members, other than Cabinet ministers, consider their representative roles to be a part-time occupation.[19] The number of seats in the legislatures is relatively large in relation to population, with Newfoundland having fifty-two, Prince Edward Island thirty-two, Nova Scotia fifty-two, and New Brunswick fifty-eight. With the exception of Prince Edward Island, which has only ten Cabinet members, the other provinces support a full load of Cabinet ministers, each with their complement of assistants and aides: Newfoundland has eighteen ministers, Nova Scotia twenty-two, and New Brunswick twenty.

The most remarkable aspects of the political party systems in the Atlantic provinces are the lack of ideological differences and the absence of any sustained third-party success. The combination of these two factors has led to long periods of one-party dominance and provided the conditions for relatively powerful premiers to operate with minimum legislative checks.

In Newfoundland, Joey Smallwood and Brian Peckford dominated their parties and the House of Assembly with a personalized style of politics that left no doubt about who was in charge. Smallwood, especially, dominated his Liberal Party to the extent of deciding who would run in which riding, and controlled the bureaucracy by appointing many of its personnel. Peckford inherited the reforms in Cabinet structure, Conservative Party apparatus, and the bureaucracy instituted by his predecessor Frank Moores, premier from 1972 to 1979, but very clearly set his own stamp on the political and economic direction of the province. Ideological issues are almost totally absent from Newfoundland politics, most election campaigns revolving around personalities or fighting the federal government. In this regard, Peckford's resignation in 1989 will likely pave the way for a less personalized and less confrontational style of leadership in the province. During Newfoundland's forty years as a Canadian province, the party in power has changed only twice: in 1972, when the Conservatives ended twenty-three years of Liberal rule; and in 1989, when the Liberals under Clyde Wells ended seventeen years of Conservative government. Although the New Democratic Party (NDP) had two members in the House prior to the 1989 election, the retirement of their leader, Peter Fenwick, helped precipitate their return to the political wilderness.

Prince Edward Island's political modernization began in earnest under Walter Shaw's Conservatives in 1959 and continued under Liberal Alex Campbell's guidance from 1966 to 1979 with little change in direction. The major issues of a fixed-link causeway to the mainland, high energy costs, and the pace and nature of development were controversial but non-ideological.[20] The past decade has seen a more rapid turnover in premiers, with Walter MacLean and James Lee leading the Conservatives until Joe Ghiz and his Liberals came to power in 1986. The relatively regular alternation in power between the Conservatives and Liberals reflects the fairly balanced two-party system in a province noted for extensive party organizations and a democratic tradition.

In September 1988, Nova Scotia's premier, John Buchanan, led his Conservatives to a fourth consecutive victory, retaining the grip on power that he has held since 1978. In keeping with his previous campaigns, Buchanan made his personality and leadership the main issue, and attempts by the opposition parties to discuss government scandals and lack of integrity failed to arouse the voters. Although the NDP under leader Alexa McDonagh held its own in terms of popular vote, it was widely perceived as the big loser in the 1988 election since it lost one of its three seats in the legislature and failed to make an expected breakthrough.[21] The Liberal Party under Vince MacLean increased both its percentage of popular vote and its legislative seats to come within 4 percent and seven seats of the winning Conservatives. Although the NDP has had more success in Nova Scotia than in the other Atlantic provinces, even there it remains very much a third party with no realistic hope of breaking that tradition in the near future.[22]

The most remarkable event in recent New Brunswick politics was the October 1987 sweep of all fifty-eight seats by Frank McKenna's Liberals. In decisively rejecting Richard Hatfield and the Conservative Party's seventeen-year rule, the voters seem to have confirmed previous indications that the traditional political divisions between the French-speaking and English-speaking areas of the province were weakening.[23]

Turning from internal provincial politics to political relations between the region and the federal government, there has been a mixture of patterns. In recent years, the three Maritime provinces have had a low-key, co-operative relationship with the federal government, regardless of the party in power. In contrast, during the early years of Newfoundland's life in Confederation, relations between the province and the federal government were good when the Liberals were in power at both levels, but deteriorated rapidly when Smallwood had to deal with the Diefenbaker Conservatives. Since the provincial Conservatives came to power in 1972, however, federal–provincial relations have been tense, frequently breaking out into open political combat, particularly during the Trudeau years in Ottawa.

In terms of voting for the winning party in federal elections, voters of the region have a mixed record. In the fourteen federal general elections from 1949 to 1988, Newfoundland has a split record, its voters giving the majority of its seats to the winning party seven times, all but one of which were Liberal victories. Residents of Prince Edward Island have also voted with the winner seven times, voted against the winning party five times, and split their vote between the parties twice. Voters in Nova Scotia have the same seven/seven record as Newfoundland, although their winning-side vote has most consistently been with the Conservatives. The voters of New Brunswick have the best record of all, voting against the winning party only twice, voting for the winner eight times, and splitting their vote in four elections.[24]

Recent interprovincial relations in the region have been marked by co-operation among the Maritime provinces, with a "go it alone" type of aloofness by Newfoundland. The formation of the Atlantic Provinces Economic Council (APEC) in 1954 was followed by annual meetings of the Atlantic Premiers' Conference. In turn, this led the three Maritime premiers to contemplate the economic and political union of their provinces, an objective that was fully endorsed in the 1970 Maritime Union Study. Political reality and caution prevailed, however, and in 1971 the Council of Maritime Premiers was established to improve communications and co-ordinate joint activities between the three provinces. A number of joint agencies now exist, such as the Maritime Municipal Training and Development Board, the Atlantic Police Academy, and the Maritime Provinces Higher Education Commission, but there is no impetus toward further economic or political integration.[25] Newfoundland pulled out of APEC in 1983 and formed its own Economic Council, although the province still participates in some of the joint activities, such as the Atlantic Police Academy.

CONCLUSION

One might like to conclude on an optimistic note by saying that the future of the Atlantic provinces looks bright, and that by the early twenty-first century the Atlantic region will not only be contributing to the "have-not" regions in central and western Canada as the result of its prosperous secondary manufacturing and export sectors, but will have maintained its unique cultures and favourable lifestyles! Unfortunately, reality suggests otherwise. Despite the anticipated revenues from offshore resources in Nova Scotia and especially Newfoundland, the structural economic problems are likely to persist. Unemployment will undoubtedly remain well above the national average, secondary manufacturing will continue to be elusive, and the provincial economies will continue to be largely dependent on the export of primary resources of fish, forestry products, and mining.

Politically, if population growth in the Atlantic region remains slower than that in the rest of Canada, the combined clout of the Atlantic provinces at the federal level will be unlikely to increase. While one united Maritime or Atlantic province might make economic sense, and might provide the region with a stronger voice at the federal level, its political acceptability is about zero. Beyond the routine replacements of party leaders and the alternation of parties in power, Atlantic Canada is unlikely to undergo any major political or economic changes in the 1990s. Fears for the collapse of the fishery will be at least partially offset in Newfoundland and Nova Scotia by the promise of revenue from offshore non-renewable resource production, but the heavy dependence on federal transfer payments is unlikely to be reduced.

NOTES

1. Many federal government departments, including Statistics Canada, employ this form of classification, as have scholars such as Mildred Schwartz, *Politics and Territory* (Montreal: McGill-Queen's University Press, 1974); Roger Gibbins, *Regionalism: Territorial Politics in Canada and the United States* (Toronto: Butterworths, 1982); and Richard Simeon and Donald E. Blake, "Regional Preferences: Citizens' Views of Public Policy," in *Small Worlds: Provinces and Parties in Canadian Political Life,* ed. David J. Elkins and Richard Simeon (Toronto: Methuen, 1980).

2. This uniqueness has been noted by scholars who have chosen to use the individual provinces as their units of analysis. See, for instance, John Wilson, "The Canadian Political Cultures: Towards a Redefinition of the Nature of the Canadian Political System," *Canadian Journal of Political Science* (September 1974): 438–83; and Michael D. Ornstein, "Regional Politics and Ideologies," in *Regionalism in Canada*, ed. Robert J. Brym (Toronto: Irwin, 1986), pp. 47–87.

3. For an excellent overview of recent politics in Prince Edward Island, see David A. Milne, "Politics in a Beleaguered Garden," *The Garden Transformed: Prince Edward Island, 1945–1980*, ed. Verner Smitheram, David Milne, and Satadal Dasgupta (Charlottetown: Ragweed Press, 1982), pp. 39–72.

4. In their recent analysis of the 1977 Quality of Life in Canada study,

Matthews and Davis found that while Newfoundland residents had the lowest identity as Canadians, more respondents from that province identified themselves first equally as Canadians and Newfoundlanders. See Ralph Matthews and J. Campbell Davis, "The Comparative Influence of Region, Status, Class, and Ethnicity on Canadian Attitudes and Values," in *Regionalism in Canada*, ed. Brym, pp. 102–3. Unfortunately, there is no study available that measures the degree to which residents of the Atlantic provinces regard themselves as being residents of the Atlantic region as compared with their province or Canada.

5. It should be noted that there is a curious contradiction in this wary attitude toward outsiders with regard to economic development. As noted below, the Atlantic provinces have been particularly susceptible to economically unsound schemes promoted by smooth-talking entrepreneurs from outside the region.

6. According to the 1986 census, of those respondents giving a single ethnic origin, 95.6 percent of Newfoundland residents are of British stock, as are 80 percent of Prince Edward Islanders, 77.9 percent of Nova Scotians, and 49.8 percent of New Brunswickers. The comparative figures for those of French stock are: Newfoundland 2.4 percent, Prince Edward Island 15 percent, Nova Scotia 9.9 percent, and New Brunswick 46.1 percent. Those stating a single ethnic origin other than French or English were 2 percent in Newfoundland, 5 percent in Prince Edward Island, 12.2 percent in Nova Scotia, and 4.1 percent in New Brunswick.

7. Wilson, "The Canadian Political Cultures," pp. 438–83; and Richard Simeon and David J. Elkins, "Regional Political Cultures in Canada," *Canadian Journal of Political Science* (September 1974): 397–437.

8. Ornstein, "Regional Politics and Ideologies," p. 78.

9. For a good summary of traditional perceptions of the province, see Rand Dyck, *Provincial Politics in Canada* (Toronto: Prentice-Hall, 1986), pp. 42–46.

10. A province-wide public opinion survey conducted in 1986 showed that only 45 percent of respondents wanted to keep the denominational system, while 56 percent favoured the introduction of one public system. Mark W. Graesser, "Attitudes Toward Denominational Education in Newfoundland," Report of Survey, October 1986.

11. Retiring premier Brian Peckford's acceptance of nearly $100,000 from a $500 per plate fund-raising "appreciation" dinner held before he left office in Spring 1989, however, is a reminder that political greed and questionable practices have not yet been eliminated.

12. See R. Young, "Teaching and Research in Maritime Politics: Old Stereotypes and New Directions," *Journal of Canadian Studies* (1986): 133–56; and James Bickerton, "The Party System and the

Representation of Periphery Interests: The Case of the Maritimes," in *Canadian Parties in Transition,* ed. Alain G. Gagnon and A. Brian Tanguay (Toronto: Nelson, 1988), pp. 461–84.

13. An overview of the political and legal disputes, along with an excellent analysis of the entire issue of offshore resources can be found in J. D. House, *The Challenge of Oil* (St. John's: Institute of Social and Economic Research, 1985).

14. Gary Burrill and Ian McKay, eds., *People, Resources, and Power* (Fredericton: Acadiensis Press, 1987), p. 4.

15. Robert J. Brym, "An Introduction to the Regional Question in Canada," in *Regionalism in Canada,* ed. Brym, p. 10.

16. Burrill and McKay, *People, Resources, and Power,* p. 4.

17. Atlantic Provinces Economic Council, *Atlantic Canada Today* (Halifax: Formac, 1987), p. 124.

18. For a good overview of the programs and problems, see *Atlantic Canada Today,* pp. 120–26.

19. The exception to this is in New Brunswick where 90 percent of the members consider their positions to be full-time. See Dyck, *Provincial Politics in Canada,* p. 144.

20. See Smitheram, Milne, and Dasgupta, *The Garden Transformed* for a good analysis of post-1945 politics and economics in Prince Edward Island.

21. For an analysis of the election, see D. Munroe Eagles, "Politics in Canada's Ocean Playground: The 1988 Nova Scotian Election," *Canadian Political News and Life* 1, no. 1 (October 1988).

22. For recent analyses of the limited success of third parties in Atlantic Canada, see Agar Adamson and Ian Stewart, "Party Politics in the Mysterious East," in *Party Politics in Canada,* 5th ed., ed. Hugh G. Thorburn (Toronto: Prentice Hall, 1985) pp. 319–33; and Robert J. Brym, "Political Conservatism in Atlantic Canada," in *Underdevelopment and Social Movements in Atlantic Canada,* ed. Robert J. Brym and R. James Sacouman (Toronto: New Hogtown Press, 1979), pp. 59–79.

23. For a brief analysis of Richard Hatfield's efforts to deal with Acadian grievances, see Adamson and Stewart, "Party Politics in the Mysterious East," p. 322.

24. These calculations are based on an analysis of the federal election results provided in the Appendix of *Party Politics in Canada,* ed. Thorburn, pp. 338–41 and results of the 1988 federal election as reported in *The Globe and Mail.* As might be expected, the analysis also showed a greater tendency in all four provinces for voters to support the winning party federally if the provincial wing of that party was in power provincially. The ratios are 5:2 for Newfoundland, 4:3 for Prince Edward Island, 6:1 for Nova Scotia, and 5:3 for New

Brunswick. Further analysis of these voting patterns and the effects they may have had on federal–provincial fiscal and political relations is being undertaken in a separate study.

25. For a recent analysis of the Council of Maritime Premiers, see Stephen G. Tomblin, "The Council of Maritime Premiers and the Battle for Territorial Integrity," Canadian Political Science Association, June 1988.

FURTHER READINGS

Adamson, Agar, and Ian Stewart. "Party Politics in the Mysterious East." In *Party Politics in Canada*, 5th ed., ed. Hugh G. Thorburn. Toronto: Prentice-Hall, 1985.

Alexander, David. *Atlantic Canada and Confederation: Essays in Canadian Political Economy*. Toronto: University of Toronto Press, 1983.

Atlantic Provinces Economic Council. *Atlantic Canada Today*. Halifax: Formac, 1987.

Bickerton, James. "The Party System and the Representation of Periphery Interests: The Case of the Maritimes." In *Canadian Parties in Transition*, ed. Alain G. Gagnon and A. Brian Tanguay. Toronto: Nelson, 1988.

Brym, Robert J., ed. *Regionalism in Canada*. Toronto: Irwin, 1986.

Brym, Robert J., and R. James Sacouman, eds. *Underdevelopment and Social Movements in Atlantic Canada*. Toronto: New Hogtown Press, 1979.

Burrill, Gary, and Ian McKay, eds. *People, Resources, and Power: Critical Perspectives on Underdevelopment and Primary Industries in the Atlantic Region*. Gorsebrook Studies in the Political Economy of Atlantic Canada, No. 1. Fredericton: Acadiensis Press, 1987.

Campbell, Alexander, Gerald Regan, and Richard Hatfield. "The Move Toward Maritime Integration and the Role of the Council of Maritime Premiers." *Canadian Public Administration* (Winter 1972).

House, J. D. *The Challenge of Oil*. St. John's: Institute of Social and Economic Research, 1986.

Smitheram, Verner, David Milne, and Satadal Dasgupta, eds. *The Garden Transformed: Prince Edward Island, 1945–1980*. Charlottetown: Ragweed Press, 1982.

Starr, Richard. *Richard Hatfield: The Seventeen Year Saga*. Halifax: Formac, 1987.

Tomblin, Stephen G. "The Council of Maritime Premiers and the Battle for Territorial Integrity." Canadian Political Science Association, June 1988.

Young, R. A. "Teaching and Research in Maritime Politics: Old Stereotypes and New Directions." *Journal of Canadian Studies* (1986): 133–56.

PART 2

THE SOCIOCULTURAL MILIEU OF CANADIAN POLITICS

8

Political Culture in Canada

DAVID V. J. BELL

THE IMPORTANCE OF POLITICAL CULTURE

Culture is a fundamental component of life because it affects how we perceive the world and how we interact with it. Culture provides a set of lenses through which people view the world. Beliefs about the world and individually held values shape both attitude and action. Culture also provides a way of doing things, a common stock of knowledge about appropriate and inappropriate behaviour in different settings.[1] As we are socialized into a culture, we learn to behave in ways that others in the same culture will find acceptable and comfortable. We learn what to wear, what to say, and how to stand. We learn to distinguish between the public and private, how to say "hello" and "goodbye," how to indicate pleasure or unhappiness.

Political life is similarly affected by "political culture": beliefs and values related to politics, attitudes to the political system and to political issues, and commonly accepted standards of political behaviour. Frequently, political values, beliefs, and attitudes are crystallized and represented by various symbols. In its simplest sense, a symbol is a kind of shorthand: something that stands for something else. In politics, symbols usually evoke both thoughts and feelings, and reflect long-standing traditions to which individuals become strongly attached.

Canadian political culture includes a number of symbols. Some, such as Parliament, the Crown, and Mounties in red coats, have been around for a long time. Others, such as the Charter of Rights and Freedoms, the Meech Lake Accord, and the free trade agreement, are much more recent. Political symbols can evoke images of consensus and co-operation—as does the idea of helping the poorer provinces, or furthering Anglo–French partnership. But symbols can also catalyze negative emotions and hatred or distrust, as does the phrase "forcing French down our throats," or the bitter accusation of eastern domination, symbolized in the phrase "freight rates" or the National Energy Program. The variety and richness of these symbols demonstrate that Canadian politics simultaneously features harmony and disunity, conflict and co-operation. Politicians invoke symbols in their speeches to rally support for their parties and policies, to quiet discontent, or to inflame bitterness directed at their opponents. Members of the general public, for their part, often appear to need symbolic reassurances, to identify with symbols manipulated in public debate by their political leaders, and to find gratification in the symbolic aspect of politics even when more practical and material aspects are less than satisfactory.[2]

Because of its impact on individuals in their capacity as both citizens and subjects, followers and leaders, political culture (including symbols) affects the content and nature of what goes on in the "black box" that we call the political system. It helps transform the inanimate machinery of government into the living organic reality of politics. The foremost theorist of the systems approach, David Easton, points out that cultural inhibitors affect "what are to be considered culturally appropriate areas for political decision."[3] In any political system, the political culture demarcates the zone of appropriate action for government, and sets other areas beyond the realm of the legitimate. Thus, for example, Pierre Trudeau announced soon after his first election as prime minister in 1968 that "the state has no place in the bedrooms of the nation."[4]

Conversely, the political culture provides a range of acceptable values and standards upon which leaders can draw in attempting to justify their policies. Unless a politically viable justification can be attached to a controversial policy, it will not usually be adopted. The political culture sets the parameters within which debate over policy justification takes place. The political culture further affects what people view as appropriate areas of governmental action. It shapes the perception of politically relevant problems, thereby affecting both the recognition of these problems and the diagnosis of their various aspects. It influences beliefs about who should be assigned responsibility for solving problems, and what kind of solutions are likely to work. This aspect of political culture is in turn related to more general notions about the general purposes of government and the kinds of processes and substantive decisions that are acceptable and legitimate.

The political culture greatly influences political discourse. In effect, the political culture serves as the language—political discourse constitutes speech. This language–speech metaphor is very helpful for understanding the day-to-day significance of political culture. It relates closely to the notion of "the universe of political discourse" developed by Jane Jenson:

> What is the universe of political discourse? At its simplest it comprises beliefs about the ways politics should be conducted, the boundaries of political discussion, and the kinds of conflicts resolvable through political processes. In the vast array of tensions, differences, and inequalities characteristic of any society, only some are treated as "political." Thus, whether a matter is considered a religious, economic, private, or political question is set by this

definition. Invisibility can exist for those questions that are, for whatever reasons, never elevated to the status of being "political."

The universe of political discourse functions at any single point in time by setting boundaries to political action and by limiting the range of actors that are accorded the status of legitimate participants, the range of issues considered to be included in the realm of meaningful political debate, the policy alternatives feasible for implementation, and the alliance strategies available for achieving change. Thus, the universe of political discourse filters and delineates political activity of all kinds. Ultimately, its major impact is to inhibit or encourage the formation of new collective identities and/or the reinforcement of older ones. Within a given universe of political discourse, only certain kinds of collective identities can be forged; for more to be done, the universe itself must be challenged and changed.[5]

When people talk about political issues and problems, they draw on symbols and concepts embedded in the political culture that provide shared definitions of the situation. The political culture privileges or favours one set of definitions over others. It thus helps establish a dominant discourse that in turn will favour the interests of particular groups in society. This in turn allows political parties that support the status quo to articulate the dominant discourse. At the same time, it forces parties that wish to achieve significant reform to challenge the dominant discourse and attempt to gain legitimacy for an alternative discourse. According to some students of Canadian political parties, the Conservatives under Brian Mulroney successfully displaced the neo-Keynesian discourse of the governing Liberal Party with a neo-conservative discourse of deregulation and privatization. Neither of these rival discourses pay much attention to class conflict and class divisions, matters essential to the political success of a true left-wing party.[6]

In some instances, political values, attitudes, and beliefs cluster together in a particular constellation called an ideology. Ideologies are more or less coherent and explicit, and tend to be held by people whose political involvement is unusually high. Such activists find ideologies useful guides to political action. Ideologies have a programmatic aspect insofar as they provide a diagnosis of the problems facing society and a prescription of solutions for these problems. Indeed, the ideology in many instances amounts to a way of viewing the world (*Weltanschauung*).

Ideologies are often derived from, or closely related to, more profound and sophisticated statements as set forth in works of political philosophy. In this respect, ideology is like the *Reader's Digest* paraphrase of a great work. Compared to political philosophies, ideologies are more simplified, and less profound. They emphasize action over thought and may stress emotions rather than cognitions.

Most of the great works on ideology assume that ideologies rest on a set of underlying interests and predispositions, often derived from one's class position in society. Thus, one speaks of the ideology of the ruling class, working-class ideology, bourgeois ideology, and so on. This awareness of the connection between ideology and interests leads inexorably to a concern to "unmask" ideologies to discover their material base in social relations.

It is evident that relatively few people have coherent and explicit ideas about politics that deserve the designation "ideology." Many individuals lack a clear, consistent set of political views. They react in an ad hoc fashion or simply avoid thinking about politics altogether. They may have low levels of information, hold contradictory opinions, misunderstand basic concepts, and so on. Still others do have politically relevant views that are, however, either implicit or contradictory. At this point the concept of political culture becomes useful. Indeed, an attempt to look at mass in addition to elite opinions and values regarding politics was a major consideration in developing the concept of political culture, which was viewed from the outset as a broader concept with wider application than ideology. A single political culture could comprise several ideologies: the Canadian political culture is thought to include the ideologies of conservatism, liberalism, and socialism.

In short, the political culture is invisibly interwoven into all aspects of politics and government. One can isolate the cultural variable for the purposes of analysis, but to do so requires a sensitive appreciation for the techniques that can render the often hidden assumptions, values, and beliefs visible and comprehensible. The study of political culture can therefore remain rather general and abstract, encompassing the broadly stated political values at their highest level; or it can be made much more specific and focused on beliefs and values related to specific issues or policies.

APPROACHES TO THE STUDY OF POLITICAL CULTURE

Most students of political culture seem to agree on one point: culture is a collective phenomenon, the attribute of a group and not of an individual. An individual cannot make or possess a culture. However, she or he can learn a culture. For this reason, the components of a political culture— values, beliefs, and attitudes among others—can be observed in the individual. Thus, one might refer to X's religious values or Y's attitudes to abortion as aspects of a culture. But what does it mean to talk about a *group* value or attitude? Is a group merely the sum of those individuals who belong to it, and its culture the average beliefs of its membership? Or is culture something different again from majority opinion or a statistical average? In grappling with these questions, social scientists tend to fall into one of two camps: some opt for a "holistic" approach, while others insist on "methodological individualism."

The *individualistic approach* to political culture assumes that values and beliefs exist only in specific individuals, who may or may not resemble one another. To generalize about the values of any group of people requires reliable information obtained from a large sample of individuals who are representative of the population as a whole. These data are almost always obtained by survey research. Once these individual-level survey data have been gathered, the problem of how to aggregate them in order to make judgments about the entire population involves the use of statistical "modal" characteristics. The term "mode" refers to that point along a continuum where the largest concentration of attitudes is found.

The first and most prominent example of the individualistic approach to political culture is Gabriel Almond and Sidney Verba's study of five countries: the United States, Britain, Mexico, Germany, and Italy.[7] The authors selected a sample of respondents from each country and administered a long questionnaire designed to elicit attitudes to the political system in general, to the role of the individual as both a citizen (i.e., a participant in the decision-making process) and a subject (i.e.,someone on the receiving end of the laws and regulations enforced by the system.[8] In analyzing their data, Almond and Verba introduced several categories that allowed them to generalize about the "modal" characteristics of each of the societies they studied. For example, they planned to use results of "citizen efficacy" and "subject competence" questions, together with questions about orientations to the system as a whole, to locate societies along a continuum from primitive political cultures, in which there is little awareness of the existence of the nation-state or of the individual's role in the national political system; through "subject" cultures, in which the individual responds positively to the system's outputs but has a low sense of personal citizen efficacy; to the most advanced "participant" cultures, displaying high measures of both efficacy and competence. Their survey results proved somewhat disappointing. The neat distinctions between participant, subject, and primitive political cultures did not materialize. Instead, Almond and Verba found a mixture of attitudes encompassing elements from all three categories. Consequently the term "civic culture" denoted the hybrid mixture of attitudes and values—some "modern," others pre-modern—found in what they believed to be the most highly developed democratic political system in their study: the United States.[9]

Although Almond and Verba did not include Canada in their five-nation study, their survey has been applied (at least in part) many times in this country. Virtually every major academic survey conducted since 1965 has included one or more items from the civic culture survey. Researchers have emphasized in particular the questions on "efficacy" and "trust."

The questions measuring efficacy and trust include various versions of the following items:

Political Efficacy
1. "Generally, those elected to Parliament (Congress) soon lose touch with the people."
2. "Sometimes politics and government seem so complicated that a person like me can't really understand what's going on."
3. "I don't think that the government cares much what people like me think."
4. "People like me don't have any say about what the government does."

Political Trust
1. "Do you think that people in government waste a lot of the money we pay in taxes, waste some of it, or don't waste very much of it?"
2. "How much of the time do you think you can trust the government in Washington (Ottawa) to do what is right?"
3. "Would you say the government is pretty much run by a few big interests looking out for themselves, or that it is run for the benefit of all of the people?"
4. "Do you feel that almost all of the people running the government are smart people who know what they are doing, or do you think that quite a lot of them don't seem to know what they are doing?"
5. "Do you think that quite a few of the people running the government are a little crooked, not very many are, or do you think hardly any of them are crooked at all?"[10]

The efficacy questions were included in Canadian national surveys done in 1965, 1968, 1974, 1979, and 1984. The trust questions were administered only in 1965, 1968, 1979, and 1984. The answers to each question were scored on a five-point scale, with one being the lowest level and five being the highest level of efficacy or trust. These scores were combined and averaged to get an overall measure of efficacy and trust. Table 8.1 summarizes these scores for the country as a whole and for each province from 1968 to 1984. In 1984 researchers added a new twist by asking respondents to express their attitudes toward the federal and the provincial governments separately.

Some interesting trends emerge. Efficacy scores rose sharply between 1968 and the 1970s, but fell back down slightly in 1984. Trust decreased over that period. Variations between provinces also decreased, indicating a homogenization of political attitudes across regions. Both efficacy and trust scores are slightly higher for provincial as compared with federal governments, indicating that Canadians feel closer to their

Table 8.1
Efficacy and Trust Scores, Canada and the Provinces

| | EFFICACY | | | | | TRUST | | |
	1968	1974	1979	Fed. 1984	Prov. 1984	1968	Fed. 1984	Prov. 1984
Canada	1.8	2.1	2.1	1.9	2.0	2.0	1.7	1.8
Newfoundland	1.2	1.6	1.7	1.6	1.7	1.4	1.6	1.7
P.E.I.	–	2.0	2.2	2.0	2.1	–	1.9	2.1
Nova Scotia	1.4	2.3	2.1	2.0	2.2	1.7	1.8	2.0
New Brunswick	1.2	2.0	1.9	1.3	1.4	1.3	1.6	1.6
Quebec	1.5	1.8	2.0	1.8	1.7	1.8	1.9	1.6
Ontario	2.1	2.3	2.2	1.9	2.1	2.1	1.7	2.0
Manitoba	2.0	1.7	1.9	1.9	2.1	2.3	1.5	1.9
Saskatchewan	1.7	2.3	2.3	1.7	2.3	2.0	1.7	2.1
Alberta	1.8	2.1	2.2	1.9	2.1	1.8	1.7	2.0
British Columbia	2.3	2.6	2.3	1.9	2.0	2.3	1.6	1.5

Source: Data provided by Jon Pammett, compiled from various National Election Surveys.

provincial government and trust it slightly more than the federal government.

One of the most useful and innovative applications of these concepts appears in the work of David Elkins and Richard Simeon. Instead of analyzing efficacy and trust responses separately, Elkins and Simeon combined them to form a new typology of orientations to politics, as shown in Table 8.2. Elkins and Simeon also used the typology to analyze political orientations in each of the ten provinces, separating out anglophones in Quebec and francophones outside of Quebec. Using data from the 1968 federal election survey, they found some rather surprising results. Only about one-quarter of the total sample of respondents fell into the "supporter" category, while fully one-third were classified as "disaffected." Striking provincial contrasts emerged. Only in Ontario, Manitoba, and British Columbia were there more supporters than disaffected. These provinces also, however, had the largest number of "critics." In the Atlantic provinces over half the respondents were disaffected.

Table 8.2
Typology of Orientations to Politics (Elkins & Simeon)

| | | EFFICACY | |
		High	*Low*
	High	Supporters	Deferentials
TRUST			
	Low	Critics	Disaffected

Nationally, and without exception in very province, the smallest group were the "deferentials."[11]

While these and similar survey results are clearly interesting and illuminating, they also have important limitations. Surveys provide a *direct* measure of political culture, and have the advantage of forcing people to make explicit what may be otherwise obscure or implicit. In doing so, however, these measures sometimes distort or twist reality in subtle ways. We cannot be sure that survey responses validly reflect what people really believe or value. Furthermore, surveys and interviews can be used only in the present or recent past, and do not illuminate the period of earlier history that contains important clues to the development of political culture. Hence indirect approaches are critical supplements to interviews and surveys.

The *indirect approaches* are far more numerous and varied in their utility and validity. A number of techniques, usually involving content analysis, allow researchers to extract from written documents or speeches the values and beliefs that are implicit in them. In the case of the political values of the elite, a highly specialized "operational code" approach has been used to reconstruct the outlook and assumptions of key individuals.[12] Biographies and autobiographies shed light not only on cognitive beliefs and values, but on life experiences that reflect how important those values are for behaviour. Indeed, by studying the behaviour of individuals, or the collective behaviour of institutions (i.e., their adoption of various policies), skillful students of political culture can excavate latent assumptions about politics and therefore create a picture of the political culture of both the present and the past.

The latter kind of indirect approach often accompanies a "holistic" conception of political culture. In the holistic approach, political culture constitutes a kind of "ethos"[13] that envelops and conditions a society. Certain values and predispositions are, figuratively speaking, "in the air." For this reason, one sometimes speaks of a "climate" of opinion. Like climate, these values influence behaviour invisibly but effectively. The individual is born into this ethos and absorbs it through a kind of osmosis. Though people may vary in the degree to which they absorb the culture, everyone is exposed to these values to a great extent. An individual's departure from the prevailing ethos, or social deviance, in no way disproves the existence of the culture, because socialization is never complete.

Descriptions of the ethos of Canadian political culture are many and varied. Sometimes geography is credited with having produced a distinctive Canadian ethos. Two years after Confederation, for example, in a lecture about Canadian "national spirit" delivered to the Montreal Literary Club, Robert Grant Haliburton stressed the formative influence of Canada's "northern" geography and climate: "...may not our snow and frost [he asked] give us what is of more value than gold or silver, a healthy, hardy, virtuous dominant race? [For Canada] must ever be...a Northern country inhabited by the descendants of Northern races."[14] Haliburton regarded the superiority of northerners as a fundamental axiom of politics. Rhetorically he asked, "If climate has not had the effect of moulding races, how is it that the southern nations have almost invariably been inferior to and subjugated by the men of the north?" From the felicitous marriage of racial inheritance and northern environmentalism, there would emerge a Canadian people worthy of the ideals of "the true north, strong and free."

Not all efforts to define a Canadian ethos are infected by the virus of racial nationalism. Nor do they necessarily emphasize the formative impact of geography. Seymour Martin Lipset explicitly posits the existence of a national ethos in the following passage: "[V]alue differences between the United States and Canada suggest that they stem in large part from two disparate founding ethos."[15] But for Lipset (as we will see below) historical events rather than geographical factors account for the variation.

The approach presented in this chapter draws on both individualism and holism. We are interested in the pattern of individually held values and beliefs, and thus examine relevant survey results such as those discussed above. We are aware, however, that the individualistic approach alone is insufficient. To appreciate the importance of the larger whole within which individuals operate (without, however, arguing that values and beliefs are somehow preserved in an invisible ethos, a kind of social formaldehyde), we draw attention to certain distinctively Canadian political institutions such as Parliament, the Constitution Act, federal–provincial conferences, the CBC, Air Canada, CN, elements of popular culture (novels, poetry, songs, films, etc.) that form part of Canada's political personality and illuminate the character of Canadian politics. They exist in important respects independent of the modal attitudes and values of individuals living in Canada at any particular moment in time. Some of these institutions present themselves to the outside world as quintessentially Canadian, frequently with explicit authorization to speak or act on behalf of Canada. Notwithstanding the range of possible variation within the country, there are times and places where a single voice speaks, and it calls itself Canadian.[16] In these settings, the individual or group that presumes to speak for the collectivity, insofar as it is effective, becomes the collectivity. Individuals who hold a different outlook become irrelevant, at least until they are able to project a dissenting voice or image. The world, in short, contains significant "institutional facts" that assume a different character and exist apart from the individuals that surround and inhabit them. Canadians, whatever their individual conceptions of value and purpose, live and breathe to some extent in a common political space dominated by institutions whose very design and functioning evolves from, and gives shape to, the complexities of Canadian political culture. Thus, it is useful to examine the values promoted by, and embodied in, these institutions. Of particular interest are institutions that explicitly undertake a role in political socialization, described in the title of a recent textbook as the "foundations of political culture."

POLITICAL SOCIALIZATION: THE LEARNING OF POLITICAL CULTURE

Political socialization is the process of transmitting political values and attitudes through time and across space. Agencies involved in the process include families, schools, churches, political parties, and perhaps most important, mass media. These and similar institutions consciously attempt to inculcate certain values and foster particular attitudes toward politics. Political socialization is especially effective during the "formative stage" in the development of the individual's values and orientations (the early teen years), but political socialization can continue beyond adolescence.[17]

Socialization and learning are not perfectly congruent. Socialization suggests a planned, controllable, linear pattern of acquiring knowledge and values. But people learn more than they are "socialized" to learn. They learn from unpredictable events in both the natural and the social environment. A flood can serve as a fundamental learning experience, as can a war, a hockey game, or even a federal election. People learn from introspection and self-education, often despite what their socializers would like them to learn instead. They learn as well from individuals and groups whose values run counter to the prevailing political culture. In short, learning, unlike socialization, is a dialectical process full of contradictions and unpredictable outcomes.

Furthermore, socialization is not always a benign process. The attempt to preserve and transmit a culture can have a nasty side. Although the following observation exaggerates the extent to which coercion is used to "socialize" people in our society, it serves to remind us that cultural continuity should never be taken for granted:

> To maintain and transmit a value system, human beings are punched, bullied, sent to jail, thrown into concentration camps, cajoled, bribed, made into heroes, encouraged to read newspapers, stood up against a wall and shot, and sometimes even taught sociology. To speak of cultural inertia is to overlook the concrete interests and privileges that are served by indoctrination, education, and the entire complicated process of transmitting culture from one generation to the next.[18]

SOCIETAL ORIGINS OF POLITICAL CULTURE: FOUR VIEWS

We may surmise, therefore, that an individual acquires political culture traits through a learning process, part of which is controlled by various socializing agencies. But where do the political culture traits embraced by these socializing agencies originate? In attempting to answer this question, students of political culture have adopted differing interpretations. One theorist, Louis Hartz, argues that societies such as Canada and the United States, founded by immigrants from Europe, develop a political culture that reflects the values and beliefs of the groups that were dominant during the "founding period." Hartz contends that the "founders" are able to dominate the political culture of a "new society" by setting up institutions and myths that imbue their values and beliefs with a nationalistic flavour, thus making membership in the nation contingent on accepting the dominant ideology.[19]

Thus, new societies, "fragments" of Europe transported to the New World, tend to have a political culture that conserves and preserves the values, beliefs, and attitudes of the founders of that society. The "fragment theory" was first applied to the United States. Hartz describes the political culture of the United States as "bourgeois," and points to its origins in British seventeenth-and eighteenth-century society. Applying the fragment theory to Canada is complicated by the fact that ours is a "two fragment" society. *La Nouvelle France* was founded by seventeenth- and eighteenth-century emigrants from feudal France. English Canada was founded by Loyalist refugees from the American Revolution, who were also largely bourgeois in outlook. Much of the present-day difference between Canadian anglophones and francophones can be traced back to the vast political culture differences between these two founding fragments.

Seymour Martin Lipset disagrees with Hartz's view that societies bear forever the cultural marks of their birth. For him cultural inheritance is less significant than the experiences that society undergoes. Indeed, he suggests that one can identify certain "formative events" in the history of a country that help mould or shape its values and consequently have a lasting impression upon its institutional practices.[20] When he applies his formative events notion to (English) Canada, however, the differences between him and Hartz shrink. For Lipset, the most important formative event in Canada's history is the obverse of that in the United States: the "counter-revolution" and subsequent migration north of the Loyalists, an event that he believes affected Canada's political culture as significantly as the American Revolution moulded the United States.

Thus, both Hartz's "fragment theory" and Lipset's "formative events" notion focus attention on the Loyalist experience as a major source of English Canada's political culture. Yet, the cultural consequences of the Loyalist migration are a subject of considerable controversy among historians and social scientists. Much of the debate has turned on defining the ideological outlook of the Loyalists. The main issue has been to what extent the Loyalists presented an "organic conservative" alternative to the "liberal" world view of the revolutionaries who expelled them and shaped the political institutions and culture of the new United States.

Lipset himself speaks of the Loyalists as "counter-revolutionaries" who helped make Canada more elitist, ascriptive, and particularist, with greater emphasis on the collectivity, than the United States. To substantiate his claims, he examines not only survey results but also data comparing crime rates, educational practices, economic policies, and even religious traditions in the two countries.

A number of scholars have criticized Lipset's interpretation of these data, and more fundamentally his failure to distinguish anglophones from francophones. Clearly, the two groups have had different cultural origins and experienced different formative events. The French Canadians were relatively unaffected by the American Revolution. For them, the major formative event was undoubtedly the Conquest (described in their history books as the Cession, a term that reveals their profound sense of betrayal by France.) French-language history books typically depict the events leading up to 1763 as a "catastrophe," and devote half of their space to the "golden age" that preceded it.

One advantage of Hartz's fragment theory is that it highlights the cultural uniqueness of the anglophone and francophone fragments. But despite a general consensus about the political culture of the francophone fragment, followers of Hartz have disagreed even among themselves about the impact of the Loyalists. Some have seen the Loyalists as primarily a bourgeois fragment, albeit "tinged with Toryism." Others have insisted that we not dismiss the "Tory Touch," which is deemed to have had an important influence on both policies and institutions.[21] While both perspectives on the Loyalists (i.e., the "liberal" interpretation and the "conservative" view) contribute important insights, they tend to ignore effects of the Loyalist migration that go beyond the usual categories of ideology. Although undoubtedly Canada's unique brand of conservative liberalism probably can be traced back to our Loyalist origins, so too can our profound identity crisis, our fascination with the mosaic, and our willingness to use the state for "interventionist" purposes that most Americans would reject. Furthermore, one can regard the Loyalist experience as having produced an "anti-fragment" insofar as it encouraged a prolongation of emotional and cultural ties to Britain instead of leading to the kind of cultural isolation that is a precondition to the "freezing" of the fragment culture. Consequently, English Canada found no difficulty importing British-style parliamentary socialism in the twentieth century, whereas both Quebec and the United States rejected it as "alien."

Although the fragment theory, enriched by the introduction of Lipset's formative events notion, illuminates the otherwise baffling history of ideologies and political parties in Canada, political culture studies need not be confined by the categories of analysis that derive from the European ideologies of conservatism, liberalism, and socialism. Much of the experience of the New World lies beyond these categories, and in any event the study of political culture can and should embrace virtually every aspect of political practice. Similarly, Almond and Verba's concern with efficacy and trust is too limiting. They chose to focus on those aspects of political culture because they were primarily interested in the problem of democracy. But the problem of democracy is not the central political problem in Canada. Therefore, there is no reason to stick with their concepts and concerns either. Instead, as students of the Canadian experience, we need to examine values, attitudes, and beliefs that relate to more fundamental and pressing problems such as Anglo–French relations, regionalism, and American domination, not merely to the problem of democracy or the problem of class and ideology that animated the work of those who pioneered in the use of political culture.

Furthermore, we need to supplement the rather idealistic approaches to political culture of Hartz and Lipset with approaches that have a much firmer appreciation of the structural bases of culture. For culture never exists in a vacuum, nor does it have an all-determining effect on politics. Rather, culture and its structural underpinnings are interrelated and interdependent. To understand this aspect of culture and trace it back to its societal origins, we need to examine the work of two additional theorists, Harold Innis and Karl Marx.

Although he did not consider himself a student of political culture, Harold Innis offers important insight into the process of cultural transmission.[22] Unlike Hartz and Lipset, who seem to treat values and beliefs as determinants of social and political structures, Innis reverses the causal arrow. It is not culture that shapes society. For Innis, cultures are heavily affected by the technology of production and distribution of ideas. Hence the culture of society is transformed when new developments take place in the technology of communication. The invention of the printing press revolutionized Western culture, according to Innis. Recent revolutionary developments, dubbed by Alvin Toffler "the third wave," include the discovery of radio and television, the introduction of inexpensive copying machines, and the still-emerging technology of the microchip, and two-way video communication such as Canada's Telidon system. Unfortunately, Innis died before most of these innovations had become widespread, and thus he did not assess how they have affected Canadian political culture. But his insight concerning the importance to culture of the underlying structure of communication remains fundamentally useful.

Innis's insights can be elaborated to explain much of the crisis of Canadian identity in the twentieth century. Cleary the means of distribution of culture (including popular culture) are important determinants of what ideas get transmitted to the general public. Canada, unlike virtually any other country in the world, has a cultural transmission system that is almost entirely in the hands of a foreign power. Most Canadian children pass into adulthood without, for example, ever seeing a Canadian feature-length film. They watch American television and even read school text-books that are produced and written in the United States. They listen to American records and eat food produced by mass-distribution food outlets owned in the United States. They see American commercials and read American advertising. Little wonder then that they grow up with a very shaky sense of Canadian identity and relatively little knowledge about their own country and political institutions, much less any sense of what might constitute Canadian culture in the mass media, the arts, music, and letters. So extreme has been the domination of our cultural networks that in a document prepared in 1977 to provide new directions for the Canadian Broadcasting Corporation, the then CBC president, Albert Johnson, commented, "Canada today faces its greatest crisis in history: the combination of national life-threatening arguments over our nationhood and the relentless American cultural penetration."[23] Whether this cultural domination leads to economic domination, or the reverse, is perhaps immaterial: the massive U.S. presence on the cultural scene is matched by an equally dominant U.S. presence in the economy, fully reinforced by the Free Trade Agreement. This leads directly to Marxist and neo-Marxist analyses of the Canadian dilemma.

According to Karl Marx, the material conditions under which a society produces its wealth is a major factor in determining the nature of the political culture. In his view, there are relatively few "modes of production": primitive, feudal, capitalist, and socialist. Each limits the kind of political structures and culture that can exist. Within a given mode of production, however, variations will occur as a result of different patterns of external trade relations and of internal control of production and distribution. Students of contemporary Canadian politics who have applied Marxist concepts to Canada emphasize the effect on our political culture of Canada's major economic structures. The fact that we are a capitalist country with a long history of economic dependence on foreign capital bears heavily on our current political difficulties.

Furthermore, the neo-Marxists have pointed out that within the dominant capitalist class are various "fractions" that have different perceptions of their interests and different orientations toward the economic system. They distinguish in particular between a mercantile/financial class fraction, which makes profits on the circulation rather than the production of goods and services, and an industrial capitalist fraction, which is more entrepreneurial and is interested in industrial development and expansion. Particularly in the crucial period of the late nineteenth century, the interests of these two class fractions were opposed. The mercantilists did not favour the development of an indigenous heavy industry in Canada, but instead sought to profit on the exchange of staple products from the hinterland for manufactured goods imported from the imperial centre (i.e., Britain and at a later point the United States). According to the neo-Marxists, the political culture of colonialism and imperial dependency was consciously fostered by the mercantile-class fraction to support their economic interests. The dominant element of Canada's capitalist class, this group could not see themselves as rulers of a strong, independent nation-state. Burdened with a colonial mentality, they opposed any efforts to develop a true Canadian nationalism.[24]

Each of the above approaches to political culture sheds light on the social origins and development of culture. A comprehensive historical analysis must therefore take account of:

a. the cultural genes implanted by the founding groups (Hartz);
b. the kinds of formative events that affected cultural values and institutions (Lipset);
c. the nature of the technology of communication (Innis);
d. the economic infrastructure of society (Marx).

These four perspectives complement each other. Any one of them alone is insufficient. Yet, taken together, they illuminate the complexity and richness of a political culture. They show as well that a variety of institutions plays a part in transmitting political culture, including the family, schools, the mass media, and work experiences.

SUMMARY

It is possible to analyze the development of Canadian political culture in more detail using the four insights mentioned above. From the Hartzian perspective, we realize that Canadian political culture developed from the cultural genes implanted by the two major founding groups, the English and the French. These two groups embodied contrasting ideologies that would never easily mix together. The absolutism and feudal tendencies of the French fragment led to a preservation of that culture and an antipathy toward the modernizing impulses of the anglophones. The anglophones for their part were a very strange mixture of elements. Irrespective of how important the Tory touch was, the anglophone bourgeois culture had the ironic and paradoxical characteristic of being simultaneously liberal and anti-American. Because the United States had made liberalism into its national culture, the anglophones were prevented from doing so: thus the origin of Canada's never-ending identity crisis and the peculiar combination of celebration of the British connection and antipathy toward a culture that was ideologically very similar to that of English Canada. Furthermore, because of the failure to nationalize the political culture of the anglophones, and because of the pattern of settlement that led to a direct importation into the Canadian West of founding groups from Europe that did not become socialized to either anglophone or francophone Canadian culture before settling there, the Canadian West featured what some have called a process of "subfragmentation" in which new groups brought with them ideologies that reflected their European origin and that were much more progressive than those of the older fragments. Thus, socialism arose in Saskatchewan. The Alberta subfragmentation reflected the influence of the United States, from which many of the founding settlers of Alberta came. In general, the political culture of the Canadian West has shown noticeable differences from that of the older parts of the country and has featured the appearance of at least two ideological variants not found in much strength elsewhere: socialism and social credit.

The Lipset emphasis on formative events is similarly revealing. Canada had no single great nationalizing formative event. The events that are significant in our history show the strong influence of the colonial powers, because in almost every instance the events were the outcome of struggles taking place between England and France or England and the United States. These events include the Conquest of New France in 1763, the American Revolution in 1776, and the War of 1812. Two other events that were significant and had more of an indigenous flavour were the uprisings in 1837 and the passage of the British North America Act in 1867. But even that latter event took place in England as a statute of the British Parliament, a fact that continued to bedevil attempts to patriate the constitution until 1982. A second insight from the formative events notion is that different regions and different cultural fragments have had a different perspective on these formative events and in effect a different kind of history.

The Innis approach suggests how important it is to have a national communications network that would be capable of binding the community together. This system would have to offset cultural fragmentation between anglophones and francophones and the enormous cultural influences from south of the border. But in several respects we have failed to carry out this task successfully. Despite the setting up of a national broadcasting network in the 1930s, the CBC has proved incapable of bringing together francophones and anglophones or of offsetting infusions of American culture. Furthermore, other important socializing agencies were not left in the hands of the federal government. Responsibility for education was assigned to the provinces, and political party organizations developed into quasi-autonomous provincial organizations with a very loose federal alliance at the top. Thus, two of the most critical socializing agencies have been under provincial control and have contributed to the development of provincial political cultures in some cases at the expense of a national culture. In the early 1980s, Canada was facing a severe crisis over the control of new communications systems such as Cablevision, pay-TV, and Telidon. The provinces, aware of the potential of the communications system in controlling the thoughts and minds of the public, are determined not to let this control pass to the federal government.

Finally, from the Marxist perspective, we see immediately the important impact on our political culture of foreign dependency and the different alignment of capitalist groups around the dominant capitalist forces in the country. We see as well the effect that uneven economic development has had on the country in fostering regionalism and leading to the growth of regional economic interests and regional perspectives. Paradoxically, however, class divisions (supposedly the major determinants of political culture in a modern society) have had only a minor effect on Canadian politics, in part because the party system and the electoral system enhance sectional cleavages.

CONCLUSION

Political culture consists of individually held values, attitudes, and beliefs concerning politics; symbols that catalyze sentiments and beliefs about politics and political action; politically relevant knowledge and perceptions, including perceptions of historical experiences and notions of identity; and finally ideologies as aggregations of values and beliefs that have coherence and internal cohesion. Political culture must be examined historically, and therefore one must use both direct and indirect techniques for measuring it. Political culture serves as an important filter affecting political action because of the way that it constrains perceptions about politics, notions of what constitute political problems, and prescriptions for resolving these problems.

Political culture is historically derived. It is affected by the cultural baggage brought to a society by immigrants, especially first settlers. It is moulded by the formative events a society undergoes in the course of its modernization. It is conditioned by such structural underpinnings as class relations, trade patterns, the flow of transportation, and communications. It changes as a result of contact with other cultures.

Political culture can be seen as the "language" of politics. Political discourse is its "speech." Through political discourse, contending groups in society attempt to shape both public perceptions and governmental responses. They proffer competing conceptions of problems that embody their interests and preferences, and privilege the outcomes they wish to see achieved. In effect, these conceptions entail both a diagnosis of the nature of the problem and a prescription concerning the appropriate response to it.

Political discourse is not always manipulated in such a conscious, deliberate manner. Sometimes the discourse reflects assumptions and values no longer obvious or explicit, but reflecting instead historical viewpoints that have sunken beneath the surface of conscious awareness. They are nonetheless potent for this. To achieve social change, these implicit conceptions must be "excavated" and made apparent.

NOTES

1. *Cf.* Clyde Kluckhohn, *Culture and Behavior* (New York: The Free Press, 1962), p. 42: "Culture is—among other things—a set of ready-made definitions of the situation that each participant only slightly retailors in his idiomatic way."
2. For a discussion of symbolism in politics, see the several books by Murray Edelman, including *The Symbolic Uses of Politics* (Urbana, Ill.: University of Illinois Press, 1964); and Lowell Dittmer, "Political Symbolism and Political Culture: Toward a Theoretical Synthesis," *World Politics* 30 (1977).
3. David Easton, *A Systems Analysis of Political Life* (New York: Wiley, 1965), p. 101.
4. The boundaries of legitimate political activity, like other elements of the political, can and do change over time. Responding in part to the growth of neo-conservatism in Britain and the United States, and in part to an indigenous concern that government had become too big and too interventionist, the Mulroney government began to "privatize" a number of Crown corporations and to "deregulate" some aspects of the Canadian economy. See Janine Brodie and Jane Jenson, *Crisis, Challenge and Change: Party and Class in Canada Revisited* (Ottawa: Carleton University Press, 1988), ch. 10.
5. Jane Jenson, "Changing Discourse, Changing Agenda: Political Rights and Reproductive Policies in France," in *The Women's Movement of the United States and Western Europe: Consciousness, Political Opportunity and Public Policy*, ed. Mary F. Katzenstein, et al. (Philadelphia: Temple University Press, 1987). See also Brodie and Jenson, *Crisis, Challenge and Change.*
6. See, among others, Brodie and Jenson, *Crisis, Challenge and Change*, ch. 10; and contributions by Janine Brodie, Jane Jenson, Neil Bradford, and Duncan Cameron to *Canadian Parties in Transition: Discourse, Organization, and Representation*, ed. Alain G. Gagnon and A. Brian Tanguay (Toronto: Nelson, 1988).

7. Gabriel Almond and Sidney Verba, *The Civic Culture* (Princeton: Princeton University Press, 1963).

8. The distinction between citizen and subject was first discussed by Jean Jacques Rousseau in his famous book *The Social Contract*, W. Kendall trans. (Chicago: Henry Regnery, 1954), p. 21. Rousseau says: "The members of a body politic call it 'the state' when it is passive, 'the sovereign' when it is active, and 'a power' when they compare it with others of its kind. Collectively they use the title 'people' and *they refer to one another individually as 'citizens' when speaking of their participation in the authority of the sovereign, and as 'subjects' when speaking of their subordination to the laws of the state"* (emphasis added).

9. Carole Pateman, and many other scholars, sharply criticized Almond and Verba's interpretation of their results. Faced with evidence that large numbers of Americans were apathetic, and that apathy correlated highly with low socio-economic status, Almond and Verba counselled complacency, apparently in the belief that modern democracy requires apathy to ensure stability. This viewpoint left Almond and Verba (and others who shared their outlook) unprepared for the "participation explosion" that erupted in the United States in the late 1960s. See Carole Pateman's "Political Culture, Political Structure and Political Change," *British Journal of Political Science* 1, no. 3 (July 1971): 291–306.

10. As summarized in Nathaniel Beck and John Peirce, "Political Involvement and Party Allegiances in Canada and the United States," *International Journal of Comparative Sociology* 18 (March–June 1977): 28.

11. In a follow-up study, Jon Pammett analyzed the 1984 data, this time separating federal from provincial citizen types. Significant changes appeared. The percentage of both supporters and deferentials had risen considerably to nearly 60 percent. Critics and disaffecteds fell to about 40 percent.

12. See, among others, Ole Holsti, "The 'Operational Code' Approach to the Study of Political Leaders: John Foster Dulles' Philosophical Beliefs," *Canadian Journal of Political Science* 3 (1971).

13. The most extensive discussion of "ethos theory" has occurred in the literature on urban politics. In 1963, Edward Banfield and James Q. Wilson in *City Politics* (New York: Vintage Books) wrote about "two fundamentally opposed conceptions of politics" (p. 234), "two mentalities" (p. 46) found in U.S. cities. These two conceptions accounted for a great deal of political behaviour in urban settings. For a critique, see Timothy M. Hennessy, "Problems in Concept Formation: The Ethos 'Theory' and the Comparative Study of Urban Politics," *Midwest Journal of Political Science* 14 (November 1970).

14. Quoted by Carl Berger, "The True North Strong and Free," in *Nationalism in Canada* ed. Peter Russell (Toronto: McGraw-Hill, 1966), p. 6.
15. S. M. Lipset, *Revolution and Counterrevolution* (New York: Anchor Books, 1970), p. 55.
16. By the same token, however, a number of important institutions are provincial, and they help foster and maintain a provincial outlook.
17. For a recent discussion on a related theme, see Jon Pammett and Jean-Luc Pepin, eds., *Political Education in Canada* (Montreal: Institute for Research on Public Policy, 1988).
18. Barrington Moore, *Social Origins of Dictatorship and Democracy* (Boston: Beacon Press, 1966), p. 486. To validate Moore's point one need only review the history of cultural contact between whites and natives in Canada. The coercion that sometimes accompanies political socialization indeed proves, as Moore argues, that cultural inertia is not inevitable. But it also shows how difficult it is to engineer cultural change. This difficulty has complicated attempts to inculcate the "official" political culture in countries such as Poland and Czechoslovakia where values from an earlier era continue to dominate. See Archie Brown and Jack Gray, eds., *Political Culture and Political Change in Communist States* (London: Macmillan, 1977).
19. Louis Hartz, et al., *The Founding of New Societies* (New York: Harcourt Brace, 1964).
20. Lipset, *Revolution and Counterrevolution.*
21. See especially Gad Horowitz, *Canadian Labour in Politics* (Toronto: University of Toronto Press, 1967).
22. See, for example, the following works by Harold Innis: *Canadian Economic History* (Toronto: University of Toronto Press, 1956); *The Fur Trade in Canada,* rev. ed. (Toronto: University of Toronto Press, 1970); *Empire and Communications,* revised by Mary Q. Innis (Toronto: University of Toronto Press, 1972). Also see James W. Carey, "Harold Adams Innis and Marshall McLuhan," *Antioch Review,* Spring 1967. See also William H. Melody, et al., eds., *Culture, Communication and Dependency: The Tradition of H. A. Innis* (New Jersey: Ablex Publishing Corporation, 1981).
23. Albert Johnson, *Touchstone for the CBC* (mimeo, 1977), p. 2. See also John Redekop, "Continentalism: The Key to Canadian Politics," in *Approaches to Canadian Politics,* 2nd ed., ed. John H. Redekop.
24. Gary Teeple, ed., *Capitalism and The National Question* (Toronto: University of Toronto Press, 1972). For a critique, see Glen Williams, "The National Policy Tariffs: Industrial Underdevelopment Through Import Substitution," *Canadian Journal of Political Science* 12 (June 1979).

FURTHER READINGS

Bell, David V. J., and Lorne J. Tepperman. *The Roots of Disunity*. Toronto: McClelland and Stewart, 1979.

Black, Edwin. *Divided Loyalties*. Montreal: McGill-Queen's University Press, 1975.

Christian, William, and Colin Campbell. *Political Parties and Ideologies in Canada*. Toronto: McGraw-Hill Ryerson, 1974.

Clarke, Harold D., et al., *Political Choice in Canada*. Toronto: McGraw-Hill Ryerson, 1979.

Elkins, David J., and Richard Simeon, eds. *Small Worlds: Provinces and Parties in Canadian Political Life*. Toronto: Methuen, 1980.

Hartz, Louis, et al. *The Founding of New Societies*. New York: Harcourt Brace, 1964.

Lipset, Seymour Martin. *Revolution and Counterrevolution*. New York: Anchor Books, 1970.

Pammett, Jon, and Michael Whittington, eds. *Political Socialization: Foundations of Political Culture*. Toronto: Macmillan, 1976.

9

Political Participation in Canada

WILLIAM MISHLER and HAROLD D. CLARKE

Few aspects of Canadian government reveal as much about its political character as the way in which citizens participate in the political life of the country. Widespread, informed, and effective participation is a hallmark of democracy. Participation provides citizens the means to influence the selection of political leaders, communicate their needs and aspirations to government, and hold elected officials accountable for their performance. It also enables citizens to express dissent and ventilate their grievances with government, thereby regulating societal conflict and promoting political stability.

Democratic theory holds participation to be important for the individual, as well. Liberal democrats believe the ability to participate effectively in important decisions gives citizens a sense of self-esteem. It enhances human dignity and self-respect and contributes to the individual's civic education and moral development. To a substantial degree, therefore, the quality of democracy in Canada is revealed by the nature and extent of citizen participation in the political system. How do Canadians participate and how extensively? Who participates and in what activities? Why do some people participate but not others? What is the quality of citizen participation? How effective is participation in influencing the course of government action? And what are the prospects for promoting higher levels of better-informed and more effective participation in the years ahead? The answers to these questions reveal a great deal about the health of democracy in Canada today, in the 1990s, and beyond.

HOW DO CITIZENS PARTICIPATE?

Political participation consists of those voluntary activities by citizens that are intended to influence the selection of government leaders or the decisions they make. In an open society such as Canada there are many ways in which citizens can attempt to influence government, directly or indirectly, individually or in groups, legitimately or illegitimately.

Voting in periodic national, provincial, and local elections is the most common and widely recognized avenue for citizen participation in Canada, as in other Western democracies. Canada does not hold as many elections as some countries, most notably the United States. Nevertheless, the federal structure of the Canada polity combined with parliamentary norms that require governments to resign and call elections whenever they are defeated on fundamental issues provide opportunities to vote in federal, provincial, or municipal elections on an average of almost once a year. Canadians also have occasional opportunities to vote in referendums or plebiscites where they have a direct influence on important decisions. Referendum elections are rare, but when used they can generate considerable political interest and activity and have significant policy effects, a dramatic illustration being the 1980 sovereignty-association referendum in Quebec.

Voting, however, is only the most visible means of citizen political action in elections. Canadian federal and provincial election campaigns invariably are expensive and labour-intensive contests. As a consequence, campaigns provide manifold opportunities for voluntary activity such as ringing doorbells, canvassing neighbourhoods, mailing campaign literature, distributing posters, telephoning potential voters, and the like. Moreover, parties and candidates are always willing to "allow" citizens to participate with their pocketbooks by contributing money to help finance campaigns.

Political parties also depend heavily on volunteer labour between elections. For a small minority, parties provide opportunities to engage in significant and oftentimes exciting activities such as screening candidates for party nominations, developing party policies, and attending party conferences and national or provincial leadership conventions. Larger numbers find that their party work is confined to a myriad of routine and frequently boring tasks such as organizing party files, updating membership lists, stuffing envelopes, and licking postage stamps.

Nor is citizen participation confined only to the electoral process. The ballot is an imprecise and only occasionally available instrument of political communication. Citizens frequently have interests that cannot be expressed adequately through the simple choices that voting for one of several political parties provide or issues whose settlement cannot be postponed until a future election at some uncertain date. Thus, in the interelection period some individuals attempt to influence government decisions directly. One way they do this is by contacting public officials to express an opinion on a pressing public issue or to request assistance with a personal or group problem. Government officials at all levels receive a steady flow of letters, telegrams, and telephone calls. Citizens also visit the offices of their federal MPs, provincial MLAs, and local councillors, or approach them at shopping centres, hockey games, beauty salons, or wherever they happen to recognize their elected representatives. Elected officials, for their part, are generally quite receptive to such communications and, indeed, regularly make themselves available in locales where this is likely to occur.

Some people find it more comfortable, or think it more effective, to try to influence government as part of a group rather than individually. Some are members of formal organizations or pressure groups that regularly employ full-time professionals to lobby government on behalf of member interests. Others belong to informal groups such as neighbourhood associations that pressure government for group or community concerns or take direct action to solve the problem themselves—for example, by cleaning up a neighbourhood park.

Ultimately, the most direct means for Canadians to influence government is by becoming part of it—by running for elected office or seeking an appointed post. However, opportunities to hold elected office are severely limited by the small number of available positions, by the time and money required for successful campaigns, and by the practical necessity of securing a party's nomination and ultimately the approval of the electorate. Appointive offices also are relatively few in number. Access to prestigious ones, such as the Senate, historically have been used as patronage for political "influentials" who have rendered long and faithful party service. Nevertheless, although the ascent to public office is a slippery slope, there are always ample volunteers to attempt the climb.

Despite having many ways to engage in election-related and other conventional forms of political activity, some Canadians choose to employ more forceful and dramatic means to register their opinions or protest government actions. Such unconventional activities may be individual or collective, legal or illegal, violent or passive. People may march in peaceful demonstrations to protest public policies; they may disobey specific laws in an effort to have them changed; they may even attempt to stop government actions directly through the use of force or violence. During the past thirty years, protests have run the gamut from bombings, kidnapping, and murder by the radical Front de libération du Québec (FLQ) to the passive resistance of the Greenpeace conservation group attempting to stop government-sanctioned hunting of baby seals.

HOW EXTENSIVELY DO CANADIANS PARTICIPATE?

Opinions vary on the extent of public political participation in Canada.[1] Some argue that Canadians are a nation of political "spectators" who are generally quite content to observe the political spectacle from the sidelines. Others maintain that Canadians are relatively active in comparison to the residents of most other democratic countries. Few deny, however, that opportunities for participation far exceed actual levels of involvement.

Those who hold that Canadians are relatively active usually point to the levels of voter turnout in federal and provincial elections. Given a

Table 9.1
Voter Turnout in Federal and Provincial Elections

Federal Elections	Percent Voting	Percent Voting
1988		76
1984		75
1980		69
1979		76
Provincial Elections		
Newfoundland (1985)		78
Prince Edward Island (1986)		88
Nova Scotia (1988)		78
New Brunswick (1987)		82
Quebec (1985)		76
Ontario (1987)		63
Manitoba (1988)		74
Saskatchewan (1986)		82
Alberta (1986)		47
British Columbia (1986)		77

Source: Frank Feigert, *Canada Votes: 1935–1989* (Durham, N.C.: Duke University Press, 1989).

chance to vote, most people do so. Over the past thirty years an average of 75 percent of those on the voters' lists have cast a ballot in federal elections, and turnout has fallen significantly below this figure on only three occasions since the Second World War. The 1953 and 1974 elections were held during summer months when many potential voters were away from home on vacation and unable to get to the polls. Turnout also was low in 1980. In addition to being held in the winter, this was the second federal election in less than a year, and it was held at a time when many voters seemed tired of the seemingly interminable partisan wrangling between the two major parties. Turnout at the provincial level also varies from one election to the next, but on the whole it is roughly on a par with that in federal contests (see Table 9.1).[2]

Excluding nations such as Australia, Belgium, and the Netherlands where voting is compulsory and enforced by legal sanctions, turnout rates in most democratic countries vary between 60 and 90 percent.[3] Canada ranks behind several of these countries, but compares favourably with others such as Japan, Switzerland, India, and particularly the United States. In the United States, only about 70 percent of those who are registered turn out for presidential elections, and fewer than two-thirds of eligible citizens are registered to vote. Still fewer Americans vote in congressional and state elections, and turnout in all U.S. elections has been declining for several decades. In 1988 only 49 percent of the potentially eligible electorate cast a presidential ballot.

Electoral turnout in Canada is even more impressive when examined over time. There are many reasons that a person may fail to vote in a particular election: bad weather, illness, the need to be out of town on business. However, voter surveys suggest that fewer than one person in ten is a habitual non-voter in federal or provincial elections. Another quarter occasionally fail to cast a ballot, but nearly two-thirds report voting whenever they get a chance. However, underlying the national averages, turnout in both federal and provincial elections varies substantially among the provinces. These differences can be explained in part by special circumstances such as the presence in one province or in one election of an especially controversial issue or unusually popular (or unpopular) leader. Differences in weather and geography also have some impact. However, the effects of such idiosyncratic factors probably are quite modest.

More important in explaining differences in turnout among provinces appears to be the relative organizational effectiveness of the parties, the levels of competitiveness among them, and public perceptions of the importance of the issues at stake. Close competition among the parties makes elections interesting and gives voters a sense that their ballot might make a difference. Moreover, party competition is associated with party efforts to bring their supporters to the polls and with the vitality of party organization more generally. Prince Edward Island and Saskatchewan, which traditionally have enjoyed the most competitive party systems, tend to have high levels of voter turnout in both federal and provincial elections. On the other hand, elections in Alberta, Quebec, and Newfoundland have been among the least competitive and historically have had the lowest turnout. Significantly, however, turnout increased dramatically in Newfoundland in the early 1970s with the rise in competition that accompanied the end of Joseph Smallwood's quarter-century domination of provincial politics. Turnout in Quebec tends to be higher in provincial elections, and it increased noticeably in the 1970s with the emergence of the Parti Québécois, whose separatist platform placed the future of the province and Canada as a whole at the forefront of the province's political agenda. Similarly, over 80 percent of Quebeckers voted in the 1980 sovereignty-association referendum.

Although a large majority of Canadians exercise their electoral franchise, substantially fewer participate in other aspects of political life. For example, despite abundant opportunities, most never work for political parties during election campaigns or participate in other ways during such contests. As indicated in Table 9.2, fewer than half engage in any campaign activity, and those who do tend to confine their efforts to "low intensity," episodic activities such as attending the occasional political

Table 9.2
The Extent of Political Participation

Type of Activity	Percent Participating		
1. Election Campaign Activities		Federal	Provincial
Percent who often or sometimes:			
a. try to influence friends' votes		18	20
b. attend political meetings		16	18
c. work for party or candidate		12	9
d. give money to party or candidate		13	10
2. Political Protest	Approve	Effective	Participate
a. sign a petition	85	71	68
b. march or rally	53	52	20
c. boycott	64	61	38
d. sit-in	26	35	5
e. demonstration/protest with chance of violence	11	23	4
3. Other Activities			
Percent who often or sometimes:			
a. read about politics in newspapers		73	
b. watch political programs on TV		69	
c. discuss politics with others		63	
d. contact politicians		20(fed) 18(prov)	
e. are active political party member		4	
f. work with others to solve community problems		34	
g. follow politics very closely		18	

Source: Harold Clarke, Jane Jenson, Lawrence LeDuc, and Jon Pammett, *The 1979 Canadian National Election and Panel Study*; Harold Clarke and Allan Kornberg, *Sources, Distribution and Consequences of Political Support in Canada Study*; Ronald Lambert, Steven Brown, James Curtis, Barry Kay, and John Wilson, *The 1984 Canadian National Election Study*.

rally or trying to persuade a friend how to vote. Political parties are even less successful attracting volunteer workers between elections. At most only 5 percent of the public are even sporadically active in party organizations and, even then, devote an average of less than an hour a week to party affairs.[4]

Part of the reason that Canadians do not participate more extensively in party organizations or electoral campaigns may be that many are unaware of the opportunities that exist. Surveys indicate that greater numbers would be willing to contribute both time and money if they were asked. In Canada, however, political parties are loosely knit organizations and are not very efficient in recruiting or mobilizing members, particularly in the period between elections. Except at the highest echelons, party organizations "hibernate" between elections. They lack public visibility and their interest in stimulating citizen political activism lies dormant until the "spring thaw" provided by a new election writ.

Among the possibilities for participation in non-electoral activities, Canadians are most likely to sign petitions, write to public officials, or work with others to solve community problems. Indeed, about two persons in three have signed a petition at some time in their lives—although the political commitment this indicates probably is minimal. Working with a group to solve a community problem requires somewhat more time and effort. As a consequence, only about half as many ever take part in such activities. Similarly, although writing a letter or making a telephone call typically takes little time or energy, less than a quarter of the public have ever contacted a public official. What makes this all the more surprising is that an overwhelming majority of Canadians—more than 75 percent according to some surveys—believe that MPS, MLAS, or other public officials would pay attention and respond to their communications.

About 60 percent of Canadians are members of one or more voluntary organizations or groups such as labour unions, professional associations, church, or fraternal groups. Many of these groups are involved in political affairs and thereby enable citizens to participate indirectly in politics by becoming involved in group affairs. In fact, however, only about one person in four ever takes an active role in the groups to which they belong. Still fewer express interest in, or are even aware of, the political activities of their groups. Most join groups for social, economic, or professional reasons rather than as a means of political expression. Thus, the number of citizens who can be said to engage in politics indirectly through the involvement of voluntary groups is quite small.[5]

Activities such as political protest and violence, though not unknown in Canada, traditionally have been much lower than in most other countries, including Western democracies such as the United States. During the 1960s, a period of relatively high political ferment in both countries, Canada experienced an estimated forty significant protest demonstrations that resulted in nearly ten deaths. In the United States by comparison, the 1960s witnessed more than seven hundred riots and demonstrations causing more than two hundred and fifty deaths. Controlling for the difference in population size, Canada experienced less than a quarter as many protests and demonstrations during that decade of discontent.[6]

Nevertheless, for a minority of Canadians, protest is, or can be, an important avenue of political expression. In a 1983 national survey, for example, 20 percent of those interviewed reported having taken part in a protest rally or march, and nearly 40 percent had participated in a boycott (see Table 9.2). Even among citizens who have not engaged in protest, the majority believes that such activities are legitimate and potentially effective. Presumably, larger numbers of Canadians would be willing to take part in such mild protest activities given sufficient cause.

In sharp contrast, very few citizens have ever taken part in more extreme, confrontational activities such as sit-ins or demonstrations where the potential for violence is substantial. Still, the potential for more of such activity in the future may not be trivial—upwards to a quarter of the public think that such activities are legitimate and 35 percent think they can be effective. More generally, political protest in Canada may be greater than these survey data suggest in that citizens may register their discontent by quietly casting ballots for extremist parties or dropping out of political life altogether.

The "participation portrait" of the Canadian public that emerges from an examination of any specific activity is not encouraging. There are few activities other than voting in which as many as half of the adult population participate even on an occasional basis. However, it is important to realize that various types of political activity appeal to different individuals. The 20 percent of citizens who write letters to public officials are not necessarily the same 20 percent who participate in protest rallies, or who try to influence their friends' votes. Different activities require disparate skills and resources and often appeal to dissimilar personalities.

When the entire range of political activities is considered, the picture that emerges is one of a moderately, if sporadically, active citizenry. It is true that upwards to 10 percent of the public are completely disengaged politically. Such individuals rarely, if ever, read about politics, talk about them, or participate in any discernible way. It also is the case that another 25 to 30 percent confine themselves to voting. What is impressive, and widely overlooked, however, is the fact that between half and two-thirds of adult Canadians participate at least occasionally in one or more political activities in addition to voting, and as we have noted, large majorities regularly cast ballots in most federal and provincial elections. Moreover, when confronted with an issue about which they feel strongly, sometimes sizable minorities become more intensively involved and choose avenues of political expression compatible with their personal abilities, needs, and resources.

WHO PARTICIPATES?

Because of the likelihood that the interests of less-active citizens will be overlooked by government, democratic theory emphasizes the importance of high levels of involvement by all segments of society. Although political activity in Canada involves individuals from virtually every social and economic group, citizens from certain walks of life enjoy greater political opportunities, possess superior political resources, and are

TABLE 9.3
WHO PARTICIPATES IN SELECTED POLITICAL ACTIVITIES 1983–84

	VOTING	PARTY WORK	GIVE MONEY	CONTACT MPS	MARCH/RALLY	SIT-IN
OCCUPATION						
PROFESSIONAL/MANAGERIAL	93	19	22	31	31	6
WHITE-COLLAR	86	14	12	19	15	3
BLUE-COLLAR	76	10	9	14	19	5
FARMER	92	13	25	32	14	4
HOMEMAKER	84	12	12	15	9	2
STUDENT	82	7	7	15	31	14
INCOME						
LESS THAN $20,000	80	10	10	17	15	4
$20,000–29,999	85	12	11	16	24	6
$30,000–49,999	87	12	12	22	26	6
$50,000 AND OVER	89	18	23	27	24	4
EDUCATION						
ELEMENTARY OR LESS	80	8	10	9	9	2
SOME SECONDARY	80	10	10	17	13	4
SECONDARY	87	11	11	18	20	5
UNIVERSITY	90	21	21	31	34	6

AGE						
18–25	72	9	7	15	24	8
26–35	85	12	8	20	31	9
36–45	90	13	15	26	21	2
46–55	91	14	17	23	16	4
56–65	88	17	20	19	10	2
66 AND OVER	90	11	14	14	7	1
REGION						
ATLANTIC	85	11	7	16	13	2
QUEBEC–FRENCH	85	12	12	17	30	8
QUEBEC–NON-FRENCH	91	14	18	15	26	7
ONTARIO	85	14	12	23	16	4
PRAIRIES	84	9	18	22	13	3
BRITISH COLUMBIA	83	10	12	14	24	6
GENDER						
MALES	86	12	13	21	24	6
FEMALES	84	13	12	18	16	4

exposed to more intense political stimuli that lead them to participate more than others. Some of the more important of these differences are illustrated in Table 9.3.

The largest and most consistent differences in political activity are those associated with citizens' positions in society. In Canada as elsewhere, the higher a person's social standing the more likely he or she will be to engage in virtually all political activities. In addition to determining the social and economic resources available for political investment, social status influences citizens' perceptions of their personal stakes in politics and their ability to influence government decisions. High-status persons also are centrally placed in important informal communication networks, being, for example, the neighbours and curling partners of public officials, high-ranking party activists, and other members of the political elite. They are more likely to know and be known by political decision makers and are viewed by the public and by politicians alike as community opinion leaders.

In advanced industrial societies such as Canada, social status correlates with a variety of factors, but especially with occupation, income, and education. Since work is a central experience of adult life, it is not surprising that occupation has important consequences for citizen participation. Generally, individuals in higher-status occupations participate more than those with lower-status jobs. Although this relationship holds broadly for all types of political activity, differences based on occupation are most pronounced for the more intensive and time-consuming forms of participation. This is illustrated most graphically for the highest-level political activities—seeking and holding elected public office. Lawyers, business executives, and other professionals constitute less than 20 percent of the work force, yet they dominate the electoral arena, occupying more than 75 percent of the seats in Parliament and the provincial assemblies.[7]

Income and education reinforce the political advantages of occupation. Education, in particular, increases political interest, expands awareness of participatory opportunities, and nurtures many of the skills necessary for effective involvement. The university experience is especially important in these regards. Given their idealism and free time, university students are particularly likely to engage in protest activities. Involvement in protests declines as individuals grow older, but the excitement generated by the protest activities frequently whets the appetite for participation in more conventional activities later in life.

Similarly, although money may not "buy" political power, it does provide access to political opportunities and resources that give the relatively affluent decided advantages in political life. Money purchases the leisure time necessary to pursue politics either as a hobby or career; it buys political information, which increases both political interest and awareness; and it facilitates contacts with party leaders and public officials, which enhance both political communication and influence. Consequently, wealthy citizens participate more extensively in all forms of political activity. The wealthy enjoy only marginal advantages with respect to voting and community work, which are not as resource-intensive as some other activities. However, they are considerably more active in party organizational and election campaign activities and virtually monopolize elected office. Interestingly, they also are more likely to engage in unconventional activities. Thus, student protesters tend to be sons and daughters of the wealthy. Students are not atypical—the leaders of protest movements, including, for example, the separatist movement in Quebec, have been drawn disproportionately from the upper strata of society, as well.[8]

Although occupation, income, and education are the principal social forces structuring participation, other factors such as ethnicity, region, religion, age, and gender also are widely believed to influence both the nature and extent of political activity. However, in Canada the importance of these other social characteristics is substantially less than that of social status and frequently disappears when status differences between groups are taken into account. With regard to region and ethnicity, for example, although there are significant differences in voter turnout among provinces and regions, there is relatively little regional variation in party or campaign work. Although residents of the Atlantic provinces rank near the bottom of every category of activity reported in Table 9.3 this is attributable almost entirely to the relative poverty of the region and the lower than average educational level of persons living in these provinces. Similarly, francophone residents of Quebec participate less in most election-related activities than do their anglophone neighbours. However, these differences, which are small in the first place, vanish in most cases when the educational and income advantages of anglophone Quebeckers are controlled. [9]

One trait that is important irrespective of social status is age. Politics traditionally has been the preserve of the middle-aged. Younger people, especially those eighteen to twenty-five, tend to be preoccupied with school and the demands of starting jobs and families. As a consequence, they are slow to take advantage of the political opportunities available to them—a phenomenon usually known as the "start-up" effect. In contrast, older citizens are subject to a much weaker "slow-down" effect. They participate somewhat less than middle-aged persons (but more than the youngest citizens) not only because of the increasing burden of poor health that is often associated with aging, but also because older Canadians on average have somewhat lower formal educations than do younger generations. The principal exception to this pattern is with respect to political protest, where activity rates are highest among students and those twenty-six to thirty-five and decline steadily among older groups.

GENDER AND PARTICIPATION

Until very recently, some of the most consistent differences in political participation were those based on gender. Politics traditionally has been a "man's world" in which women have been treated as "political inferiors." This is illustrated most dramatically in the Canadian case by the fact that women were denied the right to vote in federal elections until 1918 and in some provincial elections until 1940. Although legal barriers to the participation of women have been eliminated, a variety of informal obstacles persist today making involvement more difficult for women than for men.[10]

Explanations for male–female differences in participation are numerous. Some believe that women are less involved in most activities because of hidden discrimination (the reluctance of party leaders to select women candidates for public office or of voters to cast ballots for women). Others think the problem originates with women's roles in society. Where once women were handicapped by the expectation that they had the principal, if not the exclusive, responsibility for child rearing and home making, now women who want to "have it all," may be expected to "do it all," adding the burdens of building a career to the traditional responsibilities of home and family. Still others argue the problem is one of socialization; women learn (or are taught) as children that politics is a man's preserve and that women should be politically passive and deferential.[11]

Overlooked in the debate about causes of gender differences in political activity is the fact that male–female differences in many types of "lower level" political activities in Canada now are quite small and have been for at least a decade. For example, evidence from 1983 and 1984 national surveys (Table 9.3) indicates that no more than three percentage points separate men's and women's participation in five of the six activities examined. Data from a 1974 national survey show a similarly small "gender gap." The one exception is participation in protest activities such as political marches and rallies where men tend to be more active. What is more, most of the small differences in participation rates between men and women vanish when occupation and education are considered.

Table 9.4 compares the average number of several political activities of men and women when occupation and education are controlled. Significantly, among persons with professional occupations or those with college educations, women participate as much as men, if not more. However, among men and women without college educations or with middle- to low-status occupations, men are considerably more active.

Table 9.4
Mean Number of Political Activities of Men and Women
Controlling for Occupation and Education

	Men	Women
A. Conventional Participation[1] by Occupation		
Professional, Business, Managerial	2.87	3.02
Other, None	2.21	1.99
B. Conventional Participation[1] by Education		
Attended University	2.90	2.88
Secondary School or less	2.20	1.98
C. Protest Participation[2] by Occupation		
Professional, Business, Managerial	1.73	1.71
Other, None	1.29	1.13
D. Protest Participation[2] by Education		
Attended University	1.85	1.94
Secondary School or less	1.31	1.13

[1]Conventional activities include voting in the 1984 federal election, discussing politics, trying to influence friends' votes, attending political meetings, working for a political party or candidate, contributing money to a party or candidate, or contacting politicians.
[2]Protest activities include signing a petition, participating in a protest march or rally, engaging in a sit-in, or taking part in a boycott.

This suggests that gender differences stem more from women's early socialization experiences than from overt discrimination or even role differences. It also suggests that women's early socialization to political passivity and indifference can be reversed by later life experiences and that access to university education may play an especially critical role in liberating women from traditional political roles. Unfortunately, a smaller percentage of women attend college, and the percentage has increased only slightly since the early 1970s.[12] Thus, the small but significant advantage men have enjoyed for most of the past two decades is likely to persist into the 1990s and beyond.

Although male–female differences in many lower-level political activities are fairly small and probably do not reflect overt discrimination, gender differences in higher-level and more influential political activities are pronounced and difficult to explain in terms of socialization alone. In political parties, for example, women tend to be relegated to the bottom of the organizational hierarchy where they do much of the time-consuming and tedious organizational maintenance work but have little influence on candidate selection or policy. The proportion of women involved in the party declines sharply at successively higher levels—a phenomenon sometimes called the "law of increasing disproportion." Thus, for example, approximately 70 percent of secretaries in local constituency association ridings are women, but women constitute only about 30 percent of party convention delegates.

Women also continue to be a small, if growing, minority of candidates for public elective office. As Figure 9.1 illustrates, the percentage of women nominated as parliamentary candidates by the three major parties has increased rather steadily, if slowly, over the past fifteen years.[13] The New Democratic Party (NDP) has led the way in providing women with opportunities to run for Parliament, such that in 1988, 29 percent of NDP candidates were women. Importantly, however, many of these women NDP candidates have run in ridings where their party had little chance of success, and the Liberals and Progressive Conservatives have not nominated nearly as many women candidates. As a result, the percentage of women elected to Parliament has remained meagre. Although the percentage of women MPs more than doubled during the 1980s (from 6 to 13 percent, see Figure 9.2), Parliament remains largely a male preserve. The continuing paucity of women in the House of Commons also restricts the possibilities for representation in the federal Cabinet. Historically, very few women have been Cabinet ministers, and fewer still have held important portfolios. Nor have women fared better in provincial politics—male dominance of provincial legislatures and Cabinets remains pervasive.

In sum, although the ranks of the political activists in Canada include representatives from all segments of society, certain types of people participate more than others. In particular, the wealthy and well educated, men, and the middle-aged tend to be found in disproportionate numbers among the ranks of the politically active.

WHY DO SOME PARTICIPATE MORE THAN OTHERS?

The extent of citizen participation in political life is determined by the interplay of motivation and opportunity. Today, people become involved politically when they want to and when they possess sufficient resources to translate motivation into action. Although political opportunities in Canada once were severely circumscribed by laws restricting the participation of women, the poor and those without property, native peoples, and members of certain religions, most legal impediments to participation have been eliminated.[14] It remains true, of course, that politically relevant resources vary substantially between individuals and groups, thereby impeding the participation of some more than others. As we have noted, this is particularly true with regard to public office holding. However, if most Canadians do not have sufficient resources to become full-time politicians, they do have the wherewithal and opportunities to perform a wide range of political activities. Therefore, the differences observed in most types of political action are better explained by differences in motivations.

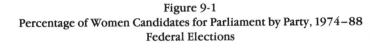

Figure 9-1
Percentage of Women Candidates for Parliament by Party, 1974–88
Federal Elections

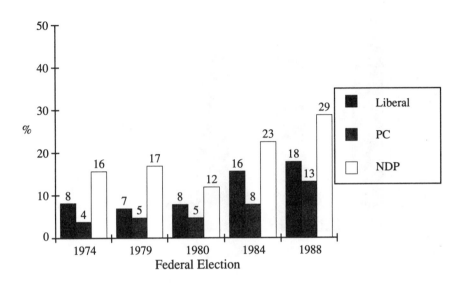

The motivation to participate is determined by a complex set of attitudes and beliefs about politics, society, and self. Among the more important of these are the individual's awareness of, interest in, and concern about government and public affairs. It should come as no surprise that political participation varies with political interest. Although even a passing interest in politics usually is sufficient to motivate most people to vote, interest of a more absorbing kind is required for other types of activity. Few persons possess an abiding interest in politics. Only about one in five reports following politics closely day to day. Political interest increases somewhat during periods of crisis or in response to highly visible events, but even election campaigns with all their conflict and excitement generate little public enthusiasm. During the 1984 federal election campaign, for example, only one person in three expressed a high level of interest in the campaign. The problem appears to be that, for many people, government and politics seem irrelevant and remote. Politics intrudes upon their daily lives every year or two when they are called upon to vote in an election, but otherwise they see little direct or immediate impact of politics on their workaday lives.

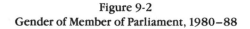

Figure 9-2
Gender of Member of Parliament, 1980–88

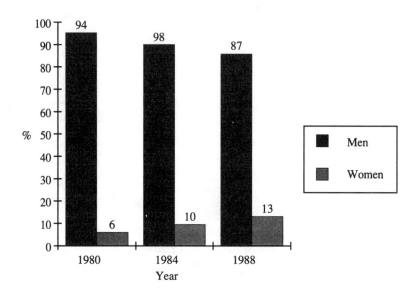

Compounding the problem of marginal interest in a seemingly remote political world is the fact that many citizens are poorly informed about politics and do not understand how government works. Political interest and information are closely related and mutually reinforcing. Just as people who are interested in politics attend more closely to public affairs and are likely to be better informed, those who understand government are more sensitive to the political messages around them and are more likely to develop strong incentives to participate. The latter also are more likely to acquire the resources needed for effective participation and to comprehend, as well, the range of opportunities available. Most Canadians, however, possess only a superficial understanding of their country's government and politics. Also, although virtually everyone can identify the prime minister and most recognize the name of their member of Parliament, knowledge of the policy and more general ideological positions espoused by leading politicians and the major parties tends to be quite meagre.

Low levels of political information have important consequences not only for the extent of participation, but also for its quality. With respect to voting, for example, the classic view is that the democratic citizen studies political issues, evaluates parties' programs and platforms, and selects the party that takes positions on important issues closest to the voter's own. Although election surveys indicate that most voters cast their ballots for the party they think closest to them on a few, highly salient issues, these studies also indicate that most voters are concerned only with one or two leading issues and that their conceptions of these issues are often vague and superficial. Moreover, expressed issue positions may be rationalizations or projections based on partisanship or feelings about party leaders or local candidates. Although issues do influence electoral choice, their role may be overshadowed by long-standing party loyalties or affective reactions to the images of the parties' leaders and candidates.[15]

For a sizable number of citizens, therefore, the motivation to participate stems from feelings of "like" or "dislike" about parties, leaders, or candidates rather than from a commitment to political ideals. Partisanship, or a sense of identification with a political party, is a prime motive for numerous political activities, especially those related to elections. Persons with strong psychological attachments to a party are more likely to vote and engage in campaign activities. They also are the ones on whom the burdens of party work disproportionately fall, since they are more likely to volunteer their services or to be easily recruited, especially when an election is in the offing.

Although few citizens hold intense opinions on political issues or possess well-developed ideologies, those who do are among the most active members of the polity. However, because political parties in Canada typically favour pragmatism over ideological consistency, citizens with strong ideologies frequently encounter difficulties finding appropriate outlets for expressing their views. Persons motivated by ideology often identify with one of the smaller, more radical or programmatic parties such as the Co-operative Commonwealth Federation (CCF) or Social Credit during the 1930s, or the NDP or Parti Québécois today. Those who cannot find appropriate parties for their points of view sometimes express their frustrations through protest activities or by abstaining from politics altogether.

Whatever the initial impetus for political activity, citizens are unlikely to act on that impulse unless they also are convinced that their involvement holds reasonable prospects for success. Political efficacy, the belief that one can influence political decisions through personal action, is a necessary if not sufficient condition for nearly all forms of participation. Although it appears that many Canadians believe that voting is a civic obligation to be performed regardless of its likely impact, few are willing to take part in more demanding activities unless they believe not only that opportunities for effective participation exist, but also that they personally are capable of exploiting those opportunities. Even the discontented must be convinced that dissent will make some difference before they are likely to express their dissatisfaction through protest.

For many citizens, however, government appears too large, too complicated, and too remote for them to understand, much less to influence, its operations and policies. In a 1984 national survey, two-thirds of those interviewed complained that government was too complicated; more than half thought that government did not care about their opinions and that MPs soon lose touch with their constituents; and a majority concluded that they did not have any real say in government. Numerous other surveys conducted over the past two decades also indicate that many Canadians in all regions of the country feel politically inefficacious.

Feelings of political powerlessness and incompetence frequently are products of more generalized feelings of powerlessness, cynicism, and distrust about society and self. These feelings of alienation, as they are called, appear to be linked, in turn, to the frustration many people feel at being excluded from significant opportunities to participate in important non-political decisions that affect their everyday lives at home, in school, and on the job. Participation in non-political institutions, it appears, provides training for political life. Citizens reared in homes where family decisions are shared and those educated in schools where student opinions are solicited and taken seriously acquire confidence in themselves, which increases their sense of personal competence and efficacy and enhances their political involvement later in life. Opportunities to engage in decision making at work appear to be even more important. Even limited involvement in workplace decisions appears sufficient to increase political interest and efficacy, to promote tolerance, and thus to enhance both the quantity and quality of citizen participation.

HOW EFFECTIVE IS PARTICIPATION?

Underlying all that has been said thus far is the assumption that citizen participation matters—that who participates, how, and how extensively have real consequences for the selection of political leaders and the substance of public policy. Democratic theory, we have noted, is predicated upon the belief that participation is the most effective means for citizens to express their interests to government. Consequently, inequalities of political participation can distort the representation of public interests and undermine the fundamental basis of political equality. The little evidence that is available regarding the consequences of participation for leadership selection and public policy in Canada suggests that participation does, indeed, matter, and that government is most responsive to the interests of those who participate most extensively and in the most demanding political activities.

Although opportunities for citizen participation are numerous, the effectiveness of certain forms of political activity is tenuous at best. This is particularly the case for election-related activities. Despite widespread involvement, the practical value of voting and campaign work is severely limited by the absence of effective competition in many elections combined with the basic homogeneity of the major parties on many fundamental political issues. Because the major parties often fail to offer Canadians meaningful choices even where competition is robust, elections too often are little more than civic rituals. They permit people to participate symbolically, but provide ordinary Canadians with little real influence in the selection of political leaders or the development of public policies. Moreover, because of the sheer number of ballots cast, even in local elections, the probability that any individual's vote will decide who wins an election is so small as to be virtually nil. This has led some theorists to conclude that voting is not a rational use of one's resources and that people would be better advised to devote the time and energy spent in voting on more productive political activities.

One problem with this logic, however, is that many of the more demanding and influential political activities are effectively monopolized by social and economic elites. Political parties, for example, play obvious and important roles in leadership selection and policy development. However, despite periodic attempts to expand their memberships and encourage wider participation by the rank and file, the major parties have been careful to ensure that the nomination of candidates, the selection of party leaders, and the formulation of party programs are dominated by high-ranking party officials and "informal influentials" who are not directly elected by the broad mass of party supporters or are not elected at all, and who differ significantly from ordinary party members in social background and political opinion.[16]

Interest groups also have substantial influence in Canadian government and politics. Even more than parties, however, interest groups are dominated by elites whose backgrounds and interests may be very different from the average group member. This frequently is true even of groups such as labour unions that represent working-class interests. Despite the formal trappings of democracy in their organizations, interest group leaders often are only nominally accountable to their membership for actions taken on the organization's behalf.[17]

Nor does political protest necessarily provide a viable alternative to elite-dominated activities. Protests frequently are exciting, even dramatic, departures from what constitutes "normal politics" in Canada. As such, they often receive widespread attention from the mass media who are hungry for a good story to "spice up" an otherwise dull news day. Although it is arguable that the publicity surrounding protests can heighten public consciousness of neglected interests and thereby lay a foundation for gradual, long-term changes in government policy, in the short run, the usual response of government has been to suppress (sometimes forcefully) protest and to resist taking actions that might be interpreted as capitulation to the demands of highly visible protest groups.[18]

Given the relative ineffectiveness of voting combined with the domination of more demanding and effective activities by social and economic elites, it is not surprising that the composition of Canada's political leadership continues to be elite (and male) dominated or that the tenor of public policy appears to many observers to manifest an elite bias. At the same time, however, although the composition of Canada's political leadership has changed very little in this century despite broad changes in the nature and extent of citizen participation, even relatively modest changes in the configuration of the politically active strata of society have been sufficient to stimulate significant changes in government policies and priorities. In particular, it appears, the gradual expansion of opportunities for working-class participation in political life has provoked somewhat greater attention to the interests of the disadvantaged, especially in those provinces where political competition has been comparatively high and where the working-class-orientated CCF/NDP has enjoyed its greatest success.

On balance, the available evidence suggests that the nature and extent of public participation do have important consequences for political accountability and responsiveness—albeit consequences that sometimes work to the disadvantage of the majority of Canadians. There also is increasing evidence that political participation has intrinsic value for individual citizens, enhancing their self-esteem and fostering more democratic personalities. The problem, however, succinctly stated by Robert Presthus,[19] is that,

> in the context of democratic participation, the going system produces some questionable consequences. Participation tends to be restricted to those groups that possess the greatest amounts of resources...The majority are unable to compete effectively in the political arena, for lack of such resources...which tend to be monopolized by those we have defined as political elites. Government in responding to the elites is placed in the somewhat anomalous position of defending the strong against the weak.

DEMOCRATIC IDEALS AND CANADIAN REALITIES

Perhaps inevitably, assessments of the democratic character of political participation in Canada depend upon one's perspective. Although it is obvious from this brief discussion that the structure of citizen participation in political life falls considerably short of the democratic ideal, it also is the case that Canada approaches this ideal more closely than all but a handful of the world's nation-states. Indeed, it is doubtful that any country provides significantly greater opportunities for participation than are enjoyed in Canada.

In many respects, the structure of citizen participation in Canada is wider and deeper than often assumed. The great majority of citizens regularly accept the responsibility to vote, and substantial numbers take part at least from time to time in more demanding political activities as well. Moreover, although many display little interest in politics and are poorly informed about both the structure of government and pressing issues of the day, there are good reasons to believe that both the quantity and quality of public participation would increase if political competition were strengthened and if more people were accorded more effective opportunities to become involved in political life and, especially, in such basic social institutions as the family, school, and workplace.

Political participation is a tonic. It is healthy for the individual and therapeutic to the state. Increased political activity in Canada would enhance citizen interest in, and knowledge of, government and public affairs, promote subjective political competence, and strengthen historically fragile feelings of membership in an overarching political community. Increases in the political activity of working-class persons, especially women, and of other politically disadvantaged groups also would foster more equitable representation of all social and economic interests and strengthen political equality.

It is highly unrealistic, of course, to expect everyone to engage intensively in every facet of political life. The number of citizens who can hold elected office in any year is limited, and the widespread resort to violent forms of political protest threatens the continuing existence of a democratic political system. Notwithstanding such limits, there remain abundant opportunities to increase public participation in a wide variety of conventional and less-conventional political activities, thereby increasing the quality of democratic citizenship in Canada in the 1990s and achieving a closer approximation of the democratic ideal.

NOTES

1. For contrasting perspectives, see Richard J. Van Loon, "Political Participation in Canada," *Canadian Journal of Political Science* 3 (September 1970): 376–99; Léon Dion, "Participating in the Political Process," *Queen's Quarterly* 75 (Autumn 1968): 437–38; and William Mishler, *Political Participation in Canada* (Toronto: Macmillan, 1979).

2. For a comprehensive report of data on Canadian elections, see Frank Feigert, *Canada Votes: 1935–1989* (Durham, N.C.: Duke University Press, 1989).

3. Ivor Crewe, "Electoral Participation," in *Democracy at the Polls*, ed.

David Butler, Howard R. Penniman, and Austin Ranney (Washington, D.C.: American Enterprise Institute, 1981), pp. 234–37.

4. Allan Kornberg, Joel Smith, and Harold D. Clarke, *Citizen Politicians—Canada: Party Officials in a Democratic Society* (Durham, N.C.: Carolina Academic Press, 1979).

5. On interest group membership and participation, see Robert Presthus, *Elite Accommodation in Canadian Politics* (Toronto: Macmillan, 1973); Robert Presthus, *Elites in the Policy Process* (Cambridge: Cambridge University Press, 1974); A. Paul Pross, *Group Politics and Public Policy* (Toronto: Oxford University Press, 1986).

6. Ronald Manzer, *Canada: A Socio-Political Report* (Toronto: McGraw-Hill Ryerson, 1974), pp. 74–84. See also Harold D. Clarke, Allan Kornberg, and Marianne C. Stewart, "Active Minorities: Political Participation in Canadian Democracy," in *Minorities and the Canadian State*, ed. Neil Nevitte and Allan Kornberg (Oakville, Ont.: Mosaic Press, 1985), ch. 16.

7. Harold D. Clarke, et al., "Backbenchers," in *The Provincial Political Systems*, ed. David Bellamy, et al. (Toronto: Methuen, 1976), pp. 216–19; Allan Kornberg and William Mishler, *Influence in Parliament: Canada* (Durham, N.C.: Duke University Press, 1976).

8. Kenneth McRoberts and Dale Posgate, *Quebec: Social Change and Political Crisis*, rev. ed. (Toronto: McClelland and Stewart, 1980), pp. 185–89.

9. Regional differences in attitudes such as political efficacy and interest, which are conducive to political participation, also largely disappear when educational and income differences are controlled. See, for example, Allan Kornberg, William Mishler, and Harold D. Clarke, *Representative Democracy in the Canadian Provinces* (Toronto: Prentice-Hall, 1982), p. 83.

10. Catherine L. Cleverdon, *The Women's Suffrage Movement in Canada* (Toronto: University of Toronto Press, 1950).

11. See, for example, Jerome H. Black and Nancy McGlen, "Male–Female Political Involvement Differentials in Canada, 1965–1975," *Canadian Journal of Political Science* 12 (September 1979): 471–98; Kornberg, Smith, and Clarke, *Citizen Politicians—Canada*, ch. 8; Barry Kay, et al., "Gender and Political Activity in Canada, 1965–84," *Canadian Journal of Political Science* 20 (December 1987): 851–63.

12. Alfred A. Hunter, *Class Tells: On Social Inequality and Canada*, 2nd ed. (Toronto: Butterworths, 1986), p. 122.

13. Sylvia B. Bashevkin, *Toeing the Lines: Women and Party Politics in English Canada* (Toronto: University of Toronto Press, 1985); and M. Janine Brodie, *Point of Entry: The Election of Women in Canada* (Toronto: University of Toronto Press, 1985).

14. Terrance H. Qualter, *The Election Process in Canada* (Toronto: McGraw-Hill Ryerson, 1979).
15. Harold D. Clarke, et al., *Political Choice in Canada* (Toronto: McGraw-Hill Ryerson, 1979), chs. 5, 7, 11.
16. Kornberg, Smith, and Clarke, *Citizen Politicians—Canada*, chs. 7, 8.
17. Presthus, *Elite Accommodation*, pp. 286–87.
18. Judith Torrance, "The Response of Canadian Governments to Violence," *Canadian Journal of Political Science* 10 (December 1977): 473–96.
19. Presthus, *Elites in the Policy Process*, p. 461.

FURTHER READINGS

Barnes, Samuel, and Max Kaase. *Political Action*. Beverly Hills, Calif.: Sage Publications, 1979.

Bashevkin, Sylvia B. *Toeing the Lines: Women and Party Politics in English Canada*. Toronto: University of Toronto Press, 1985.

Clarke, Harold D., et al. *Absent Mandate: The Politics of Discontent in Canada*. Toronto: Gage, 1984.

Clarke, Harold D., Allan Kornberg, and Marianne C. Stewart. "Active Minorities: Political Participation in Canadian Democracy." In *Minorities and the Canadian State*, ed. Neil Nevitte and Allan Kornberg. Oakville, Ont.: Mosaic Press, 1985.

Crewe, Ivor. "Electoral Participation." In *Democracy at the Polls*, ed. David Butler, Howard R. Penniman, and Austin Ranney. Washington, D.C.: American Enterprise Institute, 1981.

Kornberg, Allan, Joel Smith, and Harold D. Clarke. *Citizen Politicians—Canada: Party Officials in a Democratic Society*. Durham, N.C.: Carolina Academic Press, 1979.

Mishler, William. *Political Participation in Canada*. Toronto: Macmillan, 1979.

10

Elites, Classes, and Power in Canada

LEO V. PANITCH

"In Toronto there are no classes. . .just the Masseys and the masses." This little ditty, perhaps reflecting a centralist bias characteristic of Canadian politics itself, captures graphically the way political scientists have often approached the study of power in Canadian society. Inequalities of political and economic power are rarely denied and indeed are frequently a direct object of study. In general, however, political scientists have operated with a somewhat impoverished—and misleading—set of concepts in trying to understand these inequalities. As in the case of "the Masseys and the masses," they have tended to categorize society in terms of a gradation of rich, middle, and poor, and to examine politics in terms of elites with power and masses without. In employing such imprecise and oversimplified generalizations, social scientists have obscured and mystified the real links between social, economic, and political power in Canada.

Who, then, are these "elites" and "masses"? Occasionally, and most usually in the context of voting behaviour studies, the "masses" are divided into statistical classes grouped together on the basis of income, occupational status, or the "common sense" self-perception of individuals themselves in class terms. Insofar as actual socio-economic collectivities of people are dealt with, this has usually been done in terms of the concept of "interest groups"—formal organizations of farmers, workers, business people, etc. Those who lead such organizations are usually designated as "elites" and differentiated from the "non–decision-making" mass of their members. In this view, *power* is seen in terms of *relations among elites*. It is extended to the study of relationships between elites and masses only through the highly structured contexts of elections, opinion polls, and interest group "demands."

The problem with this approach is not that is sees politics as isolated from socio-economic structure. On the contrary, the behaviour of elites is very much seen as conditioned by the socio-economic "background" of the individuals who compose them, and by the highly structured demands coming through voting or interest groups from society. As in the celebrated political system approach, which serves as a conceptual framework for Canada's most widely used introductory political science text,[1] the determinant of politics is seen as "demands" coming from the "environment" of politics.

It is often alleged that what is wrong here is that the political system is a "black box" that reveals little of the inner workings of government, where the most salient elites make their decisions. There is something in this argument, but what is even more striking is the "black hole"—the environment. We are told that scarcity prevails here and that demands are generated by conflicts over resources, but a systematic examination of the way in which our economy is structured to cope with material scarcity, of the social relations that result between people, and thus of the concrete material clash of social forces that goes on is seldom undertaken. References to individual competition or intergroup competition, as with rich and poor, elite and mass, may give us clues, but because of their "grossness" as categories, because of their abstraction from concrete social relationships between people in a capitalist society such as Canada, they do not contribute enough to our understanding of what is acknowledged to be the determinant element of politics—the socio-economic system in which politics is embedded.

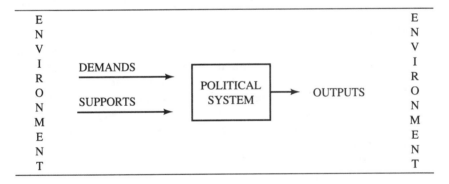

To properly understand the relationship between society and politics involves taking an analysis of society seriously, which itself entails going beyond categories such as elite, mass, and group. It involves getting down to the material social relationships between people, their common experiences in terms of these relationships, and the actual collectivities they form and the struggles they enter into in handling these experiences. This is what a *class analysis* as opposed to an *elite analysis* of society and politics is designed to do. In Canada—and even in Toronto—there *are* classes, and it is their history of contradictory relations to one another, and the balance of power that results at given periods and instances, that establishes the foundation of politics, including setting the extent and limit of the power of the Masseys, or that of any other "elite."

ELITE ANALYSIS IN CANADA

There is fairly widespread agreement among political scientists that what is meant by the term "democracy" as applied to a contemporary political system is "that institutional arrangement for arriving at political decisions in which individuals acquire the power to decide by means of a competitive struggle for the people's vote." The people themselves do not decide, and therefore power does not immediately reside with the people, but rather "the people have the opportunity of accepting or refusing the men [*sic*] who are to rule them."[2] This is an "elitist" conception of democracy that does not require or expect high citizen participation in public affairs beyond the act of choosing between competing teams of leaders. A degree of *elite-pluralism* is guaranteed in this system, at least with a view to elections and formal parliamentary opposition, by a two-party or multiparty system. Moreover, in the case of a federal system like Canada, the elite-teams compete for votes in various jurisdictions, and this further tends to multiply the extent of elite-pluralism. Finally, insofar as freedom of association prevails, it is recognized that the decision-making elites may be subject to a process of interest group competition for influence upon them.

This system of "elite-pluralism," however much it may be demarcated from broader, more mass-participatory conceptions of democracy, is not to be sneezed at as a minimal description of "actually existing" liberal democracies. It captures, albeit in too formal and unhistorical a fashion, some of the basic differences between a polity such as ours and an authoritarian regime. Yet, serious students of power in Canadian society have understandably not been willing to rest content with minimal descriptions of this sort. They have wanted to know *who* these competing teams of leaders are in socio-economic terms and the extent to which they reflect in their competition and decision making a narrow or broad range of approaches to public issues and concerns. They have wanted to know the relationship between the democratically elected political elites and those decision makers in institutional spheres, such as the private corporations that dominate our economy, which are not democratically elected. To speak of elite-pluralism properly, they have recognized, entails examining the degree of *autonomy* political elites have from, at least, the elites that exercise power (in the sense of decision making) in the economic sphere.

John Porter's *The Vertical Mosaic*[3] is the classic Canadian study that asks these questions within the elite-pluralist conceptual framework, and it is for the most part better than similar studies of other liberal democratic societies. Porter began with an examination of the broad social differentiations between people in Canada in terms of demographic patterns, occupational and income distribution, and ethnic and educational inequalities. Although he discerned persistent "class" inequalities in Canada, in keeping with the elite–mass dichotomy of his conceptual approach, he tended to treat class as merely a "statistical category" imposed on society by the researcher rather than an actual collectivity of people with real social cohesion and power. Instead, he reserved the study of social cohesion and power only to the "elites"—to those identifiable individuals who occupied decision-making positions at the top of all the major institutional orders that might be said to perform "essential tasks" for Canadian society. Society is seen to be composed of institutional power centres in the state, the economy, and the ideological sphere, with a set of elites in each (political and bureaucratic; corporate and labour; mass media, educational, and religious) that have power by virtue of the necessity of institutions to be "directed and coordinated," itself entailing "the recognized right to make decisions on behalf of a group of people." Thus turning the question of power into a matter of "authority," Porter went on to isolate the principal authority roles in each institution, to locate the individuals who filled these roles, to examine their social backgrounds, and to study the degree of elite cohesion within each power centre and among them. His test of Canada's claim to democracy rested, then, not on popular involvement in, or resistance to, the exercise of power, but rather on whether the elites came from different social backgrounds and whether they were autonomous from, and competitive with, one another.

Porter's findings, covering the 1940 to 1960 period, substantially undermined the conventional wisdom of treating Canada as an "elite-pluralist democracy." Examining the boards of directors of the 183 corporations that dominated the Canadian economy in terms of assets and sales, he found an internally cohesive and concentrated elite characterized by extensive interlocking directorships between corporations, recruitment on the basis of "upper-class" family ties and exclusive private school education, common ethnic (Anglo-Saxon) origins and religious (Anglican) affiliations, common membership in exclusive social clubs, and a shared commitment to a "free-enterprise" capitalist value system.

In contrast, the political and bureaucratic elites (federal Cabinet ministers, provincial premiers, Supreme Court and provincial chief justices in the first case, and highly paid civil servants in the second) were somewhat less exclusive in terms of social backgrounds, although still drawn from a narrow "middle class" excluding some 90 percent of most Canadians. The political elite was characterized by a high degree of co-optation from other elites, lacked a discrete internal career structure, and Cabinet membership itself often served as a stepping stone for entry into the corporate elite. In terms of values it was ideologically cohesive, but with an obsession with national unity ("From Sea to Sea" as the formative credo of politics) that was innately conservative in terms of failing to express substantive values ("Liberty, Equality, Fraternity," "All Power to the People") that could challenge the economic elite's dominant value system. As such, he saw Canada as burdened with an "avocational" political elite, particularly weak as a base for guaranteeing pluralism. As for the ideological elite, neither the mass media, nor religious leaders, nor intellectuals had the independence or the inclination to challenge critically the power of the economic elite.

Porter concluded that the Canadian system of power relations was best seen as a "confraternity of power" rather than as a set of competing, autonomous elites. The various elites were "operating more or less within the same value system, a condition brought about in part by the establishments of kinship and class. Any examination of career interchanging, the membership of boards, commissions and councils, and the structure of political parties would probably show the dominance of the corporate world over the other institutional systems."

Labour was the one elite Porter studied that was marked off from this "confraternity." Alone in being drawn from "lower-class" social backgrounds, the labour elite was questionably an elite at all in that they operated in the economic sphere as an oppositional element, excluded from decision-making positions. In any case, their role did not much extend beyond collective bargaining in the economic sphere, since they "rarely shared in the informal aspects of the confraternity of power." They were on "the periphery of the overall structure of power, called in by others when the 'others' consider it necessary, or when the labour leaders demand a hearing from the political elite." Defining democracy as entailing equality of opportunity for individuals, and competition among elites, Porter concluded: "Canada...has a long way to go to become in any sense a thoroughgoing democracy."[4]

Subsequent studies have produced similar conclusions. Wallace Clement's examination of the corporate (and mass media) elites in the early 1970s[5] found a greater degree of corporate concentration (with 113 firms now dominant in the economy), even more extensive interlocking directorships among them, and a higher degree of social exclusiveness in terms of "upper-class" family background than there had been twenty years before. Clement stressed the greater structural differentiation within the corporate elite, distinguishing between a dominant fraction of Canadian-controlled corporations in the financial, utilities, and transportation sectors, and a predominance of foreign-owned corporations in the manufacturing and resource sectors, with Canadian corporate executives located there as "compradors." But the interlocks between these "fractions" were extensive, as Canadian bankers were allied with American multinational capital. As for the mass media elite, Clement showed that they functioned as part of the corporate sphere. And he demonstrated that some 40 percent of the corporate elite themselves had, or had close relatives who had, occupied positions in the important political and bureaucratic offices.

Dennis Olsen's *The State Elite*, covering the 1961 to 1973 period, found marginal changes from what Porter had described, particularly pertaining to greater French and "other ethnic" representation. In the case of the political elite, he found that the elite had changed only "very slowly and not at all in some respects," in that it was still dominated by those from a narrow band of middle- and upper-middle-class origins and still lacked a discrete political career structure. As for the bureaucrats, he found that "the new elite is more open, more heterogeneous and probably more meritocratic, than the old," but that "the overall pattern is one of the marked persistence of both social class and ethnic preferences in recruitment." And he concluded that the "middle class state elite sees itself in alliance with business, or at least not in any fundamental opposition to its general interests."[6]

Robert Presthus's study of the accommodation between political, bureaucratic, and interest group elites in Canada, although more orientated to a survey of the attitudes of the elites, is not in sharp variance with the above findings of elite analysis in Canada with regard to socio-economic backgrounds or general ideological disposition. He too found an absence of institutional cohesion within the political system that would facilitate it acting as a counter-elite to business. He demonstrated that it is difficult for new or substantively weak interest groups to penetrate the decision-making process as "functional ties and established clientele relationships tend to crystallize existing power relationships." Significantly, he found that the senior bureaucrats showed a marked lack of enthusiasm for state welfare activities, although he still contended that the state elite "plays an equilibriating role in welfare areas." But "much of its energy is also spent in reinforcing the security and growth of interests that already enjoy the largest share of the net social product." Of particular note, in terms of the continuity of findings of elite studies, is that organized labour still "fails to enjoy the legitimacy imputed to other economic groups" and remains "marginal" vis-à-vis established elite arrangements.[7]

More recent studies continue to confirm these findings. Sometimes, following in the journalistic tradition of Peter C. Newman, these studies are directed at a more popular audience and are more anecdotal, but they contain valuable statistical data as well. Thus, Diane Francis's *Controlling Interest* demonstrates that thirty-two wealthy families, alongside five conglomerates, control about one-third of Canada's non-financial assets. This tiny "power elite" had a combined income among them in 1985 of $123 billion, whereas the federal government's total income was around $80 billion. Her conceptual analysis of what she calls Canada's "financial feudalism" is rather weak and unelaborated, however, as is her proposed solution, which is merely to call for new rules and tax breaks that will allegedly encourage more entrepreneurial competition. Indeed, Linda McQuaig's excellent study of Canada's tax policies, *Behind Closed Doors*, shows conclusively how tax breaks operate to promote the concentration of wealth and power in Canada. She shows how the rich consistently are able to veto progressive reform of the tax system and to use their political influence and the leverage that their control over the economy gives them to ensure that lower- and middle-income Canadians pay for the tax breaks for the economic elite.

These exercises in elite analysis, while not gainsaying the value of liberal democratic institutions, are valuable for piercing the myths that tend to accompany these institutions, such as equality of opportunity, competitive pluralist power relations, the state as autonomous from corporate capital or neutral between "interest groups." But while useful in this sense, the very mode of analysis also obscures many aspects of power that require study, and tends toward either viewing power as monolithically exercised at the top of our society, or suggesting that more equality of opportunity would resolve the problem of power. The mode of analysis, sometimes against the inclinations of the researchers themselves, is thus both too radical and too liberal in the conclusions it tends to produce.

There is an implicit tendency in elite analysis toward seeing power in terms of a metaphor of "representation." Social groups are spoken of loosely as being "represented," not in the sense of election, accountability, and control by the groups in question, but rather in the sense of elites having similar social backgrounds to the groups that are thus "represented." Yet, there is no *necessary* link between someone who comes from a particular class or ethnic background and the behaviour he or she will exhibit as a member of the elite. Only if a person has a social base in a given collectivity, and only if her or his position in the elite is dependent upon this base and accountable to it in some significant respects, can we properly speak of representation. Much less valid is the notion that, by virtue of state personnel being more or less recruited from "middle-class" social origins, we can speak of the middle class as a social force engaging in alliances or conflict with other classes on the basis of state elite behaviour. This is a form, not so much of "class reductionism," as of "class substitutionism," in that it substitutes individuals of certain social backgrounds for a class that is not even specified in terms of its own social relations, associations, struggles, etc.

Turning to the tendency for elite analysis to treat social, political, and economic power in relation to equality of opportunity, it should be apparent that problems of domination and subordination are not reducible simply to patterns of recruitment. Even a perfect meritocracy implies a social division of labour with people in authority and people subject to their authority. Authority positions, positions of control, set structural limits to what individuals can do in occupying decision-making roles within these institutions. If the president of INCO were to change places with a hard-rock miner, the structural position of the *place* occupied by each individual would strongly condition their behavior. Elite analysis, in general, gives too much credence to the autonomous ability of "elites" to make unconstrained decisions. An awareness of individual social backgrounds and values is not unimportant in trying to understand behaviour. But neither should one overestimate their importance. Replacing one set of politicians or bureaucrats or capitalists by another is just that, unless the *social base and purpose* of the institutions in which they are located change simultaneously.

It may be said that the main shortcoming of elite analysis is that it tends to ascribe *too much power*, indeed exclusive power, to those at the top. Restricting the concept of power, by definition, to authority in institutions obscures the fact that *power is a fluid social process* that, if stopped dead and anatomized in institutional terms, constantly evades analysis. The very private property market economy that corporate elite members seem to dominate by virtue of their institutional authority and cohesiveness is at the same time a limit on their authority and cohesiveness. Their positions are dependent on maintaining a rate of profit relatively high in relation to other corporations. Even if corporation executives don't lose their positions by the corporation going bankrupt, capital will flow from the less profitable corporations to the more profitable, and thus those in the less profitable will lose a good deal of their power. It is less institutional control than control over capital, a much more fluid thing, that is the foundation of the power of the corporate elite.

Similarly, by looking for power only among the elites one is forced to treat the masses as inert political clay, without self-activity (except perhaps in the highly structured context of elections). Yet, the ways in which collectivities outside the "confraternity of power" engage in struggles to further their interests both limit and influence the decisions of institutional office holders. Indeed, in the very definition of democracy that introduced this section it may be noted that the political elites' power finds it source in "the people's vote." This already implies that the power in question cannot be anatomized only by examining the elites, but must instead be seen in terms of a relationship between masses and elites. This would mean paying attention to the social collectivities that make up the "masses," enquiring whether these have modes of activity, of exercising power, outside of the electoral process—as indeed they do. It would also mean examining whether and where the relations between the collectivities intersect and overlap within and between the spheres of economy, state, and culture that the elite theorists only look at in terms of those at the top.

It is one of the ironies of elite theory that it often takes its intellectual root in the argument that Marxist class analysis assumes an all-powerful ruling class that does not fit twentieth-century reality. Yet, elite theory ends up seeing power much more monolithically than class analysis ever does. For class analysis entails seeing power as a *relational* concept, involving the necessity of tension, conflict, and struggle between social classes. The economy, the state, and culture are not seen here merely as hierarchically structured institutions (with the rational bureaucracy becoming the model for society as a whole), but rather as fields of competition and struggle among the social classes that compose a society such as ours. It is an approach that, despite the metaphor "ruling class," does not see power as the unconstrained prerogative of certain individuals at the top, but as a quality of conflictual social relationships that runs through society as a whole.

CLASS ANALYSIS

The concept of class which finds the significant determinant of social and political behaviour in the ability or inability to dispose of labour—one's own and others'—demonstrated its value in nineteenth-century historical and sociological analysis, but has been rather scorned of late years. No doubt it is inadequate in its original form to explain the position of the new middle class of technicians, supervisors, managers, and salaried officials, whose importance in contemporary society is very great; yet their class positions can best be assessed by the same criteria: how much freedom they retain over the disposal of their own labour, and how much control they exercise over the disposal of others' labour. Nor is this concept of class as readily amenable as are newer concepts to those techniques of measurement and tabulation which, as credentials, have become so important to modern sociology. Yet it may be thought to remain the most penetrating basis of classification for the understanding of political behaviour. Common relationship to the disposal of labour still tends to give the members of each class, so defined, an outlook and set of assumptions distinct from those of the other classes.

This does not necessarily mean that the members of a class, so defined, are sufficiently conscious of a class interest to act mainly in terms of it in making political choices. Nor need it mean that their outlook and assumptions are a conscious reflection of class position or needs as an outside observer or historian might see them.

These words by C. B. Macpherson, from *Democracy in Alberta,*[8] are as relevant today as when they were written almost thirty years ago. The central notion here is that it is people's *relationship* to property, to the ownership and control of the means of production, that is the main guide to the social composition of society and to the power relations that pertain therein. Macpherson has noted in another context that a"... somewhat looser conception of class, defined at its simplest in terms of rich, middle or poor, has been prominent in political theory as far back as one likes to go."[9] It is this looser definition of class that is employed in elite analysis in Canada. Insofar as the object of attention is the elite and its characteristics, the 80 to 90 percent of the population that is excluded from the upper or middle class (defined by elite family backgrounds, private school or university education, fathers with professional occupations, or an income above a certain level), remains an undifferentiated "mass." Thus, even though Olsen and Clement insist that "class is defined objectively by relationships to the ownership and control of capital and other valued resources,"[10] this definition stands external to their elite analysis, which rests on the categories of upper, middle, and "below middle" (the rest) as defined above. While this is appropriate to gaining a sense of limited mobility in our society, it runs counter to the way they say classes must be objectively defined. Unfortunately, they sometimes slip into referring to those who are in the "below middle" category as "working class," and it is thus often confusing to the student which operative definition of class they are working with at different points of their analysis.

A class analysis always begins with *social relationships* that people enter into, or are born into, in producing their material means of livelihood. For production to take place in any society—and without it no society can exist—three elements are necessary: producers—the people doing the work themselves; objects of labour—the natural materials to work on (land, minerals, fish, etc.); and means of labour—instruments to work with (hoes, nets, tractors, boats, machines, computers, etc.).[11] These elements may be owned by the producers themselves (collectively as in many primitive tribal societies, or individually as in the case of the family farm or the craftsperson's workshop) or by someone else, who is a non-producer. In a slave society, all the elements—including the producers—are predominantly owned by slave-owners. Under feudalism, the most important object of labour—the land—is predominantly owned by landlords. In a capitalist society, the means of labour—the machines, factories, offices, etc.—are predominantly owned by capitalists individually or as groups of capitalists (as in the modern corporation).

Thus, the relationships between owners and non-owners, producers and non-producers, vary in different modes of production. Under slavery, the direct producers are in a position of servitude to the non-producers and can be bought and sold, or born into servitude. Under feudalism, the peasants are not themselves owned and possess their own tools, but are legally tied to the land and required to pass over a portion of their produce to the landlord. Under capitalism, the producer is free, in the sense of having a proprietary right over his or her own labour, but is dispossessed of proprietary holdings of the objects and means of labour. In order to obtain the wherewithal to exist, therefore, the producer must sell his or her labour for a wage or salary to those who own the means of production and who control this labour directly—or indirectly through managers—in the production process. On this basis we can locate the predominant social classes of each society.

> Classes are large groups of people, differing from each other by the places they occupy in a historically determined system of social production, by their relation (in most cases fixed and formulated in law) to the means of production, by their role in the social organization of labour, and consequently, by the dimensions of the share of social wealth of which they dispose and the mode of acquiring it. Classes are groups of people one of which can appropriate the labour of another owing to the different places they occupy in a definitive system of social economy.[12]

It will be seen immediately that classes as approached in this fashion are not ordered in a higher and lower fashion, as rungs on a ladder, but rather in terms of people's *relationship* to one another. And it is a multidimensional relationship in that people are dependent on one another (the elements must be brought together in order for production to take place), yet it is an unequal dependence in that one class appropriates the labour of another. Because the mutual dependence is therefore one of dominance of one class and subjection of another by the appropriation of labour, the social relationship is a *contradictory* one, entailing the potential of antagonism, of conflict, between the classes. This is not to say that the permanent condition of society is one of strikes, demonstrations, revolts, and revolutions. These are but the more explosive outcomes of the contradictory relations in question. But in the sense of an irreconcilable *basis* of conflict, over how much and under what specific conditions labour will be appropriated from the direct producers, the system is a conflictual one. This has historically been expressed in struggles over control of the labour process, over the length of the working day, over remuneration, over new machines that displace labour and/or require labour to work more intensively.

But if these kinds of struggles have been more common than struggles to "change the system" itself, this reflects the balance of power between the classes. Class analysis is precisely about assessing that balance of power. This does not mean that those who sell their labour to other—the working class in capitalist society—only have power at the moment of social revolution. For it will be seen that what is operating in the relations between classes is never all power on one side and the lack of it on the other. Because the classes are constituted in terms of their mutual, contradictory dependence on one another, both sides always have power. The balance of power may be unequal, and may structurally favour those who own and control the means of production, but depending on given economic, cultural, and political conditions, the balance may change. This may alter the terms and conditions of the appropriation of labour, and it may give rise to struggles over changing the historically structured relations between classes themselves. But all this is the object of inquiry within a class analysis.

It should be stressed that in talking about classes in this way, we are talking about actual historical groups, real collectivities of people, who therefore cannot ever be examined in terms of economic categories alone. Classes, as societies, are constituted on a material basis in terms of producing the material means of livelihood, but they exist simultaneously in terms of culture, ideology, politics, consciousness. Insofar as we speak of classes in terms of statistical economic categories (so many owners, so many workers, etc.), we miss the point that we are dealing with real men and women. This is usually seen to be important—and it is—in terms of assessing the degree to which class relations as defined above are expressed in cultural, political, and ideological differentiations and conflicts. But it is important as well in terms of understanding the basis of social cohesion and stability of a society in the face of the inherently contradictory relations between classes, since the maintenance and reproduction of the relations of production is itself dependent not only on economic relations, but on the degree of cultural, political, and ideological homogeneity that keeps these contradictory relations in check. This too, then, is part of the balance of power, which means that to undertake a class analysis of society we do not just map out economic relations, but rather examine the totality of cultural, ideological, and political, as well as the economic, relations between classes as the relevant "variables" in the overall balance of power.

Elite studies have certainly provided us with a window to the constitution of the capitalist class in Canada (albeit only the most dominant fractions of it) as a social force along all of these dimensions. However, recent work in Canadian labour history has begun to reclaim for contemporary students of Canadian society the fact that it is not the "corporate elite" alone that is an active historical actor, with the "masses" but mere statistical categories. In a study of the formation of the working class in Hamilton in the latter half of the nineteenth century, Bryan Palmer has written: "Class is inseparable from class struggle. The process of confrontation conditions an understanding of class and of people's place in the larger social older, an understanding mediated by a particular cultural context. Class is thus defined by men and women as they live through the historical experience. It is class struggle and culture, not class itself, as an analytic category, that are the primary concepts upon which classes themselves arise and assume importance. One task of social history...is to address the class experience in such a way as to force consideration of the central place of conflict and culture in any historical and/or theoretical discussion of class."[13] Palmer's study shows that through baseball clubs, firehalls, benevolent societies, and above all through the union hall, skilled workers created for themselves an associational network and a discrete culture that both grew out of and sustained the conflicts they engaged in with their employers. These struggles, taking place both in industry and politics, were about the very organization of workers into their own unions, about control over the labour process, about the ten-hour working day, about wages and conditions, in short about how much and under what conditions labour would be appropriated from the workers by the capitalists.

Labour history has, moreover, increasingly been sensitive to the way that gender relations and class relations intertwine. Elite studies have often counted the (very small) number of women who have been "represented" in Canada's boardrooms or Cabinet rooms or even legislative chamber, but recent attention has also been given to the way in which women have been either marginalized from direct participation in the economy (while engaged in reproduction in the domestic sphere) or concentrated, as "working women," in particular spheres of the economy, while continuing to do a double-days work in the home. The importance of women's work, in either sphere, to generating the surplus appropriated by the capitalist class has been increasingly stressed. Research by Pat and Hugh Armstrong, Margorie Cohen, Meg Luxton, and Heather Jon Maroney might be cited here, but perhaps the most important contribution to the study of the way in which the changing pattern of class relations over the past century has changed the role of women—in a different way within each class—has been Dorothy Smith's remarkable class analysis of women's inequality and the family. It demonstrates how the changing role of women in the economy and the family has changed the internal structure of each class.

Studies such as these provide an antidote to other recent accounts of Canadian history that, while freely and loosely employing the term "class," in fact have more in common with the tradition of elite analysis than class analysis proper. In particular, Tom Naylor's *History of Canadian Business*[14] sought to locate the roots of Canada's limited and dependent industrialization in the dominance of financial capitalists over other fractions of capital and the state. Characterized by an ideology that impelled them toward making profits through commercial transactions, rather than appropriating labour directly through industrial production, these capitalists are seen to have frozen out Canadian industrial capitalists and constructed a National Policy that encouraged resource exports and branch-plant industrialization with the Canadian banks as a source of loan capital. Yet, in concentrating on the values and political power of one fraction of the capitalist class, Naylor replicates the shortcomings of elite analysis in his one-sided perception of power. And, somewhat surprisingly, so do those recent important studies that offer critiques of Naylor by stressing not the values of capitalists, but rather the structural dynamics of global capital competition, concentration, exploitation, and accumulation in their analysis of Canada's capitalist class. They emphasize the development and role of Canada's own multinational corporations (Jorge Niosi); and/or they recognize that American investment has actually encouraged the development of the industrial sector in Canada and identify the rise of a Canadian class, not of *financial capitalists* who are uninterested in industry, but of a *finance capitalism* based on interlocks between finance and industry (William Carroll). But like Naylor, they look very little at relations between classes as opposed to relations among capitalists. By looking at interclass relations, especially by examining the extent of class struggle between workers and capitalists in industry, we may discern discrete limits to the accumulation potential of Canada's indigenous manufacturers, apart from those allegedly imposed by the values and machinations of the bankers (many of whom invested in industrial production where it was profitable to do so and thus became industrial capitalists themselves).

Given Canada's later start toward capitalist industrialization than that of the United States, and given our more limited domestic market, the only way capitalists could have competed successfully with American capitalists was through a higher degree of exploitation of the working class than in the United States. Thus, the very struggles of Canadian workers, emboldened by the ready possibilities of migration to the United States and by the example of relatively high incomes in Ontario farming, put limits on the potential competitiveness of Canadian capitalists. These limits were constantly tested in struggles by both sides, but given this balance of power (as opposed to the presumed monolithic power of capitalists alone), it was scarcely surprising that Canadian capitalists (industrial and financial) and politicians turned to tariff barriers, new staple resource exports, *and* foreign investment in industry as a means of promoting economic growth in Canada. Insofar as this entailed a clear strategy at all, it was arrived at more through the push and pull of contending social forces rather than emerging from the heads of a fully conscious and cohesive class of mercantile capitalists, and its development was conditional upon its ability to mediate between interests of the full array of class forces in Canada, including those of the working class (who after all, had an interest in obtaining jobs in Canada at as low a rate of exploitation as possible). If Canada's entry to the modern world of capitalist industrialization has proved to be based on the shifting sands of resource export dependence and foreign ownership, a class analysis of the roots of this sorry state of affairs has to go beyond the mercantile mentality of our leading capitalists.

This example will perhaps help to dispel one of the major misconceptions that commonly pertains to what class analysis is about in political science—that it is a sectarian attempt to confirm Marx's famous aphorism that the state is but "the executive committee of the whole bourgeoisie." Apart from the fact that what Marx may have written on any given occasion can scarcely be taken as the last word on anything (either by proponents or detractors of class analysis), the charge is unfounded. Because capitalism is a competitive system, and because capitalists are competing with one another, for the state to pursue policies in the interest of the *whole* capitalist class entails it having a degree of *autonomy* from the dictation of particular capitalists.

But the state's "relative autonomy" from the capitalist entails more than this. It will be recalled that, whereas in a slave or feudal system class relations are *legally* constituted and hence *directly* dependent on the state's coercive force, in a capitalist society individuals are free and classes are constituted on the ability to dispose of labour in the economy. This separation of the state from the constitution of classes and from the economy is also the basis of the state's "relative autonomy." To speak of the state in a capitalist society as a capitalist state means only that, to use Porter's phrase, the "essential task" of the state is to maintain the necessary social conditions for economic growth and the reproduction of classes in a way consistent with the dynamics of an economy that is capitalistically structured. This will mean the promotion of the profitable accumulation of capital, for economic growth is *dependent* on how much capitalists invest, but also on the containment and mediation of the contradictory class relations that might give rise to disruptive social conflict. This does *not* mean that the state is to be conceived of as a perfect planner, an all-seeing "collective capitalist," which balances the provision of favourable conditions for profit against the necessity of throwing the occasional crumbs to the working class. Rather, because the state is not the preserve of one class, it means that *the state is a field of class struggle itself.*

The capitalists are a "ruling class" only in the sense that the condition for the economy's growth is conditional on private profit, on the capitalists' structural position as investors and organizers of production on which all other classes and the state are dependent. But the degree to which the state is "relatively autonomous" from the capitalist cannot be given in the abstract. It can only be assessed through a concrete class analysis. And such an analysis of the balance of class forces must not only look at the political field directly (in terms of parties, interest groups making demands on the state, etc.), but also at the economy and culture, for the balance of forces here also constrains, limits, and provides guidance to the possible choices of the state in any particular instance.

A second misconception that often arises regarding class analysis is that it only produces a bipolar, two-class model of society: workers–

capitalists, peasants–landlords, etc. For the sake of exposition in relation to the bipolar elite–mass distinction of elite analysis, I have myself given this impression to this point. But this is incomplete. Because societies are products of history, not of analytic models, the various ways in which people are related to each other in material production allow for a wide variety of relationships. Although one may still discern the predominant social relationships that mark off one stage of history from another, each stage contains within it older forms of such relations and newer developing ones.

Thus, in Canada it is commonplace to observe that for a very large part of our history, and to some extent even today, extensive groups of people have neither sold their labour nor directly appropriated the product of other people's labour through employing them, but have rather been independent producers—owning their own means of production and working on it themselves, engaging in commodity and credit exchange relations with the other classes. This is the traditional middle class, the old "petite bourgeoisie," of independent craftspeople, family farmers, etc. It is sometimes alleged that such a class exists only as an analytic category, not as a real historical actor through culture and struggle, because the independent nature of the activity begets no common bonds between these producers. Yet history, and above all Canadian history, demonstrates the contrary. From the great Rebellions of 1837–38 to the prairie radical farmer movements of this century, we have seen that this class was significant in the overall balance of social forces, with its own culture, institutions, and ideologies whose effects were very strongly felt historically and whose influence can still be felt today.

To be sure, the development of capitalism, entailing as it does an increasing concentration and centralization of production as the forces of competition tend to squeeze out the weak and less capital-intensive units, orientates class relations more and more toward a worker–capitalist dimension. In Canada, as elsewhere, the working class has been drawn, apart from immigration, from the displaced members of the class of independent producers. But Canada's history over the past century was distinctive in that the very industrialization of the country was in good part dependent on the successful exploitation of the wheat staple, which historically entailed the growth of the petit bourgeois farmer class in the western frontier simultaneously with the development of the working class (primarily located in industrial Ontario in terms of manufacturing, although more widely dispersed in relation to mineral and forest resource extraction). This multidimensionality of class in twentieth-century Canada, characterized as it was by uneven regional location and salience of the various classes, produced a cacophony of interlocking but distinct struggles in the economy, polity, and culture. Whereas an identity of class opponents sometimes united the farmers and workers, their different class experiences also divided them, as the farmers focused on conditions of credit, commodity prices, transportation costs, and the tariff itself rather than on wages and conditions of employment or control of the labour process as the main terrains of conflict. Thus, even on those occasions when farmers and workers went so far as to identify the capitalists, the capitalist parties, and even the capitalist system as their common enemy, the concrete struggles of each revealed a far more complex and ambiguous pattern of relationships at work.

At first glance it might appear that this situation has now changed, that today a bipolar set of class relations more nearly obtains. With the decline of the importance of prairie wheat in the economy as a whole, and with the stark decline in the number of independent producers over the century, wage and salary employees now constitute over 80 percent of the economically active population. But not all wage and salary earners can be unambiguously identified as working class.[15] This is not primarily due to differences in income, status, etc., between white-collar salaried employees and manual wage workers, as the stratification approach of elite analysis would have it. These differences have more and more proved ephemeral and temporary, as the clerks in the office and the steelworkers in the mill are increasingly aware. Nor is it so much because many white-collar workers are located in the state and commercial sectors that are not directly a source of the profits on which the economy continues to depend for its dynamic.

For here as well, the main criterion is the ability to dispose of labour that is at issue, and this criterion traverses the industrial, commercial, and state sectors of the economy. Indeed, the extensive unionization and militancy of so many white-collar employees would seem to suggest increasingly that they are indeed well into the process of class formation along the dimensions of culture and struggle that compose real social classes. But in terms of the disposition of labour, it is also clear that within both the private corporations and the public sector there has developed over this century a stratum of employees who, without ownership or control of the means of production, nevertheless dispose of labour in terms of managing, supervising, and controlling the labour of others. Although there is some theoretical disputation regarding the "class position" of such employees, it does seem that in the terms within which we have been speaking these people might be properly conceived of as a (for want of a better word) "new middle class," who by virtue of their function in the labour process stand in a contradictory relationship both to capital and labour, as salaried technocrats, managers, and professionals.[16]

It has indeed become one of the favourite themes of contemporary political science in Canada to identify many political changes in terms of this "new middle class" as a social force. In particular it has been seen as a dominant force underlying both the Quiet Revolution and the Parti Québécois in Quebec and the aggressive Lougheed Conservatives in Alberta. However suggestive these analyses, it must be said that there tends to be a rather cavalier attitude toward clearly delineating this class. To take the example of Alberta, in John Richards and Larry Pratt's *Prairie Capitalism* this class is variously referred to as an "arriviste bourgeoisie" and an "upwardly mobile urban middle class," which includes not only "upper-income" professionals and managers, but also indigenous Alberta entrepreneurs (capitalists) and a "state-administrative elite." There is a vague set of criteria operative here, borrowing rather indiscriminately from elite analysis and class analysis proper. It is possible that in terms of the culture and struggle that bind these groups together one might find the basis of a cohesive social force in class terms. But much more needs to be done in this respect before the case is convincing, not least involving the attempt to define more clearly the common social relationships with other classes that give this disparate "new middle class" its unity.

It is one of the ironies of *Prairie Capitalism* that it takes C. B. Macpherson to task for treating Alberta in the first three decades of this century as a "single-class society" in terms of the overwhelming predominance of the independent farmers. As against this, Pratt and Richards argue: "Alberta has never been as homogeneous and free of internal class conflict as is argued by Macpherson...in Alberta tensions among rival metropolitan centres, between urban and agrarian interests, between ranchers and farmers, mine-owners and coalminers, between indigenous and external capital, and between capital and labour are recurring, not occasional, themes in the various stages of the province's development; and they can be ignored only at the risk of distortion."[17] However, within the account of modern Alberta that Pratt and Richards give us, the broad perception of internal class conflict that they require of Macpherson is paradoxically absent. We are given an account of conflict between indigenous and external capital and, less clearly so, between urban and agrarian "interests," but little else. Are there no conflicts between capital and labour in contemporary Alberta? Are conflicts between the men on the rigs and the oil companies more or less salient than between miners and coal companies in the 1930s? What are we to make of the public sector strikes in that province in recent years, whether by nurses, teachers, or manual municipal workers? Are these people—some or all—to be assimilated to the new middle class or arriviste bourgeoisie? Presumably not, yet what is the pattern of social relations and social forces in that province?

CLASS AND PARTY

There is a tendency in much "new-middle-class" analysis, moreover, to posit a very close identity between class and party, whether it be the

Lesage Liberals, the Parti Québécois, or the Lougheed Conservatives. This has, to be sure, long been a bane of class analysis in Canada, revealing an inclination to think that class analysis only has relevance if it receives an unequivocal party political expression. A number of points may be made in this regard. Although it is easy to locate the social backgrounds of a party's leading personnel, one must be careful to avoid the trap of "sociological representation" that we saw in elite analysis. Without representation in the sense of social base, control, delegation, and accountability in the expression of common class interests, the socio-economic origins of leaders may be quite misleading as indicators of class interests. *If* the party is one of the places through which the class is united as a social and cultural entity, one may speak of it properly as a party of a certain class. It well may be, and the evidence is suggestive, that this is the case for the "new middle class" with the Parti Québérois and the Alberta Tories.

But one should still be careful of treating the party *as* the class. Precisely because parties aim at state office (and even when they get there are only a part of the state as governing parties) their project entails a relative autonomy from specific classes, since a political party, as Gilles Bourque puts it, "poses the question of power amidst the whole process of the class struggle. . . . By definition, it cannot assert itself as the unilateral, unequivocal instrument of just one class or class fragment. The struggle between parties, in liberal democracies, is not a tournament with as many teams as there are classes or fragments."[18] Bourque goes on:

> Involved in a party is social space in its totality. A party undertakes not only the promotion of specific, multiple and heterogeneous interests, but also the reproduction of the totality of the social formation. In it unfolds the whole domain of hegemony, alliances and compromises. A party seeks to create those political and ideological conditions which are most favourable to the promotion of the economic interests it defends, whether or not these interests are dominant within the social formation. While it is true that a party does not enjoy the same autonomy vis-à-vis its hegemonic class, or even subordinate classes and fragments in its midst, as the state vis-à-vis the totality of classes, a party is less directly controlled than is a corporative organization by the short-term economic interests of its members. The program of a party, much less the policy of a government, cannot be unequivocally identified with the specific interests of its hegemonic class. While the legislation of a government may be used as an indication of the class interest defended by a party in power, this is not a demonstration of the operating social force.

This issue has relevance to a broader one in the domain of class analysis. It is often argued that class analysis is irrelevant *in Canada* because there is no major working-class party (often defined as Bourque warns us not to) on the national scene, or because voting behaviour does not exhibit a distinct pervasive cleavage along class lines. But it is a major mistake to arrange parties along ideological or policy dimensions of "left" and "right" and then hypothetically assign classes to them in a bifurcated fashion. If voters are found not to conform with this procedure, this may say as much about the brittleness of the analytical construct as about the flexibility of the voters. As Bourque suggests, every party seeks to contain within it the totality of social relations in a society.

Thus, when John A. Macdonald's Conservative Party constructed a "Tory–Producer" alliance around the tariff and mildly progressive industrial relations legislation, it did so not by ignoring class (although certainly by decrying class conflict), but by incorporating working-class demands, interests, and leaders in their project, mediating them in a way consistent with the hegemony of the capitalists in the party. When the Mackenzie King Liberals constructed their industrial relations and welfare state program in 1944–45, they did much the same thing. How far a simple voting behaviour test of the relevance of class in Canadian politics departs from capturing reality may be noted in the fact that the Communist Party supported the Liberals rather than the Co-operative Commonwealth Federation (CCF) in the 1945 election. And Pierre Trudeau, seeking to end his dependence on the New Democratic Party (NDP) in a minority government, and faced with the opportunity of the Stanfield Conservatives calling for an incomes and prices freeze, went to Sudbury during the 1974 election campaign and shouted: "So what's he going to freeze? Your wages! He's going to freeze your wages!"[19] Here again was the incorporation of class, the expression and mediation of working-class interests, within the framework of the Liberal Party.

To be sure, the way in which politicians employ language and symbols is enormously important to whether the electorate itself explicitly perceives politics, and elections in particular, to be about class. People who have but recently engaged in militant and protracted strikes may very well fail to perceive that a subsequent election is about class struggle, much less connect either their strike or the election to the question of "socialism versus capitalism." It is parties that structure the symbols of the electoral battle, not the voters that do so (although the concrete promises contained within these symbols are certainly shaped by the balance of class forces). As Jane Jenson and Janine Brodie have argued in an analysis that applies as much to the CCF/NDP as to the Liberals and Conservatives:

From the beginning, mass political parties have integrated voters into a system of partisan relations but in this process of integration, parties have also provided voters with a *definition of politics*. They define, for the electorate, the content of politics and the meaning of political activity. In other words, at the level of ideology, *political parties shape the interpretation of what aspects of social relations should be considered political, how politics should be conducted, what the boundaries of political discussion most properly may be and what kinds of conflicts can be resolved through the political process.* From the vast array of tensions, differences, and inequalities characteristic of any society, political parties choose which will be treated as political alternatives in the electoral process and, thereby, how the electorate will divide against itself. This role of parties is profoundly important because before electoral cleavages come into being, a definition of what is political must exist. Whether a social problem is considered to be a religious, economic or political question is something that is set by this definition. A conspiracy of silence can exist around matters which parties, for whatever reason, choose not to elevate to the level of partisan debate.[20]

It can certainly be appreciated that the ability of a party to catalyze the working class around a class definition of politics, and reciprocally for the working class of construct a party in which it is the hegemonic class while successfully integrating other classes, is something that contributes very much to the cohesion and strength of the working class in society. But here we have to return to the balance of class forces. The inability to do so does not invalidate class analysis, but rather necessitates it all the more to cut through the veil of appearances that confronts the social scientist. (The sun *looks* like it is moving around the earth, even though we know that not to be the case. Indeed, we explain why it looks that way through scientific analysis.) It is only when class analysis is thought to be a teleological exercise that involves the claim that the working class exists only when it has full consciousness and political expression of its "revolutionary destiny" that class analysis is invalidated. But this precisely fails to grasp that class analysis entails not imposing abstract categories (whether statistical categories or pristine parties) on real social relations, but rather concerns actually examining the many ways in which contradictory social relations between people take historical expression, through culture and struggle.

In Canada it has usually been the case that the struggle of the working class finds direct expression more in the arena of work and in union struggles than in electoral politics or in the "elite accommodation" of interest groups. Although this is not immediately promising in terms of replacing capitalism with socialism, neither is social democratic electoral politics or the elite accommodation of labour leaders. For in those countries where labour leaders have indeed been assimilated to the "confraternity of power" through these mechanisms, this has often not carried the class struggle to a higher plane, but weakened it as labour leaders, as a condition of their entry into the confraternity of power, have acted as agencies of social control over working-class demands "in the national interest." If it appeared in the 1950s that such integration foretold the final "end of ideology" and the "embourgeoisement" of the working class, the resurgence of industrial militancy after the mid-1960s (of which Canada was one of the most prominent examples) belied such predictions. In Europe this rendered social democratic parties' "consensus" politics unstable. In Canada, given the lesser importance of such parties, this particular effect of industrial militancy has been less visible. But it has nonetheless had real political effects.

Let me conclude with a contemporary example of the political effects of industrial class struggles, effects that do not depend on explicit political "demands" coming to political elites from the working class. In 1981 a leaked discussion paper of the Department of Finance considered the options available to the government in fighting inflation.[21] It was a document produced by the "upper-middle-class" bureaucrats of state elite. The labour elite had not been consulted in the process of framing the document. Yet, the document was centrally about the power of the working class. This was not because the document provided an ideologically biased account of the causes of inflation. It was recognized that (unlike 1974–75) Canada was not experiencing a wage-driven inflation, as real wages had fallen over the previous few years.

Yet, on each strategy proposed, the central variable used to assess its viability was its potential to provoke future demands of workers in the public and private sectors and what their response might be to changes in economic policy by the government. Would a given policy increase militancy or weaken it? Would it contain wage pressure so as to permit higher investment through higher profits and lower taxation, or would it produce a backlash that would contradict this goal and/or undermine the popularity of the government? If stronger groups of workers could not be contained, could the government compensate for this by concentrating harder on holding down the wages of weaker, less well-organized groups of workers, such as by refusing to participate in compulsory arbitration for such groups? To what extent were capitalists in the private sector prepared, in light of the state of the economy, their competitiveness, sales, and profits, to resist workers' demands? How much would they need or appreciate supportive action by the state—whether by setting guidelines or setting an "example" by resisting the demands of public sector workers? In trying to answer such questions, the state was surveying the *balance of class forces* regarding an anti-inflation strategy. Of course, they are not the only social forces that have to be weighed on this or any other assessment of politics. But one wishes that political scientists, at least those outside the bureaucracy, and whatever their sympathies on either side, would undertake more of this essential social scientific practice in their work.

POLITICAL SCIENCE AND SOCIAL CHANGE

To see political science in this way is to stress that the study of politics is not just the study of Parliaments or bureaucracies or even a broader study of the most powerful decision makers in all spheres of society. It must be a study as well of the social forces "from below." Some will say that is the proper field of sociology, especially insofar as the activities of those below, even if they influence the decision makers, do not have enough power "to change the system." But this is an impoverished view of political science. Indeed, as Antonio Gramsci wrote half a century ago:

> If political science means science of the State, and the State is the entire complex of practical and theoretical activities with which the ruling class not only justifies and maintains its dominance, but manages to win the active consent of those over whom it rules, then it is obvious that all essential questions of sociology are nothing other than the questions of political science.[22]

There is another important dimension to political science, of course, which precisely has to do with "changing the system"; which is not just about analyzing what the state and ruling class do, criticizing it on this basis, or even coming forward on the basis of this analysis with "public policy" proposals for enabling the state to manage the system better. Rather, this other dimension of political science is about developing analyses of the processes and strategies involved in changing the system from one based on class competition, exploitation, and conflict to a different system based on the elimination of classes and the development of as fully a democratic, egalitarian, and co-operative society as possible. Here we begin to raise larger questions about what "science" is really all about. And Gramsci is again a valuable guide:

> Is not science itself "political activity" and political thought, in as much as it transforms men, and makes them different from what they were before?...If science is the "discovery" of formerly unknown reality, is this reality not conceived of in a certain sense as transcendent? And is it not thought that there still exists something "unknown" and hence transcendent? And does not the concept of science as "creation" then mean that it too is "politics"? Everything depends on seeing whether the creation involved is "arbitrary," or whether it is rational—i.e., useful to men in that it enlarges their concept of life, and raises to a higher level (develops) life itself.[23]

We can see, in this sense, the importance of a political science that is trying to know more than how to uncover how the power elites rule the world, but which also has an understanding that the majorities subjected to that rule also have power capacities, and is trying to discover how those capacities might be enhanced: not just to criticize the elites or ruling classes, not just to influence their decisions through struggles "from below," but to "transcend" the present system of power relations entirely. This is less a matter of constructing utopian visions of a "good society" than of discovering the means whereby the subordinate classes have increased their power historically and of trying to discover further and better means. Political science has a role to play in demonstrating that most people are not just passive recipients of someone else's power, that they currently exercise some power even if just in relation to the greater power of the dominant classes. It could have a larger and more creative role to play still, by discovering the limits to the ways in which subordinate classes have organized so far, and by trying to think through and offer advice on how to organize for a fundamental challenge to the powers that be. This will, above all, be a matter of discovering the kind of political organizations that enhance the intellectual capacities of working people themselves, so that they can become leaders and educators in their own communities and develop their capacities to run society and state in a fully democratic manner. To be a political scientist, in this conception, is to be someone who knows how to do more than criticize the power elite. It is to be someone who is orientated to discovering how to help those who have the potential power to change the system to realize that they have that potential—and then actually to act upon that potential. Philosophers, a great social scientist once said, have always tried to understand the world, but the point of this understanding, he appropriately insisted, was to change it.

NOTES

1. R. J. Van Loon and M. S. Whittington, *The Canadian Political System*, 2nd ed. (Toronto: McGraw-Hill Ryerson, 1976).
2. J. A. Schumpeter, *Capitalism, Socialism and Democracy*, 5th ed. (London: George Allen and Unwin, 1976), pp. 269, 285.
3. J. Porter, *The Vertical Mosaic: An Analysis of Social Class and Power in Canada* (Toronto: University of Toronto Press, 1965). For two useful critiques of Porter's approach, especially his conception of class and power, see J. Heap, "Conceptual and Theoretical Problems in *The Vertical Mosaic*," *Canadian Review of Sociology and Anthropology* 9 (May 1973), and J. Hutcheson, "Class and Income Distribution in Canada," in *(Canada) Ltd., The Political Economy of Dependency*, ed. R. M. Laxer (Toronto: McClelland and Stewart, 1973).
4. Porter, *The Vertical Mosaic*, pp. 532, 539–40, 557.
5. W. Clement, *The Canadian Corporate Elite: An Analysis of Economic Power* (Toronto: McClelland and Stewart, 1975).

6. D. Olsen, *The State Elite* (Toronto: McClelland and Stewart, 1980), pp. 82, 124.

7. R. Presthus, *Elite Accommodation in Canadian Politics* (Toronto: Macmillan, 1973), pp. 348–49, 169.

8. C. B. Macpherson, *Democracy in Alberta: Social Credit and the Party System* (Toronto: University of Toronto Press, 1st ed., 1953, 2nd ed., 1963), p. 225.

9. C. B. Macpherson, *The Life and Times of Liberal Democracy* (Oxford: Oxford University Press, 1977), p. 11.

10. Clement, *The Canadian Corporate Elite*, p. 10.

11. See J. Harrison, *Marxist Economics for Socialists* (London: Pluto, 1978), p. 30.

12. V. I. Lenin, "A Great Beginning" (1919), *Selected Works* (Moscow: 1971), vol. 3: 231. ·

13. B. D. Palmer, *A Culture in Conflict: Skilled Workers and Industrial Capitalism in Hamilton, Ontario, 1860–1914* (Montreal: McGill-Queen's University Press, 1979), p. xvi; *cf.* G. S. Kealey, *Toronto Workers Respond to Industrial Capitalism 1867–1892* (Toronto: University of Toronto Press, 1980).

14. T. Naylor, *The History of Canadian Business*, 1867–1914 (Toronto: Lorimer, 1975).

15. See L. A. Johnson, "The Development of Class in Canada in the Twentieth Century," in *Capitalism and the National Question in Canada*, ed. G. Teeple (Toronto: University of Toronto Press, 1972).

16. For important attempts to "map" the contemporary class structure in these terms see: G. Carchedi, "On the Economic Identification of the New Middle Class," *Economy and Society* 4 (1975): 1, and *On the Economic Identification of Social Classes* (London: Routledge and Kegan Paul, 1977); E. O. Wright, *Class, Crisis and the State* (London: New Left Books, 1978). For a good example of the cultural dimension entailed in the relation between this new middle class and the working class, see A. Gorz, "Technical Intelligence and the Capitalist Division of Labour," *Telos* 12 (Summer 1972), especially pp. 34–35.

17. J. Richards and L. Pratt, *Prairie Capitalism: Power and Influence in the New West* (Toronto: McClelland and Stewart, 1979), pp. 150–51. On Quebec in this vein, see K. McRoberts and D. Postgate, *Quebec: Social Change and Political Crisis*, rev. ed. (Toronto: McClelland and Stewart, 1980).

18. G. Bourque, "Class, Nation and the Parti Québécois," *Studies in Political Economy* 2 (Autumn 1979): 130.

19. Quoted in *The Toronto Star*, 18 October 1975.

20. M. J. Brodie and J. Jenson, *Crisis, Challenge and Change: Party and Class in Canada* (Toronto: Methuen, 1980), p. 8.

21. "Discussion Paper on Anti-Inflation Policy Options," 9 January 1981.

Incomplete reports of the document can be found in *The Toronto Star*, 24 March 1981 and *The Globe and Mail*, 25 March 1981.
22. Q. Hoare and G. Nowell Smith, eds., *Selections from the Prison Notebooks of Antonio Gramsci* (London: Lawrence and Wishart, 1971), p. 244.
23. Ibid.

FURTHER READINGS

Armstrong, Pat, and Hugh Armstrong. "Beyond Sexless Class and Classless Sex." *Studies in Political Economy* 10 (Winter 1983).

Carroll, William K. *Corporate Power and Canadian Capitalism.* Vancouver: University of British Columbia Press, 1986.

Clement, Wallace. *Continental Corporate Power.* Toronto: McClelland and Stewart, 1977.

Cohen, Marjorie. *Women's Work, Markets, and Economic Development in Nineteenth-Century Ontario.* Toronto: University of Toronto Press, 1988.

Cuneo, C. "Corporate Power in Canada." *Studies in Political Economy* 27 (Autumn 1988).

Fox J., and M. Orenstein. "The Canadian State and Corporate Elites in the Post-War Period." *Canadian Review of Sociology and Anthropology* 32, no. 4 (1986).

Francis, D. *Controlling Interest: Who Owns Canada?* Toronto: Macmillan, 1986.

Hunter, Alfred A. *Class Tells: On Social Inequality in Canada*, 2nd ed. Toronto: Butterworths, 1986.

Maroney, Heather Jon, and Meg Luxton, eds. *Feminism and Political Economy: Women's Work, Women's Struggles.* Toronto: Methuen, 1987.

McQuaig, Linda. *Behind Closed Doors: How the Rich Won Control of Canada's Tax System. . . and Ended Up Richer.* Toronto: Penguin, 1987.

Miliband, R. *Marxism and Politics.* Oxford: Oxford University Press, 1977.

Niosi, Jorge. *Canadian Multinationals*, trans. Robert Chodos. Toronto: Between the Lines, 1985.

Palmer, Bryan D. *Working-Class Experience: The Rise and Reconstitution of Canadian Labour, 1800–1980.* Toronto: Butterworths, 1983.

Panitch, Leo. "Capitalism, Socialism and Revolution." In *The Socialist Register, 1989*, ed. R. Miliband, et. al. London: Merlin Press, 1989.

Panitch, Leo, ed. *The Canadian State: Political Economy and Political Power.* Toronto: University of Toronto Press, 1977.

Panitch, L., and D. Swartz. *The Assault on Trade Union Freedoms.* Toronto: Garamond Press, 1988.

Porter, John. *The Vertical Mosaic.* Toronto: University of Toronto Press, 1965.

Smith Dorothy. "Inequality and the Family." In *Inequality: Essays on the Political Economy of Social Welfare*, ed. Alan Moscovitch and Glenn Drover. Toronto: University of Toronto Press, 1981.

11

Rethinking Canadian Politics: The Impact of Gender

SANDRA BURT

Even after three decades of organized feminist activity, it is difficult to find many indications in the literature on Canadian politics of how the significant changes that have taken place in women's lives have affected the pattern of political life. Canadian political science continues to be dominated by descriptions of powerful office holders and the process by which these (primarily) men sift through policy options, selectively making policy choices.[1] The focus on power holders often excludes women, who are still in the minority among decision makers both in Canada and throughout the world. The absence of women or women's perspectives from major political issues was particularly striking in the 1980s when federal–provincial relations and free trade dominated the political agenda. Since federal–provincial discussions take place primarily among political elites, most women were excluded. Certainly in the deliberations that led up to the new Constitution Act of 1982 and the Meech Lake Accord of 1987, only the federal and provincial leaders (all men) were major actors in the decision-making process. And in the free trade negotiations, Pat Carney's presence did little to focus attention on the potential effect of free trade on female workers.

When women are considered by political scientists, it is typically to determine how they fit into the *existing* pattern of political life, a pattern set by the men who have defined the meaning of the political process throughout all of Canadian history. And so, a student approaching the field of Canadian politics in the 1990s would be left to conclude from the literature that women, compared to men, participate at about the same rate in electoral activities, are somewhat less likely to be interested in the political world, and are significantly less likely to seek elected office, in particular at the federal and provincial levels. But to accept this profile of women as political actors is to ignore the rich tradition of women's political activity both in this century and the preceding one, as well as the impact of that activity on Canadian politics.

SEPARATE SPHERES

For an understanding of Canadian political life that fully includes women's involvement, we must first reconsider the boundaries of political activity. This requires a rejection of the "separate spheres" approach. We can trace the notion that the public sphere of politics is a male preserve characterized by the values of self-interest, competition, and masculine rationality as far back as classical Greek political life. According to this doctrine, the private sphere is under women's control and characterized by the values of group interest, co-operation, and feminine emotionalism. The separate spheres doctrine has informed men's thinking about women's political roles in varying degrees throughout Canadian history. It was most commonly voiced in the early years of the twentieth century. Typical was the view of Ernest Lapointe, expressed in the federal House of Commons during the 1918 debate on suffrage rights for women. Women are, he proposed, in an "exalted position as queens of the household" and generally "quite willing to leave to the men all the troubles and responsibilities of political administration."[2]

Lapointe's sentiments are rarely voiced today, and we now recognize that the activities of women and men, in industrialized societies at least, have always overlapped the boundaries separating the public from the private, just as those boundaries themselves have changed over time. Even in the nineteenth century when most women were confined to the household, men's influence extended into that household. As Carole Pateman points out, "It was (and is) only women whose power was to be separate—not separate from men, but from the exercise of power and authority. Men's sphere was to be circumscribed by few boundaries since husbands were legally and conventionally 'head of the household'."[3]

Today the blurring of the boundaries is even more apparent since over one-half of Canadian women are now working for wages outside the home. In 1985, 54 percent of women in Canada were members of the paid labour force, a dramatic increase from 38 percent in 1970 and only 16 percent in 1901.[4] With this labour force participation came demands for equality rights—for equal access to the opportunities in the public sphere that men had enjoyed for many years. In response, affirmative action, pay equity, child care, and legal equality rights were written into the policy language of the 1980s.

As a result of pressure from women's groups representing female workers, combined with appeals from these few women sitting in elected office, some important reforms affecting women's roles were enacted throughout the second half of the twentieth century. The first significant measure came in 1956 when the federal government produced equal pay legislation, forcing employers under federal jurisdiction to pay the same wages to women and men carrying out the same or similar work. This legislation was a weaker version of the 1951 United Nations declaration in favour of equal pay for work of equal value. It was passed in response to pressure from groups such as the National Council of Women and the Canadian Federation of Business and Professional Women's Clubs by a Minister of Labour sympathetic to women's claims.

By 1980 the momentum of reforms increased and the language of governments became the language of equal rights. In 1986 the federal government passed an Employment Equity Act that called for affirmative action within Crown corporations and federally regulated businesses. In that same year, at the annual First Ministers' Conference, the agenda included labour force equality for women, and the focus was on "employment equity" and "overcoming the barriers" to equality.[5] By 1977 all provinces had some version of equal pay legislation in place. In the 1980s both Manitoba and Ontario enacted legislation guaranteeing equal pay for work of equal value for some employees.

Thus, demands for what was often called simple justice have had a very real impact on the agenda of governments. And while legislators often redefined the issues in their own terms, nevertheless their recognition of the need for equality rights for women in the labour force reflected changes in their thinking about the movement of women and men between the private and public spheres.

In addition, the separate spheres notion that politics is a public activity that is distinct from life in the home has been challenged successfully by feminists. It is now clear that the personal *is* political, that the shape of people's individual lives is partly the consequence of collective social and economic conditions that often are beyond their control. When viewed in this light, women's decisions to stay out of electoral politics or to accept jobs at the bottom of the economic hierarchy are responses to social conditioning and the presence of structural barriers rather than autonomous personal choices. The recognition of this relationship between material and social conditions and personal choices has led to research that has uncovered some of the structural obstacles facing women who want to open the doors to political power. This research has contributed to the reform process within the political parties focused on improving the representation of women at the top decision-making levels.[6]

At the same time, issues such as sexual harassment and sexual assault, which used to be regarded as part of the private sphere, have been approached from new public perspectives by legislators. These issues have been on the political agenda since the early days of Canada. In the context of their belief in separate spheres in the latter years of the nineteenth century, federal policy makers passed laws to protect the chastity of young girls before marriage. These chastity laws were intended to eradicate prostitution as well as punish seducers. But the onus of proof was on the seduced, and the accused seducer could be a witness for the defence. Furthermore, these early laws stopped short of enforcing morality in the home. Legislators and the courts regarded the wife as the property and responsibility of her husband. Her duty was to remain with him—even in the face of cruelty—partly on the assumption that she must have contributed to the conditions that resulted in the offence. The wife was expected to submit to the will of her husband, and failure to do so was interpreted as provocation for violent actions. Many judges "seemed to feel that the permanency of marriage ought to outweigh the protection of battered women."[7] In the 1980s both federal and provincial governments began to take some responsibility for controlling family violence. The federal government set up a National Clearinghouse on Family Violence and a working group to study wife battering.

The altered political agenda of the latter part of the twentieth century is yet another indication of recognition that the personal is political. Just as men individually in the nineteenth century assumed responsibility for much of what went on in the private world of the family, so today does the state bear a great deal of responsibility for the private lives of its citizens. The history of Canadian public policy documents this movement of governments into the private sphere, partly as a consequence of pressure exerted by women both individually and collectively. As legislators have adopted a positive or interventionist conception of the role of the state, they have moved much of what in the nineteenth century was considered private family business onto the public agenda. They have assumed responsibility for, among other things, education, relief for the poor, medical assistance, and care of the elderly.

This assumption of responsibility by governments for some of the things formerly considered part of the private sphere began long before the second wave of the women's movement. In 1916 the Manitoba legislature put in place the first system of mothers' pensions in Canada—the forerunner of the current family allowance program. The legislation was limited in scope. It provided small monthly payments to widows with two or more children still at home,[8] and introduced the principle that the state was prepared to enter into the life of the family, in this case to provide for the well-being of needy children. In 1944 the federal government took over this program, removed the means test, and made the benefits available to all mothers with children aged sixteen or younger.

But the greatest movement of governments into family life has occurred in the 1970s and 1980s. Most dramatic has been the assumption of some responsibility for the daily care of children, through public funding of day care programs. In December 1987 the federal government announced its new strategy on child care, which would provide funding for more spaces in both non-profit and commercial child care facilities, and an increase to $4,000 in the child care expense deduction on income tax paid. While the government has been slow to pass legislation to implement this strategy, it has at least accepted the principle that child care is a public issue.

These changes have been mirrored in public opinion. Issues such as affirmative action now receive support from both women and men in the public. In the 1984 federal election study, for example, 76 percent of the respondents reported their support for affirmative action programs.[9] In a 1982 Gallup poll, 41 percent of the respondents perceived day care as a joint family–government responsibility. The difference between women and men on this question was insignificant. In another poll taken in 1982, 38 percent of respondents agreed with the proposition that even women with young children at home should find paid employment. This was a dramatic increase from only 13 percent in 1970 and 18 percent in 1975.[10] The call for "wages for housework," adopted by radical feminists in the 1960s and widely regarded then as an intrusion into family life, has now been adopted by some anti-feminists seeking to counter the economic pressures pushing women out of the home and into the labour force.

But while all of these changes are important, there have been clear limits to the reforms. Governments have improved women's access to the public sphere without at the same time redefining life there. The adoption of equal rights guarantees for women has improved the material conditions of many Canadian women. But the decision to grant women equal rights is not a manifestation of a radical restructuring of political life to reflect the special needs of women. Instead it may be viewed as a by-product of the spirit of rights-consciousness that emerged gradually in the wake of the Second World War. It has come about in the context of a general commitment by successive Canadian governments to remove obstacles to free and equal competition among individuals in the marketplace. Thus, equal rights for women, as they have developed in the second half of the twentieth century, have clear limits—the market mentality—and have been absorbed into the prevailing discourse of contemporary liberal and neo-conservative thinking.

The inclusion of equal rights for women in the 1982 Charter of Rights and Freedoms provides a good example of this pattern. The proposal to entrench equal rights for women in the new Canadian constitution was made by the Liberal government in its first Constitution Bill introduced in 1978, and was part of a section prohibiting discrimination on the basis of race, national or ethnic origin, language, colour, religion, age, or sex. As early as 1972, Prime Minister Trudeau had indicated to his Cabinet colleagues that under his leadership women would be integrated into the development of Canada "as equal partners with men."[11] In the course of the negotiations over the new constitution between the federal government and women's groups in the period from 1980 to 1982, the wording of the equal rights guarantees was improved to strengthen women's claims for equality before the courts. Disagreements focused on the legal implications of different wordings of these rights guarantees rather than on the principle of equal rights *per se*. And there is no question that the Ad Hoc Committee on the Constitution, the leading women's lobby during the Charter negotiations, won important battles on the question of wording. Most notable was the success in convincing the Minister of Justice to rewrite equality before the law to equality under the law.[12] But, in the end, women's groups were absorbed into the debate on the Charter, the limits of which were set by the federal government and did not extend beyond the principle of equal opportunity.

In much the same way, the current debate over day care demonstrates how women have succeeded in adding items to the public agenda without, at the same time, substantially altering the framework within which that agenda is set. As early as 1975, groups such as the National Action Committee on the Status of Women (NAC) and the Canadian Labour Congress were pressuring both federal and provincial governments to increase government funding for additional spaces in publicly run, non-profit day care facilities. They stressed the need for high-quality, non-profit units subsidized by tax dollars and accessible to all working parents. In 1986 a task force set up by the previous Liberal government recommended that such a system be put into place.[13] But the proposal was rejected, and in 1986 the federal Conservative government announced a new program that would assist both public and private day care operators. The subsequent legislative proposals of the government enshrined the principle of profitable day care over the principle of affordable day care. The NAC expressed the views of day care advocacy groups across the country when it labelled the government proposals a disaster. In the NAC's words, "the big winners in this charade are commercial child care operators, affluent taxpayers and Finance Department bureaucrats who wanted to put a lid on federal government spending for child care."[14]

In yet another fundamental way the altered agenda reflects the limits of the transformation in the thinking of legislators on the question of gender roles. The designation of day care, pornography, sexual assault, and the like as "women's issues" has contributed to the perpetuation of the separate spheres mentality, with women still shouldering the responsibilities for the home and family. But in the modern version of separate spheres, women may gain access to the public world of politics and work provided only that they follow the previously set rules of the game, and at the same time maintain their traditional responsibility for life in the home. In addition, the separation of "women's issues" from the general package of policy decisions has contributed to their marginalization.

Moreover, the equal rights or equal opportunity principle doesn't always work in women's favour. The application of equal treatment has resulted in the perpetuation or creation of some serious inequalities. Recent changes in child custody laws illustrate this development. Increasingly, the courts are prepared to grant custody of children to fathers as well as mothers in divorce cases, even when the father has no previous history of active child care involvement. "In the name of equality, men are now maintaining that though women still usually carry the primary responsibility for child care, they should not have seniority because of it and fathers...should have an equal crack at the job."[15] In a system that evaluates the child's best interest in terms of financial security, women with their record of earning only 60 percent of the wages men earn are decidedly not equal in these custody battles. The problem here, as throughout Canadian history, is that women have no control over these equal rights laws. They are still the subjects of policy decisions made primarily by men, often with men's interest in mind. As a society we have undoubtedly advanced beyond the mentality of the nineteenth century when, for example, rape laws were developed to protect men's property rights in their wives and daughters.[16] However, we have not yet advanced to the stage where women and men share equally in the development of legislative initiatives.

THE GENDER GAP

At another level, there have been more fundamental, but less apparent, indications that women have altered the fabric of Canadian political life. In the wake of the women's liberation movement of the 1960s with its emphasis on consciousness raising and self-discovery, some women began to question the underlying set of assumptions on which politics, and the study of politics is based. They were particularly concerned with what they saw as a male definition of power, as the ability to do things *to* other people rather than the building of capabilities among people to work together to accomplish their goals. They questioned the standard descriptions of women's political behaviour, which focused on electoral politics and compared women to men. Instead, they argued, women and men might hold different views about the meaning of democracy, and about the ways in which political power should be exercised. At first glance, this proposal seems to be in conflict with feminist critiques of the notion of separate spheres. And yet, it makes sense in view of the perpetuation of different socialization patterns for girls and boys, the reproductive function performed by women, and the perpetuation of child care as women's work.

In 1972 British sociologist Ann Oakley, on the basis of this kind of reasoning, proposed that a distinction should be made between sex as a biological term and gender as a psychological and cultural term. While this distinction is problematic—in particular in view of the tendency for women to focus on common "feminine" experiences or traits while ignoring the differences among them that are related to class, race, income, and/or age—it did nevertheless underscore the fact that the salient experiences of most women have been different from the salient experiences of men. Furthermore, these different world experiences have produced a set of attitudes that may affect political choices.

The most celebrated study that seeks to demonstrate this difference in the world views of women and men is Carol Gilligan's analysis of the moral reasoning of college students and of women seeking an abortion in the United States. Twenty-five students and twenty-nine women took part in the two studies. Since neither study used a representative sample of the population, it is not possible to make generalizations on the basis of the results. Nevertheless, Gilligan's findings can serve as a guideline for future research. She found that "men and women may speak different languages that they assume are the same, using different words to encode disparate experiences of self and social relationships."[17] Gilligan was struck by the refrain of responsibility and care in women's perception of morality. She concluded that there may be a gender difference in moral capacity, with women (according to Gilligan) tending to see "moral problems as situations that call for finding some way of maintaining connections between persons" and men focusing on the decision as to which claims are legitimate.[18] In other words, in this construct women see rights as inextricably linked to responsibilities, as opposed to men who view rights as competing claims that must be assessed.

There is some evidence in Canadian research that a significant minority of people agree that some gender differences exist. In a series of polls conducted between 1981 and 1983, researchers found that men were more likely than women to believe that a woman's place is in the home (37 percent versus 32 percent). More men agreed that women in the business world are not as capable as men in understanding teamwork (37 percent versus 27 percent), or that women are more emotional than men (53 percent versus 42 percent). And about one-third of both women and men disagreed with the proposition that, mentally and emotionally, women are as capable as men of doing a job.[19] However, research in this area is limited and we do not have a clear picture of Canadians' perceptions of gender differences.

Evidence on the existence of such differences in either the attitudes or behaviour of women and men is mixed. On questions of equality rights for women, the responses of men and women are consistently alike. Some differences have emerged on questions of social services and defence policy. For example, in polls conducted between 1981 and 1984 there were small but statistically significant gender differences on the questions of needed government action for crime prevention and for social services for women. Fewer women than men favoured increases in defence spending, foreign ownership, free trade, and free enterprise.[20]

Among party activists, the gender differences are even more apparent. Delegates to the Progressive Conservative Party convention in 1983 and the Liberal Party convention in 1984 were polled on their attitudes on policy issues. While women and men were agreed on issues such as relief for the poor and the need for day care, they disagreed on the other attitudinal questions posed. The most striking differences were on peace-related questions. Among the Conservative delegates, 75 percent of the women compared to 84 percent of the men were in favour of testing the cruise missile. Among the Liberals, the difference was greater (59 percent versus 79 percent). On most questions the gender gap was most apparent within the Conservative Party, with fewer women than men approving of President Reagan's ideas, supporting freer trade with the United States, and agreeing with the proposition that many of our social programs are unnecessary. After analyzing the data from these convention surveys, Janine Brodie concluded that the "delegates' responses clearly demonstrate that attitudinal gender gaps are found within each party. What is more striking is that Liberal and Conservative women stand closer together on some of these issues than they do to the men in their respective parties."[21]

In an earlier study of party activists conducted with a small, unrepresentative sample in the late 1970s, it was found that male and female party activists also differed in their views of their roles within the party. Men were more likely to think of party activity as instrumental—as a means either of pushing a policy position or of paving the way for a political career. Women were more likely to think in terms of the interpersonal relations established in the party offices, and the decision-making process within the party rather than in government. Most significant were the views held on the meaning of party activity. The male party activists talked about their own successes in the decision-making process, and focused on what they had done in the past or would like to accomplish in the future in the policy area. The female party activists talked about party activism as a vital part of representative democracy. They focused on their role as mediators between the elected officials and the general public, and on the importance of party activism to the functioning of representative democracy.[22]

Gender differences have appeared in other aspects of political life, notably the activities of interest groups. Since the early 1970s the number of groups working to affect policy in areas relevant for women's lives has increased dramatically. Most of the new groups began with the assistance of grants from the Women's Program of the Secretary of State. A large proportion—evidence from a 1984 survey suggests about one-half[23]—of the groups are engaged in providing services to women in transition or crisis. These groups, for instance, have set up educational counselling centres and shelters for victims of assault. The remaining groups are working for economic and political reforms to improve the status of women, or are engaged in various peace, networking, or rights-related activities.

These women's groups are unique in the world of pressure politics because of their adherence to the principles of co-operation and consensus rather than competition and hierarchy. In the 1984 survey, one-third of the groups surveyed have rejected traditional group decision-making structures in favour of consensus. Even among the more traditionally organized groups, members reported serious attempts by the executive to obtain members' views on salient issues—through polls, frequent general meetings, or study groups. The consensus approach is possible because most women's groups are small (47 percent in this study had fewer than fifty members). Significantly, consensus-style decision making did not have a negative effect on these groups' ability to influence policy outcomes.

FUTURE CHOICES

The impact of these different world views on Canadian political life has not been as significant as feminists were predicting in the early 1980s. This is partly because, with the exception of the free trade positions in the 1988 federal election, the parties have not divided on gender-significant issues. It is due as well to the emergence of an anti-feminist backlash. Among women, this has meant unrealistic calls for a return to the male-led, nuclear family in which women care for the husband and children in return for protection and economic security. Among men, anti-feminism has resulted in pressure to remove equal pay and anti-discrimination laws from the legislative books on the grounds that women's gains are men's losses. In addition, it must be recognized that the gender divisions between women and men are confounded by differences among them based on such factors as age, religion, occupation, and race.

At this point there are few indications that the impact of gender differences will increase. Indeed, with the entrenchment of classical liberal values—those same values that the Greeks deemed suitable for public sphere activity—it seems likely that in the future the public sphere will continue to be dominated by the male ethic of rationality, and the female ethic of responsibility and co-operation celebrated by Gilligan will be assigned a place even further from the mainstream of political life. There are mounting pressures on women as policy actors to conform to the rational-actor, competitive-market mentality of the 1980s. And there are some good reasons for arguing that gender differences should not form the *only* basis for thinking about future action. For the doctrine of gender differences drives us back to the argument of separate spheres, which ironically is the same argument used by anti-feminists in their campaign to move women out of the public sphere. In addition, "a feminism which emphasizes only the dangers to women from men, which insists upon the essential differences between women's and men's inner being, between women's and men's natural urges and experience of the world, leaves little or no scope for transforming the relations between men and women."[24]

At the same time, a doctrine that stresses gender similarities will, history tells us, result in the perpetuation of a system of political power and decision making in which the rules will continue to be made by men, or by women speaking with men's voices. This is a dismal prospect for feminists committed to a vision of a world in which the individual rights that have been so vigorously defended and celebrated since the end of the Second World War would be balanced with a sense of obligation to the well-being of the community and the ethic of caring within a fundamentally fair society.

There *are* differences between the economic and social conditions of women and those of men in Canadian society. In spite of the legislative reforms worked out during the past twenty years, women still earn significantly less than men who have equivalent educational qualifications. Women's potential for advancing up the occupational or political hierarchies is still limited by structural obstacles and personal prejudice. Women still bear children, although discoveries in reproductive technologies may bring changes even here.[25] And women still assume most of the responsibility for caring for these children. At what is now a turning point in gender relations in Canada, it is time to look for a way to translate the positive aspects of these differences into political action while at the same time applying the principle of fairness to the removal of inequalities. In the future, Canadian women will continue to speak with more than one voice, reflecting the divisions among them on the blueprint for the good society as well as on the differences between men and women. And it will require combined and determined action from both women and men to alter the present course of Canadian politics, to create a society in which differences can be the basis for equality, and rationality can be balanced with justice.

NOTES

1. The absence of women authors is striking in most of the standard texts on Canadian politics. One exception is Robert J. Jackson, Doreen Jackson, and Nicolas Baxter-Moore, *Politics in Canada* (Toronto: Prentice-Hall, 1986).
2. Canada, House of Commons, *Debates*, 22 March 1918, p. 97.

3. Carole Patemen, "Women, Nature, and the Suffrage," *Ethics* 90 (July 1980): 566.
4. Canada, Dominion Bureau of Statistics, *Women Who Work*, Part 2 (December 1986).
5. Canada, Annual Conference of First Ministers, "Achieving Labour Force Equality for Women: Federal Government Initiatives" (Vancouver, British Columbia, 20–21 November 1986).
6. For an excellent history of the status of women within the major political parties in Canada, see Sylvia B. Bashevkin, *Toeing the Lines: Women and Party Politics in English Canada* (Toronto: University of Toronto Press, 1985).
7. Constance Backhouse, "Nineteenth-Century Canadian Divorce Law: Shoring Up the Patriarchal Family," unpublished manuscript, rare book room, arts library, University of Waterloo, July 1983, p. 60.
8. Veronica Strong-Boag, "Wages for Housework: Mothers' Allowances and the Beginnings of Social Security in Canada," *Journal of Canadian Studies* 14, no. 1 (1979): 25.
9. Barry J. Kay, Ronald D. Lambert, Steven D. Brown, and James E. Curtis, "Feminist Consciousness and the Canadian Electorate: A Review of National Election Studies, 1965–1984," *Women and Politics* 8, no. 2 (1988): 17.
10. Monica Boyd, "Canadian Attitudes Toward Women: Thirty Years of Change," prepared for the Women's Bureau, Canada Department of Labour , 1984, pp. 45–50 and 53.
11. This is taken from a federal briefing document for deputy ministers on status of women policy, n.d.
12. Sandra Burt, "The Charter of Rights and the Ad Hoc Lobby: The Limits of the Success," *Atlantis* 14, no. 1 (Fall 1988).
13. Canada, Task Force on Child Care, *Report* (1986).
14. National Action Committee on the Status of Women, *Action* (February 1988).
15. Susan Crean, "In the Name of the Fathers," *This Magazine* 22, no. 7 (February 1989): 24.
16. Constance Backhouse, "Nineteenth-Century Canadian Rape Law, 1800–92," in *Essays in the History of Canadian Law*, Vol. II, ed. David Flaherty (Toronto: University of Toronto Press, 1983), p. 201.
17. Carol Gilligan, *In A Different Voice* (Cambridge, Mass.: Harvard University Press, 1982), p. 173.
18. Sharon Bishop, "Connections and Guilt," *Hypatia* 2, no. 1 (Winter 1987): 11.
19. These data were collected from polls conducted by Goldfarb between 1981 and 1983. Some additional results from other polls are reported in Sandra Burt, "Women's Issues and the Women's Movement in Canada Since 1970," in *The Politics of Gender, Ethnicity and*

   Language in Canada, vol. 34, ed. C. Williams and A. Cairns, studies
   commissioned for the Royal Commission on the Economic Union
   and Development Prospects for Canada (Toronto: University of
   Toronto Press, 1986), pp. 128–31.
20. Janine Brodie, "The Gender Factor and National Leadership Conventions in Canada," in *Party Democracy in Canada*, ed. George Perlin
   (Toronto: Prentice-Hall, 1988), p. 180, and John Terry, "The Gender
   Gap: Women's Political Power," paper prepared for the Current
   Issues Series, Political and Social Affairs Division, Research Branch of
   the Library of Parliament, Ottawa, 1984.
21. Brodie, "The Gender Factor and National Leadership Conventions in
   Canada," p. 183.
22. Sandra Burt, "Different Democracies? A Preliminary Examination of
   the Political Worlds of Canadian Men and Women," *Women and
   Politics* 6, no. 4 (Winter 1986): 57–79.
23. Between March and April, 1984, the author mailed questionnaires to
   the 686 groups listed in the 1982 directory of the Women's Program of
   the federal Secretary of State. The response rate was 24 percent.
24. Lynne Segal, *Is the Future Female?* (London: Virago, 1987), p. 37.
25. For a good discussion of some of the problems associated with these
   new technologies, see Rona Achilles, "Artificial Reproduction: Hope
   Chest or Pandora's Box?" in *Changing Patterns: Women in Canada*,
   ed. Sandra Burt, Lorraine Code, and Lindsay Dorney (Toronto:
   McClelland and Stewart, 1988), pp. 291–311.

FURTHER READINGS

Bashevkin, Sylvia B. *Toeing the Lines: Women and Party Politics in English
   Canada.* Toronto: University of Toronto Press, 1985.
Burt, Sandra, Lorraine Code, and Lindsay Dorney, eds. *Changing Patterns:
   Women in Canada.* Toronto: McClelland and Stewart, 1988.
Cohen, Yolande, ed. *Women and Counter Power.* Montreal: Black Rose Books,
   1989.
Segal, Lynne. *Is The Future Female?* London: Virago, 1987.
Sapiro, Virginia. *The Political Integration of Women: Roles, Socialization and
   Politics.* Urbana, Ill.: University of Illinois Press, 1983.

12

Images and Issues: The Mass Media and Politics in Canada[1]

FREDERICK J. FLETCHER AND DAPHNE GOTTLIEB TARAS

The mass media have become in modern industrial societies the primary communicators of politically significant images. The capacity of these media—newspapers, magazines, radio, film, television—to reach large audiences and to select which ideas and images will have wide popular currency gives them great potential influence. In large part, the media form our psychic environment, especially with respect to matters beyond our direct personal experience, a realm into which most aspects of politics fall. The average Canadian adult spends more than three hours watching television each day, a little less listening to radio, and more than fifty minutes reading a daily newspaper. Television viewing takes up more of the average Canadian's time than anything but work and sleep, and nearly half our population say that they stay informed by watching television news.[2]

The mass media are in the business of attracting audiences to sell to advertisers (and in the case of the Canadian Broadcasting Corporation, to demonstrate its popularity). While informing and entertaining us, "the media...define what is normal and respectable in a society, what is debatable and what is beyond discussion by decent, respectable citizens," as Anthony Westell put it.[3] In choosing among the vast array of available drama scripts, news items, and other materials, key media personnel have great influence on the beliefs and perspectives presented to the citizenry. These choices help to determine the available role models, images of reality, and definitions of what is political. Exposure to the media not only provides information on a wide range of subjects, but also generates topics of conversation and things to worry about (from environmental issues to advertiser-generated concerns about dandruff and bad breath).

MEDIA EFFECTS: GATEKEEPING, FRAMING, AGENDA SETTING, PRIMING

Thousands of potential news stories are caught in the news net and fed into an ever-narrowing funnel known as the newsroom, where newsworkers decide what stories will become news. Many will be missed because the news net tends to focus its attention on official sources, elite countries, and easily accessible locations. The importance of this gatekeeping function[4] derives in large part from the fact that gatekeepers tend to share assumptions about what makes appropriate media content. These assumptions can be traced to cultural norms, government regulations, policies of media organizations, training of media personnel, current fashion, and the requirements of media technologies. Within the boundaries of acceptability, the gatekeepers are primarily concerned about attracting audiences. While each medium has its own requirements, they all tend to prefer the immediate, the personal, and the concrete to long-term social processes or abstract ideas. Complex, technical, and difficult to research topics, as well as those from outside society's mainstream of ideas and institutions, rarely became news, regardless of their significance.[5] Media consumers are conditioned to accept these standards as well, making it difficult for messages that do not fit the media mould to get a hearing.

The news selection criteria—that the story be immediate, involve conflict, concentrate on personalities, require little background research, and for television, have good visual properties, to name the most influential—affect presentation as well as selection. Reporters are sent out to interview personalities, camera crews seek out sensational shots, and stories are written that highlight any inherent drama. This shaping of the news story for entertainment value is one aspect of framing,[6] a process that influences the way issues come to be viewed.

The effects of gatekeeping and framing on our political life are hotly debated. To paraphrase an early study of newspapers, the media may not be successful much of the time in telling people what to *think*, but they are stunningly successful in telling people what to *think about*.[7] It is becoming increasingly evident that the items that receive prominent attention on the national news, especially the leading items or those items that appear frequently, become the problems the public regards as the nation's most important. This is known as agenda setting.[8] By concentrating on free trade and polls during the 1988 federal election, the media were able to influence the agenda of public debate without necessarily having a direct effect on opinions or voting intentions.

Television is a particularly powerful shaper of values, not only because of its popularity, but also because people tend to use it non-selectively, watching whatever attracts them most at the time they want to relax. A leading American communication researcher has concluded that television viewing is a "ritual" that crosses social, religious, generational, and class lines in an unprecedented manner. Most viewers come to "share a great deal of cultural imagery," so that "the most recurrent patterns of the ritual tend to...become the assumptions we make about the world."[9]

These patterns include the stereotyping of minority groups, a great exaggeration of the amount of crime and violence in society (ten times that of the real world), and an unwarranted emphasis on conflict and risk. Portrayal of Third World issues is almost always characterized by natural calamities, riots, scandals, and political violence, with little attention to longer-term problems and achievements. Coverage emphasizes the differences among peoples, not their similarities. The line between news and entertainment shows is increasingly blurred by television. Indeed, a training manual for CBC television producers states bluntly that "news is theatre."[10] The risk is that even public broadcasters will turn from providing the news we need to the news we want (to entertain us).

Although many experts believe that television newscasts are at best a distorted mirror of society, their visuals and eyewitness quality give them great credibility. Audiences appear generally unaware of the medium's limitations—a thirty-minute newscast contains less information than the front page of *The Globe and Mail*—and beguiled by the illusion of access to news makers that television news provides. A fifteen-second clip from a twenty-minute speech is not real access. Nevertheless, a recent poll confirmed earlier studies that found television to be the most "believable" news medium.[11] The tendency to view television news as accurate, objective, and impartial means that audiences are more receptive to influence from that source, and helps to explain the attention that politicians give it.

There is growing evidence that television not only has substantial influence on the public agenda, but also helps to set the standards by which governments, policies, and candidates for public office are judged. It appears that media consumers evaluate political figures based on the information they have most recently and most frequently been exposed to on the news, a process called priming.[12] During the 1988 Canadian federal election, voters probably were primed by free trade coverage and reports on party and leader preference polls. The emphasis of the national news on party leaders has primed many voters to evaluate parties based on leaders rather than local candidates or party platforms. The question is no longer whether the media affect our lives, but rather in what ways.

SCHOOLS OF THOUGHT

In attempting to understand the role of the media in Canadian politics, analysts generally draw upon elements of two competing schools of thought: the liberal democratic and the neo-Marxist approaches. The two perspectives share the view that the mass media, though for the most part privately owned, have important political functions. Both believe that the media have significant social power and reject the argument advanced by some media people that they merely reflect the values and tastes of their audiences.

In liberal democracies such as Canada, the media are seen by many as a "fourth branch of government," meeting the needs of citizens by presenting the information necessary for effective political participation and by providing a forum for debate on public issues. In this process, they are expected to help governments disseminate vital information about public services—and government accomplishments—while providing opportunities for opposition parties to criticize government and propose alternative policies. Ideally, they provide commentary on public affairs from a wide variety of perspectives, including those of unpopular minorities. An important tradition in the Anglo-American democracies holds that the news media should serve as watchdogs, sniffing out abuses of power—especially by governments—and barking out the alarm. In a recent study of the Canadian media, Ericson and his colleagues argue that "deviance is *the* defining characteristic of what journalists regard as newsworthy....Journalists act as watchdogs, policing organizational life for deviations from their conceptions of the order of things."[13] Official ombudsmen no less than media crusaders rely on publicity to restrain government power. In short, news organizations have a duty to "help keep democracy alive in societies too populous and too complex for face-to-face exchange...."[14]

An alternative view, drawing on neo-Marxist thinking, sees the media as an important part of an ideological system that effectively promotes the dominant ideology of society, providing a justification for the economic and political status quo, thus serving the interests of the rich and powerful. By establishing the limits of debate, the media screen out radical critiques and reinforce existing values, values defined by the powerful and communicated from the top down. In North America, the mass media are seen as promoting consumerism, which supports the economic system, and the myth of "middle classness," which holds that society's advantages are equally available to all and that critics of the system are failures, with only themselves to blame, or promoters of "foreign" ideologies. Private ownership of property is presented as an inviolable norm. The inefficiencies, wrongdoings, and mismanagement of private corporations are hidden in shadow while the media searchlight is trained on corrupt or ineffectual individuals in the public sector. When criticisms of the economic and political system are presented, the approach is generally reformist rather than radical. In short, the media are seen as "a powerful ideological weapon for holding the mass of people in voluntary submission to capitalism."[15]

It has been demonstrated many times that those who control the mass media are a powerful segment of Canada's economic elite. Class analysts argue, therefore, that the owners and, thus, the media have a stake in the perpetuation of the existing power structure. "Freedom of the press," as the American media critic A. J. Liebling said, "is guaranteed only to those who own one."[16] The extent to which corporate control of media organizations actually influences content is examined below.

THE CANADIAN MASS MEDIA SYSTEM: EVOLUTION

The media system in Canada has undergone great change in audience penetration, operating philosophy, technology, and ownership over the years. From their earliest beginnings in the eighteenth century, Canadian newspapers were highly political, with close ties to government or opposition parties. In the nineteenth century, they often served as personal vehicles for editor-politicians such as George Brown, William Lyon Mackenzie, Étienne Parent, Joseph Howe, and Amor De Cosmos. During the upheavals of the late 1830s, the press was a thorn in the side of those in power, and the reformist strain of Canadian journalism was firmly established along with a tradition of press freedom. After the Rebellion of 1837 in Upper Canada, Attorney General John Beverly Robinson lamented the principle of a free press, but could do little about it:

> It is one of the miserable consequences of the abuse of liberty that a licentious press is permitted to poison the public mind with the most absurd and wicked misrepresentations, which the ill-disposed, without inquiry, receive and act upon as truths.[17]

During the nineteenth century, newspapers were small operations, locally owned and highly partisan, often relying on government patronage or party financial support. They engaged in vociferous competition and denounced political opponents with vigour, contributing much to the vitality of political debate, but often little to public enlightenment.

By the 1870s, the growth of urban centres and the emergence of new technologies—mechanized printing, cheap newsprint, the telegraph for rapid news gathering—contributed to the proliferation of newspapers and the creation of a mass press, which emphasized strictly political matters less and social issues of broad interest more. Newspapers tried to broaden their appeal to serve two distinct but related markets: readers and advertisers anxious to reach them. Newspapers were no longer primarily vehicles for political debate among competing elites, and advertisers freed the press from financial dependence on politicians. In the competition for mass audiences, many publishers fell by the wayside, and by the turn of the century, successful publishers were buying out those in financial difficulty. For example, the Southam family purchased *The Ottawa Citizen* (1897), the *Calgary Herald* (1908), *The Edmonton Journal* (1912), and the *Winnipeg Tribune* (1920). The Southam and Sifton chains were well established by 1920, and the trend toward concentration of ownership has continued to accelerate, with a handful of large corporations now controlling most daily newspapers and many weeklies, magazines, and privately owned radio and television outlets, as well as cable systems.

The quest for mass audiences, the growth of newspaper chains and absentee ownership, and the advent of wire services selling news to a wide range of clients all contributed to the decline of the partisan press. More interested in profits than politics, the larger publishers moderated their partisanship to appeal to broader audiences. Wire services were founded to sell newspaper copy across the country and throughout the world. Their reports were kept as neutral as possible, especially with regard to domestic politics, so they could appeal to newspapers of all partisan stripes. Publishers were delighted to subscribe to news services and to purchase syndicated features because they were so much cheaper than staff-written material. The costs were shared by many clients. For these reasons, the era of so-called objective journalism emerged, spreading gradually in the years following the Great Depression.

The major Canadian wire service, the Canadian Press (CP), was founded in 1917, as a national co-operative, owned collectively by the major daily newspapers. Set up as a clearing house for news gathered by Canada's dailies, CP has provided an effective, and inexpensive, mechanism for exchanging news among member papers and for bringing in up-to-date foreign news. CP remains today the primary source of non-local news for all but the largest Canadian dailies. With its own staff of reporters, it covers major stories within Canada and provides limited foreign coverage. It has been criticized, however, for relying too heavily on the central Canadian media and for importing most of its foreign news from the world's major news services. Because of its heavy reliance on American sources, especially its U.S. counterpart, the Associated Press (AP), Canadians continue to see the world "through U.S. eyes."[18]

Radio and television newsrooms, most of which lack the resources to do much news gathering on their own, also rely on CP and its subsidiaries. Television news uses the U.S. networks and Visnews, dominated by the British Broadcasting Corporation (BBC). The French media rely on these same sources, with a heavy dose of material from Agence France-Presse (AFP), the Paris-based service. While the CBC makes a real effort at independent foreign coverage, with bureaus in a few major world centres and a number of excellent foreign correspondents, its limited resources compel it to rely heavily on local feeds or news services, using voice-overs to give a Canadian interpretation to an agenda set by the sources of its pictures, usually U.S. networks.

From the beginning, the development of Canada's magazine and motion picture industries was hindered by competition from the United

States. Since the 1930s, the Canadian government has employed tariffs, tax measures, subsidies, and government agencies, including Crown corporations, to assist Canadian enterprises to survive competition from large and well-funded American corporations, which regarded Canada as a convenient secondary market. The consistent view of Canadian governments has been that to permit American-based media to dominate Canadian markets would threaten Canada's cultural identity and siphon off revenues needed by Canadian enterprises to perform their public duties. These measures included the creation of the award-winning National Film Board in 1939 and a variety of subsidy schemes that have had only limited success in countering the flood of American movies and television shows. More recently, the Broadcast Fund of Telefilm Canada has been quite successful in promoting Canadian drama on television. In the 1970s, new legislation helped *Saturday Night* to survive[19] and created room in the system for *Maclean's* to become a weekly news magazine. In recent years, Canadian magazines have flourished, but their finances remain precarious in our relatively small market. Negotiations pursuant to the 1988 free trade agreement with the United States may limit the capacity of the Canadian government to favour domestic magazines through postal and tax laws in future.

Canadian radio and television services were founded in direct response to the spillover of signals from the United States. Government intervention was made necessary not only by the need to allocate frequencies and to negotiate an agreement with the U.S. government for a share of the airwaves, but also by the high cost of reaching Canada's scattered population. Faced with a choice between a government-owned system and a U.S.-dominated commercial one with little Canadian content that would serve only the major cities, the Conservative government of R. B. Bennett opted in 1932 for a Crown corporation, which became the CBC, and now provides nation-wide signals in both French and English. The radio network was joined by a television service in the 1950s. In 1958 the Board of Broadcast Governors (BBG) was created to regulate both the CBC and the growing private sector. It oversaw the end of the dream of a single integrated broadcasting system and the growth of parallel public and private systems. The most important product of this evolution was the Canadian Television Network (CTV), a national private English-language television network formed in 1961. Since the early 1970s, a number of independent stations and regional networks have been licensed.

In 1968 a new Broadcasting Act was passed that changed the name of the regulatory agency to the Canadian Radio-Television Commission (later the Canadian Radio-television and Telecommunications Commission) or CRTC and set out some ambitious objectives for the broadcasting system:

> The Canadian broadcasting system should be effectively owned and con-
> trolled by Canadians so as to safeguard, enrich and strengthen the cultural,
> political, social and economic fabric of Canada; the programming provided
> by the Canadian broadcasting system should be varied and comprehensive
> and should provide reasonable, balanced opportunity for the expression of
> different views on matters of public concern, and the programming provided
> by each broadcaster should be of a high standard, using predominantly
> Canadian creative and other resources.

Both public and private broadcasters were expected to contribute to these
goals and the CRTC was to implement them. The new Act, it was hoped,
would "help maintain the existence of a broadcasting system intended to
serve Canadian needs despite the influence everywhere of American
television and films." Federal government objectives have also included
provision of coast-to-coast service in both official languages, reflecting
the diversity of Canadian cultural and social values and, for the CBC,
contributing to the development and maintenance of national unity and
Canadian cultural identity.[20]

In attempting to fulfil these objectives, the CRTC has promulgated
Canadian content regulations for both radio and television and has
required cable systems, which came into being to deliver clear U.S.
signals, to give priority to Canadian stations.[21] U.S. border stations have
complained that Canadian regulations removing tax deductions from
Canadian businesses advertising on non-Canadian stations and requiring
cable systems to carry only the Canadian station when a program is
broadcast simultaneously on a U.S. station are interfering with the free
flow of information. It must be noted that the border stations do not pay
program suppliers for the right to broadcast shows in Canada. Nevertheless, the issue is likely to come up in future free trade negotiations, along
with other issues, such as financial compensation for U.S. stations when
their signals are distributed via cable in Canada.

In fact, of course, station owners are primarily concerned with their
own profits. The cost of Canadian content relative to its revenue potential
is a sore point with private broadcasters. Private broadcasters argue that
they generate most of their revenues (about 70 percent) from U.S.
imports while Canadian shows absorb most of their program expenditures.[22] The American imports are usually proven winners, already promoted by the U.S. networks, and much cheaper than homegrown shows
of comparable quality because their costs have already been covered in
the U.S. market. It is this economic fact of life that has limited CTV to
producing dramatic series only as co-productions with U.S. networks,
leading to shows that have little direct relevance to Canada.

The conflict between open borders and cultural sovereignty is not
unique to Canada, of course, and in the Canadian case virtually no U.S.
network programs are denied entry to Canada. The objective is not to shut

out U.S. programming, but rather to preserve a place for Canadian content. Canadian audiences demonstrate an interesting ambivalence on the issue. While showing a strong preference for U.S. entertainment programs, they generally prefer Canadian documentaries and news and public affairs shows. Moreover, there is clear evidence from public opinion surveys that Canadians want to have a substantial amount of Canadian programming available, even if they reserve the right not to watch it.[23] The regulations have encouraged the development of good quality news and public affairs shows that are now popular money-makers. In addition, the CBC has in recent years been able to improve its audience share with an increasingly Canadian lineup, including some shows with a very high ratings.

When the CRTC licensed pay-television in 1982, having resisted cable company lobbying for a decade, it also sought to promote Canadian content through stringent requirements regarding the allocation of broadcast time, revenues, and program acquisition budgets to Canadian productions.[24] Despite the financial difficulties of the pay services, few of which survived, the commission quickly licensed a number of other specialty services, including MuchMusic, The Sports Network (TSN), and narrowcasters, such as TeleLatino and ChinaVision, and permitted the cable systems to import from the United States the Cable News Network (CNN) and Arts and Entertainment (A&E). In 1988 Youth TV and Vision TV were approved as new Canadian services to be offered on cable, along with a new pay-television service, the Family Channel. In addition, the CBC, with private sector partners, is putting together an all-news channel, NewsWorld, a non-discretionary cable service scheduled to begin operation in the Fall of 1989.[25] The goal has been to provide a wide range of choice on cable so that most Canadians will not feel the need to turn to U.S. satellite services with little Canadian content.

Despite the regulatory efforts of the CRTC and the promises of private broadcasters, Canadians continue to be inundated with the values of American commercial television. Even on Canadian stations, U.S. programs dominate prime time.[26] English-speaking Canadian children spend more than 80 percent of their television viewing time watching U.S. programs. The effect upon Canadians is both subtle and profound. The Caplan–Sauvageau Task Force on Broadcasting lamented in 1986 that "English Canadians...are virtual strangers in television's land of the imagination."[27] American images crowd out Canadian ones, and Canadians who do not pay close attention can easily become confused about our political institutions, many of which have similar names but differ markedly in theory and practice from their U.S. counterparts. Many believe, as Meisel has put it, that television "has contributed significantly to the loss of regional and national identities" and to the Americanization of Canada.[28] This pattern of communication reduces our capacity to come to grips with our own particular problems and to preserve our distinctive values (such as civility, order, compassion, community responsibility). How far can the American occupation of the Canadian imagination go without threatening the foundations of Canadian society?

MEDIA AND ISSUES OF REGIONALISM AND DUALISM

The extent to which the mass media system can contribute to promoting national unity and identity is also affected by two other enduring issues in Canadian politics: regionalism and cultural dualism. Canada's dispersed and culturally diverse population has always presented a formidable barrier to the development of national consensus. The Caplan–Sauvageau Task Force on Broadcasting concluded in its 1986 report that the broadcasting system was woefully inadequate in promoting Canadian national identity. It identified as major causes insufficient funding for the CBC and other public outlets by successive governments, the unimpressive performance of the privately owned media in explaining Canadians to one another, the CRTC's inability to pursue these objectives vigorously as a result of legislative and political constraints, and the system's insensitivity to regional differences. In its wide-ranging recommendations on the future of Canadian broadcasting, the task force attempted to find ways to promote Canadian cultural identity and the Canadian broadcasting industry without requiring unrealistic levels of government funding. The main thrust of the recommendations was to encourage increased Canadian programming through new services—such as an all-news channel and a new, non-commercial satellite-to-cable service in both official languages—and increased funding derived from mandatory cable subscription fees and a variety of tax measures. The task force also recommended tax incentives for advertisers sponsoring Canadian entertainment programming and decentralization of the CBC and the CRTC to encourage regional input.[29] While various aspects of these recommendations have already been implemented, others have fallen by the wayside or will have to await passage of a new Broadcasting Act, which has been in the works for several years.

Although important advances in cross-regional communication have been made in recent years, primarily through improved regional coverage by *The Globe and Mail*, the fifteen Southam dailies through Southam's news service (SN), and the CBC, most news still tends to originate in the Ottawa–Toronto–Montreal triangle. The news services and national syndicates, which distribute news and features, tend to draw heavily on the Toronto papers and broadcast outlets. The reporters in the regional bureau of the *Globe*, SN, and CBC write for Toronto- or Montreal-based editors. The national media—the *Globe*, *Maclean's*, CBC radio and the television networks—remain few and are limited in their penetration. The system's combination of parochialism—with most news outlets locally oriented—and central Canadian domination of national coverage has not done very much to strengthen the ties of Confederation. CBC's NewsWorld, by originating newscasts in Calgary during prime time (4 p.m. to 9 p.m.), Halifax, and Winnipeg, may help to redress regional imbalance in coverage.

Cultural dualism has been an even greater barrier to effective communication. The two language groups tend to live in separate media worlds. Attempts over the past fifteen years to integrate the CBC's French and English services have been largely ineffective, and the Caplan–Sauvageau Task Force recommended that they be permitted to focus on serving their culturally distinct audiences.[30]

Until recently, most Quebec outlets concerned themselves primarily with Quebec issues, and few had correspondents beyond Ottawa. In the late 1970s, interest in the rest of Canada increased and coverage improved, as English media coverage of Quebec had a decade earlier. Frequently, however, major political events are given sharply different interpretations in French and English media. The most striking differences occur with respect to issues involving the preservation of Quebec's distinct society: issues of language policy, constitutional issues, such as the Meech Lake Accord, and clashes between collective and individual rights in Quebec. This distinctiveness is found in all types of programming, reflecting and promoting distinct social perspectives.[31] The overwhelming Conservative victory in Quebec in the 1988 federal election reflected an elite consensus, communicated by the media to the voters, that both the free trade agreement and the Meech Lake Accord were in the best interests of the Quebec community. The debate over free trade in English Canada was not mirrored in the French-language media.

OWNERSHIP AND CONTROL[32]

The trend to large-scale corporate ownership of the media is widespread and accelerating. Most of the country's approximately one hundred and twenty dailies are owned by a handful of media conglomerates. In the English daily press, two major chains—Southam and Thomson—own some fifty-five dailies with more than half the daily circulation. The French daily press is dominated by three chains that control most of the circulation. The central features of the dominant chains in Canada are: (1) both vertical and horizontal integration, with in-house production capabilities combined with distribution facilities and ownership of outlets in more than one medium; (2) mass media holdings that are only a small part of their total operations; (3) a pattern of co-ownership among the communication giants, including media and non-media holdings; and (4) development of specialized markets so that competition among dailies (and other media) is limited. Southam, with the largest total circulation, illustrates these patterns well. In addition to its fifteen dailies and fifteen weeklies, it publishes *TV Times* and fifty-three smaller trade publications, owns a major chain of bookstores (Coles), has interests in videotex, and is partially merged with another media giant, TorStar. Thomson Newspapers Limited is a true conglomerate. In Canada, it owns *The Globe and Mail* and *Winnipeg Free Press*, thirty-eight dailies in smaller centres, and many other businesses, in travel, real estate, oil and gas, insurance, electronic publishing, and large-scale retailing (including The Bay, Simpsons, and Zellers). In most provinces, ownership of major media is concentrated in very few hands.

Business conglomerates now house "communications" divisions for which any informational or entertainment product or technology is a potential investment. Cross-media ownership carries with it potential for abuse, as it is possible that an entire point of view, advertising campaign, or political candidate could be frozen out of the media in a particular community. The Irving group is frequently accused of failing to give appropriate coverage to events that might prove detrimental to the Irving family or their business interests in New Brunswick.[33]

Another cause for concern is absentee ownership. In the three most western provinces, all of the major daily newspapers are owned by chains with headquarters in Ontario. Indeed, almost all of Canada's smaller dailies are controlled from Toronto and Montreal. The extent to which this pattern influences local coverage depends largely on the policies of the owners. Chain ownership can bring the benefits of shared resources, including national and foreign coverage far beyond what smaller, locally owned dailies could afford. It can also produce homogenization of coverage and insensitivity to local concerns. The Southam chain, for example, provides quality national and international coverage through economies of scale, whereas Thomson ownership usually means little attention to editorial quality.[34]

Over the past few decades, direct competition among daily newspapers has been declining rapidly. At this writing, there are only eight cities in Canada where there is any form of competition among dailies published in the same language. In all but three of these, the second paper trails substantially in circulation, so that such papers as the *Calgary Herald, The Edmonton Journal*, and the *Winnipeg Free Press* dominate their markets. In Vancouver both dailies are owned by Southam. Only in Toronto and Montreal (and to a lesser extent Quebec City) is there full competition, which survives mainly because the newspapers have been able to find distinct audiences.

Until 1980 two major chains—Southam and FP—competed vigorously across Canada. They had competing dailies in Vancouver, Calgary, Winnipeg, Ottawa, and Montreal and operated competing news services based in Ottawa. Not long after the Thomson interests purchased FP in January 1980, a series of manoeuvres took place that ended the competition. Several newspapers were closed—in Montreal, Ottawa, Winnipeg, Calgary, and Victoria—and ownership was consolidated. While there may have been sound business reasons for these transactions, they clearly marked the end of meaningful newspaper competition for most of English Canada and alarmed politicians and the interested public to the point that the Royal Commission on Newspapers (Kent Commission) was set up and a parallel investigation was begun under the Combines Act.[35].

Charges of conspiring to lessen competition and unlawful merger were subsequently laid against Thomson and Southam in May 1981. Although court testimony made it clear that the two giant chains had exchanged information and discussed the future of the newspapers to be closed, the court found no public detriment and the charges were dismissed in late 1983. It has proven exceedingly difficult to demonstrate harm under the Act, and in practice, it presents no real barrier to concentration of media ownership.[36]

The Kent Commission was given a tight ten-month deadline, in the hope of heading off further takeovers, and produced a detailed report and eight volumes of research. The commission viewed conglomerate ownership as a powerful threat to the public service functions of newspapers, fearing that concern for return on investment would reduce editorial quality and that corporate leaders would not live up to their promises to the commission to take a hands-off approach to their newsrooms. The Kent Commission recommended a series of measures to restrict concentration and to limit the influence of corporate owners in the editorial offices of the newspapers they owned. A series of indirect measures to encourage editorial quality was suggested, including guarantees of autonomy for editors and more self-policing mechanisms, such as press councils. When the Commission's report was released on 18 August 1981 the industry response was hysterical denunciation. Peter Desbarats, former journalist and one of the research directors of the commission (now Dean of Journalism at the University of Western Ontario), observed:

> The modern newspaper quite often says publicly that is not like the old partisan newspaper: it's a forum for expression of diverse views. But it did not follow the rule when its own industry was touched. It became a forum for a very one-sided presentation of the issue. That made any kind of intelligent debate very difficult.[37]

Whatever the role of corporate ownership, there is little doubt that the media present a rather similar picture of society. Observers agree that the media tend to reinforce the dominant institutional and cultural patterns of authority. By setting the limits for public debate, the media generally exclude serious challenges to the status quo, whether from the left or the right. Even as mild a challenge as that mounted by the New Democratic Party (NDP) is too much for most editorial boards. Editorial endorsements for the NDP are so rare as to be newsworthy. Most newspapers are reluctant to challenge in any direct way the dominant interests in their communities. However, there is a reformist thrust to the media, both privately and publicly owned, that angers some conservatives. Both business and labour tend to feel aggrieved about their coverage and can cite evidence of bias.[38] Certainly, both sides in the free trade debate of 1988 complained of biased coverage.

There is some evidence that journalists as a group see themselves as slightly left of centre,[39] yet editorial endorsements of the NDP are rare. One explanation for the status quo orientation cites the fact that all major private media are owned by members of the business community and that it is unreasonable to expect "the owners of watchdogs to let them loose on their own friends," or to provide succour for their enemies.[40] In a discussion of the Irving chain, Alden Nowlan suggests that while the Irving family may not interfere directly in editorial operations, they can hardly be expected to mount campaigns against themselves.[41] It seems that journalists do learn the limits of tolerance in their newsrooms and therefore avoid submitting materials likely to be rejected.[42]

The argument that the media elite use their outlets in any direct way for propaganda purposes under normal circumstances is discounted by many observers, who claim that return on investment is the dominant motive of the media barons. According to this explanation, the media cling to the "extreme middle" of the political spectrum not so much because their owners and managers are tied in with the country's power structure as because their profits depend upon attracting mass audiences to sell to advertisers and mass values tend to be middle of the road. By reflecting these values, the mass media reinforce them, a cycle that is most frustrating to those who seek change.

NEWS COVERAGE OF GOVERNMENT AND POLITICS

Much of what Canadians know about the political process comes from the day-to-day news coverage of government. The news and commentary from Ottawa, the provincial capitals, and city hall are important for the quality of public debate. Parliamentary debates and Question Period would be empty rituals without the media to tell the country about them. Opposition parties rarely can mobilize support to modify government policies without media attention.

The largest and most important group of political reporters is in the parliamentary press gallery in Ottawa. By the 1990s, the gallery will have about four hundred members, the majority from the electronic media. As an "adjunct of Parliament," in Mackenzie King's terms, gallery members are given special access to government documents and the activities of Parliament.[43] They have access to cable coverage of the House of Commons and press coverage, as well as clipping services and other information not readily available to the public. Gallery correspondents are a vital link between the federal government and the electorate. Their selection of events to cover helps to determine the national political agenda. Political columnists are particularly influential because they provide interpretations of events that colour the way we view the political process.

The gallery's growth and the arrival of a new generation of better-educated journalists have helped the gallery provide more and better coverage of federal politics than it did two decades ago. Yet, much government activity goes unreported as the majority of reporters concentrate on Question Period and government announcements (with opposition reactions). Because most editors give priority to routine coverage, reporters rarely have time to dig behind the scenes for the real story of how decisions are made. As Anthony Westell has observed, "The question period. . .is almost a perfect media event. *Public personalities* come into *Conflict* over current *Controversies*, providing in one neat package the basic ingredients of a news story."[44] These stories meet the standard criteria of news, but provide little information about policy development or the philosophic differences between parties. The courts, regulatory agencies, and the inner workings of the civil service and Cabinet are rarely covered adequately.

The gallery often operates according to a kind of "herd instinct," partly due to reporters' lack of expertise and partly because editors complain if their staff coverage differs in significant ways from that provided by the wire services. In fact, some of the major news organizations—CP, SN, *The Globe and Mail*, *The Toronto Star*, *La Presse*, the CBC, and one or two others—do have specialists on such subjects as finance and economic affairs, energy policy, social issues, federal–provincial relations, and so on. However, they are few and they tend to lead the press herd in their areas of expertise. The major stories of the day are generally identified collectively and often given a common interpretation. This pattern, combined with the rather narrow ideological range represented by the major columnists, means that the diversity of perspectives needed for a healthy media system is often absent.

An important aspect of political reporting is the mutual dependence of reporters and their sources. Politicians need publicity to promote themselves and their programs, and reporters need information and quotes for their stories. Even the prime minister needs media attention to maintain his political popularity, which is an important resource when he deals with his Cabinet, negotiates with provincial premiers, or tries to persuade a private group to support government initiatives. The prime minister, on the other hand, as Ottawa's chief news maker, has considerable capacity to manage the news, by timing announcements and rewarding sympathetic journalists by granting interviews, for example. He can also bypass the gallery by requesting network television time. Other prominent political figures, including the premiers, Cabinet ministers, and opposition party leaders, have similar resources, but none can match the "clout" of the prime minister.[45] In all news management situations, the government has the advantage of being able to act, while opposition parties can only react or suggest. Governments often use the media to test public opinion by leaking proposals to a reporter who will value the "scoop." A positive public response often strengthens the position of those in government supporting the policy, while a negative reaction might kill it.[46]

The advent of the electronic Hansard in the House of Commons in October 1977 has reduced the dependence of radio and television reporters on direct access to the prime minister and other leading politicians. While such access is still sought for various reasons, reporters can now obtain clips for their stories from the audio and video tapes. Politicians can expect more media exposure, but except for the relatively few citizens who watch the proceedings on cable, the focus remains on Question Period. The advent of television in the House has increased the visibility of the opposition party leaders and critics, putting them on a more equal footing with the prime minister and Cabinet.

Recently, governments have turned to advocacy advertising to bypass the gallery. Using mainly television, governments have employed spot commercials to promote everything from energy conservation and physical fitness to national unity, constitutional reform, and free trade. An ancillary objective, it seems clear, is to improve the government's image at public expense. Such advertisements played a major role in the 1980 Quebec referendum campaign and were also used heavily by the Conservative government in the immediate pre-election period once it became apparent that a concerned electorate wanted more information about free trade. The line between government information and partisan propaganda is frequently hard to draw.

While some observers feel the gallery is credulous and easily manipulated, others feel that too many journalists have come to see themselves as commentators and critics rather than reporters, rendering judgments instead of reporting the arguments of the contending parties. One study of the 1984 campaign found that most of the time devoted to coverage of the two major party leaders (127 stories in all) on the CBC national news was taken up by reporters' providing description and commentary. Only 12 percent of the time was taken up by the leaders' speaking for themselves, a total of forty-two minutes over eight weeks.[47] Perhaps responding to this study, CBC's "The National" provided considerably more direct quotes during the 1988 campaign, but of course the "sound bites" remained relatively short.

Some see the automatic hostility to authority of many gallery members as an unjustified extension of the appropriate stance of scepticism; others say that politicians have given reporters much to be cynical about. Anthony Westell argues that the parliamentary system has an institutionalized opposition and does not need an adversarial press: "The central business of the press is to facilitate communication between the institutions which do the business of democratic society and the publics which are supposed to oversee them."[48] There is a concern that journalistic cynicism and emphasis on conflict create a sense of continuing crisis that alienates citizens from the political process. However, Marxist critics argue that the conflicts emphasized are not the significant conflicts in society and that the adversarial approach to government is superficial and personalized rather than aimed at the real issues of class conflict.

From a liberal democratic perspective, election coverage is particularly important. Modern campaigns depend upon extensive media coverage. Although many daily newspapers continue to endorse candidates and parties on their editorial pages, overt partisan bias in now rare. Nevertheless, reporters and editors, through their selection and presentation of news, clearly prime the electorate by shaping the images of party leaders, defining campaign issues, and influencing the tone of the coverage.

In many respects, campaigns are contests in which media attention is the prize. In both Canadian and American elections, the roles of "media handlers"—who manage relations between politicians and media—and "spin doctors"—who try to channel media coverage of leaders, events, and policies in favourable directions—have become more and more central to election campaigns. The increasingly overt activities of these new professionals underscores the preoccupation of parties with managing the media, especially during the critical weeks of an election campaign.[49]

The dominant role of television has become particularly evident in recent campaigns, primarily because party strategists believe that it is the best medium for reaching uncommitted voters. The party leaders' tours are tailored for television, with speeches written to produce a brief clip (usually three to twelve seconds) for the television news and cameras given the best vantage point at rallies. The commitment to "image politics" also shows up in the increasing use of television advertisements, mainly thirty- or sixty-second spots, with time to communicate symbols but not arguments. The bulk of the more than $12 million spent on the 1984 election was allocated to the purchase of television time.[50] In the early 1980s, the CBC introduced "The Journal" and its French equivalent, "Le Point," forty-minute public affairs shows that follow the national news. They are regarded as vital by party strategists and, at their best, are excellent national forums for debate on public issues.

The main consequence of television's dominant role is that style tends to overwhelm substance. Campaigns become contests of television performance, favouring some leaders over others on attributes that have little significance for capacity to govern. The emphasis placed on national leaders by the national media means that voters tend to see relatively little of local candidates or potential Cabinet ministers during campaigns. Liberal leader John Turner is a good example of a politician who was initially glorified by the media, becoming something of a political legend while he was out of public life (and the glare of media scrutiny), but whose weaknesses—probing stare, nervous cough, and brittle delivery— were magnified by television. It seems likely that his "image problem" was a major factor in his two electoral defeats. Former Conservative leader Joe Clark was also victimized by a media that would not tolerate a non-telegenic leader.[51] As Cocking has put it:

> The normal journalistic reaction is not to praise but to criticize. There is a tacit understanding among journalists that to write favorably about events or people is, if not perverse, at least gutless and certain to harm one's career. Criticisms, charges and accusations produce the most jolts on television news and the biggest headlines in the papers.[52]

In the end, the campaign presented in the media is a product of the interaction of media and parties. As long as the parties play by the media rules, focusing on the leaders and a few central issues and presenting their appeals in brief and dramatic fashion, they can set the campaign agenda.[53] Only a few of the major news organizations have made any real effort to get the leaders to address issues they might wish to ignore. The 1988 election was fought almost entirely on the issue of free trade, an agenda set largely by the parties, and one that had the effect of crowding out other issues of interest to significant numbers of Canadians.

The actual effect of media coverage on election outcomes remains a matter of controversy. While it seems clear that the media cannot deliberately swing elections, there is also evidence of significant effects. For example, though there was a consistent drift of editorial support away from the Liberals after 1972, the Trudeau government was returned to office in 1974 and 1980, when only two major dailies endorsed them. While the Mulroney Conservatives were being savaged by the media prior to the 1988 campaign, they were returned to office despite four years of almost unabated negative coverage of patronage, Cabinet-level scandals, and policy problems. On the other hand, it can be argued that they recovered popular support through a well-orchestrated media campaign in the months leading up to the election and during the campaign. Given the openness of many voters to change, it seems plausible to suggest that the agenda-setting and priming effects of the media do trigger voting decisions for a good number of citizens. While only a minority of voters will acknowledge the direct effects of the media on their vote choices, most will admit that they make their judgments of leaders and party platforms at least in part on the basis of information gleaned from the media. Indirect effects on party morale and fundraising are also important. In the 1988 campaign, the televised debates and subsequent election coverage helped John Turner to revive his chances, while the Conservative media and advertising strategy appeared to reverse the tide and give them a majority.[54]

THE POLITICAL SIGNIFICANCE OF MEDIA PATTERNS

Because the effects are often long term or obscured by other influences, media effects on individual attitudes and behaviour are frequently hard to trace, as we saw with voting. Nevertheless, most observers agree that the contents of the media do set the agenda for public discussion and influence the basic value system of society. The priorities of the media do tend to become over time the priorities of the public. These priorities are largely by-products of the quest of the media for audiences and profits. Conspiracy theories that attribute vast malevolent influence to the media through subliminal advertising and deliberate slanting of the news have had to give way to those that view the process as a form of social interaction. Media priorities emerge from the organizational needs and interests of the media and from their interaction with political parties, interest groups, advertisers, boards of directors, and government regulators, as well as audiences. The political bias that excludes radical criticism of the status quo is as much a function of the perceived limits of public tolerance as of the preferences of corporate owners. The relative absence of tough-minded investigative journalism can be explained more readily by reference to the unwillingness of publishers to spend the necessary funds and take the risk of libel suits than to corporate ideologies.[55]

As we have seen, there are certain systematic biases in our media system that may well have significant political effects. For reasons of both convenience and ideology, journalists prefer official sources and established images to more unconventional approaches. While it is true that effective mass communication is difficult without reference to widely known personalities and ideas, the resulting status quo orientation means that audiences are rarely asked to question society's basic assumptions. The media's focus on public rather than private sector abuses of power lends support to the dominant ideology of "welfare capitalism." These tendencies—found in entertainment programming as well as news and public affairs—probably promote political stability at the expense of social progress.

Other patterns, such as the weaknesses in communication across regional and linguistic lines, along with the stress on conflict and the personal side of politics, may well damage the fabric of Confederation. The denigration of political leaders and institutions in the quest for media jolts may hamper their capacity to cope with the strains in the system. The crowding out of Canadian images on television by popular American programming appears to be weakening our sense of ourselves. The scarcity of journalists with the genuine expertise to gain credibility with policy makers impoverishes public policy debate in Canada. While the individual level effects of these patterns are difficult to demonstrate, the larger effects seem clear enough. As we look ahead to the twenty-first century, we must consider the implications of new technologies and global concentration of ownership for Canadian identity and democracy. The simultaneous development of small-scale alternative media and vast international conglomerates presents us with an important set of choices, choices that will help to determine the nature of our political community.

NOTES

1. This an extensively revised and updated version of "The Mass Media and Politics: An Overview," which appeared in the second edition of this volume.
2. Leonard Kubas, et al., *Newspapers and Their Readers*, Royal Commission on Newspapers, research studies on the newspaper industry (Ottawa: Supply and Services Canada, 1981), vol. 1: 11–2. See also the *Report of the Task Force on Broadcasting Policy* (Ottawa: Supply and Services Canada, 1986), pp. 82–87, hereinafter cited as Caplan–Sauvageau Report, and Michael Adams and Jordan A. Levitin, "Media Bias as Viewed by the Canadian Public," in *Canadian Legislatures: 1987–88*, ed. Robert J. Fleming (Ottawa: Ampersand, 1988), p. 5.
3. Anthony Westell, *The New Society* (Toronto: McClelland and Stewart, 1977), p. 73.
4. A useful discussion of gatekeeping and the factors affecting it may be found in Walter C. Soderlund, Walter I. Romanow, E. Donald Briggs, and Ronald H. Wagenberg, *Media and Elections in Canada* (Toronto: Holt, Rinehart and Winston, 1984), pp. 31–35.
5. Coverage of the Meech Lake Accord by television news is an excellent example of that medium's tendency to focus on the clashes and human interest aspects of the story's main characters rather than the dry technical information necessary for citizens to assess the content

of the Accord. See David Taras, "Meech Lake and Television News," and Elly Alboim, "Inside the News Story: Meech Lake as Viewed by an Ottawa Bureau Chief," in *Meech Lake and Canada: Perspectives from the West*, ed. Roger Gibbins, et al. (Edmonton: Academic Printing and Publishing, 1988), pp. 219–46.

6. Todd Gitlin, *The Whole World is Watching* (Berkeley: University of California Press, 1980), p. 7.

7. Bernard Cohen, *The Press and Foreign Policy* (Princeton: Princeton University Press, 1963), p. 13.

8. Shanto Iyengar and Donald R. Kinder, *News that Matters: Television and American Opinion* (Chicago: University of Chicago Press, 1987), pp. 16, 112–14. The authors recruited more than one thousand respondents who were shown subtly altered versions of national television newscasts. In a series of rigorous experiments, their responses to different news formats were measured and compared. The work is considered a significant advance in research on media effects. For some Canadian evidence, see Frederick J. Fletcher, "Mass Media and Parliamentary Elections in Canada," *Legislative Studies Quarterly* 12, no. 3 (August 1987): 361–64.

9. George Gerbner, "Television: A New Religion?" *London Free Press*, 24 January 1981. For a more detailed account of Gerbner's views, see G. Gerbner and L. Gross, "The Scary World of TV's Heavy Viewers," *Psychology Today*, April 1976, pp. 41–89, and a series of articles in *Journal of Communication*.

10. Quoted in Richard V. Ericson, Patricia M. Baranek, and Janet B. L. Chan, *Visualizing Deviance: A Study of News Organization* (Toronto: University of Toronto Press, 1987), p. 51.

11. Adams and Levitin, "Media Bias as Viewed by the Canadian Public," pp. 10–11. See also "TV Is Most Believable Medium," *Marketing* 93, no. 7 (15 February 1988): 5.

12. Iyengar and Kinder, *News that Matters*, pp. 63, 114–33.

13. Ericson, et al., *Visualizing Deviance*, pp. 4–5.

14. John Westergaard, "Power, Class and the Media," in *Mass Communication and Society*, ed. James Curran, et al. (London: Edward Arnold, 1977), p. 97. Westergaard sets out this view to debunk it. For a more sympathetic treatment, see Fred S. Siebert, Theodore Peterson, and Wilbur Schramm, *Four Theories of the Press* (Urbana, Ill.: University of Illinois Press, 1956), pp. 39–103. For a recent examination of these theories in a Canadian context, see Ross A. Eaman, *The Media Society: Basic Issues and Controversies* (Toronto: Butterworths, 1987), pp. 63–90.

15. Ralph Miliband, quoted in Dennis McQuail, "The Influence and Effects of the Mass Media," in *Mass Communication and Society*, ed. Curran, p. 89. The general argument is taken from Wallace Clement,

The Canadian Corporate Elite: An Analysis of Economic Power (Toronto: McClelland and Stewart, 1975), pp. 270–86.

16. Clement, *The Canadian Corporate Elite*, pp. 325–43. The quotation is on p. 343.

17. This discussion of the development of the Canadian media draws on Paul Rutherford, *The Making of the Canadian Media* (Toronto: McGraw-Hill Ryerson, 1978), and W. A. Kesterton, *A History of Journalism in Canada* (Toronto: McClelland and Stewart, 1967). The quotation is from Rutherford, p. 1.

18. Arthur Siegel, *Politics and the Media in Canada* (Toronto: McGraw-Hill Ryerson, 1983), p. 194. See also Royal Commission on Newspapers, *Report* (Ottawa: Supply and Services Canada, 1981), pp. 119–33, hereinafter cited as Kent Commission. Criticized by the Kent Commission for its weak foreign coverage, CP increased its allocation for international coverage to $500,000, less than 2 percent of its total budget. Joseph Scanlon, "Canada Sees the World Through U.S. Eyes: A Case Study in Cultural Domination," *The Canadian Forum*, September 1974, pp. 34–39. A re-examination of the issue in 1983 came to a similar conclusion. Joseph Scanlon and Al Farrell, "No Matter How It Sounds or Looks, It's Probably Not Canadian," paper presented at the Conference on Media and Foreign Policy, University of Windsor, 29 October 1983. It must be noted that the CBC, Southam News (SN), and *The Globe and Mail* maintain a number of foreign correspondents of their own and devote significant resources to overseas coverage.

19. *Saturday Night* is now owned by Conrad Black's media conglomerate, Hollinger, Inc.

20. Frank Peers, *The Public Eye: Television and the Politics of Canadian Broadcasting* (Toronto: University of Toronto Press, 1979), p. 409. See also Martha Fletcher and Frederick J. Fletcher, "Communications and Confederation: Jurisdiction and Beyond," in *Canada Challenged: The Viability of Confederation*, ed. R. B. Byers and R. W. Reford (Toronto: Canadian Institute of International Affairs, 1979), pp. 171–72.

21. For details, see Rowland Lorimer and Jean McNulty, *Mass Communication in Canada* (Toronto: McClelland and Stewart, 1987), pp. 217–19 and 224–25.

22. For further discussion of these issues, see John Meisel, "Escaping Extinction: Cultural Defence of an Undefended Border," *Canadian Journal of Social and Political Theory* 10, no. 1–2 (1986): 20. See also Caplan–Sauvageau Report, Parts 1–5.

23. See the discussion in Lorimer and McNulty, *Mass Communication in Canada*, p. 273.

24. The major services were required to: (1) devote a minimum of 30

percent of total broadcast time to Canadian content, rising to 50 percent in later years; (2) allocate 50 percent of total revenues and 50 to 60 percent of total expenditures to acquisition of or investment in Canadian productions; (3) obtain certification from government officials for content claimed as Canadian. In addition, they were forbidden to show commercials or produce their own programs. Canadian Radio-television and Telecommunications Commission, "Statement by Chairman John Meisel on CRTC Decision 82-240 (Pay-Television), Ottawa, 18 March 1982. For details of the decision, see CRTC, "Decision 82-240," Ottawa, 18 March 1982. For a useful summary, see Udo Salewsky, "Pay TV, Canadian Style," *Cable Communications Magazine* 48, no. 4 (April 1982): 11–17.

25. The CRTC requires cable companies to carry some services (non-discretionary) and permits them to offer others as part of the basic service (for which subscribers must pay if they wish any cable service) or as optional to subscribers for an additional fee.

26. While anglophone Canadians spend about five hours per week watching CBC television, they still spend more than 75 percent of their viewing time watching non-Canadian programs. But then more than 75 percent of the programs available to Canadian households are non-Canadian. See Pierre Juneau, "A Report to Shareholders," notes for an address to the Broadcast Executives Society, Toronto, 18 January 1984. The demand for Canadian programs is discussed extensively in the Caplan–Sauvageau Report; see the summary on p. 691.

27. Caplan–Sauvageau Report, p. 81.

28. John Meisel, "Five Steps to Survival," speech at Conference on Mass Communication and Canadian Nationhood, York University, Toronto, 10 April 1981.

29. Caplan–Sauvageau Report, pp. 341 and 696.

30. Caplan–Sauvageau Report, p. 217.

31. Many of the relevant studies are summarized in Andre H. Caron and David E. Payne, "Media and Canadian Politics: General and Referendum Applications," paper presented at the Duke University Conference on Political Support in Canada: The Crisis Years, November 1980. On the Quebec press, see Dominique Clift, "French Journalism in Quebec: Solidarity on a Pedestal," in *Canadian Newspapers: The Inside Story*, ed. Walter Stewart (Edmonton: Hurtig, 1980), pp. 205–18. See also Lysiane Gagnon, "Journalism and Ideologies in Quebec," and Florian Sauvageau, "French-speaking Journalists on Journalism," in *The Journalists*, Royal Commission on Newspapers, research studies on the newspaper industry (Ottawa: Supply and Services Canada, 1981), vol. 2: 19–52. Caplan–Sauvageau Report, pp. 205 and 207. The task force found that Quebec, with one-tenth the population, produces more programs than France.

32. See Kent Commission, pp. 1–14 and 87–103, and Siegel, *Politics and the Media in Canada*, pp. 110–24.

33. Alexander Bruce, "Lords of the Atlantic," *The Globe and Mail*, 21 February 1987, pp. D1–2. See also Alden Nowlan, "What about the Irvings?" in *Canadian Newspapers: The Inside Story*, ed. Stewart, pp. 63–72.

34. For discussions of "Thomsonization," see Frederick J. Fletcher, *The Newspaper and Public Affairs*, Royal Commission on Newspapers, research studies on the newspaper industry (Ottawa: Supply and Services Canada, 1981), vol. 7: 36–40; Eaman, *The Media Society*, pp. 104–5; Stewart, *Canadian Newspapers: The Inside Story*, pp. 17–18.

35. For more details, see Fletcher, *The Newspaper and Public Affairs*, ch. 1; Kent Commission, chs. 1 and 3.

36. See Kent Commission, pp. 57–60. The charges against Southam and Thomson were dismissed on 28 October and 9 December in judgments handed down by Mr. Justice William Anderson of the Supreme Court of Ontario.

37. Murray Campbell, "Requiem for the Kent Report," *The Globe and Mail*, 15 November 1984, p. 9. For a summary of industry response, see Donald C. Wallace, "The Kent Commission: The Fourth Estate Under Attack," in *Canadian Annual Review, 1981*, ed. R. B. Byers (Toronto: University of Toronto Press, 1982).

38. See E. R. Black, *Politics and the News* (Toronto: Butterworths, 1982), pp. 54–56 and 140–45, for a penetrating discussion of these issues. One observer has suggested that there is an implicit agreement between reformist journalists and generally conservative publishers that newspapers may take a reformist stance on social issues as long as economic matters are treated conservatively. Conrad Winn, "Mass Communication," in *Political Parties in Canada*, ed. C. Winn and J. McMenemy (Toronto: McGraw-Hill Ryerson, 1976), p. 132.

39. For example, in 1982, a survey of the Ottawa press gallery found that 37 percent felt closest to the NDP, compared to 17 percent who cited the Liberals and 11 percent the Conservatives. Peter Desbarats, "Eye on the Media," *The Financial Post*, 13 July 1985, p. 7, and "Media Influence on the Political Process," in *Canadian Legislatures: 1987–1988*, ed. Fleming, p. 20.

40. Ericson, et al., *Visualizing Deviance*, p. 38.

41. Nowlan, "What about the Irvings?" p. 68.

42. Special Senate Committee on the Mass Media, *The Uncertain Mirror*, vol. 1 of the *Report* (Ottawa: Queen's Printer, 1970), p. 87. For a recent description of newsroom dynamics and the values and socialization of reporters, see Ericson, et al., *Visualizing Deviance*.

43. For example, when the Minister of Finance makes his budget speech, reporters are locked up with advance copies and given full briefings

by government officials in an attempt to improve the quality of reporting.

44. Anthony Westell, "Reporting the Nation's Business," in *Journalism, Communication and the Law*, ed. Stuart Adam (Toronto: Prentice-Hall, 1976), p. 63.
45. See Frederick J. Fletcher, "The Prime Minister as Public Persuader," in *Apex of Power*, 2nd ed., ed. Thomas A. Hockin (Toronto: Prentice-Hall, 1977), pp. 86–111, and David Taras, "The Prime Minister and the Press," in *Prime Ministers and Premiers* (Toronto: Prentice-Hall, 1988), ch. 9.
46. A typical "trial balloon" was released in Ontario in 1979 when a Cabinet minister let it be known that the government was considering allowing the sale of beer in the province's ball parks. Vociferous opposition from temperance groups and residents living near the parks led to the proposal's withdrawal, but it was later proceeded with when polls showed widespread support.
47. Mary Anne Comber and Robert S. Mayne, *The Newsmongers: How the Media Distort the Political News* (Toronto: McClelland and Stewart, 1986), p. 92. The reliability of this study is difficult to assess because not enough details on methodology are given.
48. A. Westell, "The Press: Adversary or Channel of Communication," in *Parliament, Policy and Representation*, ed. Harold D. Clarke, et al. (Toronto: Metheun, 1980), p. 49.
49. These media managers even have their own professional journal, *Campaigns and Elections*, published in Washington, D.C., in which they exchange trade secrets.
50. F. J. Fletcher, "The Media and the 1984 Landslide," in *Canada at the Polls, 1984: A Study of the Federal General Elections* (Durham, N.C.: Duke University Press for AEI, 1988), pp. 163–64.
51. For an overview of media treatment of recent prime ministers, see Taras, "The Prime Minister and the Press," and Comber and Mayne, *The Newsmongers* pp. 43–53.
52. Clive Cocking, *Following the Leaders: A Media Watcher's Diary of Campaign '79* (Toronto: Doubleday, 1980), p. 111.
53. Fletcher, "Mass Media and Parliamentary Electronics in Canada," pp. 341–72.
54. Fred Fletcher and Bob Everett, "Television and the 1988 Campaign: Did It Make a Difference," *Scan*, January 1988. See also *Maclean's*, 8 December 1988. For a general perspective on voting in Canada, see Harold D. Clarke, Jane Jenson, Lawrence LeDuc, and Jon H. Pammett, *Absent Mandate: The Politics of Discontent in Canada* (Toronto: Gage, 1984), especially pp. 84–89 and 117–23.
55. The proposition that the absence of hard-hitting (and costly) investigative journalism is more a reflection of tight editorial budgets than

political timidity as such is supported by a wide range of anecdotal evidence. See "No Virginia, There is no Lou Grant," in *Canadian Newspapers: The Inside Story*, ed. Stewart, pp. 17–18. In the end, the entire FP news service was closed down. See also Ericson, et al., *Visualizing Deviance*. There are, of course, notable exceptions, such as the 1988 series of stories in *The Globe and Mail* on land developers and development issues in communities surrounding Toronto, which consumed more than a year and cost more than $200,000. Others could be cited.

FURTHER READINGS

Audley, Paul. *Canada's Cultural Industries: Broadcasting, Publishing, Records and Film*. Toronto; Lorimer, 1983.

Black, Edwin R. *Politics and the News*. Toronto: Butterworths, 1982.

Eaman, Ross A. *The Media Society: Basic Issues and Controversies*. Toronto: Butterworths, 1987.

Ericson, Richard V., Patricia M. Baranek, and Janet B. L. Chan. *Visualizing Deviance: A Study of News Organization*. Toronto: University of Toronto Press, 1987. This is the first of three volumes on the media and social order in Canada.

Fletcher, Frederick J. "Mass Media and Parliamentary Elections in Canada." *Legislative Studies Quarterly* 12, no. 3 (August 1987): 341–72.

Lorimer, Rowland, and Jean McNulty. *Mass Communication in Canada*. Toronto: McClelland and Stewart, 1987.

Lorimer, Rowland, and Donald Wilson, eds. *Communication Canada: Issues in Broadcasting and New Technologies*. Toronto: Kagan and Woo, 1988.

Report of the Task Force on Broadcasting Policy. Ottawa: Supply and Services Canada, 1986.

Royal Commission on Newspapers (Kent Commission). Ottawa: Supply and Services Canada, 1981.

Rutherford, Paul. *The Making of the Canadian Media*. Toronto: McGraw-Hill Ryerson, 1978.

Siegel, Arthur. *Politics and the Media in Canada*. Toronto: McGraw-Hill Ryerson, 1983.

Singer, Benjamin D., ed. *Communications in Canadian Society*. Toronto: Addison-Wesley, 1983.

Soderlund, Walter C., Walter I. Romanow, E. Donald Briggs, and Ronald H. Wagenberg. *Media and Elections in Canada*. Toronto: Holt, Rinehart and Winston, 1984.

PART 3

CANADA'S POLITICAL STRUCTURES

13

The Party System

JANINE BRODIE AND JANE JENSON

Canada's federal party system provides a somewhat perplexing case for students of politics in liberal democracies. Some sociological theory, drawing on Western European experiences, claims that changes in social structure induced by urbanization and industrialization eroded the traditional electoral cleavages of religion, language, and region and created the politics of class. In so-called "modernized" party systems, a class cleavage differentiates the electoral support of the parties and contributes to policy differences. From this perspective, the Canadian federal party system does not appear to have "modernized." Instead, religion, language, and especially region continue to differentiate the Canadian electorate's support for political parties much more than class does. Studies of federal voting behaviour consistently depict an electorate that does not divide its support for political parties according to occupational position or even according to the location that voters think they occupy in a status ranking. Both major parties, moreover, depict themselves as guardians of the "national interest," thereby denying the importance of class distinctions.

This is not to say, however, that Canadian electoral politics has not witnessed at least some of the symptoms of a modernizing party system. There have been social democratic or socialist parties active in the federal party system, yet all these parties, including the New Democratic Party (NDP), have never enjoyed anything near a majority of the support of their claimed constituency, the Canadian working class. Therefore, the federal party system remains an anomaly, a party system that has never passed through a stage of class-divided electoral politics.

PARTY AND CLASS IN CANADA

There are several popular explanations for the absence of pervasive class-based voting in federal politics. Following the language of politics used by the major federal parties themselves, this absence has been attributed, by different authors, to the social diversity of Canada resulting both from the existence of two separate cultures within a single state and from distinct regional variations in economic and political orientations, which are reinforced by the institutions of federalism. A second theme in the literature then stresses the need for consensus amid diversity. This consensual view argues the irrelevancy of class conflict in a country with rich resources and opportunities. These themes have penetrated deeply into the country's political consciousness, have been reinforced in election after election, and have served as substitutes for a class-based understanding of politics.

These popular explanations also concur that the Liberals and Conservatives, and to a lesser extent the NDP, act as "brokers," offering the electorate an aggregation and accommodation of the myriad of conflicting interests that inevitably arise in any society. The parties' primary concern, according to this analysis, is to accommodate diverse interests sufficiently to build an electoral coalition large enough to capture power. Instead of organizing the electorate around class interests, the major parties are said to engage in politics of moderation that minimizes differences and restrains divisive tendencies. It is further argued that a beneficial consequence of such brokerage parties is that they can knit together diverse interests in a polity that is otherwise weakly integrated.

As appealing as these theses may be, there are a number of factors that challenge their validity as explanations for the absence of class voting in Canada. If, for example, the major parties are solely concerned with accommodating social conflicts, then the federal party system is witness to their failures. For decades, large regionally based third parties occupied their own space on the partisan landscape, citing the neglect and biases of the supposedly brokerage parties as their reason for entering the electoral fray. Their existence suggests that not all interests were equally accommodated by the two major parties. Moreover, there is much evidence to suggest that brokerage parties are themselves class-based organizations. Their major sources of campaign financing, their patterns of recruitment of members and candidates, and their policy orientations all suggest that the Liberals and Progressive Conservatives have a decidedly status quo and frankly pro-capitalist bent. Yet, paradoxically, these parties find much of their electoral support among workers. Thus, we must return to the question of why there is so little evidence of class-based voting in Canada's federal party system.

In addressing this question we should remember that analyses of the party system as a brokerage one are popular because they do rather effectively *describe* how parties have behaved in federal elections. The Liberals and Progressive Conservatives have had similar platforms and have changed them from election to election. The Liberals and Tories often have abandoned promises once the exigencies of office seemed to demand something else, and they have not emphasized ideological differences in their perennial search to construct a winning coalition. Although sometimes these parties have momentarily developed quite coherent and even principled positions, such constructions have always been fragile and easily reversed when conditions changed.

Nevertheless, even if parties are part of an ongoing brokerage system, we must still ask what reproduces this partisan formation. We must explain *why* parties have followed a brokerage strategy and *why* the party system has taken a brokerage form. In order to do this we must explore theoretically and historically the links between social relations and politics in capitalist societies. In doing this, it is important from the outset to reject any notion that there is a necessary and easy link between the form of social relations in any country and its politics. Too often political sociologists have assumed that the stage of development of a particular society determined its partisan politics. They have argued that industrialization was followed by the emergence of class-based parties in which the line of demarcation in the electorate ran between those who, according to the laws of the economy, controlled the production process and those who, according to the laws of liberal democracy, could gain some political control over production and distribution of profit. A corollary of this argument was that politics in advanced capitalist societies would focus primarily on questions of control over production, distribution, and consumption. It is, obviously, this particular organization of partisan relations that is missing in Canada.

Yet, such a deterministic analysis is far too simplistic. An examination of the last hundred years of the history of industrial capitalism leads to the following perspective: while capitalism has proceeded in all countries in similar—although not always exactly the same—directions toward centralization, the growth of large monopolistic corporations, and an increase in state intervention in the economy, the political expression of class conflict has varied in important ways. Such variation suggests that it is necessary to entertain the possibility that political parties—as organizations that pursue strategic goals—have a crucial effect on whether class conflict is mobilized in party politics.

If the political formation of classes is not an automatic consequence of social conditions, we must ask what role parties themselves play in shaping class identities. Through their everyday actions and pronouncements, all parties in liberal democracies integrate individuals into an ongoing system of partisan relations. In this process of integration, parties provide voters with a *definition of politics*. In other words, political parties help to *shape the interpretation of which aspects of social relations should be considered political, how politics should be conducted, what the boundaries of political discussion most properly may be, and which kinds of conflicts can be resolved through the political process.* From the vast array of tensions, differences, and inequalities characteristic of any society, parties treat only some as alternatives in the electoral process and thereby influence how the electorate will divide against itself. This activity of parties is profoundly important because before electoral cleavages come into being, a definition of what is political must exist. Whether an issue is considered to be a religious, economic, private, or political question is set by this definition. Matters that do not achieve the status of "worthy of partisan debate" will remain invisible and absent from the political realm.

From this perspective we can say, then, that while elections are events of conflict and competition, the substance of electoral politics is not automatically given. For example, politics may be described as the expression of conflict between classes or between ethnic groups or as the aggregation of individual preferences. Economic conditions, such as the level of industrialization, set parameters around the range of the possible in any society, but they can never guarantee that particular classes will be politically active. Subordinate classes will not spontaneously recognize the political implications of their disadvantaged location in capitalist relations of production and vote according to their class position. Members of particular occupational sectors in capitalist society—whether they are farmers, blue-collar workers or office workers—do not and will not act cohesively as a class until they become aware that they are members of a class. The nurturing of this awareness demands, as a prerequisite, ideological and organizational activity. Classes as active and self-conscious social actors must be *created*, and in turn the extent to which they live politically as classes is largely the extent to which they behave as classes in elections.

At a very minimum, then, class-based voting must be preceded by the development of a class-based organization that challenges existing definitions of politics and that interprets social and political relations in non-class terms. If the existence, characteristics, and partisan implications of class conflict are exposed by the activities of a well-developed trade union movement or a powerful and influential party of the left, then there will be evidence, at the level of voting, of class-based politics. Without these prior conditions, class cleavages will be submerged, distorted, and rarely visible in voting behaviour.

Since the late nineteenth century, socialist parties have existed that have defined politics as the expression of conflict between classes and not as neutral aggregations of individual or group preferences. They have precipitated a conflict over definitions of politics as well as governmental policies. The existence of such a debate over definitions means that voters have been offered alternative bases for electoral alignment, and some of these threaten the very existence of one or more of the bourgeois parties. Not surprisingly, then, the threatened parties struggle hard to maintain and re-create a definition of politics that denies the centrality of class differences and relations in capitalist systems. Time and again, confronted with a class-based definition of politics advanced by socialist parties, bourgeois parties have retorted that this definition is inappropriate and that politics is really about race or religion, and moreover that politics is not about conflict at all but about finding consensus so that the capitalist system can be managed successfully to benefit all.

If alternative ways of organizing the electorate are possible under the same economic conditions, and the nature of this organization affects the manner in which classes and individuals behave in electoral politics, we begin to see a way of unravelling the perplexity of the Canadian party system. The extent to which capitalist relations of production are debated politically depends in large part on how successfully either socialist or bourgeois parties organize the electorate behind their respective points of view. If politics is defined as conflict between language groups, it is more difficult to unite for partisan actions members of the same class who have different linguistic backgrounds. In other words, some political cleavages are likely to be incompatible with others, as the dominance of one cleavage generally inhibits the growth of others. By examining this contest over the definition of politics, it is possible to arrive at a better understanding of the background of the contemporary Canadian party system, which is divided along lines of language and region.

ORIGINS OF THE FEDERAL PARTY SYSTEM

In the early years of Confederation, Canada did not have a fully operative two-party system. For the first forty years, the federal government engaged in a complex process of nation building around the development strategy known as the National Policy, seeking three goals. First was the promotion of railway construction from the centre to the peripheries. Railways linking all parts of the country would transport western products to the East and vice versa. The second goal was to foster immigration to the West, expanding the number of agricultural exporters and providing an internal market for eastern manufactured goods. Finally, the National Policy imposed tariffs on imported goods, thereby protecting the Canadian manufacturing sector, concentrated in the central provinces, from foreign, especially American, competition.

These aspects of the National Policy formed an integrated and mutually reinforcing whole. As the policy unfolded, however, it induced class-based tensions and the mobilization of partisan opposition that persists to the present day. In order to trace the growth of this opposition, it is necessary to understand the ways in which the party system organized relations between classes in the post-1867 years, by examining the definitions of politics, the kind of political agenda, and the conflict that emerged.

The bourgeoisie was the moving force behind the establishment of the Canadian state, and this class was quite united in its support for the goals of the National Policy. In fact, there was little ground for partisan competition among manufacturing, merchant, and financial interests. All vigorously pursued in both their business and political dealings a strategy of nation building and railway building that facilitated further exploitation of an export-orientated, resource-extracting, staple-based economy. Westward expansion and the marketing of wheat were profitable to merchants and railway investors; tariffs encouraged expansion in the manufacturing sector; and economic growth, in part stimulated by immigration, promised good returns for all, but especially for the financial community. In the early years of Confederation, these interests found their political home in the Conservative Party of Sir John A. Macdonald, which held power for more than two decades.

There were isolated pockets of opposition to this particular strategy of economic development, but these disparate forces were unable to forge a cohesive partisan alliance against the "nation-building" Conservatives. In fact, it was not until the 1890s that the Liberal Party managed to build a national party capable of competing on an equal footing with the Conservatives. It did this, however, not by contesting the Conservatives' vision of the national dream, but rather by embracing it and by emphasizing religious and linguistic differences within the electorate.

The transfer of the federal government in 1896 from the remnants of Macdonald's coalition to Laurier's Liberals is a watershed in Canadian partisan history. It marks the entrenchment of a definition of politics that has enabled the Liberal Party to dominate federal politics for most of the twentieth century. It was never obvious in the first elections after Confederation what the substance of electoral conflict would be—whether class, language, religion, or some other social differences would characterize the support base of the federal parties. The Conservatives, as nation builders, had a clear position to advance, so the Liberals had to find a viable way of distinguishing themselves from their competitors. In other words, they had to define and create their electorate. Eventually, the Liberal Party came to realize the electoral potential of religious and linguistic allegiances as a basis for electoral cleavage.

Macdonald had recognized the need to defuse differences between English and French by forging strong links with the leadership of Quebec, through George-Étienne Cartier, and with the hierarchy of the Roman Catholic Church. In terms of its electoral support, then, the original Conservative Party was an amalgam of Protestant and Catholic, English and French. But by 1896 the party was unable to overcome the tensions that had erupted in its own ranks and that were a boon to the Liberals searching for an electoral base. Capitalizing on the hanging of Louis Riel, conflict over religious schools in the West, and increasingly vocal anti-French and anti-Catholic rhetoric in Ontario, the Liberals finally identified their issue, created their electorate, and formed a competitive national party. In essence, they presented themselves as the only party still able to represent Quebec and thus guarantee the Confederation project.

The emergence of a bicultural definition of politics had a profound influence on subsequent patterns in the federal party system. By the 1890s the two federal parties agreed about the strategy of economic development implied by the National Policy, so the same bourgeois interests that had supported Macdonald's Conservatives easily could— and did—shift their allegiance to the Liberal Party. They did this not because of any particular identification with the religious or language controversies of those years, but because the Conservatives had lost their electoral majority and, thus, their ability to govern.

This particular form of partisan conflict also emerged partially as a result of an early decision on the part of Canada's trade unions, following the example of their American co-unionists, not to sponsor a workers' party. By this decision they withdrew from the process of "creating" a working class at the level of electoral politics. In direct consequence, little expression of class conflict emerged in federal campaigns, at least not until the western farmers mobilized to contest the costs of the National Policy and the bourgeois interests that sponsored it.

When the two major parties first looked westward to the new provinces, there was ample reason to believe that a two-party system revolving around bicultural politics might be successfully transplanted there. A number of factors, however, made this transfer less than perfect. First, the eastern-based definition of "the political," emphasizing nation building and the dual religious and linguistic composition of the new country, was largely out of tune with the western social and economic fabric. More important, the western electorate—especially farmers—grew increasingly disaffected with the National Policy embraced by both parties.

Western farmers had only to compare the prices of their farm machinery and other products with the prices paid by their neighbours in the American Midwest to realize that a large portion of the burden of tariffs (designed to encourage Canadian manufacturing by raising prices of imported goods) fell on them. Transportation policy was also a source of mounting irritation. The federal government permitted railways to charge higher rates on the less-competitive western lines and lower ones in the East where competition from other modes of transportation seemed to make them an economic necessity. The level and characteristics of tariffs and freight rates became burning political questions as western farmers began to press the two federal parties for adjustment of both.

Additional explanatory factors must be added to help us understand how this potential for protest was mobilized. The complaints of the farmers had to be transformed into partisan differences, either within the existing two-party system or in the form of a separate party devoted to advancing the needs of farmers as a class. Farmers' organizations were crucial centres for both educating and organizing western discontent against the economic development strategies of the federal government. These farmers' organizations provided the foundation for opposition to the prevailing development strategy, an opposition that did not break along language and religious lines. The British-born, the anglophone Canadian, the German, and the Eastern European farmers in unison criticized the eastern-based political parties for their preoccupation with cultural issues to the exclusion of western economic grievances. Nevertheless, it was not until 1921 that these independent commodity producers, led by farmers' organizations, actually challenged the dominant cultural definition of politics by creating their own party.

The Progressive Party is significant in the history of Canadian partisan relations because it was a class party with a class-based definition of politics challenging the consensual definition that had dominated federal campaigns to that point. Yet, the form of class-based politics that emerged was different from that predicted by the deterministic sociological theories described above. Canadian development, structured as it was by the National Policy, encouraged the expansion of two subordinate classes—industrial workers, primarily concentrated in the centre, and farmers in the West. It was the latter group that first mobilized against the bourgeois parties and their definition of the political. It was, in other words, a class conflict between forms of property rather than between capitalists and workers; but class conflict it was, and it threatened the very basis of electoral support of both major parties.

The Progressives' critique put the other two parties on the defensive and they attacked the new party's conception of politics and its class biases. Prime Minister Arthur Meighen, for example, described the Progressives as a misinformed class party that threatened to upset the fiscal balance of the country. The new leader of the Liberals, William Lyon Mackenzie King, urged voters not to invite the awful unknown by experimenting with a discourse of class in matters of government. The western electorate and rural Ontario in 1921, however, remained unconvinced by these warnings. The Progressives won sixty-five seats, thirty-seven of them in the West. The Conservatives did not win any seats in Manitoba, Saskatchewan, or Alberta, while the Liberals won only two. The prairie provinces, it seems, had rejected almost unanimously the politics of biculturalism and class consensus.

Perhaps because of their relatively short life and because the Ontario electorate soon returned to the two-party fold, the Progressives have often been viewed as an isolated episode, a short-term regional deviation from the two-party system. Yet, the Progressive experience was of fundamental importance in shaping the later federal party system, which had been fractured regionally into two distinct components—one in the East revolving around the politics of language and religion and one in the West informed by the politics of class. After 1921 the Liberals and Conservatives would never be able to re-establish fully their preferred definition of politics.

The experience of the Progressives left two other distinct legacies. First, the success of the party in 1921 reflected the mobilizational potential of a class-based definition of politics, by an actor with strong organizational resources. The Progressives claimed that the major parties' insistence that they represented the "national interest" was only a convenient myth that really protected and advanced the interests and needs of eastern capital, often at the expense of farmers and workers. In this way, the Progressives offered a redefinition of federal politics. The second legacy of the Progressive experience was that a space was opened for class-based politics in the federal party system. During the 1930s the Co-operative Commonwealth Federation (CCF) filled this space. One of the curious anomalies of Canadian politics is that the most enduring party of the left emerged with support drawn from farmers located in an economic hinterland rather than from urban workers. While the CCF has its own organizational and ideological history, its success in the prairie provinces cannot be isolated from the Progressive experiment, whose legacy was an electorate disengaged by cultural politics and open to the mobilizational efforts of a party utilizing a discourse of class politics.

THE CONTEMPORARY PARTY SYSTEM

During the late 1930s and the war years, it appeared as if the CCF might successfully challenge, with the politics of class, the two major parties and their definition of politics. Some forty years later, however, it is apparent that neither the CCF nor its successor, the NDP, has succeeded in this goal. The Liberal Party, kept afloat by the politics of language, has won most of the federal elections since the Second World War, and it has been the Progressive Conservative Party rather than the CCF/NDP that has won the rest. Confounded by a seemingly insurmountable electoral arithmetic, the CCF first moderated its policies, later forged an organizational alliance with the trade union movement, and finally changed its name and formal structure in 1961 by reconstituting itself as the New Democratic Party. Each strategy was designed to enhance the electoral fortunes of social democracy in Canada. Yet, rather than expanding the space for class politics, they tended to close it, leaving the NDP today relatively weak and uncertain about its definition of the political.

The reorientation of the NDP's socialism began during the Second World War when the party cautiously redefined its nationalization policy goals so as to avoid alienating potential voters. This strategy of moderation accelerated until, in 1956, the party adopted a new statement of principles, the Winnipeg Declaration, which provided the theoretical foundation for the NDP. An essential element of the NDP's moderation was its view of the state's role in social change. Departing from its earlier and more radical advocacy of state ownership of key sectors of the economy (in order to guarantee that production would reflect the public interest), the party increasingly proposed only Keynesian economic solutions. It promised to pursue anti-cyclical policies to stabilize the economy and maintain full employment as well as to provide a comprehensive net of social programs to improve the lives of the disadvantaged. The Liberals and Conservatives, as did most bourgeois parties in other countries in the post-war years, also promised most of the same policies. The CCF/NDP, therefore, did not represent a position sufficiently different from either the Liberals or the Progressive Conservatives to allow the electorate to distinguish its policies from what the other parties were offering.

The CCF's, and later the NDP's, failure to impose a new definition of politics following from a distinctive strategy meant that the party did not constitute a clear alternative for the voters. With its liberal view of a basically neutral state, the NDP had only a single argument to rally support behind it—vote NDP for more honest and fair government. In consequence, the NDP had few policy alternatives to propose once full employment and investment policies came into conflict with each other. When the continued economic growth on which these policies were premised grew more and more difficult to achieve, the NDP was as confounded as the other parties. It moved from "more Keynesianism" to an "industrial policy" to state-directed "investment programs," but none of these presentations appeared credible to the voters of the 1970s and 1980s. It found itself competing with the two bourgeois parties, especially the Liberals, more or less on their terms.

A second factor accounting for the failure of the NDP to inject a viable alternative definition of politics into the federal party system followed from the strategic decision to construct a particular kind of organizational base for the party. In the 1950s the CCF thought that its decline could be halted only if it followed the example of the British Labour Party and constructed a formal organizational link with the trade union movement. Together with the newly formed Canadian Labour Congress (CLC), the CCF created a new social democratic party, the NDP, in 1961. The anticipated surge of electoral support toward the NDP from Canadian workers did not materialize, however. Overall, the union links with the party remained more formal and financial than directed toward mobilization of the union membership in support of the NDP. The new party was largely a marriage of notables—designed by the leadership of the old CCF and the new CLC. Therefore, the NDP did not replicate the successes the British

Labour Party enjoyed after the Second World War. The obsession with bringing about union affiliation that dominated the CCF in the 1950s also meant that the new party accepted the union movement as it was— without political class consciousness, without a history of struggle for socialism, and without partisan experience. This meant that the CCF/NDP felt compelled to moderate its program so as to gain the support of union leaders who, in turn, recognized the conservatism of their rank and file or who were politically conservative themselves.

What consequences did this moderation in response to the union movement of the 1950s have for the NDP? With the Liberal Party actively implementing a social program, NDP "moderation" meant more of the same. However, the Liberals were a major party, while the NDP was the newcomer. Therefore, there was little reason to expect union members to support the NDP when they could have almost the same thing with the Liberals. As such, the problem of building a strong and effective party did not go away, and the experience of the NDP since the early 1960s has been one of almost constant internal party conflict over economic and electoral strategy. These conflicts reflect the mobilization of criticism by NDP members who reject their party's moderation, criticize its focus on winning parliamentary office as *the* major goal, and regret its inability to react satisfactorily to the new conditions that the Canadian economy faces and that have led the other two parties to respond with neo-liberal retrenchment of the welfare state and continentalism.

The first of these internal conflicts came in the late 1960s, as the Waffle wing emerged within the NDP to propose a vision of Canada's future based on the fundamental importance of an autonomous and, therefore, less continentalist economic development strategy. But in addition, the Waffle advocated more participatory politics and less electoralism and parliamentarism. It promoted, in other words, a more radical definition of politics in which party actions extended well beyond trying to win elections and, indeed, paid attention to class formation. The NDP expelled the Waffle in the early 1970s, as unionists within the party realized that the Waffle's nationalistic enthusiasms might extend to encouraging Canadian unions to break away from international ones. This was too much of a threat to the organizational integrity of the union movement, and its leaders weighed in on the side of others within the NDP who rejected the Waffle's vision of the world.

It is somewhat ironic, then, that by the late 1970s and 1980s, trade union leaders were in the forefront of criticisms of the NDP's response to economic crisis. As politics in most industrialized countries turned away from the Keynesianism and welfare state politics that dominated the first twenty-five years after 1945, the NDP struggled to develop and offer an industrial strategy for Canada that would prevent it from being swallowed by the continuing move toward continentalism. The task was not easy for the NDP, any more than it was for the other social democratic parties of the advanced industrial world, which also confronted fundamental economic and political restructuring. But because electoralism continued to dominate the party's strategy, the discovery that Ed Broadbent was, throughout the 1980s, the most popular of the party leaders meant that internal policy confusion often translated into disjointed discussions of policy alternatives or even of relative silence on the major economic and social questions of the day. The NDP often offered "Ed" to the electorate in place of a strong economic policy package, hoping that in that way that it would not "frighten" the voters and its electoral fortunes would improve.

Union leaders and rank-and-file members were vocal participants in policy discussion inside the NDP pressing for a coherent alternative development strategy. Nevertheless, the majority of the NDP remained drawn to the elusive promise of electoral success "if only" the right appeal could be found. Thus, as federal politics in the late 1980s became increasingly conflictual, the NDP increased its popular support in the interelection periods and then suffered losses. Throughout these years, however, the NDP eschewed a strategy that might have contributed to the construction of a class-based coalition and contributed instead to the sustenance of brokerage politics based on populist themes. The NDP presented itself as the only "honest broker" in a brokerage party system shaken by deceit and corruption, and as the only alternative to the "Bay Street" orientations of the two major parties. Playing the brokerage game was not without costs, however. Without the stable anchors of partisan loyalty based on differences among the parties, the Canadian electorate remained volatile, easily swayed by appeals of leadership at one moment and divided by regional or national loyalties the next.

In this way, brokerage politics with a populist tinge strained and weakened the NDP's ties with organized labour and other progressive forces, because the NDP's populism meant that the labour movement had no privileged position in party doctrine or as a constituency. As a result, in the popular mobilizations around the patriation of the constitution in the early 1980s and the free trade debate in the last years of the decade, individual unions and the CLC often found more sympathetic allies in representatives of other social movements—such as the women's movement or the nationalist movement—or in organizations opposed to economic restructuring via the free trade agreement than it did in the NDP.

When the NDP did not mobilize subordinate classes behind a new definition of the political, federal elections continued to revolve around the politics of religion and culture. For most of the history of the federal party system there has been space for only one party of "the national interest" and only one strategy of national development. The Liberals claimed that space in the post-war years through a winning combination of economic and cultural politics. They gained a partisan advantage with their wartime recognition that Keynesian demand-management techniques and specific social programs could increase consumption and stabilize capital accumulation, thereby avoiding a recurrence of the 1930s Great Depression. To this welfare state, the Liberals added intensified continentalism, soliciting foreign investment in both the manufacturing and resource sectors.

For the most part the Tories accepted the same positions, although they suffered immensely as the Liberals played more and more successfully to the politics of culture. The result was that the Progressive Conservative Party throughout the first three post-war decades sought to create its own electoral space, but was defeated by Liberal bloc support from Quebec. Moreover, the continuing search for a viable electoral strategy was a constant source of tension for the Tories, a tension that was perhaps best exhibited in their decision in the 1940s to change the party's name. Ironically, while the choice—Progressive Conservative—was obviously contradictory according to common ideological usage, it did in fact offer a relatively correct representation of the tension at the heart of the party. While there was widespread support for the development strategy defined by the Liberals, lack of electoral success sometimes allowed populist positions, which promised victory, momentarily to take over the party.

Therefore, at times the Progressive Conservatives have used a populist appeal designed to mobilize the electorate awakened by the Progressives in the 1920s and suffering from the continuing inequities produced by the post-war development strategy. John Diefenbaker's time as leader represents a major essay into this strategy, but his subsequent troubles with Canadian and American business, the bureaucracy, and his own party members testify to the difficulties of attempting to redesign a bourgeois party by inserting strands of critical populism. Something different was needed, then, and the opportunity for the Progressive Conservatives came with the shocks sustained by the post-war development strategy after 1973 and especially in the 1980s.

From the end of the war until the early 1970s the three-pronged strategy of a growing welfare state, Keynesian macro-economic management, and continental economic integration continued to show promise. There were, however, a few disturbing signs on the horizon that soon became chronic problems. Relative productivity rates were slowing; exports formed a larger proportion of the Gross National Product than in other countries; and unemployment rates were rising slowly but perceptibly. These negative economic indicators were the symptom of a contradiction at the heart of post-war economic strategies. Keynesian politics had been based on the assumption of expansion, allowing capital accumulation to go forward at the same time as worker's wages rose and state-organized social programs grew. Without expansion, the edifice trembled and threatened to tumble.

At the same time, throughout the 1970s the Liberals, in particular, were kept busy with the politics of biculturalism, which had spawned a major nationalist movement in Quebec that demanded independence for—and thus isolation of—a large portion of the industrial heartland and domestic market. The political difficulties accumulating during this period were acute. On the one hand, the politics of culture was available to the major parties to distinguish themselves and, for the Liberals, to construct a winning partisan coalition. On the other hand, its continued use had left space for the mobilization of new nationalist movements, the growth of which required real adjustments in the relations between the two cultural groups. Quebec was rapidly organizing for independent linguistic and economic action. The major preoccupation of the governing party was to quell the rising nationalist fervour.

When the economic downturn became more severe in the 1970s and 1980s, none of the parties came easily to a substitute for the post-war development strategy. Nevertheless, the combination of economic and political crisis finally opened the space that the Tories needed to reorganize their terrain. They did this by developing an increasingly coherent position on economic development for the new international conditions and by successfully merging this with the politics of culture so that they could dislodge the Liberals from their hegemony in Quebec.

Nevertheless, the politics of a brokerage party system continued to make the debate about alternative futures hard to follow through, although never irrelevant to, electoral politics. One alternative future was a new development strategy of state-encouraged, and even state-led, industrial restructuring. The other was neo-liberal retrenchment of state spending and a greater reliance on market forces, which by the mid-1980s included accelerated continentalism through free trade. The call for a coherent state-centred industrial strategy arose as the costs of branch-plant industrialization became a growing source of concern for government officials, economists, and some voters. The focus of new policy instruments—such as the Canadian Development Corporation (CDC), the Ministry of State for Science and Technology, the Foreign Investment Review Agency (FIRA), and Petro-Canada—was foreign (American) investment. By the mid-1970s, proponents of an industrial strategy were concerned about both the *fact* of foreign investment and the *form* that future investment in the industrial sector might take. Demands appeared that the government not simply think of "buying back" industry, but that it also actively launch and support the specific industries likely to prosper in the new international economy. Proponents of this position began to argue that the most appropriate industrial strategy for Canada would involve the state "picking winners," specifically industries with a high value-added component and research and development potential.

But not everyone shared this enthusiasm for new state action. The Liberal Party, in fact, continued to harbour strong supporters of greater continentalism and less government intervention. More threatening than its internal party divisions, however, was the fact that the Liberals found themselves losing the support of powerful elements of the business community. At the same time, the Canadian government accepted the line of the Bonn Economic Summit that government spending lay at the root of the economic difficulties all countries were experiencing. So the Liberals were only partly interested in an industrial strategy, and indeed the Liberal Party had tentatively embraced fiscal conservatism in the late 1970s.

This interpretation of the economic future was being fully elaborated in other quarters. The neo-liberal Margaret Thatcher won election in Britain in 1979 and Ronald Reagan became president of the United States in 1980. In Canada, a powerful coalition of conservative "think tanks," provincial and federal politicians, and business leaders adopted this viewpoint, clothing it in support for continental free trade. According to the neo-liberal othodoxy, the crisis of advanced capitalism derived from over three decades of Keynesianism, which had pushed capitalist economies to the brink of collapse. Governments, through social welfare programs and extensive growth in the public service, had become too large, fiscally irresponsible, and oppressive to the "creative elements of society" (read capitalist) with increasingly onerous taxation. Given these truisms, the solution was simple: reduce the size of government and let the private sector resume its supposedly historic role as the creative, efficient, and productive engine of capitalist growth. This coalition urged Canadian policy makers to minimize the role of the state, cut back social welfare policies, reduce regulation, and allow trade liberalization to proceed.

During the late 1970s, this vision was increasingly interwoven into the positions of the Progressive Conservative Party. The party's transformation began during the leadership of Joe Clark, who brought together an unstable coalition of western capital and its supporters, province-building politicians, and some progressive elements in the party (the so-called "Red Tories") in 1976. This coalition self-destructed during the short-lived Clark government of 1979, but was recast—largely without the progressive faction—behind Brian Mulroney in 1983. It was the rise of Clark to the leadership of the Conservative Party, however, that revealed to Tory strategists an apparently winning formula in the federal arena.

For most of the post-war period, the Conservatives had been relegated to the status of the party of the peripheries, the party of those dispossessed by the post-war development strategy. By the late 1970s the western provinces were powerful actors in the Canadian economy and increasingly frustrated with the continuing centrist orientation of the federal Liberal Party. The growing western malaise, however, was not, as it had been in the past, tied to progressivism. Rather, it was increasingly informed by neo-liberalism. The western premiers utilized the combined themes of regionalism and neo-liberalism—with their call for decentralization and a return to free enterprise—throughout the 1970s. They used the notion of less state intervention as a shorthand for no *federal* intrusion in provincially orientated and state-directed provincial developmental policies.

For a few years at the beginning of the 1980s there was uncharacteristic conflict in federal party politics. The Liberals and Conservatives, for the first time in many years, disagreed over three fundamental orientations that had formed the basis of consensus for much of the post-war period. The first was decentralization of economic policy making. The post-war interparty consensus favoured federal power. By 1979, however, the federal Conservatives began to articulate a different conception of Canada, with the ambiguous phrase "community of communities," while the Liberals held fast to the notion that the federal power should not be surrendered to the provinces.

The proper role for government in the economy was the second point of contention between the two major parties. The Liberals, while cutting back state activities during the late 1970s, maintained a positive orientation toward an activist state, but the Tories increasingly adopted the "buzz-words" of the "new right."

The third major area of interparty disagreement was economic nationalism. For most of the post-war years the Liberals had been continentalist, an orientation that was consistently opposed by the NDP and by the Conservatives under Diefenbaker. Throughout the 1970s, however, the Liberals had taken a few tentative steps in the direction of economic nationalism, while the Conservatives argued that regulatory instruments such as FIRA were unnecessary restrictions on the private sector and that discouraging foreign investment was a luxury the economy could ill-afford.

The policy effects of these differences appeared quickly after the 1980 election defeat of the Tories and the success of the *Non* position in the Quebec referendum. A confident Liberal government put together a package of unanticipated policy initiatives, to halt the regionalizing forces in Canadian politics and to provide a new vision of a single community—a Third National Policy. Central to it was patriation of the British North America Act and entrenchment of a Charter of Rights and Freedoms, implementation of the National Energy Program, unveiling of a resource-driven industrial strategy, and introduction of the Western

Development Fund. These initiatives were both nationalist and centrist. The Charter of Rights and Freedoms, for example, stressed individual rights over those of provinces, while the National Energy Program and the Western Development Fund strengthened federal goals for economic development. Both the provinces and the Tories were obviously suspicious of, if not downright opposed to, these actions.

The Third National Policy collapsed, however, under the joint pressure of American protest and flaws in its own design. Like its predecessors, it was a resource-driven strategy, which meant that its success was tied to the vagaries of the international commodities market. The whole plan depended on rising energy prices, but only months after the federal government announced its vision of Canada's prosperous future, oil prices began their downward spiral, reducing federal (and provincial) revenues and making many proposed megaprojects much less feasible.

The Liberals' Third National Policy thus resembled a "shooting star," visible at one moment but gone the next, as the global economy entered the recession of 1981. Not only had the Liberals failed to imprint an overarching national design on the balkanized provincial economies of the country, but they had alienated significant segments of the electorate and the capitalist class in the process. The government had run out of ideas and options to cope with the growing economic crisis. Thus, in the fall of 1982, it appointed Donald Macdonald to head the Royal Commission on the Economic Union and Development Prospects for Canada and charged it to recommend "appropriate national goals and policies for economic development." Before the commission could report, however, Brian Mulroney displaced Joe Clark as Leader of the Opposition, Pierre Trudeau retired, and the new prime minister, John Turner, led his party to a resounding defeat at the polls.

But the Liberal government had already begun to beat its retreat from interventionism in the last years of its tenure, and its legacy to the new Tory government was the political space to institute a Canadian variant of neo-liberalism. In the 1984 federal election both major parties hugged the centre of the political spectrum, avoiding controversial policy debates. It was much more a fight between two new leaders, who were depicted as the "Corporate Clones" and "Bobbsey Twins of Bay Street." In fact Mulroney and Turner *were* very similar candidates in terms of economic philosophy, background, and support networks. Both promised better management of the economy, trade liberalization, more jobs, and more co-operative federalism. The difference was that Turner was saddled with a legacy of Liberal policy failures, a weak organization, and a party with a dubious reputation for patronage appointments.

The first Mulroney government made it clear that its major concern was economic recovery and promised to employ the policy instruments of neo-liberalism to achieve this goal. It unveiled a fourfold approach to recovery: reorientating public policies to encourage entrepreneurship, investment, and risk taking; rationalizing the management of government resources and programs; balancing the budget; and reducing both the size and role of government. But the keystone to this whole construction was free trade with the United States. The Conservatives unexpectedly found support for their agenda in the Macdonald Commission, which concluded that a market-driven approach, including free trade with the United States, was the only viable option available to Canadian policy makers. Indeed, on each of the issues that had momentarily distinguished the Liberals and Conservatives in the early 1980s, the commission appeared to side with the latter's position.

The Macdonald Commission and the Mulroney government presented free trade as if it were governed by the neutral mechanisms of the market, but it was anything but neutral. It harmonized well with the neo-liberal political agenda and strategy for industrial restructuring, which entailed a market-driven approach to economic growth, continental rationalization, government cutbacks in social services, reduced rights for workers, and a lesser role for the state in the economy. While the Liberals opposed the specific deal cut by the Tories with the United States in 1987–88, it was also clear even in the midst of the 1988 election campaign that the weight of opinion in the Liberal Party was in favour of freer trade.

There are several lessons to be learned from an examination of the party system in the last decade of the twentieth century. It looks very unlikely that the federal party system will pass through the "modernized" stage of class politics mobilized around a social democratic party. If the NDP since 1961 has not succeeded in mobilizing a class-based constituency, the legacy of that absence is likely to be, at least in the foreseeable future, various forms of populism. The NDP's own appeal to "ordinary Canadians" distressed by the chicanery of the two major parties is one kind of populism. The politics of province-building premiers who play on the we/they sensitivities of their populations, fanned to greater heat when it seems that Ontario might be making gains, is another form of populism, long familiar in Canadian politics. And, finally, the mobilization of two coalitions in the free trade debate—the so-called "popular sector" of a loose alliance of representatives of a variety of social movements versus the business community—produced another form of populism. The free trade debate exposed the real potential of defensive populism directed against the loudly advertised hopes of the business community. But whether that populist defence of an ill-defined mélange of "social programs," "Canadian distinctiveness," and medicare-as-the-essence-of-Canadianism will translate in the future into a political movement of positive proposals remains the open question for the Canadian party system as it moves into the 1990s.

FURTHER READINGS

Bashevkin, Sylvia B. *Toeing the Lines: Women and Party Politics in English Canada.* Toronto: University of Toronto Press, 1985.

Brodie, Janine. *Women and Politics in Canada.* Toronto: McGraw-Hill Ryerson, 1985.

Brodie, Janine, and Jane Jenson. *Crisis, Challenge and Change: Party and Class in Canada Revisited.* Ottawa: Carleton University Press, 1988.

Clarke, Harold D., Jane Jenson, Lawrence LeDuc, and Jon H. Pammett. *Absent Mandate: The Politics of Discontent in Canada.* Toronto: Gage, 1984.

Gagnon, Alain G., and Brian Tanguay. *Canadian Parties in Transition: Discourse, Organization, and Representation.* Toronto: Nelson, 1988.

Smith, David. "Party Government, Representation and National Integration in Canada." In *Party Government and Regional Representation in Canada,* ed. Peter Aucoin. Toronto: University of Toronto Press, 1985.

Thorburn, Hugh G., ed. *Party Politics in Canada,* 5th ed. Toronto: Prentice-Hall, 1985.

Wearing, Joseph. *Strained Relations: Canadian Parties and Voters.* Toronto: McClelland and Stewart, 1988.

14

Elections

JON H. PAMMETT

Although the idea that the suffrage for elections should approach the universal is a product of very recent times, the notion that leaders should be chosen by voting is an ancient one. In the Athens of 500 BC, an assembly of citizens elected generals and voted on numerous policy questions. Republican Rome operated an elaborate system of voting assemblies, electing consuls, tribunes, and many other officials. Medieval city-states such as Florence and Venice developed very complex structures of government, where officials were chosen by combinations of election and selection by lot.[1] Elections, then, are one of humanity's most ancient political institutions.

Elections have reached the status of virtually omnipresent institutions in nations of the modern world, no matter how authoritarian the actual regime is.[2] Elections are so popular because they serve a multiplicity of functions for almost everybody connected with them, as well as for the political system that sponsors them. Whatever complaints are registered about the time they take, the expense they involve, the choices they present, or the results they produce, they are vital to the image that almost every country wishes to present to the rest of the world. And whether they are perceived to be "meaningful" or not, few individuals anywhere have recorded their wishes to do away with them altogether.

Impressive catalogues of functions performed by elections may be compiled on all levels of analysis. For the *political system*, elections fulfil at the outset a recruitment function by providing an orderly way of choosing the rulers or elites that govern the society. Because of the complexities involved in so doing, the institution of elections facilitates grouping within the system, and thus participates in the creation and maintenance of a system of political parties. We have already mentioned the fact that elections are perceived to be symbols to the rest of the world about the democratic nature of the country concerned; within the bounds of the system, however, this legitimation function is also important. By the very fact of their having taken place and produced a result, elections create support for the political system (providing the result is seen as having been fairly arrived at) and a certain amount of legitimacy for the resulting government. "The people," it is often said, "have spoken." Not to be neglected is the important political socialization function discharged by elections. An election centres attention on the political system and provides opportunities for learning about it. It is often one of the few genuine communal experiences that people in a diverse country go through together, and simple participation in the same activity can be integrative for the system as a whole.

Political parties, for their part, are served by elections. They provide a ready-made occasion for a party to build or renew its internal organization; such activity can take place around an agreed-upon, short-term goal and thus galvanize all efforts. In some cases, elections may perform the function of allowing competing party elites to resolve internal power relationships and strategic conflicts within the party.[3] Elections can also provide the parties with policy guidelines or parameters, depending on how issues are seen by politicians as having affected the election result. These messages range from very specific policies that may be seen as having been accepted or rejected along with the party, to more general philosophical or ideological approaches to governing. Finally, the result of an election provides the party with a claim to the legitimacy of the status it achieved therein, whether that of victor, official opposition, major or minor party.

For *individuals*, elections serve the function of forging a link between them and the political system. This connection can foster a sense of support for the system, or sense of efficacy, a belief in the potential of provoking a response of the system to personal or group demands. It has been suggested that elections function as a protection for the individual, giving people control over those in power and "a voice in their own affairs."[4] Elections facilitate the socialization function by providing education and information about politics to individuals, as well as by affecting the partisanship they hold. Elections can also serve certain ego-enhancement functions for the individual personality by providing an opportunity to make a political statement, to impress others with political knowledge or disdain, and to feel in general infinitely superior to those politicians attempting to curry favour. Finally, political participation, stimulated by the election context, may advance a variety of functions, ranging from direct personal gain and advancement, to ego-identity formation, to satisfaction in the involvement with other people.[5]

In keeping with the foregoing division of the functions of elections, analysis by political scientists takes place at both the level of the individual and the political system, and includes, as well, a considerable number of studies of the internal operations of political parties. The individual-level analysis consists of explanations of voting behaviour and of how individuals arrive at their decision to support one party or another at a particular time. Those working in this field have carried out numerous pieces of survey research to amass the interview data necessary to test their theories. The system-level studies have been less common and have generally been of two types. The first has been an effort to study intensively the "context" of a particular election—the party platforms and activities, the media coverage, the events of the campaign, the patterns of the results, etc.[6] The second has involved the attempt to use survey data to explain the outcomes of particular elections. We will explore this subject further after we examine some aspects of individual voting behaviour in Canada.

VOTING BEHAVIOUR IN CANADA

The fact that elections perform a variety of functions for the individuals who vote in them would lead us to expect considerable diversity in their reasons for casting ballots in any given election. All indications we have from the National Election Studies, which are conducted after most Canadian federal elections, are that this expectation is easily met.[7] The evidence from these studies shows that virtually any short-hand explanation of why Canadians vote is bound to be correct for only a portion of the electorate. Thus, one should be highly suspicious of the generality implied by such interpretations as "Canadians rejected wage and price controls in 1974," "Pierre Trudeau's unpopularity led to the Liberal defeat in 1979," "the country voted against the Crosbie budget in 1980," "Brian Mulroney won the 1984 election," or "Canadians provided a mandate for free trade in 1988." Wage and price controls were cited by some as the main reason for their 1974 vote, a group of voters in 1979 thought Trudeau was "the issue," the budget was important in 1980, Brian Mulroney was more popular in 1984 than other PC leaders had been in the past, and many people evaluated the free trade agreement in 1988, but none of these factors produced the election result by itself, or even came close to doing so.

Rather than being some monolithic entity, the Canadian electorate is composed of subgroups of people acting for a panoply of different reasons. Some people say they are voting for the party as a whole, either because of long-standing loyalty or newfound conviction that it is time a new lot of politicians was given a chance to run the country. To another set of voters, the comparative evaluation of the leaders is a major factor; for some others it is the local candidate from their riding who makes the difference. A wide variety of different issues is cited, some of long-standing concern (e.g., the problems of inflation and unemployment) and others that emerge as important in one election but are scarcely mentioned in another (e.g., the national unity question, which dominated a lot of the election rhetoric in 1979 but was not a major issue five years earlier or five years later).

The question of the importance of issues in individual voting decisions has long interested political scientists. Because the electoral process involves decisions made by masses of people, and therefore by numbers of people who are low in political information or interest, there has always been scope for charges that voting decisions are not being taken for the "right reasons." Usually this involves assertions that voters decide on the basis of the personality or images of the leaders or candidates, or unthinking party loyalty, but not on "the issues." This kind of debate often includes questions about the extent of "rational voting," voting on the basis of a reasoned consideration of the issues important to the voter. It does not seem particularly profitable to engage here in a discussion of whether Canadians vote rationally or not (and it would seem even less advisable to take a position on just what constitutes a rational motive for voting choice in the first place). It is possible to state, however, that in Canada a considerable amount of voting does take place for issue-related reasons.

The extent to which voting choice is motivated by issue concerns can be seen more clearly if we look at the voters' rankings of the four factors of leaders, candidates, parties, and issues in terms of importance to their vote decisions. To prevent setting up a direct choice between issues and these other factors in people's minds (we felt that the number citing issues might be artificially high since voting on the issues is a more socially approved answer), respondents to the National Election Surveys were asked to choose among the three factors of party, leader, or candidate, and then asked whether or not there was an issue basis to their choice. The percentage of people ranking the four factors important in the 1980 and 1988 federal elections is shown in Table 14.1. When offered a choice between party leader, local candidate, and party taken as a whole, the last emerges as the most important factor at both elections. Interestingly, however, there is considerable variation between the two elections in the number who declared there was an issue basis to their choice of party. While less than half of those citing party as the most important factor in their voting choice declared there was an issue basis to this choice in 1980, more than half did so in 1988, reflecting the enhanced importance of issues, particularly free trade, on the latter occasion. Similarly, the number reporting an issue basis to choice of leader or candidate as most important to them rose substantially in 1988. In Canadian elections, a majority of the electorate, or close to it, reports an issue basis for their voting decision, in contrast to glib media commentary that sometimes asserts that elections are just popularity contests between the leaders.

One fact that emerges from the evidence about the reasons for voting contained in the National Election Studies is that a large proportion of such motivating factors is distinctly "short-term" in nature. Leaders and candidates are subject to frequent change, especially if saddled with the stigma of having lost an election or two, and the importance of issues can

Table 14.1
"Most Important Reason" for 1980 Vote
(percentages)

Party Leader		Local Candidate		Party as a Whole	
36		20		44	
Issue Stand	Personal Qualities	Issue Stand	Personal Qualities	Issue Positions	General Approach
53	47	40	60	43	57

"Most Important Reason" for 1988 Vote
(percentages)

Party Leader		Local Candidate		Party as a Whole	
20		27		53	
Issue Stand	Personal Qualities	Issue Stand	Personal Qualities	Issue Positions	General Approach
71	29	57	43	57	43

vary a lot from one election to the next. Although Canadians are by no means bereft of general images of, and loyalties to, the political parties, a majority claim to make up their minds at each election on the basis of short-term factors operative at the time.

This picture of the Canadian electorate is supported by the evidence we have about the nature of partisanship in this country. A majority of voters develop party loyalties that are either weak, changeable over time, or different at the two levels of the federal system. All three of these factors contribute to the *flexible* partisanship that characterizes the link of about 60 percent of Canadian voters to the federal political parties. Thus, for many, when we ask, "To which party do you feel closest?" the answer we get may be different from the response we would have received to the same question last year or at the time of the last election.

Several facets of the political culture contribute to the flexibility of ties to political parties. The most basic is that Canadian political culture is relatively apolitical. While Canadians are moderately interested in politics, this interest does not translate for most into substantial political involvement. The amount of political information possessed by the average Canadian is low, reflecting both a general lack of desire for detailed knowledge and the inadequate presentation of political news in the public media. Studies of children's political learning, or socialization, show a relatively weak transference of preference for a political party from parent to child. Such transmission of enduring partisan ties from generation to generation is not the norm because these feelings may not be strongly or persistently held in the adult "socializer." Children are accordingly less likely to develop such feelings for themselves, and a culture is perpetuated in which partisanship is not strongly held, or is changeable.

Canadians are not often content with being apolitical; in many cases they are downright anti-political. In the 1974 national survey interview, the respondents were handed a blank map of Canada and asked to "write in five words or phrases which best describe politics in Canada." The replies revealed a considerable degree of negativism toward almost everything associated with the political system.[8] In particular, the public feels negatively about political parties and politicians; ratings of them after the 1988 election were lower across the board than at any time since such surveys began. In such an atmosphere, it is no wonder large numbers of people are unwilling to stick with "their party" in perpetuity. When those people who changed their partisanship were asked their reasons, more talked of the negative qualities of the party they were changing from than mentioned the positive qualities of the party they were changing to. It is not hard to foresee that many may soon become disillusioned with their new party as well.

Because of the conflicts and regional loyalties associated with its founding and development as a nation, Canada is governed by an extremely complex federal system. By the 1990s it is clear that a complete understanding of our system of government requires information about, and orientations toward, several different political systems, as well as sophisticated notions about their interrelationships. While most people have a basic understanding of the constitutionally established functions performed by the various actors of the federal system, it would be unrealistic to expect detailed knowledge of intergovernmental relations on the part of the mass public. Lack of knowledge begets lack of interest. Further, the image of conflict surrounding the Canadian federal system contributes to the general public mood of exasperation with, and cynicism about, the political process.

Every Canadian except for those resident in the Northwest Territories is a member of a political community that possesses two systems of political parties. This situation does not necessarily further complicate the individual's political world, since in some areas those party systems are for all intents and purposes the same. For example, the provincial Liberals and Conservatives in Nova Scotia are really the same parties as their federal namesakes. In several provinces, however, this is not the case. In British Columbia, the only party common to both federal and provincial party systems that has any continuity in terms of its strength is the New Democratic Party (NDP). Quebec has contained several major provincial parties that have not existed in any form at the federal level. In other provinces, such as Ontario, parties have different competitive positions at the two levels, and there are different strategic choices involved in casting votes.

This complex situation has produced the Canadian phenomenon of the "split identifier," where persons may consider themselves provincial Liberals and federal Conservatives (a common pattern now in Ontario and Quebec), etc. The proportion of Canadians who can be classified as split identifiers has increased over the last twenty years, largely due to identification with provincial-only parties in Quebec and British Columbia. By the 1980s over a quarter of those identifying with parties in Canada chose different parties at the two levels of the federal system. By some complicated psychological process, being a split identifier seems to make it easier to change parties and votes within each level as well, and contributes to the overall flexibility of partisanship.

Those whose ties to political parties are flexible have an enhanced potential to shift their votes from one election to the next, though only a minority of them do so at any given time. The reasons that influence such partisans, particularly those who switch their votes, are predominantly short-term in nature: liking for a political party at that particular time, feelings about a leader or candidate, concern for an issue, or some combination of these factors. We can pinpoint further types of flexible partisans who will be influenced by different factors if we subdivide them on the basis of their political interest. About one-third of the electorate is flexible in its partisanship while having a lower degree of interest in politics, while just over a quarter of the electorate is flexible in its partisanship with a higher degree of political interest. It is this flexible higher-interest group who will give relatively heavy weight to political issues in determining their voting choice; the parties aim to appeal to this group with their issue-oriented campaigns. The flexible lower-interest group, on the other hand, pays less attention to issues and more to general images of leaders and parties; the personal appeal of leaders like Trudeau or Mulroney works well with this group.

The flexibility of partisanship in Canada and the tendency for voting decisions to be determined by short-term considerations of the parties, issues, leaders, and candidates active at any given time has meant that social cleavages that are sometimes thought to form enduring loyalties in the population and divide them in important ways are not very influential in affecting people's votes. One of these cleavages, religion, can still be discerned in voting patterns, specifically in that Roman Catholics have tended to vote for the Liberals. Overall, however, the relationship between religion and vote has not been very strong and is seen by many analysts as either being in decline or being so difficult to explain in modern circumstances that it should be treated as a relic of the past.[9] Studies have consistently found that another important cleavage, social class, has very little relationship to voting choice at the federal level in

Canada, though there is more connection between the two variables in some provincial elections.[10] Ethnic factors affect voting behaviour to the extent that there was a tendency for francophones to favour the Liberals until 1984 and, thenceforth, to vote Progressive Conservative. The overall effect of this factor is mitigated, however, since these parties get a lot of English-speaking support as well, particularly in Quebec where the tendency for anglophones to vote for them is even stronger than it is for francophones. The votes of Canadians, then, are not heavily "preordained" by social or demographic factors as they evaluate an electoral situation, just as they are not predetermined by durable party loyalties.

One major consequence of this situation is that election campaigns can be of major importance in affecting the outcome. Over half the electorate claims to make up their minds which way to vote during the campaign period, and one-fifth of the respondents to the National Election Studies say they decide during the last week of the campaign or on election day itself. Given the short-term nature of the factors that are important in many voting decisions, and the potential impact of the campaign and its events, the Canadian electorate is a very volatile group of people. The potential for dramatic swings in election results is always present. We will turn our attention in the next section to why they have so seldom occurred.

THE OUTCOMES OF ELECTIONS

It may seem anomalous that a political system in which the electorate is characterized by such volatility appears so stable at the aggregate level of federal election results that it has at times been referred to as a one-party dominant system. The Liberal Party, "the Government Party" as it was called, won the bulk of federal elections until recent years, with the Conservatives forming governments in the twentieth century only under Borden (1911–20, part of which was a wartime Unionist government), Meighen (1926), Bennett (1930–35), Diefenbaker (1957–63), and Clark (1979–80). With the Progressive Conservative victories under Brian Mulroney in 1984 and 1988, analysts are already talking of a potential long-term dominance of that party in government, replacing the Liberals as the "Government Party."

The resolution of the apparent paradox between individual volatility and aggregate stability lies in our ability to differentiate between the effects of electoral conversion and electoral replacement, and plot the patterns of the "vote flows" related to them. *Conversion* involves the extent of vote switching among those who are members of the "permanent electorate," people who are already in the electorate and who can be counted on to vote in every election. All parties, through their campaign appeals, attempt to get voters to switch over to them from a previous vote for some other party. We have seen that the potential for such conversion is high, since the incidence of durable party loyalty is relatively low. *Replacement,* in contrast, is the impact on the result that newly eligible voters will have, as well as a group of "transient" voters, who do not turn out in every election. The impact of the transient vote will be determined by the difference in behaviour of those leaving the electorate (who voted last time, but not this time) and those mobilized into the electorate from a past abstention. In the past, the success of the federal Liberal Party has been achieved because, whatever the patterns of conversion in any given election, it consistently gained through the process of electoral replacement. And indications are that the Progressive Conservative Party was sustained in power in the 1988 election in part for the same reason.

The three Canadian federal elections held in 1974, 1979, and 1980 illustrate the operations of the patterns of conversion and replacement to the Liberals' benefit.[11] In 1974 the Liberals were able to increase their overall popular vote from 1972 and win enough seats to form a majority government. However, if the process of conversion had been the only one operating, the result of the 1974 election would actually have been *worse* for the Liberals than 1972. This is because vote switching from 1972 to 1974 among members of the permanent electorate favoured the Conservatives. The process of electoral replacement, however, worked quite differently from 1972 to 1974. The Liberals won the bulk of the votes of young voters who became newly eligible in 1974, and also the majority of support from transient voters who had not gone to the polls in 1972. Thus, because those who did not vote in the previous election, either through choice or through lack of eligibility, favoured the Liberal Party by wide margins, the party's losses through vote switching were more than offset.

In determining the outcome of the 1979 election, in which the Conservatives came close to forming a majority government, conversion and replacement again operated differently. There was substantial vote switching of 1974 Liberals away from that party toward the Conservatives. Fully 8.2 percent of the 1979 electorate switched from the Liberals to the PCs, whereas only 1.5 percent went the other way. In addition, the Conservatives gained slightly from switches between their party and the NDP, a better performance than they had managed in 1974. Once again, however, electoral replacement was the Conservatives' Achilles' heel. They did manage to win a slight plurality of the transient vote, important because of the high turnout in 1979. Newly eligible voters, on the other hand, still favoured the Liberals by a substantial margin, and this new-voter group was particularly numerous in 1979 because of the five-year interval since the previous election, and because the electorate is still mirroring the effects of the high post–Second World War birth rate. Almost two and a half million new voters had come of age since the previous election. The Liberals' ability to retain their appeal to this group, therefore, reduced the magnitude of their 1979 defeat, and the Conservatives' inability to win this new-voter group was to have disastrous consequences for them in terms of denying them majority government status as well as the opportunity to renew their support among the young.

In the 1980 election held a scant few months later, the processes of conversion and replacement worked in the same direction, favouring the Liberals. The Liberals showed a net benefit in vote switching with the PCs and the NDP, and also regained their edge among transient voters moving into the electorate from a non-voting stance in 1979. Similarly, since voting turnout in 1980 was down from 1979, it is relevant to note that the Conservatives suffered disproportionately from the 1980 abstention of voters who had favoured them a year earlier. Thus, even though the Liberal Party in government often lost voters through conversion (which is only natural since it was so often in a position to disillusion voters), it made up for that through infusions of new and transient voters, thereby creating a kind of "past through" effect, forming a new electoral coalition of voters at each election.

Tables 14.2 and 14.3 present the conversion and replacement patterns for the last two pairs of elections. The 1984 federal election, which resulted in a Conservative landslide, came about because of extreme voter dissatisfaction with the Turner and Trudeau regimes,[12] and shows what happens when both factors operate strongly in the same direction. The proportion of the total electorate switching to the Conservatives from a 1980 Liberal vote totals almost as much as that remaining with the Liberals (Table 14.2: 13.4 percent versus 15 percent). Similarly, transient voters entering the electorate from a 1980 abstention favoured the Conservatives by a wide margin, as did newly eligible voters by a not-so-wide margin.

The 1988 election reflects a different scenario. As we were used to seeing in the years when the Liberals were in power, vote switching went against the government. Table 14.3 shows that, although the differences between those abandoning the Tories and those attracted to them were not overwhelming, they were consistent. The Tories lost voters to the Liberals, the NDP, and a series of small parties, such as the western Reform Party. That the Conservatives managed to win the election was due to two factors. First, their victory in 1984 had been so overwhelming that they could afford to lose more votes than they gained and still survive comfortably. Second, however, the PCs gained from electoral replacement, winning a plurality of transient voters and newly eligible voters. Once again, we see emerging a pattern whereby these latter groups are more likely to favour an incumbent government (in the absence of a public consensus on the need to replace it) and offset the effects of vote switching away from it. It is too soon to say whether the mechanism of electoral replacement will sustain the Conservatives in power in the 1990s.

Table 14.2
Electoral Turnover, 1980–84
(diagonal percentages)

		1984 Behaviour				
		Liberal	PC	NDP	Other	Not Voting
1980 Vote/Status	Liberal	15.0	13.4	2.2	0.5	3.6
	PC	1.0	23.9	0.7	0.4	1.8
	NDP	0.4	2.0	7.8	0.1	1.3
	Other	–	0.6	0.1	0.4	0.1
	Not Voting	2.0	4.4	1.1	0.3	5.3
	Not Eligible	2.8	3.9	1.0	0.2	3.6

100%

Source: 1984 Canadian National Election Study.

The jury is still out on the prospects of a new Conservative hegemony in federal elections for one basic reason. To understand it, we need to look back at the success of the federal Liberals in winning elections in this century. One reason for this success has had to do with the kind of political issues that emerge in Canadian elections. More than any other party, the Liberals managed to adopt as their own a cluster of political issues that can affect an election *outcome,* as opposed to simply affecting a number of individual voters. This distinction may not be immediately apparent, but it is extremely important if elections are to be analyzed as political events. An issue can affect an individual's vote simply by being

Table 14.3
Electoral Turnover, 1984–88
(diagonal percentages)

		1988 Behaviour				
		Liberal	PC	NDP	Other	Not Voting
1984 Vote/Status	Liberal	12.2	4.2	1.7	0.6	1.8
	PC	7.0	29.4	3.7	2.2	2.8
	NDP	1.8	1.4	8.9	0.2	0.4
	Other	0.2	0.9	0.3	0.3	0.2
	Not Voting	1.8	2.0	0.9	0.3	3.3
	Not Eligible (estimate)	2.2	3.3	2.3	0.3	3.7

100%

Source: 1988 follow-up interview of 1984 Canadian National Election Study respondents.
Behaviour of newly eligible voters estimated from other surveys.

important to that particular voter. To affect an election outcome, however, an issue must meet three conditions. First, an issue must be salient to an appreciable number of people—if few people think it is important they are not likely to act on it. Second, an issue must have a "skewed" distribution; in other words, it must be *valenced* in a certain direction, so that people are generally in favour of it or against it. If people are split on the general desirability of something like free trade, to take an example from the campaign of 1988, then any shift of votes to one party on the basis of that issue is likely to be offset by a countervailing shift away from that party of those who do not care for the party's position. Third, an issue position must be linked to one party in the electorate's perception. If no one party is particularly preferred on an issue, then even if the voters consider the issue to be important to their individual decisions, their voting behaviour will be unlikely to benefit any one party. In this case, even a very important issue may not affect the election outcome. This was the case with the inflation issue in 1974 and the energy issue in 1980. Lots of voters thought they were important, and they were agreed that inflation was bad or that plentiful, cheap energy was good, but no one party was perceived to have the solution to either the inflation or the energy problem, and therefore no party was differentially favoured.

It is difficult for economic issues, such as those cited previously, to meet all three conditions for an effect on an election outcome. Although the public usually considers them to be important, they are often either not linked with a particular party (as with general problems such as inflation or unemployment) or not valenced (as with specific economic issues such as wage and price controls, or free trade, which had strong contingents both pro and con). The Liberal Party, however, has managed in this century to meet the three conditions on a set of Confederation issues, which include national unity, bilingualism, constitutional questions, and issues involving Quebec. These issues, at least in their "national unity" manifestation, are valenced in that most people are concerned with keeping the country together and reducing conflict, and have been historically linked with the Liberal Party in that the Liberals have been seen as the one party with enough appeal to both English and French Canada to be able to work out solutions to the problems with Confederation.

The question for the 1990s, therefore, is whether the federal Progressive Conservative Party under Brian Mulroney has managed to change the public's mind about which party is positively linked to such Confederation issues. If people outside Quebec continue to view the Conservatives as the party that can best "deal with Quebec," and those in Quebec continue to view the party as the one that can best "represent Quebec," the prospect of future Conservative dominance is enhanced. Much depends on leadership choices, government performance, and economic conditions in the 1990s. All we can say with certainty is that the demonstrated volatility of the Canadian electorate allows for a multiplicity of possible outcomes.

CONCLUSION

If we return to consider some of the major functions of elections referred to at the beginning of this chapter, it is apparent that federal elections in Canada perform some of these functions much better than others. Recruitment, for example, is reasonably well served; each election produces the requisite cadre of leaders to operate the ministries, though the scarcity of representatives from certain regions often causes concern to the parties. The function of creating support for the political system and legitimizing it in the eyes of its citizens is another matter. Because many federal elections have produced in recent years highly regionalized patterns of support for the parties, there has been a tendency to regard governments as primarily representative of certain parts of the country at the expense of others. This situation has the potential to affect the amount of support given to the central government, and thus to the present structure of the Canadian political system, but there is really very little evidence that discontent has penetrated as deeply yet. Although many Canadians might favour some rearrangement of the existing federal system, particularly if some such proposal promised to alleviate the constant bickering between governments, very few favour basic changes to the system's structure or a serious weakening of the federal government. The 1980 referendum in Quebec was defeated largely because sovereignty-association was perceived as posing a serious threat to the overall Canadian political community.[13] The country is split evenly on the desirability of the Meech Lake Accord for much the same reasons.[14] A considerable amount of system support *is* being created in Canada, and elections play a part in this process; the continuity implied in the simple conduct of federal elections may in the long run be more important than the patterns of particular results.

Elections, we noted previously, perform functions for political parties as well. They certainly enable parties to revive and re-establish their organizations; since the Liberals and Conservatives (and also, to a large extent, the NDP) exist as political parties primarily for the purpose of contesting elections, these events are their *sine qua non*. With regard to the proposed function of setting policy parameters for the parties, or sorting out the specific policies they will have a mandate to enact, the Canadian election system does not perform very well. This is partly because parties often seek to avoid specific policy stands during election campaigns, knowing they would usually alienate as many voters as they attracted by such pledges. Even if specific policies are proposed, recent

Canadian history shows that parties rarely feel themselves bound by them. During the 1974 campaign, for example, the Liberals fought strenuously against the idea of wage and price controls, and then promptly introduced them once re-elected. Similarly, the short-lived Clark government spent much of its tenure in office searching for ways to alter or abandon its 1979 campaign promises on such matters as moving the Canadian embassy in Israel, allowing mortgage interest charges to be deducted from income tax, selling Petro-Canada, etc. And the turnabout from opponents to proponents of free trade characterized the behaviour of the Mulroney government from 1984 to 1988. Not only does this behaviour of parties in power mean that elections provide little opportunity for the public to affect policy, it also damages the credibility of politicians, increases political cynicism among the population, and may have some negative impact on support for the political system.

Finally, with regard to serving functions for individuals, elections also produce mixed results. They do affect the development of the individual personality in many different ways, though whether these effects contribute to a "healthy" personality is a judgment that had perhaps better be left to psychologists. As to whether the institution of elections contributes to people feeling they have a say in controlling their own affairs or a sense of efficacy in dealing with government, we can, at the present time, agree only partially. Most Canadians are not very confident that they can understand and influence the political system, and many are quite cynical about the possibility of producing any significant change through elections. This situation may be mitigated somewhat by the feeling on the part of most that their satisfaction with their lives and material standard of living is not greatly affected by government. Thus, the feeling that elections do not really accomplish very much does not manifest itself in rage and destructiveness, but rather in a bemused detachment from the whole political process, in the apolitical political culture we noted earlier. Some people have argued that this situation has been, on balance, beneficial in that elites are free to govern and to implement some policies that might have been more vigorously opposed in a more politicized society. That may be true, but there are also inherent dangers in having a public so divorced from, and cynical about, the political process in a country that depends so heavily on politics to negotiate solutions to its numerous problems.

NOTES

1. These and other examples of ancient elections are discussed in Jon H. Pammett, "A Framework for the Comparative Analysis of Elections Across Time and Space," *Electoral Studies* 7, no. 2 (1988): 125–42.
2. In the early 1960s, data collected by Yale University showed that out

of one hundred countries for which information existed, ninety-two had held elections in the past six years. See Richard Rose and Harve Mossawir, "Voting and Elections: A Functional Analysis," *Political Studies* 15 (1967): 180.

3. Primary elections in the United States are an obvious example of this; however, it also takes place in other contexts. See Jane Jenson, "Strategic Divisions within the French Left: The Case of the First Elections to the European Parliament," *Revue d'integration européene/Journal of European Integration*, September 1980.

4. Norman D. Palmer, *Elections and Political Development* (Durham, N.C.: Duke University Press, 1975), p. 87.

5. Jon H. Pammett, "Adolescent Political Activity as a Learning Experience: The Action-Trudeau Campaign of 1968," in *Foundations of Political Culture: Political Socialization in Canada*, ed. Jon H. Pammett and Michael Whittington (Toronto: Macmillan, 1976), pp. 160–94.

6. This tradition in Britain produced the "Nuffield" series of election studies, such as David E. Butler, *The British General Election of 1987* (Basingstoke: Macmillan, 1988). In Canada, examples are John Meisel, *The Canadian General Election of 1957* (Toronto: University of Toronto Press, 1962) and Howard Penniman, ed., *Canada at the Polls: The Canadian Election of 1984* (Washington: American Enterprise Institute for Public Policy Research, 1988).

7. Large national surveys have been conducted after seven Canadian federal elections. The studies of the 1965 and 1968 elections were organized by John Meisel, and the studies of the 1974, 1979, and 1980 elections by Harold D. Clarke, Jane Jenson, Lawrence LeDuc, and Jon H. Pammett. The most complete report of the 1974 data can be found in Harold D. Clarke, Jane Jenson, Lawrence LeDuc, and Jon H. Pammett, *Political Choice in Canada* (Toronto: McGraw-Hill Ryerson, 1979). For 1979 and 1980, see *Absent Mandate: The Politics of Discontent in Canada* (Toronto: Gage, 1984) by the same authors. The 1984 study was organized by Ronald Lambert, Steven Brown, James Curtis, Barry Kay, and John Wilson. The 1988 survey used in this article is a follow-up interview with the 1984 respondents organized by Ronald Lambert, Steven Brown, James Curtis, Barry Kay, Lawrence LeDuc, and Jon Pammett. A 1988 National Election Study is being conducted by Richard Johnston, Andre Blais, and Jean Crete.

8. The replies are analyzed in considerable detail in Chapter 1 of Clarke, et al., *Political Choice in Canada*.

9. See William Irvine, "Explaining the Religious Basis of Partisanship in Canada: Success on the Third Try," *Canadian Journal of Political Science* 7 (1974): 560–63. Also John Meisel, "Bizarre Aspects of a Vanishing Act: The Religious Cleavage and Voting in Canada," in his

Working Papers in Canadian Politics, 2nd rev. ed. (Montreal: McGill-Queen's University Press, 1975), pp. 253–84. Also see Richard Johnston, "The Reproduction of the Religious Cleavage in Canadian Elections," *Canadian Journal of Political Science* 18, no. 1 (1985): 99–114, and the ensuing comment by William Irvine in the same issue.

10. For a survey analysis of class and vote in Canada, and an extensive bibliography, see Jon H. Pammett, "Class Voting and Class Consciousness in Canada," *Canadian Review of Sociology and Anthropology* 24, no. 2 (1987): 269–90.

11. A complete analysis of the outcome of the 1974 federal election can be found in Clarke, et al., *Political Choice in Canada*, ch. 12, and of the 1979 and 1980 elections in Clarke, et al., *Absent Mandate*, ch. 7.

12. For analyses of the 1984 election, see Alan Frizzell and Anthony Westell, *The Canadian General Election of 1984* (Ottawa: Carleton University Press, 1985), as well as Penniman, *Canada at the Polls*.

13. Jon H. Pammett, Harold D. Clarke, Jane Jenson, and Lawrence LeDuc, "Political Support and Voting Behaviour in the Quebec Referendum," in *Political Support in Canada: The Crisis Years*, ed. Allan Kornberg and Harold D. Clarke (Durham, N.C.: Duke University Press, 1983).

14. The 1988 survey used in this article showed that one-third of Canadians favoured the Meech Lake Accord, one-third opposed it, and the remaining third had no opinion.

FURTHER READINGS

Beck, Murray J. *Pendulum of Power*. Toronto: Prentice-Hall, 1968. Gives accounts of Canadian election campaigns to 1968.

Clarke, Harold D., Jane Jenson, Lawrence LeDuc, and Jon H. Pammett. *Political Choice in Canada*. Toronto: McGraw-Hill Ryerson, 1979, and abridged edition 1980. The most extensive treatment of Canadian voting behaviour and partisanship. Now out of print, but copies are available from the authors.

——— . *Absent Mandate: The Politics of Discontent in Canada*. Toronto: Gage, 1984. An analysis of voting behaviour and election outcomes in the climate of economic decline of the 1970s and 1980s. A new edition covering elections through 1988 should be available by 1990.

Frizzell, Alan, Jon Pammett, and Anthony Westell. *The Canadian General Election of 1988*. Ottawa: Carleton University Press, 1989. A companion volume on 1984 is also available.

Meisel, John. *Working Papers on Canadian Politics*, 2nd enlarged ed. Montreal: McGill-Queen's University Press, 1975. A series of perceptive, empirical analyses on Canadian elections.

Penniman, Howard, ed. *Canada at the Polls: The General Elections of 1979 and 1980*. Washington: American Enterprise Institute for Public Policy Research, 1982. Articles by Canadian scholars on the campaigns waged by each of the parties, as well as such topics as campaign finance, nomination of candidates, mass media coverage, and the participation of women. Companion volumes on the 1974 and 1984 elections are also available, but cover fewer topics.

Regenstrief, Peter. *The Diefenbaker Interlude.* Toronto: Longmans, 1965. Based on the author's own polling during the Diefenbaker years, many of the conclusions about Canadian voting behaviour in this book have stood the test of time.

Schwartz, Mildred. "Canadian Voting Behaviour." In *Electoral Behaviour: A Comparative Handbook*, ed. Richard Rose. New York: The Free Press, 1974. An overview of voting behaviour, the electoral system, and the nature of Canadian society.

15

Pressure Groups: Talking Chameleons

A. PAUL PROSS

The most difficult of all governmental tasks is that of communicating with the public. Despite the millions of words expended in public debate every day, modern governments have great difficulty finding out what the public wants and needs, and what it feels about the work that the state is already doing. Equally, although its payroll is laden with press officers, writers, and others skilled in the arts of communication, government has immense problems in explaining itself to the public, in reporting back to it, and in persuading and leading it.

Pressure groups are one of three communications systems used by most modern states to overcome these problems. The other two are the internal apparatus of the government itself, such as the press officers and writers mentioned above, and the party system. Political parties are best equipped to transmit the demands and views of individuals and of groups of individuals concerned about specific localities. This is because political parties tend to be built around an electoral system created to fill a legislature that is territorial or *spatial* in orientation; i.e., each member represents the people who live in a specific area, or constituency.

Pressure groups have become prominent because they are effective where parties fail. They can identify and articulate the views and needs of individuals who may live far apart but who share common interests. In modern society, with its interdependent economy, its multinational corporations, and its very large and specialized government bureaucracies, this sectoral approach of pressure groups is an essential complement to the spatial orientation of political parties. Even so, as we shall see later, the rapid growth and rising influence of pressure groups gives concern to many observers, some of whom feel that democratic government is threatened thereby.

Pressure groups are organizations whose members act together to influence public policy in order to promote their common interests.[1] Unlike political parties, they are not interested in directly wielding the power of the state, though sometimes a group representing a particularly large socio-economic block (the Acadians are a good example) will decide to transform itself into a political party. In general, pressure groups are interested in exerting influence and in persuading governments to accommodate the special interests of their members.

To achieve this, pressure groups have to be more than mere assemblages of people. Their members have to be organized; brought together in structured relationships with one another and dragooned into identifying and expressing their common interests. Pressure groups are consequently distinct, clearly identifiable elements in the body politic. While their chief role, as far as the political system in concerned, is to provide a network for policy communication, in the following paragraphs we shall see that they have several other functions as well.

Pressure groups are also very adaptable members of the polity—so adaptable, in fact, that we can use their structure and behaviour as a guide to charting the policy process in a particular political system. We cannot look at this aspect of pressure group life in great depth here, but we shall try to use it to draw some comparisons between the manner in which policy is made in Canada and in the United States. Furthermore, we shall use our understanding of the adaptive behaviour of pressure groups to set out a theory that explains the day-to-day relationship of pressure groups and their members to the policy system. Finally, we shall look at a couple of the very large issues raised by the growing influence of pressure groups in the policy system.

THE FUNCTIONS OF PRESSURE GROUPS

Whenever we try to set down precisely what it is that pressure groups do, we have to remember that, like most institutions, they are different things to different people. Leaving aside for the moment those who feel that pressure groups are a curse and an abomination, let us look briefly at the ways in which government officials and group members relate to them.

Most of us are unaware of the number of pressure groups we belong to. Because we join many associations in order to share our interests and concerns with others, we tend not to think of them as pressure groups. Each September, as Canadian universities resume classes, thousands of students pay dues to their campus student associations. Most of that money supports local campus activity that has nothing to do with politics, but some of it is channelled to provincial and national federations of student associations, which in turn devote considerable time and money to lobbying governments concerning matters such as tax breaks for students, university funding, tuition fees, student loans, and national and international issues that have pricked the conscience of the university community. Acquiring a university degree is a serious business, and if government is to be deeply involved in education we should expect student associations to act as pressure groups.

We do not expect our leisure associations to camp as regularly on the doorsteps of government, yet they are among the most active pressure groups to be found in Canada. For instance, many a rural politician has trembled as provincial legislatures have debated hunting and fishing legislation; game laws have often been the most hotly contended items on legislative agendas, and provincial associations of hunters and anglers have been slow to forget the transgressions of politicians who have opposed their ideas. Similarly, associations of camping enthusiasts, naturalists, bird watchers, and wilderness buffs have a surprising degree of influence with government agencies, such as Parks Canada, that cater to their interests. In fact, the wilderness orientation of Canada's national parks system is in large part a reflection of the strength of this lobby.

These examples illustrate a basic point: very few pressure groups exist simply to influence government. Their members have joined in order to obtain some special benefit that each organization alone can offer. Yet, because government intrudes so much into our daily lives, these associations become a very convenient vehicle for communicating with government. While most associations inevitably develop some capacity in this role, the members often only very grudgingly allow this to happen—lobbying governments is an expensive business. But as the need to express their views becomes more urgent, they hire consultants, undertake studies, appoint "government liaison officers" meet with officials and politicians, and generally join the babble of tongues that surrounds the policy process.

From the group members' point of view, then, the lobbying activities of their associations are first and foremost intended to *communicate*. People in government also see pressure groups in this light, though not always happily. Communication may take many forms, some of them violent, many of them distinctly noticeable to the general public—and therefore usually embarrassing. However, the great majority of them are unobtrusive, involving the careful negotiation of technical and regulatory details of policy. Although often unwelcome—after all, no official or politician likes to be told that a pet project or policy is faulty—pressure groups are frequently the most reliable and the best-informed link between government agencies and the portions of the public that they particularly serve. Indeed, so important is this function that governments have often gone out of their way to encourage the creation of special-interest groups. In the Atlantic provinces the federal and provincial governments did exactly this in the late 1970s when they encouraged independent fishermen to form bodies able to participate in developing policies for managing Canada's newly expanded fishery. "If I had to write the manual for dealing with government," federal Fisheries Minister Romeo LeBlanc told one group, "I would put two main rules of the road: carry a flag—that is, have an organization—and sound your horn. Let people know you are there." By the early 1980s, the Eastern Fishermen's Federation, the chief product of the exercise, was a recognized actor in the fisheries policy community.[2] Similarly, core funding from the federal government was an important factor in developing the modern Canadian Indian movement.[3]

Nor does communication flow in only one direction. Most lobbying organizations present governments with a convenient means of reaching a special audience. Annual meetings can be addressed by ministers and senior officials intent partly on flattering and winning over a special clientele or constituency, but also on conveying various messages: a hint at policy change, an explanation of action, warnings, encouragement, and so on. Eyes watering from cigar and cigarette smoke, perspiring under the television lights, wondering whether they can be heard above the clatter of coffee cups and the hum of comment, guest speakers drone through their after-dinner jokes, their compliments, and their pious reminders, knowing that alert minds in the audience will soon have interpreted the speech's central message and passed it on to the less discerning. Similarly, organization newsletters, regional meetings, and informal get-togethers offer government spokespersons networks for the rapid transmission of information.

If communication is the primary function of pressure groups, *legitimation* is not much less important.[4] That is, pressure groups play a very significant part in persuading both policy makers and the general public that changes in public policy are worthwhile, generally desired, and in the public interest. Because pressure groups frequently speak for a significant proportion of the public that will be affected by a change in policy, governments find it reassuring to have their proposals endorsed by the relevant groups. As Romeo LeBlanc told fishermen in the speech previously quoted, "Push the officials...they like it." Cabinet ministers know how helpful it is to have a pressure group leader tell a legislative committee, as one did in 1975, that "we provided extensive comments... with respect to the first draft. When we saw the new bill most of the corrections, changes or criticisms we had found with the first draft had been corrected, modified or vastly improved."[5] In a similar way, group leaders sell their members on the desirability of policy changes.

On the other hand, officials are aware that a disaffected group can use its many connections with the media, the opposition parties, and perhaps other governments to attack policy and so undermine its legitimacy. The mining industry did this between 1967 and 1972 when it disagreed with the federal government over tax reform. Using a combination of general appeals to the government and behind-the-scenes lobbying with provincial governments, the mineral industries eventually forced the federal government to revise its proposals. One of the reasons for their success lay in their ability to persuade the public and the provinces that the new laws would discourage investment in the mining industry and so hurt the economy. In other words, they undermined the legitimacy of the proposed changes.[6] Similar interest group reactions to Finance Minister Allan

MacEachen's 1981 budget had the same effect, ultimately leading to a number of changes and an attempt on the part of the finance minister, and his successor, to reform the budget-making process so that interests would have an opportunity to discuss possible tax changes before they become government policy. Fear of the embarrassment caused by such incidents, to say nothing of the disruptive effect on policy, gives government agencies a powerful incentive to consult with pressure groups that has become more pressing as our policy process has become increasingly diffuse.

Administrative and regulatory activities are much less prominent functions than communication and legitimation, but they occur often enough to deserve mention. Provincial administration of social services is often supplemented by the work of groups such as the Children's Aid Society or church-affiliated organizations. In the years when Canada was receiving large numbers of immigrants, voluntary associations provided many facilities that helped newcomers move to, and settle at, their destinations.[7] Today, as tight budgets constrain governments' ability to pay for services we once took for granted, we have begun to revive the practice of encouraging voluntary associations to provide supplementary services, particularly in support of food banks and in home care for the elderly. Often the groups involved in these activities are not thought of as pressure groups, but because they often do contribute to the development of policy in their areas of interest, we are justified in thinking of them in this way.

Groups perform administrative functions for several reasons. Often, as we have suggested, governments cannot afford to offer the services that they provide through a combination of volunteer and paid help. Sometimes governments are not willing, for policy reasons, to provide special services, though they are willing to help voluntary associations provide them. The community is so divided over many issues related to birth control, for example, that some governments prefer to support birth control counselling indirectly through general grants to organizations such as Planned Parenthood rather than to advocate directly one position or another. Finally, many groups administer programs that could as easily be carried out by government officials, simply because they have traditionally offered such services. Periodically, as in the case of the Children's Aid Societies in Ontario, these roles come under review and sometimes they are taken over by government.[8]

Regulatory functions are delegated to groups for quite different reasons. Lawyers, doctors, chartered accountants, and other professional groups have been given considerable authority to govern themselves through their associations, largely because governments are reluctant to thrust themselves into the complicated and often treacherous debates that surround professional accreditation and ethics. As well, though, some professional groups have a great deal of influence, and quite probably that has been exerted to keep government at arm's length. Even so, we see governments increasingly cutting back on this autonomy—for instance, forcing the medical profession, by and large, to accept publicly approved fee schedules or, as in Quebec, by imposing a high degree of regulation on all professional groups.[9]

In summary, we have argued that as far as the political system is concerned, pressure groups serve four functions: they communicate, legitimate, administer, and regulate, though to their members these are often the least important roles that they play. We have suggested that the communications function is the most important. In the following comments we shall concentrate on this aspect of pressure group life, looking especially at the way in which factors such as the need to communicate with government, the amount of resources available for communication, and the level of understanding of policy systems combine to affect both the structure and behavior of such groups.

STRUCTURE AND BEHAVIOUR

The functions that pressure groups perform have much to do with both the organizational form they take and the way they behave. We might be tempted to claim that their form follows their function, were it not for the fact that structure is also greatly influenced by such things as the kind of resources made available by the group's members, their determination to promote their common interest through exerting influence and, always, the characteristics of the political system itself. We shall return to these influences after we have looked at the more fundamental aspects of pressure group structure and behaviour.

Earlier, we defined pressure groups as "organizations whose members act together to influence public policy in order to promote their common interest." The fact that they are *organizations* is crucial. In political life there are many interests and over time a considerable number exert influence in the policy process, but unless they have access to more resources than most individuals and the majority of companies, they lack the ability to sustain their influence. Unaggregated demand, as political scientists call the political demands of individual persons and corporations, tends to occur sporadically and on a piecemeal basis. Often it is sufficient to achieve or avert specific decisions, such as a spot rezoning in a city plan, but it rarely influences public policy. This is because the process of policy formation is extremely complex, involving many participants, taking place over a long period of time and usually consisting of innumerable decisions.[10] For most of those who want to take part in this process the only feasible way to do so is to band together, to share costs, to deploy at appropriate times the different talents that participation requires, even simply to maintain continuity as the process unfolds—in other words, to organize.

Not all pressure groups organize in the same way or to the same extent. Much depends on what they want to achieve by engaging in the policy process, on the resources they can put into lobbying, and on their understanding of the mechanics of policy making. Since the way in which all these factors come together has a lot to do with the policy consequences of the work of pressure groups, it is important to try to understand the relationship between the levels of organization pressure groups attain and their behaviour in the policy process.

Our goal here is not simply to understand the behaviour of pressure groups; the way in which they behave can also tell us a great deal about policy making in specific political systems and even about the political system itself. For example, as the introduction to this chapter implied, studies of Canadian pressure group behaviour have led some students to conclude that administrators in Canadian governments have a far greater influence in policy making than our earlier work on political parties, parliamentary institutions, and legal frameworks had led us to believe.

To understand these aspects of pressure group life we must arrange what we know about them in meaningful patterns. There are various ways to do this. One that is used by many scholars is to classify all groups according to the *kinds of causes* they promote. This usually results in two broadly defined lists: in one, the groups that pursue the self-interest of their members; in the other, the groups that pursue more general, public interests. Some important insights have come from using this approach. For example, as a result of the debate triggered by studies such as *The Logic of Collective Action,*[11] which argues that interest groups only survive if they can offer their members advantages (selective inducements) that can be obtained nowhere else, we now know a great deal about the internal forces that motivate pressure group behaviour and we appreciate more than we ever have before the problems that beset public interest groups. A practical consequence of this improved understanding has been the trend in several countries toward giving public interest groups special assistance in arguing for the public interest before regulatory and policy-making bodies.[12]

Useful though this approach is, it has serious weaknesses. In the first place, the classification system itself is "messy," for there are far too many groups that work simultaneously for both selective benefits and the public interest, and it is often difficult to categorize them; there is often a very fine line between self-interest and public interest.[13] More important, however, this method takes a one-sided view of the relationship between pressure groups and governments. Although it admits that pressure group activity is often triggered by government action, such as the creation of a new program or the ending or an old one, it tends to explain the subsequent behaviour of such groups either in terms of competition between rival groups or in terms of what one writer has called their "interior life." In other words, the approach focuses on the effort group members are willing and able to make to convince policy makers of the rightness of their cause. This concern is very necessary, but it has to be put in perspective. The other partner in the relationship—government—affects pressure group behaviour just as much as does membership commitment, organizational sophistication, and so on. In fact, most pressure groups are *chameleons*: those that take their lobbying role seriously adapt their internal organizations and structure to suit the policy system in which they happen to operate. That is why pressure groups working only at the provincial level in Canada are often quite different from those that concentrate their efforts at the federal level, and why both differ dramatically from their counterparts in Eastern Europe, the Third World, and even the United States.[14]

Several years ago this writer developed a conceptual framework that does try to look at pressure groups from the perspective of the *influence of government* as well as from that of the internal dynamics of groups. This approach starts with the assumption that pressure groups have functions to perform that are as necessary to the development of government policy as those performed by political parties, bureaucracies, executives, and courts. However, the way in which they perform those functions is as much determined by the shape of the policy system as it is by the knowledge, the enthusiasm, the financial capacity, and the other internal characteristics of individual groups.[15] For example, a policy system like Canada's, in which legislatures do not have a large say in policy development, will encourage pressure groups to develop quite differently from those that emerge in a system such as found in the United States, with its emphasis on congressional power.

Institutionalization, this approach argues, gives us the key to understanding pressure group behaviour. If we can come to understand how it is that some groups survive in a political system and become influential and organizationally sophisticated, while others quickly disappear, then we can learn a great deal about their interior life and about their particular policy environment.

An institution is a sophisticated entity, one that not only works to achieve the goals laid down for it, as any organization should, but that actually embodies the values it is built around. Like any organization, it begins life as a collection of individuals gathered to achieve certain objectives. Sometimes such groupings have organizational shape—the members have structured relationships with one another that permit them to carry out specialized tasks—but often they are simply a group of people who want to accomplish something. Gradually, if they stay together, they elaborate an organizational structure, and if they are successful their organization develops into an institution, "a responsive, adaptive organism" that, to its members and many of those it deals with, has a philosophy, a code of behaviour, and sense of unity related to the values it has come to embody. The Greenpeace Foundation is a good example of such an organization. It is not only sophisticated as an organization with an international structure, but it stands very firmly for certain beliefs and acts accordingly. As a pressure group it is highly institutionalized, even though it is not popular with governments.

When we apply the concept of institutionalization to pressure group analysis we must be very aware of a point made by an early student of institutions, Philip Selznick. "As institutionalization progresses," he maintains, "the enterprise...becomes peculiarly competent to do a particular kind of work."[16] In the case of pressure groups this means that they must become "peculiarly competent" to carry out the four functions we have already discussed, especially the function of communication. The institutionalized group knows what government is thinking about, what it needs to know, and how to get that information to it at the right time, in the right place, and in the most acceptable form. This means a great deal more than simply button-holing politicians at cocktail parties. It means the group must have an expert staff—or a helpful, well-informed membership—able to communicate with government officials at bureaucratic as well as elected levels, on a continuing basis. The need for this particular competence has led this writer to claim that one of the defining characteristics of institutionalized pressure groups is "an extensive knowledge of those sectors of government that affect them and their clients." In its entirety that definition describes institutional pressure groups as:

> groups that possess organizational continuity and cohesion, commensurate human and financial resources, extensive knowledge of those sectors of government that affect them and their clients, a stable membership, concrete and immediate operational objectives associated with philosophies that are broad enough to permit [them] to bargain with government over the application of specific legislation or the achievement of particular concessions, and a willingness to put organizational imperatives ahead of any particular policy concern.[17]

We cannot explain this definition completely here, but we should note several things about it. First, it is very unlikely that any real group could be described in these particular terms. It is an idealized version of a certain kind of group; it is a model with which to compare the various types of groups we come across. Second, because the idea of institutionalization suggests a progression and because this particular model can be used as a bench mark against which other groups can be compared, it becomes possible to think of pressure groups as falling along a continuum. At one extreme we can place institutional groups like those in our model, and at the other we can put those groups that have the opposite characteristics. These, we would argue:

> are governed by their orientation toward specific issues. . .[and have] limited organizational continuity and cohesion, minimal and often naive knowledge of government, fluid membership, a tendency to encounter difficulty in formulating and adhering to short-range objectives, a generally low regard for the organizational mechanisms they have developed for carrying out their goals, and, most important, a narrowly defined purpose, usually the resolution of one or two issues or problems, that inhibits the development of "selective inducements" designed to broaden the group's membership base.[18]

We call these "issue-oriented" groups and can readily identify them. They spring up at a moment's notice, usually in reaction to some government action or a private sector activity that only government can change. (They are often seen in city politics confronting developers, highway builders, and planners.) Usually, they disband when their goals are either won or convincingly lost, but occasionally they keep on playing a part in politics and slowly become recognized voices in policy making. In order to do this, they have to become more highly organized, developing their "peculiar competence" to communicate their policy views to government. Since the early 1970s, a number of environmental groups have done this, in effect engaging in the process of institutionalization. They do not, of course, become institutional groups overnight. In fact, very few achieve that status, and most we could describe as either fledgling or mature, depending on how closely they seem to conform to the models at either end of our continuum.

Figure 15.1 sets out a visual guide to this continuum. In it we have tried to show how the organizational development of each kind of group helps define its relationship to the policy process. For example, the issue-orientated group with its supporters participating out of concern for a particular issue usually has a small membership that tries to make up in devotion to the cause what it lacks in resources or staff. Lack of staff is this type of group's most serious deficiency, at least in the Canadian setting, because it generally means that the group does not have expert knowledge about what government is doing or thinking about the issue of concern. Its members tend, therefore, to work in an information vacuum. Not only do they not know what government is thinking, they tend not to know who in government thinks about their particular issue. Their reactions, therefore, tend to be gut reactions directed at the most likely figure in sight, usually a politician, and expressed vociferously in the media.

In the long run these methods do not work. A specific decision may be turned around, but to change policy—which is a mosaic of many decisions—groups need to be close to government thinking, able to overcome the barriers created by administrative secrecy, and knowledgeable about where and when to intervene. In Canada, particularly, where public information legislation was until recently quite antiquated and group participation in policy making has been considered a privilege, not a right, government officials have in the past been able to undermine any groups too inclined to publicly attack policy simply by withholding vital information. It may be that recent changes in the policy process, particularly in the diffusion of power that has become the norm in Ottawa, is altering this condition. Nevertheless, for many years the authority of information control made government agencies the dominant partner in their relations with pressure groups and forced those issue-orientated groups that did survive to follow a pattern of institutionalization that took them very rapidly from the placard-carrying stage to the collegial and consultative relationship favoured by government.

Yet, though confrontation has been, and perhaps still is, dysfunctional for groups in the long run, in their early life it can be very important, sometimes essential. Since they generally emerge in response to a policy issue, new groups cannot, by definition, have participated in the deliberations that led to the decision they are concerned about. Thus, they enter the policy process at a stage when events are moving beyond their ability to stop them, and only the most drastic measures will have any effect. In these circumstances, confrontation may be the best available strategy, as it makes use of the media's ability to influence the only decision makers who may still be able to change the course of events—the politicians.

The group that outlives this early "placard-carrying" stage generally has done so by changing its relationship to its members and by adapting to the policy system. One of the first steps in this adaptation is that the organization must stop being concerned with only one issue and instead take up several causes. Many environmental groups took this route, starting up to prevent the destruction of a particular natural amenity, then switching their concern to large issues. With a broader range of interest the group attracts a wider membership. While the new members may lack the fervent sense of commitment of the group's founders, and may be less inclined to sound a strident ideological note when the group tries to communicate with government, a wider membership base usually broadens the group's financial resources, bringing stability and a strengthened capacity to engage in the information game. Here again

Figure 15.1
The Continuum Framework

Categories	Group Characteristics							
	Objectives				Organizational Feature			
	single, narrowly defined	multiple but closely related	multiple, broadly defined, & collective	multiple, broadly defined, collective & selective	small membership/ no paid staff	membership can support small staff	alliances with other groups/staff includes professionals	extensive human and financial resources
Institution-alized				■				■
Mature			■				■	
Fledgling		■				■		
Issue-Orientated	■				■			

group-oriented and policy-orientated developments may take place in tandem. With a steady budget the group may take on a modest staff, a move that usually ensures that finances are better managed and that the members are served more consistently. Financial capacity usually also means that the group can afford to hire professionals—lawyers, public policy experts, public relations specialists—who can help it acquire the information it needs to participate in the policy process. These are the first steps in institutionalization. From this point on, the nature of the organization does not change a great deal. It simply becomes more complex, more capable of adapting to changes in the policy system, and to the disappointment of founding members, more remote and professional, guided increasingly by its paid staff.

Once started on the road to institutionalization the pressure group more readily wins the attention of government officials and, at the same time, is more apt to adapt to meet shifts in government policy processes. This largely follows from the decision to hire professionals. Because they are familiar with the way in which policy is made, these people guide the group away from some lines of action and encourage others. In Canada and most European countries this generally means that groups become more and more intimate with the details of bureaucratic decision making and less and less inclined to use the media except when formal hearings necessitate the presentation of rather general briefs that are intended to create an image rather than promote a specific policy. In the United States, on the other hand, lobbyists can expect to have to argue both in public and in private. With these differences in strategy go differences in organizational structure.

As these comments suggest, the processes of pressure group institutionalization offer us a particularly useful way of discovering the differences between policy systems and even tracing the evolution of our systems over time. In Canada, for example, because we have pressure groups, we often mistakenly think that they behave in the same way as American pressure groups. This sometimes leads to the notion that our policy system is becoming more like that of the United States. It is quite true in some respects, particularly when issue-oriented groups exploit the media, that there is more than a superficial resemblance between Canadian and American pressure group behaviour. As soon as we look at the behaviour of more established groups in both countries, however, we see major differences. For example, even well-established American groups readily take part in public debates over policy, while their counterparts in Canada see an appeal to public opinion as a last resort.[19]

Why the difference? In the American system congressional politics plays a large part in policy development, with policy tending to be formed by the congressional committees responsible for a particular field, the administrative agencies carrying out policy, and the interest groups affected by it. Much policy discussion is conducted in private, but there is also an important public element involving committee hearings where rival demands are vigorously presented and where even the most secure, discreet, and established lobby must put its case to the general public as well as to the policy makers.[20]

Canada has had no such public forum. Debate in Parliament has been tightly controlled by the government, and even committee hearings have offered few opportunities for airing grievances, much less changing policy. The basic form of public policy has been worked out between the political executive and senior administrators. Consequently, lobbyists and others wishing to influence public policy have chosen to do so by approaching and persuading civil servants and Cabinet ministers rather than parliamentarians. There are innumerable consequences to this, some affecting pressure groups, others the policy process itself, most of which we cannot discuss here. Suffice it to say that the end effect of this system is that "legitimate, wealthy, coherent interests, having multiple access to the legislative process, would tend to be more influential than less legitimate, poor, diffuse interests, having few sources of access to the legislative process."[21]

It may be that changes in parliamentary procedure, in the structure of policy making, in the availability of government information, and in our constitutional framework are causing important modifications in this system of pressure group politics, making groups less dependent on bureaucracy and more capable of engaging in open and public debate. At the moment, we have only a few hints that this is the case and no very clear idea as to what the future may bring. However, probably we can assume that a tendency for pressure groups to become more numerous and more publicly active will continue to grow.[22]

PRESSURE GROUPS IN THE POLICY PROCESS: THE ROLE OF POLICY COMMUNITIES

We sometimes think of pressure groups in the singular, acting alone to bring off a policy coup or to thwart some scheme cooking in the "policy shops," as government policy analysis units are often called. At other times they are described en masse: collaborating, competing, and generally rampaging across the policy stage. In general, however, their participation in the policy system is continuous, discreet, and multifaceted.

The first responsibility of any pressure group is to attend to the immediate needs of its clients. This usually means dealing with quite routine problems: alleviating the too stringent application of regulations, negotiating a minor shift in policy, bringing about the slight extension of a service. Such minor irritations along the public sector–private sector interface bring pressure group representatives into daily contact with government officials and, while not inspiring in themselves, familiarize them with the subtle changes in administrative routine and attitude that eventually crystallize into a change in policy.[23] When formal policy discussions begin, the understanding developed through these routine contacts is of immense value.

The policy process itself is hard to define: the origins of policy are often obscure and the roles of those who take part are seldom exactly the same from debate to debate. Even so, we do have some general notions as to how the key policy actors—politicians, bureaucrats, and lobbyists— relate to one another, and this helps us develop a rough picture of the part pressure groups play in the process.

The first point that we must bear in mind is that the entire political community is almost never involved in a specific policy discussion. Specialization occurs throughout the policy system. The existence of pressure groups gives us the most obvious evidence of this, but special- ization occurs elsewhere as well. Government departments, however large and multifaceted they may appear to be, are confined to a precisely defined territory. Even the political executive finds that only the really big issues are discussed by the entire Cabinet. All the rest are handled by individual Cabinet ministers or by specialized Cabinet committees. Rich- ard Crossman, once a member of the British Cabinet, remarked in his dairy that "we come briefed by our departments to fight for our depart- mental budgets, not as Cabinet ministers with a Cabinet view."[24] Only prime ministers and presidents play roles that encourage them to con- sider policy in the round, and they live with such tight schedules that only the most urgent and significant issues come to their attention.

Out of specialization come what we call "policy communities"— groupings of government agencies, pressure groups, media people, and individuals, including academics, who for various reasons have an inter- est in a particular policy field and attempt to influence it. Most policy communities consist of two segments: the subgovernment and the atten- tive public. To all intents and purposes the subgovernment is the policy- making body in the field. It processes most routine policy issues and when doing so is seldom successfully challenged by interlopers. The subgovernment is what has been called "the durable core of any policy arena."[25] It consists of the government agencies most directly engaged in setting policy and regulating the field and a small group of interests— generally associations but occasionally major corporations—whose power guarantees them the right to be consulted on virtually a daily basis. Their power wins them a place at the policy table, but government also needs their expert knowledge of the technical aspects of policy.

The power of the inner circle is used to limit the participation of others in policy debate. Those who are excluded congregate in the "attentive public." This outer circle includes those who are interested in policy issues but do not participate in policy making on a frequent, regular basis. The academic community often plays this role, as do journalists working for specialized publications and, of course, a range of organizations and associations whose interest is keen but not acute enough to warrant breaking into the inner circle.

The attentive public lacks the power of the subgovernment, but it still plays a vital part in policy development. Conferences and study sessions organized by professional and interest associations offer opportunities for officials at various levels to converse with the grass roots of their constituency and with journalists and academics who have been studying public policy. Most have views on government performance and are quick to put them forward. Though most are heard sceptically, sometimes patronizingly, they contribute to the process through which government and people gradually amend, extend, and generally adapt policies and programs to the changing needs of the community. Similarly, the newsletters, professional journals, and trade magazines that circulate through the policy community give both the subgovernment and the attentive public plenty of opportunity to shore up, demolish, and generally transmogrify the existing policy edifice. In this turmoil of theories and interests, officialdom—which is almost never monolithic, nearly always pluralistic, and seldom at peace with itself—discerns the policy changes government must make if it is to keep nearly abreast of circumstance. The main function of the attentive public, then, is to maintain a perpetual policy review process.

In Figure 15.2, we have described the kind of policy community that might be active in a field in which the federal government is prominent. At the heart of the community are the key federal bodies involved: the agency primarily responsible for formulating policy and carrying out programs in the field, Cabinet with its co-ordinating committees and their support structures, the Privy Council Office, the Treasury Board, and so on. None of these are located at the very centre of the figure because no agency is ever consistently dominant in the field. On average, though, because so much of policy making is routine, the lead agency tends to be most influential over time. Clustered around it are the pressure groups and provincial government agencies to which we have already referred, keeping a sharp eye on "the feds" and generally participating in the subgovernment. Also involved are other federal agencies whose mandate overlaps that of the lead agency. These usually review agency policy, working through interdepartmental committees to do so, and often greatly alter it. For example, Canadian fisheries policy has often been influenced by External Affairs, worried about our relations with trading partners who fish off our coasts. Hovering on the edge of the subgovern-

Figure 15.2
The Policy Community

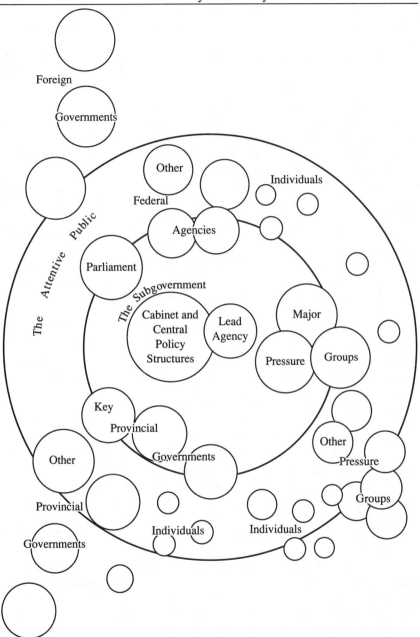

ment is Parliament, perennially interested, intermittently involved, sometimes influential.

Also hovering on the edge of the subgovernment are other provincial governments. Some of these might wish to be part of the subgovernment but lack the resources to maintain a presence; others are simply not interested and are content to observe the activities of the subgovernment, interfering when necessary. In the final analysis, they may be no more influential than some of the major pressure groups active in the community. Some of the pressure groups are depicted as overlapping one another, because in fact they do overlap. They share membership, are often put together on advisory boards, and frequently combine their efforts to present a common stand to government and the public. Finally, we should note that foreign governments must also be included in Canadian policy communities. Canadian politicians and officials are great travellers, always aware of changing trends and conditions abroad— sometimes more alert to developments elsewhere than to developments in parts of Canada—and ready to import new ideas and approaches to the Canadian scene.[26]

The figure suggests an orbital movement around the lead agency and the federal executive, but that would be too static. Rather than revolving around the key agencies, the other members of the policy community are in constant motion. As governments and key personnel change, provincial government participation varies, or changing economic factors compel provincial agencies to retreat or advance into the subgovernment. In the energy field, for example, Alberta became prominent after the Leduc discovery, and Newfoundland after Hibernia. Similarly, pressure groups come and go from the centre.

Pressure groups, along with individual members of the attentive public, are the most mobile members of the policy community. With their annual meetings, their newsletters, their regional organizations, and above all, their informal networks, they have an ability to cross organizational lines denied other more formal actors, such as government departments. They can, therefore, act as go-betweens, provide opportunities for quiet meetings between warring agencies, and keep the policy process in motion. These services, together with their ability to evaluate policy and develop opinion, make pressure groups integral members of the policy community.

Before we conclude our comments on the policy community, we have to remember that the most prominent of its members are not primarily interested in making or reformulating policy. Rather, for them, the policy community is a protective device, limiting rather than expanding the opportunities for the public at large to achieve major policy changes. Thus, it is the goal of the subgovernment to keep policy making at the routine or technical level. If it achieves this, the subgovernment can keep interference to a minimum. Often, however, circumstances outside its control—economic changes, the development of new technologies, changing public concerns—are more than the subgovernment can handle through its system of formal communications and informal networks. Controversy develops, new issues emerge, and more and more interests want to take part in policy making. Policy debate broadens as levels of conflict rise, so that eventually central issues are taken out of the hands of the subgovernment and policy community and resolved at the highest political levels—by Cabinet and by the First Ministers' Conference.[27] When this occurs, the policy community, as well as policy, is often vastly altered.

PRESSURE GROUPS AND DEMOCRACY

Many people feel that pressure groups are a threat to democratic government. They distrust "special-interest groups," arguing that their special pleading circumvents the legitimate authority of elected representatives and unfairly competes with the average citizen who approaches government as an individual. They fear that the special-interest state is more easily corruptible than one that debates and settles policy in the open forum of Parliament. "It is one thing," Robert Stanfield argues,

> For individuals to pursue their own interests as they always have: it becomes a qualitatively different kind of society when individuals organize to pursue their individual interests collectively. National life has become a struggle for advantage among large and powerful organizations—not simply corporations and trade unions. Organized pressures abound.[28]

Stanfield sees pressure groups supplanting political parties as the citizen's chief vehicle for communicating with government. John Meisel shares this view:

> Pressure groups are often unwilling to permit their interests to be expressed and transmitted only by parties, but wish to participate directly in making their voices heard and their influence felt....Their numbers and means permit them to become rivals of political parties. These rapidly proliferating groups and institutions can gain access to the decision-making process without having recourse to parties which thus become bypassed in the vital area of mediation between individual and group interests and the state.[29]

Not only does democracy suffer as the political party is undermined, but the country also loses "the only organization whose nature forces them to work towards a national consensus."[30] "National political parties are the only mass organizations we have which are forced to try to see the country as a whole and to reconcile regional and other differences."[31] Unless we act to check the spreading influence of pressure groups, Stanfield warns, we shall lose our capacity to discern the national interest. Similar fears have been expressed in other countries, particularly in the United States, where criticism of "interest group liberalism" suggests that pluralism, the touchstone of American government, has bred a monstrous, competitive, and eventually self-destroying system.[32]

We cannot lightly dismiss these fears. There is no doubt that interest groups have proliferated in recent years, nor that the influence of political parties has abated. Nor does long study of their behaviour banish the suspicion that special-interest groups are capable of corruption and, however unwittingly, of destroying democracy. Ultimately, special interests want special favours, and the logic of the relationship between groups and their clients countenances the unscrupulous use of influence.

The fact is, pressure groups have become necessary. In Canada and elsewhere, governments have needed pressure groups so badly that they have encouraged their growth. They have given them moral encourage-ment and financial assistance, they have made places for them on advisory boards and regulatory agencies, they have created regulations that inten-tionally push those who are regulated into associations, and they have made many groups a part of the administrative process. None of these steps has been taken in order to destroy democracy, and although some challenged political patronage, they attacked corruption, not the party system.

The decline of the political party as an instrument for developing policy has come about because government itself has changed, not because of effete party leadership, rapacious pressure group activity, or a declining sense of community among the public. The modern state delivers innumerable services, manages vast resources, and attempts to direct complex economies, and to do all of these things it has organized itself into massive, functionally orientated, specialized bureaucracies. These agencies have great difficulty dealing with human beings. They deal with cases, with the partial needs of individuals. To develop policy they must talk with the public—not the public in general, but with the public they serve: their special public. What could be more natural than to persuade this public to organize itself, to adapt to the structure of modern government in order to communicate more effectively with it?

Nor does the trend to special-interest representation stem solely from the growing complexity of modern government. Equally important are the changes that have taken place in the economy over the last two centuries. The world of small enterprises whose fortunes were associated with the fortunes of particular places gave way during this century to a world economy vastly influenced by the giant corporation. Whether it is a multinational or not, the giant corporation is not very interested in what happens in specific localities. It has plants in many places, draws its resources from around the world, and markets its products everywhere. In its own way it is just as concerned with specialized issues as are government agencies, and it is no accident that these two forms of human organization have achieved complexity together.

Equally, it is no accident that as these structures have evolved, political parties have declined. Political parties in most Western nations, at least, have a territorial basis. They are designed to win control of legislatures, and thus political power, and as most legislatures are based on territorially demarcated constituencies, party organization must follow suit. This is in many ways anachronistic, for the reasons we have outlined: governmental bureaucracies and their clients deal with sectoral issues, not the local concerns that disturb constituency organizations. Hence the decline of party influence. Yet the party system is not as outdated as it may seem. Despite decades of organizational conditioning, human beings still exhibit tremendous attachment to specific places. Consequently, the spatial basis of political party organization provides an important antidote to the sectoral bias of the administrative arm and the machinery of the economy.

With the legitimacy of government rooted in a spatial orientation to political communication, and its effectiveness depending on sectoral organization, the modern democratic state contains a tension that is the most fascinating, most disturbing feature of modern political life. Out of it has come the decline, but certainly not the demise, of the political party and the rise of the pressure group, the ideal instrument for sectoral, specialized communication. With the rise of pressure groups has come a tendency for institutionalized groups—the majority representing business interests—to dominate debate within policy communities. As William Coleman has pointed out, because policy making has become so diffuse, it is difficult to compel these interests to consider the general welfare or to be accountable to the public. Equally, it is extremely difficult for other interests to participate effectively—let alone on equal terms with business—in public debate.[33] Public interest groups are especially disadvantaged by this imbalance. Such developments threaten democratic discourse, as recent concern over lobbying and over business-interest participation in the free trade debate demonstrates.[34]

During the 1990s, we will hear increased public discussion of these issues. Some reform proposals have already been put forward. In 1987, for example, a parliamentary committee recommended the registration of lobbyists, and in 1988 a weak registration law was passed.[35] In another publication I have argued for lobbyist registration, for strengthening the capacity of parliamentary committees to use and encourage interest group discussion of policy, and for providing more resources to public interest groups.[36] Most recently Coleman has made a similar plea for parliamentary reform and has suggested that Canada follow the lead of small European states and restructure business interests so that the entire spectrum of business can be represented by "a very few organizations that can give voice to the diversity of interests resulting from territorial and sectoral factors."[37] He also argues that labour groups should be strengthened so that they will acquire both a capacity to speak to general concerns and an acknowledged responsibility to do so.

Some of these changes are in progress. Parliament, in particular, has used procedural reforms to encourage more open and vigorous policy debate. We can expect the regulation of lobbying to take firmer hold during the 1990s. We may even see greater government support for public interest groups. There is less likelihood that business interests will be reorganized in the fashion that Coleman recommends. Despite similarities between Canada and small European states, Canada is physically a very large and regionally diverse country. It is, therefore, doubtful whether even a highly democratic organizational structure for business interests can offset the pull of regional tensions within interest communities. Similarly, it is unlikely that the most prominent public interest groups—such as environmentalists, consumer activists, and women's groups—would be willing to voice their concerns solely through the labour movement. In other words, public supervision of pressure group activity will proceed incrementally in Canada during the decade. Whether it will be either sufficient or appropriate is not clear.

NOTES

1. This definition was first presented in "Pressure Groups: Adaptive Instruments of Political Communication," in *Pressure Group Behaviour in Canadian Politics*, ed. A. Paul Pross (Toronto: McGraw-Hill Ryerson, 1975), pp. 1–26 and has been elaborated in my *Group Politics and Public Policy* (Toronto: Oxford University Press, 1986).
2. *Lunenburg Progress-Enterprise*, 5 April 1978, p. 16.
3. J. Hugh Faulkner, "Pressuring the Executive," *Canadian Public Administration* 25, no. 2 (1982): 240–44, 248.
4. See David Kwavnick, *Organized Labour and Pressure Politics* (Montreal: McGill-Queen's University Press, 1972) for a useful discussion of this aspect of pressure group life.
5. W. L. Canniff, Technical Director, Canadian Chemical Producers' Association, House of Commons, Standing Committee on Fisheries and Forestry, *Minutes of Proceedings and Evidence*, 17 April 1975, p. 18:4. (Re: "An act to protect human health and the environment from substances that contaminate the environment.")

6. See Arthur Drache, "Improving the Budget Process," *Policy Options* 3, no. 5 (1982): 15–19 and Douglas Hartle, *The Revenue Budget Process of the Government of Canada* (Toronto: Canadian Tax Foundation, 1982).

7. Freda Hawkins, *Canada and Immigration: Public Policy and Public Concern* (Montreal: McGill-Queen's University Press, 1972), p. 301.

8. The role of Children's Aid Societies in Ontario has been vigorously debated in the past. See particularly *The Globe and Mail*, 16 December 1977, and the debate over the provincial government's intervention in the operation of the Kenora District Office of the Children's Aid Society, in the provincial legislature. See also National Council of Welfare, *In the Best Interests of the Child: A Report by the National Council of Welfare on the Child Welfare System in Canada* (Ottawa: The Council, 1979).

9. See René Dussault and Louis Borgeat, "La reforme des professions au Québec," *Canadian Public Administration* 17, no. 3 (1974): 407.

10. For example, in June 1983, officials in Ottawa sat down with representatives of the Canadian Chamber of Commerce, the Business Council on National Issues, and the Canadian Manufacturers' Association to discuss revisions to federal competition legislation. On six previous occasions since 1971 government proposals to change the legislation had been set aside in the face of fierce opposition from business groups (*Kingston Whig-Standard*, 21 June 1983). The story of the long attempt to reform competition policy can be found in W.T. Stanbury, *Business Interests and the Reform of Canadian Competition Policy* (Toronto: Carswell/Methuen 1978) and Irving Brecher, *Canada's Competition Policy Revisited: Some New Thoughts on an Old Story* (Montreal: Institute for Research on Public Policy, 1981).

11. Mancur Olson, *The Logic of Collective Action* (Cambridge, Mass.: Harvard University Press, 1965).

12. See Peter H. Schuck, "Public Interest Groups and the Policy Process," *Public Administration Review* 37, no. 2 (1972): 132–40.

13. Terry M. Moe, *The Organization of Interests* (Chicago: University of Chicago Press, 1980).

14. Suzanne D. Berger, ed., *Organizing Interests in Western Europe* (Cambridge: Cambridge University Press, 1981).

15. A similar view is put forward by Henry W. Ehrmann in *Interest Groups on Four Continents*, ed. Henry W. Ehrmann (Pittsburgh: University of Pittsburgh Press, 1958).

16. Philip Selznick, *Leadership in Administration* (New York: Harper and Row, 1957), p. 139.

17. A. Paul Pross, "Canadian Pressure Groups in the 1970s: Their Role and Their Relations with the Public Service," *Canadian Public Administration* 18, no. 1 (1975): 124.

18. Ibid.
19. For a fuller discussion of this point, see W. T. Stanbury, *Business–Government Relations in Canada* (Toronto: Methuen, 1986), ch. 7.
20. See Randall B. Ripley and Grace A. Franklin, *Congress, the Bureaucracy and Public Policy* (Homewood, I11.: Dorsey Press, 1976); Robert Presthus's two-volume comparative study on Canada and the United States, *Elite Accommodation in Canadian Politics* (Toronto: MacMillan, 1973) and *Elites in the Policy Process* (Cambridge: Cambridge University Press, 1974); and Mildred A. Schwartz, *The Environment for Policy-Making in Canada and the United States* (Montreal: C. D. Howe Institute, 1981).
21. Fred Thompson and W. T. Stanbury, "The Political Economy of Interest Groups in the Legislative Process in Canada" (Montreal: Institute for Research on Public Policy, Occasional Paper No. 9), p. viii.
22. The recent evolution of the Canadian policy process has caused a good deal of debate, which probably can best be followed in the journals *Canadian Public Administration* and *Policy Options*.
23. There are useful descriptions of these relationships in Kwavnick, *Organized Labour and Pressure Politics*.
24. Quoted in J. J. Richardson and A. G. Jordan, *Governing Under Pressure: The Policy Process in a Post-Parliamentary Democracy* (Oxford: Martin Robertson, 1979), p. 26.
25. John E. Chubb, *Interest Groups and the Bureaucracy: The Politics of Energy* (Stanford: Stanford University Press, 1983), pp. 8–10, quoted in William D. Coleman, *Business and Politics: A Study of Collective Action* (Montreal: McGill-Queen's University Press, 1988), p. 277. Coleman presents case studies of a number of policy fields in which the workings of the policy community can be discerned. For an elaboration of the concept itself, see my *Group Politics and Public Policy*. Susan McCorquodale and I have looked at a specific policy community in *Economic Resurgence and the Constitutional Agenda: The Case of the East Coast Fisheries* (Kingston: Queen's University, 1987).
26. For example, Canadian minimum wage policy has been influenced by the experience of other countries and the work of international organizations. See Chris Parke, "The Setting of Minimum Wage Policy in the Maritimes" (Halifax: Dalhousie Institute of Public Affairs, 1980).
27. This paragraph adapts to the Canadian scene concepts developed in E. E. Schattschneider, *The Semi-Sovereign People: A Realist's View of Democracy in America* (New York: Holt, Rinehart and Winston, 1960). The Canadian variant is looked at more fully in Pross, *Group Politics and Public Policy*.

28. Robert L. Stanfield, the Fifth George C. Nowland Lecture, Acadia University, 7 February 1977 (mimeograph).
29. John Meisel, "Recent Changes in Canadian Parties," in *Party Politics in Canada*, ed. Hugh G. Thorburn (Toronto: Prentice-Hall, 1967), pp. 33–54.
30. Stanfield, Fifth George C. Nowlan Lecture.
31. Ibid.
32. Theodore J. Lowi, *The End of Liberalism* (New York: Norton, 1979).
33. Coleman, *Business and Politics*, pp. 261–65.
34. See, for example, John Sawatsky, *The Insiders: Government, Business and the Lobbyists* (Toronto: McClelland and Stewart, 1987) and Hyman Solomon, "Business Got its Feet Wet in Public Policy," *The Financial Post*, 5 December 1988.
35. I have given an account of this in "The Business Card Bill: The Debate Over Lobbyist Registration in Canada," in Grant Jordan, ed., *Commercial Lobbying* (forthcoming).
36. Pross, *Group Politics and Public Policy*, pp. 261–72.
37. Coleman, *Business and Politics*, p. 169.

FURTHER READINGS

Coleman, W. D. *Business and Politics: A Study of Collective Action*. Montreal: McGill-Queen's University Press, 1988.

Dion, L. *Société et politique: la vie des groupes*, 2 vols. Québec: Les Presses de l'Université Laval, 1971.

Kwavnick, D. *Organized Labour and Pressure Politics*. Montreal: McGill-Queen's University Press, 1972.

Lang, R. W. *The Politics of Drugs: A Comparative Pressure-Group Study of the Canadian Pharmaceutical Manufactures' Association and the Association of the British Pharmaceutical Industry, 1930–1970*. Lexington, Mass.: Saxon-House and Lexington Books, 1974.

Presthus, R. *Elite Accommodation in Canadian Politics*. Toronto: MacMillan, 1973.

———. *Elites in the Policy Process*. Cambridge: Cambridge University Press, 1974.

Pross, A. Paul. *Group Politics and Public Policy*. Toronto: Oxford University Press, 1986.

Schwartz, M. A. *The Environment for Policy-Making in Canada and the United States*. Montreal: C. D. Howe Institute, 1981.

Stanbury, W. T. *Business–Government Relations in Canada*. Toronto: Methuen, 1986.

Thorburn, H. G. *Interest Groups in the Canadian Federal System*. Toronto: University of Toronto Press, 1985.

PART 4

STRUCTURES OF CANADIAN GOVERNMENT

16

Canada's Constitutional Odyssey

DAVID MILNE

After the extensive constitutional wanderings of the 1980s, it may now be appropriate for Canadians to take stock: to see whence we have come and where we appear to be going. The decade began with the defeat of a government-led referendum on Quebec independence, followed shortly by a constitutional agreement among all first ministers except Quebec's to patriate the Canadian constitution and to incorporate in it a Charter of Rights and Freedoms. By mid-decade, the courts found themselves inundated with Charter cases, forcing them to rethink older constitutional principles and practices and to redefine their role in Canadian politics.

Hardly before the country had absorbed the measure of these profound changes, several constitutional conferences ensued, driven to focusing on ways to entrench in the constitution the idea of aboriginal self-government and to give constitutional protection to negotiated self-government agreements. No sooner had Canada retreated unsuccessfully from that journey in March 1987 than the country began a new series of talks among first ministers aimed at healing the earlier constitutional rupture with Quebec. That particular undertaking led to Meech Lake, where in April 1987 another major constitutional agreement was announced. The long trek in pursuit of ratification of that agreement continues today.

So much for this bare sketch of the nation's most recent constitutional outings. What of their meaning and logic? Presumably, there should be some underlying political explanation for the choices the country has already made or is now making, some link between past and present. It is the theme of this chapter that Canada's recent constitutional ventures do reflect a longer historical odyssey, though our current constitutional adaptations may be so large and so novel that they call into question some of the older images we have inherited from the past.

FROM IMPERIAL CONSTITUTIONAL ROOTS TO NATIONAL INDEPENDENCE

Doubtless every Canadian student has read the less-than-stirring historians' tales of Canada's march "from colony to nation." The essentials of the story are familiar enough: we see a picture of loyal Canada, spurning the

American revolutionary tradition, deciding instead to take a slower, evolutionary—but nonetheless inevitable—path to nationhood. While the image represses much of the actual violence in Canada's history, it bears a remarkable and reliable likeness to its subject. For Canada's political culture is rooted in an imperialism that Canadians appear over time to have wanted simultaneously to retain and to throw off. This is true not only for both French and English Canadians alike, but also for Canada's aboriginal peoples.

Since it was Britain that ultimately triumphed in the struggle for the northern half of North America, it is to British constitutional practices that we must turn to discover the essential foundations of Canada. Long before Confederation, for example, the people of the different colonies of British North America had adopted many of the cherished elements of British constitutionalism: the Crown, Parliament, Cabinet and responsible government, an independent judiciary, and even the rudiments of party politics. Much of this heritage took the form of constitutional conventions, practices, and rules that had evolved over a much earlier period of political experimentation in Great Britain. In addition, it is to Westminster one must turn to find the legislation creating and expanding upon so much of Canada's constitutional life, both pre- and post-Confederation. So many of the great landmarks in Canada's constitutional evolution are simply proclamations of the British Crown or statutes of the United Kingdom: the Royal Proclamation of 1763; the Quebec Act of 1774; the Constitutional Act of 1791; the Act of Union passed in 1840 and proclaimed in 1841; the British North America Act (now Constitution Act, 1867) establishing the Dominion of Canada; and many later acts of constitutional amendment, of which the most important is the Canada Act and Constitution Act of 1982 providing for final constitutional independence from Britain, a domestic amending formula, and a Charter of Rights and Freedoms. It is wholly characteristic that Canada remained committed to that process of imperial creation and adaptation of its constitution right to the end.

It is this British imperial heritage that has shaped the constitutional life and imagination of Canadians to the present day. English-speaking colonists carried with them a fondness for representative elected legislative assemblies, while their French-speaking compatriots learned very early of the value of such institutions in the defence of their own unique way of life. The Quebec Act of 1774 guaranteed to the inhabitants of what had been New France freedom of religious worship and their own civil law, while the Constitutional Act of 1791 gave them an elected assembly and a territory in Lower Canada in which to begin their practice of constitutional democracy. Despite the fact that these assemblies were often in conflict with the members appointed by the governor to legislative and executive councils, Canadians did not opt for American republicanism when offered the chance of rebellion during the American Revolution, the War of 1812, or the Rebellions in Upper and Lower Canada in 1837. United Empire Loyalists who had fled to the British North American colonies from the American Revolution by the tens of thousands clearly did not relish American practices, while the powerful Church in Lower Canada preferred the political accommodations it had managed to work out within the British Empire to life in the great secular republic to the south.

Widespread dissatisfaction with a system of elected assemblies on the one hand and appointed executives on the other led Lord Durham to recommend responsible government for the colonies in his 1839 report to the British government. The Rebellions of 1837 led by William Lyon Mackenzie in Upper Canada and Louis-Joseph Papineau in Lower Canada had precipitated Durham's study and underlined the urgency for Britain to act upon his recommendations. Responsible government meant that the governor general ought to appoint and take advice from executive members who sat in the elected assembly and held the confidence of the members of the assembly. In this way, the old power struggle between an appointed clique of governors' favourites and the elected assemblies of the colonies was resolved in favour of the popularly elected leaders in the assembly. Students of Canadian history will recall this victory symbolized in a reluctant Lord Elgin signing the Rebellion Losses Bill in 1849 on the advice of his popularly elected ministers, and a conservative opposition venting its rage in the burning of the Parliament buildings in Montreal.

While the winning of responsible government appeared to enshrine democratic values by requiring the governor to appoint elected leaders to the executive, it also ironically laid the foundations for later Cabinet domination of the legislature.[1] Now the political leaders in the assembly, able to dominate proceedings there, were also granted executive powers; with the withdrawal of the governor from its meetings as early as 1854 and with the later development of a disciplined party under its control, the Cabinet under the direction of the prime minister was able to serve as the effective centre of power in the system. In effect, an older, weaker form of executive domination over the legislature gradually was replaced by an even stronger form. But this too was completely in the spirit of the British parliamentary tradition.

And so it went with very many other features of Canada's constitution, later carried forward into the British North America Act: the vesting of legal executive power in the Queen (though by convention effectively controlled by her ministers), and an appointed, propertied second House for "sober second thought" modelled loosely on the House of Lords. Canada's constitution was expressly designed to be "similar in principle to that of the United Kingdom." Provision was made for the creation of an independent court system, with final appeals heard by the Judicial Committee of the Privy Council, a circle of legal councillors tendering advice to the British monarch on appeals from Empire and Commonwealth Courts. That committee would serve as Canada's final court of appeal until 1949, and through its decisions played a vital role in shaping the nature of Canada's constitutional evolution in those first critical years.

There was not even a domestic amending formula in the Constitution Act, 1867. This too would be provided for by the imperial connection. Since the United Kingdom Parliament was the effective legal author of Canada's constitution, changes could be made to the British statute, as deemed appropriate, on request of the Canadian Parliament. This was the route that was in fact followed for so many significant amendments to Canada's constitution: the 1871 amendment granting Parliament the power to create new provinces out of the territories, hence legitimizing the earlier establishment of Manitoba in 1870 and the subsequent additions of Saskatchewan and Alberta in 1905; the final granting of rights over natural resources to the western provinces in 1930; the virtual achievement of full sovereignty under the Statute of Westminster in 1931; the transfer of provincial powers over unemployment assistance to Ottawa in 1940; the addition of Newfoundland in 1949; acceptance of a federal role in pensions in 1964. These and even the Canada Act of 1982 are all merely U.K. legislative enactments.

The same dependence upon the imperial connection was carried forward in the field of foreign affairs and shaped the peculiar nature of Canada's legal powers over external relations with other countries. The British North America Act made no express provision, for example, for a treaty-making power for the Canadian Parliament, except as it may relate to responsibilities that it might assume as part of the British Empire. As a result, no thought was given to what powers Ottawa might eventually exercise in this area its own right. That left the courts, in particular the Judicial Committee of the Privy Council in Britain, with the uneasy task of filling in that constitutional hole in a later judgment in 1937. Although that decision appeared to leave Ottawa without power to implement treaties it had signed with other countries when the subject matter lay in provincial jurisdiction, that result owed as much to the blind arrogance of our imperial history as to judicial heavy-handedness. The legal architecture arose on an imperial foundation that scarcely even contemplated the emergence of an independent Canadian state.

While continuing to exercise virtual autonomy respecting internal matters, Canadians for their part were not especially eager to move onto the road of full national independence. English Canadian nationalism, in particular, was a long time extricating itself from the lure of mother country and empire. Economic patterns also continued to reinforce dependency. It was not until 1931 with the Statute of Westminster that practical sovereignty arrived with British acknowledgment that no law from the Dominions would be struck down on the grounds of repugnancy to British statutes. However, even here, Canada deliberately decided to leave legal control over its constitution in British hands, with the requirement that Britain effect changes only on the request of Canadian authorities. This decision was taken because Canadians could not agree on an amending formula by which changes could be made in Canada; it was the only legal deficiency in the assumption of Canadian sovereignty. The retention of this colonial anomaly, however, underlined the extent to which Canadians continued to look to Britain as an ultimate protector and guarantor of their constitution.

Despite repeated efforts to correct this anomaly dating as early as the 1930s, Canadian ministers failed to agree on any domestic procedure for amendment of the constitution until after Prime Minister Trudeau forced the issue by deciding to take unilateral action in 1980.[2] That decision, after a long battle with the provinces for public support and in the courts, eventually led to renewed federal–provincial negotiations in the fall of 1981. A settlement was finally reached on 5 November, despite the vigorous opposition of Premier René Lévesque of Quebec. In the past, when Quebec had alone dissented from proposed amendment procedures, as in 1964 and 1971, no action was taken. This time, with the Supreme Court of Canada judgment declaring that only "substantial agreement" and not unanimous provincial consent was required, the federal government proceeded without delay. The constitutional resolution was passed by the Canadian Parliament on 8 December and transmitted to Westminster for its approval on 29 March 1982. Proclamation of the Canada Act and Constitution Act, 1982, by Queen Elizabeth followed in Ottawa on 17 April.

This recent exercise underlines how respectfully Canadians have observed the strict requirements of legal and imperial form. Even though Canada had, as a practical matter, long enjoyed legal sovereignty, it asked British consent for change for one last time and even kicked off its celebration over "patriation" of our constitution with a visit by the Queen. Even the new Charter of Rights and Freedoms was legally authored by Great Britain on Canada's behalf. During the struggle between Ottawa and the provinces, provincial governments made continuous appeals to Great Britain for it to exercise its discretion to refuse a request of the federal Parliament to amend Canada's constitution without their consent. Once again, they showed themselves quite ready to accept an imperial umpire on contentious matters of Canadian concern. This was particularly true of Quebec when it repeatedly and unsuccessfully appealed to Great Britain to block patriation. It was also true of the leaders of native peoples in Canada who campaigned vainly for a continuing British supervisory role over Canada, until their own issues of concern had been finally and properly dealt with.

Although patriation did block any future application of British law to Canada, Canada showed in other provisions of the 1982 Constitution Act its continuing commitment to the elements of British constitutionalism. Most striking in this respect was the decision to place the offices of the Queen, the governor general, and the lieutenant-governor of a province first on the list of specially "protected" subjects that would require the consent of Parliament and every provincial legislature for any change. This decision, of course, reflects more than mere sentimental loyalty, but rather the firm commitment of the first ministers to protect the legal basis of their own prime ministerial powers within a Cabinet system of government in the British parliamentary tradition.[3] That same determination can be seen in the vigorous speeches of many premiers in defence of parliamentary sovereignty as against a constitutional Charter of Rights and Freedoms over several years of negotiations with Ottawa. In the end, loyalty to that tradition probably accounts for the presence of the notwithstanding clause in section 33 of the Charter, permitting Parliament or legislatures to override the Charter and the courts whenever they expressly choose to do so for renewable periods of five years.[4]

In short, recent Canadian constitutional discussions show the continuing power of Canada's earlier history in many illuminating ways. The political institutions that Canadians enjoyed during their colonial period continue to endure and exercise their influence over the political allegiances and loyalties of Canadians. Those political forms have now been even more firmly entrenched in the constitution as a result of the 1982 constitutional amendments. Even the conventions supporting parliamentary supremacy, such as the principle of responsible government, have been set out and championed by the Supreme Court in its judgment of 28 September 1981 on the patriation reference.[5] It may come as some comfort to the conservative to acknowledge that, even with all of the frenetic constitutional activity of the 1980s and with the many recent changes, the British parliamentary tradition remains the bedrock upon which Canadians build their own constitutional arrangements.

QUEBEC, FRENCH CANADIAN NATIONALISM, AND THE CANADIAN FEDERAL UNION

It would certainly not surprise a Canadian historian to discover that recent constitutional politics in this country continues to be dominated by the perennial question of how to make appropriate arrangement for the "distinct society" of Quebec within a wider, largely English-speaking Canada. This issue, after all, was the first item of business after the British Conquest in the mid-eighteenth century, and it has not ceased to occupy centre stage ever since.

The debates over the "distinct society" clause of the recent Meech

Lake Accord and of the other constitutional provisions specifically designed to make Quebec feel more at home in Canada are merely the latest in a continuous series of adaptations to the presence of a concentrated French-speaking society that has lived on the shores of the St. Lawrence for several centuries. A French-speaking colony had existed there for almost one hundred and fifty years before the link with Paris came to an abrupt end with the British Conquest of New France in 1759. Then the former colony began a new life within the framework of an alien empire.

It was the brutal realities of British imperialism that focused the minds of all Quebeckers on the impossibility *either* of retaining the older ties with France or of striking out on their own. Accordingly, Quebec looked to the new imperial centre to see whether it could extract some minimum guarantees for its continuing collective existence. In effect, that social contract was struck with the Quebec Act of 1774 recognizing the colony's Roman Catholic religion, its French civil code, and its right to expand westward into the Mississippi Valley. Although language was not itself touched upon in the Act, the English conquerors clearly accepted the continuing use of the French language. This victory was followed up by another. The Constitutional Act of 1791 gave the French-speaking people of Lower Canada control over their own elected assembly. Even though the British grant of lands in the American West had been frustrated by the successful American Revolution in the intervening years, Quebeckers still had a defined territorial base within which they could expect to live out their distinctive way of life.

While English-speaking Canadians have always looked upon these arrangements as evidence of unusual generosity on the part of the British conqueror, they were dictated by certain sober realities. Quick assimilation was out of the question in any case, and the threatening atmosphere marking relations between Britain and the United States made the adoption of this kind of imperial policy a question of simple prudence. Nonetheless, this social contract was the beginning of the French Canadian reliance upon the imperial connection to check threats and abuses that might arise from the English-speaking colonists who arrived in increasing numbers after the Conquest. Certainly, as stated earlier, it blocked any Quebec flirtation with revolution or of complicity with the American rebellion. At the same time, it did signify from the very outset that Canadian constitutional statecraft must somehow take account of *dualism*, the simultaneous presence of both French- and English-speaking peoples within British North America.

The assimilation option, ruled out on practical grounds earlier, was nonetheless considered and recommended by Lord Durham in 1839 as a long-run solution to the dilemma. By uniting Upper and Lower Canada into a single state, he hoped over time to merge the French Canadians into a dominant English-speaking society. When the British acted on his recommendation with the passage of the Act of Union in 1840, the assimilation experiment failed. Instead, French-speaking politicians from Lower Canada used their power to hold their own with their English-speaking counterparts within the new united Province of Canada. Dualism again raised its head, this time with dual premiers and several dual ministries complete with dual bureaucracies. Where this pattern did not apply, there developed other variations on dualism: alternating of portfolios between ministers from Canada East and Canada West; effective use of two languages in government; equality of representation in the lower House between Canada East and Canada West; even the doctrine of the *double majority* whereby no government measure would be valid unless it had received majority support from the representatives of Canada East and Canada West. These adaptations made political life complicated and often unstable, but they demonstrated very early on how inventive Canadians could be in their constitutional arrangements.

When Confederation arrived, it was accepted largely because it carried forward some of this intricate constitutional legacy. On the one hand, French-speaking Quebeckers would recapture control of their own elected assembly within their own province, an arrangement they had enjoyed from 1791 until the ill-fated experiment with political union. On the other hand, the new federal Parliament would incorporate some of the accepted practices that had developed since 1840, including prominent roles for French-speaking politicians in the new Houses of Parliament and acceptance of the equal right to use either language there. These arrangements indicated that complicated versions of dualism were being etched onto the Canadian body politic: provision for a majority French-speaking province within a larger mostly English-speaking federal union and provision for bilingual guarantees in Parliament and in the courts and legislature of Quebec. This legal architecture added yet another component of the ongoing social contract: recognition of the continuing distinct French-speaking society in the St. Lawrence Valley, alongside respect for its language in the common institutions of the new Canadian state.

There was, therefore, reason to think that the new experiment in federalism was, at least in spirit, something of a compact between the French- and English-speaking peoples, built on an older working set of conventions and understandings. While strictly speaking the compact theory of Confederation is not convincing from a legal point of view, it became customary to assume that Canada could function only within some moral bargain or social contract between the two major language communities. Certainly, there was precisely this kind of *modus vivendi* struck on Manitoba's entry into Confederation in 1870. Here, bilingual guarantees were accepted for the new province of Manitoba in deference both to English-speaking settlers and to the majority Métis population. Not only were denominational school rights as they were obtained by law and practice at the union secured, but English and French were equally protected as languages of use in the legislature and courts of the province. Both languages could appear in the records and journals of the province, and all statutes would be printed in both French and English. Similarly, amendments to the original North-West Territories Act of 1875 provided for the equality of the two languages in the government and courts of the region that would become the provinces of Saskatchewan and Alberta and the Northwest Territories and Yukon.

This structure of bilingual arrangements seemed to imply that, in the Canadian northwest, there would be ample opportunity for both language groups to expand and live in mutual respect in these territories under these arrangements. Similar protections existed, as noted, in the federal Parliament and in Quebec. Although extended no further at that time, this was the embryo for the later development of Canada as a bilingual state. Although motivated by the same pragmatic considerations that had forced the earliest accommodations with the French-speaking peoples living in Canada, it was seen nonetheless as another significant step in the developing moral bargain between the French- and English-speaking peoples of Canada.

As it turned out, Canadians proved unready for, and unworthy of, this legal edifice. As Confederation proceeded and settlement developed rapidly along predominantly anglophone lines in the Canadian West, it was not long before provinces there began to ignore or overturn these provisions. In Manitoba in 1890, the constitutional guarantees to the French-speaking minority were summarily dismissed in legislation declaring English the only official language. Lower court judgments declaring this legislation unconstitutional shortly afterward were flatly brushed aside by the government of Manitoba. The provinces of Alberta and Saskatchewan, created in 1905, simply ignored the provisions of the old North-West Territories Act and proceeded to construct an English-only constitutional regime.

Attacks on denominational school rights had begun even earlier in New Brunswick in 1871 when new legislation on education removed state support for sectarian schools, many of which had been operating exclusively in the French language for a long time. These assaults appeared to contradict the spirit of the Confederation bargain to protect the rights of the denominational schools and hence, indirectly, the linguistic minorities. It outraged opinion in Quebec, but the federal government respected the constitutional rights of the provinces in the field of education and refused to intervene. The same dismal procedure went on elsewhere in the English-speaking provinces, causing Quebec itself to turn increasingly toward provincial rights.

Therefore, the anglophone attacks on the structure of bilingualism in Confederation had the effect of reinforcing Quebeckers' sense that Quebec was their only true homeland, the only place where the French language would be respected and secure. Ultimately, this history, together with other deeply divisive events such as the hanging of Louis Riel and the conscription crises of the two world wars, provided the bitter ground upon which the seeds of Quebec separatism or of "special status" could take root. In short, the case for a *territorial dualism* was reinforced and the way prepared for its later assertion during the more confident period of Quebec nationalism after 1960.[6]

On the other hand, Quebec was forced equally by these attacks on the linguistic minorities elsewhere in Canada to define more sharply its broader sense of Confederation.[7] In this task, the other side of Canada's longer historical understanding of dualism—as a pattern of arrangements between the French- and English-speaking peoples *within* a broader polity—received more attention. One of the most celebrated spokespersons for this new portrait of Canada was Henri Bourassa, who drew upon and extended the existing structure of agreements between the French and the English until he had fleshed out a picture of Canada as a truly bilingual country. He called for recognition of the equality of the French and English languages across Canada, for respect for linguistic minorities, and for a shared building of a common land by the two founding peoples. This, too, was a critical intellectual development for what would follow almost a half century later during the prime ministership of Pierre Elliott Trudeau.

It was only after the unleashing of Quebec nationalism during the 1960s that the country once again had to reckon with its own past and with francophone demands for changes to the constitutional status quo. As it turned out, there were conflicting demands for recognition of *both* kinds of dualism: on the one hand, struggle for a righting of old wrongs and expansion of French-language rights throughout Canada in the tradition of Henri Bourassa; on the other, insistence either upon increased powers for Quebec as the francophone homeland or for outright independence. There were French Canadian spokespersons from Quebec for each of these options, often competing bitterly with one another for the opportunity to shape the Canadian state in the image of their own brand of dualism. Although there were also other constitutional actors during recent years with agendas of their own to pursue—particularly premiers from western and eastern Canada seeking solutions to regional discontents; aboriginal leaders seeking self-government for their peoples; public rights groups seeking protection of their liberties—they were all riding on the coattails of Quebec nationalism. It was this explosive force that compelled Canadian leaders to begin again and attempt to devise a new, more satisfactory definition of dualism.

From the 1968 Confederation of Tomorrow constitutional conference until the 1987 Meech Lake Accord, Quebec concerns have dominated the constitutional agenda. However, it took an unusual combination of events for one of these dualist options to be enshrined in a constitutional amendment in 1982: terrorist bombings, kidnappings, and the like in Quebec up to 1970; statutory approval of bilingualism as a policy by Ottawa; the coming to power of a separatist party in Quebec in 1976; a declaration of official unilingualism for Quebec under Bill 101; an unsuccessful referendum in Quebec on sovereignty-association; federal unilateral action to amend the constitution and to grant Canadians a Charter of Rights and Freedoms; and a Supreme Court judgment requiring only "substantial" provincial support for a last request to Britain to amend the constitution. The story is long and complicated.[8] But in the end, so we have seen, an agreement was struck between all first ministers, except Premier Lévesque of Quebec, to bring home the constitution with a Charter of Rights and Freedoms, containing much of Trudeau's bilingual vision within it. The Charter

- declared French and English the official languages of Canada;
- declared New Brunswick an officially bilingual province; and
- guaranteed minority-language educational rights in the provinces.

Although by no means complete, it did appear as though Canada was moving decisively toward adoption of the style of dualism expounded by Henri Bourassa years earlier. Even more heartening in this respect was the great success that French-language immersion programs were having throughout English-speaking Canada and the other statutory promotions of bilingualism by Parliament and many provincial governments.

These successes were reinforced by decisions of the Supreme Court repudiating many of the provincial policies of unilingualism. In 1979 Manitoba's 1890 bill making English the only official language was finally struck down, and on 13 June 1985 all of the English-only statutes passed by the province since 1890 were ordered to be translated into French. Quebec's French-only provisions for statutes in the Quebec Assembly under Bill 101 were overturned in 1979, while in July 1984 the barriers placed against Canadian anglophone entry to their own school system in Quebec were removed. In February 1988 even the provinces of Alberta and Saskatchewan learned that the old bilingual guarantees in the North-West Territories Act continued to apply, unless expressly repealed. Finally, the Supreme Court struck down the French-only signs provision of Quebec's Bill 101 on 15 December 1988. Hence, in a curious dialectical fashion, Canadians were made to return to their past and once again wrestle with the uglier side of the politics of dualism.

Unfortunately, in every case except in Manitoba where the bilingual guarantee was binding and in Quebec where the rights for the English-speaking minority in the legislative assembly and in the schools were mandatory, the provinces used their legislative might under the parliamentary tradition to roll back these court victories for the linguistic minorities. In effect, the notion of territorial dualism (namely the idea that the French fact be expressed in Quebec, the francophone homeland, and the English fact be pre-eminent elsewhere) prevailed. Modest improvements to the linguistic status quo were made in these provinces as face-saving compromises, but it was clear that the bilingual vision of Canada, despite its partial constitutional protection in 1982 and its successes elsewhere, was experiencing great difficulty in winning full acceptance. Resistance came not only from disgruntled anglophones in many parts of English-speaking Canada, but increasingly from nationalist francophones in Quebec.

Certainly, on a number of levels, it is hardly surprising that separatists would not welcome bilingualism. Not only would such a program deflect francophone nationalism away from the idea of Quebec as the exclusive homeland of francophones and retrieve a united Canada within which French- and English-speaking peoples might live, but the policy's protection of the anglophone minority in Quebec itself would be a constant threat and irritant. Only an independent, unilingual French Quebec would satisfy their sense of linguistic security and national pride. This option, however, was defeated in the 1980 referendum, in the constitutional negotiations in 1981, and in the provincial election of 1985. Yet, it remains a still-active choice on the political menu in Quebec in the Parti Québécois under the leadership of Jacques Parizeau.

Even the advocates of special status for Quebec, while accepting the idea of Quebec within a broader Canadian federation, share the separatists' concerns over the application of bilingualism in Quebec. These leaders, elected to power under Premier Robert Bourassa, have chosen to stress the other side of dualism: the preoccupation with expanding the powers and dignity of Quebec as the francophone homeland. Their constitutional program, unveiled prior to the December 1985 provincial election, included the following demands as conditions for Quebec finally acceding to the 1982 constitutional amendments:

- recognition of Quebec as a distinct society, homeland of the francophone element of Canada's duality;
- restrictions on the use of the federal spending power;
- a veto for Quebec over constitutional amendments affecting federal institutions and full compensation on opting out of transfers to provincial jurisdiction to Ottawa;

- guarantee of extended powers for Quebec in the field of immigration; and
- participation by Quebec in the nomination of judges to the Supreme Court of Canada.

These elements formed the substance of a new round of constitutional discussions among officials and first ministers in 1986 and 1987, leading ultimately to the Meech Lake communiqué on 30 April 1987.[9] With its announcement, it became clear that *both* of the traditional forms of dualism (strengthened bilingual guarantees across Canada in 1982; and a strengthened Quebec as homeland) were seeking constitutional satisfaction in the same decade.

The subsequent vigorous public debate over the wisdom of the Meech Lake Accord has indicated that there was by no means a clear consensus in the country for the entrenchment of this territorial version of dualism. While francophone opinion in Quebec was generally supportive of the idea of declaring Quebec "a distinct society within Canada," there were very serious reservations elsewhere. Not only did this part of the constitutional agreement appear to undermine the bilingual strategy of accommodating the French and English-speaking peoples, but in many respects it seemed but another springboard toward Quebec nationalism and independence. While there was an attempt in the Meech Lake Accord to balance this concession to territorial dualism with a modest expression of support for the preservation of the linguistic minorities, there was little doubt that Quebec was receiving unusual constitutional recognition. This symbolic gesture was also being backed up with some real devolution of power along lines very similar to those requested by Quebec at the outset of the negotiations. Even more important, there was a firm constitutional commitment by Ottawa and all the provinces to continue constitutional discussions indefinitely into the future.[10]

However, ratification of the Accord had in fact become problematic within eighteen months of its conclusion. Not only was there stiff political resistance throughout the country, but with the subsequent electoral defeat of the premiers from Manitoba and New Brunswick who had been signatories to the deal, neither province could now be counted on to carry out its terms. Unless this state of affairs can be changed, there will remain a firm legal roadblock to ratification.

The issue had become yet more complicated by the decision of the Bourassa government on 18 December 1988 to invoke the notwithstanding clause to override the Charter of Rights and Freedoms with respect to the use of any language other than French on exterior commercial signs in Quebec. This gesture was reminiscent of the tactics of Saskatchewan and

Alberta, which earlier in the same year had chosen to override court-recognized language rights in those provinces in order to retain officially English-only regimes. These developments show that the politics of territorial dualism could once again lead Canada away from the bilingual course, despite the successes achieved earlier under Trudeau and the federal Liberals. On the other hand, the extension of the idea of territorial dualism—and especially of Quebec as a distinct and more powerful French-speaking society—was making very slow and uncertain headway. By the end of the 1980s, there was understandable confusion about the status and endurance of any newer modern strategies of accommodation of the French- and English-speaking peoples within Canada.

DEMOCRACY, LIBERALISM, AND THE CHARTER

Even if the issues demanding constitutional resolution in the 1980s seemed so typically Canadian and even if the methods being used to negotiate and ratify them are so reminiscent of our past, changes were nonetheless occurring. In effect, the same fact of a largely French Quebec within a predominantly English-speaking Canada had forced Canadians into rethinking not only the older social contract between the two founding peoples, but also the whole question of renewed legitimacy for the Canadian state. It was the Charter that for many Canadians seemed to offer a means for addressing these needs simultaneously.

Even though the idea of an entrenched Charter of Rights for Canadians found a bad fit with the dominant notion of parliamentary sovereignty inherited from Great Britain, Canadians seemed to cleave to it despite repeated attacks upon it by the premiers in their rear-guard struggle against Trudeau's constitutional plans. In the end, when a compromise Charter finally was agreed to by first ministers and ultimately enacted by the U.K. Parliament in 1982, its provisions reflected the compromises that grew out of this curious struggle. Although in one sense a constitutional innovation, the Charter in a second sense actually was a unique blend of old and new. Seemingly American in inspiration, it actually grew out of Canadian political culture and preoccupations. Although legally and symbolically a new element in Canadian constitutional life, it was still a *graft* onto an existing body politic.

In what senses, then, does the Charter in its provisions still reflect this paradoxical leaning both backward and forward? First, there is evident throughout the Charter an attempt to strike an appropriate balance between the *old* tradition of relying upon parliamentary government for promoting the public good and preserving rights and the *new* doctrine that rights must be protected by a neutral judiciary against government infringement. This balancing exercise begins in section 1, which expressly "guarantees" all the rights and freedoms in the Charter, but then suggests that, nonetheless, they may be "subject to reasonable limits prescribed by law as can be domonstrably justified in a free and democratic society." Similarly, in another section, the Charter grants citizens the liberal right to move and work freely within the country, and then qualifies that right by granting legislatures the power to discriminate on behalf of their residents whenever the employment rate in that province is below the Canadian average. The results of the same balancing act can be seen in the equality clause of the Charter, which contains bold declarations of equality for every individual, but also includes exemptions for government programs for "disadvantaged individuals or groups."

The paradoxical balance is most striking of all, of course, when the Charter provides for vigilant defence of all rights and freedoms by a judiciary armed with the power to order remedies for government violations under section 24, and then proceeds to grant Parliament and provincial legislatures untrammelled power to override the courts and expressly infringe upon certain of those rights under the notwithstanding clause. Nor does this legislative override extend to freedoms at the margins of the Charter. On the contrary, it applies to the most fundamental freedoms traditionally at the core of any liberal bill of rights. Such grant of authority to override the Charter is unrestricted, apart from the qualification that it may extend for a five-year period only and must then be renewed to continue to be effective. Hence, Parliament remains legally sovereign, within the bounds of the federal division of powers and certain other exceptions, despite the apparent victory of a liberal Charter of Rights restricting state power on behalf of the individual. The cynic, familiar with Mackenzie King, would perhaps dismiss this paradox in typical Canadian fashion: "Fundamental freedoms if necessary, but not necessarily fundamental freedoms."

Certainly Saskatchewan workers, who discovered their ability to use the Charter against provincial back-to-work legislation blocked by the invoking of section 33, would have had reason to ponder this paradox. So too would thousands of anglophone Quebeckers who discovered on 18 December 1988 that their rights to use of their language on public signs in Quebec, so recently recognized by the Supreme Court, would nonetheless be stripped away by the Quebec legislature. Section 33 had turned out to be a triumph for parliamentary government, a clause that could and would be used as a political counterpoise to the courts. There was even a corresponding language of "rights" to be used in defence of the legislature having the final word: the "collective rights" of the people must, it was said, prevail over the merely individual rights spelled out in the Charter.

Yet, it would be misleading to overdramatize the grip that Canada's older parliamentary tradition continues to exercise and, consequently, to underplay the significance of the arrival of the Charter. For one thing, there were important areas where the rhetoric of a Charter actually binding the legislature held true: revealingly, this applied primarily to bilingual obligations and to *collective* rights for members of minority-language communities. What could be more Canadian? But for another, despite the presence of the legislative override—perhaps even *because* of it—the courts have taken seriously their duty to apply the Charter. Hence, over the first few years, when hundreds of new Charter cases appeared in court dockets, there were provisions in many duly enacted federal and provincial laws struck down by the Supreme Court. In practice, then, a new balance was being struck, and advocates of parliamentary sovereignty were having to make room for an activist court wielding much more power than in the past.

No longer would the Supreme Court merely be concerned with umpiring disputes over which level of government might legislate with respect to which subject matters under the constitution. Now the court was forced to set laws passed by elected legislatures alongside the Charter and decide whether they infringed upon the rights and freedoms protected therein; and if so, it was also called upon to judge whether such infringements were nonetheless "reasonable," "prescribed by law," and "demonstrably justifiable in a free and democratic society." If such laws failed these tests, the court would strike them down and refuse to apply and enforce them. This would, by no means, be a merely technical exercise. At best, it called for an exercise of delicate political judgment by the courts. They would shape the actual meaning of the Charter's generally worded provisions, develop the tests that the governments must meet for violating rights, and generally give what force and purpose to the Charter it would have.

Despite repeated denials that it was only "interpreting" the constitution, the Supreme Court was in fact forced to play an increasingly political role in the Canadian constitutional system. This was true in a double sense. Not only did it have to make broad political judgments concerning laws and policies and their acceptability under the Charter, but many of the issues themselves were politically controversial. For example, citizens' groups quickly decided to press the courts directly into the political spotlight by raising Charter challenges over cruise missile testing, abortion policy, language rights, and the like. Under these circumstances, even if the Supreme Court had wished to proceed circumspectly with its new power under the Charter, there was no way in which it could escape operating within a highly volatile and charged political environment. There was also growing public interest in the philosophy of members of the bench, and increasing provincial interest in sharing the power of appointment of new justices with the federal government.[11]

While most of the laws overturned during the early years of Charter litigation were not politically momentous, concerned as they were with procedural questions in the criminal justice field, they were important indicators of the determination of the Supreme Court to give a strong and purposeful reading to the Charter. Government powers to search and seize under the Combines Investigations Act were curbed, as were its powers to place the burden of proof of innocence upon accused drug dealers. There were many other modest defences of legal rights both for refugees and for other Canadians. In most of these cases, the Supreme Court deliberately followed American precedents and expounded a vigorously liberal view of the Charter. Accordingly, the limitation clause of section 1 was given a restrictive reading and the governments put on notice that a very stringent test would be applied for any limitations to be considered "reasonable" and "demonstrably justified." This was a popular and defensible posture for the courts.

However, on decisions concerning broader social issues, such as the Morgentaler case on abortion and several landmark labour cases, the way was not so easy. The abortion decision showed that the Supreme Court was ready to use a broad interpretation of section 7 of the Charter to overturn Parliament policy on abortion, leaving the federal government with the thankless task of trying to draft a new policy on the subject in the absence of a public consensus. Moreover, the court had in its judgment probably ruled out a number of other options; indeed, there was considerable doubt as to whether *any* legislative restrictions on the right of a woman to an abortion during the first trimester of pregnancy would be acceptable to the court. While this political result pleased pro-choice advocates, it thoroughly dismayed right-to-life groups.

There was political division as well over several court rulings that indicated a much less vigorous interpretation of other Charter rights, particularly those in the sensitive labour field. The court, for example, refused to recognize a right to strike as part of freedom of association under the Charter, and took an equally narrow view of the right to secondary picketing. These decisions left most of the elements of the collective bargaining system to find what protection they could in statutory law. This was not the protection that labour lawyers had hoped would come with the advent of the Charter. Indeed, to the extent that the Charter did not confer any constitutional sanctity upon these economic rights, it made them even more vulnerable. Yet, there were other important labour cases pending, including decisions on mandatory retirement and the broader question of the acceptability of using labour funds for broader political purposes. Lower court decisions on these issues were often not encouraging to the labour movement. It appeared that the Charter's playing field had its own political winners and losers.

DEMOCRACY AND CONSTITUTIONALISM

There were other elements in the 1982 Constitution Act, including the entrenchment of a new amending formula, recognition of the principle of equalization, and expansion of provincial powers over natural resources. These were, in effect, part of the price paid by the Trudeau government to secure a deal with the nine anglophone premiers over a Charter of Rights and Freedoms. The amending formula was probably the most important, since it enshrined both the principle of provincial equality and also the right of provinces to opt out of amendments transferring provincial powers to Ottawa.[12] Except for a relatively short list of subjects on which the consent of every province would be required, the formula provided for no veto for the province of Quebec; there was no expression of dualism in the formula, except for the provision that Ottawa would provide compensation to an opting-out province if there were any transfer of provincial powers over education or other cultural matters. This concession was aimed at matters sensitive to Quebec.

Yet, the amending formula was one of the first areas that Quebec wished reviewed in the round of discussions leading to Meech Lake in 1987. In the end, the premiers upheld their earlier position that no province ought to have a special veto and refused Quebec's demand in that respect. However, they did concede to Quebec and to every other province a right to block changes to federal institutions such as the Senate and Supreme Court by adding these and other subjects to those matters requiring unanimity. In addition, first ministers agreed to extend compensation to provinces opting out of transfers of provincial powers on *all* subjects, not just those in education and culture. These concessions were widely criticized for making Canada's amending formula even more inflexible and for setting back the prospects of Senate reform. These reasons, among others, were in part responsible for resistance to ratification of the Meech Lake Accord.

In fact, throughout the 1980s, there had been growing disquiet over the whole process of constitutional reform. Critics, for example, had been quick to denounce the constitutional negotiations leading to the 1982 Constitution Act for their failure to seek public ratification of these changes. Although the public had been extensively involved in commenting on the federal constitutional resolution and winning important changes to the final draft, they were quite left out when the final compromise was struck between first ministers in November 1981. Though some subsequent changes were made restoring aboriginal rights and guaranteeing sexual equality following a successful lobby effort by women's groups, the public had little real say on the essential compromises struck by first ministers. Hence, though the notwithstanding clause in the Charter was much criticized, as were the amendment procedures, the public watched from the sidelines as Parliament proceeded with the resolution and the U.K. Parliament finally adopted it. Public exhaustion with the process and resigned acceptance, after years of bitter battle, accounted for this result. But the public had at least helped shape many of the details of the Charter, and they drew satisfaction from the fact that the Charter was now a part of Canadian law.

It was the subsequent meetings over aboriginal self-government that for the first time opened up the direct negotiating process to actors who were not first ministers of the Crown. Here, Canadians witnessed other Canadian leaders sitting at the conference table, seeking constitutional redress of their problems. Yet, in the end, there were no agreements, primarily because some premiers refused to go along with entrenching the principle of aboriginal self-government in the constitution. Native peoples had no leverage over any of the other parties, other than the broad public sympathy for their cause, and therefore they were not bargaining from a position of strength. After a third unsuccessful aboriginal conference in 1987, the process once again reverted back to its "normal" exclusive character, as first ministers began to consult with one another, this time over Quebec's grievances. Moreover, these discussions, culminating in the Meech Lake Accord, were more exclusive and secretive than ever before.

The federal government had decided to adopt a quiet behind-the-scenes approach to these negotiations. Discussions between a select group of officials and first ministers took place behind closed doors in every capital in the country for approximately a year before a constitutional conference was called at Meech Lake in Quebec. Even then, the drafts and documents upon which discussions were based were not made public, nor was there any expectation that a deal was about to be struck. Worse still, after announcement of an agreement and publication of a draft text in April followed quickly by a secret meeting over the final legal document in early June, the public was confronted with a *fete complis*. First ministers promised to defend its terms and to ensure approval of it in their respective legislatures. It was flatly declared that the Accord would not be reopened short of discovery of "egregious errors": only these would cause the exclusive circle of eleven first ministers to renegotiate its terms. Only in Quebec was there even a gesture toward public consultation prior to the making of this fateful pact.

This arrogant display of solidarity among first ministers respecting the constitution prompted critics to ask whether the constitution was somehow thought to be "owned" by the first ministers of the Crown.[13] The public, disturbed over many of the terms of the Accord, had become increasingly incensed over the proprietary control exercised by first ministers over *their* constitution. After the long public struggle over the Charter, and the people's increasing identification with it, this reliance upon executive power vested in the parliamentary tradition was regarded as an affront in a democratic society. Since first ministers virtually controlled their Cabinets and legislatures through party discipline, there was little effective check against the imposition of their own constitutional terms.

Even if constitutional politics had been traditionally the work of small elites in colonial days and with Confederation itself, it is no longer an acceptable practice.[14] The battle over Meech Lake has exposed the cracks in the legitimacy of the prevailing system of prime ministerial negotiation, followed by dutiful legislative compliance. Even in Canada there are limits to public patience with the concentration of power of a modern parliamentary system. As Alan Cairns has argued, the arrival of the Charter has brought with it a new consciousness of the vested interest that citizens of Canada have in the constitution. The discussions on aboriginal rights have underlined the same fact. Even the defeated Quebec referendum had taught the public the lesson that they could be constitutional actors too.

In short, the time has long past when governments can argue that constitutional politics are essentially their own affair.[15] There is more to the agenda than governmental institutions and powers, but even these are rightly seen by the public as more than the exclusive property of today's politicians. The debate over Meech Lake has shown that the people want to assume ultimate responsibility for the constitution, including the question of rights for women, for residents of the Northwest Territories and Yukon, and for native peoples. Though Canada's amendment formula makes no formal room for this public role and instead leaves the subject in the intergovernmental arena—Prime Minister Trudeau's plan for ultimate referendums having been dropped in the compromises of 1982—the issue will not go away. In these and other ways, Canadians are beginning to understand the deeper changes that have accompanied recent constitutional reform.

NOTES

1. This is a widely argued thesis in the literature on parliamentary legislatures that is developed extensively in R. I. Cheffins and P. A. Johnson, *The Revised Canadian Constitution: Politics as Law* (Toronto: McGraw-Hill Ryerson, 1986). This text is also very useful in briefly tracing the pre-Confederation period of Canadian constitutional development.

2. There are many useful accounts of this process, including Roy Romanow, John Whyte, and Howard Leeson, *Canada Notwithstanding: The Making of the Constitution, 1976–1982* (Toronto: Cars-

well/Methuen, 1984), and David Milne, *The Canadian Constitution*, 2nd ed. (Toronto: Lorimer, 1989).

3. This decision, in effect, "entrenches" Cabinet government without change and "freezes" a constitutional system that is often charged with being highly centralized and unresponsive. See, for example, Cheffins and Johnson, *The Revised Canadian Constitution*, p. 74. Apart from these initiatives, it is also worth noting that both in 1982 and in the proposed Meech Lake amendments in 1987, first ministers begin to appear in the constitutional language in their own right as actors, committing themselves to First Ministers Conferences on the constitution or the economy and to particular agendas. Although the term "first minister" hadn't appeared until recently in official documents on federal–provincial relations, the concept itself is a venerable one, reaching back into our past.

4. The question of the notwithstanding clause has become an even more controversial subject since its use by Premier Bourassa to protect a new French-only sign law after that section of Bill 101 had been struck down by the Supreme Court on 15 December 1988. The matter will be taken up later in this chapter. For a brief account of its role in the negotiations in the early 1980s, see Milne, *The Canadian Constitution*, pp. 67–68.

5. *A.G. Manitoba, et al. vs. A.G. Canada*, [1981] 1 S.C.R. 753.

6. See Kenneth McRoberts, "Quebec: Province, Nation, or 'Distinct Society'?" ch. 6 in this volume.

7. One of the finest works to trace the development of this part of French Canadian nationalism during the late nineteenth century is A. I. Silver's *The French-Canadian Idea of Confederation, 1864–1900* (Toronto: University of Toronto Press, 1982). He shows that the bilingual idea of Canada was much more sharply defined and understood after the assaults of the anglophone provinces on the French-speaking minorities, though it never effectively dislodged the idea of Quebec as the French Canadian homeland.

8. See Milne, *The Canadian Constitution*, for an overview of these and other constitutional events in the 1980s. See also Romanow, Whyte, and Leeson, *Canada Notwithstanding*.

9. See Milne, *The Canadian Constitution*, for more detail on the process leading to the Meech Lake agreement. For a trenchant critique of that process, see Alan C. Cairns, "The Limited Constitutional Vision of Meech Lake," in *Competing Constitutional Visions: The Meech Lake Accord*, ed. Katherine E. Swinton and Carol J. Rogerson (Toronto: Carswell, 1988).

10. For my analysis of the Meech Lake Accord in substance and process, see "Much Ado about Meech," in *Canada: The State of the Federa-*

tion, 1987–88, ed. Peter M. Leslie and Ronald Watts (Kingston: Institute of Intergovernmental Relations, Queen's University, 1988), pp. 97–115. Much more extended analysis from a critical perspective can be found in Bryan Schwartz, *Fathoming Meech Lake* (Winnipeg: Legal Research Institute of the University of Manitoba, 1987). See also Peter W. Hogg, *Meech Lake Constitutional Accord Annotated* (Toronto: Carswell, 1988); Swinton and Rogerson, *Competing Constitutional Visions*; and Roger Gibbins, et al., eds., *Meech Lake and Canada: Perspectives from the West* (Edmonton: Academic Printing and Publishing, 1988). See also the special issue on the Meech Lake Accord in *Canadian Public Policy* 14 (September 1988).

11. That, of course, was one of the required elements in Quebec's demands during the Meech Lake discussions, and the principle was accepted in the final draft. It provided for provincial nomination of judges to the court, with a federal right to appoint candidates that they found acceptable. Quebec was the only province that had an exclusive right to advance names for the three required judges from that province, while other provinces would presumably compete with one another for nominations as openings developed.

12. There have been a variety of commentaries on Canada's amending formula, including Garth Stevenson, "Constitutional Amendment: A Democratic Perspective," in *Socialist Studies* 2 (1984): 269–84; Stephen A. Scott, "Canadian Constitutional Amendment Process," in *Reshaping Confederation: The 1982 Reform of the Canadian Constitution*, ed. P. Davenport and Richard Leach (Durham, N.C.: Duke University Press, 1984); and D. Marc Kilgour and T. J. Lévesque, "The Choice of a Permanent Amending Formula for Canada's Constitution," *Canadian Public Policy* 10 (September 1984).

13. See Cairns, "The Limited Constitutional Vision of Meech Lake."

14. The suggestion that the public must be involved in constitutional change prior to any first ministers' agreement was heard repeatedly in hearings and commentary. Indeed, that was the considered recommendation of several committees that reported to legislatures on the subject, particularly in Ontario.

15. This argument is best laid out in the thoughtful article by Cairns cited earlier.

FURTHER READINGS

Banting, Keith, and Richard Simeon, eds. *Redesigning the State: The Politics of Constitutional Change*. Toronto: University of Toronto Press, 1985.

Cheffins, R. I., and P. A. Johnson. *The Revised Canadian Constitution: Politics as Law*. Toronto: McGraw-Hill Ryerson, 1986.

Gibbins, Roger, et al., eds. *Meech Lake and Canada: Perspectives from the West*. Edmonton: Academic Printing and Publishing, 1988.

Hogg, Peter W. *Meech Lake Constitutional Accord Annotated*. Toronto: Carswell, 1988.

Mandel, Michael. *The Charter of Rights and the Legalization of Politics in Canada*. Toronto: Wall and Thompson, 1989.

"The Meech Lake Accord" (special supplement). *Canadian Public Policy* 14 (September 1988).

Milne, David. *The Canadian Constitution*, 2nd ed. Toronto: Lorimer, 1989.

———. "Much Ado about Meech." In *Canada: The State of the Federation, 1987–88*, ed. Peter M. Leslie and Ronald Watts. Kingston: Institute of Intergovernmental Relations, Queen's University, 1988.

Monahan, Patrick. *Politics and the Constitution: The Charter, Federalism and the Supreme Court of Canada*. Toronto: Carswell, 1987.

Romanow, Roy, John Whyte, and Howard Leeson. *Canada Notwithstanding: The Making of the Constitution, 1976–1982*. Toronto: Carswell/Methuen, 1984.

Schwartz, Bryan. *Fathoming Meech Lake*. Winnipeg: Legal Research Institute of the University of Manitoba, 1987.

Swinton, Katherine E., and Carol J. Rogerson, eds. *Competing Constitutional Visions: The Meech Lake Accord*. Toronto: Carswell, 1988.

17

Parliamentary Government in Canada

MICHAEL M. ATKINSON

Parliament poses a problem for those who are comfortable only with clear, unambiguous categories. What, after all, is "Parliament"? Should the term be used to refer to the 295 MPs and 104 senators drawn together to oversee the conduct of the nation's business? Presumably, but how does Cabinet fit into this definition? Are ministers simply MPs who have a slightly exalted status? Perhaps the term "Parliament" should refer to everyone except ministers of the Crown: this would recognize the ancient distinction between legislative and executive functions. But what would Parliament be without a ministry—an executive to guide its activities?

To sort out this maze it is useful to begin by recognizing that there are two fundamentally opposing perspectives on the nature of parliamentary government in Canada.[1] In the Parliament-centred (or liberal) model, the most important unit of parliamentary government is the individual MP. The rights of MPs to speak on behalf of their constituents and to give expression to personal opinions is understood to be one of the critical features of democratic governance. Reforms that are premised on this view seek to enhance the ability of MPs to control Parliament's agenda, to appoint or elect its officers, and to shape the content of legislative debate. There will always be room for leadership in the Parliament-centred view, but that leadership must be responsive to the will of the House and never allowed simply to retreat behind a parliamentary majority. Indeed, political parties in the Parliament-centred view become the servants of MPs, useful for expressing broad programs with which MPs might associate, but never encroaching seriously on the freedom of individual expression.

In the second perspective on parliamentary government—the Cabinet-centred (or Westminster) model—strong, executive leadership is understood to be the *sine qua non* of effective government. Parliament, in this view, consists of leaders and followers. The role of parties is to provide a vehicle for communication between them and a mechanism for distributing rewards and sanctions. The use of patronage and other tested methods for rewarding supporters is considered a legitimate means of securing the authority of the parliamentary party leadership. This view of parliamentary government expects discretion on the part of leaders and deference on the part of followers. Members of Parliament are not law makers in anything but the formal sense of the term. Parliament is a deliberating assembly, an arena in which Cabinet outlines and defends it proposals before an organized, sceptical opposition. It is the Cabinet and individual ministers, acting in the name of the Crown, who exercise effective political authority.

The development of the Canadian Parliament has been strongly influenced by this second, Cabinet-centred perspective. This Westminster model of parliamentary government has found favour both among Canadian politicians and academics.[2] The Canadian public, on the other hand, has been alternately confused, bemused, and offended by the practices it engenders. The first part of this chapter outlines those practices and comments critically on the capacity of the Westminster model to deliver on its promise of effective government. The second part of the chapter examines relations between Cabinet and Parliament other than those emphasized by the Westminster model. It discusses the 1980s reforms, most of which flow out of the Parliament-centred model, and the competing views about what these reforms have achieved.[3]

THE FUNDAMENTALS OF THE WESTMINSTER MODEL

From the gallery of the House of Commons the scene below is a bewildering mixture of ritual and routine, humour and solemnity, camaraderie and incivility. Most observers are unaware of the most important formal rules that govern procedure (the Standing Orders) let alone the established, if informal, norms that govern personal conduct. Yet a careful study of these rules and norms is not the place to begin to understand parliamentary government in Canada. The rules are important, of course, but primarily because they give expression to more profound principles and conventions upon which the Westminster model is based. In this section we examine two of these principles. They may strike readers as so elementary that little more than a brief mention is necessary. But as we shall see, problems arise when we are forced to give these principles some meaning. Not only are they at odds with one another, but they often give rise to behaviour that many find inimical to good government. Moreover, these fundamental principles make demands on politicians, public servants, and the electorate that are, in the context of the modern administrative state, quite unrealistic.

1. The Cabinet is in charge of, and responsible for, the conduct of parliamentary business. During the nineteenth century ordinary members of Parliament assumed much of the initiative for legislation by offering proposals in the form of private bills and private members' bills.[4] Even then, however, it was the government-sponsored public bill that was used to change the general laws of the country.[5] Now almost all of the bills that Parliament finally adopts are government bills; that is, they have been introduced by ministers of the Crown. Moreover, only ministers are permitted to introduce bills that authorize the raising or spending of money. Parliamentary procedure has gradually tightened to give the government sufficient time to enact its legislative program and to curtail lengthy debates. The government relies on the Speaker to dispose of dilatory or frivolous motions.

The government has responsibilities other than the sponsoring of a legislative program. Every year, on or before March 1, the government lays before the Commons a request for funds to conduct business. This request appears in the form of "estimates" followed by supply bills needed to give them legislative authority. Supplementary estimates and further supply bills are tabled as required during the remainder of the fiscal year. The Minister of Finance introduces a budget, usually in the spring of each year, which announces the government's overall financial plan and intended tax changes. Major policy announcements often accompany the budget.

The government house leader is responsible for orchestrating all of this activity, ensuring that deadlines are met, that important government bills are not postponed indefinitely and that the opposition is satisfied with the time that has been made available to discuss these measures. The week-by-week and month-by-month planning of the parliamentary session is in the hands of the parliamentary party leadership. The prime minister is responsible for calling Parliament and requesting that the governor general dissolve it. From the narrowest of details to the broadest of constitutional responsibilities, the government is in charge.

How does the government acquire and retain these responsibilities? The formal (and rather uninformative) answer is that the Cabinet enjoys the confidence of the House of Commons and is therefore able to offer advice to, and act on behalf of, the Crown. But behind this expression of confidence lies the machinery of the electoral process and the politics of party organization and cohesion. The support that the Cabinet possesses has been garnered in the electorate, not in the House of Commons. The electorate has given one party more seats than the others. That party's leader usually (but by no means necessarily) becomes prime minister and chooses a Cabinet. As individuals, members of Parliament have no special role in any of this. They seek election, of course, but the support they receive cannot easily be interpreted as a personal endorsement.

Small wonder that once they arrive in Ottawa, the Westminster model assigns MPs a rather prosaic task. If they sit on the government side of the House their job is to express confidence in the leadership by voting for government-sponsored measures; if they are opposition members they are expected to oppose those measures, at least if directed to do so by the opposition party leadership. The team spirit that this exercise engenders is reinforced by the "confidence convention," the erroneous notion that the defeat of any government-sponsored bill requires the government's resignation.[6] No such requirement exists, except perhaps in the minds of MPS. Many appear to be convinced that given the circumstances of their own election, namely the role played by the party's leadership, an overt expression of independence is tantamount to a renunciation of that leadership. The result is that rigid party discipline, punctuated (on the opposition side at least) by leadership crises, is the standard behavioural dynamic in the House of Commons.

Called upon to extol the virtues of this system, one would surely point out that it concentrates authority and responsibility in the hands of elected representatives. A government created and sustained in this manner is able to act decisively and can accomplish a great deal without delaying and equivocating until problems have reached crisis proportions. Professor Ned Franks has argued that medicare, and the social programs to which Canadians often point with pride, have emerged not because of broadly based social democratic parties, but "through the electoral dialectic of a powerful, centralized cabinet and a mass electorate."[7] The Westminster model, it appears, is well suited to the development of integrative, national programs, rather than the cultivation of narrow, special interests. By the same token, the concentration of responsibility implicit in this model presumably aids in the assignment of blame. Since political parties remain cohesive parliamentary actors, the governors are easily identifiable and electors are able to sanction poor performance. It is not surprising that this type of system, with its focus on the effectiveness of centralized decision making, in often referred to as Cabinet government.

In spite of these advantages, certain problems have arisen in the practice of Cabinet government in Canada. In the first place, our single-member plurality electoral system has often failed to produce a majority of seats for the governing party in the House of Commons. To have the confidence of the House in a minority situation, the government must attract and retain the support of at least some members of the opposition. Confidence motions, under these circumstances, are no longer routine demonstrations of party solidarity. Moreover, the assignment of responsibility for government actions is not as clear cut. It has been suggested, in their defence, that minority governments are likely to be sensitive to the House of Commons. What is lost in the concentration and certainty of authority is supplanted by an added responsiveness to Parliament. But there is nothing to guarantee this outcome, and during the Pearson and Diefenbaker years there was very little evidence of it.[8] Minority governments have their virtues, but the point is that they are not the same as those used to justify the Westminster model.

The second problem is that of ministerial responsibility. The fiction that ministers can comprehend the activities of enormous government departments to the point of resigning in the face of administrative failure has been almost universally abandoned. Ministers simply will not accept personal responsibility for errors and omissions that occur at the hands of public servants. They retain effective responsibility for actions undertaken in accordance with their instructions or with their policies, but determining which actions are encompassed in this understanding can be a very difficult task.[9] The Federal Court of Appeal sought to make that task easier in 1988 by finding two ministers—Joe Clark and Flora MacDonald— personally responsible for the failure of their public servants to obey a court order. This decision sent a message to officials and politicians, but it did not produce resignations. Ministers continue to behave as if individual ministerial responsibility requires little more than a willingness to appear in Parliament to answer questions and promise investigations.

In their attempt to make someone responsible for government actions, MPs and others have suggested that deputy ministers might accept responsibility for administrative matters and politicians responsibility for questions of policy. This would shake, but by no means topple, the accepted doctrine of ministerial responsibility, which contains the provision that senior officials offer politically neutral advice in exchange for anonymity.[10] Deputy ministers, and perhaps others, would be required to explain and justify how departments were managed, but they would not be held responsible for policy direction. Of course, this formula for accountability rests on the assumption that policy and administration can be neatly separated, and both observers and participants are quick to agree that complete separation is impossible.[11] Besides, the policy role of deputy ministers and other senior officials is widely acknowledged. Avoiding comment on the political aspects of policy is a difficult chore for any public servant. Nonetheless, deputy ministers are routinely forced to make fine distinctions in the realm of politics, policy, and administration. The accountability system has become highly dependent on the deputy ministers' ability to do so at the same time that their organizational responsibilities are increasing and when the rapid rotation of deputies within the public service has limited their capacity to become familiar with departmental programs and practices.[12]

The fact that deputies are governor-in-council appointees who offer private policy advice to ministers but accept no political responsibility has become an increasingly worrisome feature of the modern administrative state. This, plus the growth of central agencies, Mr. Mulroney's practice of appointing bureaucratic outsiders (such as Stanley Hartt and Dalton Camp) to senior public service positions, and his willingness to pluck public servants (such as Derek Burney) out of the bureaucracy and assign them high-profile political posts (in Burney's case, chief of staff in the Prime Minister's Office), has fuelled suspicions that the senior ranks of the public service have become highly politicized. No one questions the government's right to obtain the best advice possible, but perhaps something is amiss when the chief architects of government policy are able to avoid the questions of parliamentarians. Has ministerial responsibility become merely a polite subterfuge used to protect the senior officials and "superbureaucrats" who silently and covertly govern?

The answer is almost certainly no. Politicians still wield significant power, especially in the setting of priorities, and Mr. Mulroney's appointments have been no more remarkable than those of his predecessors. On the other hand, there is ample evidence that senior bureaucrats and ministers do form a policy-making oligarchy in which the differences between them are sometimes hard to detect. Senior Canadian bureaucrats, for example, are far more tolerant of politics than their junior colleagues, and they work heavily within contact networks that include only ministers and other senior public servants.[13] Under the circumstances, some politicization of the bureaucracy and some blurring of lines of responsibility is bound to occur. The Westminster model therefore, in spite of its stress on centralized political decision making, cannot resolve the problem of accountability.

Another problem the model seems unable to resolve is the diffusion of power in Ottawa's policy system. Although the Westminster model is supposed to supply strong executive leadership, and has been defended as the source of national programs, many observers detect a leaching of power to individual departments where technical expertise resides and interest group contacts are frequent.[14] The resulting bureaucratic pluralism stands squarely in the way of strong central direction.

This diffusion of power within the bureaucracy is compounded by the willingness of politicians to devote large chunks of time and vast amounts of money to programs that are fashioned to meet the territorial realities of Canadian politics. The system of regional ministers has survived in spite of the efforts of Prime Ministers Trudeau and Mulroney to do without these political agents of Cabinet. In addition to being responsible for patronage, regional ministers have succeeded in mobilizing their department's resources behind provincial and local projects.[15] Lloyd Axworthy has acquired perhaps the biggest reputation in this regard, but others, including Don Mazankowski and John Crosbie, have had little difficulty securing Cabinet approval for projects of dubious economic value such as the Husky oil upgrader and Hibernia. Of course, a Parliament-centred approach might make matters worse, inviting all MPs to concentrate on nothing but locally tailored programs. But it should be acknowledged that we do not have to endorse a Parliament-centred view of government before we can witness the diffusion of power. It is, in many ways, already upon us.

The final problem with the operation of the Westminster-style Cabinet government is perhaps the most important of all: it offers individual members of Parliament very few opportunities for personal initiative and achievement. Unless MPs are fortunate enough to be a elevated to Cabinet, they must be content with the vicarious experience of power and the satisfaction that comes with performing countless tasks on behalf of constituents. In debating the McGrath Report on parliamentary reform, government backbenchers expressed their frustration with this role. They decried the chains of party discipline, severely criticized the conduct of private members' business, and described the legislative process in general as a charade. A respected opposition member, Keith Penner (Lib: Cochrane–Superior) summed up the mood: "We have a parliamentary system in Canada which is underdeveloped, immature, retarded and defective. . . . In what other Parliament of the world are members referred to as sheep or trained seals?"[16] Still, the Westminster model does not countenance institutions or procedures that encourage independent behaviour or the achievement of non-partisan consensus.

This was not always the case. Before parties had secured their grip on elected representatives, responsible government in Canada meant that, if provoked, the assembly could, and would, dismiss a government and install another without the benefit of a general election. From 1848, when responsible government was first introduced in British North America, to 1864, when Confederation discussions began in earnest, a series of governments were made and unmade in this way. After Confederation, the term "responsible government" lost this meaning.[17] Between 1867 and 1873 John A. Macdonald suffered several defeats in the House of Commons but refused to resign. As political parties became cohesive in the electorate and in Parliament, the threat of defeat itself diminished considerably. Even the emergence of third and fourth parties and, in the 1960s and 1970s, a series of minority governments did not spell immediate defeat for the governing party. And when defeat came, the government either refused to treat it as a matter of confidence (e.g., February 1968; December 1983) or called an election immediately (May 1974; December 1979). Whatever responsible government meant in pre-Confederation Canada, it does not mean, in the 1990s, that the House of Commons can choose the government.

In the 1990s the Cabinet is responsible, through the party system, to the electorate. This does not imply that Parliament and parliamentarians are irrelevant. Parliament's chief task is to ensure that the government behaves appropriately. It performs this task through the political parties around which Parliament is organized. The spectacle of a vigilant House of Commons constantly questioning and criticizing the government is sufficient assurance for some that this task is being performed. But it is the actions of political parties, including the party in power, that determine how much of this is show and how much is substance. In this respect a great deal of emphasis is placed on the role of the opposition as an alternative government and a constant source of sceptical and critical pronouncements. We turn now to the consideration of a second principle of parliamentary government in Canada and an evaluation of the opposition's ability to hold governments accountable between elections.

2. The opposition must have the right to criticize the government openly and the ability to make the criticism felt. In Parliament the government explains and justifies its action (or inaction), not to an audience sympathetic and anxious to offer assistance, but to an organized, institutionalized opposition bent on demonstrating the inappropriateness and inefficiencies of government policy. Though it may never have the votes necessary to defeat the government, the opposition is nonetheless charged with ensuring that the responsibility of the government to the House of Commons is more than a formality. As John Stewart has put it, "It is this public testing of governance, with the government and the opposition as institutionalized adversaries, that is the hallmark of contemporary Responsible Government."[18]

The idea of opposition was not always so compatible with parliamentary government. Parliaments in Britain were originally meetings of nobles called to offer advice to the king and, it was hoped, to support the Crown in its (mostly military) ventures. Although an offer of advice often implied criticism, outright opposition could easily be construed as treason. In the seventeenth and eighteenth centuries, by which time Parliament had made good its claim to supremacy, the idea of opposition-in-Parliament was still resisted, this time by those who saw it as divisive—an expression of greedy factionalism. But by then efforts to create governments composed of the "best men" had failed, and observers had come to recognize that, while opposition to the government might be denounced as factional, the government itself was a "party."[19] Parties, moreover, might prove advantageous if they could be used as a bulwark against the danger of concentrated power. This bulwark would take the form of a recognized and legitimate opposition eager to secure office.

With the government facing the opposition in Parliament and two teams of party leaders struggling for support in the electorate, have we at last defined the essence of responsible government? Defined perhaps, but this system has to work before anyone can feel completely satisfied, and there are several obstacles to its effective operation.

First, the opposition in Parliament, because it is not in control of the parliamentary agenda, cannot insist that pressing issues be addressed immediately on the floor of the Commons. Because of this, and the demands of government business, many issues of general concern are not debated in Parliament for weeks or months after they have come to the attention of the public. Thus, for instance, the Ocean Ranger tragedy was never properly addressed in Parliament and the McDonald Commission on the RCMP received no statement from ministers or any debate until months after its report was tabled. Too often Parliament appears to be very ponderous, unable to react quickly or to act at all as a forum for serious debate of important public issues. Yet, it is in this environment that the opposition must do the work assigned to it under the Westminster model.

Second, the opposition must compete with other bodies capable of offering compelling criticism of government policy. The C. D. Howe Institute, the Economic Council, the Frazer Institute, and the Canadian Labour Congress are all capable of supplying policy analyses that are more stimulating and informed than those produced by the opposition. The opposition can use these studies, but in spite of over a million dollars allocated to caucus research units, opposition parties have been unable (or unwilling) to generate their own economic analyses. They are without the information and expertise the government is able to marshal on virtually any specialized subject, and they appear to be convinced that the resources they do have ought to be used to exploit short-term partisan opportunities.

No where is the irrelevance of opposition criticism more apparent than in the realm of federal–provincial relations. For instance, because provinces own and control the development of most natural resources, debates on the floor of the Commons about the price of oil have the quality of a side show compared to the negotiation and debate that take place between the federal government and the producing provinces. The major issues of centralization and decentralization in the Canadian federation are also debated outside of Parliament. In Canada it is possible for first ministers to meet behind closed doors and present the opposition with a constitutional *falt accompli*, such as the Meech Lake package, to which no amendments are permitted. In these cases opposition to federal policies emerges from the governments of the provinces. They become the counterbalance on which the Westminster model depends.

The third problem faced by the opposition in Canada is that of achieving policy distinctiveness. The institutionalization of opposition in Parliament was originally premised on an agreement among all participants not to question the foundations of the parliamentary system. Opposition parties have added to this their tacit agreement not to question the fundamentals of the social and economic order. Securing power, therefore, has become a matter of piecing together a coalition, consisting of regional and linguistic interests, sufficient to produce a majority of seats in the House of Commons. For the greatest part of Canadian history the opposition has been comprised of those elements left out of the governing coalition.[20] With little to unite them other than antipathy toward the government, both the Liberal and Conservative parties in opposition have experienced wrenching divisions over policy and leadership. They have seized opportunities, such as the free trade debate, to distance themselves from government policy, only to experience strong pressures for conformity once the debate was over. Only the New Democratic Party (NDP) has succeeded in supplying an ideologically consistent critique of the governing parties, but (ironically perhaps) at the expense of appearing unnecessarily rigid and uncompromising.

In Canada, an opposition committed to the present means of distributing economic resources, to the existing system of representation, to the preservation of linguistic duality, and to the structures of federalism faces an electorate deeply divided on regional linguistic grounds. Achieving policy distinctiveness under these circumstances is, understandably, an uncommon occurrence and one that is fraught with electoral dangers. Yet without policy innovations the opposition begins to surrender to interest groups and provincial governments the task of offering creative responses to government policy. Bernard Crick has described Parliament as, ideally, a "permanent election campaign";[21] but to make Parliament work that way requires a capacity to define acceptable alternatives, a capacity that Canadian parties in opposition have not had in abundance.

Finally, what strength the opposition in Canada possesses is derived primarily from the fact that the government cannot ignore it. Ministers may make announcements and speeches outside Parliament (much to the consternation of the opposition), but it is Parliament that must eventually approve legislation and appropriate funds. In the course of doing so, opposition members engage in lonely debates in the hope that their ideas and reservations will be communicated beyond the chamber to an alert and interested public. Is this a reasonable expectation? Is electoral choice influenced by the performance of the opposition on the floor of the House of Commons? A strong affirmative answer is impossible. In spite of the televising of Parliament (which is selective in content and distribution) there is no evidence that the electorate has an improved awareness of opposition policies and attitudes. The press gallery persists in concentrating on spectacular developments, scandals, and human interest stories, while election campaigns continue to be contests among party leaders, not alternative ministerial teams. Opposition parties exacerbate the process by resisting the creation of a small and stable shadow Cabinet in favour of balancing regional claims to positions of prominence on the opposition front benches.

These observations on the opposition in Canada should not be interpreted simply as criticisms of opposition parties, the government, or the media, whatever their shortcomings may be. The point is that the Westminster model of parliamentary government requires a great deal of the parliamentary opposition. Yet this opposition must work under severe institutional and political constraints not at all anticipated by the model.

In summary, the Westminster model promises decisive government, political accountability, and the open debate of legislative changes, spending decisions, and controversial government actions. It promises political stability in the form of a government-in-waiting should the present one falter. Unfortunately, as we have argued above, the Westminster model is unable to deliver on all of these promises. Of course, a model of parliamentary government based on a Parliament-centred, rather than a Cabinet-centred, approach will have liabilities as well. But this has not deterred parliamentarians from pressing for Parliament-centred reforms. They recognize that the overwhelming authority of the Westminster model makes it unlikely that it will be replaced altogether. In the next section we consider some of these reforms and relationships between Cabinet and Parliament that are largely ignored in the Westminster model.

Before leaving our discussion of fundamental principles, however, it is necessary to make mention of a new challenge to the Westminster model—the Charter of Rights and Freedoms. The Charter, introduced into the constitution in 1982, implies that both legislative and executive actions will now be subject to the scrutiny of the courts. Without the Charter, the nature and extent of the rights possessed by Canadians was made concrete by the actions of Parliament and the provincial legislatures. With the Charter, a portion of this task has been passed over to the courts. In 1988 the Supreme Court of Canada, using section 7 of the Charter, struck down that part of the Criminal Code that restricted the availability of legal abortions. The abortion issue, which Parliament had avoided for decades, was suddenly returned to the political realm. It is unlikely that this decision will herald a period of unbridled judicial law making. But the courts are now a factor in the constitutional balance and those who claim that the Westminster model can deliver decisive government must now come to terms with another potent institution.

EXECUTIVE–LEGISLATIVE RELATIONS

The Westminster model rests heavily on the clash of government and opposition forces. But to expect the opposition to assume the entire burden of ensuring a responsible government is, as we have argued, no longer realistic. In this section we explore relations between the government and the House of Commons that carry us beyond government–opposition confrontation. The work of members of Parliament, either as individuals or in concert, can complement the dominant adversarial style of politics in the House and supplement the work of the opposition. In fact, the activities of Parliament should be understood as a process of conflict and concession involving the government on the one hand and, on the other, three elements: the opposition, taken as a whole; small groups of MPs, both formal and informal; and private members, or MPs acting as individual representatives. Each of these relationships exists within Parliament, although at different times and in different forums.

The Government vs. the Opposition

On 30 September 1986 the House of Commons, for the first time, met to elect a Speaker. At 3:00 a.m. the next day, twelve hours and eleven ballots later, John Fraser, a former Conservative Cabinet minister, emerged victorious. It was a remarkable event.[22] Previous Speakers had been chosen by the prime minister in consultation with the leaders of the opposition parties. Dissatisfaction with that procedure had been brewing for years, but it took the bell-ringing incident of 1982 (in which Parliament was effectively suspended two weeks), and the resultant demands for reform, combined to finally make the Speaker the choice of the House of Commons.

The election of a Speaker was one of a number of reforms introduced in the 1980s to provide MPs with greater control over the internal affairs of the House of Commons. Indeed, the 1980s was a reform decade: speeches were shortened to twenty minutes, the parliamentary calendar was readjusted to allow MPs to meet all of their responsibilities, parliamentary committees were strengthened and given the power to review order-in-council appointees, and a new system for private members' bills was introduced.

Nonetheless, the House has found it hard to shake its "bear-pit" image. The Chamber is still the stage on which the ritual and theatre of partisan antagonism is performed. It is the primary battleground of government and opposition forces, which usually means ministers or parliamentary secretaries, on the one hand, and members of the opposition front bench, on the other. The dominant style of debate is oratory, and backbenchers on both sides of the House are expected to provide an appreciative audience.

There are three important activities that take place on the floor of the House and have these combative and partisan qualities. Question Period is, by a considerable margin, the most successful, at least from the point of view of the party leadership. During the 1980s the opposition parties developed a systematic approach to Question Period in which questions were orchestrated and ordinary backbenchers were discouraged from interrupting the flow until the front bench was finished. But this did little to improve decorum or enhance respect for the Speaker or parliamentary traditions. More than any single institution, Question Period has created the impression that the only political test of importance is survival in combat conditions on the floor of the House of Commons. Members of the media, often untutored in the ways of the House or the substance of policy, gravitate to these stylized confrontations because they offer the sound bites demanded by radio and television. Unfortunately, this overattention to Question Period has diminished the significance of other debates and left the impression that adversarial politics is all that the Commons is about.

A second occasion on which opposition and government traditionally confront one another is the second reading stage of government-sponsored legislation. First reading is nothing more than parliamentary approval to allow the bill to be printed and placed on the order paper. Second reading is the stage at which Parliament debates "the principle" of the bill; no amendments are permitted and strict rules of relevance are enforced. It is here that the minister appears in the House to defend the legislation and the opposition spokesperson mounts a challenge. The government prefers to believe that once the second reading stage has been successfully completed, Parliament is obliged to concentrate on the details of the bill, the main battle over principles having been fought. This interpretation of second reading is entirely in keeping with the idea that legislation is a government–opposition affair.

A similar quality of partisanship is found in the special debates that are scattered throughout the parliamentary year. The Speech from the Throne and the Budget Debate are opportunities for the opposition to criticize, and the Cabinet to defend, the government's vaguely worded legislative program and its more precisely formulated tax proposals. In addition, twenty-five "Opposition Days" are set aside in each parliamentary session during which motions proposed by the opposition parties form the basis for debate. These normally take the form of general critical pronouncements on government policy.

Unfortunately, none of these debates can be considered a splendid success from anyone's perspective. Franks puts the matter bluntly: "The action is slow, the dialogue is ponderous and interminable, the scene is sparsely populated and the wit has all the subtlety but none of the force of a Mack truck."[23] The Special Committee on Procedure (Lefebvre Committee), created after the bell-ringing incident, succeeded in persuading the House to adopt a set of reforms that have improved the circumstances of debate. There are now shorter speeches (normally twenty minutes) followed by a brief exchange. There are no more evening sittings, no more votes on Friday, and the government has agreed to announce its legislative intentions on a trimester basis. But the essential problem of parliamentary debate—the absence of any media interest—remains. This problem cannot be solved by procedural reforms. Until MPs exercise sufficient independence in their own speech making to attract media attention, their efforts will be lost in the larger picture of government–opposition confrontation.

If all the business of Parliament were conducted on the floor of the Commons, there would be little more to add to this picture of executive–legislative relations. But with the growth of government activity and an increase in annual government spending to over $120 billion, the government has found it expedient to transfer some of its own business to parliamentary committees. In 1968, changes were made to the Standing Orders to require that detailed, clause-by-clause consideration of legislation be accomplished in standing committees. At the same time the opposition, somewhat reluctantly, agreed that the scrutiny of departmental spending estimates, previously considered under the heading of "Supply" on the floor of the House, could also be transferred to the committee system. Committees hold out the prospect of conflict as well, but not always on a strictly partisan basis.

Even without these changes to parliamentary rules, it would still be a distortion to think of Parliament simply in terms of government–opposition relations. Some of the most important political activity in Parliament takes place away from the floor of the House in the caucuses of the governing and opposition parties. It is in forums such as these—caucus and committees—that conflicts over policy are refined or redefined, that agreement is often achieved, and that truly controversial matters are subject to a measure of conciliation.[24]

The Government vs. Formal and Informal Groups of MPs

For the government, one of the most important sources of criticism is the government backbench. Normally quiescent and polite in public, in private the backbench supporters of the government frequently clash with Cabinet on matters of policy. Open rebellion, though rare, can take the form of abstentions on important votes, minor media campaigns, and cross-voting.

The disapproval of backbench supporters is a serious matter for the government. Occasional expressions of personal disgruntlement can be tolerated and many potentially disruptive issues can be assuaged by appeals to party loyalty. But when backbenchers refuse to respond to threats (e.g., no trips to Europe), to inducements (e.g., the possibility of a parliamentary secretary position), or to the rallying cry to party solidarity, the viability of the government itself is at stake. The opposition preys on suspected rifts within the governing party, and while cross-votes may not lead directly to government defeats, when a government has lost the confidence of its own backbenchers then it has lost the confidence of the House of Commons.

Government members, ministers included, meet in caucus every week when Parliament is in session. Because these meetings are always held *in camera* and MPs are very reluctant to expose to the public any sign of divisiveness in the party, the impression is sometimes one of Cabinet control and caucus deference. The reminiscences of MPs from the Diefenbaker and Pearson years have helped to confirm this image: denied any knowledge of the government's pending legislative program, MPs were forced to content themselves with issues such as parking spaces on Parliament Hill. In 1969, however, the Liberal caucus insisted that it be consulted on legislation and other expressions of government policy before these were announced in the House of Commons. A system of ad hoc caucus committees was created to implement this consultative arrangement, and since 1970 the Liberal caucus has elected its own officers, including the caucus chairperson, without the direct interference of the parliamentary party leadership. Since then regional caucuses and caucus task forces have proven to be successful vehicles for mobilizing caucus opinion and forcing the party leadership to be responsive to their backbench supporters.

Caucus meetings are as closed as ever, but the noise of battle can occasionally be heard in spite of the secrecy. There is no doubt, for example, that many members of the Liberal caucus strongly opposed changes to the Unemployment Insurance Commission throughout the 1970s. Several amendments to the Liberal government's Crow Rate legislation in 1983 were accomplished at the insistence of caucus. In April 1980, members of the Quebec caucus announced their support for General Dynamic's bid in the New Fighter Aircraft Program. It required a four-and-a-half-hour meeting with officials to convince the caucus to support the government's preference for the MacDonnell-Douglas offer.

On the Conservative side, members of the parliamentary party expressed dismay over the return of Sinclair Stevens to caucus after a judicial inquiry determined that he had permitted serious conflicts of interest to exist while he served in the Mulroney Cabinet. Mr. Mulroney declined to sign his nomination papers for the November 1988 election. Shortly before that election, division over amendments to the Official Languages Act forced Mr. Mulroney to fire one of his parliamentary secretaries, whose opposition to the government's measures had aroused the Conservative Party's Quebec caucus.

As these cases illustrate, the government must attempt to anticipate and answer caucus opinion. Caucus is not a decision-making body, however, and the outcomes of caucus meetings are frequently a mystery even to participants. The committee systems do not always work, regional input does not always find expression in national caucus decisions, and the party leadership almost always has the last word.[25] In spite of these structural problems a veteran of the Liberal caucus, Mark MacGuigan, came to the following (perhaps overly emphatic) conclusion: "From the beginning of my years in Parliament it has been apparent that strong caucus opposition to any government proposal imposes an absolute veto on the proposal."[26]

Like the meetings of caucus, committees of the Commons are means by which smaller groups of MPs acting in concert can influence the direction of government policy. The potential of committees in this regard lies primarily in their ability to study specific topics in depth and offer detached, and sometimes non-partisan, assessments. Unlike caucus, however, Commons committees are comprised of representatives from all parties, and with some exceptions they conduct their hearings in public. The present committee system is the product of two decades of reform, most of it aimed at enhancing the role of private members of Parliament and much of it inspired by the Parliament-centred view of parliamentary government. The last set of reforms, contained in the McGrath Committee reports,[27] have been the most dramatic and have set the stage for a much stronger system of parliamentary committees.

There are now four types of committees: legislative committees, created to give clause-by-clause consideration to bills that have passed second reading; standing committees, which give continuous considera-tion to broad policy areas; special committees, which normally have a specific task and seldom last beyond a session; and joint committees composed of senators as well as MPs.

Legislative committees are a recent experiment. They are ad hoc, in the sense that they are struck to consider a limited number of legislative items, and the chairperson is drawn from a panel composed of members from all parties. Initially, the experiment received mixed reviews: there were too many legislative committees and they were too large. These problems have been remedied, however, and legislative committees seemed destined to stay. Since their task is normally the consideration of government legislation, Cabinet ministers naturally prefer that party lines be respected and that government supporters on each committee accept the direction of the minister (even though he or she is not a member of the committee) and the parliamentary secretary. This does not mean that changes to legislation cannot be accomplished, only that the government is normally the final arbiter.[28]

Much of the time of standing committees is consumed in the scrutiny of departmental spending estimates. Since committees cannot change these estimates, except to lower them (which has happened on occa-sion), both government and opposition members spend most of their time directing questions to the minister and his or her officials. It is when standing committees begin to investigate problem areas on their own initiative that the partisan mould is often broken and committee members begin to act as a unit. During the 33rd Parliament (1984–88) standing committees produced an impressive number of studies, including reports on substance abuse, broadcasting policy, misleading advertising, the equality provisions of the Charter, and the government's White Paper on Tax Reform. These investigations have been made much more effective by the McGrath Committee reforms. Most standing committees consist of only seven members, all are now free to choose their areas of study, they are unencumbered by parliamentary secretaries, they are able to hire research staff, and the government must (eventually) respond to their reports.

Governments are ambivalent toward the launching of general investigations by parliamentary committees. On the positive side (from the government's point of view) public inquiries give the appearance of action without the substance. They ascertain the reactions of interest groups to government proposals without requiring that a formal commitment be made to introduce changes. MPs, particularly government backbenchers, are kept busy and given an opportunity to prove themselves.

On the negative side (once again from the government's point of view) committees eventually present reports, and committee members, not surprisingly, are usually eager to have their proposals discussed. Moreover, these reports are not always what the government wants to see. The Standing Committee on Finance and Economic Affairs, chaired by Don Blenkarn (PC: Mississauga South), produced a report on bank charges that was highly critical of the banking community, and another on tax reform that suggested the middle class would bear the brunt of the tax changes. If reports are tabled with the unanimous approval of committee members, the government will be facing a small body of informed opinion, usually supported by interest groups, which it might find difficult to ignore. The situation is all the more uncomfortable since appeals to government supporters on the basis of party loyalty are less compelling when reports are the product of considerable research and discussion among committee members. The opposition party leadership, for its part, is similarly reluctant to have opposition party supporters drawn heavily into investigations of this type lest unanimous committee reports compromise the opposition leadership in its struggle to establish itself as a viable alternative to the government.

In spite of the problems that committees pose for traditional government–opposition confrontation as sanctified in the Westminster model, it is safe to predict that throughout the 1990s governments will be called upon to respond to the studies and recommendations of small groups of MPs. How far can this be permitted to go? Critics of an expanded committee system have warned that once committees cease behaving as little replicas of the Commons, we can look forward to the decline of parliamentary traditions and a weakening of party ties that can only culminate in congressionalism. In short, the Westminster model will ultimately be undermined.

It is not at all clear, however, that this is the only path that Parliament must tread. Several years after the McGrath Committee reforms, the government does not appear to have lost control of Parliament. Cross-voting has not increased and government MPs are as loathe as ever to criticize party policy in public. On the other hand, MPs are now better able to make a timely contribution to the government's policy agenda and parliamentarians on both sides of the House have acquired a measure of control over the procedures, personnel, and precincts of Parliament. Developments such as these suggest that there is another dimension to responsible government. The responsibility of a vigilant assembly to monitor closely the actions of a government need not be borne exclusively by the united opposition. Other groups of MPs, including the government caucus, standing committees, and task forces of MPs, can reasonably be expected to share that responsibility.

The Government vs. the Private Member of Parliament

In a government apparatus that spends enormous sums of money and employs hundreds of thousands of people, the private member of Parliament cuts a lonely figure. The vast majority of MPs owe their electoral victory to regional and national trends in the popularity of their party and its leaders. The machinery of party politics is such that very few of them will have made a critical contribution to their own election.[29] Once in Parliament they still have those privileges earned by their predecessors in the British House of Commons, but private members are no longer the source of legislative initiative that they were in the nineteenth century. A few hours every week are set aside for the consideration of private members' business, but attendance is generally poor and, until recently, the vast majority of private members' bills have not been voted on at second reading. The arrival of cohesive political parties and the government-sponsored public bill long ago set the stage for the departure of the private member as law maker.

But neither the House of Commons as a whole nor private members should be judged as initiators of policy. While it is true that many items in the government's legislative program have as their precursors private members' bills, the task of private members, like that of the opposition and groups of MPs, is to prod, encourage, question, and occasionally castigate the government with the intention of forcing it to justify in public its actions or inactions. For a certain range of matters the private member is in an excellent position to do that.

Each member of Parliament represents, on average, about 60,000 electors. Representation implies, among other things, responsiveness to the needs of individual constituents, and many MPs spend most of their working time attending to their constituency caseload. This includes unemployment insurance programs, immigration cases, and countless other instances in which the personal intervention of a member of Parliament is requested. While some MPs come to resent this combined role of social worker and ombudsperson, a 1983 Gallup poll showed that over 60 percent of respondents believed that looking after constituents should be the first priority of the MP. Moreover, this type of activity keeps members in touch with the concerns and problems of their constituents. For people who feel aggrieved in some fashion, the government *is* the post office that has curtailed its service or the fishery officer who refuses to open the capelin season. The tendency to judge the House of Commons solely on the strength of its ability to affect the broad strokes of policy does a disservice to those MPs who labour to make sure that their constituents receive justice at the hands of the federal bureaucracy.

There are, in addition, those MPs who wage personal campaigns to secure a particular policy objective. Bill Domm (PC: Peterborough) has worked tirelessly for the restoration of capital punishment in Canada, and the name of Jed Baldwin (PC: Peace River) will always be associated with the battle for freedom of information legislation. The efforts of these MPs have been assisted by the introduction of a new system for handling private members' bills. Twenty such bills are chosen at random at the beginning of a session and an all-party committee selects six for debate in the House. These six are permitted to come to a vote at second reading. It was through this procedure that Lynn McDonald (NDP: Broadview–Greenwood), in 1988, successfully sponsored a bill to eliminate smoking in all federally regulated buildings.

Anthony King has described these personal campaigns as the "private members' mode" of executive–legislative relations. MPs who adopt it, in his words, "come to see themselves simply as backbench Members of Parliament, concerned with investigating the quality of the performance of the executive (of whichever party), with protecting the rights of the citizen against the executive (of whichever party) and with asserting the prerogatives of backbench MPs (irrespective of party)."[30] Very few MPs can stand up to the demands imposed by this style of operation. Parliament is about political parties, not private members. Nonetheless, members of Parliament frequently feel the need to make manifest their legislative aspirations, sometimes to fulfil a personal mission, sometimes to demonstrate their political talents. For these reasons alone the government will always be confronted by the private member of Parliament.

CONCLUSION

The importance of Parliament does not lie in its capacity to be a centre for the detailed construction of public policy, for this capacity is meagre indeed. Parliament is, instead, a forum where the ideas and concerns of the government, the opposition, groups of MPs, and individual representatives meet. According to the Cabinet-centred view, the government should always be in charge: its ideas and policies should form the basis for the most important debates. But the government must also listen. To be out of touch with the sentiments of backbench supporters or the opposition is to court disaster.

Reform proposals inspired by the Parliament-centred view will continue to find articulate supporters on both sides of the House. If the norms and rules that underpin responsible government continue to grow in complexity, and Parliament is strengthened in its ability to question and prod, governments will have to listen more closely to MPs. This will undoubtedly occasion some loss of flexibility, and demands on governments to inform and explain will tax ministerial and bureaucratic resources. But it is surely not too much to ask that a government that listens so closely to the pronouncements of the provinces, interest groups, OPEC, and Washington also remain in touch with the country's elected representatives.

It is essential, however, that these representatives have something to say that merits attention. While strengthening Parliament's side in each of the relationships discussed above will help, it will also be necessary to challenge the fundamental principles of the Westminster model with a view to guiding its evolution. If ordinary MPs remain in splendid isolation, entirely neutralized by strictures of party discipline that very few Canadians understand, Parliament will increasingly become an irrelevant and obscure institution.

NOTES

1. For excellent discussions of the history of these perspectives and their contemporary relevance, see Gordon T. Stewart, *The Origins of Canadian Politics: A Comparative Approach* (Vancouver: University of British Columbia Press, 1986), and C. E. S. Franks, *The Parliament of Canada* (Toronto: University of Toronto Press, 1987), especially ch. 2.
2. For the argument that academic infatuation with this view is the product of a colonial mind set, see Mark Sproule-Jones, "The Enduring Colony? Political Institutions and Political Science in Canada," *Publius* 14 (Winter 1984): 93–108.

3. Although Canada's Parliament is a bicameral legislature, consisting of the Senate as well as the House of Commons, this chapter will confine itself to the latter. Senate reform is a perennial topic, but for those who wish to become more familiar with the Senate's internal operation, consult Colin Campbell, *The Canadian Senate: A Lobby From Within* (Toronto: Macmillan of Canada, 1977).

4. On the various types of bills and the distinction between private bills and private members' bills, see Robert J. Jackson and Michael M. Atkinson, *The Canadian Legislative System*, 2nd rev. ed. (Toronto: Gage, 1980), pp. 89–92.

5. John B. Stewart, *The Canadian House of Commons: Procedure and Reform* (Montreal: McGill-Queen's University Press, 1977), p. 201.

6. Eugene Forsey and Graham Eglinton, "Twenty-five Fairy Tales about Parliamentary Government," in *Politics: Canada*, 6th ed., ed. Paul W. Fox and Graham White (Toronto: McGraw-Hill Ryerson, 1987), pp. 507–13.

7. Franks, *Parliament of Canada*, p. 260.

8. Linda Geller-Schwartz, "Minority Governments Reconsidered," *Journal of Canadian Studies* 14 (Summer 1979): 67–79.

9. Kenneth Kernaghan, "Power, Parliament and Public Servants in Canada," in *Parliament, Policy and Representation*, ed. Harold D. Clarke, et al. (Toronto: Methuen, 1980), pp. 128–29.

10. Thomas d'Aquino, G. Bruce Doern, and Cassandra Blair, *Parliamentary Democracy in Canada: Issues for Reform* (Toronto: Methuen, 1983), pp. 45–46, and Canada, Royal Commission on Financial Management and Accountability, *Final Report* (Ottawa: Supply and Services, 1979), p. 374.

11. Colin Campbell and B. Guy Peters, "The Politics/Administration Dichotomy: Death or Merely Change?" *Governance* 1 (January 1988): 79–99.

12. Timothy Plumptre, "New Perspectives on the Role of the Deputy Minister," *Canadian Public Administration* 30 (Fall 1987): 376–98.

13. Michael M. Atkinson and William D. Coleman, "Bureaucrats and Politicians in Canada: An Examination of the Political Administration Model," *Comparative Political Studies* 18 (April 1985): 58–80.

14. A. Paul Pross, "Parliamentary Influence and the Diffusion of Power," *Canadian Journal of Political Science* 18 (June 1985): 235–66, and Michael M. Atkinson and William D. Coleman, *The State, Business and Industrial Change in Canada* (Toronto: University of Toronto Press, 1989), ch. 3.

15. Herman Bakvis, "Regional Ministers, National Policies and the Administrative State in Canada: The Regional Dimension in Cabinet Decision-Making," *Canadian Journal of Political Science* 21 (September 1988): 539–67.

16. *Debates*, 4 December 1985, p. 9157.
17. The transition is outlined in Thomas A. Hockin, "Flexible and Structured Parliamentarism," *Journal of Canadian Studies* 14 (Summer 1979): 8–17.
18. Stewart, *The Canadian House of Commons*, p. 21.
19. Ghita Ionescu and Isabel de Madariaga, *Opposition* (Harmondsworth: Penguin, 1972), ch. 2.
20. Franks, *Parliament of Canada*, pp. 40–44
21. Bernard Crick, *The Reform of Parliament* (New York: Anchor Books, 1965), p. 201.
22. See Gary Levy, "A Night to Remember: The First Election of a Speaker by Secret Ballot," *Canadian Parliamentary Review* 9 (Winter 1986/87): 10–14.
23. Franks, *Parliament of Canada*, p. 155.
24. The role of legislatures in the management of conflict is often underemphasized. See the comments of Gerhard Loewenberg and Samuel C. Patterson, *Comparing Legislatures* (Boston: Little, Brown, 1979), pp. 59–60.
25. Paul G. Thomas, "The Role of National Party Caucuses," *Party Government and Regional Representation in Canada*, the Collected Research Studies of the Royal Commission on the Economic Union and Development Prospects for Canada, ed. Peter Aucoin (Toronto: University of Toronto Press, 1985), pp. 69–136.
26. Mark MacGuigan, "Parliamentary Reform: Impediments to an Enlarged Role for the Backbencher," *Legislative Studies Quarterly* 3 (November 1978): 676.
27. House of Commons, *Report of the Special Committee on Reform of the House of Commons* (Ottawa: Queen's Printer, 1985).
28. Paul G. Thomas, "The Influence of Standing Committees of Parliament on Government Legislation," *Legislative Studies Quarterly* 3 (November 1978): 683–704.
29. William Irvine, "Does the Candidate Make a Difference? The Macro-Politics and the Micro-Politics of Getting Elected," *Canadian Journal of Political Science* 15 (December 1982): 755–82.
30. Anthony King, "Modes of Executive–Legislative Relations: Great Britain, France and West Germany," *Legislative Studies Quarterly* 1 (February 1976): 11–36.

FURTHER READINGS

Aucoin, Peter, ed. *Institutional Reforms for Representative Government*. The Collected Research Studies of the Royal Commission on the Economic Union and Development Prospects for Canada. Toronto: University of Toronto Press, 1985.

Clarke, Harold D., Colin Campbell, F. Q. Quo, and Arthur Goddard, eds. *Parliament, Policy and Representation.* Toronto: Methuen, 1980.

Courtney, John C., ed. *The Canadian House of Commons.* Calgary: University of Calgary Press, 1985.

Franks, C. E. S. *The Parliament of Canada.* Toronto: University of Toronto Press, 1987.

Jackson, Robert J., and Michael M. Atkinson. *The Canadian Legislative System: Politicians and Policymaking,* 2nd rev. ed. Toronto: Macmillan, 1980.

Kornberg, Allan, and William Mishler. *Influence in Parliament: Canada.* Durham, N.C.: Duke University Press, 1977.

Special Issue on Legislatures in Canada. *Legislative Studies Quarterly* 3 (November 1978).

Special Issue on Responsible Government. *Journal of Canadian Studies* 14 (Summer 1979).

Stewart, Gordon. *The Origins of Canadian Politics: A Comparative Approach.* Vancouver: University of British Columbia Press, 1986.

Stewart, John B. *The Canadian House of Commons: Procedure and Reform.* Montreal: McGill-Queen's University Press, 1977.

18

The Federal Cabinet in Canadian Politics

DAVID E. SMITH

In the year of Confederation, Walter Bagehot described the Cabinet as "a combining committee—a *hyphen* which joins, a *buckle* which fastens the legislative part of the state to the executive part of the state." Buckle and hyphen have proved durable metaphors with which to open discussions of Cabinet government despite the fact that the functions and structure of modern Cabinets are significantly different from those of Bagehot's time. The executive he had in mind, the Crown, has faded into obscurity in the public consciousness. For most Canadians, the Cabinet's central importance lies in its *governing and representative* functions, while its role as advisor to the Crown is seldom considered and, when regarded, scarcely understood. Nevertheless, we should keep in mind that the Cabinet, through the prime minister, still formally advises the chief executive officer, the governor general, who always, or almost always, takes that advice, for not to take it would create a constitutional crisis.

Metaphors like Bagehot's are attractive when facts are hard to find, and with notable exceptions, studies of the Federal Cabinet are rare. There is no encyclopedic Canadian work comparable to Sir Ivor Jennings's *Cabinet Government* in Great Britain, nor are there even very many less ambitious exercises.[1] Personal accounts of those in command at the Cabinet table go unwritten; of the eighteen prime ministers to date, only two (Diefenbaker and Pearson) have published their own memoirs, and these tell disappointingly little about Cabinet decision making or about the respective influences on Cabinet of the bureaucracy, interest groups, political parties, or the parliamentary opposition.[2] In the twenty years after Lester Pearson formed a government, just two Liberal ministers (Walter Gordon and Judy LaMarsh) wrote memoirs, though the revelations about Cabinet business contained in them are cause for regret that other ministers did not follow suit; unfortunately four accounts written by former Trudeau ministers, and published in 1985 and 1986, do not meet this earlier standard.[3] This reticence to "talk" on the part of past ministers is not new. Mackenzie King's extraordinary tenure as prime minister for twenty-two years proved no more productive of published accounts. If Pearson is excluded, only one of King's seventy-three other ministers dictated his memoirs.[4] In the first half-century of Confederation, when

Cabinets were smaller and responsibilities less extensive, the selection is no better.[5]

The absence of memoirs is certainly unfortunate for academics or for citizens who would like to know how government works. However, it also points to a political system that produces politicians who are uncommunicative and incurious and who, according to David Hoffman and Norman Ward in their study *Bilingualism and Biculturalism in the Canadian House of Commons*, also lack ambition: "Only 24 percent [of the backbench MPs interviewed in that 1964–65 survey] indicated that they would be interested in a cabinet post at some time in the future; 50 percent said that they had no interest in any public office(s) in the future."[6] This reign of political silence and passivity stands in marked contrast to the situation in Great Britain, where a former prime minister, Harold Wilson, once had to resort to the courts in an attempt to stop his ministers from publishing their memoirs (although some cynics suggested the prohibition had less to do with alleged violations of the Official Secrets Act than with allowing the prime minister to publish first!).

Thus, while we may not know as much as we might like about the inner operation of the Cabinet, we can begin our investigation by locating the process of Cabinet government within the context of the Canadian political tradition. This will prepare us for a subsequent examination of the role of Cabinet according to its two principal and historic functions: as an instrument of governance and as a vehicle for representation.

CABINET AND THE CANADIAN POLITICAL TRADITION

Pragmatic Politics

Whatever label might be applied to the two political parties that have formed Canada's federal governments, "doctrinaire" is not one of them. Debates between these parties in Parliament and in the country do not reflect differences of principle so much as differences over how to implement policies of economic growth or social security (in this respect, the single issue "free trade" election of 1988 was unusual). Within Cabinet as well, this value consensus generally holds, and only very occasionally are there intraparty divisions where the alignment of sympathies is as clear as it was between economic nationalists and contintentalists in the Liberal Party of the 1960s and the early 1980s. Significantly, one of the rare ex-ministerial authors of memoirs was Walter Gordon, the gadfly of economic nationalism who held several portfolios in the Pearson government of the 1960s.

Walter Gordon was unusual less for the policy he advocated than for the arguments he used. He urged economic nationalism for its long-run concrete benefits, but he promoted it first as a principle. From the studies of Cabinet that do exist, the impression gained is that ministers are normally pragmatic in the positions they take. While pragmatism might seem inevitable in a country as large and diverse as Canada, one must be careful not to underestimate the latent importance of values in Canadian politics. Walter Gordon was distinctive not so much because he had firm principles, but because he publicized his position. Most ministers do not, and in fact they may act embarrassed when it is suggested that they might hold a position on some ideological issue. But the PC leadership contest in 1983 and the Liberal leadership contest in 1984, for instance, demonstrate that candidates are sometimes forced to declare their position on such ideologically charged questions as medicare, Petro-Canada, and bilingualism. Nevertheless, it is clear that at least one reason Canadians are not used to thinking ideologically about subjects is that their politicians have also been reluctant to treat them this way.

The absence of a doctrinaire approach within the old political parties is revealed paradoxically enough in the resignations of ministers from the federal Cabinet. Not only do few resignations occur (the half dozen Tory Cabinet ministers who either resigned or were fired after being accused of poor judgment in 1984, 1985, and 1986 are unusual), but those that do are seldom attributed to policy differences. There are exceptions, of course. For example, Israel Tarte (Public Works) was ejected from the Cabinet in 1902 for publicly disagreeing with the government's tariff policy; Clifford Sifton (Interior) resigned in 1905 from the same government because he dissented from the original educational provisions of the Alberta and Saskatchewan acts; J. L. Ralston (National Defence) was fired by Mackenzie King in 1944 for advocating military conscription for overseas service before King, who long resisted this policy for fear of its detrimental effect on national unity, was ready to accept it; and Douglas Harkness (National Defence) resigned from the Diefenbaker government in 1963 because he supported the arming of BOMARC missiles with nuclear warheads and his leader did not.

But even in instances such as these, the effect of the resignations has never been to extend the political debate very far or for very long.[7] Much more typical is a resignation like that of John Turner (Finance) from the Trudeau government in 1975, which was publicly described as being for "personal reasons." Although Turner was subsequently labelled as more conservative than Trudeau on economic and social issues and although he was even then widely viewed as a major contender for the Liberal leadership when Trudeau retired, his resignation prompted little public debate over political principle either inside or outside the party. Certainly there was no massing of Liberal support behind competing interpretations of Liberalism.

To conclude, one consequence of this reluctance to inject policy differences into either public debate or Cabinet deliberations is to depreciate the intellectual level of political discourse within political parties and within the country, to the detriment of politics as an educative activity. In its place, the cult of personality seizes the attention of the media, the public, and the politicians, and this is not, as we shall next see, an attitude conducive to the growth of professionalism in politics.[8]

Avocational Politics

Arguably, political debate is pragmatic because the politicians who take part in it are not professionals. Twenty years ago, in *The Vertical Mosaic*, John Porter wrote that a model political career implies

> a professionalizing of political roles where the individual devotes his life to politics and in the process develops a "love" for political institutions. . . .[But] where the political career is unstable and taken up for an interstitial period only, during a career devoted to something else, the political system will probably be strong in administration and weak in creativity.[9]

In the period he studied, Porter discovered that life at the top was peopled by ministers frequently co-opted from other careers (for example, business or the public service) or after brief experience in the House of Commons, and that in either case their period in Cabinet was surprisingly short. In 1960, 47 percent of the ministers had served for less than six years. Porter's findings here were confirmed in a 1973 study by Dennis Olsen that found that 52 percent had served for five years or less and that 95 percent had served fewer than eleven years.[10] Moreover, given a House of Commons where the turnover rate is usually around 40 percent (in 1988, 43 percent of those elected had not sat in the previous Parliament) and where, generally, another 20 to 35 percent of the MPs have less than five years' experience, Cabinet "timber" nurtured in a parliamentary environment is never a commodity in great supply when a prime minister sets about constructing a government.

There are other reasons why the Cabinet is deficient in political experience. The most important is the imperative of sectional representation, which will be discussed in more detail later. At this point, it is enough to say that the practice of ensuring representation from all the provinces in Cabinet is now so strong—it is a convention or binding rule of prime ministerial behaviour—that it overrides considerations of political experience where the two criteria conflict. The depressing effect of this practice on those MPs who aspire to ministerial office but are excluded for geographic reasons needs to be recognized when explaining why Porter's model political career is infrequently seen in Canada. Conversely, the size of the Cabinet (thirty-nine in September 1988) increases the problem of finding sufficient personnel with satisfactory parliamentary experience.

One final word on the absence of professionals in federal politics concerns the party leaders themselves. During the Progressive Conservative leadership race in 1983, the Liberals liked to point out that one of the front-runners, Brian Mulroney, who eventually won, had no parliamentary experience. But Liberal leaders in this century since Mackenzie King have been remarkably innocent of backbench experience themselves: King had less than a year, St. Laurent none, Pearson none, and Trudeau seventeen months, fifteen of them as a parliamentary secretary. Norman Ward once wrote that "one excellent way of ensuring that one will not rise to the top of the Liberal party is to start at the bottom."[11] As well, one effect of leadership conventions in Canada has been to favour non-parliamentary over parliamentary experience, and this seems almost as true of the Progressive Conservatives as of the Liberals. Since 1942 and John Bracken's selection, the PCs have had six leaders, four of whom have had no federal parliamentary background.

Thus, the Cabinet is not the kindergarten of political leadership in Canada that it is in Great Britain. (While no one knows, for example, who will succeed Margaret Thatcher, the probability that he or she will come out of the Cabinet's ranks is extremely high.) The fact that the Cabinet is not seen as the training ground of leadership, coupled with the pragmatic nature of its politics already alluded to, helps explain the nature of Cabinet government in Canada. But there is a third factor, related to those already mentioned, that needs to be considered and that is the process by which major interests reach agreement through bargaining—brokerage politics.

Brokerage Politics

Brokerage theory, which has dominated Canadian political science, argues that national political parties must encompass all the essential interests in the country if a majority is to be secured and if minority rights are to be guaranteed. This theory is both empirical and prescriptive. It purports to describe how parties actually practise their art, and it defends that practice. Parties, it is believed, are supposed to act as agents of consensus and as aggregators of interests rather than as instruments of choice. But despite its dominance, the theory has its critics, most notably John Porter, who charged brokerage politics with stultifying "creative" political debate. The search for the middle ground in politics, Porter argued, too often excluded rather than included interests. The result was that parties and governments seemed always to pay undue attention to professional, commercial, middle-class concerns. "Seemed" was the operative verb, for as he noted: "We have in fact very little information about what interests political leaders take into consideration in making up cabinets."[12]

Unfortunately, we still lack the concrete information necessary to confirm Porter's judgment on the mechanisms of Cabinet selection.[13] But the belief that interests must be balanced, especially regional ones, remains strong, and this belief can be seen currently in support for proposals to reform the electoral system and the upper house so as to bring to the centre a greater range of regional interests. More will be said about these proposals later. At this point, it need only be stated that institutional reformers assume the validity and utility of brokerage politics and, in the case of proponents of proportional representation, believe it would strengthen the Cabinet by presenting the prime minister with more choices when selecting ministers.

Brokerage politics cannot be fully discussed in this chapter for the scope of the discussion would go far beyond its effect on the Cabinet. However, it is necessary to recognize what its assumptions imply for a study of the Cabinet. Inevitably they suggest an analysis of the Cabinet in terms of how faithfully its members reflect the "elemental" divisions of the country. It is for that reason that so much research on the Cabinet presents in detail the geographic and socio-economic characteristics of its members. But it is also the case that very few of these same studies explain why such "representation" is significant. Instead, it is assumed rather than demonstrated that *balanced Cabinet representation leads to balanced policies.*

An alternative theory to appear recently in Canadian political discourse is the theory of *consociational democracy*, developed in small European countries like the Netherlands where the interests of strong subcultures require accommodation if national unity is to exist.[14] In the European experience, accommodation takes place at the elite levels and requires for its success integrated subcultures with clear patterns of leadership. From this brief description, the appeal of the theory of consociationalism in Canada can be appreciated, especially since the 1960s, when the Canadian polity became increasingly fragmented as the Quiet Revolution spread in Quebec and as the other provinces increased their demands on Ottawa for greater financial and political control over economic and social policies. In addition, consociational democracy as a theory of bargaining among subcultural elites gave a new respectability to brokerage politics. However, in the past, political party elites had been the brokers while, in the modern period, governmental elites under the rubric of executive federalism have gained the upper hand.[15]

Having mapped the essential topography of the federal Cabinet process within the Canadian political tradition in terms of its pragmatic, avocational, and brokerage boundaries, we are now ready for a closer examination of its governing and representative functions. Because the history of the federal Cabinet is the history of Canada's evolution as an independent parliamentary democracy, we must now trace the changing role of Cabinet from the achievement of responsible government in the 1840s.

CABINET AS AN INSTRUMENT OF GOVERNMENT

A Colonial and Imperial Past

Colonial origins and imperial models determined the evolution of Cabinet government. The idea that the Crown should heed the advice of those who command the support of the popularly elected chamber (which in the United Canadas was recognized in 1848 by Lord Elgin's acceptance of the Rebellion Losses Bill) implied more than a new parliamentary democratic value, as important as that was. It also signified a new organizing principle for the British Empire, and Lord Durham's recommendation of a decade earlier that colonies should be responsible for their internal affairs was now to be implemented. The importance of this development for Canada cannot be underestimated. The conflict between Parliament and the king, which had seen Parliament prevail in Great Britain a century before, was now to be repeated in the colonies with the same result. However, there was something more here as well. To the extent that colonial Parliament prevailed over the king's representative, so did Canada prevail over Great Britain—responsible government thus ultimately led to independent government.

All of this is history, but it is history with a point as far as the development of the Canadian Cabinet is concerned. For it would be misleading to discuss the federal Cabinet's growth solely in terms of domestic politics, since the Cabinet and its leaders also gained strength and unity out of the colonial situation. Not only did external matters occupy Cabinet attention (especially military questions and their effect on domestic harmony—the Boer War and Laurier, the First World War and Borden, the Second World War and King), but the evolution of the British Empire into the Commonwealth was accompanied by a transfer of power from imperial to Canadian authorities (in such forms, for example, as the power to make treaties, to declare war and, finally, to amend the constitution at home). Questions of status—colonial, dominion, national, and international—have traditionally bulked large for prime ministers because of their implications for Canada's developing autonomy and prestige. This explains why until 1946 the prime minister acted as his own Secretary of State for External Affairs and why even afterwards, in contrast to their British counterparts, Canadian prime ministers continued to play a leading role in foreign affairs.

If over time Canada's developing colonial status conferred new

responsibilities on its Cabinet and enhanced the power of its prime
minister, there were other influences derived from its colonial origins
that affected the Cabinet right from the start. Indeed, some of these were
pronounced well before Confederation. Responsible government arrived
in the St. Lawrence lowlands when the Canadas, united since 1840 by a
single set of political institutions but by little else, were already an
embryonic federal system. In order to operate this unwieldy structure,
practical adjustments were necessary, and from early on the Cabinet
proved especially useful as a mechanism for accommodating the social
diversities of the colony. There were several reasons for this development. The myriad of interests—religious, linguistic, legal, economic, and
military among others—that jockeyed for attention in the colony evolved
through a period when they looked to the executive (the governor and his
Council) to protect them. And there were no modern disciplined political
parties. Instead, factions based on regional or social groupings were in a
seemingly continuous process of formation and dissolution. The result
was a series of coalition governments throughout the history of the
United Canadas whose authority was frequently rejected by the elected
legislators but who could look to their executive power as the Crown's
advisors to give them the legitimacy they needed.

Old Traditions and Modern Practice

From the outset, Canadian Cabinets were large because of the number of
interests to be accommodated in a culturally bifurcated society, and
because of the breadth of territory to be represented. The pressure to
include rather than exclude affected the conduct of business too. From
colonial days, the preferred practice was to confer rule-making power on
the Council and not on individual ministers. In the modern era of
expanded delegation from Parliament to the executive the same is true,
for to do otherwise would favour with power or information some
ministers over others—an act of discrimination that the sectional dimension of Cabinet membership particularly discourages. As an indicator of
this volume, in 1976 there were 3,326 orders-in-council, of which the
three largest categories concerned appointments (22.5 percent), regulations (19.6 percent), and property transactions (14.5 percent).[16]

   A related effect has been to minimize traditional British distinctions
as, for example, between Cabinet and Council or between Cabinet and
Ministry. In Great Britain, where rank is one of life's organizing principles, such distinctions are accepted, but in Canada, where society is both
more open and more heterogeneous, they are not. Here the governor's
old Executive Council (after July 1, 1867, it was called the Privy Council)
evolved into Cabinet with minimal distinction between the two. (By
convention, membership in the Council is retained for life along with the

designation "Honourable," but even for ceremonial purposes the Council rarely convenes.) The Cabinet as a Committee of Council is a "masquerade," according to R. MacGregor Dawson, which it adopts "when it desires to assume formal powers."[17]

It is only since the Second World War and particularly after Trudeau became prime minister that the Privy Council Office began to have a life of its own. Although there has been a clerk of the Privy Council since Confederation, the office was (with rare exceptions) from Laurier through Diefenbaker seen as the fiefdom of the prime minister. Since Pearson's time the office of president of the Privy Council has been held by the leader of the House, and the Privy Council Office itself has become one of the so-called "central agencies," whose influence is derived from its position in the decision-making process and whose operation is described in more detail elsewhere in this volume. [18]

There was a similar reluctance, and for the same reasons, to follow British precedent and distinguish between Cabinet and Ministry. For although the number of ministers has always appeared large in comparison to the needs of a relatively small population, any attempt to introduce efficiency by streamlining structures (which usually has meant reducing numbers) has been resisted because of its exclusionary effect. In Great Britain the Ministry may be in excess of one hundred members and the Cabinet a quarter that number with an Inner Cabinet within that. By contrast, in Canada, except for the occasional exclusion of the solicitor general, the controller of Customs, or the controller of Inland Revenue (all before 1926), *all* members of the Ministry have also been members of the Cabinet. Moreover, until the late 1960s when Cabinet committees were introduced, there has been nothing resembling an Inner Cabinet. Practically, that ceased to be true after the early 1970s when creation of a Priorities and Planning committee by Trudeau introduced an approximation of an Inner Cabinet, and formally, in 1979 when Joe Clark restructured Cabinet committees to create an Inner Cabinet. It should be remarked that parliamentary secretaries (twenty-eight as of September 1988), who have existed on a regular basis since the 1940s, when they were called parliamentary assistants, have never been considered part of the Ministry).

These changes notwithstanding, it is true that Cabinet government in Canada has meant, since Confederation at least, government by the full Cabinet—a body large in number and chosen to reflect the country's geographic diversity and cultural duality, although more recently its social base has broadened to include women (1957), someone not from one of the two founding cultures (1957), a non-Christian (1968), and a native Canadian (1976), a tendency that can be expected to continue as society changes.

The principal functions of the federal Cabinet are to direct the business of Parliament, to administer the individual departments of government, to formulate and discuss policy, and to pass orders-in-council. Most importantly, it is "to furnish initiative and leadership" for the country and Parliament.[19] Essentially this is a joint enterprise of the Cabinet and the prime minister, but in truth how well it is done and what character it assumes is the responsibility of the prime minister alone. In the Canadian system the prime minister enjoys inordinate powers by tradition and as a result of innovations in technology (e.g., television) and institutions (e.g., leadership conventions), which elevate the position vis-à-vis the Cabinet to the point where the off-repeated claim that the prime minister is only *primus inter pares* (first among equals) is no more descriptive of the position than Bagehot's buckle-and-hyphen metaphor is of the Cabinet.[20]

Three Models of Political Leadership

The Canadian system of government is party government, or more precisely party-in-government. The telescoping of these two features confers exceptional power on the leader of the legislative party that controls the House of Commons, but how that power is used is at his or her discretion. Since Confederation it is possible to identify three broad approaches to political leadership, each of which has not only implied a different role and function for the Cabinet, but also has affected the image Canadians have of themselves. For brevity's sake the three may be labelled as the personal, the accommodative, and the pan-Canadian approaches. While historical events never fit exactly into time periods, it is possible to see each approach as the dominant characteristic of political leadership in the following major eras of Canadian history: personal (Confederation to First World War), accommodative (interwar and immediate post–Second World War), and pan-Canadian (mid-1950s to the present).

The personal approach, in place up to the First World War, can be identified with the leadership of Macdonald and Laurier. Although of different political parties, each was concerned with national expansion: Macdonald basically with rounding out the Union by incorporating new provinces and territories and by welding the whole into one economic unit through his National Policy with its protective tariff, transcontinental railway, and accelerated immigration; and Laurier by furthering that expansion through more aggressive immigration and settlement of the West. But although their policies were national, their political practices were local. As Gordon Stewart has shown, they pioneered patronage politics to create a national party system that was intensely local in its interests and profoundly personal in its management by the party leader.[21].

Under them, the Cabinet became a collective through which to channel gifts in the form of jobs and contracts from the government, which in this period was among the largest businesses (in terms of expenditure and employment) in the country. Unlike the United States, Canada had no giant capitalist corporations of national breadth, excluding perhaps the Canadian Pacific Railway, itself scarcely independent of the federal government. In the process Macdonald and Laurier created an "effective party structure," but not a "modern" one, and the First World War, with its economic and social dislocations, revealed just how inadequate the system was in adjusting to change. The rise of a strong third party in the form of the Progressives, who captured 65 of 235 seats in the 1921 election, vividly demonstrated the need for a new political response. That response had to come from the Cabinet and its leader, for among the functions of the Cabinet not listed earlier but of crucial significance to Canadian politics is its role as the "managing committee for the party in power."[22]

The new accommodative approach, initiated by Mackenzie King, became the hallmark of his long tenure as party leader and prime minister (as well as of Louis St. Laurent's prime ministership) and differed from the Macdonald–Laurier style in several important respects. King was unusually alive to the divisive forces in Canadian society, in part because of his experience as a labour conciliator and in part because of events that preceded and accompanied his rise to office—the conflict in English–French relations from 1890 onward, culminating in the conscription crisis in Quebec, and the farmers' revolt on the prairies, which up to 1917 had represented safe Liberal territory. These factors and others, such as the civil service reforms of the former (Union) government that moderated patronage in federal politics and thus conformed more closely to King's personal disposition and political decision to be less directly involved in these matters than Laurier, help explain the source of King's consensual approach to leadership.

There is no dispute that King had no peer in the art of accommodation or compromise. Nor is there doubt that he used the Cabinet as one of his instruments and that he was supremely skilled in its use. He deflected the Progressives in the 1920's in part by co-opting two of their leaders (Forke and Crerar), and he similarly blunted the threat of the Co-operative Commonwealth Federation (CCF) in part by taking in labour spokesman Humphrey Mitchell. Further, he defused a Quebec explosion over conscription through the help of his Quebec ministers, two of whom eventually resigned over this drawn-out question, and by the dimissal of the Minister of National Defence (not from Quebec) who advocated conscription for overseas service before King believed the country was ready for it.

Under King and St. Laurent, the Cabinet became not only the locus for resolving domestic tensions, but the directing arm of the Liberal Party. The ministers, when they were not former partisan opponents, were the chief Liberals of the day. A former provincial premier like J. G. Gardiner from Saskatchewan, for example, was as close to being a "proconsul" in that province, and on occasion in the neighbouring prairie provinces, as could be found in Canadian political history. King and St. Laurent respected departmental autonomy, and thus their ministers gained unprecedented independence at the same time as the growth of the Canadian government's activities and responsibilities increased their powers. But with power came costs. In the period of Macdonald and Laurier, party had penetrated the bureaucracy through patronage, and now the bureaucracy penetrated the party by transmitting its values, objectives, and procedures to the politician. In the end the Liberals became what Reginald Whitaker has called "the Government Party,"[23] and if the parties and governments of Macdonald and Laurier grew out of touch with national economic and social trends, the Liberal Party and governments of King and St. Laurent did the same, this time by failing to comprehend the growth of regionalism.

The pan-Canadian approach to leadership represented a response to this rise in regionalism, first by creating federal programs and departments to deal specifically with regional questions, and then, more distinctively, by promoting pan-Canadian policies—that is, policies that overarched constituency or group interests and touched individual Canadians wherever they might live in Canada. John Diefenbaker's "One Canada," his appeal to "unhyphenated Canadianism," his Bill of Rights, his national social policies (such as hospitalization), and other responses in the late 1950s and early 1960s took as their premise "equal rights for all, privileges for none." It was Diefenbaker who used the prime minister's appointment power to "recognize" distinctive groups in society, by placing the first woman and the first Canadian of Ukrainian origin in the Cabinet, by appointing the first Indian to the Senate and the first French Canadian as governor general.

But this initial attempt at a pan-Canadian approach of governing was cut short by the Quiet Revolution, for Diefenbaker's vision of his country did not sanction treating Quebeckers any differently from the rest of Canadians. However, the vision of his successors, Lester Pearson and Pierre Trudeau, did accept at as a first principle that Canada was composed of two founding peoples. From this premise flowed a host of policies aimed at touching all Canadians through the medium of one or other of two official languages. Mr. Diefenbaker never accepted this Liberal view of Canada and, indeed, continued to fight it all of his political life in part because of what he interpreted as its anti-British connotations. But he did accept the implementation of other pan-Canadian policies, applauding, for instance, the federal government's national medical care and pension plans. In its National Energy Program, constitutional reforms, and entrenchment of a Charter of Rights and Freedoms, Mr. Trudeau's government when further than either Diefenbaker's or Pearson's breaking the consensual mould of national politics created by Mackenzie King. One cost of this approach for the Liberals was the loss for over two decades of major electoral support in the West, a region of the country where there had once been significant Liberal sympathy. The long-run implications for Canada of these policies remain unknown, but in the short run the benefits to French Canadians of opening wider the institutions of the federal government are substantial. Nowhere else was this clearer than in the Cabinet itself. Under Pearson and Trudeau the number of French Canadian ministers rose as did the importance of the portfolios they held. In this century until 1963, the proportion of Cabinet ministers of French ethnic origin never exceeded 30 percent, after that it stood consistently above 40 percent, and while as late as 1970 it could be said that no French Canadian had ever held the Finance, Trade and Commerce, or Labour portfolios, by 1984 French Canadians either did hold or had held all three.

Significantly, the election of a Progressive Conservative majority government in 1984 (and again in 1988) did not lead to abandonment of this most recent approach to leadership. On the one hand, Mr. Mulroney sought to reduce conflict with the provinces by opting for conciliation rather than accepting confrontation, going so far in the Meech Lake Accord as to tolerate ambiguity between Charter guarantees and recognition of a "distinct society" in Quebec. On the other hand, the PC prime minister aggressively promoted official bilingualism, vigorously used his appointment power to bring representatives of visible minorities onto national boards and commissions, and tirelessly sought to promote the careers of prominent francophones within the Tory party and especially in his Cabinet. In this last regard, Mr. Mulroney's efforts were initially frustrated not because of lack of will, but due to the calibre of some of the fifty-seven freshmen members of his party from Quebec who were swept to victory in the PC tidal wave of 1984.

This summary of models of leadership indicates the importance of political personality, but also the different uses to which the Cabinet can be put, for as an instrument of government it is more than a body that passes orders-in-council or that superintends the administration of government. Because it combines political and governmental power, it occupies a unique position from which a leader can initiate and direct policies. What policies are chosen and how they are implemented is a function of many variables, but crucial among them is that leaders depend on the power they possess at the head of a disciplined party, caucus, and Cabinet.

CABINET AS A VEHICLE FOR REPRESENTATION

The Cabinet is the pre-eminent institution of sectional representation in the Canadian parliamentary system. In practice that has meant the sectional representation of the provinces and the historic linguistic and religious communities of Canada. Other minorities have been present in Cabinet, but the term "sectional presentation" customarily refers to the foregoing interests. Whatever the expectations of the Fathers of Confederation, the Senate has never played this role. Appointment by governor-in-council, allocation of equal numbers of senators by regions and not provinces, separation from the executive that sat in the lower house, and infrequent membership in the Cabinet all saw to that. A province or a group (the English-speaking Protestants of Quebec or the Irish Catholics of either Quebec or Ontario, for example) who wanted to take part in the decisions of the day or to protect their special interests had to be represented in the Cabinet. Of course, there was not equal representation there either, since generally two-thirds of the ministers came from Ontario and Quebec, but a seat at the Cabinet table was believed to be more influential than any other federal office.

The Traditional Cabinet: A Federal Structure

The conviction that provinces must be represented was shared by leaders as well as followers, and the history of Cabinet building by any prime minister reveals the strength of this particularly Canadian article of faith. Where the electorate of a province was thoughtless enough to return no members to Parliament from the party that formed the government, then the prime minister had to perform as a political gymnast twisting his way around an inconvenient election result in order to fulfil one of the first commandments of Cabinet making—that all parts of the whole must, if at all possible, be represented in the finished product. Generally speaking, he has had two alternatives: to run those who cannot get elected in their home province in a safe seat elsewhere (when the Liberals were shut out of Alberta in the 1921 election Mackenzie King brought the former Liberal premier of that province, Charles Stewart, into the Cabinet as Minister of the Interior by opening a Quebec seat for him), or to resort to the Senate route, where there are usually several Cabinet aspirants per province.

The former route is out of fashion today (although it was used in Canadian history to bring into Cabinet such outstanding ministers as Charles Dunning to Finance and Angus MacDonald to Naval Services, who were not electoral liabilities by any stretch of the imagination but for whom a federal seat elsewhere than in their home province was at the time convenient to them and the prime minister). The latter route is the preferred modern method (in 1980 Mr. Trudeau took in three senators from the three most western provinces where no Liberals had been elected), though it has little to recommend it other than its simplicity.[24] While the Senate continues to do some fine investigative work, it is not an institution in which the principle of democratic accountability is strong, and its members as Cabinet ministers experience and cause frustration. Senators are appointed to Cabinet where the governing party is weakest in electoral favour, yet the process does nothing to build the party and can indeed divide it by creating antagonisms and jealousies. The fact that recent prime ministers have resorted to this alternative in spite of its disadvantages is evidence of the strength of the convention that Cabinet must encompass representation from all provinces.

Sectional representation is not an abstract notion of symbolic value only, though this is not an unimportant consideration. In regard to certain matters, ministers *from* individual provinces are seen as ministers *for* those provinces. This is true particularly with respect to appointments, but also to discussions of policy and its potential effect on provincial interests. It is misleading to depict the Cabinet as no more than a collection of sectional "veto groups"—some policies, labelled above as "pan-Canadian," are less regionally specific than others, and therefore are less susceptible to regional bargaining—but it is equally erroneous to ignore the durable effect of a federalized Cabinet on policy formulation.[25] Canada is still a country of sharply defined regions, with geographic and cultural boundaries that enclose distinctive ways of life, and the Cabinet continues, as it always has, to reflect this fact.

For much of the country's history particular portfolios were identified with particular regions or provinces. With the opening of the West, responsibility for agriculture went to a westerner until 1965. But the Liberals' dismal electoral record in that region altered this tradition, and in only four of the next twenty years did a westerner hold that portfolio. As compensation, responsibility for the Canadian Wheat Board, the agency in charge of the prairies' staple industry, was assigned either to a western minister with another portfolio or, in 1980, to a minister of state who was a senator. Since the change in government in 1984, a specific minister has again had responsibility for the Wheat Board or, more recently, for grains. The old Department of the Interior, which disappeared shortly after the transfer of the prairie provinces' natural resources from the federal government in 1930, was even more closely identified with that region's settlement and expansion. The prominence of that endeavour, which has been described as the most "far-reaching activity" in this century except for the prosecution of the wars, is indicated by the calibre of those who held the portfolio, among whom were Edgar Dewdney, Clifford Sifton, Frank Oliver, Arthur Meighen, Sir James Lougheed, Charles Stewart, and T. A. Crerar.[26] Contrarily, Transport is seen as a portfolio associated with any province but Ontario. George Hees, who was given this portfolio in 1957 by John Diefenbaker, has commented that "a central Ontarian is not very much interested in Transport," and the list of ministers who have had this responsibility in the last half-century would bear him out. Only three other Ontario ministers for a total of seven years have held this portfolio. Transport has been the bailiwick of Quebec or the eastern and western hinterlands.

The above comments concern portfolios that have a specific regional impact; there are others (Fisheries is an example) of which the same could be said. But there are more portfolios, indeed including the great departments of state—Finance, Trade and Commerce (and its modern equivalents), Justice, and External Affairs—that are marked by their lack of obvious geographic specificity. And yet, these too have historically been allocated to ministers distinctive in part for their provincial origins but also for their language group. Finance until very recently has always gone to an English-speaking minister, and more often than not to one from Ontario, but sometimes from Quebec and occasionally from elsewhere. Justice, on the other hand, has tended (though not since 1984) to go to French-speaking Quebeckers. The concentration of the business community in Toronto and Montreal and the dual legal systems of Canada help to explain this distribution of portfolios in the same way that other reasons can be found for additional discernible patterns of portfolio allocation. What is perhaps most significant in the last two decades, however, is the decline in the boldness of geographic and cultural patterns. Sectional representation remains an indelible part of Canadian political practice; the segregation of portfolios to specific types of ministers does not.

The Modern Cabinet: A National Institution

The politics of the federal Cabinet, like the politics of the country, are more national than they once were. Ministers are less likely to be the party chiefs in their provinces than used to be the case in the time of Mackenzie King and St. Laurent, and one looks in vain to find a Cabinet minister who can play the role of proconsul as J. G. Gardiner did in Saskatchewan, or Stewart Garson in Manitoba, or Angus MacDonald in Nova Scotia. Canadian federalism has witnessed major changes since those days, none more significant than the growing separation between federal and provincial politics in the last quarter-century. The effect on political parties has been immense, not least on their claim to be institutions of national integration. The old structures of federated parties—national leaders dependent on a provincial base—require reform, and the Liberals more than the others (because by 1984 they were in power in no province) experimented with pan-Canadian structures to conform to their pan-Canadian policies. The Cabinet may remain the managing committee of the party, but the party it manages looks very different than it once did.

Federal–provincial relations are less a matter to be resolved through intraparty bargaining and more a subject for negotiation among governments. All ministers, but particularly the prime minister, find themselves meeting on a regular basis with their provincial counterparts (and, if the Meech Lake Accord is ratified, annual meetings on the constitution will be required). The description of Cabinet as party-in-government is still true, but in the federal–provincial realm the emphasis must today be placed more on the government side of this unique entity than on the party side. It is for this reason that federal governments in the modern period are so particularly concerned to have within their ranks authoritative spokespersons for the provinces with which they must negotiate. But it is because of the deterioration of the old party structures that they regularly find themselves deprived of this representation in some parts of the country. Here is the attraction of proportional representation, for under whatever guise it was implemented it would in all probability produce from each province at least a minimum of one popularly elected member of Parliament who, once admitted to the Cabinet, would confer on that body the imprimatur of a national government. Proportional representation was once promoted as a system of election preferable to plurality voting because it would make easier the representation of muliple interests in national legislatures. The national legislature would become a congress of more varied opinion than is produced by a system of election such as Canada at the federal level has always had. It is a measure of the strength of the belief in Cabinet—as an instrument of government and as a vehicle for sectional representation—that proportional representation has been turned on its head so that it is advocated not to make Parliament more diverse in the interests it embraces, but to make Cabinet more powerful for its task of governing Canada.

CONCLUSION

Political attitudes and practices affect the operation of political institutions. In this chapter three attitudes and practices have been singled out for attention as regards the Cabinet: a reluctance to inject ideology into politics, an inclination to view politics not as a career in itself but rather as a temporary occupation into and out of which significant numbers of key personnel move, and a belief that the primary aim of politics is to balance conflicting geographic and cultural interests. As an instrument of government the Cabinet has been crucially influenced as well by Canada's history, especially its colonial origins. By tradition, the Cabinet as a collective body has been favoured over its ministerial parts, a fact that, in turn, has made Canadians place a great premium on leadership. At different times different models of leadership have dominated. In chronological sequence, these have been identified as personal, accommodative, and pan-Canadian models. But while the Cabinet might be seen over time to have adjusted to a succession of leadership styles, at all times it has been expected to function as a vehicle of sectional representation, although here too an evolution in practice has occurred. Where once the Cabinet was pre-eminently a federalized structure, more recently this guise has been subsumed by a new emphasis on the Cabinet as a national institution.

NOTES

1. The most useful Canadian sources are Thomas A. Hockin, ed., *Apex of Power: The Prime Minister and Political Leadership in Canada* (Toronto: Prentice-Hall, 1971), and W. A. Matheson, *The Prime Minister and the Cabinet* (Toronto: Methuen, 1976).

2. From this count are excluded biographies, "life and times" studies, Henry Borden, ed., *Robert Laird Borden: His Memoirs*, 2 vols. (Toronto: Macmillan, 1938), and Mackenzie King's mammoth diary. The diary's importance is incalculable for the long period King was in office, but in published version it is available only in extracts as, for example, in the four-volume *The Mackenzie King Record* (Toronto: University of Toronto Press) covering the period 1939 to 1948. Volume 1 is edited by J. W. Pickersgill; the remaining volumes are jointly edited by him and D. F. Forster.

3. See Walter L. Gordon, *A Political Memoir* (Toronto: McClelland and Stewart, 1977), and Judy LaMarsh, *Memoirs of a Bird in a Gilded Cage* (Toronto: McClelland and Stewart, 1968); the others are Jean Chrétien, *Straight from the Heart* (Toronto: Key Porter Books, 1985); Donald Johnston, *Up the Hill* (Montreal: Optimum Publishing International, 1986); Roy MacLaren, *Honourable Mentions: The Uncommon Diary of an M.P.* (Toronto: Deneau, 1986); and Eugene Whelan (with Rick Archbold), *Whelan: The Man in the Green Stetson* (Toronto: Irwin, 1986).

4. Norman Ward, ed., *A Party Politician: The Memoirs of Chubby Power* (Toronto: Macmillan, 1966).

5. The best is Sir Richard Cartwright, *Reminiscences* (Toronto: William Briggs, 1912).

6. David Hoffman and Norman Ward, *Bilingualism and Biculturalism in the Canadian House of Commons*, Royal Commission on Bilingualism and Biculturalism, Study No. 3 (Ottawa: Queen's Printer, 1970), p. 125.

7. An exception among defectors was H. H. Stevens who resigned from R. B. Bennett's Cabinet because he believed Bennett was too soft on

capitalists. He then formed the Reconstruction Party, which was devoted to the reform of capitalism and which in the general election of 1935 won 9 percent of the popular vote and one seat, Stevens's. See J. R. H. Wilbur, *H. H. Stevens* (Toronto: University of Toronto Press, 1977).

8. "In the adversary confrontation on the floor of the House, psychological issues may be more important than substantive ones." J. R. Mallory, "The Two Clerks: Parliamentary Discussion of the Role of the Privy Council Office," *Canadian Journal of Political Science* 10 (March 1977): 18.

9. John Porter, *The Vertical Mosaic* (Toronto: University of Toronto Press, 1965), pp. 405–6.

10. Dennis Olsen, *The State Elite* (Toronto: McClelland and Stewart, 1980), p. 130.

11. N. Ward, "The Liberals in Convention: Unrevised and Unrepentant," *Queen's Quarterly* 45 (Spring 1958): 1.

12. Porter, *The Vertical Mosaic*, p. 397.

13. An exception with a specific focus is Frederick W. Gibson, ed., *Cabinet Formation and Bicultural Relations: Seven Case Studies*, Royal Commission on Bilingualism and Biculturalism, Study No. 6 (Ottawa: Queen's Printer, 1970).

14. See Kenneth D. McRae, ed., *Consociational Democracy: Political Accommodation in Segmented Societies* (Toronto: McClelland and Stewart, 1974).

15. The literature on executive federalism is large. The best place to start is Richard Simeon, *Federal–Provincial Diplomacy: The Making of Recent Policy in Canada* (Toronto: University of Toronto Press, 1972).

16. Canada, House of Commons, *Debates*, 17 October 1977, p. 8259. The durability of this practice is confirmed in Canada, House of Commons, *Third Report of the Special Committee on Statutory Instruments* (1968–69) pp. 35–37; though as the *Fourth Report of the Standing Joint Committee on Regulations and Other Statutory Instruments* notes: "Very few draft regulations are actually considered by the Cabinet as a deliberative body. By far the greater number...is recommended...by the Special Committee of Council which consists of ten Ministers with a quorum of four." Canada, Senate, *Debates*, 7 July 1980, pp. 757–91 at 761.

17. R. M. Dawson, *The Government of Canada* (Toronto: University of Toronto Press, 1947), p. 201 in J. R. Mallory, "Cabinets and Councils in Canada," *Public Law* 2 (Autumn 1957): 244.

18. See Richard J. Van Loon and Michael S. Whittington, "Kaleidoscope in Grey: The Policy Process in Ottawa," ch. 22 in this volume. See, too, Colin Campbell, *Governments Under Stress: Political Executives*

and Key Bureaucrats in Washington, London, and Ottawa (Toronto: University of Toronto Press, 1983), pp. 83–90.

19. Dawson, *The Government of Canada*, p. 233.
20. The prime minister's extensive powers are codified to some extent in a minute of the Privy Council (P.C. 3374, 25 October 1935), reprinted in Paul Fox, ed., *Politics: Canada*, 3rd ed. (Toronto: McGraw-Hill Ryerson, 1970). These include, among others, the calling of Cabinet meetings, recommendations for the dissolution and summoning of Parliament, and recommendations for the appointments of Cabinet minister, lieutenant-governor, and senator.
21. "Political Patronage under Macdonald and Laurier, 1878–1911," in *American Review of Canadian Studies* 10 (1980): 3–12, and "John A. Macdonald's Greatest Triumph," *Canadian Historical Review* 43 (March 1982): 3–33.
22. Richard Van Loon, *The Structure and Membership of the Canadian Cabinet* (Internal Research Project of the Royal Commission on Bilingualism and Biculturalism, October 1966), p. 27.
23. R. Whitaker, *The Government Party: Organizing and Financing the Liberal Party of Canada, 1930–58* (Toronto: University of Toronto Press, 1977).
24. The Senate route is more popular now than at any time since Macdonald's day: "In the period 1867–1896 every cabinet portfolio except Finance, Railways and Canals, and Customs, was held at one time or another by a member of the Senate." Norman McL. Rogers, "Evolution and Reform of the Canadian Cabinet," *Canadian Bar Review* 11 (April 1933): 233.
25. The idea of the veto group is in J. R. Mallory, "The Two Clerks," p. 240.
26. Chester Martin, *"Dominion Lands" Policy*, ed. with introduction by Lewis H. Thomas (Toronto: McClelland and Stewart, 1973), p. xiv.

FURTHER READINGS

Aucoin, Peter. "Trudeau and Mulroney: Rationalism and Brokerage as Prime Ministerial Leadership Styles." *Canadian Journal of Political Science* 19, no. 1 (March 1986).

Foster, Sir George. "Getting Into the Cabinet." From *The Memoirs of the Rt. Hon. Sir George Foster, P.C., G.C.M.G.*, ed. W. S. Wallace. In *Politics: Canada*, 4th ed., ed. Paul Fox. Toronto: McGraw-Hill Ryerson, 1977.

Fox, Paul. "The Representative Nature of the Canadian Cabinet." In *Politics: Canada*, 4th ed., ed. Paul Fox. Toronto: McGraw-Hill Ryerson, 1977.

Gibson, Frederick W., ed. *Cabinet Formation and Bicultural Relations: Seven Case Studies*. Studies of the Royal Commission on Bilingualism and Biculturalism. Ottawa: Queen's Printer, 1970.

Hockin, Thomas A. *Apex of Power: The Prime Minister and Political Leadership in Canada*, 2nd ed. Toronto: Prentice-Hall, 1977.

Matheson, W. A. *The Prime Minister and the Cabinet*. Toronto: Methuen, 1976.

Presthus, Robert. *Elite Accommodation in Canadian Politics*. Toronto: Macmillan, 1973.

Public Archives of Canada. *Guide to Canadian Ministries Since Confederation, July 1, 1867–February 1, 1982*. Ottawa: Supply and Services, 1982.

Rogers, Norman McL. "The Introduction of Cabinet Government in Canada," "Federal Influences on the Canadian Cabinet," and "Evolution and Reform of the Canadian Cabinet." *Canadian Bar Review* 11 (January, February, and April 1933).

19

Federalism and Intergovernmental Relations

GARTH STEVENSON

Canada has had federal institutions since 1867, but the importance of intergovernmental relations is a fairly recent development, and one that has little or no explicit basis in Canada's written constitution. It is also at odds with the traditional theory of federalism, at least as federalism is understood in those countries that have been heavily influenced by British and American political thought. According to the traditional theory it is possible, and desirable, to distribute the functional fields of public policy between two levels of government in such a way that each level will have full power and responsibility to act within its own fields of jurisdiction without reference to the other level. Provincial governments may be assigned responsibility for education, natural resources, and municipal affairs, while the federal government is assigned responsibility for banking, trade, and the criminal law, but each can and should act unilaterally within its own sphere as though the other level of government did not exist. Once a constitution has divided up the spheres of jurisdiction, the only mechanism needed to maintain this harmonious equilibrium in virtual perpetuity is a Supreme Court that can decide in doubtful cases whether a particular policy or action falls within the federal or the provincial sphere.

This is not, of course, how Canadian government really works, but to a large extent the Constitution Act of 1867 did attempt to follow this model. Parallel institutions of government were established, insofar as they did not already exist, at the federal and provincial levels. Each was given access to certain sources of revenue. The types of laws that could be made by Parliament and the provincial legislatures were listed in exhaustive detail, with no less than forty-eight enumerated categories. All but three of the forty-eight were assigned exclusively to one level of government or the other. According to the Colonial Laws Validity Act of 1865, neither Parliament nor the legislatures could legislate contrary to the terms of any imperial statute applying to them, and since the British North America Act (as it was formerly called) was an imperial statute, this meant in practice that the Judicial Committee of the Privy Council would act as an arbiter in cases of disputed jurisdiction.

Insofar as the Constitution Act of 1867 deviated from this model, it did so by enabling the federal government to exercise power over the provincial ones, even if the latter remained within their own fields of jurisdiction. Thus, the federal government appoints the judges to provincial superior and county courts, and also appoints the lieutenant-governor who is formally the chief executive officer at the provincial level. In the early days of Canadian federalism lieutenant-governors exercised real power: sometimes dismissing their ministerial advisors, refusing their assent to acts of the legislature, or reserving such acts for a final decision by the federal government on whether they would be allowed to come into operation. In addition, the federal government can disallow any provincial act within a year of its adoption, although this power was used very rarely after 1911 and has not been used at all since 1943. The federal government can also interfere in the provincial jurisdiction over education to protect the rights of certain minorities, although the one attempt to exercise this power in 1896 probably demonstrated that it was unusable in practice.

These admitted departures from the pure theory of federalism have little importance for modern intergovernmental relations. The powers of disallowance and reservation are unlikely ever again to be used. While provincial governments certainly complain loudly and frequently about federal "intrusions" into what they regard as their spheres of authority, it is usually the federal government's economic and fiscal policies that give offence, not the appointment of judges and lieutenant-governors. Moreover, and in complete contrast to the centralist preferences of the Fathers of Confederation, the provincial governments themselves now possess impressive means of complicating, frustrating, and interfering with policy making at the federal level, means that they are far less hesitant to employ than the federal government is to employ its virtually abandoned power of disallowance. Finally, a variety of institutional machinery not provided for in the formal constitution has been developed to facilitate interaction between the two levels of government.

Much of the change that the constitution has accommodated has been in the direction of increasing the power and importance of provincial governments, the larger of which now exercise powers that would be the envy of many supposedly sovereign members of the United Nations. Admittedly the power and importance of the federal government has expanded enormously as well, and it too performs functions that it was not expected to perform a century ago, but the growth of provincial power is more striking, whatever value judgment one may make about it.

The growth of the state is a ubiquitous phenomenon in the modern world, but Canada is unusual, and perhaps unique, in the extent to which that growth has taken place at the subnational level. Economic development and external relations, the state functions that were considered most important in 1867 and probably still are today, were originally placed for the most part beyond the reach of provincial jurisdiction, yet today the provincial governments seek with some success to influence federal policies in these areas and with even greater success to conduct policies of their own.

Provincialists will respond that this change is counterbalanced by increasing federal involvement in such areas as health and welfare, environmental policies, or the protection of consumers, but this response is unconvincing for two reasons. In the first place, these functions were not so much left to the provinces in 1867 as they were left to the private sector, so that the expansion of federal government activity has not really been at the expense of the provincial governments. Second, while these functions are certainly important, most observers would still consider them less fundamental to the *raison d'être* of the modern state than the more traditional functions of developing the economy and managing relations with the rest of the world. It is the performance of those traditional functions to some extent at the provincial level and to some extent at the federal level, but in consultation with the provincial governments, that seems to distinguish Canada from most other modern states. The involvement of the central government in policies related to health, welfare, and the "quality of life," while it too contributes to the complex pattern of Canadian intergovernmental relations, is a phenomenon not unique to Canada.

Neither the increased importance of the provincial governments nor the increased complexity of intergovernmental relations is the result of formal amendments to the constitution. Until 1982 formal amendments were usually of a minor character and the more significant ones, providing for unemployment insurance in 1940 and for pensions in 1951, increased the powers of Parliament rather than those of the provincial legislatures. The changes made by the Constitution Act of 1982 were more substantial, but their impact on federal–provincial relations was limited and somewhat ambiguous. The Charter of Rights and Freedoms restricted the powers of both levels of government, while increasing the influence and importance of the judiciary. The new amending formula entrenched what was already accepted practice, namely the involvement of the provincial legislatures in the amending process. Provincial powers over natural resources were increased to some extent, and the poorer provinces secured constitutional entrenchment of equalization payments, which they had actually received from the federal government since 1957. Yet, important as these changes were, they were less important than the non-constitutional developments that have transformed Canadian federalism in the twentieth century. The causes of those developments must now be explored.

CAUSES OF DECENTRALIZATION

Although John A. Macdonald's hope that the provincial governments would dwindle away into insignificance was shown to be fallacious even before his death in 1891, it is only since about 1960 that the growth of provincial powers and the relatively limited capacity, or willingness, of the central government to act unilaterally in most areas of public policy have appeared to distinguish Canada from other modern states. During that time various Canadian political scientists, including the present writer, have attempted to explain these phenomena, although no real consensus has been achieved. Some observers, particularly in Quebec, continue to deny that the Canadian central government is significantly weaker than those of other federal countries. Even among those who recognize that it is, opinions differ as to which are the most significant reasons why this is so. Probably few would argue that any single explanation is significant. The main categories of explanatory factors that have been suggested may be summarized as follows:

Institutional

Some observers attach primary importance to certain features of Canada's federal constitution as explanations for the growth of provincial power, even though the Fathers of Confederation apparently designed it with quite a different intention. There are a number of specific explanations within this category. The adoption of British parliamentary government and an appointed upper house, rather than institutions on the American pattern, limited the ability of the central government to accommodate provincial interests and thus encouraged the growth of strong provincial governments to speak for such interests. The explicit enumeration of provincial legislative powers, although designed to limit them, actually facilitated their expansion in practice by provincial governments and the judiciary, particularly since they included such broad categories as "property and civil rights." The very fact of having provincial governments at all facilitated "province building" and the development of separate identities. Provincial ownership of natural resources, although considered insignificant in 1867, strengthened provincial governments, most obviously in Alberta but in other provinces as well. Health, education, and welfare, all entrusted to some extent to the provincial governments, proved to be more important areas of public policy than had been anticipated.

Geopolitical

Mackenzie King once observed that Canada has "too much geography."[1] Although sometimes taken for granted, Canada's vast physical extent, small and scattered population, and geographical barriers such as the Canadian Shield, the Rocky Mountains, and the Gulf of St. Lawrence tend to weaken national integration and perhaps to encourage emphasis on the provincial level of government as a supplier of services. The relatively small number of provinces in contrast to the fifty American states, the extremely large size of Quebec and Ontario that enables them to challenge federal power if they so desire, and the absence of metropolitan areas (apart from Ottawa–Hull) that spill across provincial boundaries may also be significant.

Sociocultural

Particularly in recent years, the literature on Canadian federalism has tended to emphasize, and often to celebrate, the allegedly distinctive cultural "identities" of Canadians in the different provinces. It is said that Canadians in different provinces are objectively different in terms of such categories as ethnicity and religion, and also that they are subjectively different in that they feel attachments to their respective provinces or "regions" more strongly than to Canada as a whole. According to this view, the provincial governments are strong in Canada because Canadians have distinctive needs and interests that cannot be accommodated within a single national government, and also because Canadians actually want strong provincial governments and a relatively weak federal one. This belief is often used as an explanation for the present state of Canadian federalism, but also as an argument for further weakening the central government through formal constitutional change.

In his classic analysis of Canadian society, *The Vertical Mosaic*, John Porter described the belief that the provinces had distinctive cultures as "hallowed nonsense" unsupported by any evidence, except perhaps in the case of Quebec.[2] Even if it were true, it would not necessarily explain the power exercised by provincial governments; American states are at least as culturally distinctive as Canadian provinces, but American federalism has evolved in quite a different direction from Canadian federalism.

Quebec, however, is undoubtedly a special case. Not only is it large enough to have a considerable influence on Canadian federalism, but it has most of the characteristics of a distinct nation. In particular, it is the only part of North America where French is the predominant language. The legal system, the schools, and even financial institutions in Quebec are quite different from elsewhere. Although there are important ethnic minorities, most Québécois are descended from French settlers who came to the province during the reign of Louis XIV, and the overwhelming majority of persons born in Quebec remain there throughout their lives. Quebec nationalism has grown more intense since Confederation, partly in response to the ungenerous treatment of francophone minorities in the other provinces and more recently out of resentment against the anglophone domination of Quebec's economy. Public opinion polls consistently show more support in Quebec than elsewhere for the view that provincial powers should be increased. The referendum of 1980 suggested that 40 percent of the population of Quebec were inclined to support political independence, if economic ties with Canada could be retained. Thus, some observers believe that the existence of Quebec is a sufficient explanation for Canada's failure to develop a more centralized form of government. The fact that the centrifugal tendency in Canadian federalism became most apparent after 1960, when Quebec was undergoing a process of social and political change known as the Quiet Revolution, gives some credence to the argument.

Political

While it may be more a symptom than a cause of the difficulties of Canadian federalism, the peculiar character of the party system seems to be associated with them. Parties in a federal system are supposed to accommodate all the divergent interests of the provinces and regions, but Canadian parties have considerable difficulty in doing so. In some provinces one or both of the major federal parties is very weak or non-existent at the provincial level. Exclusively provincial parties, such as Social Credit in British Columbia or the Parti Québécois in Quebec, have sometimes been strong enough to win office. In several provinces the provincial and federal wings of the Liberal Party are completely separate from one another. Quebec's Liberal premier, Robert Bourassa, even gave tacit support to the Progressive Conservatives in the federal election of 1988. The weak links between federal and provincial politics have the consequence that very few politicians with provincial experience seek election to the House of Commons. Federal and provincial politicians live throughout their careers in separate environments, interacting only in the formal, and usually conflictual, setting of a federal–provincial conference.

Another aspect of Canada's fragmented party system is the fact that the strength of the federal parties is very unevenly distributed across the country. The New Democrats have never won a seat in Quebec. The Liberals have been very weak in western Canada since the rise of John Diefenbaker more than thirty years ago, although in 1988 they did quite well in Manitoba. The Progressive Conservatives were traditionally weak in Quebec, although their fortunes there have dramatically improved under Brian Mulroney. The danger of unevenly distributed support is that a federal government with little support in a province may lack legitimacy there and may even have difficulty in giving that province its usual quota of representation in the Cabinet. This, in turn, may give credence to claims by the provincial government that only it can speak for provincial interests. Some observers have suggested that proportional representation, either in the House of Commons or in an elected Senate, might overcome this problem. Under the present electoral system a party that receives 20 percent of the vote in a province may elect no members at all from that province.

Economic

Many features of Canadian economic development might help to account for the relative weakness of the federal level of government and the corresponding strength of the provincial level. Mainly for natural reasons, but perhaps partly because of federal economic policies, the provinces differ considerably from one another in the structure of their economies, the predominance of particular industries, and the nature and extent of their trading and investment ties with foreign countries. Business interests concentrated in a particular province may encourage the strengthening of that province's government and the weakening of the federal government. Interprovincial disparities of wealth and income are very pronounced, and the rank ordering of the provinces in this regard has changed very little since the 1920s.

The importance of mining, petroleum, and forestry in the Canadian economy reinforces the provincial level of government, which owns and controls these resources in accordance with the constitution. The relatively slow and limited development of secondary manufacturing has restricted the mobility of population and thus reinforced provincialist sentiments. The dominant influence exercised by the United States over the Canadian economy has weakened the effectiveness of, and lessened the support for, the Canadian federal government. The domination of Quebec's economy by anglophones, at least until recently, stimulated Quebec nationalism and caused resentment to be directed against the federal government. The influence exercised over the federal government by financial, mercantile, and transportation interests caused business people associated with other industries to prefer the provincial level of government. Social and economic changes in Quebec and Alberta have produced new and powerful classes in those provinces dedicated to strengthening the provincial level of government at the expense of the federal.

All of these types of explanations are of some value, although all have their weaknesses. The institutional and geopolitical explanations fail to explain why Canadian federalism has developed so differently since 1960 from the way it operated previously. The sociocultural explanation is undermined by the important diversities that exist within the provinces, the increasingly homogeneous character of Canadian society, including to some extent even Quebec, at the very time when demands for more power to the provinces are most strident, and the fact that, except in Quebec, provincial politicians appear far more committed to provincial autonomy than it does the general public. The latter fact should be disconcerting to supporters of the sociocultural explanation since the politicians, unlike the general public, are predominantly urban, upper middle class, Protestant, and of British ancestry. Finally, the economic explanations, while the present writer finds them the most persuasive, are sometimes guilty of circular reasoning or of surreptitiously borrowing arguments from the other explanations.

In any event, and regardless of which explanations are preferred, the provincial level of government is clearly strong enough to ensure that there will be no uncontested supremacy by the central government, even within many of the fields of jurisdiction assigned to the latter under the constitution. The federal government apparently cannot disregard the provincial governments and must bargain with them almost continuously in order to achieve its own objectives. The curious expression "the eleven senior governments," which has recently found its way into Canadian political discourse, is symptomatic of this factual equality of bargaining power, whatever the constitution may say to the contrary. The remaining sections of this chapter will describe the actual, as opposed to formal, division of responsibilities between the two levels, the areas of conflict, and the mechanisms of interaction, before turning to an evaluation and critique of the system.

AREAS OF CONFLICT

As an aid to understanding how responsibilities are actually divided between the two levels of government, the Constitution Act of 1867, with its detailed and seemingly precise division of jurisdictions, is of very limited value. The categories overlap considerably, many subjects that preoccupy governments in the latter part of the twentieth century are not listed at all, and both levels of government have expanded their activities without much regard for the constitution.

The actual functional areas of public policy can be classified into areas occupied exclusively by one level of government with little or no objection by the other, areas where both levels of government are active but apparently without much conflict, and areas that give rise to federal–provincial conflict. The last category includes some areas that the Constitution Act of 1867 assigns primarily to the federal level, some that it assigns primarily to the provincial level, and some that it does not assign at all because they were insignificant or unknown at the time of Confederation. Naturally the extent to which particular subjects are shared or give rise to conflict changes over time: emphasis will be placed here mainly on the situation at the time of writing.

An examination of the names of departments in the federal and provincial governments suggests what further investigation confirms: that very few areas of policy are now occupied exclusively by one level of government. The only exclusively federal areas appear to be military defence, veteran's affairs, Indian affairs, and monetary policy. The only exclusively provincial areas appear to be municipal institutions, elementary and secondary education, and some areas of law related to property and other non-criminal matters.

Some fields of jurisdiction are partially occupied by both levels of government but are not areas of serious conflict, at least for the moment. These include agriculture and immigration, both areas where the constitution says either level can legislate, and pensions, which were placed in the same position by subsequent amendments. Both immigration and pensions were the source of serious conflicts between the federal and Quebec governments in the not too distant past, but both seem now to have been resolved. Other areas of harmoniously shared jurisdiction, not mentioned explicitly in the federal constitution, include scientific research, cultural and recreational activities, tourism, and protection of the environment.

A number of areas assigned to federal jurisdiction have become sources of federal–provincial controversy, either because provincial governments have succeeded in becoming involved in them or because some of them are dissatisfied with federal policies and would like to do so. Freight rates and other aspects of railway transport policy have always been controversial in the hinterlands of Canada; the governments of Manitoba, Saskatchewan, and Alberta took vociferous, although not identical, positions on the Western Grain Transportation Act of 1983, which revised the so-called Crow Rate. More recently several provinces have expressed concern about the abandonment of railway branch lines, which has been encouraged by the federal policy of deregulation. The government of Newfoundland received generous financial compensation in return for withdrawing its objection to the termination of railway service on the island in 1988. Prince Edward Island immediately demanded similar compensation for the impending demise of its railway service, but its prospects may have been adversely affected when, later in the year, its voters sent four opposition members to the House of Commons.

Trade and commerce, including the external aspects of commercial policy, is another field of federal jurisdiction that has seen increasing provincial involvement and intergovernmental controversy. Provinces have established a variety of informal barriers to interprovincial trade, a few of which have been struck down by the Supreme Court, and have tried to become involved in foreign trade policy by influencing the federal government or even, on occasion, by direct dealings with foreign governments. When the Mulroney government, in 1986, began to negotiate a comprehensive free trade agreement with the United States, several provincial governments expressed concern that the agreement might affect areas of provincial jurisdiction. Most withdrew their objections because of their support for the general aims of the negotiations, and because the federal government was careful to keep them informed as the negotiations progressed. Ontario's Liberal government, both before and after the agreement was concluded, suggested on various occasions that the federal government might lack the legal authority to conclude an agreement that would bind the province. These remarks caused some concern in Washington, but Ontario did not actually do anything to block the agreement, perhaps because its legal case was weak and perhaps because the Ontario business community generally supported free trade with the United States.

The provinces have also become interested in macro-economic policy, particularly since the temporary imposition of wage controls by the Trudeau government in 1975. Although that initiative was supported by the provincial governments, which co-operated by limiting wage increases in their own bureaucracies, the price of their acquiescence was a federal commitment to convene First Ministers' Conferences on the management of the economy, a useless practice that has continued long after its original justification disappeared. On these occasions, which have been annual since 1984, provincial premiers can be counted on to seek easy popularity by irresponsible demands for lower interest rates. They can offer this unsolicited advice knowing that it will probably not be adopted and that, even if it were, the resulting inflation would be the federal government's problem.

Some intergovernmental conflict involves clashes between federal and provincial jurisdiction. Federal responsibilities for the aboriginal peoples, and for trade and commerce in sources of energy, conflict with provincial ownership and control of public lands and natural resources south of the 60th parallel. The administration of justice, a responsibility shared in a somewhat ambiguous but usually effective way between the two levels of government, has led to conflict over federal efforts to prosecute offences under the Narcotics Control Act, the Combines Investigation Act, and the Food and Drugs Act. The provinces, which prosecute ordinary criminal offences, argued that the federal government was trespassing on their jurisdiction, but the Supreme Court ruled that it was not.[3]

Some of the most intractable areas of federal–provincial conflict are fields of jurisdiction that were not envisaged in 1867. A leading example would be the complex and arcane matter of "communications," which has grown increasingly contentious as technological change has blurred the once-familiar distinctions between telephones, telegraphs, and broadcasting, while adding new and anomalous categories such as cable television and pay television. The situation is complicated by provincial ownership of some telephone systems, the use of broadcasting (declared a federal responsibility by the Judicial Committee of the Privy Council in 1932) for purposes of education, and Quebec's desire to protect its language and culture.

Other "new" areas of jurisdiction that have led to conflict include occupational training programs (regarded as part of economic development by the federal government, but as part of education by some provincial governments) and income support programs such as family allowances. Still more recently, legislation to protect the consumer has become a source of conflict, with both levels of government understandably wishing to occupy this politically popular (and financially inexpensive) area of jurisdiction.

A particularly important area of intergovernmental conflict, and one that exists to some extent in all federal countries, is that of finance and taxation. The constitution allows the federal government to impose any kind of taxation, while the provinces are restricted to "direct" taxation and to revenues from their natural resources. The Constitution Act of 1867 also provided for modest federal subsidies to provincial governments, but while these are still paid, they have been overshadowed since 1957 by massive "equalization" payments to provinces with below-average ability to raise revenue, a program whose annual cost to the federal treasury now exceeds $6 billion. Since 1982 the obligation to make these payments has been entrenched in the constitution.

Since both levels of government have constantly increasing needs for revenue, and since both ultimately rely on the same taxpayers to provide it, the need for co-ordination and the scope for conflict are obvious. Since the Second World War elaborate arrangements have been devised, and modified at five-year intervals, for sharing revenue from personal and corporate income taxes, which are now the most important sources of revenue. While these arrangements have been reasonably successful, there have been some eruptions of conflict, particularly involving the larger provinces, in the course of negotiating the five-year agreements. Additional conflicts can be anticipated as the Mulroney government proceeds with its plan to impose a broadly based federal sales tax on goods and services, a policy foreshadowed by the White Paper on Tax Reform in June 1987. The government would like the new tax to be harmonized, and perhaps collected jointly, with provincial retail sales taxes. This may require changes in the provincial taxes, which are imposed at varying rates and do not cover all kinds of goods and services. Exemptions vary from province to province, and Alberta has no sales tax at all. Apart from its obvious purpose of providing revenue, taxation is now viewed by governments as a tool for manipulating, regulating, and stimulating the economy. Moreover, tax concessions to both individuals and corporations are important means of winning and keeping political support. Thus, the "stakes" in financial negotiations are high.

Intergovernmental conflicts over energy resources between 1973 and 1984 had important financial implications, although there were other issues as well. As oil and gas prices rose, both levels of government tried to capture the economic rents that resulted by imposing taxes or, in the provincial case, by increasing the royalties that the province collected as the owner of the resource. The producing provinces claimed that their ownership rights entitled them to reap the financial benefits of higher prices, while the federal government argued that its powers to regulate trade and commerce entitled it to control domestic prices and to tax exports to the United States. An additional problem was that increasing resource revenues in a few provinces increased the federal government's obligation to make equalization payments. By 1977 even Ontario would have received equalization had not the formula hastily been changed to preclude this possibility.

Another source of controversy, particularly with the governments of Quebec and Ontario, has been federal spending in the areas of health, education, and welfare, which fall under provincial jurisdiction. The federal government initially offered to share the costs of certain programs in an effort to encourage provinces to establish them. After the programs were established, and as their costs began to escalate, the federal government would try to impose a ceiling on its own expenditure or even to withdraw from the field altogether. Provincial governments argued that these conditional grants put pressure on them to alter their spending priorities (which was precisely the federal government's intention), that the terms and conditions of federal support prevented them from designing programs that fitted their own needs, and that subsequent federal efforts to restrict federal spending placed an unfair burden on the provinces. These issues have become increasingly complex over the years and have become entangled with the issues of tax sharing as discussed above. In 1965 Quebec was allowed to "opt out" of certain programs, meaning that federal grants and federal taxes were both reduced, allowing Quebec to increase its own taxes and run the programs without federal interference. In 1977 all provinces were given a combination of cash payments and additional tax room in place of the payments previously received in support of health insurance and post-secondary education, an innovation known as Established Programs Financing (EPF). In 1984 strict federal conditions regarding the design of health insurance programs were reimposed by the Canada Health Act. In 1987 the prime minister and the ten premiers signed the Meech Lake Accord, a package of constitutional amendments that would allow any province to opt out, with appropriate financial compensation, from any new federal spending program in an area of provincial jurisdiction, provided the province established a program that met federal objectives. (To take effect, the Meech Lake Accord must be ratified by all provincial legislatures before June 1990, an event that now seems unlikely.)

While it is increasingly fashionable to speak of "the provinces" as a collectivity, it should be remembered that the ten provincial governments are not identical in their interests, demands, or behaviour. Indeed, if they were the system would probably be unworkable, since their differences enable the federal government to make alliances with some against the others, and thus win more of the battles than it could hope to do otherwise.

The sources of these differences are various, and like the explanations for Canada's lack of unity, to which they are closely related, they may vary in importance according to the viewpoint and preference of the observer. While institutional self-interest (the tendency of any government to maximize its power at the expense of other governments) produces some common patterns of behaviour, its effect is lessened by differences in economic and social structure, size, level of affluence, party affiliation, the state of public opinion, and even the personality of the provincial premier. Rich provinces, and those undergoing rapid economic growth, are generally more truculent than poorer provinces. Quebec is traditionally sensitive to any restriction on its autonomy, and the western provinces, particularly Alberta, have a long history of opposition to the economic policies of the federal government. Large size, distinctive and specialized economic interests, and an overwhelming majority in the provincial legislature tend to make provincial governments intransigent and uncooperative, while the contrasting attributes seem to encourage more accommodating behaviour.

In resisting or opposing federal initiatives, provincial governments make use of a variety of arguments. Sometimes they say that the provincial level of government is "closer to the people" and better able to understand their needs, sometimes that the federal government is seeking to impose "bureaucracy," centralization, and excessive spending, sometimes that their province's allegedly distinctive "way of life" is in danger, and sometimes (more rarely in recent years) that the terms of the constitution are being violated. Western provincial governments often argue that federal policies discriminate in favour of Ontario and Quebec, while Quebec governments argue that federal policies discriminate in favour of Ontario and the West. As the great economic historian Harold Innis commented in 1946:

The hatreds between regions in Canada have become important vested interests. Montreal exploits the hatred of Toronto and Regina that of Winnipeg and so one might go through the list. A native of Ontario may appear restive at being charged with exploitation by those who systematically exploit him with their charges of exploitation, but even the right to complain is denied to him.[4]

Behind the rhetoric the interests at stake are often more specific than appears at first sight. Provincial politicians may need votes to win an election or provincial officials may want to expand the budget and clientele of their own "shop" by excluding the federal government from a contested field of policy. Interests in the private sector are also influential. Alberta's demands for higher oil prices and natural gas exports reflect the interests of the petroleum industry as well as the government. The Ontario government often lobbies against federal initiatives that are opposed by secondary manufacturing firms, such as tougher restraints on corporate mergers and combines that were contemplated in the 1970s. The differing positions of Alberta and Saskatchewan regarding the Crow's Nest freight rates reflected the predominance of ranchers in the former province and of grain farmers in the latter. Prior to the deregulation of air transport, several provinces supported locally based regional air carriers in opposition to federal policies that were perceived to favour Air Canada. Federalism provides regionally concentrated interests with a powerful defence against the possibility of being overriden by a national majority.

INTERGOVERNMENTAL MECHANISMS

Because of the many ways in which the two levels of government affect one another's freedom of action, a variety of mechanisms and processes have developed for co-ordinating policies and resolving conflicts. A common characteristic of these mechanisms and processes is that none of them is provided for in the constitution. Those institutions that were provided for, the lieutenant-governors and possibly the Senate, have proved to be insignificant as means of facilitating the operation of the federal system.

As in most other federations, the judiciary is an important mechanism for resolving questions of jurisdiction. Established in 1875, the Supreme Court of Canada did not actually become the highest court of appeal until 1949, when Parliament abolished the right of appeal to the Judicial Committee of the Privy Council in London. The Judicial Committee's interpretations of Canada's constitution had tended to restrict the powers of the central government and to enhance the status of the provinces, and were thus deplored by Canadian nationalists. For two decades after the abolition of appeals the Supreme Court did not strike down any federal statutes, and it was also quite permissive in regard to provincial statutes, so that it attracted little controversy. From about 1973 onward, the Supreme Court was much more in the limelight as it struck down provincial statutes in relation to agricultural marketing, taxation and management of natural resources, and Quebec's efforts to regulate cable television.[5] Critics, particularly in Quebec and the prairie provinces, charged that the Supreme Court had a "centralist" bias, perhaps because its members were appointed by the federal government. In 1978 Saskatchewan's governing political party won re-election largely by campaigning against Chief Justice Bora Laskin, one of the most distinguished persons ever to sit on a Canadian court. The critics, however, ignored the fact that the Supreme Court struck down a number of federal statutes in the same period. Even its decision upholding federal wage controls in 1976 did so on such narrow grounds that the scope of federal power was arguably diminished.[6] In 1979 the Supreme Court also ruled that the reform of the Senate involved provincial rights and was thus not within the powers of Parliament.[7]

The Supreme Court's interpretations of the constitution may arise out of litigation in which an individual or a corporation challenges the constitutionality of a federal or provincial statute. Until the Charter of Rights and Freedoms was enacted in 1982, such a challenge could only be made on the grounds that the statute trespassed on the powers of the other level of government. Judicial interpretations may also arise out of reference cases, in which a government seeks an advisory opinion on a question of constitutional law. A government may do this either to forestall litigation directed against its own legislation, as a means of challenging another government's legislation, or simply to clarify an uncertain situation. The federal government can submit reference cases directly to the Supreme Court. Provincial governments can submit them to their own supreme courts, whose decisions can be appealed to the Supreme Court of Canada. Governments that are not directly involved frequently intervene in important constitutional cases, whether these arise as references or as ordinary litigation.

Politicians generally prefer political solutions, in which they can split the difference and provide partial satisfaction to both sides, to the clear-cut, "either-or" decisions produced by the judicial process. For some provincial politicians, this preference is reinforced by the belief, as noted above, that the Supreme Court has a centralist bias. In fact, a great variety of informal political mechanisms for arriving at solutions are available. Federal and provincial governments interact at a number of different levels, ranging from relatively junior officials to premiers and the prime minister. Intergovernmental relations may also be distinguished in terms of which governments are involved: bilateral contacts between the federal government and one provincial government are a part of the process, and there are also interprovincial relations not involving the federal government.

During the two decades that followed the Second World War, as the two levels of government began to have a greater and greater impact on one another's activities, there was a rapid development of collaborative relationships, including semi-formal and semi-permanent committees with representatives of both levels. Most of these involved officials, sometimes of relatively junior rank. Most were concerned with a few functional areas of policy in which there was a large amount of intergovernmental interaction: finance, health, welfare, agriculture, renewable resources, and statistics. This pattern of intergovernmental relations came to be designated by the term "co-operative federalism." In many cases it was related to programs that were jointly financed by the two levels of government, though primarily administered by the provincial. It was characterized by a fragmentation of intergovernmental relations within each government, since departments with specific responsibilities were given a largely free hand to conduct their own relations with counterpart departments in other governments. Most of the officials involved were more concerned with resolving problems and running effective programs than they were with scoring points for their level of government in relation to the other level. In fact, it is not easy to be certain, even in retrospect, whether co-operative federalism was centralizing or decentralizing in its overall impact. At the time, no one much cared.

Beginning in the 1960s, and continuing in the 1970s, this pattern of intergovernmental relations was transformed into a new pattern for which the more recent term "executive federalism," rather than "co-operative federalism," is more appropriate. Conditional grants, in which the federal government pays a fixed percentage of the cost of provincially administered programs that meet federally determined criteria, became unpopular as both levels of government sought to tighten control over their expenditures. Central agencies such as the Privy Council Office and its offshoot, the Federal–Provincial Relations Office, began to play a greater role in intergovernmental relations, riding herd on the activities of the functional departments. Political leaders, as opposed to appointed officials, also played an increasingly prominent role. For all of these reasons, there was an increasing tendency, among both federal and provincial participants, to assign the prestige and power of "their" level of government a higher priority than the resolution of conflicts or the success of programs in delivering services to the public.

These changes were partly associated with the growth of Quebec separatism and with the energy crisis, developments that led to more conflict and less collaboration in federal–provincial relations. They were also encouraged by the popularity of "rational" approaches to decision making, which were based on the premise that each government could and should arrange its "priorities" in a centralized fashion and exercise a tight grip over its expenditures. Central agencies and elected politicians are more inclined than specialists in health, welfare, or resource development to think in terms of maximizing their government's power in relation to other governments.

A characteristically Canadian institution that has assumed great prominence is the First Ministers' Conference, which brings together the federal prime minister and the ten premiers, assisted by numerous officials. The building that served as Ottawa's railway station until 1966 has been remodelled into a conference centre where these and other federal–provincial meetings take place. The date perhaps reflects a not entirely accidental coincidence between the end of the age of steam and the rise of executive federalism. Until the 1960s First Ministers' Conferences occurred only occasionally, usually in connection with proposed amendments to the constitution or major changes in fiscal arrangements between the two levels of government. Since 1963 there has been at least one such meeting in most years, and in some years more. The Meech Lake Accord would entrench in the constitution the requirement that there be at least two First Ministers' Conferences every year, one on the economy and one on the constitution.

While First Ministers' Conferences, particularly those dealing with the constitution, are the most publicized aspect of executive federalism, there are also frequent meetings at the ministerial level, which involve almost every field of public policy. Other meetings include non-elected officials, rather than politicians, and may be designed either to prepare for the executive sessions or to implement agreements concluded by the politicians, or simply to exchange information. Since 1960 the provincial premiers have also held an annual meeting with the prime minister not present, followed by a communiqué that usually criticizes an assortment of federal policies and initiatives. From 1980 to 1984, when no provincial government had the same party label as the federal government, these communiqués were exceptionally strident and hostile in tone. More typically, they are toned down in deference to the sentiments of premiers who may be political allies of the prime minister.

Despite all the advance preparation, expense, and ballyhoo, the record of First Ministers' Conferences in reaching agreements or solving problems is poor; in fact, it would be difficult to devise a worse way to carry on the nation's business. Provincial premiers often have no strong incentive to reach an agreement and may even gain popularity by being as unreasonable and intransigent as possible. The federal prime minister, on the other hand, is expected both to defend the national interest and to satisfy the demands of all the provinces, two objectives that may be totally incompatible. The prime minister, rather than the premiers, will be blamed if an agreement is not concluded, and the temptation is therefore strong to sacrifice the national interest to provincial demands.

A majority vote at a First Ministers' Conference would have little meaning, because the prime minister represents Canadians in every province and should logically have as many votes as all of the premiers combined. The premiers themselves are not equal except in a formal sense. Ontario's population is seventy-three times that of Prince Edward Island, and almost equal to the total of all the western and Atlantic provinces combined. Only Alberta can cut off the nation's supply of oil and gas, and only Quebec can plausibly threaten to secede from Canada and become a sovereign nation. All of the Atlantic provinces depend on federal grants to maintain even a semblance of provincial status. Thus, agreement must be on a basis of consensus or, at the very least, include the federal government and eight or nine provinces. (Some constitutional amendments can be made by seven provinces, including either Ontario or Quebec, but the provinces that did not agree would have the right to opt out if the amendment affected any of their "rights or privileges.")[8] Consensus, whether on constitutional amendments or on more mundane matters, is not easily achieved among governments representing different regions, political parties, and jurisdictional interests. If it is achieved, it will probably be because the prime minister has given the premiers everything they asked for. Parliament, not to mention the provincial legislatures, will then be told that it must give automatic approval to the agreement or else run the risk of a dire threat to national unity. This, of course, makes a mockery of responsible government. In any event, opposition parties in the House of Commons are often reluctant to criticize intergovernmental agreements involving premiers with whom they share a party label, or agreements popular in a province where they hope to win votes.

CONCLUSION

While Canada's problems may be slight compared to those of many other countries, and while the federal state has survived through a number of decades in which its future appeared less than assured, there is nonetheless some cause for concern about its present situation and prospects. Contrary to the myth propagated in some provincial capitals, the picture that Canada presents to the outside world is that of an increasingly loose collection of semi-sovereign provinces, with a central government unable or unwilling to exercise much control over the economy or to carry out coherent policies even within its own fields of jurisdiction. Compared with almost any other modern state, or with Canada itself as recently as the 1950s, the extent of provincial power and the passivity of the central government are remarkable.

The conspicuous and frequent intergovernmental conferences since the early 1960s have possibly accustomed many Canadians to regard the central government as only one government among eleven that are more or less equal in status—a serious misreading both of Canada's constitution and of the requirements of a healthy political system. Harold Innis once wrote that provincial control over lands and resources was a survival of "feudalism" and a source of weakness for Canada.[9] Certainly the effort that the central government must devote to bargaining with quasi-independent provincial potentates both lessens its ability to function effectively and undermines its authority in the eyes of the public. The federal–provincial conference does resemble a meeting of a medieval king with his feudal barons more than it does the government of a modern state. The implicit assumption that regional divisions and interests are the most significant ones in Canada, and that only the provincial governments are capable of representing them, calls into question the authority and usefulness of the federal Parliament, which must often rubber-stamp the results of intergovernmental agreements and which is prevented from legislating even in the areas assigned to its jurisdiction without interference by the provinces.

Particularly in Quebec and Alberta, some persons continue to propagate what former federal Cabinet minister Jim Fleming once called "the myth of the power-hungry centralizers" and to argue that the provincial governments should be given more influence over federal policies and more freedom to pursue their own.[10] The reality is that Canada is already the most decentralized country in the industrialized world. Provincial revenues have been greater than federal revenues in every year since 1977, although they were only half as large as federal revenues in 1960.[11] Federal powers have been whittled away by judicial interpretation or have simply fallen into disuse; the power to declare works and undertakings for the general advantage of Canada has not been used since 1961. Labour relations (apart from those of the railways and airlines), post-secondary education, highway transport, and the regulation of trading in securities have become exclusively provincial fields of jurisdiction *de facto*. Since 1974 the provinces distribute family allowances according to their own criteria, although the federal government provides all the funds. The larger provinces maintain permanent diplomatic missions in foreign countries.

Contrary to a widespread belief that is incongruously shared by its opponents and by many of its supporters, the Constitution Act of 1982 did not give the federal government any additional powers, either in theory or in practice. The Charter of Rights and Freedoms limits provincial powers in certain respects, but most of its provisions can be overriden by the notwithstanding clause, to which two provinces have already resorted. The bizarre amending formula, originally devised by the Alberta government, makes it easier to transfer federal powers to the provinces than vice versa. The Meech Lake Accord, if it is ratified, would give the provincial governments some additional powers, including the power to nominate senators and justices of the Supreme Court. This may be an acceptable price to pay for enhancing the legitimacy of federalism in Quebec, but the same cannot be said for the Canada–U.S. free trade agreement, which came into effect at the beginning of 1989. That agreement severely weakens federal powers over energy, broadcasting, foreign investment, financial institutions, regional development, industrial strategy, and various other areas, as well as the whole rationale for having a federal government at all. It is surely significant that former Alberta Premier Peter Lougheed and Parti Québécois leader Jacques Parizeau were among the most fervent supporters of the free trade agreement, and both suggested that it would make their provinces more independent of the federal government. Quebec and Alberta, the two provinces most obsessed with provincial autonomy, were also the only two in which a majority of the voters in the 1988 election supported the Progressive Conservative Party and the free trade agreement.

Canada is a relatively small, industrialized country in a world where most of its competitors are larger, stronger, and more centralized. If it is to survive in this environment and to overcome the divisive effects of its geographical barriers and its closeness to the United States, it may require a stronger central government than it has enjoyed in recent years, and a corresponding reduction in the powers of provincial governments. Moreover, a lessening of the Canadian obsession with provincial interests and jurisdictional controversies might direct attention to more significant issues, such as the unequal distribution of wealth, power, and opportunity among the population.

NOTES

1. Canada, House of Commons, *Debates*, Session 1936, p. 3868.
2. John Porter, *The Vertical Mosaic* (Toronto: University of Toronto Press, 1965), p. 382.
3. *R. vs. Hauser*, [1979] 1 S.C.R. 984; *A.G. Canada vs. CN and CP Transport*, [1983] 2 S.C.R. 206; *R. vs. Wetmore*, [1983] 2 S.C.R. 284.
4. Harold A. Innis, *Political Economy in the Modern State* (Toronto: Ryerson, 1946), p. xi.
5. *Burns Foods Ltd. vs. A.G. Manitoba*, [1975] 1 S.C.R. 494; *CIGOL vs. Saskatchewan*, [1978] 2 S.C.R. 545; *Central Canada Potash vs. Saskatchewan*, [1979] 1 S.C.R. 42; *Dionne vs. Public Service Board of Quebec*, [1978] 2 S.C.R. 191.

6. *Reference re Anti-Inflation Act,* [1976] 2 S.C.R. 373.
7. *Reference re Legal Authority of Parliament to Alter or Replace the Senate,* [1980] 1 S.C.R. 54.
8. Constitution Act, 1982, section 38.
9. Harold A. Innis, *Essays in Canadian Economic History* (Toronto: University of Toronto Press, 1956), pp. 277–78.
10. Jim Fleming, "The Myth of the Power-Hungry Centralizers," address to the Empire Club, Toronto, 19 February 1981.
11. Canadian Tax Foundation, *The National Finances, 1987–88* (Toronto, 1988), Table 3.6.

FURTHER READINGS

Banting, Keith G. *The Welfare State and Canadian Federalism,* 2nd ed. Montreal: McGill-Queen's University Press, 1987.

Black, Edwin R. *Divided Loyalties: Canadian Concepts of Federalism.* Montreal: McGill-Queen's University Press, 1975.

Cairns, Alan C. *Constitution, Government and Society in Canada: Selected Essays.* Toronto: McClelland and Stewart, 1988.

Leslie, Peter. *Federal State, National Economy.* Toronto: University of Toronto Press, 1987.

Milne, David A. *Tug of War: Ottawa and the Provinces under Trudeau and Mulroney.* Toronto: Lorimer, 1986.

Simeon, Richard. *Federal–Provincial Diplomacy: The Making of Recent Policy in Canada.* Toronto: University of Toronto Press, 1972.

Simeon, Richard, ed. *Intergovernmental Relations.* Toronto: University of Toronto Press in co-operation with the Royal Commission on the Economic Union and Development Prospects for Canada, 1985.

Smiley, Donald V. *The Federal Condition in Canada.* Toronto: McGraw-Hill Ryerson, 1987.

Stevenson, Garth. *Unfulfilled Union: Canadian Federalism and National Unity,* 3rd ed. Toronto: Gage, 1989.

20

City Politics in Canada

JACK LAYTON

City politics in Canada is characterized by contradictory faces. Some cities struggle with the painful problems of economic decline, while others grapple with the headaches of boom economies. A decade ago, many of these cities were elsewhere on the boom/bust cycle. Cities once wanting to control unbridled growth in the early 1980s are now looking for ways to promote flagging economies and create jobs. Others, bursting at the seams with the congestion and pollution resulting from unbridled expansion, are trying desperately to pull in the reigns.

While the urban bounty of the 1950s and 1960s provided many crumbs to distribute to the poor, the economic stagnation that struck many cities in the late 1970s or early 1980s left fewer resources to be divided among a much larger needy population. The recovery of the past few years has simply emphasized a growing gap between rich and poor. Desperate attempts to divert attention by constructing civic monuments like domed stadiums or convention centres had Canadian big city mayors falling over one another in a competition for prestige. Perhaps, it was hoped, the people would be distracted from the ills of city life.

Recent years have seen a resurgence of interest in urban affairs and a renewed criticism of pro-development policies in several cities. Local politicians had become too cavalier in their abuse of community interests and were beginning to suffer the consequences. Canada's two largest cities both saw the defeat of many establishment council members and the election of reform-orientated majorities. After a decade of floundering, the urban reform movement appears to be on the rise again. The question for the 1990s is simple. Can the reformers cope with the increasing contradictions of Canadian urbanism: wealth with growing poverty; prosperity with environmental degradation; success with increased violence; free trade with economic dislocation; freedom with alienation?

THE MYTHOLOGY

The mythology of city politics revolves around two misperceptions: "Local government isn't important. It's little more than pothole politics," and "City politics is probably the most democratic form of government we have in Canada."

We need to clear up these seriously flawed conceptions. The mythology is that city hall merely offers mundane services such as garbage collection, roads, and sewers. Accordingly, local government is seen as a level of government to be taken less than seriously. But imagine living without adequate sewers, garbage collection, running water, or fire protection. Many of the world's millions of urban residents do without these. City governments are actually responsible for making urban areas physically habitable. This is not to say they have always succeeded: increased concern about the serious environmental consequences of growth and the increasing frequency of toxic disasters in urban areas is highlighting the fact that the physical livability of cities is threatened. Equally important is the trend of the past four decades that has seen municipalities spending more of their resources on facilities and services of unquestioned importance: public transit, social services, policing, schools, housing, and urban planning. If there ever was a time when city councils were restricted to trivial responsibilities, that day is long gone.

The second myth concerns the supposed highly democratic nature of city government. We often hear local politicians touting the unique nature of city hall government because it is so accessible to local residents and even encourages citizen participation. This view cannot be totally discounted—there is some truth to the contention. Local politics is certainly more open to input from the average citizen than either federal or provincial governments. After all, the municipal councillors spend most of their time right in the community. City hall is usually a short distance away from homes and workplaces. At first glance, this is the most accessible level of government.

It is also true that, in most cities, individuals or group delegations are given the opportunity to stand before the council or its committees and give their views, looking their politicians right in the eye. This is not possible for most of us when it comes to federal or provincial governments. Hence the fanfare about how "government by the people" flourishes in city politics.

This view hides much of the reality of municipal politics, and there are good reasons why we should be sceptical of it. First, a pervasive combination of apathy, confusion, and alienation among voters serves as a real obstacle to local democracy. Voter turnout at municipal elections is very low. On average, 30 to 40 percent of eligible voters cast ballots in local elections, in contrast to the 70 to 80 percent turnout at other levels.

Second, the electoral system in cities produces results that very poorly reflect the diverse socio-economic makeup of urban areas. The majority of local politicians are businessmen, lawyers, or other professionals. Very few are unionists, immigrants, women, or people who have been unemployed. A thoroughgoing democracy would likely see a much closer reflection of the demography of a city in its elected representatives.

Worse than this, however, is the disturbing reality that many local politicians are not elected at all. Rather, they are appointed to their posts, and sometimes these posts are very powerful indeed. Until recently, the best example of this arrangement was the chairman of the regional government in Metropolitan Toronto. One powerful incumbant of this position, Paul Godfrey, held this position for well over a decade without having to face the electorate. Other examples can be found in the many special boards that make up the local government structure: transit authorities, police commissions, hydro boards, harbour commissions, or public housing companies. Often the appointments are not even made by the local councils but by the provincial governments, far removed from the local scene but very well connected to the elite power structure from whom the selected few are usually chosen. The end result is a process in which the voter has virtually no say, removing that basic public accountability essential to a democratic system.

There are further problems. All politicians, including those at city hall, are subject to pressure from special interests. Some pressure groups have considerably more resources than others, giving rise to an imbalance in the decisions made by local councils—an imbalance that favours the most powerful sectors, most notably business.

There is a final limitation on local democracy that cannot be overemphasized: Canada's constitution gives provincial governments full control over their municipalities. The provinces can create or eliminate local governments, decide what powers municipalities exercise, prescribe procedures for local elections and decision-making processes, dictate how local taxes are to be raised, and as if all this weren't enough, a province can ultimately veto municipal laws or policies.

All of this calls into question the traditional view that local politics is democratic, but not particularly important. Indeed, the reverse proposition seems to be more accurate. With this in mind, we will now turn to a discussion of the current state of city politics including the context within which city hall operates, the responsibilities of city governments, the organization of local government, the various forces at work in Canadian cities and the major issues that confront city politicians. We will conclude with an analysis of political power in urban political systems.

THE CONTEXT OF CITY POLITICS

We do not often think of municipal government as a revolutionary phenomenon, but Canada's early city governments were born in the struggle to transform Canada from a colony to a self-governing nation. The idea that townspeople should be able to control their own affairs and not be subject to arbitrary dictates from the British Colonial Office was a central feature of reform movements in various parts of Canada throughout the nineteenth century.[1]

The "victories" of the reformers were not, however, resounding ones. While many city councils were incorporated between the 1840s and the turn of the century, they were not what one could call models of local democracy. The first restriction, which as we have seen persists even today, was the dictate that municipal governments would be "creatures of the Province." The reformers of the day were advancing the theory that "the right of the community to govern itself arose directly from the people."[2] Senior governments took a different view, arguing that local governments should only be mechanisms for administering certain delegated responsibilities and for the arbitration of selected disputes under the authority of sovereign provincial governments.

Perhaps more disturbing from today's perspective is the limitation that was imposed upon those who could vote in municipal elections. Because the role of local government was traditionally restricted to servicing property by providing and maintaining such services as roads, sewers, and bridges, only male property owners were to enjoy the franchise. Women (who normally didn't own property) and tenants were not granted the right to vote, and while women were given the vote in the early twentieth century, it has only been relatively recently that tenants have been permitted to participate in local elections.

However, local governments are now involved in much more than servicing property. The advent of programs such as welfare, day care, public housing, mass transit, and public health policies, to name just a few, have expanded the work of local politicians and bureaucracies dramatically. Since the Second World War, municipalities have become increasingly preoccupied with these issues and with the constant search for funds to pay for the new services. Of course, their traditional role as suppliers of services to property (often called "hard services") has remained, but federal and provincial governments have begun to rely on the local level to deliver social services (or "soft services") because they are "closer to the people" and because it is an easy way to pass on some of the costs that provinces would have to bear themselves.

As we will subsequently explain, one of the reasons for this expansion of the municipal role was the introduction of "welfare state" policies by the senior federal and provincial governments, but another cause has simply been the burgeoning population of urban areas. The larger the population of a municipal territory, the more complex its service needs become. Services to property quickly became entangled with services to people. Roads were built near new factories to move workers to and from work and also to provide the factories with the means of bringing in raw materials and shipping out finished goods. Neighbourhoods were planned, renovated, torn down and rebuilt, in part as a social welfare measure and in part as a means of supplying services to private property. The point here is that municipalities are now involved in servicing both property interests and people generally. The extent and complexity of this mix is very directly related to the population and territorial size of the local government in question.

RESPONSIBILITIES OF CITY GOVERNMENTS

The responsibilities of local government can be listed in several general categories. While there is some variation from province to province, the list that follows is generally applicable to all Canada's municipalities. First are *protection services*. Police and fire services have long occupied an important position as one of the more visible and pervasive functions of local government. Local police forces enforce federal, provincial, and municipal laws. Together these laws prescribe a socio-economic order for the society, and it is the municipality's job to ensure that this order (or status quo) is maintained. Policing is a mechanism for *social control*, a central function of the state in a capitalist society. Lines of officers at worker picket lines or demonstrations as well as controversies about police treatment of minorities illustrate the phenomenon. Fire departments fulfil another important state function, the protection of private property and human life.

In any developed society the state is also called upon to provide the physical infrastructure required for the processes of production, distribution, and exchange that are essential to the proper functioning of the economy. In a capitalist society, the state provides the infrastructure while the private sector by and large provides for production, distribution, and exchange. In this context, *transportation services* are key elements of local responsibilities. The expressways, road networks, bus routes, and subway lines that are built and maintained by city governments are nothing less than the production lines and distribution networks of the urban economy. The efficient movement of raw materials, finished products, workers, and shoppers is constantly sought by the city's corporate interests. Consequently, a major proportion of the capital spending by every city hall is devoted to the discharge of this responsibility. Some of the most famous urban political battles have centred on transportation issues, for example, the construction of expressways or rapid transit lines through established neighbourhoods (the Spadina Expressway or the Vancouver LRT).

Another local responsibility designed to provide physical infrastructure is captured under the polite designation *environmental services*: sewers, garbage disposal, and water supply. Initially established to respond to serious public health concerns, these services have become increasingly important as a response to urban growth. Some might consider these matters rather mundane, but the conflict between an economy that generates phenomenal quantities of waste (close to three kilograms of solid waste per person per day in Canadian cities) and the livability of the environment is becoming increasingly severe. The location of huge landfill sites, incineration of waste, the disposal of toxics, and the need for recycling, reduction, and reuse of waste are all controversial and critical issues on the municipal agenda of the 1990s.

Aside from physical infrastructure, cities have moved into the field of what we might call "social infrastructure." This move has been accelerated in the latter half of the twentieth century as the "welfare state" has been added to the inventory of government responsibilities. The post-Depression Canadian state found that social welfare policies were essential to maintain the capitalist social order in the face of mounting popular discontent. Municipalities have taken on the administration of a great many programs designed to keep the lid on the political fallout of urban poverty.

This category of municipal responsibility can be labelled *social and health services* and includes welfare payments, day care, and homes for the aged, as well as public health programs. In most of these categories, provincial governments maintain particularly strict control over the activities of city politicians, leaving little scope for creative or independent municipal action. Indeed, some provinces, such as British Columbia, have kept the welfare system under their own jurisdiction entirely. On the other hand, local politicians and city staff are the ones who come into direct contact with the heavy economic and personal fallout suffered by disadvantaged communities and individuals. Poverty and its associated ills are all-too-common characteristics of Canada's urban centres. Families unable to pay their rent find themselves evicted and usually contact city hall, desperate for assistance. Inadequately fed children struggle through inner-city schools. Economic tensions breed wife-beating and child-beating crises. Most such sad situations leave city councillors at a loss; there is little beyond emergency band-aid treatment that can be provided, because provincial governments have not permitted municipalities to develop adequate policy tools to respond. Some cities have worked at the margin of existing policy to develop innovative responses to urban poverty, but because several million Canadians live below the poverty line, most of them in cities, these efforts have had limited significance.

The economic crises of the late 1970s and early 1980s aggravated the situation, but even cities that experienced huge growth spurts in the mid-1980s found homelessness and food banks on the rise at the same time. Social services are without question a vital but frustrating area of responsibility for city governments. All too often, the problems are simply left unattended because the poor have so little political clout.

In this same category, but with growing importance, is the realm of public health. Once a guiding force behind municipal policies, for instance when sewer systems were constructed as a public health measure to curb urban diseases of the early twentieth century, public health slipped into the background after the Second World War. It was overtaken by the era of modern medicine and the "magic bullet" concept of dealing with health problems with drugs instead of preventing the ills through public health strategies. With the advent of AIDS, public health was once again given a high profile by local governments. Controversial public health measures such as needle exchanges for drug addicts, explicit sexual material teaching safer sex, and workplace smoking controls found their way onto city council agendas. Broader health promotion strategies to tackle the root causes of ill health such as inequality, poverty, bad housing, and poor nutrition are now being taken up under the rubric of the "healthy cities" movement.

An ancilliary element of the "social infrastructure" is the city's responsibility for *recreation and cultural services*. Parks, community centres, municipal swimming pools, golf courses, nature trails, tennis courts, and the like have become important components of urban community services. A traditional pattern of inequity has developed in most cities, however. Neighbourhoods with lower-income residents seem to receive fewer such services than the rest of the city. In part, this is due to the tendency for wealthy areas to provide private recreational facilities, but the imbalance also reflects an unequal distribution of political power between a city's neighbourhoods.

Recently, local politicians have become infatuated with "grand projects." Perhaps the first and most famous incarnation of this preoccupation was Montreal's former mayor, Jean Drapeau. Projects such as Expo '67 and the Olympics required massive public investments in facilities, often at the expense of needed services such as sewage treatment or housing. The pursuit of monument building in recreational planning seems to have captured the imagination of most city governments. In part, this trend is a distorted reflection of the long-standing interurban competition for prestige and economic development. The effects of this new mania on the politics of Canada's cities will be felt during the next decade and may well precipitate a reaction by overtaxed citizens who question the benefits of these megaprojects. In this regard, the Montreal Citizens' Movement rallied to win a sweeping majority in 1984 with new Mayor Jean Doré and a reform agenda. Some have suggested that unhappiness with Toronto's domed stadium project and the kind of philosophy that it represented was at least partly responsible for the election of a NDP-reform coalition majority in the 1988 civic elections.

The next responsibility in our list is perhaps the most important of all: *land use planning*. The deceptively small portion of municipal budgets allocated to planning (1 to 2 percent of the operating budget) belies the vital role played by the planning function. Indeed, decisions about the use of land in cities are by far the most politically contentious questions facing local governments.

Even with the huge geographic mass of Canada, urban land remains a scarce commodity. This is because, as we have seen, *urban* land must be extensively serviced with roads, buses, sewers, water, street lighting, parks, schools, and much more. Without these services, land cannot be used for urban purposes such as housing, offices, factories, universities, or shopping centres. Land use planning essentially consists of determining the appropriate uses for particular parcels of land and providing required services according to the use.

Needless to say, most land in cities is already being used for one purpose or another; so planning focuses on *changes* in land uses and tries to determine which changes are appropriate and which are not. And here is the rub: there is often considerable disagreement about what should happen to a particular piece of property. The owner of the land will want to establish a use that can maximize its value. Adjacent owners will advocate a use that will enhance the value of their properties. People elsewhere in the city might have views as well. Perhaps there is a group arguing that there is a desperate shortage of affordable housing and that the land in question should be devoted to that purpose irrespective of the desires of the owner. Sometimes residents in a neighbourhood far removed from the contentious land might perceive a threat to their lifestyle. For instance, if the development of some downtown land as office towers produces a requirement for a new expressway into the heart of the city, passing through existing residential areas, opposition can be expected.

City hall has not always been involved in land use planning. Prior to the Second World War, the urban structure of most Canadian cities was determined by the private decisions of land owners. While the city engineer might have specified a street pattern, virtually no further controls were available. However, the haphazard pattern of urban growth, combined with its post-war rapidity, highlighted the need for some sort of "rationale" for the distribution and intensity of the land use. Planning acts, adopted by provincial governments, gave cities the power to regulate land use through mechanisms known as "official plans" and "zoning by-laws."

Business interests were sceptical about these measures, though the need for planned growth was generally acknowledged. Indeed, an important role of the state in a capitalist society is to manage growth in the interests of *all* capitalists, not exclusively that of a particular business. The problem for business, particularly land developers, was that planning law permitted government to interfere with what they believed to be their sacrosanct rights to do whatever they wished with their property. In this sense, the advent of urban planning constituted a dramatic intervention by the state into the affairs of private enterprise.

There was an obvious solution to this problem that was not lost on the major land developers. Clearly, they needed to ensure that the planning process produced decisions that were favourable to their objective of maximizing profit from land development. It has therefore been necessary for the property industry to attempt to "capture" control of the land use planning process. When city governments tackle land use issues in planning reports, public hearings, and council debates, they are subject to tremendous and usually successful pressure from developers. We will examine these pressure tactics as well as their implications later in this chapter.

A final point on planning must be made. City councils have not been able to force a private land owner to actually build a certain sort of building. Their governing legislation does not give them this power, although some are seeking to have this situation changed. The best that politicians have been able to do is to prohibit certain uses and permit others. Accordingly, there has been no guarantee that a project desired by the politicians will ever be built by the private sector. The ball always ultimately finds itself in the property owner's court where the private decision "to build or not to build" presents a clear handicap to achieving public objectives.

One solution to this problem, recently adopted by some cities, is for the municipal government itself to purchase land and build projects. In the Canadian experience, this has been done primarily for the purposes of building low and moderately priced housing. The 1970s saw several major cities approach their provincial governments for permission to set up city-owned housing companies. The provinces have generally agreed, and the responsibility for housing production has now been added to the inventory of municipal responsibilities.

A similar initiative is now taking shape as cities try to reverse the flight of industry from their central cores. Toronto, for instance, is establishing a municipal corporation to purchase land and build industrial buildings in an attempt to bring industry back to the downtown. It remains to be seen if this strategy can reverse the tendency of multinational industrialists to shift production to suburban areas or, worse, to low-wage Third World countries. In all likelihood a much larger "carrot" or, more likely, a "stick" will be required to reverse this trend.

A final strategy is to establish the concept of "exactions" or levies on private developments. Some municipal reformers are looking to set up linkages whereby, in order to build a certain number of square feet of office space, a developer would also be required to construct a specified number of square feet of housing, perhaps to be turned over to the municipality for non-profit operation. All these techniques are designed to mitigate the negative effects of purely market-driven urban growth.

This brings us to the last item on our list of municipal responsibilities: *administration*. A city government is a large bureaucracy designed to *produce decisions*. Accomplishing this requires a number of administrative components: a decision-making structure, personnel to fill the spots in the structure, funds to pay for the services provided by the city, and a management system to permit an efficient and effective operation. We will examine the structures of city government in the next section of this chapter.

The most controversial aspect of administration, as far as the public is concerned, is the financing of local government. With budgets in the billions of dollars, urban governments are faced with major problems in funding their services. Unlike federal and provincial governments, cities are not permitted to use deficit financing, virtually eliminating fiscal flexibility. Property tax, the basic source of municipal revenue, is an unfortunate instrument because of its regressive character (as incomes drop, the percentage of income paid in property tax usually increases, putting the heaviest burden on lower-income groups, including tenants).

Grants from provincial governments ease this burden to some extent, but bring with them strict conditions that force city councils to spend money according to provincial priorities rather than their own. This situation has led the Federation of Canadian Municipalities to describe local governments as "puppets on a shoestring."[3] The battle between municipalities and provinces on this matter has raged for years, with little prospect of resolution. Without independent status in Canada's constitution, local governments are left without an independent financial lever to deal with urban problems.

THE NUTS AND BOLTS: STRUCTURES AND PROCESSES

For the purposes of our discussion, we might consider the institutions of city government as a machine for transforming raw materials (issues, problems, and demands from citizens, businesses, labour, or the media) into products (decisions and policies). When we examine the machinery and internal processes of a city council, wherever it may be found in Canada, a number of common characteristics can be found. While the individual structures and positions have different nomenclature, the essential elements are the same: an elected council, headed by a mayor and composed of a number of councillors or aldermen; a series of committees of council; and a number of bureaucratic departments. To illustrate the basic processes of decision making, an outline of the life cycle of a typical decision follows.

The machinery is fired up whenever a problem arises. The identification of this problem can come from any one of a number of sources. Perhaps a land developer wants to proceed with an office complex not permitted in the current land use legislation; or a citizen has complained about snow-clearing arrangements; or the local daily has criticized the city's policy on housing. The most frequent sources are found within city hall itself—the bureaucracy which has uncovered some issue requiring a policy decision by council or the politicians who have been prompted to raise some matter with their colleagues. No matter which of these sources provides the initiative, the process that follows is roughly the same, though its results can be dramatically different.

The first step is to present the issue to a committee of council. The committee will consist of a portion of the council members and will be responsible for a certain policy territory such as planning, hard services social services, parks, or finance. Usually, the committee will request a report on the matter from the appropriate department of the bureaucracy. This issue will come back to the committee when the report is ready. In it the staff will present an analysis of the problem and suggest an appropriate course of action in the form of a number of recommendations.

Prior to the committee meeting, the members will have received a long agenda containing the reports from staff on the assortment of issues before it. Sometimes these agendas are hundreds of pages long, and only the most diligent councillors will have studied all the material thoroughly. The most common practice is to assume that the bureaucratic recommendations are appropriate. First-time observers at these meetings are often stunned by the hundreds of recommendations that are approved without discussion. At a typical meeting, only a few items are debated. These tend to be the controversial matters, involving situations where the bureaucrats are suggesting a solution that is opposed by constituents, businesses, or some councillors.

In most cities, procedures have been developed to allow people to address the committee when they disagree with proposals from the city staff. These public deputations can become lively exchanges. Whether the deputations are successful in convincing the politicians to adopt a different position from the bureaucracy will depend on the political effectiveness of the deputants. Indeed, often these deputations are mere exercises in "legitimation" through giving people the impression that their voice has been heard. Community groups are permitted to come to city hall and have their say, but few councillors listen to the representations of citizens. On the other hand, some deputants, developers and their lawyers for example, seem to be remarkably successful in their efforts to convince councillors.

Next, the decisions of the committee are sent along to the legal department to be cast into by-law form. A by-law is the term used to describe municipal legislation, like a "bill" in Parliament. These by-laws are constructed in the specialized language of lawyers, which means that citizens who cannot afford legal counsel are at a real disadvantage when dealing with the complexities of by-laws.

Ultimately, all committee decisions and by-laws are forwarded to the whole city council for discussion. The members of council have a number of options: they can approve the recommendations (which they do 95 percent of the time); they can reject the proposals (which hardly ever happens); they can amend the recommendations (a more regular occurrence); or they can delay controversial matters by referring them back to the bureaucracy for further study (a common ploy when politicians are in trouble).

With the decision of council made, the issue may still face further hurdles. Provincial governments have the power to veto municipal decisions, and while this is rare on routine matters, some major questions may provoke provincial intervention. Most provincial governments have institutionalized a process for automatic review of municipal decisions, usually through a review board with the power to turn down or amend local by-laws. These boards are not elected but are appointed by the provincial Cabinet. Needless to say, it is most frustrating for a city council to have its decisions rejected in this manner. A more effective reminder of the subservient status of local government would be difficult to imagine.

Councils, committees, and bureaucratic departments form only part of municipal government structure. In addition there is a plethora of special agencies, boards, and commissions (ABCs) designed to deal with particular policy matters. There are usually dozens of these: parking authorities, school and library boards, transit and police commissions, advisory committees on a wide range of subjects. This institutional fragmentation of decision making makes matters most confusing for the average resident. Designed initially to ensure that specialists were in charge of specific aspects of local government, these bodies have usually become repositories for political patronage appointments and have served to remove policy decisions one step further from public accountability. Despite regular recommendations from academics and formal reviews of local government structures aimed at reducing the number and variety of these special-purpose bodies, little reform has been accomplished to date.

A relatively recent development in urban government in Canada has been the introduction of "super-governments," regional governments that incorporate a number of cities, boroughs, and towns under one umbrella structure. Metropolitan Toronto, established in 1954, was the first of these. The concept of regional governments has been promoted as a means of dealing with urban growth. During the post-war expansion boom, which lasted until the mid-1970s, suburban housing developments proceeded rapidly. Local councils, often little more than rural townships, found themselves faced with massive costs for the physical infrastructure to support this growth. Roads, sewers, water supply, hydro, schools—all these had to be provided to meet the needs of the new suburbanites. Developers of subdivisions were frustrated at the inability of the small municipalities to service their land quickly. Some mechanism had to be developed to utilize the strong financial base of the urban core to pay for suburban expansion, otherwise growth could well grind to a halt. Regional governments provided this mechanism, marshalling the tax base of the developed urban centre for the benefit of the surrounding suburbs, while retaining some autonomy for the various municipalities within the region.

One problem with these regional systems is that they have added yet another layer to the complex urban governments. This has created further confusion among the electorate. Indeed, the regional governments are not usually directly elected by the public. Their members are selected from among local councils. This removal of decision making from the control of the electorate has seriously undermined the democratic operation of local politics in Canada's cities.

As well, the politics of regional governments have proven problematic. The interests of the suburbs have frequently come into conflict with the urban base. Whether in Montreal, Ottawa, Toronto, Hamilton, or Vancouver, downtown politicians have had great difficulty convincing their suburban counterparts to deal with many urban problems, simply because the suburbs have not yet experienced these problems directly. Neighbourhood destruction from downtown development and expressways, the need for expanded social services to deal with disadvantaged groups, and the demand for expanded public transit to reduce automobile commuter congestion have all created sharp conflicts within regional governments.

The most recent phenomenon in urban development may create a base for common interests between suburbs and central cities. Continued urban growth is gradually transforming former suburbs into more complex urban municipalities. As industry, office developments, and public housing move into the suburbs, the previous power of traditional middle-class single-family suburban homeowners is being undermined. Suburban politicians find themselves confronting problems such as poverty, congestion, and redevelopment schemes that were formerly exclusive to inner cities. Perhaps this trend will eventually mitigate the tensions within regional governments. There is no doubt that the politics of the "suburbs" will be quite different ten years from now.

In fact, the 1990s will bring whole regions together into single megalopolis phenomena. The famlands that once separated competing cities are rapidly giving way to suburban sprawl. Lost self-sufficiency in food production is only one of the many costs of growth. Another is the increasing conflict between the sprawling local governments. Provincial governments will no doubt consider redefining boundaries in order to rationalize the situation, but this may further reduce possibilities for local democracy through citizen participation as local government becomes bigger and bigger. Those who see the city as a money-making machine may welcome the trend because local opposition to unpopular development schemes will be diluted in the process.

POLITICAL FORCES IN CITIES

In trying to understand the politics of Canada's cities, it is never enough to examine only the formal structures of local government. These are, after all, simply the components of the machine. The essential questions are: what flows into the machine, who operates it, and what is done with the products?

Six major forces operate in urban politics: business, community groups, labour, the media, bureaucrats, and politicians. The most influential of these, business, has, for obvious reasons, a long history of involvement in city politics. City hall makes a great many decisions about land use, hard services, and taxation that affect business interests directly. While the overt corruption of past relationships between business and city officials has largely been eliminated with conflict-of-interest legislation, there are other, more subtle and powerful techniques that have been developed to ensure that these interests are well served by civic policy makers. Indeed, the power of capitalist interests grew in the early 1980s because of the depressed state of urban economies. The conventional wisdom that "what is good for our city's businessmen is good for our city" is a particularly attractive dictum in the context of recession and decline. Any policy that can encourage investment by the private sector is automatically ranked high because of its short-term benefits in increasing the tax base.

If there are negative long-term consequences of such a policy raised by critics, these are discounted. This amounts to a basic ideological congruity between the private sector and most municipal politicians and bureaucrats and constitutes the most powerful weapon in the arsenal of political power available to business. Consider the impact of a corporate executive stating to a municipal council: "If city hall won't co-operate with me, I'll simply have to find another town that will!" Cities are highly dependent upon the investment decisions of those in control of private capital.

When it comes to specific political tactics, there are many resources available to the business sector. Most important are the funds available to hire experts, lawyers, and lobbyists. These funds are also diverted into the political campaign warchests of sympathetic politicians, enhancing the likelihood of a council's positive response to business needs. While a small number of Canadian municipalities and a smaller number of provinces have implemented election expense legislation requiring the disclosure of campaign donors, this has simply produced a more complex form of corporate donation where funds are funnelled through a number of corporate officers in small denominations less likely to be noticed.

The availability of expertise and lobbyists is actually much more significant than the relatively crass practice of campaign donations. Match a corporate lawyer against the city's own professional staff and against the wits of local politicians and the business interest is likely to come out on top. Perhaps most skilled in this area are the land developers. Practice, in this case, has made perfect. The lucrative results of a successful official plan change or rezoning has produced a small elite of lawyers, planning consultants, and lobbyists in each city who have become highly skilled at extracting favourable decisions from city councils.

A final crucial political resource is "organization." No group can begin to extract what it wants from government if it is not effectively organized. Business is able to develop successful political organization because it has identified and agreed upon objectives and it can develop strategy to achieve them. The corporate sector is highly organized to deal with municipal government, through broad organizations such as boards of trade, chambers of commerce, and certain specific industrial organizations such as the Urban Development Institute or the Housing and Urban Development Association of Canada. Even the individual corporation is an organization that can be used in this way.

Thus, when the powerful political and economic resources of the private sector are combined with the predominant ideological support for business initiatives, there can be no question that capitalists receive top rank in the hierarchy of urban political power. But this is not to say that there are no instances of political loss for land developers or their colleagues elsewhere in the business world. They suffer "defeats" of two types. The first type of "defeat" occurs with sufficient frequency to be considered "normal": defeat through competition with other corporations. Occasionally the local state will be called upon to mediate these disputes within the capitalist class, with developers using their influence at city hall to try to convince local politicians to accept their proposals over those of competitors.

A second, but rare, type of "defeat" for business comes at the hands of community or citizen groups. Attacks on urban neighbourhoods by capitalist expansion and major development projects spur residents to attempt to protect their cities. The regular success of business proposals at Canadian city halls, especially those of the major developers, became so frustrating for communities who were opposing developer plans that the phenomenon of the urban reform movement emerged in response. Reformers and citizens' groups have become much more active, and in some cases successful, during the past decade. While their political resources have been much less daunting than those of their business opponents, they have had a number of important cards to play.

Not all citizen or community groups have been reformist or progressive, though. Citizens' groups come in a wide variety of shapes and sizes. Political resources and impact vary a great deal. A wealthy neighbourhood association has many of the same political advantages as a business, while a community organization in a poor neighbourhood will have few of these traditional instruments.

The last two decades have given new meaning to the political clout of neighbourhoods in Canada's big cities. A wave of opposition to unbridled growth and developer-dominated councils has led to alliances and new political parties. Many neighbourhoods were determined to elect politicians with community-based agendas. There were successes, sometimes even majorities. John Sewell, activist and ultimately mayor of Toronto, was a leader of this wave in that city in the 1970s, but his defeat in 1980 put reform into a deep-freeze until the 1988 reform upset. In Montreal, Jean Doré and the Montreal Citizens' Movement capped over a decade of careful organizing with a sweep of fifty-five of fifty-seven seats on the city council in 1986. Factions began to develop within a year, however, as the tensions of the coalition began to generate fissures. Vancouver's Committee of Progressive Electors (cope) failed in its 1986 mayoralty bid as Harry Rankin went down to defeat. The 1988 civic elections saw further losses for Vancouver's reformers. So, there's an ebb and flow to the involvement and success of citizens' groups intervening in direct election campaign strategies to achieve their objectives.

Most important was the emergence of *community* organizing as a strategy to face off against business organizations. From Halifax to Vancouver, residents were organizing to resist the destructive consequences of rapid urban growth—particularly on downtown communities. The battles were often fierce. Creative strategies were used to attract media attention and to influence politicians through the fear of the electorate's vote. While on occasion civil disobedience was added to the more traditional tactics of mass meetings, protest marches, petitions, and like methods, there was a certain "properness" that pervaded these protest efforts, perhaps partly due to the fact that the movement was an alliance of middle- and working-class elements, with the middle class providing the leadership and the major portion of the movement's membership.

As a political force, community groups have had sufficient victories to qualify as a significant factor in urban politics. However, if we were to break down these groups and victories, we would find a clear pattern. The rate of success varies directly with the class status of the group involved. A wealthy neighbourhood can often count on success at city hall while a poor neighbourhood can almost always count on defeat. Of course, even these disadvantaged corners of our cities are allowed the occasional success, thus helping to "prove" that the political process is fair to everyone, giving all an equal chance. (This is somewhat like calling an 8 to 1 hockey game score a "tie" because both sides scored.) This, again, is the "legitimation" function of the local state apparatus.

The middle-class reform movements in Canada's cities have emphasized the need for open and participatory processes in their local governments. Many of these goals have been achieved. Decisions once taken in private meetings are now discussed in public, with public deputations being heard. Of course, the improved process by no means guarantees the ultimate decision will be any different than it would have been under the previous arrangements. Indeed, many communities experience the remarkable frustration of presenting their views to a politely attentive council committee, views that are then summarily ignored. The citizen upheavals of the 1970s and 1980s have actually done little to change the popular attitude in working-class neighbourhoods that "you can't fight city hall."

Movements with special concerns have sometimes focused their efforts on city hall. Tenant organizations, women's rights or health groups, environmental alliances, peace groups, and gay activists often find that city hall is the best focus for their demands. In some cases, the demand is to change a city policy, perhaps with respect to minority hiring, policing policy, or waste collection. Quite often, the goal is to recruit the support of the city council for a national or provincial cause. It's as though the town hall concept is still alive—that local government is a place where issues of importance can be discussed and where the citizens of a city can let their collective opinion be known to the "higher authorities." The strategy can work. It was, for example, city governments, under pressure from tenants' groups, that called for and achieved rent controls in Ontario.

What about labour as a political force? If workers are not successful in influencing city politics using their neighbourhood organizations, could it be that their power lies in workplace trade union organizations? Labour is not listed with the traditional list of urban political forces, but it should be. There are three ways in which unions become involved in local government. First, municipal workers in Canada's cities are unionized. They deal with city politicians as their employers, and the results of contract negotiations have a major impact on the city's budget and delivery of service. Indeed, recent cutbacks in various municipal services have met with stiff union opposition, occasionally sufficient to maintain the service. The most powerful weapon of civic employees, as with other unions, is the strike. Whenever teachers, sanitation workers, or police (who cannot strike legally in most jurisdictions in Canada) walk off the job, they are able to put considerable pressure on decision makers. Most often, though, public outcry against the strike is so strong, fanned by politicians and the media, that the provincial government will step in and "legislate" the workers back to work, often with little having been gained. Nonetheless, the unionization of municipal workers, a relatively recent phenomenon, has had a decidedly positive effect on wages and working conditions.

A second way in which labour has exercised influence at city hall is through municipal labour councils, which have existed for many years in Canadian urban areas. Composed of the union locals in a particular city, labour councils are labour's watchdog on local government. Policies on a wide range of issues are developed by these councils. Economic development and jobs, housing, planning, social services, labour relations, public transit policy, property tax reform, and human rights issues are among the matters most commonly raised at the meetings of labour delegates. Acting much as any other pressure group might do, though usually with considerably fewer political resources than business groups, labour spokespersons will attempt to catch the attention of the public or the ear of the politicians in an effort to produce policies that will be more favourable to working people. Nevertheless, having, as they do, few strong allies among city politicians, the success rate of the labour movement in its efforts to change the pro-business direction of urban policies has been low.

The third device that labour has used to influence city politics is the electoral process. Indeed, labour has sometimes joined forces with citizens' groups to bring forward a "united front" in contesting local elections. Most major Canadian cities have experienced this phenomenon in recent years, and despite ups and downs, these coalitions are having a major impact on the shape of urban political debate. Unions and community groups have assisted in polarizing the issues, clarifying the conflicting positions, and offering voters a recognizable choice. There are many examples, some quite successful: the Montreal Citizens' Movement, the Committee of Progressive Electors in Vancouver, or the municipal wing of the NDP in Toronto, Ottawa, Hamilton, and Winnipeg.

Thus, if there is a single trend during the 1980s that we can identify with some certainty, it is the gradual shift toward some form of overt party politics in Canadian cities. Labour is playing a major role in this process. If it is successful in establishing party politics in Canadian city halls, the local arena will have received a promotion in the voters' eyes, from "pothole politics" to the serious business it really is.

Media influence on Canadian federal and provincial politics is generally acknowledged to be quite impressive. In urban politics as well, the media has helped to shape the agenda. To begin, most media outlets relegate city hall to a low status in their coverage. Given that these are *mass* media interested in maximizing sales and profit, it is not surprising that stories with the widest geographical interest, like international or national news, will receive top or front-page billing. City issues can be found, with some searching, deep inside the newspaper or near the end of the newscast. All of this has had a serious effect on public attitudes toward local politics and politicians by reinforcing people's general apathy with respect to issues in their city.

However, certain types of local news are covered. Major private developments and public megaprojects are usually greeted with unbridled enthusiasm by the media. Whether it is a new high-rise office tower, a convention centre complex, or a domed stadium, the corporate and civic booster mentality dominates news stories and commentaries. A close look at the interconnections between the boards of directors of major press and electronic media outlets reveals the origin of this enthusiasm. Development companies, banks, mortgage companies, and other major industries have been remarkably successful in placing their directors on these boards, effectively guaranteeing reportage consistent with their interests. The natural scepticism of reporters is often curtailed by editors not wishing to print negative stories about such pro-business ventures.

Media moguls do, however, provide one outlet for their reporters' cynicism. There is a manifest delight in presenting reports of the interpersonal attacks and sometimes silly debates between local politicians. The public quickly draws the conclusion that all municipal politicians, and city politics in general, are nothing more than trivialities, worthy of little attention and much ridicule. As a contribution to the democratic process, this tendency is extremely negative because it convinces people that there is little point in becoming concerned about the urban issues addressed at city hall. This helps to reduce meaningful and informed citizen participation, leaving a vacuum into which other pressure groups, such as business interests, can successfully flow.

Finally, the media usually dubs critics of development "radicals" and alleges that they have adopted a "stop the world, I want to get off" approach to urban growth. This belittling of alternative viewpoints has placed a major obstacle in the path of citizens and communities in their efforts to urge different priorities on their city governments. One encouraging trend has been the emergence of alternative, community-based newspapers and co-operative radio stations. These news outlets have limited circulation because their access to corporate advertising dollars is almost nil. Nonetheless, for those willing to scout their newsstands for these fly-by-night community gems, the rewards can be substantial.

CONCLUSION: UNCERTAIN PATTERNS OF POLITICS

There is a marked imbalance of forces in the urban political matrix. The tools of political power are unequally distributed. Fortunately, there are shifting sands that redistribute some of the power some of the time. There is nothing to indicate that a fundamental restructuring of the Canadian urban power structure is underway, but there has been significant change.

The 1970s and 1980s recast the stable control of local government maintained by an effective alliance of business and the municipal state for over half a century. An awakening resistance among neighbourhoods of all classes brought real debate into council chambers across the country. New notions of the importance of community preservation and of participatory democracy spread. The alliances pushing for change were powerful ones because they usually crossed class boundaries and therefore had serious political clout. Powerful local incumbants were toppled in some extraordinary elections. Most of the defeated forces were not absent for long, but the reform interludes have left lasting impressions on their cities. Most often, shrewd elements of the establishment recognized that positive responses of some kind were necessary to reform demands. Concessions were made so as to transform radical policies into much more mild-mannered reforms.

Increased power for municipalities to confront their problems directly has been the most important legacy of recent reform trends. Cities were faced with the frustration of provincial and federal government inaction in fields such as affordable housing, local economic development, day care, and public health initiatives such as workplace smoking control or AIDS defence). Therefore, they simply tackled these problems directly: the housing crisis through local non-profit housing companies, day care through centres built by the regional governments, urban growth through new zoning measures, loss of affordable housing through demolition control, environmental toxics through right-to-know laws, and the ubiquity of the automobile through major public transit improvements.

Shifts in the business cycle have proved particularly difficult for the reform movement to manage and have resulted in a regular return to traditional corporate control of city halls. Economic recessions, which hit different cities at different times, have led a concerned public to take more seriously the tantalizing visions of construction booms dangled by pro-development politicians. The monuments are taken out and dusted off and presented again for public approval: the domed stadiums and opera centres. Such vacillation, of course, weaken the prospects for long-term change. This is in part because the gains of reformers' efforts are often more symbolic than real, given that they have little time (usually one electoral term) in which to establish themselves.

What then is to be the appropriate basis upon which to construct a movement for fundamental change: for a city of equals, a just city, a healthy city, a green city, a friendly city without violence and fear? The general, but highly unequal, decline of living standards in the contemporary Canadian city is the clear starting point. And no longer is this decline a matter of high-rise towers casting unpleasant shadows on sedate back yards. Rising poverty, a serious housing crisis, the worst evidence being found in the numbers of homeless in downtown streets, and significant unemployment, particularly long-term joblessness among the young, are the new characteristics of the contemporary urban situation.

One problem in establishing these issues as the basis of a new urban reform movement in any city is that they are not traditionally seen as problems for city governments to address. The policy instruments and fiscal resources necessary to tackle them lie with provincial governments—at least that is what we are told. On the other hand, poverty, housing problems, and unemployment are experienced by individuals, families, and communities *in cities*. And these problems manifest themselves in particular, distinctly urban situations: racial tension in public housing projects, plant shutdowns, large rent increases in apartment blocks, homeless youth on downtown streets.

Accordingly, instead of trying to pull together the old alliances of reform, progressive community organizing must now orient itself around the pressing and painful circumstances of the 1990s: increased inequality, extremes of poverty and wealth, deteriorating living conditions for many, and environmental degradation. Distinctions between those who benefit from the urban economy and those who do not should be sharpened. A more profoundly ideological approach is needed. Powers currently thought to be unavailable to the city halls of Canada must be developed and used directly at the local level to confront these problems. The new movements will have to be more self-consciously socialist and class-based. Urban conflict must be defined as having a broader social base—beyond one's own, often rather comfortable street and neighbourhood.

NOTES

1. For a review of the history of local government in Canada, see Warren

Magnusson and Andrew Sancton, eds., *City Politics in Canada*
(Toronto: University of Toronto Press, 1983), pp. 3–57; Donald H. J.
Higgins, *Urban Canada: Its Government and Politics* (Toronto:
Macmillan, 1977), pp. 15–44.
2. Magnusson and Sancton, *City Politics in Canada*, p. 7.
3. Canadian Federation of Mayors and Municipalities, *Puppets on a
Shoestring: The Effects on Municipal Governments of Canada's System of Public Finance* (Ottawa, 1976).

FURTHER READINGS

Dear, Michael, and Allen J. Scott, eds. *Urbanization and Urban Planning in Capitalist Society.* London: Methuen, 1981.
Gerecke, Kent, ed. *City Magazine.* Winnipeg, Manitoba. A quarterly magazine with news and analysis of cities across the country. Good central themes for each issue; the best way to stay current.
Higgins, Donald. *Local and Urban Politics in Canada.* Toronto: Gage, 1986. This volume serves as a good introduction to institutions and processes of local government in Canada. Differences between municipal organization in various provinces are illustrated.
Magnusson, Warren, and Andrew Sancton, eds. *City Politics in Canada.* Toronto: University of Toronto Press, 1983. This book has excellent chapters on the politics of each of seven major Canadian cities as well as useful introductory and concluding chapters by the editors.
Roussopoulos, Dimitrios, ed. *The City and Radical Social Change.* Montreal: Black Rose Books, 1982.
Tindal, C. R. *You and Your Local Government.* Toronto: Ontario Municipal Management Development Board, 1988.

21

The Size and Scope of Government: Robin Hood Sent Packing?

ISABELLA BAKKER

> Government is not only too big, it also reaches too far into almost every corner of the economy. It over-regulates some industries and over-protects others. In trying to facilitate investment, government too often distorts it. Instead of encouraging strength, many actions perpetuate inefficiency. Too often, government frustrates entrepreneurship and discourages initiative.
> –Michael Wilson, Budget Speech, 23 May 1985

> Under the Mulroney government, Robin Hood hasn't actually disappeared; he's working for the other side.
> –Linda McQuaig, commenting on the Tory tax changes in her book on the history of Canadian tax reform *Behind Closed Doors*

The past two decades have been marked by competing visions of the proper role of government in the economy. Government increasingly came to be seen as the problem, the market as the solution. However, as this chapter suggests, there are many political and institutional factors that determine whether public sector activity will be good or not for the economy. To simply assume that the state, redistributive policies, and social spending are bad for the economy is to ignore a great deal of the evidence from other countries.

During the 1970s, the debate over the role of the public sector was generally dominated by two competing schools of thought: Keynesian and monetarist. The Keynesian school sees a legitimate role for government intervention in the workings of the market. It recognizes a need for government intervention in times of recession and unemployment in order to overcome shortfalls in aggregate demand. During the Great Depression and after the Second World War, Keynesians were generally those who argued for active government fiscal and monetary policies as well as regulations aimed at curbing the excesses of corporate concentration and abuses of consumers. In addition, some Keynesians embraced the proposition that redistributive measures such as social security and income supplements such as unemployment insurance were effective safeguards because they gave workers money to buy the goods the economy produced even during economic downturns. Keynesianism was dominant in the development of Canada's post–Second World War economic strategy.

Monetarists such as University of Chicago economist Milton Friedman advocate a purely self-regulating market regime wherein all production, allocation, distribution decisions, as well as the prices of goods, services, and income are determined by the market. Public sector activities, including taxation, are viewed as disincentives to investment that distort the decision-making process of individuals and firms. Monetarists are strong advocates of the need for a sharply curtailed size and role for the public sector and a strict control of the money supply. By the 1980s the Keynesians had been chased from the spotlight and the monetarists, champions of the free market, moved beyond their preoccupations with monetary policy to assume a new guise as neo-liberals.[1] In the 1990s the economic priorities of the "free market" continue to fight it out with the political priorities of the public sector. Some hope that the election of the Tories to a second term means that the prizefighter with the "invisible hand" can deliver a knockout punch.

The recent intensity of these debates about the size and role of the government and the Keynesian welfare state can be linked to political and economic developments originating out of both domestic and international pressures. This chapter begins by examining the breakdown of political regulation of the capitalist economy in the 1970s. Up to that point, continuous economic growth had fostered a set of institutional arrangements and social policies that muted distributional conflicts between labour and capital. The retreat from universalistic and redistributive welfare measures paved the way for the rise of new economic orthodoxies that rejected public intervention in the economy. This monetarist agenda was initially set by the Liberals in the mid-1970s, but has been accelerated by the Tories' accession to power in 1984.

In a sense, the early success of Keynesianism in promoting economic growth was also its downfall. Once recession tested the Keynesian compromise between labour and capital the way was paved for the monetarist resurgence. Part and parcel of this resurgence was the increasing visibility of the role of the state. With the breakdown of the Keynesian welfare state compromise, distributional conflicts were exacerbated and the state became, once again, a subject and a site of struggle. This translated into a greater awareness of, and concern about, the size and scope of government.

The size of government spending became identified by the monetarists and neo-liberals as one key source of the country's economic woes in the 1970s. This chapter will analyze Canadian expenditure trends both in the international context and by the various levels of government (federal, provincial, local) in light of this argument. We will find that, from

1970, the share of Canadian government spending relative to Gross Domestic Product (GDP) is not extraordinary when compared to other advanced capitalist countries. And when one turns to an examination of all levels of government within Canada, it becomes apparent that provincial and local governments have realized a more rapid growth in expenditures than the federal government. This in large part reflects the introduction of new layers of welfare programs (mainly in the jurisdiction of these subnational levels of government) in the late 1960s.

Public spending levels are frequently correlated with the size of deficits. The section of this chapter on revenue will reject this argument. In large part, the Canadian deficit can be attributed to the failure of the federal government to bring its revenue-raising capacity in line with expenditures. This is due to a number of factors, including increasing interest payments on the debt, increases in cyclical expenditures such as unemployment insurance, and various tax breaks and deferrals that have resulted in a significant loss of federal revenues relative to GDP. It remains to be seen whether extra revenues will be captured through Finance Minister Michael Wilson's tax reforms, but all indicators point to any recaptured revenue coming out of regressive consumption taxes as opposed to corporate taxes. The chapter concludes with the argument that trends on the revenue side, in conjunction with the free trade initiative and its impetus toward harmonization, point to intensified pressures on social programs and the public sector in the 1990s. Efforts to reduce social spending represent an attempt by monetarist or neo-liberal forces to emphasize economic efficiency rather than equity. Their arguments for spending cutbacks are particularly effective when federal deficits are at a high level. Rejecting government expenditures as the source of deficits, this chapter represents an attempt to clarify the high stakes of this political debate.

THE DECLINE OF POLITICAL REGULATION AND THE RISE OF THE NEW ORTHODOXY: TOWARD A NEW SYSTEM OF DISTRIBUTION

The recession of the early 1980s capped a decade of uncertainty for state policy makers. The economic prosperity of the "golden era" following the Second World War had come to a sudden halt in the early 1970s with the simultaneous appearance of high levels of unemployment and inflation (stagflation). Keynesian policies and the construction of the welfare state had been widely viewed as the foundation of this post-war prosperity. However, Keynesianism represented more than an economic doctrine; it represented a *political regulation* of the market economy and included state efforts to harmonize opposing interests through a series of economic and social policies. In the aftermath of the Great Depression and the Second World War, Keynesian principles of demand management and fiscal stabilization were harnessed to the traditional Canadian staples-led approach to economic development. When the underlying political and economic conditions that allowed Keynesian policies to flourish changed, the entire Keynesian approach came to be questioned. This was especially the case with the Keynesian welfare state.

The Keynesian welfare state was constructed in order to address the social policies and the pressures coming from a growing labour movement and the political parties that spoke for it: the Co-operative Commonwealth Federation and the New Democratic Party (NDP). Although never warmly embraced in Canada, the Keynesian welfare state was tolerated as long as it was financed out of increased economic growth and higher marginal incomes; it was deemed acceptable and muted distributional conflicts between capital and labour. The Canadian welfare state was to ensure the continuity of income over the ups and downs of the economy much in the same way as Keynesian macro-economic policies were to secure the smooth flow of profits during economic upswings and downturns. Through this dual approach Keynesianism managed to address both the concerns of labour and capital. The fiscal burden of the Keynesian welfare state was acceptable in the particular context of workers' rising standard of living and rising corporate profitability stimulated by the high level of demand for Canadian resource exports in the international economy. However, the stable economic environment that had fostered this post-war development strategy began to crumble in the late 1960s and early 1970s. In addition, the tax burden of corporations and the wealthy was beginning to be reduced through a series of tax measures that shifted the increased cost of the Keynesian welfare state onto working-class and middle-income earners.

With the onset of recession in the early 1970s and the collapse of the post-war economic strategy, new economic orthodoxies that reaffirmed economic growth through market forces emerged. By 1975, with the announcement of reductions in the growth of the money supply by the governor of the Bank of Canada and the advent of wage controls, monetarist principles were replacing earlier Keynesian-style approaches to macro-economic policy. Constant attempts by the Bank of Canada to protect the value of the Canadian dollar meant high interest rates. In 1981 interest rates were at 20 percent, and by 1989 they had only fallen to 12.5 percent. High interest rates, reduced investment, and a withdrawal of the federal government from direct job creation are part of the monetarist approach to federal government policy. The new monetarist economic orthodoxy also questioned the role of the state in harmonizing the production of wealth with its distribution by arguing that allocation and distribution should be left to the market.

State policy makers were at the same time grappling with the declining international economic status of the United States. The position of the United States has been affected by a decline in its share of world exports (from 22 percent in 1950 to 10 percent in 1980), reduced technological superiority, competition from the newly industrializing countries in the Pacific Rim and South America, and the formation of powerful trading blocs such as the European Economic Community. This trend poses a particular problem for Canada because its post-war development had relied heavily on American investment in Canadian domestic manufacturing and resource development. Canada's branch-plant industrialization compounds the already difficult task for governments of coping with productivity declines and the accelerated application of technological innovation to production. Branch plants do not control their own technology, nor do they undertake much research and development. As a result, many Canadian companies rely on responses to world-wide economic restructuring made south of the border. This makes it difficult to set a clear and independent policy direction in Ottawa.

Furthermore, in the Canadian context, the growth of provincial fiscal power also complicates federal government responses to international economic shifts. Indeed, as we will soon see, many of the fiscal tools of the federal governments are slowly being turned over to the provinces. Canadian federalism, contrary to other federal states, has been moving toward greater decentralization.

In the 1970s an alternative vision of decentralized economic development took hold among the premiers of the western, resource-producing provinces. Tired of servicing central Canada and having the status of an economic hinterland, the premiers began to emphasize market-driven economic development, greater north–south integration, and a decentralization of the federal government's economic prerogatives. They were to clash with the central Canadian economic interests who sought to preserve existing Canadian manufacturing sectors and advocated new state-directed development of the industrial and service sectors. However, the federal Progressive Conservatives had largely embraced the vision of the western premiers by the mid-1980s.

The Mulroney government came to power inclined toward the pro-market liberalism of Reagan and Thatcher. In their November 1984 mini-budget and the May 1985 budget, the Tories set out an objective of "economic renewal" employing neo-liberal policy instruments to realize that goal. This meant reorientating public policies to encourage entrepreneurship, investment, and risk taking; rationalizing the management of government resources and programs; restoring fiscal balance in how Ottawa spends and taxes; and reducing both the size and role of the federal government.[2]

Neo-liberal policy initiatives, however, have been limited by the unique features of Canada's geography and economic structure and by elements within the Conservative Party itself.[3] For example, so-called "Red Tories" in the Cabinet, such as Flora MacDonald and Joe Clark, sought to protect the universality of social programs and did not support extensive deregulation. Canada's regional and cultural diversity along with the regionally based support of the two main political parties also tempered the ideological attack on government and the Keynesian welfare state.

THE INTERNATIONAL CONTEXT

The neo-liberal view that associates levels of welfare spending with negative economic performance has not been supported by the empirical evidence. Comparative research shows that many of the countries that have a large Keynesian welfare state also have the healthiest economies. In fact, countries that spend more on health, education, and welfare also exhibit higher growth rates in manufacturing productivity. Similarly, there is no simple correlation between government deficits and the Keynesian welfare state. While the Canadian government's share of Gross National Product (GNP) has remained fairly static since 1975, the share of government expenditures for social programs has dropped from 46 percent in 1976 to 40 percent in 1982.[4] This is precisely the period during which the deficit became a source of economic and political concern. As we will discover, the source of the deficit lies in the reduced revenue-generating capacity of the federal government rather than with uncontrollable welfare spending.

Canadian expenditure and revenue trends demonstrate that Canada is relatively close to the averages of the Organization for Economic Co-operation and Development (OECD). Nevertheless, there are considerable variances in government expenditure and revenue levels across countries. Table 21.1 shows the share of total government revenues and expenditures as a percentage of GDP from 1975 to 1987 in the so-called Group of Seven (G7) countries. In 1975 the level of revenues relative to GDP ranged from a low of 24 percent in Japan to a high of 43 percent in Germany. By 1987 Japan still exhibited the lowest government share of revenues at 33 percent, while France had the highest level at 49 percent of GDP. Canada has consistently been among the middle range of countries, with neither particularly high nor low levels of government revenues. In 1987 the Canadian government revenue share was at 41 percent.

The same extremes among the G7 countries are reflected in government expenditures. Japan is again at the low end of the scale with expenditures at 27 percent of GDP in 1975 and 33 percent in 1987. This contrasts with Germany's expenditure share of 49 percent in 1975 and France's expenditure share of a little over 51 percent in 1987. Sweden, a country that is not part of the G7 but is well known for its high level of

Table 21.1

International Comparisons of Total Government Revenues and Expenditures as Percentages of GDP, 1975–87

	Weighted Average*	Canada	United States	United Kingdom	France	Germany	Italy	Japan
Revenues								
1975	33.1	37.4	31.2	39.8	41.2	43.3	27.8	24.5
1980	35.7	37.5	33.2	39.7	46.1	45.3	33.3	28.2
1981	36.7	39.8	34.1	41.8	46.7	45.5	34.3	29.7
1982	37.1	40.4	34	42.3	47.6	46.2	36.5	30.1
1983	37.1	40	33.7	41.7	48.2	45.7	38.5	30.4
1984	37.3	40	33.7	41.6	49.2	45.7	38.2	31.1
1985	37.8	39.8	34.5	41.5	49.3	46	38.8	31.8
1986	37.7	40.6	34.5	40.5	48.8	45.2	39.7	31.9
1987	39.1	40.7	35.5	39.9	49.1	44.8	40.4	33.2
Averages								
1970–1974	32.3	36.6	31.7	37.4	39.1	41.1	27.3	22.6
1975–1981	34.6	37.6	32.6	39.1	43.8	44.9	31.2	26.2
Expenditures								
1975	37.5	39.9	35.2	44.4	43.4	48.9	40.2	27.3
1980	38.2	40.3	34.4	43.1	46.1	48.2	41.9	32.6
1981	39.4	41.3	35.1	44.3	48.6	49.1	45.8	33.6
1982	41.1	46.3	37.5	44.7	50.3	49.5	47.8	33.7
1983	41.2	46.9	37.5	45.1	51.4	48.2	49	34.1
1984	40.7	46.5	36.5	45.5	52	47.6	49.9	33.2
1985	41.1	46.8	37.8	44.3	52.1	47.1	51.5	32.6
1986	41	46.1	38	43.2	51.8	46.4	51.4	33
1987	40.8	45.3	37.8	41.3	51.4	46.5	51	33.4
Averages								
1970–1974	32.8	35.9	32.2	38.1	38.5	41.2	33.7	21.9
1975–1981	37.4	39.9	33.9	42.9	45	48.2	41.3	30.3

*GDP/GNP weights expressed in U.S. dollars based on 1980–81 averages of exchange rates and GDP/GNP figures.

Source: Canada, Department of Finance, Quarterly Economic Review, June 1988, Table 95.

government expenditures (67 percent in 1982), also has the highest level of government revenues (60 percent in 1982).[5] Again, the Canadian government share of expenditure relative to GDP is in the middle range at 45 percent in 1987 compared with 38 percent of the United States, 41 percent for the United Kingdom, and 51 percent for Italy. Canada's increase in spending over the two previous decades, however, has been relatively large; from the mid-1960s to the early 1980s, the share of GDP absorbed by government spending expanded by about 40 percent in Canada, compared to increases of 25 percent in the United States and France, and 33 percent in Britain. For all seven countries over this period of time, revenues rose by less than expenditures. While the 1970 to 1974 average shows a balance between revenues and expenditures, governments increasingly became net borrowers, and budget deficits became the norm by the early 1980s.

Several other significant shifts in public sector activity of the OECD countries (including Canada) occurred in the period from the 1960s to the 1980s. First, there was a movement away from defence and public administration to welfare state expenditures on education, health, and income maintenance. Second, by the early 1980s, government consumption in Canada, Britain, and Australia—in contrast to most European nations—was greater than transfer payments to individuals. This means that spending on goods, services, and labour consumed by government to carry out its various programs and activities such as health care, police protection, and day care surpassed social subsidies, social security, welfare payments, and pensions.

Some observers have suggested that this particular policy mix has fuelled public resentment about the growth of government. Comparative studies confirm that welfare states that rely heavily on services rather than transfers open themselves up to a greater degree of public criticism about bureaucracy and public sector wage demands.[6] If this is the case, Canada's public sector may be particularly open to public scrutiny given that it is relatively generous in its provision of services such as health care and education while less resources are put into programs involving direct transfer payments to individuals.

GOVERNMENT SPENDING TRENDS IN CANADA

By Level of Government

In order to understand fully the nature of government spending, it is necessary to disaggregate total government expenditures into federal, provincial, and local categories. Table 21.2 provides the proportions of GDP in 1951, 1961, 1971, 1976, 1981, and 1987 that are represented by total current expenditure, government consumption expenditure (on goods and services), and transfer payments of all levels of government.

Spending trends in Table 21.2 indicate that provincial and local governments have realized a more rapid growth than the federal government. This no doubt reflects the rapid expansion of provincial services in the education and health care fields initiated by Mackenzie King and successive social Liberal governments. It appears that the provinces and municipalities provided a disproportionate share of the personnel necessary to deliver services of the Keynesian welfare state and a disproportionate share of the increment in personnel and services as well. Roughly three-fifths of the total increase in spending of subnational governments

Table 21.2
Expenditure as a Percent of GDP at Market Prices: All Levels of Government,
1951-87

	Current Expenditures on Goods and Services	Transfer Payments to Persons	Interest on the Public Debt	Total Current Expenditure
All Levels of Government*				
1951	12.6	4.6	2.7	20.7
1961	15.1	6.7	2.9	25.7
1971	18.7	8.5	8.3	32.4
1976	19.3	9.8	4.1	35.7
1981	19.3	9.8	6.3	38.7
1987	19.6	12.2	8.2	43.1
Federal Government				
1951	7.3	2.6	2.2	13.9
1961	6.3	4.9	1.9	16.9
1971	5.1	4.8	2.0	17.4
1976	4.9	5.8	2.3	19.1
1981	4.6	5.2	3.9	20.1
1987	4.5	6.3	5.1	22.0
Provincial Government				
1951	2.1	1.9	0.4	5.3
1961	2.6	1.6	0.4	8.3
1971	4.9	3.2	0.9	15.5
1976	5.5	3.3	1.2	17.0
1981	6.1	3.5	1.7	18.5
1987	6.5	4.0	2.4	20.5
Local Government				
1951	3.2	0.1	0.2	3.6
1961	4.7	0.2	0.5	5.6
1971	6.3	0.3	0.7	7.5
1976	6.3	0.2	0.6	7.2
1981	5.9	0.1	0.6	6.8
1987	5.7	0.2	0.6	6.7

*Intergovernmental transfers are not included in this total since in the consolidation of the government sector such transactions cancel out. Note that percentages by level of government are not net of transfers and therefore sum to a higher total than the consolidated accounts of all levels of government.
Source: Statistics Canada, National Income and Expenditure Accounts.

from 1961 to 1987 involved the direct purchase of goods and services as opposed to transfer payments to individuals.

Figure 21.1 presents the same data as Table 21.2 revealing the more pronounced increases in government spending that occurred at the provincial level. The growth in spending at the subnational levels of government is clearly a reflection of the fields of governmental jurisdiction that were most significant to the Keynesian welfare state—education, health care, and social services. These policy areas fell under provincial responsibility, and the provinces became increasingly important as suppliers of new programs and services. The 1960s witnessed the introduction of the Canada and Quebec Pension Plans, national medicare, the Canada Assistance Plan (which provided an umbrella for various social assistance programs), the progressive expansion of unemployment insurance and workers' compensation, and large public expenditures on schools, universities, and colleges.

This spending pattern fuelled a growing resentment by the Trudeau governments of the 1970s, which had committed themselves to contributing to the cost of provincial social programs but received little political credit in the eyes of the electorate. Increasingly, the growth of government in the social field led to intergovernmental friction concerning federal intrusions into the provincial domain and discrepancies among provinces in their ability to render services to their citizens. These concerns eventually led to a complex set of federal–provincial fiscal agreements in the late 1970s and throughout the 1980s.

Federal Transfers to the Provinces

The extent to which federal funds have contributed to provincial budgets is reflected in Table 21.3. Federal transfers to the provinces represent about 4 percent of GDP and one-fifth of federal expenditures. In 1987 approximately one-fifth of provincial revenues were derived from federal transfers. Since the 1970s, the federal government has reduced its fiscal transfers to the provinces, reflecting its concern with federal budget deficits.[7]

Given the variation in revenues among the provinces, federal transfer payments may, depending on the wealth of the province in question, play a relatively important role (e.g., the four Atlantic provinces) or a minor role (e.g., Ontario) in supporting programs. In contrast to considerable interprovincial variation on the revenue side of budgets, the expenditure side is relatively uniform. Greater variation on the revenue side is due to differences in provincial wealth, income bases, and the amounts received through transfers from the federal government. There is a tendency toward greater uniformity on the expenditure side given political pressures of federalism to equalize the provision of services in health care, education, and social welfare.

Transfers from the federal government can generally be categorized as being conditional or unconditional. Conditional grants involve shared-cost programs in which Ottawa pays for half the cost of provincially

Figure 21.1
Percentage of GDP Spent by Federal Government,
by Type of Expenditure, 1951–87

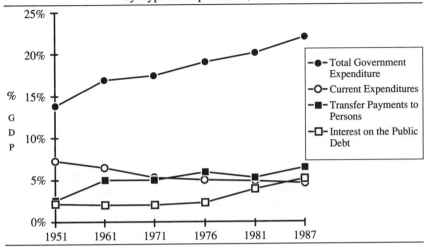

Percentage of GDP Spent by Provincial Government,
by Type of Expenditure, 1951–87

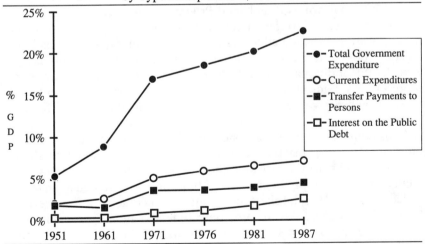

Table 21.3
Federal Transfer Payments to the Provinces

	As % of GDP	As % of Federal Expenditure	As % of Provincial Revenue
1951	1.2	8.3	19.3
1961	2.7	15.9	31.2
1971	4.3	25.0	27.1
1976	4.2	22.1	24.9
1981	3.9	19.3	20.7
1987	4.0	18.3	20.3

Source: Statistics Canada, National Income and Expenditure Accounts.

administered programs provided that minimum national standards are observed. Conditional grants programs in such areas as health care and post-secondary education were first established to ensure a fairly equal provision of services between the "have-not" provinces and the "have" provinces. In particular, they were meant to stimulate public expenditure in areas that do not contribute directly to business expansion such as health, welfare, pensions, and culture. Rhetoric against government spending is most often directed against these expenditures in contrast to spending on infrastructure or regional subsidies.

The two decades since the Second World War saw a proliferation of shared-cost programs and conditional grants. In 1977, however, a new arrangement known as Established Programs Financing (EPF) replaced the old cost-sharing arrangements for health insurance and post-secondary education. This signalled a federal retreat from direct responsibility for social policy. In effect, the EPF transfer, like equalization grants, is now virtually unconditional. Unconditional grants, or equalization payments, represent a system of payment out of federal government revenues to those provinces whose *tax* capacity is less than the average for five representative provinces. This is so that all provinces can provide their citizens comparable levels of basic services. These payments are unconditional in the sense that there is no direct connection between the size of a payment and what the province chooses to do with it. Recent developments in federal–provincial block-funding arrangements may be reshaped by the Meech Lake Accord, but the outcome is far from certain. Under the Meech Lake Accord, new federal/national programs will require the approval of seven provinces. In addition, any province that undertakes its own program initiatives that meet national objectives must be given reasonable compensation by Ottawa.

Federal Transfers to Individuals and Businesses

Federal subsidy and assistance payments to business during the past two decades have grown faster than the share devoted to social program spending. The amount spent on transfer payments to business as a percentage of GDP increased to a peak of 2.5 percent in the mid-1980s from less than 1 percent in 1970. While the share slipped to 1.6 percent in 1987, it still represents double the share of 1970. By contrast, spending on persons has declined as a proportion of GDP from a peak of about 7 percent to about 6 percent. Since 1970, the growth in federal transfer payments to persons has been below the growth in transfers to business.[8] At the same time, the tax burden of business has also been getting lighter through a series of tax reforms and hidden tax measures.

Debt-servicing Costs

The steady growth of debt-servicing costs since the 1970s is a final important area to consider in an examination of government spending trends (see Table 21.2). In part, this trend reflects the unwillingness of the federal government to initiate tax increases while continuing to maintain both social and automatic stabilization programs, such as unemployment insurance. In effect, programs are now being financed through the public debt. Also, since 1982, very high interest rates have contributed to the rapid growth in debt charges. Increasing interest costs were partly a reflection of the inability of federal policy makers to intervene to lower international interest rates, especially those of the United States. The maintenance of high interest rates, as we have seen, is one of the strategies practised by the monetarists in their attempt to keep inflation down. However, higher interest rates have become a growing burden on government finances, absorbing a rising share of government budgets. While monetarist interest-rate policies have increased the size of government expenditures required to service the debt, their fiscal policies (tax deferrals and exemptions) have reduced a number of important sources of revenue. Before we pursue this question in greater detail, it is useful to review some of the explanations of the increase in government spending.

EXPLANATIONS FOR RISE IN GOVERNMENT SPENDING

Explanations for the rise in government spending are numerous. The most cogent analyses of expenditure growth in Canada situate the discussion within the context of economic and political developments.

First, it is important to highlight that modern governments have grown for many reasons quite apart from the emergence of the Keynesian welfare state. For example, in the United States, much of the increase is due to rising military expenditures. As well, many services would not be efficiently provided for on a pure market basis. Market provision of education, health care, housing, energy, and communication would mean that many people would be excluded. Many public services are delivered efficiently. Through the provision of public health care, governments reduce the costs to firms of private health insurance and ensure a healthy labour force. For example, the Canadian health care system, which is publicly run, is more efficient and uses less resources than its American counterpart, which is privately financed and run. This is not to deny that there are public services that are inefficient. However, simply privatizing these services is also not the solution. The challenge lies in providing high-quality, efficient services that benefit all income groups.

Critics of government spending often ignore the positive direct and indirect effects of public expenditure on the private sector. Public enterprises and services have historically absorbed many of the expenses that private corporations did not wish to pay given the high start-up costs of infrastructural projects, such as the Canadian Pacific Railway or the James Bay hydro-electric project, or which otherwise would have to be paid by the private sector as part of its costs of production. In many instances, state spending on economic infrastructure—such as highways, mass transit, airports, and electrical, gas, and water utilities—allows private companies to produce and market their goods efficiently. In a sense, the state has provided enormous amounts of the risk capital that was needed for these investments, and these investments have in turn benefited the private sector through provision of efficient transportation and cheaper power. A recent American study confirms the importance of government investment in infrastructure for economic growth. The study points to the slowdown in public capital growth as contributing significantly to the slowdown in that country's private productivity growth.[9]

In addition to establishing the economic infrastructure required for the private sector, there are a number of other necessary functions performed by the public sector that have contributed to increased spending over time. Government absorbs the costs of creating a well-educated and technically trained labour force. Although business bears part of the taxation and spending burden, the incremental costs to employers are frequently outweighed by superior productivity of the labour force.

The peculiar nature of Canadian economic development has also demanded a vital role for the public sector. Canada is highly trade dependent and has a weak manufacturing sector that is very reliant on American capital and technology. Empirical evidence, based on cross-national studies, suggests a strong relationship between the "openness" of an economy (measured by the proportion of GDP devoted to exports) and government spending. In open economies such as Canada, changes in the international economy may lead to sudden adjustments in employment, production, and consumption, and this translates into a greater likelihood of government compensating the affected sectors, firms, and individuals.

There are also a series of political factors that affect the level of public spending. These are: (1) federal state structures that tend to limit the expansion of public spending; (2) the ideological orientation of governments, with leftist governments generally being more expansionary; and (3) the strength of organized labour, with highly unionized labour forces and strong labour federations contributing to government spending.[10] Canada is a federal state; the two main parties have successfully excluded the "party of the left," the NDP, from governing at the national level; and, compared to most European nations, the labour movement is more fragmented, with the system of collective bargaining being highly decentralized. While cross-national findings cannot offer definitive explanations for the particular pattern of growth of government spending in Canada, they may be suggestive of why the Canadian public sector has grown more slowly relative to other nations.

A number of more general socio-economic factors have also been identified in the literature as contributing to public expenditure growth. The growth in population and resulting demographic changes have been important determinants of public spending levels in all of the OECD countries, not just Canada. In particular, health care, education, and pension programs have expanded with the size and age of the population. Aside from coverage extensions, increases in service and benefit levels have also been a contributing factor. The degree to which coverage and benefit levels have expanded will, aside from economic resources, depend on political factors such as the strength of organized labour and other social movements concerned with improvement in the standard of living of the working population, and the extent to which financing of social expenditures is centralized. In political systems where collective bargaining and the allocation of resources are relatively centralized, such as Austria and Sweden, social program coverage tends to be more secure and extensive.

Some have argued that government spending will increase over time because the demand for public expenditures rises with upward movements in real personal disposable income. Once basic needs are met, the argument goes, then public demand for "leisure" services, such as parks and cultural facilities, that require government spending will increase. Inflation can also be identified as an influence on government spending levels. For example, if total government expenditures in current dollars are "deflated" to take into account price increases, then the "real" rate of government growth declines significantly.

Finally, some critics offer institutional arguments that blame the rise in public expenditures and the resulting tax increases to pay for them on the expansionary tendencies of the bureaucracy and the "empire build-ing" of individual bureaucrats. Where bureaucracy is measured by the number of public employees, data do not confirm this constant growth. Federal employment as a percentage of the labour force has stayed quite constant over the two decades of the 1960s and 1970s. Employment in government services currently represents approximately one-fifth of total employment.

CANADIAN GOVERNMENT REVENUES

In the 1960s discussions about taxation were motivated largely by the search for equity, fairness, and the redistribution of income. The most eloquent expression of these sentiments was contained in the 1967 report of the Royal Commission on Taxation (Carter Commission), which pressed for the elimination of tax breaks and special privileges. By the late 1970s, however, tax reform had been effectively "hijacked," to be replaced by concerns about the manner in which the existing tax struc-ture crippled market forces. In the 1980s tax reform regained a high public profile and became a key vehicle in the effort of the Progressive Conservatives to control government spending by limiting the revenue side. In effect, the new spate of tax reforms will make it increasingly difficult to finance existing programs because the burden of taxes will be shifted even more onto the middle and lower classes. There is, however, a limit to the amount of additional revenue that can be squeezed out of this group of taxpayers. This has important implications for social programs and the welfare state. With ballooning deficits and increasing fiscal restraint, a retreat from universal social programs will be the only "choice" open to a fiscally responsible government. The additional impetus of the free trade agreement to harmonize tax rates and provision of benefits with the United States will intensify pressures to cut back in the public sector in the 1990s.

The Deficit and Shrinking Revenues

Many accounts of government growth tend to concentrate on government spending, neglecting the revenue or tax side. This is unfortunate since it leads to a clouded view of the deficit. Discussions of the deficit are most frequently about the appropriate size and role of the state in the contem-porary economy and not about the deficit *per se*. This debate is not a new one in Canadian economic history, but it had been largely laid to rest in the post-war period. Deficits are one of the main indicators of political and economic trends, as well as the subject of considerable debate. In the period between the Second World War and the early 1970s, deficits were generally small. During this post-war "golden" era it was relatively easy to accept the Keynesian view that good fiscal policy called for deficits in recessionary periods in order to stimulate the economy and surpluses in expansionary periods that would cool the economy down. The resurgence of concern about the deficit in the 1970s echoes arguments voiced in the pre-Keynesian 1930s: problems about the crowding out of private sector investors and unbridled government growth financed through high levels of borrowing.

There is, in fact, no overwhelming empirical evidence to support these arguments. Cross-national studies have found no direct relationship between public spending levels and the size of deficits. Paradoxically, it is the countries of centre-right governments that have run the largest deficits. These governments were less able to implement tax policies to finance their expenditure requirements due to the political constraints imposed upon them by their business constituencies.[11] As noted earlier, governments of the left have been associated with high levels of public spending, but they have also been able to maintain lower deficits through the imposition of higher taxes.

In applying this comparative observation to the Canadian case, one notes that the centrist Liberal Party has ruled, with some Conservative interludes, for most of the post-war period. Government of both these parties have been reluctant to turn to taxes as a way to support their major spending programs. It is this discrepancy between revenues and spending that accounts for a substantial proportion of the deficit that emerged in the second half of the 1970s and was compounded by the effects of the recession of the early 1980s. The growth of national debt has meant that the annual burden of interest payments further contributes to the "fiscal crisis."

A number of contributing economic and political factors have been isolated by writers focusing on the causes and consequences of the deficit. Generally, the deficit is divided into its structural and cyclical components. The term structural deficit refers to the deficit that would prevail if income were at full employment, with a corresponding level of full-employment revenue being collected. Cyclical expenditures are related to upswings or downswings in the level of economic activity. With the onset of a major recession in 1981, the cyclical component of the deficit rose dramatically. Falling incomes, high unemployment, and reduced trade all meant a loss of government revenues and increased government expenditures in social welfare areas, especially unemployment insurance. This was compounded by historically high interest rates (thus, high debt-servicing costs) and a drop in petroleum revenues because of a decline in world prices.

Explanations of the increase in the underlying structural deficit must take into account the evolution of the revenue system over this period of time. There are a number of tax measures that to varying degrees can be blamed for revenue shortfalls. The partial indexation of the personal income tax system in 1974 resulted in a loss of federal revenues relative to GNP because indexed exemptions and tax brackets meant that the government could not capture income gains if they were attributable to inflation. On the expenditure side, a number of payments were indexed—old age pensions and family allowances—which led to lower revenues for the federal government.

There are a series of tax breaks or tax "expenditures" to individuals and corporate taxpayers that are a particularly significant drain on potential federal revenues. Tax breaks in effect are expenditures made by the government; government gives up revenue and in this sense spends it. Linda McQuaig, in her study on the politics of taxation in Canada, provides a good illustration of tax expenditures:

> In 1985, the Reichmanns were able to win from Ottawa a $500 million tax break to facilitate their takeover of Gulf Canada Ltd. When the tax concession became public, it caused a minor stir in Parliament. Imagine, however, if the Reichmanns had come to Ottawa seeking a *grant* of $500 million to assist them in their takeover of Gulf. Imagine if the finance minister had had to stand up in the House of Commons and explain why it was in the national interest for the government to dip into the federal treasury and come up with a half a billion dollars to hand over to one of the richest families in the country, a family whose assets are valued at $6.2 billion.[12]

This illustration highlights not only the massive amounts of money involved in tax expenditures, but also underscores the lack of public scrutiny through the press and Parliament that is given to such government measures. Even when a tax break is deliberate government policy, most of the dialogue over the measure is restricted to the narrow community of tax experts and their clients of business people and investors.

The hidden nature of tax breaks has, as McQuaig puts it, "allowed them to escape the scalpel of government restraint." In addition to the hidden nature of tax expenditures is also the question of who they benefit. Maslove, in a detailed 1979 study, concluded that the benefits of tax breaks received by upper-income Canadians were roughly one hundred times greater than those received by low-income Canadians. Such disparities are largely out of the realm of public debate. From the 1970s, successive federal governments have limited direct spending on federal programs and Crown corporations, but little has been done to restrain tax expenditures. While government spending grew by 30 percent between 1976 and 1979, tax expenditures grew by 42 percent over the same period. By the 1980s, tax expenditures were almost 40 percent of total government spending, or to put it another way, tax expenditures were costing Ottawa $36 billion a year.[13] Governments could give the appearance of being fiscally responsible while simultaneously pursuing tax expenditures. At a time when concerns about "big government" were at the forefront of politicians' consciousness, tax expenditures were an acceptable form of hidden spending. Paradoxically, many corporate interests do not regard tax incentives as acts of government intervention.

Tax deferrals were an additional way for corporations to reduce their tax burdens. Tax deferrals occur where government allows companies to deduct investment in plant, equipment, research, development, and exploration at a faster rate, thereby reducing profit levels for taxation purposes. In most cases, taxes are deferred indefinitely, so the term deferral is rather misleading. In addition, tax deferrals have benefited a relatively small number of companies; 82 percent of deferrals have gone to a small number (13 percent of the 450,000 firms in Canada). For example, Bell Canada deferred taxes of $129 million in 1980 bringing its total deferred taxes to $1.2 billion; in 1982 Imperial Oil deferred $322 million in taxes bringing its total deferred taxes to $1.29 billion.[14] The result of increasing deferments has been that the total corporate tax bill deferred has grown. Overall, as Table 21.4 illustrates, there has been a significant reduction in the corporate tax contribution to government revenues since 1951. The resulting shift of the tax burden to individual Canadians may be one factor contributing to public resentment about the size and scope of government since individual taxpayers are responsible for an increasing share of the burden of government financing.

Tax Reform or Deform?

The various attempts at tax reform by the Liberal Party beginning in the early 1970s are important factors to link to both a discussion of the deficit and to the determination of overall spending priorities. There was a protracted effort at the beginning of the decade at tax reform in light of the previous decade of major social reform. Additional pressure came from the United States, which had introduced major new tax incentives for U.S. corporations in 1971. The Canadian government felt compelled to match the U.S. incentive package in its 1972 budget because of the fear that future investment by U.S. subsidiaries in Canada would otherwise be undermined.

Similar pressures were to operate on the Tory government in the mid-1980s following another U.S. move to lower its tax rates. This movement for tax reform differed from early movements, such as the one initiated by the Carter Commission, that had been motivated by equity and fairness concerns. The neo-liberal version of tax reform simultaneously pushed for elimination of tax breaks (on the grounds that they were

Table 21.4
Government Revenues as a Percent of GDP at Market Prices: All Levels of Government, 1951–87

	Direct Taxes Persons	Direct Taxes Corporations	Indirect Taxes	Investment Income	Transfers from other levels	Other Revenue*	Total Revenues
All Levels of Government							
1951	5.7	6.4	12.0	1.3	0.0	0.6	26.1
1961	7.2	4.0	12.5	1.8	0.0	0.9	26.4
1971	13.4	3.4	13.3	3.3	0.0	1.4	34.8
1976	14.4	3.6	12.5	4.3	0.0	1.0	35.7
1981	14.8	3.6	12.9	5.9	0.0	1.1	38.3
1987	17.1	2.8	12.8	5.5	0.0	1.0	39.3
Federal Government							
1951	5.2	5.6	6.7	0.6	0.0	0.3	18.4
1961	6.4	3.3	5.4	0.9	0.0	0.3	16.3
1971	8.5	2.5	4.6	1.5	0.0	0.3	17.5
1976	9.1	2.6	1.3	1.3	0.0	0.3	17.7
1981	8.2	2.6	5.3	1.5	0.0	0.3	18.0
1987	9.7	2.0	4.2	1.7	0.0	0.2	17.8
Provincial Government							
1951	0.5	0.8	2.6	0.5	1.2	0.3	6.0
1961	0.8	0.7	3.1	0.7	2.7	0.5	8.6
1971	3.7	0.9	4.7	1.2	4.4	1.1	16.0
1976	4.1	1.0	4.6	2.2	4.2	0.7	16.9
1981	5.5	1.0	4.3	3.3	3.9	0.7	18.7
1987	6.1	0.8	5.4	2.6	4.1	0.7	19.8

Local Government

1951	0.0	2.7	0.1	0.9	0.0	3.8
1961	0.0	4.0	0.1	2.1	0.1	6.3
1971	0.0	4.0	0.2	3.7	0.1	7.9
1976	0.0	3.5	0.2	3.7	0.0	7.4
1981	0.0	3.3	0.3	3.7	0.0	7.3
1987	0.0	3.3	0.2	3.7	0.0	7.3

*Other revenue includes: withholding taxes (federal), and transfers from persons.
Source: Statistics Canada, National Income and Expenditure Accounts.

not available to all investors and therefore "distorted" market decisions) and advocated a reduction for those in the higher tax brackets. At the same time, the emphasis was on a less interventionist tax system, away from redistribution of income to "economic neutrality."

The Wilson tax reforms, introduced in June 1987, proposed to reform the system in two stages: the first stage involved the personal and corporate income tax; the second, the federal sales tax. It is the sales tax that is of greater interest. Since the Conservatives came to power in 1984, corporate taxes increased by only 8 percent, income taxes by 45 percent, and the sales tax by 67 percent. It remains to be seen if the extra revenue to fund the first-stage rate reductions on income tax will come from heavier corporate taxes. But given the post-war trend of declining corporate taxes as illustrated in Table 21.4, a sustained reversal seems unlikely. In the second stage of tax reform, the trend toward taxing people on their consumption as opposed to their income will become even more pronounced. Consumption taxes are regressive because they apply to everyone, rich or poor, at the same rate, thereby affecting the poor much more than the rich. It can be concluded that the current movement to tax reform has little to do with making the system fairer to individual Canadians. As Neil Brooks and Linda McQuaig suggest:

> What is really at stake here, in the long run, is our ability to finance Canada's social programs. Once the second stage of Wilson's tax reform has been phased in, with its increased emphasis on sales taxes and decreased emphasis on income tax, the burden will be shifted from the rich and from corporations onto the middle and lower middle class. Quite apart from questions of fairness, this shift will limit Ottawa's ability to finance social programs. There just isn't that much more to be squeezed out of these middle-income groups, which have limited resources to begin with. This will narrow the boundaries within which future political struggles will be fought. The prospect of ever larger annual deficits will make some social welfare programs seem impractical. Under these circumstances, fiscal restraint won't appear nasty or mean. It will simply be the only choice open to responsible governments faced with the reality of limited resources.[15]

CONCLUSION

As we move into the 1990s it seems certain that the Mulroney government in its second term will be much more vigorous in its pursuit of spending cuts. The designation of the Inner Cabinet to control the government's purse strings is a clear indicator of this trend. The direction of tax reform, however, remains largely an issue debated by "experts" and powerful economic interests. These key players in the policy process will, with free trade, be even more effective in making their case against shouldering their share of the tax burden.

The free trade agreement's promise to create "a level playing field" raises fundamental questions about the viability of differential tax levels on different sides of the border. In the face of competition with the United States for investment in production and jobs, Canadians will be told that they have little choice except to follow the American lead. The imperatives of the level playing field and competition with their American counterparts will likely mean that the tax burden will continue to be shifted away from corporations. In this scenario, the tax burden will either be forced upwards for the individual tax payer or services will have to be cut back drastically. Canadians in the 1990s may be paying more taxes for less government services and transfers. The threat to the government's ability to tax must then be seen as a threat to Canada's historically more generous social welfare and regional assistance programs.

Free trade, as envisioned by the Macdonald Commission and the Mulroney government, harmonizes perfectly with the neo-liberal political agenda and strategy for industrial restructuring as it incorporates a market-driven approach to economic growth, continental rationalization, government cutbacks in social services, reduced rights for workers, and a lesser role for the state in the economy. Can the neo-liberals actually carry out this agenda? So far no clear challenger has appeared to push the champions of the free market from the arena. The neo-liberals are, however, beginning to show the strain of trying to grapple with the massive changes taking place in both the world and domestic economies. Just at a time when governments are concertedly trying to follow their ideology and withdraw from the market, the market is in turn making new and more strident demands propelled by the forces of international restructuring. In the end, there may not be less government in the 1990s, only increased favouritism for the wealthy and the large corporations that benefit from market-orientated government.

NOTES

1. Monetarists are now subsumed within the more general school of neo-liberalism. The neo-liberal umbrella includes a wide range of perspectives, all of which argue for the full liberation of the market from the fetters of almost all forms of government intervention. Neo-liberals consistently argue that the growth of welfare state expenditures necessitates higher rates of taxation and that this in turn discourages productive investment and overall economic well-being. See Fred Block, "Rethinking the Political Economy of the Welfare State," in *The Mean Season: The Attack on the Welfare State*, ed. Fred

Block, et al. (New York: Pantheon, 1987), for a critical evaluation of this position. The earlier debates that pitted supporters of a proactive government against advocates of a particular type of inactive government have already been analyzed extensively. See Cy Gonick, *The Great Economic Debate* (Toronto: Lorimer, 1987).

2. Michael Prince, ed., *How Ottawa Spends, 1986–87: Tracking the Tories* (Toronto: Methuen, 1986), p. 10.

3. Bruce Doern, Alan Maslove, and Michael Prince, *Public Budgeting in Canada: Politics, Economics and Management* (Ottawa: Carleton University Press, 1988), p. 7.

4. David Wolfe, "The Politics of the Deficit," in *The Politics of Economic Policy*, ed. G. Bruce Doern (Toronto: University of Toronto Press, 1985).

5. OECD, *The Role of Public Sector*, Special Issue of OECD Economic Studies, no. 4 (Spring 1985), p. 29.

6. Keith Banting, "Images of the Modern State," in *State and Society: Canada in Comparative Perspective*, ed. Keith Banting (Toronto: University of Toronto Press, 1986), p. 6.

7. It is understandable that the federal government would focus on grants to the provinces as a target of deficit reduction since under current federal–provincial fiscal arrangements the state's fiscal crisis is disproportionately borne by the central level of government.

8. Marion Wrobel, *Federal Spending: Changing Trends* (Research Branch, Library of Parliament, November, 1988).

9. Alan Blinder, "Are Crumbling Highways Giving Productivity a Flat?" *Business Week*, 29 August 1988. See also Samuel Bowles, David Gordon, and Thomas Weisskopf, *Beyond the Wasteland* (New York: Basic Books, 1983).

10. David Cameron, "The Growth of Government Spending: The Canadian Experience in Comparative Perspective," in *State and Society*, ed. Banting, pp. 27–31.

11. Wolfe, "The Politics of the Deficit."

12. Linda McQuaig, *Behind Closed Doors: How the Rich Won Control of Canada's Tax System...and Ended Up Richer* (Toronto: Penguin, 1987), p. 8.

13. Ibid., p. 10.

14. Gonick, *The Great Economic Debate*, p. 121.

15. Neil Brooks and Linda McQuaig, "Taxing Our Intelligence: Michael Wilson's Great Reforms," *This Magazine* 21, no. 6 (November 1987).

FURTHER READINGS

Banting Keith, ed. *State and Society: Canada in Comparative Perspective*. Toronto: University of Toronto Press, 1986.

Calvert, John. *Government Limited: The Corporate Takeover of the Public Sector in Canada*. Ottawa: The Canadian Centre for Policy Alternatives, 1984.

Doern, Bruce, Alan Maslove, and Michael Prince. *Public Budgeting in Canada: Politics, Economics and Management*. Ottawa: Carleton University Press, 1988.

Gonick, Cy. *The Great Economic Debate*. Toronto: Lorimer, 1987.

McQuaig, Linda. *Behind Closed Doors: How the Rich Won Control of Canada's Tax System. . . and Ended Up Richer*. Toronto: Penguin, 1987.

Musgrave, Richard, Peggy Musgrave, and Richard Bird. *Public Finance in Theory and Practice*. Toronto: McGraw-Hill Ryerson, 1987.

Stevenson, Garth. *Unfulfilled Union: Canadian Federalism and National Unity*, 3rd ed. Toronto: Gage, 1989.

Wolfe, David. "The Politics of the Deficit." In *The Politics of Economic Policy*, ed. G. Bruce Doern. Toronto: University of Toronto Press, 1985.

22

Kaleidoscope in Grey: The Policy Process in Ottawa

Richard J. Van Loon and Michael S. Whittington

The centre of the political process is the making of public policy. In turn, at the core of the policy process lies the requirement to select priorities from among the myriad of demands made upon government by society. It is the prime minister and the ministers in Cabinet who must determine which of society's demands are to be satisfied, and it is they who are accountable to Parliament and ultimately to the electorate for what they have done. It is the purpose of this chapter to describe and explain the evolution of the federal Cabinet system and of the central agencies that have been established to assist the Cabinet in this process.

The complexity of modern society makes the selection of priorities a difficult business indeed. Such decisions, affecting millions of Canadians, must be made on the basis of information that is always and inevitably incomplete, for despite the most sophisticated methods of gathering data, we are never certain we have all the facts or even the right facts. Yet, paradoxically, the complexity of the world we live in, and our ability to generate vast amounts of information, faces the political executive in the Cabinet with a second problem—that of *too much* information. To deal with this twin problem, the political executives in Ottawa and most provincial capitals have experimented endlessly over the past two decades with the aim of improving the ability of government to select the right information and to process it so as to make the "best" choices among competing policy alternatives.

Our title refers to a kaleidoscope. To a casual observer, the process and the constellation of organizations involved appears kaleidoscopic indeed, for the past two decades have seen several major reshufflings of the Cabinet system and processes. However, the nature and direction of this change derives from attempts by government to impose self-discipline on a system that had grown rapidly and often with few constraints— an attempt that is parallelled by many provincial governments in Canada and by the governments of all other Western industrialized nations.

Everywhere in the Western world, the quarter century following the end of the Second World War was a time of extremely rapid growth of government. The "positive state" expanded its role in society, displacing an older economic, social, and cultural order and creating entirely new forms of public activity. However, early in the 1970s the feeling began to emerge that the growth of government should slow. It followed that the loose planning systems that suited a period of largely unrestricted expansion would also require change. The changes have been kaleidoscopic because the current generation of decision makers, nurtured during a period of rapid government growth, is still experimenting with various ways to operate a system that is, by the 1990s, expanding very slowly, if at all.

The changes are kaleidoscopic as well because of two additional factors. First, there has not always been agreement that restraint is required. As is usual in democratic politics, a rolling compromise seems to have been struck in Canada between those who believe in a restriction of government activity and those who believe that its continued growth is desirable. But such compromises are inevitably unstable. As the balance of power within a government moves back and forth, between pro-constraint and pro-growth factions, the institutions that give effect to that balance will also change.

Second, there is more than one kind of rationality that can inform the process. Bureaucratic rationality emphasizes efficiency and systematic approaches and depends on maximum amounts of "hard" or quantifiable information. It thrives on concrete objectives and clear directions. By contrast, political rationality emphasizes the provision of maximum satisfactions for voters in the relatively short run. It utilizes "soft" information such as public opinion polls and thrives on flexible objectives. Politicians are often uncomfortable with bureaucratic rationality and bureaucrats are often discomfited by political rationality. Yet, the attempt to impose more order on the system of political choice is generally implemented by bureaucrats "serving" politicians. The conflict engendered by this situation is probably inevitable and perhaps even useful since it may result in the striking of a reasonable balance. But the balance is bound to be a shifting one, and the result is bound to be kaleidoscopic changes in the structure and process of political choice.

CABINET AND CABINET COMMITTEES

While Cabinet committees have been used to conduct government business since at least the First World War, the creation of a permanent committee structure for Cabinet is generally considered to have begun under Lester Pearson in the 1960s. The use of committees was fully developed and formalized under Pierre Trudeau during the 1970s. Key to the committee structure from the early 1970s right up to the present has been a core co-ordinating committee or "Inner Cabinet," composed of the most important ministers, and generally called formally the Committee on Priorities and Planning. In the late 1980s the Priorities and Planning Committee (P&P) shares the responsibility for overall co-ordination of the business of government with the Treasury Board, a statutory committee of the Privy Council, and since early 1988, with the Committee on Operations (Ops.). Treasury Board, as well as carrying out a number of management functions assigned to it under the Financial Administration Act, acts as the Cabinet's financial management board and is the employer of record of public servants for purposes of collective bargaining. The Committee on Operations is responsible for overseeing the agenda for Cabinet and for assigning responsibilities to the various subject-specific "standing" committees, or "policy committees." Although P&P retains its formal preeminence, in mid-1988 and particularly after the 1988 election, power over day-to-day selection of priorities may have moved from it to "Ops."

Under the Liberals, during the 1970s, the Cabinet had nine standing committees, each of which met regularly, usually once a week (see Figure 22.1). Ministers then, as now, were normally members of two or three committees. Each committee has a small permanent secretariat, which is provided by the Privy Council Office (PCO) and which controls the flow of committee paper work, helps to set committee agendas, writes the committee decisions, acts as the prime minister's antenna for that sector of the government's activity, and generally facilitates the flow of information from the line departments of government and the other executive support agencies to the Cabinet.

In addition to the standing committees, there are also special or ad hoc committees of the Cabinet established from time to time to deal with specific policy problems. For example, until the Mulroney government there was a semi-permanent Labour Relations Committee that dealt with particularly serious national strikes, and from 1980 onward the Liberals had an "Ad Hoc Committee on Western Policy," which attempted to redress some of the problems attendant on the lack of Liberal support in the West. In 1989 the Conservative government had an ad hoc committee on tax reform and formed and disbanded others as the need dictated.

In the Trudeau Cabinet between 1975 and 1979, the normal flow of Cabinet business was from the sponsoring minister to the PCO to be placed on the agenda of the appropriate Cabinet policy committee. Discussion there usually produced a "Committee Recommendation," which then went to the Treasury Board, in its role as the budgetary watchdog, for consideration of the financial and personnel implications. The Treasury Board recommendation, together with the committee recommendation, then would be presented to the full Cabinet. More often than not, recommendations of the policy committees were confirmed, though major discussions might take place in full Cabinet, and policy committee recommendations could be overturned, particularly when the Treasury Board and the policy committee differed in their opinions.

Figure 22.1
The Committee Structure of the Cabinet
(1979 Trudeau Version)

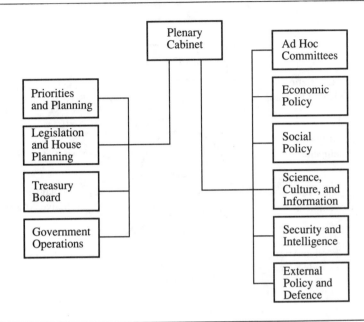

The structure and operations of Cabinet were changed in May 1979 by the Progressive Conservative government (see Figure 22.2). The major structural innovations were the creation of an Inner Cabinet and of two Ministries of State, for Social and for Economic Development, while the major change in process was the creation of what came to be called the "envelope" system of financial and policy management. The Ministries of State and the envelope system will be described in more detail below. However, the normal flow of Cabinet business under this system was from the sponsoring department to a committee of deputy ministries. Following its discussion there, the item might be aborted, but more likely was forwarded to the appropriate Cabinet committee by the sponsoring minister. After Cabinet committee discussion, a decision, again called a "Committee Recommendation," was prepared and forwarded to Inner Cabinet. These recommendations were nearly always approved, for a very important feature of the system was the delegation of real decision-making authority to the committees of Cabinet with the stipulation that these committees must not exceed a preset annual level of expenditures assigned to them by the Inner Cabinet. The full Cabinet seldom met, and

Figure 22.2
The Committee Structure of the Cabinet
(1979 Clark Version)

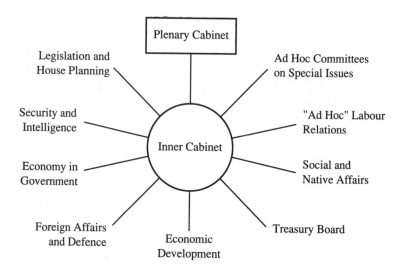

at the time of the Conservative government's defeat in December 1979 seemed to be well on the way to *de facto* extinction.

The reincarnated Liberal government of 1980 retained the basic outlines of this structure and process, though the Priorities and Planning Committee was substituted for the Inner Cabinet, and weekly meetings of full Cabinet were reinstated (see Figure 22.3).

Both the Conservative Inner Cabinet and the Liberal Committee on Priorities and Planning had memberships of about twelve ministers. The prime minister acted as chair. The Minister of Finance, the President of the Treasury Board, the chairs of the standing committees, and some other ministers assumed to be particularly close to the prime minister or particularly strong in other respects made up the rest of the group.

During his brief stint as prime minister, John Turner abolished the Ministries of State for Social Development and for Economic and Regional Development, and reduced the number of Cabinet committees by one. When he came to power in 1984, Brian Mulroney kept essentially the same Cabinet committee structure that he inherited from John Turner. However, upon earning a second term as prime minister in 1988, Mulroney made some extensive changes to the structure of the Cabinet

Figure 22.3
The Committee Structure of the Cabinet
(1980 Trudeau Version)

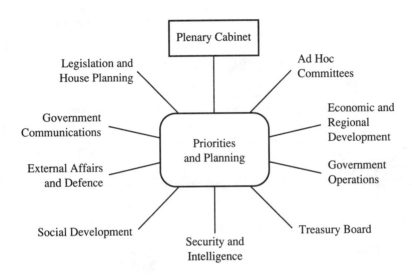

(Figure 22.4). He increased the total number of committees from ten to fourteen plus Treasury Board, and reduced the membership of the policy committees to between seven and twelve ministers. They meet bi-weekly when the House is in session and less regularly when it is not. He also increased the size of Priorities and Planning to nineteen, and clarified its responsibility to confirm all decisions of other Cabinet committees. With this restructuring of the committee system, the full Cabinet retains executive power in only a formal sense.

The Committee on Operations, which had come into informal existence early in 1988, was confirmed after the 1988 election as a central part of the Cabinet process. It is chaired by the deputy prime minister and has a small membership chosen from among senior P&P ministers who also chair other committees. It is responsible for overseeing the agendas of the policy committees and may itself handle any item of business if the appropriate policy committee is not soon to meet or if the "Ops." ministers so choose. Since it effectively sets the agenda of the Cabinet, and since he or she who sets the agenda gets to control priorities, "Ops." is a powerful committee indeed.

During the 1988–89 restructuring, the prime minister also created,

Figure 22.4
The Structure of the Cabinet
(1988 Mulroney Version)

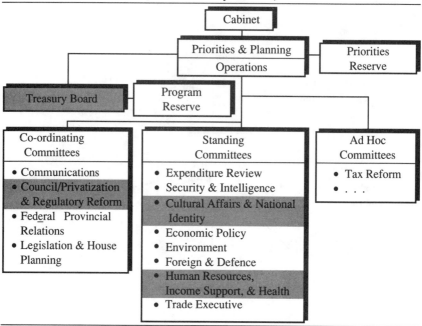

and occasionally chaired, a committee called Expenditure Review. This committee, known to some more or less affectionately as "Chops," was responsible for the major review of government expenditure that led to the 1989 budget. The combined clout of the Expenditure Review and Operations Committees in the period after the 1988 election led to the general description of executive processes in Ottawa as "Ops and Chops." In the May 1989 version of the Cabinet system, ERC screens all policy proposals which have expenditure complications before they can be discussed by policy committees. In combination with Ops. it therefore acts as a major gatekeeper in the system.

A further feature of the 1989 restructuring was the elimination of "policy reserves" or pools of funds left with policy committees for new expenditures. In the new system policy committees may make policy recommendations, but whether their decisions will receive any financial support is left for large items—probably over $20 million—in the hands of P&P, and for smaller items, in the hands of Treasury Board. In Figure 22.4 these arrangements are reflected by attributing the "Priorities Reserve" to the Priorities and Planning Committee and the "Program Reserve" to Treasury Board. Moreover, whether policy committees ever get to see the item at all will depend on the deliberations of "ops and chops." These changes effectively terminate the Policy and Expenditure Management System (PEMS) of the early 1980s and have led many observers to conclude that the influence of policy committees has been very greatly reduced.

The Priorities and Planning Committee performs four major roles. First, it is generally responsible for the determination or ratification of the most general priorities of government. Second, it reviews all committee decisions. Though this often amounts simply to ratification and referral to Treasury Board where expenditures are small, it is a more serious matter for more costly items where P&P actually controls the final expenditure allocation. Third, it deals directly with particularly big or important issues or those that cut across the line of responsibility of other committees. And finally, it has had program responsibilities of its own, such as equalization payments to the provinces.

Through all these system changes, the normal input to a Cabinet committee has been a "Memorandum to Cabinet" (MC). In its current form, the memorandum consists of a three-page "Ministerial Recommendation" (MR) and a more detailed "Analysis." The MRS are not made public, but the analyses, which contain the same information as the MR, often amplified with considerable technical detail but without the "political considerations," are public documents under Freedom of Information legislation. These documents are written within the bureaucracy. They may express demands arising within the bureaucracy (for example, when officials ask for changes in the departmental terms of reference or programs), they may result from demands that have been communicated from outside through bureaucratic channels, or they may represent departmental responses to ministerial requests generated by political communication channels such as caucus, the party organization, or the minister's own contacts.

A more recent addition to the Cabinet paperwork has been one paper notes to Ops. or ERC to support their deliberations on items which they are considering for refund to policy committees. These "one-pagers" are prepared by the sponsoring department and are essentially advocacy documents intended to secure a place on the agenda.

Not every item discussed by Cabinet committees is accompanied by an MC. At the top of most Cabinet committee agendas is an item entitled "General Discussion." This may be used for nothing more (or less) than a quick bit of chatter about the government's current political standing. It may be used by the chairperson to communicate truths from on high: P&P, Ops., ERC, or the prime minister. Or it may be used to discuss any urgent or politically sensitive item. In the latter case, the minister most directly responsible may deal with the question orally without submitting written documents. Major policy decisions are usually not made in this way.

In summary, the creation of a committee structure for Cabinet was begun under Lester Pearson in the mid-1960s. The structure was slowly elaborated and the procedures gradually formalized during the pre-1979 Trudeau government. The creation of an Inner Cabinet, of the "envelope" or PEMS system, the delegation of much effective final decision-making power to committees, together with the virtual elimination of full Cabinet as a decision-making body marked a second major step in the evolution of Cabinet structures.

When Brian Mulroney came to power in 1984, the basic structures remained the same, but over the four-year period between elections, a new and different philosophy of government policy making was gradually brought to bear on the actual process of Cabinet decision making. This approach was characterized by less formality, more centralization within Cabinet, and possibly, more application of political as opposed to bureaucratic rationality. With a second electoral victory in 1988, the Progressive Conservative government has brought the formal Cabinet structures into line with its vision of the policy process, and although this system had not jelled by mid-1989, it is appropriate to characterize this as a third major version of in the Cabinet system for choosing priorities.

SUPPORT AGENCIES: THE CABINET'S ADVISORS

Figure 22.5 presents a taxonomy of the various agencies that provide support to Cabinet. The agencies are classified by their primary and formal roles, but in practice all of them are concerned to a greater or lesser degree with all of the functions. In particular, political considerations colour all of their deliberations; since their job is to provide support for political leaders, it could hardly be otherwise.

It is important, however, to differentiate between partisan considerations and political considerations. The Prime Minister's Office (PMO), ministerial staffs, the party structures, and caucus provide advice and support to ministers because those ministers are of a particular partisan stripe. If the government changes, these people lose their jobs. Indeed, even if the incumbent of a position changes without a change of government, partisan advisors are likely to find themselves either jobless or moving with their own boss. Their loyalty is thus to a very particular set of people within a particular political party.

By contrast, all of the other executive support agencies provide advice for the government of the day regardless of its partisan stripe. When one government is defeated, they provide similar support for the next. They are employed on a permanent basis by the public service and not by a particular party, and while, being human, they will inevitably have their private preferences as to parties and incumbents, they will generally serve as well as they are able, regardless of personal feelings. The conviction that it is in place to serve the government of the day, regardless of its partisan colour, is part of the corporate culture of the federal bureaucracy.

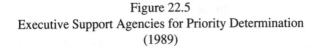

Figure 22.5
Executive Support Agencies for Priority Determination
(1989)

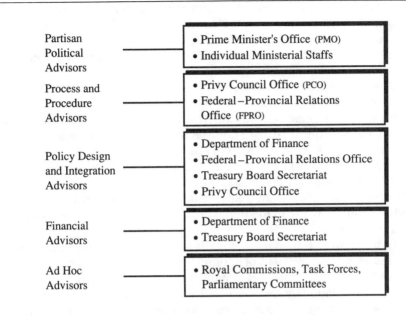

Partisan Political Advisors	• Prime Minister's Office (PMO) • Individual Ministerial Staffs
Process and Procedure Advisors	• Privy Council Office (PCO) • Federal–Provincial Relations Office (FPRO)
Policy Design and Integration Advisors	• Department of Finance • Federal–Provincial Relations Office • Treasury Board Secretariat • Privy Council Office
Financial Advisors	• Department of Finance • Treasury Board Secretariat
Ad Hoc Advisors	• Royal Commissions, Task Forces, Parliamentary Committees

PARTISAN POLITICAL ADVISORS

It has been a popular catch-phrase of political science for over one hundred years to describe the prime minister in a parliamentary system as "first among equals." For many issues he or she may well be, but in determining tne major priorities of government, the prime minister sits, in the end, far above all other ministers; what the prime minister declares to be the top priority is, by definition, the top priority. A consequence of this is that the prime minister's closest personal advisors, one or two top ministers plus those at the top of the PMO, have very great power indeed in determining priorities.

The choice of the top people in the PMO is purely a prime ministerial prerogative. At times, a prime minister will populate the top ranks of the PMO with long-standing personal associates, at other times with partisan advisors from the ranks of his political party, and at still other times with people having broad experience inside government. No one formula seems to be best, but the apparent general consensus is that at least some of the top people should have broad experience in the business of government. Beyond that, the choice is very much a matter of prime ministerial taste and experience.

The PMO staff has grown rapidly over the last twenty years and currently numbers over one hundred. By contrast, R. B. Bennett had a staff of about twelve during the 1930s, while Mackenzie King, Louis St. Laurent, and John Diefenbaker had about thirty staff members and Lester Pearson about forty. However, the number of top policy advisors within the PMO has not increased nearly as quickly as these figures might imply; about half the staff of the PMO is there only to handle the vast volume of prime ministerial mail.

The personal staff of individual ministers also can have a significant impact on partisan political decisions. The ministerial assistants grew significantly in number during the Trudeau years, so that by the early 1980s it was not unheard of for a minister in an important portfolio to have as many as forty individuals working full-time. When the Conservatives came to power in 1984 the government immediately instituted the position of chief of staff. Each minister was to hire a very senior person, paid up to the same level as an assistant deputy minister, to head up the minister's office. While in the initial period some ministers seem to have hired chiefs of staff purely on the basis of political loyalty, by 1989 most chiefs of staff were skilled professionals who, while true to the party, were selected as well on the basis of administrative and analytical ability.

Another practice that was begun by the Liberal governments of the 1970s and continued by the Conservative governments of the 1980s is the selection of some ministerial aides from within the department. While these "departmental assistants" are intended to advise the minister on substantive issues and to give the minister a direct conduit into the day-to-day affairs of his or her department, in fact many of them blossom into trusted political advisors as well. Because they often have long experience in dealing with the clientele served by the department, such departmental assistants are sensitive to "what the traffic will bear" in the policy issues that flow out of the portfolio.

PROCESS ADVISORS: THE PRIVY COUNCIL OFFICE

The PMO and its non-partisan first cousin, the Privy Council Office, share prime office space in the nineteenth-century "Langevin" office block just across Wellington Street from Parliament Hill. This symbolizes their role of serving the prime minister, and in the case of the PCO, its role of servicing the Cabinet committees that meet on the Hill. Since the late 1960s the role of the PCO has evolved from that of an agency almost entirely concerned with moving paper to Cabinet, through an attempt to co-ordinate all aspects of government policy, to a position as arbiter of much of the machinery and process of government in Ottawa and as briefer of the prime minister on the activities of the government. These latter tasks are now combined with the function of providing major logistical support for the Cabinet.

The PCO contains secretariats to service the Cabinet committees. Normally these consist of some four to eight officers headed by an assistant secretary to the Cabinet. They may provide support for more than one committee. There are also secretariats or directorates responsible for the machinery of government and for senior personnel. The whole structure is headed by Canada's highest-ranking public servant, who holds the titles of Clerk of the Privy Council and Secretary to the Cabinet.

To understand the recent evolution of the Privy Council Office and to set other support agencies in context, it is necessary to understand the general evolution of planning processes and the interrelationships among central agencies in Ottawa. We will start with the years prior to 1968, when the bureaucratic establishment dominated the formulation and implementation of policy details and when a small group of senior bureaucratic "mandarins" played a major—some would claim dominant—role in the process of policy choice.

The influence of the mandarins over the determination of priorities was based on a number of factors, some related to structural features of the system and others to the personal characteristics of the individuals involved. The most important of the structural factors was simply that government was smaller and less complex. There were very few "old Ottawa hands," and it was possible for them to know each other well. When this was combined with the deputy minister's control over the flow of information within the system, and with the fact that deputies normally held office over a considerably longer time than ministers, the potential for very powerful influence existed.

It is probable that the heyday of the mandarins would have passed of its own accord. As government grew more complex, the structures of government became increasingly formal and elaborate, the number of deputies grew too large for easy direct communication, and bureaucratic power became more diffused. Moreover, informal structures of power often vanish simply because they are powerful; their power eventually makes them visible and their visibility makes them a mark for others—such as ministers and members of Parliament—who may hold a more formal title to control over the system and who jealously guard their own authority from encroachment.

All of this coincided with, or perhaps led to, the avowed intention of the Trudeau government of 1968 to temper the influence of the senior public service by providing alternative sources of policy advice. To this end, Prime Minister Trudeau and his advisors hypothesized that the most effective counter for one institution is another with parallel responsibilities. The political advisory power of the mandarins was to be attenuated through the increase in size and influence of the PMO. Their planning functions were to be faced with competition from a revamped PCO using a more systematic approach to the divination and implementation of political priorities.

The Privy Council Office and its planning system never quite fulfilled the hopes (or fears) expressed for it in the 1970s. In part, the problems derived from a tendency by the members of departments and other central agencies to view the revamped PCO as an organization of "upstarts" and "outsiders." Although, in fact, it was composed of regular public service personnel, this resentment was probably inevitable; any agency with a new and powerful mandate will be viewed in that light by the old hands. While that is a problem that can be overcome by time, there were larger problems internal to the PCO itself. While a considerable amount of broad system-orientated planning capacity was added to the PCO, rather little in the way of more specialized types of technical expertise was put in place. Thus, its ability to conduct independent analyses and critiques of specific policy proposals emanating from departments remained limited.

The causes of most of these difficulties may well have lain simply in good intentions. The other central agencies of the early 1970s, the Treasury Board Secretariat and the Department of Finance, already conducted independent appraisals of most major policy proposals, albeit based upon different sets of premises that those used by the PCO. Thus, the pursuit of efficiency would seem to have argued against too greatly expanding another central agency even if the dictates of establishing an alternative planning system based upon political priorities might have demanded it. But whatever the reasoning, the successive heads of the PCO exhibited a definite reluctance to create another central agency "monster" in Ottawa.

Another problem also plagued the PCO planning efforts of the 1970s. Plans were to be based on ministerial priorities, yet the PCO found it could not effectively implement the statements of priorities that it got from the Cabinet. It was simply impossible to sort out the diverse proposals emanating from departments and to identify by reference to Cabinet priorities what should be accepted or rejected. It may be that the ephemeral nature of Cabinet's political priorities doomed such an effort to failure before it started. However, the problems were compounded by the lack of an institutional mechanism, which would force ministers to trade off one proposal against another in such a way that no matter what anyone said, the real priorities of government would emerge. Combined with difficulties of different sorts faced by the Department of Finance and the Treasury Board—problems to which we will turn later—the result was a predictable dispersion of government activities and a lack of coherent strategies in fields such as industrial development, social programs, or cultural policy.

POLICY DESIGN AND INTEGRATION ADVISORS

Among earlier attempts to solve problems created by both a lack of information and the difficulty of defining priorities was the creation in the early 1970s of Ministries of State for Science and Technology and for Urban Affairs. These were to collect information and, if necessary, conduct research, and they were to use the power of superior knowledge to provide program integration. However, they had no direct control over departmental budgets, no large budgets of their own, and no sympathetic Cabinet committee through which to report or to block unacceptable proposals. Unfortunately, contrary to the old adage, it turned out that knowledge is not power—at least not enough of it to move a large department or a determined minister and no Ministries of State have survived the 1980s.

The next stage in this evolution unfolded on the economic development front. By 1978 it appeared that if Canada was to compete successfully in the world of international trade, some coherent, national industrial strategy was required. Consequently, a Board of Economic Development Ministers was created under the chairmanship of Robert Andras, one of the most powerful Cabinet ministers of the late 1970s. The board met regularly over several months, but faced persistent problems because, while it discussed policy and its deliberations were supported by a strong deputy minister and secretariat, there was still no institutional mechanism to force either the integration of policies or restraint.

The solution to that problem was deceptively simple—give the board (soon to be reconstituted as the Cabinet Committee on Economic Development) responsibility for control of the entire economic development budget. The possibility of the creation of separate budgets for various policy sectors had been considered in Ottawa on and off since at least the early 1970s. However, that implied a significant institutional realignment and, given the rigidities inherent in all large institutions, could not be implemented until the appropriate conjunction of forces appeared. This conjunction was afforded by the arrival of the new Progressive Conservative government in 1979. Newly appointed ministers, without long-established turf to defend, were much more likely to accept a new expenditure management system than was a set of ministers long in place.

The new separate budgets or "envelopes" had to be administered, and more important, Cabinet committees had to be given support in the making of tradeoffs necessary to stay within the limits of the budget envelopes and in ensuring the integration of policy. Thus, two new agencies in the form of the Ministry of State for Economic and Regional Development (MSERD) and the Ministry of State for Social Development (MSSD) were created.

The ministries, created as an integral part of this new process, were relatively small, containing fewer than two hundred staff members. Each performed long-range planning functions for its sector, administered the budgets for new programs within its area of responsibility (with the budgets for ongoing programs being managed by the Treasury Board), and was responsible for ensuring policy co-ordination through its sector. While the earlier versions of the Ministries of State did not survive because they were too weak, the demise of MSERD and MSSD may be attributed, in some part, to the fact that they became too powerful. Not only did they control an important part of the complicated envelope system of budgeting, but they also came to assume functions heretofore the exclusive domain of the PCO. They also had the function of providing critiques of ministers' policy proposals: hardly something to endear them to ministers. Thus, while these organizations survived the return of the Liberals in 1980, they were abolished by John Turner when he became prime minister in 1984 and have been allowed to rest in peace by subsequent Conservative governments.

Overall policy integration with respect to intergovernmental affairs is the responsibility of the Federal–Provincial Relations Office (FPRO). The fortunes of the FPRO have waxed and waned at the whim of prime ministers since the 1960s, beginning as a part of the PCO, and evolving into a separate Cabinet secretariat headed by a minister in the 1980s. Today the FPRO plays a major co-ordinating role in intergovernmental relations and has taken the lead in the various constitutional conferences during the 1980s and in the embattled passage of the Meech Lake Accord. It also serves as the secretariat to the Cabinet Committee on Federal–Provincial Relations.

FINANCIAL ADVISORS

Figure 22.5 shows the Department of Finance and the Treasury Board both as policy design and integration advisors and as financial advisors. It is in the latter role that Treasury Board and Finance are pre-eminent, but the increasing integration of financial management and policy determination means that both also have important policy integration functions.

The Treasury Board is a statutory committee of the Cabinet. The board itself is composed of the President of the Treasury Board, who is its chairperson and is also the minister in charge of the secretariat, the Minister of Finance (*ex officio*), and four other ministers. The Financial Administration Act, which is the legislation governing the expenditure process, delegates to Treasury Board responsibility as the overseer of the budgetary process. In support of this role, the Treasury Board Secretariat keeps tract of current and projected expenditures within departments according to a common set of rules and advises the Policy and Priorities Committee on total expenditure requirements from year to year. Moreover, the Treasury Board is coming to function more and more as the board of management for the government, having responsibility for labour relations, for many aspects of personnel policy, for "person-year" allocations to departments, and for administrative and financial policy. Finally, in the 1989 version of the Cabinet expenditure management system, Treasury Board will have final authority to make allocations to new policy thrusts from the Program Reserve provided the expenditures are relatively small (probably below $20 million). The net result of all this is to make the Treasury Board and its large (four-hundred-person) secretariat highly influential in both financial management and policy co-ordination.

The Department of Finance retains primary responsibility for advising the government on economic policy in general, for the bulk of transfer payments to the provinces, and for the effect of government policies on the economy. It is the primary advisor to the Committee on Planning and Priorities when major expenditure allocations are made and to the Expenditure Review Committee in its determination of which among those proposals with financial implications are to be forwarded for policy committee consideration. Finally, it is responsible for the raising of revenues. This gives it authority over all aspects of the taxation system, including those devices intended to provide financial inducements to people and corporations to behave in certain ways—the so-called "tax expenditures."

HANDLING POLICY PROPOSALS

Perhaps one way of understanding the processes that involve this plethora of agencies is to consider the main questions that might be asked before a major proposal could become a policy. Initially, an assessment of the quality of public demand for the proposal is required. Alternately, since some proposals are generated largely from within the bureaucracy, an assessment of the amount of public support for the policy may be what is called for at this stage. This assessment would be carried out partly by the departments and ministers most directly involved, partly by the political advisors in the PMO, and often in discussions in caucus.

Some of the most important questions involving a major policy decision concern the financial feasibility and the macro-economic effects of such a step. This financial assessment constitutes the second stage in the assessment of a policy proposal. Information from economic forecasts, projections of government revenues, and consequent allocations of funds will thus become a vital part of the data required to make any major priority decision, and here the Department of Finance becomes pre-eminent. If Finance is forecasting declining government revenues, or a bleak outlook for the deficit, then the amount of "new" money allocated will be small, and barring the availability of some large expenditure reductions, government will be unable to take on a big new program, however desirable it may otherwise be. Similarly, if the Department of

Finance opines that a program will create critical economic problems, the Cabinet may be reluctant to assign a high priority to it. Since Cabinet ministers are not normally economists, and since they are too busy to be able to engage in extensive searches for alternative information, they are rather at the mercy of the Department of Finance when dealing with such matters. Nevertheless, countervailing opinions may be advanced by other agencies or by individual departments, and a healthy scepticism about economic projections prevails.

Closely connected to the foregoing questions are the problems of how such a program could be co-ordinated with current government activity in other fields and whether there are sufficient funds available to finance the program either within a department or from "central sources," a euphemism for an allocation by the Minister of Finance. The now-defunct MSSD and MSERD working within their policy sectors and within the constraints of their budgetary envelopes used to play a key role in this part of the process. Now, with an overall commitment to fiscal restraint being imposed by the government and with a restructuring of the policy machinery, the overall co-ordinative role is the combined responsibility of the Committee on Priorities and Planning and the Expenditure Review Committee, advised by the Department of Finance and with smaller expenditure issues delegated to Treasury Board. The Conservative government elected in 1988 has indicated its intention to take a more "hands on" and more "political" approach to such questions.

In addition to these financial considerations, the line departments, which ultimately would implement the new policy, must apprise Cabinet of any administrative problems they see in the proposal. In this latter role, Cabinet will be advised as well by the Treasury Board Secretariat, which also retains the right to advise Cabinet independently through its minister if it feels its "management board" concerns have not been adequately addressed.

The administrative issues as well as a general question—"Is this a wise policy, in keeping with our approach to government?"—are dealt with by policy committees. There, in addition to the more technical concerns, ministers will ask the hard political questions about political marketability. The final decisions will result from this balancing of the political and technical issues. Thus, although bureaucratic rationality informs the consideration of the technical questions in the policy process, political rationality has the initial and especially the final say.

THE BUDGETARY CYCLE

We have indicated that the trend of the last decade has been to create a closer relationship between budgetary processes and the determination of policy priorities; hence the budgetary cycle is the final part of the policy process that requires our consideration. Until the late 1970s, the budgetary process looked only eighteen months ahead and was used much more as an administrative tool than as an instrument to bring financial considerations into priority determination. The result was a start–stop system of policy making: if revenues were rising, almost any policy proposed would be accepted by Cabinet, but when "restraint" hit, as it did periodically, no new policies would be accepted at all and adjustments could not easily be made.

In an attempt to smooth out this situation, more recent attempts have been made to lengthen the budgetary cycle to a multiyear process and to place priority determination within this cycle, while still leaving sufficient flexibility to deal with emergency situations as they arise. The cycle begins with the preparation of four-year projections of economic conditions and hence of government revenues by the Department of Finance and the parallel preparation of expenditure forecasts by the Treasury Board Secretariat in consultation with departments. On the basis of these projections of the overall "pie" available and of the requirements to finance ongoing commitments, the Minister of Finance prepares a budget, complete with new taxes or program reductions intended to reduce the seemingly inevitable disparity between revenues (too low) and expenditures (too high). The making of economic projections is, of course, a risky business at best, while expenditure projections, which themselves depend on economic projections, are equally difficult to make with any accuracy. Nonetheless, if the basic objective is to indicate relative priorities and to make them more explicit by assigning dollar values to them, the exercise can still be effective as long as common assumptions are adhered to throughout the system. Moreover, the revenue and expenditure forecasts are updated as time passes, and the final budgetary assessments for fiscal year made fairly close to its start can be quite accurate.

The four-year expenditure cycle contains within it a more sharply focused twenty-four-month cycle. Approximately twelve months before the start of a fiscal year, the Secretary of the Treasury Board requests that all departments and agencies prepare five-year "multiyear operating plans" (myops). The myop suggests what expenditures departments think will be necessary to cover their ongoing activities (their A-base) during the period. A process of bargaining and negotiation ensues between the Treasury Board (interested in keeping overall expenditures down) and operating departments (interested in keeping expenditure levels up for their activities and in maintaining maximum amounts of discretionary funds in their own budgets). The bargaining goes through numerous stages, the net result being the completion, by the end of December preceding the April 1 start of the next fiscal year, of the Main Estimates. These, in the form of a metropolitan-telephone-book-sized "Blue Book," are tabled in the House of Commons early in the new calendar year, considered in parliamentary committees, and passed, usually unchanged, in the form of expenditure "votes," which constitute authority for departments to actually spend money.

In practice, this is a very complex process, and it is accompanied by procedures for supplementary estimates and for the audit and evaluation of expenditures. It is further complicated by the fact that the whole system is properly described as a "rolling cycle." As the Main Estimates are being tabled, the multiyear operating plans are being rolled forward one more year and the future years' plans updated. New policies with attendant expenditures can be added to the system at any time. In order to cope with cost overruns during the year, Treasury Board maintains an operating reserve that can be used to cover the statutory program cost increases encompassed in the supplementary estimates.

CONCLUSIONS

The image that emerges from all this is one of considerable complexity and of an expenditure management system in a state of considerable flux as governments attempt to grapple with the problem of maintaining enough flexibility to permit the selection of new policies in an era when social and financial pressures appear to preclude any substantial increase in expenditures.

As we enter the 1990s, it seems that the past two decades of grappling with these complexities have been dominated by two rather different philosophies of governance. The first, introduced and nurtured under the prime ministership of Pierre Trudeau, stood on the pedestal of technical rationalism. Trudeau was the first prime minister to grapple directly with the implications of a technological society, and he structured the policy process in a manner that attempted to allow it to cope with vast amounts of technical information. The policy-making paradigm of the 1970s was thus one that began with a presumption that Canadian political life could, and should, be *planned* on the basis of the best technical information available. The main problem to Trudeau was essentially one of effectively and rationally organizing the technical and intellectual resources of the public service. Governance was, in essence, a question of organization.

Where the legacy of the Trudeau years can be viewed as a policy system that strained to be rationalist and non-political, the later 1980s may be characterized by a different philosophy of governance. In his first five years in power, Prime Minister Brian Mulroney has put in place a policy process that assumes that political rationality is essential to government planning. This system by no means precludes technical information, but it is more likely to temper it with considerations of political support. The Conservative government of 1989 gives far more attention to remaining attuned to the shifting moods of the public than its immediate predecessors, and it would make no apology for that.

It is impossible to predict how the policy process will evolve in the

1990s. However, if the current trends continue, we can expect to see an enhanced role for the partisan political advisors to the Cabinet and an increasing concentration of power in the central committees within the Cabinet itself. The Priorities and Planning Committee has more formally taken over the executive functions of government, and even it may be declining in influence in favour of the smaller Operations and Expenditure Review Committees.

Indeed, about all that can be predicted with certainty is that no system is forever: as actors come and go, new positions of power and new systems evolve. Thus, any description of planning processes in Ottawa has only an ephemeral value, making it incumbent on the wise reader to consult sources such as newspapers, magazines, and journals for the latest grey pattern of the kaleidoscope.

FURTHER READINGS

Doern, G. B., and P. Aucoin. *Public Policy in Canada.* Toronto: Macmillan, 1979.
Doern, G. B., and R. Phidd. *Canadian Public Policy.* Toronto: Methuen, 1983.
French, R. *How Ottawa Decides.* Toronto: Lorimer, 1984.
Hockin, Thomas A., ed. *Apex of Power,* 2nd ed. Toronto: Prentice-Hall, 1977.
Maslove, Allan M., ed. *How Ottawa Spends.* Toronto: Methuen. Published annually.
Phidd, R. W., and G. B. Doern. *The Politics and Management of Canadian Economic Policy.* Toronto: Macmillan, 1978.
Report of the Royal Commission on Financial Management and Accountability. Ottawa: Supply and Services Canada, 1979.
Wilson, V. S. *Canadian Public Policy and Administration.* Toronto: McGraw-Hill Ryerson, 1981.

23

Regulatory Agencies

RICHARD SCHULTZ

Regulation and regulatory agencies have lost some of their glamour since the first edition of this book was published in 1981. At that time, the importance of regulation as one of the primary instruments by which Canadian governments sought to influence, direct, and control social and economic behaviour had been discovered. Consequently, a host of studies, governmental and academic, were undertaken on the purposes, the mix of costs and benefits, and the institutions of regulation. Since that time interest has waned somewhat, suggesting that, as with individuals, so with public policy issues, everything can be famous for at least fifteen minutes. It would be unfortunate, however, if regulatory agencies were allowed to return to languish, as previously, in the "underbrush" of the political system. Important issues remain to be resolved about both regulation and regulatory agencies. Such issues involve not only the function of regulation within the armament of governing instruments, but perennial concerns about accountability and control of the use of such instruments. Perhaps most significantly, the politics of regulatory agencies reveal important aspects about the relationships between society, economy, and the state in Canada.

DEFINITION OF REGULATION

Despite the extent of interest and the number of academic studies undertaken over the past decade, it is of some significance that there still remains considerable conceptual and definitional confusion about the nature of regulation.[1] At one extreme, regulation subsumes everything government does and therefore is almost synonymous with government itself. At the other extreme, regulation is far more narrowly defined as "the policing of a private activity with respect to a rule prescribed in the public interest." The problem with the former definition is that it effectively precludes a meaningful focus and set of boundaries for research on regulation. There are substantial problems with the latter definition as well. In the first place, where do the activities of public corporations such as the CBC or Alberta Government Telephones or Air Canada, at least until its recent partial privatization, fit? Second, is the presumption that regulation is "in the public interest" reasonable given the common allegation that regulatory agencies are routinely "captured" by the firms they regulate? If they are captured, then presumably it is the private, or at least corporate, in the case of public enterprises, interests that benefit. Finally, the concentration on "policing" in the second definition as the function of regulation may unduly constrain and distort our understanding of the role of regulation in our political system.

In the various contending definitions of regulation there is a confusing mix of intentions, consequences, objectives, tools, targets, and processes. For our purposes here it is not particularly necessary to resolve the many problems that exist as a result; accordingly, we will limit ourselves to stipulating the definition that we will use. Economic regulation has the following characteristics. First, it involves a government or public role in restricting or restraining the economic behaviour or choices of individuals or firms. Second, although economic behaviour can, and at times should, be viewed broadly, we limit it to three specific areas: (1) entry into, and exit from, a specific economic activity, i.e., a licence to provide, or permission to discontinue, a service; (2) the prices, commonly called fares, tariffs, or rates, charged for the regulated services; and (3) the conditions or standards that are to govern the relations between regulated firms and their customers. The quality of service standards imposed on Bell Canada by the Canadian Radio-television and Telecommunications Commission (CRTC) are an example of standards regulation. Third, although regulators may have other powers such as suasion or subsidization, at the heart of regulation is coercion. Regulation involves government by "command and control" rather than incentive. Although some may find such terms as coercion or command and control unsettling, they are used in a strictly neutral, Weberian sense.[2]

The advantages of this definition of economic regulation are several. It does not restrict the scope of regulation to private firms, but encompasses Crown corporations such as CN Railways, Ontario Hydro, and the Manitoba Telephone System. Second, it does not assume a single objective, the public interest. Regulation, all too often, frequently furthers private interest objectives of both firms and customers and does so at the expense of any identifiable public interest. Third, although in this chapter we will limit our subsequent analysis to issues surrounding regulation by independent regulatory agencies such as the CRTC, the National Energy Board, or the Newfoundland Board of Commissioners of Public Utilities, there is no automatic link between economic regulation and a specific form of government organization. Throughout our history such activities have been undertaken by Cabinets, individual ministers, and legislatures, as well as independent agencies. The province of Saskatchewan, for example, recently abolished the independent agency it had established only a few years earlier, the Public Utilities Review Commission, and reverted to regulation of its telecommunications sector by Cabinet.

Finally, and most significantly, our definition does not assume that regulation is limited to a specific function such as policing the behaviour of economic actors. Indeed, one of the primary reasons why regulation has received so much attention in the past few years, and should continue to do so, is that it is such a pliable, multipurpose or multifunctional instrument. Regulation is commonly used to police or constrain the behaviour of economic actors so that they do not engage in activities or practices that violate public concerns. Telephone company profits, for example, must not exceed a range set by a regulator; or railway companies may not unfairly discriminate between customers. But regulation has also been employed for more positive, prescriptive objectives. It may be used to promote or protect the economic interests of a particular firm or an industry. Air regulation, for example, in its first forty years had as its primary objective the promotion of a viable, economically healthy Air Canada. Trucking regulation, in most provinces, similarly was justified by the argument that too much competition would be "destructive" of the competitors and therefore should be controlled by limiting the number of firms and the nature of their operations.

Regulation has also been employed in Canada for much more ambitious goals, in effect to plan a sector of economic activity. Perhaps the most obvious example is the broadcasting industry where from 1932 to the present the objective has been to use regulation to further a broad set of cultural and other policies by co-ordinating the activities of the different actors, be they within the same medium, e.g., AM and FM radio or public and private television, or different forms of media, e.g., cable and off-air broadcasting. This sector has been conceived as a "single system" in which the various forms and firms are supposed to be complementary, not competitive. The role of the regulator, the CRTC, is to assign roles and responsibilities for each sector and the firms within them so that together they attain the public policy objectives deemed appropriate to the broadcasting industry, such as "to safeguard, enrich and strengthen the cultural, political, social and economic fabric of Canada."

Our purpose in developing the preceding definition of economic regulation, particularly as it pertains to the emphasis on the three different functions for which regulation may be employed, is to suggest that the politics of regulation can vary substantially depending on the nature of the regulatory function. Economic regulation is an instrument by which governments seek to influence or control both consumer and corporate economic decision making. In the case of regulation as policing, where boundaries are set within which economic decision makers must operate, regulated firms play the primary role in establishing corporate goals and the related strategies for their attainment. On the other hand, a move to regulation as promoting and particularly as planning entails a considerable shift in the relationships between regulated actors and public authorities. Specifically, it transfers to public authorities a greatly enhanced power to make strategic choices or decisions for regulated actors. One way of conceptualizing this shift is to see policing regulation as constituting *firm-led* or *firm-dominant* economic decision making. Planning regulation, on the other hand, is characterized by *state-led* or *state-dominant* decision making. The significance of such a distinction lies in the implications of adopting one function of regulation or another for understanding and analyzing the role of political intervention in the economy and the politics associated with intervention. Using regulation as a planning, as opposed to a policing, instrument, for example, means a greater role for public authorities in the allocation of resources and in directing the production and distribution of goods and services. By definition this means an enhanced role for public, at the expense of corporate, decision makers in determining the winners and losers in economic activities. It is this fact that largely accounts for the degree of political salience attached to the process and instruments of economic regulation.

REGULATORY AGENCY CONTROL AND ACCOUNTABILITY

The political salience of economic regulation can be demonstrated by reference to the continuing debate over the degree of independence that regulatory agencies exercise and how, and to what extent, that independence should be circumscribed. Although, as indicated above, regulation need not be assigned to independent agencies, and at different times has not been, today in many sectors—transportation, energy, communications—the major regulatory functions are performed by such agencies. For most of this century, such independence has not been the cause of much concern. One explanation for this is that regulators, such as those in the transport sector for the first six decades in this century, found it the better part of wisdom to interpret their mandates as narrowly and technically as possible, to emphasize their quasi-judicial nature, and to shun efforts to lure them into larger political conflicts. Another reason is that politicians reserved for themselves what were perceived to be major "political" regulatory powers. Broadcasting and airline licensing, for example, were the prerogatives of Cabinet or an individual minister until only twenty years ago when these powers were delegated to independent agencies.

Recently, however, regulatory agency independence has been the object of considerable public attention. This attention has concentrated on a number of crucial questions. Why are regulatory agencies independent? How independent are they? How can one justify conferring political power on appointed decision makers subject to minimal control by elected authorities? How should the exercise of such power be constrained and supervised?

Regulatory agencies are one group of non-departmental governmental bodies that Hodgetts labelled "structural heretics," although with the increasing number of such bodies the heresy threatens to supplant whatever constitutes the orthodoxy. The agencies are deemed to be heretics because they involve at the minimum the attenuation and at the maximum the avoidance of ministerial responsibility. The objective of such responsibility is to ensure the accountability of the government, and its individual members, to the House of Commons. Ministers are not responsible, however, for the actions of independent agencies; for their part, the agencies are largely free from direct ministerial control. This freedom or independence is, as we will soon see, relative and not absolute.

Regulatory independence has two basic dimensions. In the first place, the appointed members of regulatory commissions have tenure for fixed terms, usually ranging from five to ten years. A member cannot be removed prior to the end of his or her term except "for cause," which is essentially limited either to an incapacity to perform his or her responsibilities or to malfeasance in office. This contrasts with the appointments of deputy ministers and other appointees who serve "at pleasure" and can be summarily removed from their positions by prime ministerial or Cabinet decision. The fixed tenure of regulatory appointments, as in the United States, is perhaps the most fundamental attribute of regulatory independence and is comparable in some respects to that conferred on members of the judiciary.

Naturally, independent tenure would not be politically all that significant if those so endowed were not delegated important decision-making power. The independence of the members of the Air Transport Board, for example, from 1943 to 1967 was irrelevant because the board was solely an advisor to the minister and not an independent decision maker. It is clearly what an agency can do, and the extent of its freedom from direct political control, that determines whether its independence is a political issue. Although we cannot survey all their powers here (the Administrative Law Series of the Law Reform Commission provides very useful and informative studies of several individual agencies as well as some general analyses of the issues), we can outline the four major types of powers that they usually exercise. The first is an adjudicative power; that is, the power to approve specific applications for the approval of rates or fares or to grant, deny, or remove licences. Second, an agency may have legislative powers authorizing it to establish general rules or regulations governing not only its procedures, but the behaviour of firms subject to its jurisdiction. The CRTC's Canadian content regulations for radio and television are an example of a regulatory agency's legislative power. The third power an agency usually possesses is a research or investigative power to inquire into any matter within its jurisdiction. Finally, an agency may be delegated responsibility to administer governmental subsidy programs.

Regulatory agency independence is, as indicated, relative and not absolute; there are a number of control mechanisms, both informal and formal. One of these is the appointment power of the Cabinet. Another is the power to approve agency budgets, which can be very useful, away from the glare of publicity, if the government or an individual minister wishes to persuade an agency to adopt an alternative policy. While these are not insignificant control powers in themselves, they are rather blunt and their effectiveness is limited. In particular, once an appointment is made, if the views of the appointed individual change during incumbency there is little a government can do.

By far the most important of the direct political controls over the exercise of agency adjudicative powers are those colloquially known as political appeal powers. These powers have two broad characteristics. They can be active or passive, positive or negative. Active-passive refers to the power to initiate a review of regulatory adjudicative decisions. The power is an active one if elected authorities can review at their own discretion; it is passive if such review is dependent on an appeal by a third party. Positive-negative refers to whether such authorities can substitute in whole or in part their decisions for those of the regulatory agency or whether they are limited to rejecting or vetoing such decisions. The possible combination of such appeal powers is shown in Figure 23.1.

The significance of this classification system is twofold. In the first place, despite the common assumption that regulatory agencies are subject to political control, it demonstrates that there is no uniform system of such control over regulatory decisions. Cabinet, for example, exercises active power over the National Energy Board (NEB) in that all major decisions on pipeline certificates and licences require Cabinet approval before they are valid. Yet, Cabinet's power in this instance is also negative in that it cannot substitute or vary such NEB decisions, but is limited to rejecting them completely. Such a constraint was found to be very significant, for example, in the early 1970s in the debates over licensing of a pipeline in northern Canada when the NEB chose a firm for the licence that was not the apparent favourite of Cabinet. When this happened Cabinet found its options severely restricted. With respect to telecommunications regulation, however, Cabinet possesses both active and positive powers inasmuch as it can not only reject regulatory decisions but substitute its own. In the case of broadcasting licences, Cabinet is confined to entertaining appeals and to vetoing licences; no change in them is permitted.

The more important aspect of the existing non-uniform system of political controls is that the degree of political power over individual

Figure 23.1
Alternative Political Appeals

	Positive	Negative
Active		
Passive		

agencies varies depending on the nature of the political appeal powers. Cabinet, for example, can subject the telecommunications regulator to far greater control than it can the broadcasting or energy regulator. This means simply that some agencies, for some of their decisions, are more independent of political control than others.

As we have suggested, although the agencies have possessed independence for some time, it has only been in the past two decades that controversy has emerged over the exercise of such independence. We would argue that the primary reason for this can be traced to the use of regulation for much more positive, prescriptive purposes such as promoting a firm or industry or attempting to plan the activities of a whole sector such as broadcasting. Such uses of regulation dramatically affect the politics of regulation in two ways. In the first place, the nature and range of interests or actors with a stake in regulatory outcomes expands with a move from narrow policing to broad-gauged planning regulation. In the former, participants are usually limited to a very restricted set of interests, usually the regulated firm and groups of its customers. In the latter, more interests want to participate because regulation has direct and indirect consequences for their well-being. In addition to regulated firms and their customers, other interests such as potential competitors, provincial governments, and indeed government departments will normally partici-pate. The political significance of this is that it makes regulatory decision making much more difficult in that the regulatory agency has to balance and find compromises for a much wider set of affected interests.

The second consequence for the politics of regulation is that such expanded interest participation leads to a decrease in the traditional insulation of the regulatory arena from wider political processes and institutions. Although it always was an exaggeration to say that regulatory agencies depoliticized or "took the politics" out of some issues—they really only transferred them to another, less partisan, political forum—nevertheless, using regulation for positive public purposes results in a much closer integration of a regulatory agency with, rather than insula-tion from, other political processes such as those involved in lobbying Cabinet, members of Parliament, and departments.

In recent years, one of the consequences of the positive use of regulation flowing from the consequent broadened set of interests fight-ing political battles before regulators and the decline in regulatory insulation has been the demand that the policy making of regulatory agencies should be subject to enhanced political control. Traditional control mechanisms, such as those described above, it is argued, are inadequate in themselves. One of the preferred instruments for enhanced political control has been the policy directive. Such an instru-ment is premised on a recognition that regulatory statutes are normally far too vague or contradictory to provide sufficient policy guidance to regula-tors, thereby limiting their policy-making potential.

The proposal to grant Cabinet a policy directive power, or to expand its scope where it currently is in place, would grant Cabinet the power to issue authoritative interpretations of existing statutory policy statements that an agency would be "bound" to accept when it decided individual cases or developed sets of regulations. There would be safeguards to limit such directives to general policy matters, and Cabinet would be prohib-ited from issuing a directive that dealt with individual adjudicative cases before the agencies.

There is widespread support for the idea, although such a measure has not been without controversy, particularly because of the fear that it will enhance the power of those with greater access to Cabinet, namely the large regulated firms and departmental officials (see Andrew Roman's article listed in the Further Readings, which makes the strongest case against it), and to date it has only been introduced, in its expanded form, in the transportation sector. Most supporters, however, have argued that safeguards must accompany the measure not only to protect the indepen-dence of the regulatory agency in those areas where independence is justified, but also to ensure that, in addition to Cabinet's power being enhanced, the interests of other affected concerns such as Parliament and intervenors before regulatory agencies including the regulated firms are not sacrificed or unduly harmed.

It is clear that whether or not the directive power is included in all regulatory agency statutes, the question of the extent and appropriateness of independent agencies engaged in policy making will not disappear in the 1990s. In this respect, these agencies are only part of a more general problem associated with the growth of complex, activist government. In the words of Emmette Redford, regulatory agencies exhibit a central characteristic of the modern liberal democratic state where "policy is made for and applied to us by minorities composed of men occupying strategic positions in specialized organizations operating only in part under directives from organizations directly representative of the people."[3]

WHY REGULATE?

One of the perennial questions raised by political scientists is why governments choose to regulate economic decision making. As we shall see, the conflicting answers given to this question have provoked almost as much conflict as regulation itself. The traditional answer was that economic regulation by the state was justified on public interest grounds. According to this approach or theory, government intervention in the market was required by what are known as "market failures," that is, instances where market or economic forces cannot act as an effective regulatory instrument. The most obvious case of market failure is that involving a monopoly such as traditional telephone service. According to this argument, regulation is necessary to prevent the monopoly firm from exploiting its economic power to earn excessive profits or engaging in what is deemed to be socially unacceptable behaviour such as discrimination between customers.

Although this explanation for regulation was routinely accepted for decades, considerable doubt has been expressed recently about the validity of the public interest rationale. Starting in the 1950s, particularly with the influential work of the American political scientist Marver Bernstein, students of regulation argued that while regulatory agencies may have been created to serve the public interest, over time they become "captured" by the very interests they are meant to control. Such capture, it is argued, results in an undermining of the public purposes of regulation and the use of public instruments to promote private or corporate interests. In Canada, for example, Hershel Hardin has suggested that the CRTC as broadcasting regulator provides an excellent example of regulatory capture.

One of the weaknesses of the "capture theory" is that it ignores instances where regulation was created for the very purpose of protecting or promoting the interests of the regulated firm or industry. Air regulation in Canada, for example, was introduced in 1938 for the explicit purpose of protecting Air Canada, as it is now known, from competition. The rationale for such regulatory protection was that competition might make the public airline unprofitable and thereby force it to turn to the government for financial assistance. Similarly, in broadcasting, regulation was introduced not to serve the interests of existing private broadcasters, but to further the interests and goals of the public broadcaster. Indeed, so concerned was the government about protecting the CBC, in order to further its goals, that it made the Crown corporation the regulator of the private sector from 1936 to 1938.

More recently, economists have sought to refine the "capture theory" by contending that there is a simple explanation for regulation: it is demanded by the regulated. According to this approach, which despite the gloss that economists sometimes put on it is little more than an expanded version of conventional political science interest group theories, some firms seek regulation for the economic benefits, including a relatively quiet, non-competitive life. To obtain this goal they offer politicians votes and regulators support for their budgets and post-regulatory employment.

This is not the place to offer extended critiques of the various theoretical explanations for the introduction of regulation. In the case of the interest group explanations, there is evidence in several areas that some groups are indeed effective in persuading politicians to introduce regulation or subsequently to persuade regulators to tailor the regulatory system to serve their interests. There is also evidence, however, that regulation has been introduced to advance societal interests that go well beyond, indeed conflict with, the objectives of private or corporate actors. There is also evidence in the transportation and communications sectors that suggests that state officials in both departments and public enterprises have had considerable autonomous influence in determining the structure, goals, and processes of regulation. Both the public interest and the various private interest theories that seek to explain why and how Canadian governments regulate do not pay sufficient attention to this aspect of the political process. What is particularly significant in the Canadian context, given the rich diversity of theoretical explanations for the introduction and evolution of regulation, is that there are very few empirical studies of individual regulatory agencies.

THE POLITICS OF DEREGULATION AND REGULATORY REFORM

One of the most interesting developments in the late 1980s that was largely unanticipated at the beginning of the decade has been the emergence of deregulation and regulatory reform as viable policy options in Canada. When the first edition of this book was published, I noted that, notwithstanding the fact that the first significant act of deregulation in North America was undertaken in Canada in 1967 in the railway sector, extensive deregulation did not appear to be likely.

In the past five years, however, we have witnessed extensive deregulation in the energy, air, and financial sectors. In the rail industry, there has been a simultaneous lightening of some regulatory requirements with an increase in others. In the broadcasting sector, although the current government appears committed to a heavy reliance on traditional regulation, nevertheless, the new Broadcasting Act includes a novel technique, an incentive tax system, designed to encourage private broadcasters to fulfil their Canadian content commitments. If this should fail, it is not improbable that future governments may conclude that the effort is not worth the result and move away from any reliance on regulation that serves primarily to guarantee high profits for private broadcasters with no corresponding public gain.

For our purposes here, the significance of the emergence of deregulatory or reform policies rests in the incapacity of existing political science theories to explain fully such developments. Clearly, they are contrary to the predictions of the capture theory or the economic private interest theory. Why would regulated firms who presumably are the prime beneficiaries of existing regulatory regimes advocate their end? The answer is that they did not; indeed, in the air sector, for example, only when deregulation was clearly inevitable did the industry endorse it. Nor is it clear that the traditional public interest theory offers a better explanation. Although explanations will vary depending on the individual sector, it would appear that satisfactory explanations for these political outcomes will require, just as they did to explain the introduction and evolution of regulation, complex explanations that address technological, cultural, economic, political, and intragovernmental factors. One potentially rewarding line of research is to explore the politics of deregulation to analyze the relative influence of societal and intrastate actors. A related line of research would be to examine Canadian deregulation from a comparative perspective, particularly what it may tell us about the forces that shape the capacity of the state to intervene successfully in the economy.

CONCLUSION

The past decade has witnessed significant developments in the politics of regulatory agencies. Although they continue in some sectors such as broadcasting and telecommunications to be primary instruments of governing, in other areas their functions have been reassessed, reassigned, and in a few major instances removed completely. They remain, however, worthy of public attention and academic analysis. They constitute one of the set of "structural heretics" within our institutional system, and debate will continue on the appropriateness of their independence, the nature of their powers, and the instruments to subject them to legitimate control. Perhaps even more important, the nature of their functions and how they are performed provide a particularly instructive arena for the analysis of the relative power of private and public actors and larger questions about the limits of the modern Canadian state and its role in the economy.

NOTES

1. In this section, I draw heavily on Richard Schultz and Alan Alexandroff, *Economic Regulation and the Federal System* (Toronto: University of Toronto, Press, 1985), especially ch. 1.
2. See Theodore Lowi, "The State in Politics: The Relation between Policy and Administration," in *Regulatory Policy and the Social Sciences*, ed. Roger Noll (Berkeley: University of California Press, 1985), in particular for a defence of the Weberian concept of coercion as it pertains to regulation.
3. Emmette Redford, *Democracy in the Administrative State* (New York: Oxford University Press, 1969) p. 196.

FURTHER READINGS

Bernstein, Marver H. *Regulating Business by Independent Commission*. Princeton: Princeton University Press, 1955.

Economic Council of Canada. Regulation Reference, *Responsible Regulation* (1980) and *Reforming Regulation* (1981).

Law Reform Commission of Canada. *Administrative Law Series*. Various titles that include studies of individual agencies such as the Canadian Transport Commission, the National Energy Board, and the Canadian Radio-television and Telecommunications Commission as well as "issue" studies on political control and public participation.

Lowi, Theodore. "The State in Politics: The Relation between Policy and Administration." In *Regulatory Policy and the Social Sciences*, ed. Roger Noll. Berkeley: University of California Press, 1985.

Roman, Andrew J. "Governmental Control of Tribunals: Appeals, Directives and Non-Statutory Mechanisms." *Queen's Law Journal* 10 (1985): 476–97.

Schultz, Richard. "Regulatory Agencies and the Dilemmas of Delegation." In *The Administrative State in Canada*, ed. O. P. Dwivedi. Toronto: University of Toronto Press, 1982.

———. "Regulating Conservatively: The Mulroney Record, 1984–1988." In *Can-*

ada Under Mulroney: An End-of-Term Report, ed. Andrew B. Gollner and Daniel Salée. Montreal: Véhicule Press, 1988.

Schultz, Richard, and Alan Alexandroff. *Economic Regulation and the Federal System.* Toronto: University of Toronto Press, 1985.

Stanbury, W. T. "Reforming Direct Regulation in Canada." In *The Age of Regulatory Reform,* ed. K. J. Button and D. Swann. (Oxford: Oxford University Press, 1988.)

INDEX